Qualitative ... for the Social Sciences

Qualitative Research for the Social Sciences

Marilyn Lichtman

Virginia Tech

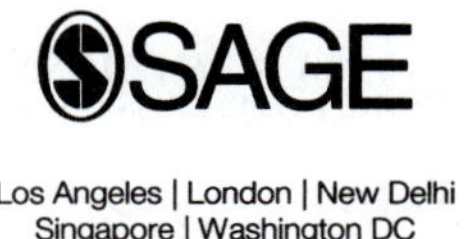

Los Angeles | London | New Delhi
Singapore | Washington DC

Los Angeles | London | New Delhi
Singapore | Washington DC

FOR INFORMATION:

SAGE Publications, Inc.
2455 Teller Road
Thousand Oaks, California 91320
E-mail: order@sagepub.com

SAGE Publications Ltd.
1 Oliver's Yard
55 City Road
London EC1Y 1SP
United Kingdom

SAGE Publications India Pvt. Ltd.
B 1/I 1 Mohan Cooperative Industrial Area
Mathura Road, New Delhi 110 044
India

SAGE Publications Asia-Pacific Pte. Ltd.
3 Church Street
#10-04 Samsung Hub
Singapore 049483

Acquisitions Editor: Reid Hester
Editorial Assistant: Sarita Sarak
Production Editor: Olivia Weber-Stenis
Copy Editor: Erin Livingston
Typesetter: C&M Digitals (P) Ltd.
Proofreader: Caryne Brown
Indexer: Diggs Publication Services
Cover Designer: Michael Dubowe
Marketing Manager: Nicole Elliott

Printed in the United States of America

Library of Congress Cataloging-in-Publication Data

Lichtman, Marilyn.
Qualitative research for the social sciences / Marilyn Lichtman, Virginia Tech.

pages cm
Includes bibliographical references and index.

ISBN 978-1-4129-9864-2 (alk. paper)

1. Qualitative research. 2. Social sciences—Research—Methodology. I. Title.

H62.L482 2014
300.72′1—dc23 2013009318

This book is printed on acid-free paper.

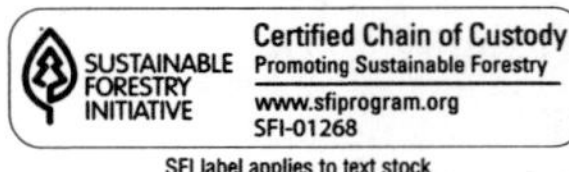

SFI label applies to text stock

13 14 15 16 17 10 9 8 7 6 5 4 3 2 1

Contents

Preface xxi

The Audience xxiii
Structure of This Book xxiii
Additional Features xxiii
Ancillary Materials xxiv

Acknowledgments xxv

References xxvi

About the Author xxvii

PART I. CONCEPTUAL AND HISTORICAL CONTEXT 1

Chapter 1. Introduction 3

Focus Your Reading 3
Qualitative Research Is Used in Many Disciplines 4
Quantitative or Qualitative? 6
How Are Qualitative and Quantitative Research Complementary? 7
What Is Qualitative Research? 8
Level of Specificity—General, Specific, or Somewhere in Between 8
Specific Discipline 10
A Working Definition 11
What Makes Research Qualitative? 12
Overview of Common Elements 12
Additional Components 13
The Growth of Qualitative Research 14
Why Qualitative Research? 16
Comparing Qualitative and Quantitative Research 16
Theoretical and Philosophical Foundations of Qualitative Research 18
What About Validity? 18
Check Yourself 21
Key Discussion Issues 22
Module 1a. Developing a Blog 22
Module 1b. Identifying Key Elements of Qualitative Research 22
Notes 23
References 23
Student Study Site 25

Chapter 2. Qualitative Research—A Reflexive Stance 27

Focus Your Reading 27
Purpose of Research and Research Questions 28
People 28
Concepts 29
Places 30
Events 30
Human Interactions, Social Processes, and Phenomena: Identification of Research Questions 30
Role of Self—Reflexivity and Subjectivity 31
Reflexivity and Its Meanings 32
Current Practice of Reflexivity 33
Illustrations of Reflexive Practice 35
Subjectivity and Its Meanings 36
Thinking About Subjectivity 36
Illustrations of Subjectivity 36
Critical Elements of Qualitative Research 37
Purpose Is to Describe, Understand, and Interpret Human Behavior 38
Qualitative Research Is Dynamic 38
Studying Culture in New Ways 39
Dynamic Aspects of Interviewing 39
Fluid Environment 40
Plan May Be Modified 40
No Single Way of Doing Something 40
Reality Interpreted by the Researcher 41
Qualitative Research Is Inductive 41
Qualitative Research Deals With the Whole 42
Qualitative Research Occurs in Natural Settings 42
Role of the Researcher 43
In-Depth Study 44
Words, Themes, Narratives, and Writing 45
Nonlinear 46
Challenges of Doing Qualitative Research 47
Check Yourself 47
Key Discussion Issues 48
Module 2. Developing Research Questions and Being Reflexive 48
References 48
Student Study Site 51

Chapter 3. Ethical Issues in Qualitative Research 53

Focus Your Reading 53
Ethical Behavior: Definitions and Background 56

Major Principles Associated With Ethical Conduct 57
Do No Harm 57
Privacy and Anonymity 57
Confidentiality 59
Informed Consent 59
Truthfulness and Accuracy in Reporting Data 60
Rapport and Friendship 61
Intrusiveness 61
Inappropriate Behavior 62
Data Interpretation 62
Data Ownership and Rewards 62
Inclusion and Social Justice 62
Other Issues 63
Misconduct in the General Scientific Community 64
Misconduct in the Qualitative Research Arena 65
Concerns for the Qualitative Researcher 66
Studying Vulnerable Participants 69
Children 69
Persons With Limited English or Other Challenges 70
Setting and Maintaining Standards 71
Problems With Review Boards 74
Check Yourself 76
Key Discussion Issues 76
Module 3. Examining the Principles of Ethical Conduct 76
References 77
Student Study Site 80

Chapter 4. Conceptualizing Research Approaches **81**

Focus Your Reading 81
Thinking About Qualitative Research 81
History of Qualitative Research Approaches 85
Generic Versus Specific Approaches 88
Problems With Research Approaches 90
Paradigm Wars 90
Mixed-Methods Approaches 91
Combined Qualitative Approaches 92
Meta-synthesis 92
Check Yourself 93
Key Discussion Issues 94
Module 4. Developing a Personal Viewpoint Regarding How to Conduct Research 94
References 94
Student Study Site 96

Chapter 5. A Detailed Examination of Common Approaches 97

Focus Your Reading 97
Qualitative Research Approaches Revisited 97
What Should a Research Approach Be Able to Do? 100
Ethnography—A Study of Cultures or Subcultures 100
History and Meaning 100
Distinguishing Features 101
Special Issues 102
Culture 102
Gaining Access 102
Participant Observation 103
Total Immersion 103
Power 103
Examples From the Field 103
Blogs and Beyond 104
Words of Caution 104
Grounded Theory—Developing Theory From Context 105
History and Meaning 105
Distinguishing Features 106
Special Issues 107
Deciding on Participants 108
Theoretical Saturation 108
Coding 108
Examples From the Field 108
Blogs and Beyond 109
Words of Caution 109
Theoretical Sampling 110
Determining True Grounded Theory 111
Theoretical Saturation 111
Theories 111
Following the Coding Rubric 111
Phenomenology—The Study of Lived Experiences 111
History and Meaning 112
Phenomenology in Today's World 112
A Variety of Disciplines 113
Growth Worldwide 113
Reinterpretations of Phenomenology 114
Phenomenology as a Philosophy and as a Method 114
Distinguishing Features 116
Special Issues 116
Translating Philosophical Ideas Into a Research Approach 116
Uncommon Terms 116
Specifics Missing 117
Complex Ideas 117
Examples From the Field 117

Blogs and Beyond 118
Words of Caution 118
Phenomenology in Name Only 118
Seems So Easy 118
Case Study—An Examination of a Particular Person, Program, Event, or Concept 118
History and Meaning 119
Distinguishing Features 120
Special Issues 120
Selecting Cases 120
What Makes a Case Study 122
Defining Limits 122
Going Beyond a Particular Case 122
Examples From the Field 122
Blogs and Beyond 123
Words of Caution 123
Utility of Case Studies 123
Is Case Study a Research Approach? 123
Narrative Inquiry—Focus on Telling a Story 124
History and Meaning 124
Distinguishing Features 125
Special Issues 125
Gathering Sufficient Information 125
Who Owns the Stories? 126
Retelling the Stories 126
Examples From the Field 126
Blogs and Beyond 127
Words of Caution 127
More Than a Story 127
Understanding the Context 127
How to Get Information 127
Fact or Fiction 127
Ethics, Anonymity, and Ownership 128
Summary of Research Approaches 128
Check Yourself 129
Key Discussion Issues 129
Module 5. Identifying Questions, Selecting an Approach, Planning and Implementing, and Connecting 130
References 130
Student Study Site 134

Chapter 6. A Review of Additional Research Approaches 135

Focus Your Reading 135
Interrelatedness of Research Approaches, Research Topics, and Participants 136

Action Research/Participatory Action Research—Solving a Particular Problem 138
History and Meaning 138
Distinguishing Features 139
Special Issues 139
Getting the Buy-In 139
Maintaining Academic Integrity 139
Changes over Time 139
Examples From the Field 140
Arts-Based Approaches 140
History and Meaning 140
Distinguishing Features 141
Special Issues 141
Attaining Legitimacy in a Scientifically Oriented World 141
Seeking Alternative Presentation Forms 141
Examples From the Field 142
Autoethnography—Exploring the Experiences of Life 142
History and Meaning 142
Distinguishing Features 143
Special Issues 143
Little Has Been Written About How to Conduct an Autoethnography 143
Reflexivity Plays an Important Role 143
Personal Story or Something More 143
Examples From the Field 144
Feminist Research 145
History and Meaning 145
Distinguishing Features 146
Special Issues 146
Definition of a Feminist Study 146
No Universal Definition of Feminist Research 147
Poststructural and Postfeminist Viewpoints 147
Examples From the Field 147
Mixed-Methods Research 149
History and Meaning 149
Distinguishing Features 149
Special Issues 150
Inconsistencies in Terms of Worldviews 150
Triangulation 150
Examples From the Field 150
Postmodernism and Critical Theory Research 151
A Summary of Research Approaches 152
Selecting a Research Approach 152
Select a Research Topic and Question 154
Select a Research Approach 154

Develop a Research Study 154
Determine Your Role as a Researcher 155
Check Yourself 155
Key Discussion Issues 155
Module 6. Read About Mixed-Methods Research or Arts-Based Methods 155
References 156
Student Study Site 159

PART II. THE QUALITATIVE RESEARCH PROCESS **161**

Chapter 7. Planning and Conceptualizing a Qualitative Research Study **163**

Focus Your Reading 163
Innovations From the Field 164
Traversing the Lonely Road by James Bernauer 164
Transparent Technology by R. A. Dibbs, David Glassmeyer, and Maria Lahman 168
Photovoice in Practice by Laura Lorenz 173
Life in the Social Sciences—An Alternate View by Christine Brooks 179
Turning Research Into Film by Kip Jones, With Trevor Hearing 184
Jumping Outside Your Comfort Zone—Painting 101 189
Developing a Qualitative Research Proposal 191
Purpose 191
Research Question and Conceptual Framework 192
Start My Review 193
Review Qualitative Research Elements 193
Select a Qualitative Research Approach 194
Explain Elements of Approach 194
Trustworthiness 195
Researcher Role 196
Practicalities 196
Qualitative Research Proposal Outline 196
Institutional Requirements 197
Qualitative Research Proposal Elements 197
Final Considerations in Writing a Proposal 200
Check Yourself 201
Key Discussion Issues 201
Module 7. Developing a Mini-IRB Protocol 201
References 202
References for Individual Contributions 202
Student Study Site 204

Chapter 8. Social Media, the Internet, and Technology 205

Focus Your Reading 205
What Are Social Media and Social Networking? 206
Definitions 207
Popular Social Networking Sites 207
Advances in Technology 208
Definitions 208
Internet Tools 209
Browsers 209
Application Software (App) 209
Cloud Computing 210
Visual Tools 210
Location Tools 210
Tools for Rapid Communication 211
Organizing and Analyzing Information on the Web 212
Types of Hardware 213
Definitions 213
Popular Devices 213
Research Related to the Internet 214
Privacy, Ethics, and Informed Consent 215
Ways to Use Tools 216
Virtual Learning 216
Research on Hardware and Tools 217
Summary 218
Check Yourself 218
Key Discussion Issues 219
Module 8a. Interact in a Virtual Community 219
Module 8b. Combine Visual and Textual Information 219
References 219
Student Study Site 221

Chapter 9. A Review of Research Literature 223

Focus Your Reading 223
Introduction 224
The Question of Why 226
Value of a Review 226
Potential Limitations of a Review 227
When Should You Conduct a Review? 227
What Are You to Do? 228
The Process of How 228
Conducting a Review of Related Research—Critical Steps 228
Identify a Topic of Interest 229
Determine Search Terms 229
Search for Information 229

Select Relevant Information 231
Review Critically 231
Modify Topic If Necessary 231
Keep Track of Things 231
Avoid Hard Copies and Printing Things 231
What Do You Write? 232
Completeness and Accuracy in References 232
Software Programs for References 232
Using Proper Form for Unusual References 232
What Do Others Say? 232
Incorporating Review in Your Work—Critical Steps 234
Using the Information 234
Decide on a Type of Review 234
Contextual 234
Historical 235
Theoretical/Conceptual 235
Methodological 235
Integrative 235
Decide on a Style of Review 235
Organize the Review 236
Locate Your Own Research 236
Relate Your Research to Existing Research 236
What Do Others Do? 236
Check Yourself 237
Key Discussion Issues 237
Module 9. Conducting a Mini-Literature Review and Writing It Up 238
References 238
Student Study Site 240

Chapter 10. Interviewing **241**

Focus Your Reading 241
Introduction 241
Purpose of Interviewing 246
Types of Individual Interviews 247
The Structured or Standardized Interview 248
The Semi-Structured or Guided Interview 248
The Unstructured or In-Depth Interview 248
The Casual or Unplanned Interview 250
General Issues in Individual Interviewing 250
Identification of Participants 250
How Many? 251
Developing Rapport 252
Selecting a Setting for the Interview 252
Observing Surroundings 253

Recording the Interview 253
Transcribing the Interview 253
Interviewing Adolescents and Children 254
Interviewing Males With Limited Verbal Skills 254
Interviewing Elites 254
Power 255
Reflexivity—Researcher as Instrument 255
Interviewer and Participant Gender 256
Emotions and Interviewing 256
Alternatives to Direct Questioning 256
Quality of the Interview 257
Collecting Data Using Internet Technologies 258
Interviewing Online 258
Preparing for an Online Interview 258
Issues and Challenges With Online Interviewing 259
Other Technologies 260
Knowing About Issues 260
The Interview Process for In-Depth Interviewing 261
Advance Planning 261
Preliminaries 262
The Body of the Interview 262
The End of the Interview 263
Post-Interview Tasks 263
Developing Interview Techniques 263
Types of Questions 263
Grand Tour 264
Concrete Questions 265
Comparison/Contrast 266
New Elements/Topics 266
Closing 267
Strategies for Questioning 267
Elaboration 268
Probing 268
Using Stimuli 269
Neutrality 269
Single Question 269
Wait Time 270
Special Areas of Concern 270
Questioning Strategies to Avoid 270
Leading Questions 270
Complex Questions 271
Double-Barreled Questions 271
Questions With Jargon or Technical Language 271
Chattiness 271

Developing an Interview Guide 271
Example of an Interview 272
Summary 274
Check Yourself 275
Key Discussion Issues 275
Module 10. Group and Individual Activities 275
References 276
Student Study Site 278

Chapter 11. Additional Methods of Gathering Data 279

Focus Your Reading 279
Observing in Natural Settings 281
Purpose of Observations 282
Issues Regarding Observations 284
Deciding Who Is to Be Studied and in What Situations 284
Types of Groups 284
Gaining Access 285
What to Study 285
Frequency and Length of Time 286
Your Role 286
How to Conduct an Observation 286
Planning 286
Conducting the Observations 287
Other Issues 287
Four Scenarios for Practice 288
Scenario 1 288
Scenario 2 289
Scenario 3 290
Scenario 4 291
Focus Group Interviews 292
Purpose of Focus Group Interviewing 294
Issues Regarding Focus Groups 294
Deciding on the Size of the Group 294
Deciding on the Number of Groups 295
Deciding the Composition of Groups 296
Focus Groups with Challenging Populations 296
Deciding the Role of the Moderator 297
Locating Facilities and Arranging for Recording 297
Transcribing 297
Online Focus Groups 297
Example of a Focus Group Interview 299
Images and Visuals 301
Purpose of Images 302
Issues Regarding Images/Video 302

Privacy and Facial Recognition Software 302
Quality of the Image 303
Manipulation of the Image 303
Relationship of the Image to Words 303
Selecting Framing for Recordings 303
Examples of Image Usage 303
Mapping 304
The Written Word 305
Issues Regarding Written Material 306
Extracting the Essence 306
Technology 307
Smartphones 307
GPS Technology 308
Skype 308
Google Products 308
Issues Regarding the Use of Technology 308
Technical Limitations 309
Recruiting Participants 309
Participant Behaviors 309
Programming Apps 309
Managing and Analyzing Data 309
Institutional Review Board Approvals With Human Subjects 309
Challenges for Researchers 309
Examples of Technology Use 309
Check Yourself 310
Key Discussion Issues 310
Module 11. Use of Apps for Gathering Data 311
References 311
Student Study Site 314

PART III. THE FINAL PRODUCT 315

Chapter 12. Drawing Meaning From the Data 317

Focus Your Reading 317
When to Do Your Analysis 323
Gaining Meaning: Themes/Concepts or Narratives 323
Looking at Themes/Concepts 323
Looking at Narratives 324
Moving Ahead 325
Conducting an Analysis for Themes/Concepts 326
Getting Started 326
Preparing and Organizing Your Data 327
Reviewing and Recording Your Thoughts 328

Looking for Concepts/Themes—The Three Cs: Coding, Categorizing, and Concepts 328
Six Steps in Coding 329
Strengthening the Process 331
Looking for Narratives or Stories 332
Qualitative Research Approaches and Data Analysis 335
Additional Qualitative Analysis Techniques or Procedures 336
Generic Approach 336
Constant-Comparative Method 336
Content (Textual) Analysis 337
Conversation Analysis 337
Discourse Analysis 337
Interpretative Phenomenological Analysis 338
Qualitative Comparative Analysis 338
Issues in Analysis 338
What About Transcribing? 338
How to Know When You Are Finished 339
Philosophical Stance 340
Data Analysis With Computer Software 340
Other Issues 343
Summary 344
Check Yourself 344
Key Discussion Issues 345
Module 12a. From Coding to Concepts 345
Module 12b. Narrative Analysis 345
References 346
Student Study Site 348

Chapter 13. Communicating Your Ideas 349

Focus Your Reading 349
First Steps 351
Guidelines for Writing and Presenting Qualitative Research 352
Your Audience: What Does It Expect? 352
What Are You Trying to Say? 353
Against the Simplified and Mechanical 353
The First Person 354
General Guidelines for Writing 354
The Voices of Others 354
Writing With Others 355
The Use of Metaphors 356
Creative Nonfiction 358
Fiction 361
Structure—A Good Thing 362
Opening Section 362

Methods and Procedures 362
Profiles of Participants 363
Concepts and Supporting Evidence 363
Self-Reflection 363
Research Literature 364
Alternative Presentation Formats 364
Social Sciences and the Arts 364
Ethnographic and Autoethnographic Narratives 364
Photography 365
Ethnodrama 365
Poetry 365
Magazine 366
Subjective Maps and Children's Drawings 366
Performance Film 366
Alternative Writing Presentations 366
Student's Examples of Qualitative Writing 367
Disseminating Your Ideas and Learning From Others 369
Selected Journals 370
Online Open Access Journals—General and Specific 370
Online Subscription Journals—General and Specific 371
Other Avenues of Distribution 371
Publishers 372
Summary 372
Check Yourself 372
Key Discussion Issues 373
Module 13a. Simple Writing Task 373
Module 13b. Reinforcing Writing Ideas 374
References 374
Student Study Site 376

Chapter 14. Judging the Research Process and Product 377

Focus Your Reading 377
Personal Criteria 381
Researcher's Role: Revealing the Self-and-Other Connection 381
Convincing Arguments 382
What Was Studied 382
What Was Found 383
Rich in Detail: How the Study Was Done 384
Communication: How Convincing Is the Presentation? 384
What Others Have to Say 385
Criteria for Reviewing Traditional Quantitative Research Approaches 385
A Brief History 386
Prior to 1990 386

The 1990s 386
The Early 2000s 388
Current Thinking 391
Summary 394
Check Yourself 394
Key Discussion Issues 394
Module 14a. Compare Lincoln and Guba's Four Criteria 394
Module 14b. Learn How to Add Your Voice 395
References 395
Student Study Site 396

Epilogue: Social Science and the Future of Qualitative Research **397**
The Digital Age 398
Globalization, Political Activism, and Social Justice in Troubled Times 398
Communicating—The Written Word and Beyond 399
Change and Resistance 400
References 400

Glossary **403**

Index **409**

Preface

In the second decade of the new millennium, it is clear that many disciplines in the social sciences have accepted some types of qualitative research (QR) as a reasonable alternative or complement to quantitative research. Although QR (specifically ethnographic methods) had long been used by anthropologists as they studied distant cultures and some sociologists (especially the Chicago school) used field methods as they studied newly arrived immigrants to the United States, some philosophers relied on methods of phenomenology and hermeneutics to study the lived experiences of individuals. For the most part, prior to the 1990s or so, many social scientists approached the conduct of research in the same way as their colleagues in the natural sciences: through experimental designs and statistical analyses.

It is helpful to look at comments by the editors of the major books of readings in the field of QR. Denzin and Lincoln (2000) observed that over two decades (referring to the 1980s and early 1990s)

> a quiet methodological revolution had been occurring in the social sciences; a blurring of disciplinary boundaries was taking place. The social sciences and humanities were drawing closer together in a mutual focus on an interpretive, qualitative approach to research and theory. (p. ix)

Commenting about the 1990s, they remarked,

> The transformations in the field of qualitative research that were taking place in the early 1990s continued to gain momentum as the decade unfolded. By century's end, few looked back with skepticism on the narrative turn. . . . There is a pressing need to show how the practices of qualitative research can help change the world in positive ways. (p. x)

Just a short decade later, Denzin and Lincoln (2011) commented about the explosion and proliferation of interest in QR. No longer a quiet revolution, but perhaps not with such a lofty goal as changing the world, they suggested that we are in the "midst of a social movement of sorts, a new field of inquiry; a new discourse had arrived . . . and it flourished" (p. ix). No longer passive and neutral, they suggested that

> it is time to move forward . . . to find new ways of connecting persons and their personal troubles with social justice methodologies. We need to become better accomplished in linking these interventions to those institutional sites where troubles are turned into public issues and public issues transformed into social policy. (p. ix)

We have come a long way since these early days. In the 1980s, teaching about QR was truly a challenge. Few texts were available. Most journals did not publish research of a qualitative nature. Editors were unclear about appropriate criteria for evaluating the worth of QR. In the second decade of the 21st century, the challenge is different but just as great. Now there is a proliferation of materials. Some journals are specifically targeted at research of a qualitative nature. Some have reached compromises by combining elements of both quantitative and qualitative. The globalization of our world, the immediacy of information, the availability of technology, and the voices of those who in the past were silenced or dismissed have all opened up the field to a myriad of interpretations and perspectives about what QR is, what it should be, and how to teach it.

This brings me to my purpose in writing this new text. My goal is to provide a book that takes students on the journey to learn about QR, what its antecedents are, and how to conduct a QR study. Further, I take the position that the role of the researcher is critical in all aspects of QR. Accordingly, I emphasize reflexivity and self-disclosure. I cannot say enough about the importance of the role of the researcher. Listen to one blogger's comments:

> One of the most powerful graduate school experiences I had drove home the point that we all "see" the world through our own filters. . . . The precision with which the qualitative researcher identifies him or herself reveals several of the lenses and the degree of sensitivity with which the researcher may collect, view, analyze, and report the data. (AMF, 2011)

This researcher is aware that each decision throughout the research process is influenced by the researcher.

Recognizing that QR is not a single entity and that there is considerable disagreement about what constitutes good QR, I offer a balanced and nuanced approach that covers the range of viewpoints about the field. I also address the role of social media in the field, in particular, using social media as a tool to facilitate the research or as a venue to study. I grapple with the sticky parts of determining appropriate criteria for judging research as well as the ways Institutional Review Boards both facilitate and hinder researchers in the process.

I have taught QR methods for some thirty years to students from many disciplines—family therapy, business, communication, education, adult learning, early childhood, architecture, and psychology, among others. I have also taught quantitative research methods, including statistics, to these same students. I have been an early pioneer in using the computer for online teaching. Students know me as a good listener, accessible, and approachable. My own experience and training informs me as I write and teach, and I model behaviors in this text that are useful in the QR domain. I write in a user-friendly style, I reveal information about myself, and I explain my own thinking and why I believe a particular thing—all as part of the reflexive stance I mentioned. I have watched this field grow and change with the times—and I have changed along with it. I write in the first person and encourage students to write that way as well. I also include examples of alternative ways of presenting information, such as artistic expressions, film, or photovoice.

My experiences in the field of art—as a docent for twenty years, as a keen observer of art, as a student in the academic side of art, and recently as a student in the studio aspect of art—have led me to think outside the box, to appreciate the creative side of QR, and to question long-held assumptions about what constitutes good art (and good QR) and who is to be the judge.

QR is about the study of humans. It is not a single entity. It is many things to many people. I have organized this book so that students will be exposed to a variety of viewpoints. At the same time, I recognize that who I am and what my experiences are influence what I write and the positions I take. In that same way, who and what you are as an instructor influences how you teach QR and what you believe, and who and what students are will influence what they take away with them. Having an open mind is critical.

The Audience

I have written this text for advanced undergraduates or graduate students in a first course in QR. They can be in any discipline—health, education, psychology, family therapy, sociology, business, or communication. It is intended as a survey that covers the history and philosophy behind QR, research approaches, and various ways of gathering and analyzing data. It adopts a reflexive position and urges that students take risks as they plan, conduct their own research, and find ways to share with others what they have learned.

Structure of This Book

The book is divided into three parts. It is organized around a typical semester class. It can also be adapted for online teaching or compressed teaching.

In Part I, I consider the conceptual and historical context and major research approaches. I review foundational and historical concepts in Chapter 1. Since QR is inductive in nature, I want you to move from the particular to the general. I also introduce the issue of validity. In Chapter 2, I introduce the idea of becoming a reflexive qualitative researcher. I address ethical issues in Chapter 3. Chapters 4, 5, and 6 examine various QR approaches.

In Part II, I consider the QR process. Chapter 7 is about innovation and planning and conceptualizing a QR study. I offer various examples from those in the field who are doing innovative things. Chapter 8 deals with social media and the Internet. I consider reviewing the literature in Chapter 9. Chapter 10 focuses on qualitative interviewing. Chapter 11 addresses other methods of gathering data.

In Part III, I deal with the final product. In Chapter 12, I consider how to extract meaning from the data. Chapter 13 centers on the communication and presentation of ideas. Chapter 14 addresses judging the research process and product. The Epilogue considers the future.

Additional Features

- Focus Your Reading—an advance organizer designed to highlight the important and key points of the chapter
- Did You Know?—a relevant tidbit or fact related to ideas in the chapter
- Check Yourself—a section with key information related to the Focus Your Reading section

- Key Discussion Issues—questions to stimulate discussion relating to important topics in chapter
- Modules—activities for practicing and extending new ideas for each chapter
- References—citations for information in the chapter, including information in print and online
- Student Study Site—links to relevant readings for each chapter
- Glossary—key terms are highlighted and defined at the end of the book

Ancillary Materials

Instructor Teaching Site

A password-protected site, available at http://www.sagepub.com/lichtmanqrss, features resources that have been designed to help instructors plan and teach their courses. These resources include an extensive test bank, chapter-specific PowerPoint presentations, sample syllabi for semester and quarter courses, and links to SAGE journal articles.

Student Study Site

An open-access study site is available at http://www.sagepub.com/lichtmanqrss. This site includes eFlashcards and links to other resources.

Acknowledgments

A few short years ago, Diane McDaniel, my editor from SAGE, suggested to me that I expand my ideas that I had developed in my text *Qualitative Education in Research* to the larger field of the social sciences. I was just in the process of preparing my third edition of that text; I thought, why not? I had taught many students in various social science disciplines; many of the issues concerning QR were the same. I agreed that my ideas about QR could be broadened to the larger social science domain. It was her faith in me and her encouragement that stimulated me to produce this book. While competing interests of art, travel, opera, bridge, and exercise were pulling at me, I was drawn to thinking about QR and how I could communicate it to others. I am always up for the challenge and love learning new things. Thank you, Diane. You continue to challenge me to keep me up with new ideas and ways of doing things.

These last two years developing this text have been challenging and exciting. I have now completed my fourth art course—a second painting course almost cured me of trying to venture into something new. I felt so humbled trying to do something I knew so little about in actuality. I learned that reading and learning about something are very different from actually doing it. I kept these ideas in mind as I thought about how I would present information to you that might be unfamiliar or difficult. Thanks to John Erik Swanson from the Corcoran Gallery of Art, from whom I learned so much. I am reminded of Gopnik's (2011) account of how he learned to draw—"helplessness" and "despair" were terms he used.

To my students: Thanks to all my students, from whom I have learned so much. I think you have taught me as much as I taught you. We challenged each other to try something new, to think in ways that might be different, and to be mindful of others. While I am no longer in contact with most of you, I want to thank especially Judy Barokas, my dear friend, shining student, and colleague—you and your family have been in my life for so many years, and I value our times together and our shared experiences. And to Satomi Izumi Taylor—your caring and thoughtfulness and creativity are immeasurable. And thanks to Facebook and LinkedIn, I have heard from other students as well. I have not forgotten any of you.

To my colleagues: Writing is a lonely activity. No longer actively teaching, I need the stimulation of new ideas to keep me going. Thanks especially to Jim Bernauer from Robert Morris University in Pittsburgh, who is available to answer a question or bounce an idea off of. And thanks to some new colleagues: to Kip Jones, my Facebook friend from Bournemouth University in the UK—I continue to be excited by your novel ideas of QR and performative social science; to David Glassmeyer from the University of Northern Colorado—your ideas about technology are so forward-looking; to Laura Lorenz from the Heller school for social policy and management at Brandeis University—you introduced me to photovoice; to

Christine Brooks from the transpersonal psychology department at Sofia University in Palo Alto—you got me thinking about alternative ways of seeing QR. Thanks also to Valery Keibler, a doctoral student in instructional management and a graphic designer at Robert Morris University, who shared her journey of writing a dissertation proposal. Thanks to Gunter Mey and Katja Mruck from *Forum: Qualitative Social Research* (*FQS*) in Berlin—you are always in the forefront with new ideas. Thanks to Ron Chenail for sparking an idea about QR research almost thirty years ago and for maintaining such a presence in the QR community.

Thanks to all the professionals at SAGE and to Reid Hester and Sarita Sarak, who have undertaken to pick up this text as Diane moves up in the SAGE hierarchy. Thanks also to Megan Koraly, who worked with me earlier as the book developed. Thanks as well to Olivia Weber-Stenis. Thanks to the following peer reviewers who offered helpful suggestions and recommendations as this book developed: Duane L. Dobbert, Florida Gulf Coast University; Lillie M. Fears, Arkansas State University; Gesine Hearn, Idaho State University; John P. Bartkowski, University of Texas, San Antonio; Kebba Darboe, Minnesota State University; William "Ted" Donlan, Portland State University; Warren Hope, Florida A&M University; Jack M. Schultz, Concordia University; Heather Dillaway, Wayne State University; Helen Potts, University of North Texas; and Debra Scrandis, University of Maryland.

To family and friends: To my three children: To my eldest, Ellen—you are an amazing daughter who shows strength, resolve, and creativity, even when times are challenging; to my son, David—you are grounded, a rock, with an incredible sensitive streak in your heart; to my youngest, Judith—you are the sounding board I need, whether we are talking about cooking shows, design ideas, or just life. To my brother, Lee—you are brilliant, caring, and always there for me. To my sister-in-law, Claire—you are even-keeled, thoughtful, and sweet. To my daughter-in-law, Margaret—you are sensitive, smart, fashionable, and extremely thoughtful. To my son-in-law, Jim—you challenge me with your ideas about art, spirituality, and religion. To my grandson, Michael—you are reaching adulthood and learning about life and the world. To my granddaughter, Lilah—you are creative, smart, artistic, and have such a sweet nature. To all of you—the most important people in my life—your caring for me and belief in me and love keep me going on this journey of life and learning. To Marty's family—Jan, Ed, and Melanie—you are always part of my life.

To all my dear friends from various walks of life: to my Corcoran friends and the beach bums —you are the best. To my bridge buddies—you are always up for some good games. To my opera-loving and music-loving friends, to my exercise friends, and all my dear friends, both old and new—all of you help me keep a balance in my life.

And lastly, but still uppermost in my mind, to my dear husband, Marty Gerstein, gone now almost ten years—your spirit will be with me forever.

Marilyn

References

AMF. (2011, November 13). Qualitative methods: The role of the researcher. *Research Salad*. Retrieved from http://researchsalad.wordpress.com/2011/11/13/qualitative-methods-the-role-of-the-researcher/

Denzin, N., & Lincoln, Y. (Eds.). (2000). *Handbook of qualitative research*. Thousand Oaks, CA: SAGE.

Denzin, N., & Lincoln, Y. (Eds.). (2011). *The SAGE handbook of qualitative research*. Thousand Oaks, CA: SAGE.

Gopnik, A. (2011, June 27). Life studies: What I learned when I learned to draw. *The New Yorker*, p. 56.

About the Author

Marilyn Lichtman is a retired professor of educational research and evaluation from Virginia Tech at both the main campus in Blacksburg, Virginia, and at the graduate campus in Falls Church, Virginia. After attending the University of Chicago as an undergraduate, she moved to Washington, DC. She completed all her degrees at the George Washington University, receiving her doctorate in educational research. She taught both qualitative and quantitative research courses while at the Catholic University of America and Virginia Tech. Her students came from many social science disciplines. She is a regular user of the Internet and social media and was an early contributor to teaching qualitative courses online. She is currently on the editorial boards of *The Qualitative Report* and *FQS*, online journals devoted to qualitative issues. She has served as a consultant to many school systems, private companies, and government agencies. Currently, she serves on the docent council at the Corcoran Gallery of Art in Washington, DC. Expanding her interest in art, she has recently taken up painting and drawing at the Corcoran. She has traveled extensively throughout the world. Her SAGE text, *Qualitative Research in Education,* is now in its 3rd edition. Her edited book of readings, *Understanding and Evaluating Qualitative Educational Research*, was published by SAGE in 2011.

PART I

Conceptual and Historical Context

CHAPTER 1

Introduction

Focus Your Reading

- Many disciplines use qualitative research
- Some combine qualitative research and quantitative research
- Definitions
- Common elements
- Growth of qualitative research
- Comparisons between qualitative research and quantitative research
- Validity

It is the first week of the new semester, and you are inundated with things to do. If you are like many students, you are juggling numerous components of your life: your family, your work, and your education. You might have teenage children or aging parents, or you may just be out of undergraduate school. You might be taking one course in the evening, or you might be enrolled in an online course; you might be taking several courses. Your major could be psychology, business, social work, or nursing. Or you could be studying family therapy or political science. You might be working, or you might have taken some time off for your schooling. Whatever your circumstance, I hope you find that the study of **qualitative research** (QR) will open your eyes to new ways of asking and answering questions about the world in which you live.

This is a particularly exciting time to study QR. As a way to explore human behavior, QR is being used in many innovative ways. Researchers take advantage of access to news events as they are happening and as they become available through YouTube or Facebook. Others use technology, such as smartphones or tablets, as an alternative way of collecting **data**. New ideas for what to study and how to study appear almost daily.

QR is the perfect approach to use if you want to learn more about human interaction. By the time you have completed this QR book, you will be well on the way to answering many questions about human beings. I was with a friend last week, and she asked me, "What is qualitative research?" I tried to give her a simple answer by turning the question back on her. I knew that she had been a teacher of children. We talked about different kinds of questions we might ask about children, schooling, and learning. I provided a simple scenario: Suppose she was interested in determining a way to teach reading that might lead to greater proficiency. Suppose one group of kids was taught the sounds of letters while another group was asked to memorize simple words. Then all the kids were given a reading test. Which group did better? You could compare the test scores of each group to answer that question.

Let me be clear: This example is about traditional experimental or quantitative research (QN). It is a simplified example designed to illustrate how many people think about research: two groups, two ways of teaching reading, and test scores. This type of research is the foundation of QN. It is basically very simple: An experiment is designed that involves one group that receives a treatment (a drug or, in this case, a particular reading program). The other group does not receive the treatment. The question is asked, how does the treatment affect the outcome? In this example, the outcome is test scores. If those who received the particular reading program have higher test scores than those who received a different program, a researcher might conclude that it was the treatment (or program) that caused the scores to be higher. This is the foundation of experimental research, albeit a very simplified illustration. It involves variables, treatment, and hypothesis testing.

Qualitative researchers address different kinds of questions. They go about answering them in different ways. They do not deal with variables, treatment, or hypothesis testing. For the moment, let's stay with an educational setting. Gray (n.d.) studied a Saskatoon English language arts teacher to understand how he provided instruction. The researcher did not collect any test scores. Gray spent time in the teacher's classroom and described it in detail in her study. It is fascinating to read this qualitative study, which reports her findings in a **narrative style**. You can see, then, that QR is of a different nature than QN.

Qualitative Research Is Used in Many Disciplines

It is safe to say that in 2013, QR as a way to answer questions is no longer a new idea. While various fields accept or value QR to a greater or lesser extent, it is clear that QR is not the stepchild that it was in the last millennium. Whether in journalism, urban studies, social work, or behavioral sciences, QR is used and will continue to be used by researchers. Brinkmann (2011), in his keynote address to the 17th Qualitative Health Research Conference in Vancouver, BC, stated that within the last two decades, QR has become generally accepted as a legitimate **scientific** way of working. Birkinshaw, Brannen, and Tung (2011) introduced a special issue of the *Journal of International Business* by suggesting that QR can "reclaim its position as an integral part of international business research" (p. 573). A call for "a day in qualitative psychology" at a preconference event at the 8th International Congress on Qualitative Inquiry, held in May 2012, acknowledged the concern by some psychologists (e.g., Benozzo from Italy, Brinkmann from Denmark, Puebla from Mexico, and Geignani from the United States) that psychology has, by and large, remained outside the wave of QR. These psychologists urged that others come together to reflect on the status of QR in psychology in the twenty-first century.

The above ideas are relatively recent. But things were brewing in 1994, in the health field, for example. Black's (1994) editorial in the *Journal of Epidemiology & Community Health* concluded,

> More frequent use of qualitative methods will greatly enhance both aetiological and health services research. Failure to use them more has retarded the advance in medical knowledge and at times led to false trails being followed. This has partly arisen because of skepticism on the part of quantitative scientists about the objectivity and rigor of qualitative methods. While this view may be justified occasionally, it is not a valid reason for ignoring the potential use of qualitative methods. As the statistician J. W. Tukey pointed out, 'far better an approximate answer to the right question . . . than an exact answer to the wrong question.' If such advice is ignored we run the risk of pursuing the measurable rather than the relevant. This would have serious consequences for our understanding both of the causes of diseases and how to improve health services. (p. 426)

Initially, the social sciences in U.S. universities adopted **research methods** drawn from the natural sciences. (It was not the case with **anthropology** or some branches of sociology, however.) There are several reasons for this. The natural sciences were of a higher status than the social sciences; ergo, if the social sciences used methods that those in the natural sciences did, that elite status might rub off on them. Another reason is that, with few exceptions, the departments were dominated by White men. In these early days, the voices of women and people of color were not heard. Accordingly, issues related to feminism or power disparities were not considered. It was the academy of European universities that dominated the development of thinking as colleges and universities developed in the U.S. But as I mentioned in the Preface, by the 1980s, various social science disciplines began to consider QR methods. Growth over the last thirty years and into the new millennium has been steady and pervasive.

Did You Know

In the painting academy in France, there was also a hierarchy in painting, just as in research. The highest forms of painting were considered historical, religious, or mythological. Next came portraits. Landscapes and genre paintings followed. The lowest form of painting was the still life. You guessed it—views were dictated and dominated by White European men.

Today, you can find numerous examples of QR studies across the social sciences. Here are just a few I culled from various publications: Dawson and Hjorth (2012) used **narrative analysis** in their study of the succession process in a family business. White and Green (2011) used **case study** research to explore how social networks influence young people's access to employment and training. Lugosi et al. (2010) relied on **participant observation** and semi-structured interviews to explore hospitality and culture in bars in dilapidated buildings in Budapest. Their article is enhanced with wonderful visuals of some of the venues. You should get a chuckle out of the furniture constructed from reclaimed bathtubs. Matusik and Mickel (2011) employed a **grounded theory** approach in their study of users' experiences with connective technology. They briefly described the features of grounded theory. Their study used a traditional approach to data analysis and used a technique taken from traditional research: inter-coder reliability. For an alternative look at how grounded theory can be used, you can read stories of medical professionals and new technologies (Korica & Molloy, 2010). We learn about host-country nationals working in American companies in Romania from Caprar's (2011) ethnographic research. Although the prevailing wisdom is that we can understand this group based on knowledge of the local culture, Caprar's work illustrates that these workers are not always interchangeable with locals. He suggests that we need a more sophisticated view of culture. It is through an ethnographic eye (one type of QR) that we gain such insight. In Chapter 5, I explain case study, grounded theory, and other **research approaches**. Subsequently, I will discuss techniques qualitative researchers can use to gather data.

Some researchers face special challenges in developing their designs. Ozturk's (2011) study employed open-ended, unstructured, and probing interviews to study the sensitive topic of workplace discrimination in Turkey based on sexual orientation. As he dealt with an atypical population, he was faced with the problem of how to identify people for his study. He used a technique called **snowball sampling**. I will discuss this technique, as well as other ways to identify **participants** for a study, in Chapter 10. Elsbach (2009) studied creative workers who developed toy cars. What better than to use qualitative methods? Her engaging style makes for an interesting read, although I wish she had included some visuals. Manghani (2009) was interested in the topic of love messaging. He studied mobile phone messaging or *txting* through Japanese tanka poetry. Given the unusual nature of the problem, he was faced with a unique challenge. Rather than using a specific research technique, his research is informed by a philosophical postmodern viewpoint associated with QR. These are just a few of the numerous examples of the use of QR techniques in various disciplines published after 2000.

■ Quantitative or Qualitative?

A number of disciplines have considered whether QR is a viable alternative to QN and in what ways. In the field of comparative politics, we learn from Mahoney (2007b) that beginning in the 1990s, there was a wave of publications of a qualitative nature. Reporting from Sydney, Fitzpatrick (2011) commented that in the field of suicidology, there was tension between qualitative and quantitative approaches and that a growing number of researchers advocated for greater use of qualitative methods in the field. As with many fields, this first wave employed qualitative methodology as a kind of last resort. However, Mahoney (2007b) further asserted that more recently, the advantages of QR have been accepted. "Students of comparative politics frequently turn to qualitative methods instead of or in *combination* with alternative techniques because they believe that qualitative methods are essential for addressing many substantive questions of interest" (p. 122).

Mahoney (2007a) used data from QR as a counterpoint to Munck and Snyder's (2007a, 2007b) work on the state of comparative politics. Munck and Snyder relied on large samples and data-driven research—basically, QN. In contrast, Mahoney used QR methodology. In his article, Mahoney described a system in which he identified relevant journals and articles and coded them as to research type. I was surprised to read, "I would caution that readers not jump to the conclusion that qualitative research dominates even the subfield journals, especially when we take into consideration issues of prestige among these journals (2007a, p. 34). He continued that "the most prestigious journals publish almost entirely quantitative work, while *Comparative Politics* publishes mostly qualitative articles" (2007a, p. 35). You might find the article interesting as well as Mahoney and Goertz's (2006) article that contrasted the two types of research.

How Are Qualitative and Quantitative Research Complementary?

Within the past few years, a number of researchers have moved toward combining QR and QN approaches. Some say yes—it is reasonable to include both in the same study. As Mahoney (2007a) suggested, a recent trend in the field is to combine QN and QR approaches. This combination has become known as **mixed-methods research**. Nielsen, Randall, and Christensen (2010) did just that in their study. Their work strongly emphasized the quantitative nature of the design and, in fact, relied on a highly structured observational study. In a study of gentrification-induced displacement among social services, de Verteuil (2011) used longitudinal numerical analysis and qualitative interviews in a multisite case study. Creswell (2011) and Teddlie and Tashakkori (2011)—all proponents of mixed-methods research—write about some controversies. In my experience, those who combine QN and QR often emphasize QN and briefly mention QR, almost as an afterthought. This is less true today than previously. I explore this idea in greater depth in Chapter 6.

While acknowledging that mixed-methods social research is acceptable, Howe (2011) investigated the relationship of mixed methods and conceptions of causation. He developed the idea that there are two kinds of causes: intentional and natural. He suggested that *intentional causation* is related to QR, while *natural causation* is related to traditions rooted in experimental research.

Westerman and Yanchar (2011) take us on an unusual pathway. They ask us to consider how quantitative methods can contribute to interpretive inquiry in psychology. In fact, the April 2011 issue of *Theory & Psychology* is devoted to this topic. The special issue addresses a number of dimensions. One is how QR can be informed by quantitative methodology. Morawski (2011) observed that the field of psychology currently asks for a détente rather than continued antagonism and warfare about which approach is better (p. 260). Other topics covered in this special issue have to do with **conversation analysis** (Westerman, 2011) and theoretical foundations of **subjectivity** (Højgaard & Søndergaard, 2011).

Brito, Ribeiro, and Machado (2011) concluded that "the best decision for the beginning researcher [in education] is indicated as joining four principles: balance, knowledge of the multiple facets of reality, ability in articulation and discernment before the plurality of options." A sociologist, Patel (2011), argued that the old debates about the merits of either qualitative or quantitative approaches have been superseded by "the evolution of a creative, interdisciplinary combination of both qualitative and quantitative approaches" (abstract). Feminists also weighed in on the topic. Westmarland (2001) concluded that there is no need for the dichotomy between the two approaches.

In addition to looking at published research, I explore views offered by bloggers. From Marta, a blogger in geography, we have the view that a particular method that is better or produces more desirable results is outdated and antiquated. Marta (2011) stated, "I hope that my generation of geographers can move past this outdated and rather pointless debate." From Mumbai, India, Bachwani-Paritosh (2011) has been posting a very interesting blog. A recent post addresses the need for unisex bathrooms on airplanes. Carr's (2011) blog is very interactive. He speaks about his thoughts on global change from a qualitative perspective. McGuire's (2011) blog is posted from New Zealand. In a post from September 2011, he sends you to some qualitative journals he discovered.

■ What Is Qualitative Research?

I have used the term *qualitative research* in a number of places already. In fact, the book's title uses the term. Do you know what it means? Let's try a simple activity. Before you read further, complete this sentence: "Qualitative research is . . . "

If you do this in a face-to-face class or an online class, you can share your responses with others. If you do it in the quiet of your home or office, you can look online as to what others have said.

Below, I provide definitions of QR offered by prominent authors in the field and those I found in my online search using three search engines.

Some definitions are very general, while others are specific. Some are associated with a particular discipline; others are more general. I organize these definitions along two dimensions: level of specificity and discipline. Here are some examples:

Level of Specificity—General, Specific, or Somewhere in Between

A standard reference book is *The SAGE handbook of qualitative research.* Edited by Denzin and Lincoln (2011), this book draws from numerous authors in the field. Here is their definition:

> Qualitative research is a situated activity that locates the observer in the world. Qualitative research consists of a set of interpretive, material practices that make the world visible. . . . This means that qualitative researchers study things in their natural settings, attempting to make sense of or interpret phenomena in terms of the meanings people bring to them. (Denzin & Lincoln, 2011, p. 3)

I have to admit that the definition seems somewhat cumbersome to me. The phrase "situated activity" seems obtuse.

Another widely used source of information about QR comes from the work of John Creswell, one of the early writers in the field. I take this definition from his book (2007) on the topic.

> Qualitative research begins with assumptions, a worldview, the possible use of a theoretical lens, and the study of research problems inquiring into the meaning individuals or groups ascribe to a social or human problem. To study this problem, qualitative researchers use an emerging qualitative approach to inquiry, the collection of data in a natural setting sensitive to the people and places under study, and data analysis that is inductive and establishes patterns or themes. The final written report or presentation includes the voices of participants, the reflexivity of the researcher, and a complex description and interpretation of the problem, and it extends the literature or signals a call for action. (Creswell, 2007, p. 37)

This definition seems unduly long, although it contains many important components.

Berg and Lune (2011) stated that "qualitative research properly seeks answers to questions by examining various social settings and the individuals who inhabit these settings." They continued: "[qualitative researchers are] most interested in how humans arrange themselves and their settings and how inhabitants of these settings made sense of their surroundings through symbols, rituals, social structures, social roles, and so forth" (p. 8). In my view, this definition is quite limiting in its focus on a study of culture. Of course, some QR does look at culture through the lens of an ethnographer. But much of it takes a very different approach.

According to Anderson (2012), in her review of Yin's book on QR, QR offers multiple interpretations of the human events studied and considerable methodological variation.

I also consulted the web. I conducted a search using three search engines: Google, Bing, and DuckDuckGo. I searched for the term "qualitative research definition 2011." I looked at ten screens each for Google and Bing. DuckDuckGo adds new sites immediately, so it is not easy to tell how many you have looked at. I was surprised at the little overlap I found. I found some links on Bing that I had not seen on Google. Similarly, I found some on DuckDuckGo that were not on either of the other two. Here are some definitions that I found:

> Qualitative research is not simply the collecting of statistics, but focuses on reasoning and cultural and social factors, which are researched and then analysed. (MediaDictionary, 2011)
>
> Qualitative research is based on finding the opinions and attitudes of respondents rather than any scientifically measurable data. (Glossary of Marketing, 2011)
>
> Qualitative researchers aim to gather an in-depth understanding of human behavior and the reasons that govern such behavior. (Wikipedia, 2011)
>
> Research that aims to understand the phenomenon of what is experienced by research subjects such as attitudes, perceptions, motivations, actions, etc., holistically, and by way of description in the form of words and language, in a particular context that naturally and by utilizing a variety of natural methods. (Deniborin, 2010)

> Quantitative research involves the analysis and interpretation of numerical data, while qualitative research involves the analysis and interpretation of observational data. (Hamilton, 2011)

As you can see, many of the definitions I located on the Internet are very brief and somewhat incomplete.

Specific Discipline

I also decided to expand my search by examining specific disciplines.

From the nursing field:

> Qualitative research is a type of scientific research which has its roots in philosophy and human sciences. (Nursing Planet, 2011)

From information systems:

> Qualitative research involves the use of qualitative data, such as interviews, documents, and participant observation data, to understand and explain social phenomena. In Information Systems, there has been a general shift . . . away from technological to managerial and organizational issues, hence an increasing interest in the application of qualitative research methods. (Myers, 2011)

From education:

> Research providing detailed narrative descriptions and explanations of phenomena investigated, with lesser emphasis given to numerical quantifications—methods used to collect qualitative data include ethnographic practices such as observing and interviewing. (Education.com, 2011)

> It is a way of knowing in which a researcher gathers, organizes, and interprets information obtained from humans using his or her eyes and ears as filters. It often involves in-depth interviews and/or observations of humans in natural and social settings. It can be contrasted with quantitative research, which relies heavily on hypothesis testing, cause and effect, and statistical analyses. (Lichtman, 2013, p. 6)

From business:

> Qualitative researchers study things in their natural settings attempting to make sense of, or interpret, phenomena in terms of the meanings people bring to them. (Asian Societies, 2011)

From the law:

> Qualitative research is a subjective form of research relying on the analysis of controlled observations of the researcher. (U.S. Legal, 2011)

From finance:

> A type of market research, especially in the form of interviews or group discussions, that aims to find out people's attitudes or opinions about something, where the results cannot be shown in numbers. (Financial Times Lexicon, 2011)

From social work:

> Qualitative research is referred to by a variety of terms, reflecting several research approaches. Field research is often used interchangeably with qualitative research to describe systematic observations of social behavior with no preconceived hypotheses to be tested (Rubin & Babbie, 1993). . . . Qualitative research is also referred to as naturalistic research (Greenhalgh & Taylor, 1997) or inquiry into everyday living. (McRoy, n.d.)

From psychology:

> Hawes (n.d.) created an online qualitative research resources page. She includes a number of MegaSites with links and brief descriptions. In addition to this site, there are links to bibliographies, creating manuscripts, institutions, journals, methodology, social science, and software.

From speech and language:

> Specifically, qualitative methods can be used "to understand the complexity of social phenomena through a set of systematic and interpretive practices designed to seek answers to questions that stress how social actions and social experiences are created and sustained" (Damico & Ball, 2010, p. 15). In other words, they can be used to situate the communicative lives of the children and the adults whom we serve in social and cultural contexts. (Hammer, 2011)

After completing this task, I found myself in a position similar to how I might feel if I had collected a lot of data through interviews. How could I organize what I had and come up with something meaningful? One way to do this is to look for common elements or **themes**.

■ A Working Definition

I have uncovered a wealth of information. In the definitions above, I identified some common elements. A number of researchers consider what is studied—human, cultural, or social interactions or behaviors. Another key element is that the settings are naturally occurring. The

role of the researcher in interpreting and generating meaning from the data is also important. The type of data collected is another key element.

Here is my working definition:

> QR is a way to study the social interactions of humans in naturally occurring situations. The researcher plays a critical role in the process by gathering data and making sense of or interpreting the phenomena that are observed and revealed.

What Makes Research Qualitative?

Moving from my definition, I am now able to determine what kinds of questions QR might answer. One type involves humans and their interactions. Think about the elderly woman who is going through beginning stages of Alzheimer's. What is she feeling? How does this affect her life and those around her? Or imagine a case worker's struggle in a new agency with clients who are disruptive or noncompliant. How does a new program the agency has put into place support this case worker's efforts? An organization discovers considerable unrest during downsizing. How does the cultural climate facilitate transitioning? Groups foment uprisings and are filmed on YouTube. How do these individuals react during tumultuous times? These kinds of questions focus on individuals or groups and the worlds in which they live and work. These are some of the types of questions to which QR is especially suited.

Another aspect of QR is that individuals are studied in their natural settings. The elderly woman, the agency, the organization, or the groups—all would be studied as they are, whether in their own homes, at a clinic, in a business, or online. Individuals would not be studied in a setting that was part of an experiment.

The researcher's role is critical in QR. It is the researcher who gathers and organizes data. It is the researcher who makes meaning from the data, who interprets the data, and ultimately who makes the world visible to others (Denzin & Lincoln, 2011, p. 3). Further, the **reflective researcher** acknowledges the role he or she plays and is reflective about that role. As such, then, the researcher's stance moves from one of objectivity to one of subjectivity.

Overview of Common Elements

I think you might find it helpful if I review some of the common elements that are often associated with various ways of doing QR.

- Its purpose is to understand and interpret the meaning of human interaction and social phenomena. This is in contrast to QN, which involves hypothesis testing and generalization.
- It considers questions that involve the *what* and *why* of human behavior. This is in contrast to those involving results.
- It is a study of humans in natural settings. This is in contrast to QN, which occurs in a laboratory, involves experiments, or surveys large groups of people.
- Its method is dynamic and fluid. As such, details of the collection and analysis of the data often evolve as the research progresses. This is in contrast to an advanced and detailed plan of research.

- It involves inductive thinking—movement from the specific to the general. This is in contrast to QN, which moves from the general to the specific.
- It looks at the whole of a situation rather than specifics. This is in contrast to the isolation and manipulation of variables.
- The role of the researcher is critical. It is through the researcher's eyes and ears that data are collected and analyzed. The researcher often takes a reflective stance. This is in contrast to a researcher's role of objectivity.
- Reality is constructed by the researcher. As such, there is not a single interpretation of reality but multiple interpretations. This is in contrast to the identification of an objective reality.
- It uses in-depth study, often of a small number of individuals or settings. It goes deep rather than broad. This is in contrast to studying large numbers.
- It involves a search for themes or a narrative story. Data are usually presented as words and/or pictures. This is in contrast to statistical analysis and tables.
- It encourages the author's voice in the context. This is in contrast to staying removed from the system (Bansal & Corley, 2011).
- It encourages presentation of findings in alternative styles. This is in contrast to a fixed method of presentation of results.

Additional Components

In my working definition, I included three critical components: study of human/social interaction; natural settings; and the researcher's role. You might also consider some additional components related to QR.

As you read and learn about the field, you will come to see that QR is not a single thing; however, we use the term as though it is. In fact, the term can be seen as an umbrella under which many ways of asking and answering questions can be used. This causes much confusion for those new to the field and also for those who have practiced it a long time. My emphasis in this book is to inform you about current practices and meanings. I caution you to check the dates of the journal articles and books you read, since viewpoints that were prevalent just a few years ago may no longer be in the mainstream now.

Qualitative researchers may be guided by a particular research approach. You might have read about an ethnographic approach. Borrowing from anthropology, ethnographers study the culture of an organization, a group, a community, or a religion. Or you may have encountered **phenomenology**. These researchers are interested in lived experiences of individuals. Some of the approaches have explicit processes and guidelines; others are somewhat general. In later chapters, I will talk in greater detail about various research approaches.

Whatever research approach is followed or whether a generic approach is used, the qualitative researcher gathers information from those studied. The most common ways to gather information are through interviews or observations. In later chapters, I will discuss these ways of gathering data, along with many others.

Another way to think about QR is based on the perspective and viewpoint of the researcher. Does the researcher support a **feminist** perspective, where issues of power and representation are considered? Is the researcher an activist, where issues of social change and politics are involved? Does the researcher take a **critical theorist** viewpoint? Does the researcher adopt a pragmatic approach in which both qualitative and quantitative data are collected and used to answer questions?

Yet another way is to think about a group you intend to study. Are you interested in studying workers, those who are planning to retire, or elite athletes? Do you want to know more about children who live in rural areas or who have recently moved from rural to urban areas?

It is also helpful to examine what is *not* included in QR. It does not involve hypothesis testing, experiments, or statistical data. It is not useful for generalizing from samples to populations. It does not assume that the researcher remains objective. It does not involve independent or dependent variables—in fact, it does not involve variables at all.

■ The Growth of Qualitative Research

QR (specifically **ethnographic methods**) had long been used by anthropologists as they studied distant cultures. Some sociologists (especially the Chicago school) used **field methods** as they studied newly arriving immigrants to the United States. Some philosophers relied on methods of phenomenology and **hermeneutics** to study the lived experiences of individuals. But there was little cross-fertilization among these disciplines.

One field in which there is a considerable amount of human interaction is the field of education. Groups of individuals come together regularly to attend school. For many years, educators relied on the methods of the natural sciences as they studied education. Many experiments were conducted, data were collected using test scores, and hypotheses were tested.

It was toward the middle of the 1980s that educators ventured into the realm of QR. Most adopted ethnographic methods from anthropology for the study of schools and classrooms. In fact, *Qualitative Research for Education* (Bogdan & Biklen, 1992) centered on ethnographic methods. The nursing profession found that grounded theory and phenomenology were useful in answering some of the questions in their field. In the 1990s, other social science disciplines experimented with using various **QR approaches**.

I vividly recall the **paradigm wars** of the 1980s (Gage, 1989). This was basically a fight against **positivism**. It was the **positivists** (the QN group) (and later, the **post-positivists**) who were being challenged by the **constructivists** or **interpretists**. This latter group represented QR. The issue related to **ontology** and **epistemology**—what is the nature of reality and how do we know it? The constructivists (many in the qualitative camp) believed that reality was constructed by the researcher and known through the researcher's lens. On the other hand, the positivists/post-positivists (mostly quantitative researchers) believed that there is an objective reality (or an approximation of that reality) out there, and researchers can know it by designing a study in such a way as to determine it. It seemed to me that you were in either one camp or the other. For me, I had to rethink my entire framework of what research was and how it was done. No longer were statistics and experimental research the best or only way to do things. Perhaps there were other ways to think about conducting research. In Chapter 7, Christine Brooks writes about her own orientation from a humanities viewpoint. For her, the qualitative-quantitative dichotomy was outside her frame of reference.

For many researchers who were trained as quantitative researchers, it was difficult to let go of the deeply held assumptions (whether explicit or implied) of what constituted good research. One solution was to aspire toward **triangulation**. A term taken from surveying, triangulation is a way to locate a point from the angles of three known points. In research, it came to be applied by using three known sources of data to verify or make credible data from a single source. Denzin (2010) described it as an "emerging fad" (p. 419) in the social sciences in these early times. But some traditional qualitative researchers (especially those applying mixed methods) use this concept.

During the 1980s and 1990s, critical theorists and **feminist researchers** struggled to acquire power for those who had been left out of the dialog and discussion (e.g., women, people of color, gays, and the poor). These newly emerging voices had a powerful impact on what was happening in the QR community.

Teddlie and Tashakkori (2003) expanded the discussion to include two additional conflicts. They suggested that between 1990 and 2005 there were conflicts among post-positivists, constructivists, and critical theorists. In essence, they added critical theorists into the mix. I would also add **postmodernism** to this latter group. Critical theorists and **postmodernists** are concerned with the role of the researcher to a greater extent than others. In the humanities and the art world, **critical theory** is also an important topic. Witham and Bensimon (2012) discussed how contemporary (post-2000) teachers use different critical theories to interpret literature and art.

Before I get too far in my discussion, let me provide you with some simple definitions. A positivist believes that there is an objective reality that can be known (the ontology) by the researcher. A post-positivist believes that there is an approximation of an objective reality that can be known by the researcher. In both cases, the researcher's role is to remain objective so as not to influence that reality. A constructivist or interpretist, on the other hand, believes that a reality is constructed by the researcher, and because of that, the researcher's role is critical in such construction. Critical theorists and postmodernists derive their stance from several intellectual movements.[1] Critical theorists are concerned with a critique of culture and society. One idea associated with critical theorists is that they should improve the understanding of society. A postmodern critical theorist is concerned with the crisis of representation and rejects the idea of objectivity that positivists and post-positivists had. The role of the researcher is especially critical, then, as a researcher reflects about the politics of the research. Lindlof and Taylor (2011) speak of the embodied, collaborative, dialogic, and improvisational aspect of QR.

According to Teddlie and Tashakkori (2003), we are currently engaged in a third war—that between those who believe in **evidence-based** work and those who accept a mixed-methods, interpretive, or critical theory[2] viewpoint. I see a conflict between several groups: those who believe in the **gold standard** of research; those who adopt many varied and wide-ranging alternative qualitative approaches; and those who compromise with a mixed-methods pragmatic approach to conducting research. For me, these three ideas (evidence based, gold standard, and scientific) represent the same thing: a return to objectivity with little regard for the role of the researcher or the need to be inclusive and expand our dialog. Denzin (2010) urged that we extend the call for paradigm expansion and that we move toward a spirit of cooperation (p. 421). I agree with him. I recognize that these arguments are a little difficult to understand, but they will become clearer as you learn more about the field.

Because there are different views of what constitutes good research, there are different expectations of various aspects of the research process. I will address some of these later, when I talk about the role of the researcher, the need for **reflexivity**, alternative forms of research presentation, and how data are collected and analyzed. What is clear to me, however, is that QR (in various forms) now plays a major role in the conduct of research in the social sciences.

■ Why Qualitative Research?

Packer (2011), in his thoughtful treatise on the science of QR, asked that we focus on why we should conduct QR. Although he might be overstating its impact somewhat, he suggested that "qualitative research has the potential to change our attitude of domination because it is sensitive to human forms of life in a way that traditional research cannot be" (location 203). Packer sees QR as a new way of conceptualizing social inquiry.

We should listen to Packer, as he reminded us that looking for objective observations about humans is not the same as studying humans as beings who live in a particular cultural and historical setting. He continued that it is not that objectivity is abandoned in favor of relativism. Rather, such a science would adopt a moral and epistemological pluralism. In a review of Michelangelo Antonioni's trilogy of films from the early 1960s (*L'Avventura, La Notte*, and *L'Eclisse*), Gariff (2012) compares Antonioni and Jackson Pollock. He concludes, "They opened the door for others to work in a more subjective and abstract manner and taught all of us new ways to see and understand art, ourselves, and the world in which we live" (p. 10). I contend that QR is moving in just this direction.

So, on a practical level, we conduct QR to answer certain kinds of questions that can better be answered in this way. On a political or moral level, we conduct QR to foster social change not through violence but ultimately by changing who we are.

Hopper (2011) suggested that by using QR, we can see how general forces affect specific circumstances. A more important point that he makes, I think, is that we ask questions that can't easily be studied using numbers. As I clarified in my working definition, QR focuses on the nature of social reality.

■ Comparing Qualitative and Quantitative Research

You should not be surprised that there have been various comparisons made between the two ways to do research. At the surface level, it should be apparent to you that quantitative researchers rely on numbers, while qualitative researchers use words and visuals. Accordingly, if you have numerical data, you can use statistics to test hypotheses. If you have words or visuals, you tend to interpret the data either by searching for common themes or by telling narratives. You may have read about qualitative researchers who choose to take their data and place it into categories and then report frequencies of occurrences of particular elements. However, this type of comparison is one that is at the direct and obvious level. I think it results in superficial interpretation of the data. I like Mitchell's (2011) straightforward approach.

> The issue of qualitative versus quantitative methods is rooted first and foremost in the character of the phenomena investigated and not in an investigator's methodological preferences. If the phenomenon under investigation is non-quantitative, then it cannot be studied successfully by attempting to use quantitative methods because trying to impose quantitative concepts upon qualitative phenomena misrepresents them. (p. 139)

Another way you can think about comparing the two types is to develop a list of elements and then compare those for qualitative elements, for quantitative elements, or for a combination of the two. Neill (2007) offered such a comparison. Although Neill's work is dated 2007, it reflected thinking from earlier times. Siegle's (n.d.) table is somewhat broader and informative. It compares two types of paradigms: positivist (quantitative) and naturalist (qualitative). One more table might help you see how comparisons between QR and QN are made. The International School of Prague's (2010) psychology course in qualitative theory and practice compared a positivist paradigm with a phenomenological paradigm.

Here is my example:

Table 1.1 Comparison of Qualitative and Quantitative Methods of Research

Element	*Qualitative*	*Quantitative*
Purpose of research	Describe and understand human and social phenomena	Test hypotheses; provide descriptive information
Types of research questions	Why and what	How many and who
Assumptions about the world	Subjective interpretation	Objective reality
Setting	Natural	Experimental; laboratory
Role of researcher	Key role; reflective	Outside of the system; neutral
Size of group studied	Tends to be smaller; nonrandom	Tends to be larger; randomly selected
Selection of group	Purposeful sampling; snowball sampling; volunteers	Random or stratified sampling
Variables	Study of the whole rather than specific variables	A few variables studied; some manipulated; some controlled
Type of data collected	Interview; observational; visual	Outcomes; scores
Type of analysis	Thematic or narrative	Statistical
Presentation format	Experimental format—may include alternatives such as performance	Traditional format

NOTE: Table omits mixed methods.

Theoretical and Philosophical Foundations of Qualitative Research

Since *qualitative research* is a general term with many meanings, I cannot directly state what its theoretical and philosophical foundations are. QR is not designed to test theory. It moves from an inductive approach rather than deductive. Its goal is to understand the *why* of individuals in a social world. However, one tradition associated with QR—grounded theory—is designed to generate theory from the data. In practice, the theories that emerge are rather weak. Robin (2011) describes how theory and concepts can be integrated and woven into the literature at the conclusion of a qualitative study.

Some approaches to QR have a philosophical base. For example, phenomenology is based in theories developed by Husserl. I will say more about this in Chapter 5. Other ways of conceptualizing QR are theoretical in nature. For example, we can think of a **feminist theory** or a postmodern theory of research. These are discussed in Chapter 6.

We can learn again from the writings of Packer (2011). He provided in-depth discussions of emancipatory research from the viewpoint of Habermas. He also developed information about Bourdieu's reflexive sociology. Most important, he elucidated the work of Foucault, whom he calls the hero of his text. I leave you with Foucault's three central questions as espoused by Packer: How are we constituted as **subjects** of our own knowledge? How are we constituted as subjects who exercise or submit to power relations? How are we constituted as moral subjects of our own actions? (location 412).

What About Validity?

Validity is a topic about which so much has been written, and that causes much confusion. As times and conceptions have changed, so too have ways in which validity has been addressed. We can think about judging or evaluating and criteria for doing so. I talk about this topic extensively in Chapter 14.

Validity. How can I know that this research is any good, or how can I believe it, or how can I trust it? From the time QR began to take hold in the 1980s or so, this question has been raised. Traditionally, the internal validity of a **research design** could be accomplished by designing an experiment and controlling for various factors that might affect the study. For example, if I administer a particular drug to control blood pressure, I would want to make sure that I took into consideration other things that might affect blood pressure (such as changes in diet or exercise). If I had a true experimental design, then I could say my study had *internal validity* if I controlled for these other variables.

Now, another part of validity has to do with whether I can say that the results could be applied to other situations than my own. This type of validity is called *external validity*. In traditional research, a design is said to have external validity if the sample on which it is done is random. In my example about drugs and blood pressure, I would need to make sure that I didn't select a group that was biased in some way.

Other factors also affect validity of the study. These include objectivity of the researcher, reliability of how variables are measured, and so on.

Initially, some qualitative researchers tried to be responsive to these concerns. They recognized that their designs would not have the controls that traditional designs had. For example, researchers were part of the system and so, by design, not objective. Variables were not controlled; in fact, most QR did not consider separate variables but looked at things as a whole. Initial responses were to develop parallel criteria to account for validity. This group of individuals came from a perspective called *post-positivism*. A post-positivist recognized some limitations of positivism but tried to design studies as close to this viewpoint as possible. Another group of researchers took a different position. They can loosely be grouped into the category *postmodernism*. For the latter group, adopting criteria that were parallel to those of traditional researchers did not make sense. Their research—in fact, their worldview—was fundamentally different from the **traditionalists**, and so the criteria were inappropriate.

Personally, I lived through this time period. My own background and training was in experimental design and statistics. I thought I knew which designs were the best. I knew how to control for extraneous variables. So did all of my colleagues. But QR had arrived. Some of us came to it via eye-opening experiences about how QN might not be suitable for answering all questions we had. For me, as I studied family therapy, I came to see that alternatives to experiments and statistics were needed; but that is another story for another time.

That these two umbrella groups (post-positivists and postmodernists) existed with very different worldviews led to something called the *paradigm wars*. Lincoln, Lynham, and Guba (2011) remind us that in the early days—mid-1990s or so—"we focused on the contention among various research paradigms for legitimacy and intellectual and paradigmatic hegemony" (p. 97). During that time, there were essentially two camps—the positivists and post-positivists constituted one group, while those in the postmodern camp were the other group. Post-positivists tried to fit into the mold and so looked for ways that were parallel to traditional research, while postmodernists discarded these ideas and said they were coming from some other place. Each camp wanted to occupy a place of legitimacy. What were they to do? A word or two about these two camps. While there were many differences between the two, the most important ones were in three areas: What about the nature of reality or what we can know (*ontology*)? What about the process of how we come to know? What is the relationship between the knower (researcher) and what is known (*epistemology*)? What about the ways of knowing? How do we seek new knowledge (*methodology*)?

What does all of this have to do with validity in 2013? While the wars have ended for most people and mixed methods (joining both QR and QN) have been adopted by others, the question still remains: How can I know that this research is any good, or how can I believe it, or how can I trust it? What are the criteria for judging and assessing the worth of QR?

The question has become much more complicated today. In fact, Northcote (2012) states that over one hundred sets of qualitative criteria have been identified (Stige, Malterud, and Midtgarden, 2009, agree). So how do you, as a student in the field, know what to do? One option is to apply some criteria; but if so, which ones? I know you want this to be a simple answer, but it can't be. One reason why is that different disciplines have different expectations. According to Northcote (2012), "The challenge of how to assess qualitative research is evident in many fields including psychology . . . , engineering . . . , health . . . and industrial marketing" (p. 102).

Further, different QR approaches or designs have different criteria. Ellis, Adams, and Bochner (2010) state that validity for **autoethnography** "means that a work seeks verisimilitude" and evokes a lifelike experience for the reader (para. 34). Rouse (2012), a European psychology student, posts a detailed and insightful blog. She recommends Yardley's (2011) core principles—sensitivity to context, commitment and rigor, coherence and transparency, and impact and importance. Those conducting participatory research face similar dilemmas of inappropriate evaluative criteria (Bergold & Thomas, 2012, para. 78). On the other hand, those using grounded theory (Hardman, 2012) are more likely to apply traditional criteria.

In order to illustrate current practice, I examined how several authors handled validity related to their particular research. The following are illustrations drawn from published research in *Qualitative Inquiry* for 2012:

Jewkes (2012), in a study of prison research using autoethnography, introduces the study thus: "There is an unspoken understanding that if we disclose the emotions that underpin and inform our work, our colleagues will question its 'validity' and perhaps even our suitability to engage effectively in criminological research" (p. 63). She remains silent on the topic after this remark.

Mikecz (2012), in his study of interviewing elites, commented that

> It is impossible to achieve perfect reliability and validity, although they are very important in social science due to the often-ambiguous nature of social constructions. . . . In qualitative research, the incorporation of rigor as well as subjectivity into the research process raises difficulties in developing validity standards. . . . Creswell . . . defines validation as the compilation of "bits and pieces of evidence to formulate a compelling whole." . . . However, evidence is not the equivalent of truth and objectivity. Because life as we live it is not static enough to allow for this kind of certainty: It is much more fluid, contextual, and relational. . . . Because we cannot separate ourselves from what we know, our subjectivity is an integral part of our understanding of ourselves, of others, and of the world around us. Thus, validation in qualitative research is a "judgment of trustworthiness or goodness of a piece of research." (p. 491)

I am not sure what he means by perfect validity, since he seems to draw away from the concept as he talks about the relationship of the knower to what is known.

Razon and Ross (2012), in their study about alliance building while interviewing in Israel comment on validity:

> We acknowledge that discussions about the collaboration between researcher and participant are not new in academic research, particularly scholarship informed by feminist, postcolonial, and science and technology studies' theories. Patty Lather . . . for example, argues eloquently about the importance of participants taking an active role in the collection and publication of data, suggesting that the absence of their voice creates issues of validity in qualitative research. (p. 496)

Holliday's (2012) research concerned interaction with an executive in a large British institution. With regard to validity, she writes, "The rigor and validity of the research thus shifts to a management of subjectivity in which researchers become conscious of their presence and use disciplines to deal with it" (p. 506). Managing subjectivity seems to be her central concern.

What can we learn from these snippets? There is a lack of clarity on what is meant by *validity*. There is lack of agreement on what is meant as well. Most authors do not address the topic. When they do, they seem to be vague or unclear.

Let me make my position clear on the topic: Validity criteria associated with traditional QN are inappropriate in today's understanding of QR. Review boards and other agencies are not necessarily the official arbiters of suitable or appropriate criteria. Criteria differ depending on one's own sensibilities and worldview. Criteria also differ depending on one's academic discipline. At times, you may find yourself out of step with others. I think that is a good thing. Here are some things that I find helpful when I read journal articles; to me, they speak about the worth of a project: (1) acknowledging that those we study are not just subjects or samples, but real people with real needs, ambitions, and foibles, and (2) involving oneself in all aspects of the study; this is critical for good QR. Thus it would not make sense to reflect concern about being too subjective or not being sufficiently objective.

Some pet peeves that irk me when I read an article include (1) apologizing because a sample is too small or not representative; this makes no sense, since the goal of QR is to describe, understand, and take action. It is not to test hypotheses or draw conclusions; and (2) seeking rigor in terms of data interpretation, as this is also inappropriate. Thus it would not make sense to look for ways to affirm the data that a researcher collects by asking others to agree with an interpretation.

So it has come to this. I adopt a position based on my own view of the world. Rigid, traditionalist criteria do not work for me. My worldview says that a piece of research meets my standards if the topic is important, the method used makes sense, the information provided about the study is sufficiently convincing, and new knowledge has been gained and/or action can be taken for the common good. The study can be about one or many individuals, groups, or organizations; it can be presented in written form or in a play; it can identify important themes or tell a story. All are possible.

Sometimes we just do research because we are required to by the nature of our job or our educational requirements. We just want to get it out of the way. But other times, we do research to make a difference in the lives of others and ultimately in our own lives.

I hope you will find the way that works for you. My intention is to help you on that journey.

CHECK YOURSELF

- Many disciplines use QR. Examples of QR are offered from a variety of disciplines in the social sciences
- Some disciplines combine QR and QN. Although some researchers use either QR or QN, others adopt a pragmatic approach, combining both in the same study.
- There are many definitions of QR. They differ in terms of how specific they are and in terms of the discipline. My definition combines many elements: QR is a way to study the social interactions of humans in naturally occurring situations. The researcher plays a critical role in the process by gathering data and making sense of or interpreting the phenomena that are observed and revealed.
- Common elements of QR include understanding human interactions in natural settings, the dynamic nature of the process, an inductive approach, and the important role of researcher.

- Table 1.1 highlights the major differences between QR and QN.
- There are different positions about validity. In part, they are connected to whether the researcher adopts a post-positivist viewpoint, an interpretist viewpoint, or the viewpoint of a critical theorist. The discussion is ongoing about what makes for good QR and who should decide about the criteria.

KEY DISCUSSION ISSUES

1. What are examples of the types of research conducted in different disciplines? How can you characterize the type of research you have just read about?
2. QR and QN seem to be different. In what ways can both be used in one study? Does that seem incompatible to you?
3. What is a good working definition of QR? What are three key elements? Are there differences by discipline?
4. What additional elements are also found in QR?
5. Why might you use QR?
6. What are key comparisons between QR and QN?

MODULE 1A

Developing a Blog

Begin a blog about being a student of QR. This can be a group project or one you do alone. Write in the first person. Include some information about yourself. Write your thoughts about QR.

Here is one way to get a blog started. Go to http://www.blogger.com. You first need to create an account on blogger.com. Choose a template from the blogger homepage and follow the directions. That's all there is to it.

MODULE 1B

Identifying Key Elementws of Qualitative Research

Working with two others, identify key elements of QR. Narrow your separate lists so that you construct one master list.

Then select two articles to review. Identify one article from a recent issue of *Qualitative Inquiry*. Identify a second article from a recent issue of the *Journal of Mixed Methods Research*. If you use the Student Study Site, I have selected articles for you to use.

Read each article to determine whether and to what extent the key elements you identified are included in each article. What other elements did you find? Comment on the relationship between the qualitative and the quantitative component in the mixed-methods article.

NOTES

1. Critical theory was originally associated with the "Frankfurt School," which described thinkers associated with the Institute for Social Research founded in 1923 in Frankfurt, Germany. Theodor Adorno, Erich Fromm, and Herbert Marcuse were prominent in the group.
2. Critical theory has been linked with art and creative research. The Pacific Northwest College of Art is accepting candidates for a master of arts in critical theory and creative research. It looks at the intersection of art, theory, and research. More information can be found at http://www.pnca.edu.

REFERENCES

Anderson, N. (2012). Book review: Qualitative research from start to finish. *Qualitative Health Research, 22*(11), 1591–1593.

Asian Societies. (2011). *The definition of qualitative research.* Retrieved from http://savoeunbusiness.blogspot.com/2011/04/definition-of-qualitative-research.html

Bachwani-Paritosh, R. (2011). *The qualitative research blog.* Retrieved from http://onqualitativeresearch.blogspot.com/2006_02_01_archive.html, http://onqualitativeresearch.blogspot.com/2011_05_01_archive.html.

Bansal, P., & Corley, K. (2011). The coming of age for qualitative research: Embracing the diversity of qualitative methods. *Academy of Management Journal, 54*(2), 233–237. Retrieved from http://www.aom.pace.edu/amj/editorials/Apr11_Bansal_Corley.PDF

Berg, B., & Lune, H. (2011). *Qualitative research methods for the social sciences* (8th ed.). Boston, MA: Pearson.

Bergold, J., & Thomas, S. (2012). Participatory research methods: A methodological approach in motion [110 paragraphs]. *Forum Qualitative Sozialforschung/Forum: Qualitative Social Research, 13*(1), Art. 30. Retrieved from http://www.qualitative-research.net/index.php/fqs/article/view/1801

Birkinshaw, J., Brannen, M., & Tung, R. (2011). From a distance and generalizable to up close and grounded: Reclaiming a place for qualitative methods in international business research. *Journal of International Business Studies,* 42, 573–581. Retrieved from http://www.palgrave-journals.com/jibs/journal/v42/n5/full/jibs201119a.html

Black, N. (1994). Editorial: Why we need qualitative research. *Journal of Epidemiology & Community Health, 48,* 425–26.

Bogdan, R., & Biklen, S. (1992). *Qualitative research for education: An introduction to theory and method.* Boston, MA: Allyn & Bacon.

Brinkmann, S. (2011). *Current dilemmas in qualitative research.* Keynote address at the 17th Qualitative Health Research Conference in Vancouver, Canada.

Brito, R., Ribeiro, O., & Machado, M. (2011). *Quantitative versus qualitative: Paradigmatic and epistemological perceptions that guide the decisions of the beginning researcher.* INTED 2011 Proceedings, 3039–3047. Retrieved from http://library.iated.org/view/BRITO2011QUA

Caprar, D. (2011). Foreign locals: A cautionary tale on the culture of MNC local employees. *Journal of International Business Studies, 42,* 608–628. Retrieved from http://www.palgrave-journals.com/jibs/journal/v42/n5/full/jibs20119a.html

Carr, E. (2011). The qualitative research challenge to RCT 4D: Part 2. *Open the echo chamber: A blog about development and global change.* Retrieved from http://www.edwardrcarr.com/opentheechochamber/2011/05/25/the-qualitative-research-challenge-to-rct4d-part-2/

Creswell, J. (2007). *Qualitative inquiry and research design: Choosing among five approaches.* Thousand Oaks, CA: SAGE.

Creswell, J. (2011). Controversies in mixed methods research. In N. Denzin & Y. Lincoln (Eds.), *The SAGE handbook of qualitative research* (4th ed., pp. 269–283). Thousand Oaks, CA: SAGE.

Damico, J. S., & Ball, M. J. (2010). Prolegomenon: Addressing the tyranny of old ideas. *Journal of International Research in Communication Disorders, 1,* 1–29.

Dawson, A., & Hjorth, D. (2012). Advancing family business research through narrative analysis. *Family Business Review, 25*(3), 339–355.

Deniborin. (2010). *Qualitative research definition.* Retrieved from http://www.deniborin.com/2010/11/qualitative-research-definition.html

Denzin, N. (2010). Moments, mixed methods, and paradigm dialogs. *Qualitative Inquiry, 16*(6), 419–27.

Denzin, N., & Lincoln, Y. (2011). (Eds.). *The SAGE handbook of qualitative research* (4th ed.). Thousand Oaks, CA: SAGE.

de Verteuil, G. (2011). Evidence of gentrification-induced displacement among social services in London and Los Angeles. *Urban Studies 48*(8), 1563–1580.

Education.com. (2011). *Qualitative research.* Retrieved from http://www.education.com/definition/qualitative-research/

Ellis, C., Adams, T., & Bochner, A. (2010). Autoethnography: An overview [40 paragraphs]. *Forum Qualitative Sozialforschung/Forum: Qualitative Social Research, 12*(1), Art. 10. Retrieved from http://nbn-resolving.de/urn:nbn:de:0114-fqs1101108

Elsbach, K. (2009). Identity affirmation through 'signature style.' A study of toy car designers. *Human Relations, 62*(7), 1041–1072.

Financial Times Lexicon. (2011). *Qualitative research.* Retrieved from http://lexicon.ft.com/Term?term=qualitative-research

Fitzpatrick, S. (2011). Looking beyond the qualitative and quantitative divide: Narrative, ethics and representation in suicidology. *Suicidology Online, 2,* 29–37. Retrieved from http://www.suicidology-online.com/pdf/SOL-2011-2-29-37.pdf

Gage, N. L. (1989). The paradigm wars and their aftermath: A "historical" sketch of research and teaching since 1989. *Educational Researcher, 18*(7), 4–10.

Gariff, D. (2012). *The psychological landscapes of Michelangelo Antonioni (1912–2007): A centenary tribute.* Washington, DC: National Gallery of Art.

Glossary of Marketing. (2011). *Qualitative research. Definition.* Retrieved from http://www.glossaryofmarketing.com/definition/qualitative-research.html

Gray, A. (n.d.). *Constructivist teaching and learning* (Master's thesis summary). University of Saskatchewan, Saskatoon, Canada. Retrieved from http://saskschoolboards.ca/research/instruction/97-07.htm

Greenhalgh, T., & Taylor, R. (1997). How to read a paper: Papers that go beyond numbers (qualitative research). *British Medical Journal, 315,* 740–743.

Hamilton, S. (2011). *Definition and description of qualitative research.* Retrieved from http://www.ehow.com/info_8698327_definition-description-qualitative-research.html

Hammer, C. (2011). Expanding our knowledge base through qualitative research methods. *American Journal of Speech-Language Pathology, 20*(3), 161–162.

Hardman, H. (2012, June 15). The validity of a grounded theory approach to research on democratization. *Qualitative Research,* 1–15. doi: 10.1177/1468794112445526

Hawes, S. (n.d.). *Online qualitative research resources.* Retrieved from http://websearch.about.com/gi/o.htm?zi=1/XJ&zTi=1&sdn=websearch&cdn=compute&tm=39&f=10&su=p284.12.336.ip_p504.1.336.ip_&tt=11&bt=0&bts=1&zu=http%3A//duckduckgo.com/%3Fq%3D%26t%3Di

Højgaard, L., & Søndergaard, D. (2011). Theorizing the complexities of discursive and material subjectivity: Agential realism and poststructural analyses. *Theory & Psychology, 21*(3), 338–354.

Holliday, A. (2012). Interrogating researcher participation in an interview study of intercultural contribution in the workplace. *Qualitative Inquiry, 18*(6), 504–515.

Hopper, J. (2011). Why do qualitative research? *MethodLogical.* Retrieved from http://methodlogical.wordpress.com/2011/02/16/why-do-qualitative-research/

Howe, K. (2011). Mixed methods, mixed causes? *Qualitative Inquiry, 17*(2), 166–171.

International School of Prague, Psychology Department. (2010). *Quantitative or qualitative?* Retrieved from http://cranepsych.edublogs.org/files/2009/07/quantitative-or-qualitative.pdf

Jewkes, Y. (2012). Autoethnography and emotion as intellectual resources: Doing prison research differently. *Qualitative Inquiry, 18*(1), 63–75.

Kaler, A., & Beres, M. (2010). *Essentials of field relationships.* Walnut Creek, CA: Left Coast Press.

Korica, M., & Molloy, E. (2010). Making sense of professional identities: Stories of medical professionals and new technologies. *Human Relations, 63*(2), 1879–1901.

Lichtman, M. (2013). *Qualitative research in education* (3rd ed.). Thousand Oaks, CA: SAGE.

Lincoln, Y., Lynham, S., & Guba, E. (2011). Paradigmatic controversies, contradictions, and emerging confluences, revisited. In N. Denzin & Y. Lincoln. *The SAGE handbook of qualitative research* (4th ed., pp. 97–128). Thousand Oaks, CA: SAGE.

Lindlof, T., & Taylor, B. (2011). *Qualitative communication research methods* (3rd ed.). Thousand Oaks, CA: Sage.

Lugosi, P., Bell, D., & Lugosi, K. (2010). Hospitality, culture and regeneration: Urban decay, entrepreneurship, and the "ruin" bars of Budapest. *Urban Studies, 47* (14), 3079–3101. Retrieved from http://usj.sagepub.com/content/47/14/3079.full.pdf+html

Mahoney, J. (2007a). Debating the state of comparative politics: Views from qualitative research. *Comparative Political Studies, 40*(1), 32–38.

Mahoney, J. (2007b). Qualitative methodology and comparative politics. *Comparative Political Studies, 40*(2), 122–144.

Mahoney, J., & Goertz, G. (2006). A tale of two cultures: Contrasting quantitative and qualitative research. *Political Analysis, 14,* 227–249.

Manghani, S. (2009). Love messaging: Mobile phone texting seen through the lens of tanka poetry. *Theory, Culture & Society, 26*(2–3), 209–232.

Marta. (2011). Quantitative or qualitative, seriously who cares????. *The geography of things.* Retrieved from http://www.geographyofthings.com/articles/QuantitativeQualitativeseriouslywhocares

Matusik, S., & Mickel, A. (2011). Embracing or embattled by converged mobile devices? Users' experiences with a contemporary connectivity technology. *Human Relations, 64*(8), 1001–1030.

McGuire, M. (2011). Qualitative research—journal, institutes, conferences. *MarkMcGuire.net.* Retrieved from http://markmcguire.net/2011/09/12/qualitative-research-journal-institute-conferences/

McRoy, R. (n.d.). *Qualitative research.* Retrieved from http://www.uncp.edu/home/marson/qualitative_research.html

MediaDictionary. (2011). *Qualitative research. Definition.* Retrieved from http://www.mediadictionary.com/definition/qualitative-research.html

Mikecz, R. (2012). Interviewing elites: Addressing methodological issues. *Qualitative Inquiry, 18*(6), 482–493.

Mitchell, J. (2011). Qualitative research meets the ghost of Pythagoras. *Theory & Psychology, 21*(2), 241–259.

Morawski, J. (2011). Our debates: Finding, fixing, and enacting reality. *Theory & Psychology, 21*(2), 260–274.

Munck, G. L., & Snyder, R. (2007a). Debating the direction of comparative politics: An analysis of leading journals. *Comparative Political Studies, 40*(1), 5–31.

Munck, G. L., & Snyder, R. (2007b). Visions of comparative politics: A reply to Mahoney and Wibbels. *Comparative Political Studies, 40*(1), 45–47.

Myers, M. (2011). *Qualitative research in information systems.* Retrieved from http://www.qual.auckland.ac.nz/

Neill, J. (2007). *Qualitative versus quantitative research: Key points in a classic debate.* Retrieved from http://wilderdom.com/research/QualitativeVersusQuantitativeResearch.html

Nielsen, K., Randall, R., & Christensen, K. (2010). Does training managers enhance the effects of implementing team-working? A longitudinal, mixed methods field study. *Human Relations, 63*(11), 1719–1741.

Northcote, M. T. (2012). Selecting criteria to evaluate qualitative research. *Education Papers and Journal Articles.* Paper 38. Retrieved from http://research.avondale.edu.au/cgi/viewcontent.cgi?article=1038&context=edu_papers

Nursing Planet. (2011). *Qualitative research in nursing.* Retrieved from http://nursingplanet.com/research/qualitative_research.html

Ozturk, M. (2011). Sexual orientation discrimination: Exploring the experiences of lesbian, gay and bisexual employees in Turkey. *Human Relations, 64(*8), 1099–1118.

Packer, M. (2011). *The science of qualitative research.* Cambridge, UK: Cambridge University Press. Kindle iPad edition.

Patel, N. (2011). *"For a ruthless criticism of everything existing": Rebellion against the quantitative/qualitative divide.* Presentation given at EPIC2011 Conference. Retrieved from http://epiconference.com/2011/program/papers/for-a-ruthless-criticism-of-everything-existing-rebellion-against-the

Razon, N., & Ross, K. (2012). Negotiating fluid identities: Alliance-building in qualitative interviewing. *Qualitative Inquiry, 18*(6), 494–503.

Robin. (2011, February 18). What is a theory? *Qualitative research field journal.* Retrieved from http://qrfj.blogspot.com/2011_02_01_archive.html

Rouse, L. (2012). Evaluating qualitative research: Are we judging by the wrong standards? *JEPS Bulletin.* Retrieved from http://jeps.efpsa.org/blog/2012/07/01/evaluating-qualitative-research/

Rubin, A., & Babbie, E. (1993). *Research methods for social work* (2nd ed.). Pacific Grove, CA: Brooks/Cole.

Siegle. (n.d.). *The assumptions of qualitative designs.* Retrieved from http://www.gifted.uconn.edu/siegle/research/Qualitative/qualquan.htm

Stige, B., Malterud, K., & Midtgarden, T. (2009). Toward an agenda for evaluation of qualitative research. *Qualitative Health Research, 19*(10), 1504–1516.

Teddlie, C., & Tashakkori, A. (2003). Preface. In A. Tashakkori & C. Teddlie (Eds.), *Handbook of mixed-methods in social and behavioral research* (pp. ix–xv). Thousand Oaks, CA: SAGE.

Teddlie, C., & Tashakkori, A. (2011). Mixed methods research. In N. Denzin & Y. Lincoln, *The SAGE handbook of qualitative research* (4th edition, pp. 285–299). Thousand Oaks, CA: SAGE.

U.S. Legal. (2011). *Qualitative research law and legal definition.* Retrieved from http://definitions.uslegal.com/q/qualitative-research/

Westerman, M. (2011). Conversation analysis and interpretive quantitative research on psychotherapy: Process and problematic interpersonal behavior. *Theory & Psychology, 21*(2), 155–178.

Westerman, M., & Yanchar, S. (2011). Changing the terms of the debate: Quantitative methods in explicitly interpretive research. *Theory & Psychology, 21*(2), 139–154.

Westmarland, N. (2001). The quantitative/qualitative debate and feminist research: A subjective view of objectivity [28 paragraphs]. *Forum Qualitative Sozialforschung/Forum: Qualitative Social Research, 2*(1), Art. 13. Retrieved from http://nbn-resolving.de/urn:nbn:de:0114-fqs0101135

White, R., & Green, A. (2011). Opening up or closing down opportunities? The role of social networks and attachment to place in informing young people's attitudes and access to training and employment. *Urban Studies, 48*(1), 41–60.

Wikipedia. (2011). *Qualitative research.* Retrieved from http://en.wikipedia.org/wiki/Qualitative_research

Witham, K. A., & Bensimon, E. M. (2012). Creating a culture of inquiry around equity and student success. In S. D. Museus & U. M. Jayakumar (Eds.), *Creating campus cultures: Fostering success among racially diverse student populations* (pp. 46–67). New York, NY: Routledge.

Yardley, L. (2011). Demonstrating validity in qualitative research. In J. A. Smith (Ed.), *Qualitative psychology: A practical guide to research methods* (pp. 234–251). London, England: SAGE.

STUDENT STUDY SITE

Visit **http://www.sagepub.com/lichtmanqrss** to access additional study tools, including eFlashcards and links to SAGE journal articles.

CHAPTER 2

Qualitative Research—A Reflexive Stance

Focus Your Reading

- Human interactions, social processes, and phenomena; research questions
- Role of self—reflexivity and subjectivity
- More on reflexivity

It has been my experience that one of the best ways to learn how to do something is to get involved in doing it. John Dewey advocated learning by doing. I believe that as well. In qualitative research (QR) in particular, it is crucial that the researcher have many opportunities for practice. The role of the researcher in this endeavor is critical, for it is through his or her eyes and ears that data are taken in, examined, and processed. It is the researcher who brings meaning and interpretation to all aspects of QR. That the researcher adopt a self-reflective mode is important as well.

One of my favorite stories is about how a class of mine practiced observations. There were about a dozen of us. We wanted to get into the field but didn't want to become involved in obtaining permission to observe in a clinic or classroom. We knew that going down that road would take a considerable amount of time and involve jumping over several hurdles. What we were interested in was practicing our observation skills. Living in a campus environment, we knew that one readily available location was a large supermarket. We certainly did not need permission to enter the market. Our plan was to enter the market, identify a parent and child shopping, and try to follow them—surreptitiously, of course. We thought this would be easy. Each student would get a shopping cart, find someone to follow, and take a few items in the cart as we wandered from one aisle to another. I chose to remain in the front of the store, browsing paperback books in a rack.

Two things happened that were unexpected. One of the students observed a shoplifter and felt the need to report it to me and subsequently to the manager. At about the same time, the manager became suspicious of me and the other students. I guess it looked as if we didn't belong. He actually thought that I was from corporate headquarters checking up on how things worked in the store. I explained what we were doing, and we were able to complete our observations. When our planned time ended, we returned to class to discuss our experiences.

We learned several lessons. We learned that we needed to reflect on who we were and what we were doing. Were we correct in surreptitiously observing individuals just for the sake of avoiding obtaining their permission? How was what we saw influenced by who we were? What was the political stance of the student who witnessed the shoplifter? Did he actually have all the facts? Perhaps we should have involved someone from the store so that they would know what was happening. We found it very difficult to try to look and listen to someone else and felt we were intruding. We were also hampered because we could not take notes. But most important, we did not really know what to look for when we observed. Should we listen to the spoken words, look for nonverbal cues, or both? We were not sure how we could move from these observations to make meaning or gain understanding of how humans interact. But we all agreed on one thing—getting into the field was very important, and we wanted to do it again. But this time, we would be better prepared. We needed an overall research question. We needed to focus our attention on some aspect of interaction. And we needed to acknowledge our own role in the study.

■ Purpose of Research and Research Questions

The purpose of QR is to explore, describe, understand, or explain a phenomenon. It is about the what, how, and why of something. For some, the purpose is to take political or social action. The purpose is not to test a hypothesis or make predictions about outcomes. It is not about how many or what kinds of test scores are received. It is not about theory testing. It is not about cause and effect.

Research questions, then, emanate from a study's purpose. I know how very difficult it is to come up with a suitable research question. Here are some ways that might be helpful to you. I have constructed a table so you can think about this more clearly. Begin by thinking about different categories: people, concepts, places, and events. Let's look more closely at each of these categories.

People

Many qualitative researchers begin with what type or kind of person they want to study. Sometimes qualitative researchers are interested in exploring individuals who are disadvantaged, homeless, deviant, or in trouble. In a very early qualitative dissertation, Liebow (1967) studied men who were unemployed and living on a street corner in Washington, DC. Several decades

Table 2.1 Formulating Research Questions

People	*Concepts*	*Places*	*Events*
students	power	classrooms	hurricanes
teachers	leadership	playgrounds	pep rallies
parents	loneliness	malls	parties
adult students	mentoring	coffee houses	athletics
administrators	gender differences	homes	assemblies
high-achieving girls	violence	lunchrooms	concerts
children at risk	cooperation	schools	parades
gangs	friendships	adult centers	flood
pregnant teens	mentoring relationship	places of worship	holidays
beginning teachers	teacher burnout	online chat rooms	mealtimes
students in same-sex classes	aggression	rural classrooms	elections

later, Liebow (1993) studied women who lived in a homeless shelter. Some researchers conduct **ethnographies** on specific groups of individuals. Correll (1995) studied a lesbian online "bar." Although you would expect that who is studied follows the general question, in my experience, researchers sometimes decide they want to study individuals with whom they identify. Some of my students did their dissertation research by studying individuals with certain characteristics. Repass (2002), thinking about retiring herself, studied professional women as they planned their retirement. Glass (2001), a parent of a child with autism, studied families with an autistic child. Snyder (2003), a consultant to the military, studied a military organization's adoption of an innovative technique. Others may choose to examine people different from themselves. This is not always easy, as Butera (2006) discovered. She describes the extreme challenge she encountered in getting men to participate in a study of cross-gender friendship.

Concepts

Another way to develop a potential research question is to think about concepts or topics of interest. Concepts that researchers address are very wide ranging. Qualitative researchers have studied surviving a heart attack, living with AIDS, power relationships in hospitals and schools, or experiences of female school superintendents. They have asked questions about forming friendships, about successful minority students, about reading programs that work, or about the politics of identity. The topics are very often close to their own hearts. In keeping with the participatory paradigms of QR, some have chosen areas in which they could intervene and make social change. Some have chosen topics that led to political action.

Places

I believe that most researchers begin with either the kind of person they want to study or the concept they want to investigate. Yet I think it is important to also consider the places where a study might take place. Without getting too complicated, you can think about it in this way: If your study is conducted in an open and public place, you do not need permission to conduct it, nor do you need to provide anonymity. For example, if you decide to conduct a study in a shopping mall and you choose to sit in an open corridor and observe people around you, you should be able to do this without encountering a problem. I would warn you, however, that in this time of heightened awareness and security, you might be approached by someone from the facility and be asked to identify yourself and what you are doing. To the extent that the place in which you plan to conduct your study is open to all, you should not face any problems of seeking permission of assuring anonymity. Places that fit into this category include sports arenas, libraries, playgrounds, amusement parks, beaches, fast food restaurants, and museums—in other words, places where adults and/or children gather that are open to all. There have been a number of studies using social media as a place where individuals congregate. Looking at interactions in chat rooms or on LISTSERVs has become popular.

As the place in which you plan to conduct your study moves to the more private, you will need to be aware of having to obtain permission to conduct the study both from the organization and the individuals within it. There are often challenges to conducting QR in certain settings. Belousov and his colleagues (2007) describe the incredible difficulties they faced in a study of health and safety regulatory enforcement in the shipping industry in Russia. Sadly, one of the fieldworkers was murdered. They talk specifically about particular social spaces and the frontier-like nature of certain settings. In all these examples, issues about privacy, confidentiality, and permission need to be addressed.

Events

The last category you might consider as you think about formulating a research question is an event. It might be a major or unique event (such as the 9/11 devastation or the Mars landing of 2012 or a political convention) or a more general event (such as a holiday celebration or a 4th of July parade). For the most part, you will find it easier to concentrate on more general events. But if you happen to be in a position to study a major and possibly unique event, I encourage you to think about that.

Of course, the examples in Table 2.1 under each category are those I have thought about. You can substitute any you wish. Very often, researchers begin by identifying individuals of interest to them. Some find it helpful to select a particular concept to study. I think this helps you to focus your ideas as you begin your study. Once you have selected whom and what you plan to study, you need to determine where the study will take place. I have listed some places for you to consider. Lastly, some people find that they are motivated by a particular event and want to study the event itself.

■ Human Interactions, Social Processes, and Phenomena: Identification of Research Questions

Research begins with a question: something we want to answer, something we are interested in studying, something the literature points to as needing further investigation. There is a vast array of questions you might want to investigate. Some of them can be answered using QR approaches. Often those approaches target questions about humans and the social world. Further, QR is concerned with how people make sense of and give meaning to their lives. Some qualitative researchers stress communities of people, while others are interested in the experiences of individuals and the meaning attached to those experiences. We can also think of QR as a study of organizations or programs. Here, the emphasis is on the program rather than the participants.

We realize the importance of beginning with a research question, topic, or statement of the purpose of our research. You can get some ideas about the range of topics that have been explored in the examples I list below drawn from recently published research:

- interactions between a White teacher and his Black students and the way race is co-constructed therein (Wamsted, 2011)
- methodological barriers of a study of women trafficked for sexual exploitation and attempts using feminist methods to resolve them (Bosworth, Hoyle, & Dempsey, 2011)
- layers of censorship related to the publication of QR studies (Ceglowski, Bacigalupa, & Peck, 2011)
- bullying in neoliberal universities as an intra-active process (Zabrodska, Linnell, Laws, & Davies, 2011)
- the influence of violent trauma on communities and emotional memories (Reilly, 2011)
- displacing the problem of power in research interviews with sociologists and journalists (Plesner, 2011)
- a study about home-based care volunteers of AIDS patients in South Africa (Naidu, 2011)
- integration of qualitative evidence: evidence toward construction of academic knowledge in social science and professional fields (Major & Savin-Baden, 2011)
- ethnography goes online: researching interpersonal communication on the Internet (Beneito-Montagut, 2011)
- using fictional narratives in social and educational research (Watson, 2011)
- online community discussion of Food and Drug Administration (FDA) recommendations (Mackert, Love, Donovan-Kicken, & Uhle, 2011)
- support for fathering from online dads (Fletcher & St. George, 2011)
- lived experiences of students doing phenomenology (Pascal, Johnson, Dore, & Trainor, 2011)

You can see that these questions cover a broad range of topics. Many focus on specific populations to study, while others deal with methodological issues.

Role of Self—Reflexivity and Subjectivity

I cannot stress enough how important the qualitative researcher is to the entire research enterprise. The qualitative researcher plays critical roles in all phases of the research process. All phases of research are impacted by the researcher. Especially important is the idea that it is through his or her eyes and ears that questions are formulated and data are identified, collected, analyzed, and interpreted. Holloway and Biley (2011) concluded that "qualitative inquiry is still the most humanistic and person-centered way of discovering and uncovering thoughts and action of human beings" (p. 974).

Let me help you see this more clearly. Imagine you are going to do a study about how creative enterprises nurture creativity within an organization. Preliminary steps would be to identify such an organization and seek permission to conduct such a study. Okay. You have your foot in the door. It is these next steps that are so crucial for the success of the study. What do you do once you get in? In using QR techniques, you will spend some time observing and talking to various individuals within the organization. Here is where you play an important role. In many forms of quantitative research (QN), you can rely on formal tests or questionnaires or observation scales to collect your data. Not so in QR. Here, you need to rely on yourself. It is through your lens that participants to study are chosen, that various interactions of individuals are observed, that interviews are conducted, and that records and prototypes are reviewed. It is through your lens that videos are made or that photos are taken. You are the one who asks the questions, listens to the answers, and probes for hidden meanings. You are the one who does the looking. You are the one who sets a schedule of when to look and what to look at. You are the one who tries to determine what makes this organization tick. And for this research question, you are the one who tries to decipher what it is about the organization's culture that fosters and encourages creativity.

At the same time that you are collecting a wide variety of data, you begin a process of analyzing the data. This dynamic, circular approach is important to QR. Rather than following a linear model, qualitative researchers often move back and forth between collecting data and analyzing data. Preliminary analyses help guide you as you pursue data collection. Seamlessly moving back and forth between data collection and data analysis strengthens your study.

Your role is further extended when you move into the phase of QR that involves interpreting or drawing meaning from the data you have collected. Again, your role is crucial here, because there are no statistical analyses to perform. You will have a vast amount of data in various forms. Some might be video; some might be from a recording; some might exist in your notes. While you may make use of computer software to facilitate processing and organizing the data you collect, your role is critical in identifying important themes or developing a narrative. What you do with all these data will become clearer as you read Chapter 12 on drawing meaning from the data.

Did You Know

Emma Burnett, a lecturer and researcher in infection prevention at the University of Dundee, writes about a lecture she attended on reflexivity that inspired her to work on her diary and her blog. She speaks specifically about subjectivity within a particular philosophical stance. Blogging since 2011, Emma addresses many topics near and dear to the QR student.

■ Reflexivity and Its Meanings

Think about reflexivity in this way: A researcher is tied to all aspects of the research. A reflexive researcher understands that a reflective stance is critical. I have identified at least three different types of reflexivity. Personal reflexivity refers to a researcher's values. Epistemological reflexivity refers to a researcher's view of how the world is known. Contextual and ethical reflexivity refer to issues related to appropriateness of doing research with some groups and issues related to informed consent. Doucet (2008) takes a different viewpoint. For her, reflexivity involves three sets of relationships—with the self, with the research participants, and with the readers or audience. She used the metaphor of "gossamer walls" to amplify these relationships.

Writing from a social work position, McCormick, Tempel, and Probst (2011) suggested that a reflective viewpoint is both ethical and accountable. Another social worker, Gilgun (2010, 2011), asked that researchers acknowledge the idea of awareness of how they affect the research process and are affected by it. Ben-Ari and Enosh (2011) amplified the reflective process. Willig (2001), in discussing QR and psychology, identified two types of reflexivity: personal and epistemological. *Personal* refers to the way in which our values have influenced and changed us, while *epistemological* addresses assumptions about the world. Griffiths (2009), writing as an educator, expressed her thoughts on the subject:

> In general, reflexivity is an explicit self-consciousness about the researcher's (or research team's, and/or the research funder's) social, political and value positions, in relation to how these might have influenced the design, execution and interpretation of the theory, data and conclusions. . . . Such self-consciousness needs to acknowledge that the self is not fully transparent to itself, so enough description of the researcher needs to be given for the audience to make judgments about his or her social and political positionality. (p. 17)

Bishop and Shepherd (2011) used a narrative paradigm to examine how reflexivity creates more ethical research. They commented that postmodern viewpoints see the self as fragmented, incoherent, and multiple; in contrast, those who espouse narrative theories see the self as coherent and unified. I believe there is still quite a bit of confusion about reflexivity. On the one hand, qualitative researchers acknowledge that the researcher's role is critical. However, I see in some writing that researchers look for ways of minimizing their role. For these individuals, they equate this reflexive stance with some kind of bias—the bias associated with more traditional types of research. You might come across some of these issues as you read or interact with your colleagues or professors.

Current Practice of Reflexivity

Not only is reflexivity here to stay—it should stay. It is an important element associated with QR. You might understand this more clearly if you examine some of the thinking during the last decade.

Contemporary qualitative researchers encourage researchers to be reflexive about themselves and what they are doing. Two research approaches have been particularly sensitive to the issue: feminist and queer methodologies. Early on, researchers practicing these disciplines acknowledged the importance of practicing reflexivity to retain a sense of their own subjectivity and to further nurture the relationships and foster mutual exchanges. By 2013, many of the research approaches acknowledge the importance of reflexive practices. Bott (2010) reminds us that there is a danger in disclosure and reflexive behavior when a study involves an unequal relationship between the researcher and the person being studied.

> These considerations are important to recognizing and negotiating the danger of constructing unequal or hierarchical power relationships in social research. Often, disclosures can be problematic for researchers and research participants alike; they carry potential risks to integrity, safety and privacy for both and it is among the many duties of the researcher to take responsibility for how they are handled, not only in the field but also during writing up. (Bott, 2010, pp. 159–160)

Reavy (2011), in her edited volume on visual methods in psychology, includes critical reflections on the research process related to using such methods. Crawford (2012), an emeritus psychology professor and feminist researcher, believes that "psychology needs much more of this kind of self-scrutiny" (p. 248).

In the early 2000s, *Forum: Qualitative Social Research* (*FQS*) devoted two special issues to the subject (2002 and 2003). The two volumes address three topics: foundational and theoretical aspects, the meaning of subjectivity and reflexivity in the research process, and reflections on the subjective nature of scientific knowledge. Breuer, Mruck, and Roth (2002) set the stage. They asserted that it is a fiction that social science research has an objective character. All the standardized procedures still do not make for objectivity. To examine further the idea that social science is or should be completely objective, they proposed to elicit articles on the topic both from a theoretical and practical viewpoint. They took the position that qualitative researchers become reflexive about the research process. You might find it helpful to read both issues to understand some of the thinking from a decade past. Macbeth (2001) stated that "In the rush of interest in qualitative research in the past 15 years, few topics have developed as broad a consensus as the relevance of analytic 'reflexivity'" (p. 35).

By 2010, Bott considered some of the dilemmas surrounding researcher subjectivity and reflexivity. Bott's setting was British migration to Tenerife. She used ethnographic data collection related to two types of employment: lap dancing and timeshare sales. One issue she addressed was the power that researchers hold as they construct the meaning. She raised the concern expressed by social scientists as to how those they study are represented, especially when those they study are so different from themselves. She asked the question of how we should deal with growing differences between the self and those we study and our own political reactions to data we find offensive (p. 161).

The Graduate School of Social and Political Science at the University of Edinburgh (2011) conceptualizes reflexivity in QR in their course of the same title. Their course description is informative:

> Building on a prior foundation in qualitative methods in social science, this course aims to provide students with an in-depth, applied understanding of the principles and practices of reflexivity. It is relevant to students whose research involves direct or indirect interaction with people's lives, including via documentary sources and internet methodologies as well as via interviews and participant observation. The course will emphasise the value of careful and critical reflection on researchers' own experiences in their interactions with the lives of others.

The learning outcomes emphasize the dynamic interplay between self and others in **fieldwork**, the power dynamics of research encounters as well as the emotional dimensions, and key moments in research encounters.

Galindo (2011), a Bolivian graduate in sociology, made a plea for reflexivity in writing dissertations. He suggested that using research diaries as part of a dissertation **biography** is reflective of the tension between the process and product. He reflected on what he learned from the process. I like his suggestion that the researcher account for reflexive practices rather than arguing for or against them (p. 22). As a student, you should find this detailed account enlightening. In fact, he concluded with an invitation to doctoral students to write dissertation biographies (p. 23). I note that he wrote the diary in 1999 and completed his degree in 2002, more than ten years earlier than this essay was written.

Pillow (2010) offered an alternative view about reflexivity. She suggested that there are four problem areas with current thinking about the topic: "reflexivity as recognition of self, reflexivity as recognition of other, reflexivity as truth, and reflexivity as transcendence" (p. 175). She recommended a move away from these comfortable uses practiced by critical, feminist, race-based, or poststructuralist theories. For her, moving toward uncomfortable practices leads to obtaining better data. Although you might not agree with her, she challenges us to think about reflexivity in new ways.

Illustrations of Reflexive Practice

How do researchers write about and put reflexivity into practice? Now that you have an idea of what reflexivity is and its impact on the social sciences, I want to suggest that you see what researchers actually do to illustrate such practice. Arber (2006) reported on her dual role as a practitioner and researcher in an ethnographic study of a hospice. She explored challenges faced by researchers with dual roles and how reflexive accounting enhanced the credibility of her study. Carrington's (2008) emphasis is on race, athletics, and identity and the use of reflexive autobiography. He explained how autoethnography is a way to explain how locating the researcher as an embodied participant in the research process is a political act. Shaw (2010) described how adopting a reflexive attitude in terms of data generation and **interpretative analysis** is important and useful to the field. Yüksel (2011) discussed a study involving post-observational reflective feedback on teaching beliefs.

I recognize that to say "be reflexive" is a first step. But to actually help others to be reflexive is challenging. One way I do this is to model reflexivity. That is why I described for you some details about my own background and experience. Modeling behavior is an important way to teach this skill. It is also a useful way to get your participants to be more open as you study them. Lambe (2011) described ways to develop such practices among preservice teachers.

Some bloggers express their views about reflexive practice. Keefer (2011) provides ongoing examples of such practice in his Silence and Voice blog and his Tweets. He posts daily on these. If you read these, you can get a sense of the way in which his reflections influence all aspects of his research life. Voutier (2011) is also an active blogger. Her comments about **reflective practice** are posted on her blog. She stated that she does not actually sit down and think about being reflective but practices it on an ad hoc basis.

Subjectivity and Its Meanings

I have chosen to separate the terms *reflexivity* and *subjectivity* even though you will find them inextricably tied together in much of the thinking and writing. Often, the term *subjectivity* is used as a counterbalance to *objectivity*. In traditional research approaches, the researcher is admonished to remain objective—to remain aloof and outside the system so that an approximation of reality can be obtained. Peshkin (1988) helped us understand this concept in his thoughtful piece appearing more than twenty years ago. At the time, his thoughts were groundbreaking. He suggested that researchers should seek out their subjectivity during the time of their research. By so doing, they would become aware of how that subjectivity might shape the outcomes. Sounds like reflexivity, doesn't it? In her blog about qualitative inquiry, White (2010), a professor of literacy, recommended Peshkin's related article. In a later article, Peshkin (2000) addressed the journey of interpretation. His purpose was "to show the way a researcher's self, or identity in a situation, intertwines with his or her understanding of the object of the investigation" (p. 5). Subjectivity, then, is not a dirty word.

Sullivan (2002) discussed the connection between reflexivity and subjectivity in relation to psychology. His study used philosophical biography and the philosophy of Wittgenstein. He concluded that exploring reflexivity-subjectivity issues does not "lead to paradox, indecision or conceptual morass" (abstract).

Thinking About Subjectivity

Qualitative researchers do not strive to eliminate subjectivity—they acknowledge it and move with it. Smith (2006) reminded us to use reflexivity that embraces and exploits subjectivity of the researcher in writing about QR. Brinkmann (2011), a professor of psychology at the University of Aalborg in Denmark, in his keynote address at the 17th Qualitative Health Research Conference, identified several dilemmas in QR. He asked the following questions: "How should qualitative researchers respond to the current call for evidence? Should they seek legitimacy by accepting the dominant politics of evidence, or should they play by their own rules with the risk of increasing marginalization?" He suggested that the way to deal with this issue is to conceive of QR as a craft and in so doing enable us "to transcend the subjective-objective dichotomies."

Illustrations of Subjectivity

To say that the researcher is the instrument is an idea that comes directly from my earlier statements about subjectivity and reflexivity. Contemporary views about QR acknowledge the importance of these two key ideas. Since it is the researcher who designs the research, collects the data, analyzes the data, and writes up the results, it behooves us to think about what the researcher thinks about the meaning of knowledge and how it is made known to him or her. In the early days, there was much discussion about two concepts: ontology and epistemology. *Ontology* is concerned with what is known or exists out in the world. *Epistemology* is concerned with how we come to know what is out there and how we influence what we know. It is certainly acknowledged today that even in the natural sciences, the researcher's influence on what is known can be felt. This is also true in the social sciences. So seeing the researcher as an instrument—deciding what is studied, how information about this topic comes to the researcher, the meanings to be made of that information, and what can be done with the information—is critical.

Janesick (2011) tackled the issue directly. She reminded us that the researcher needs to rely on the self as the research instrument and, as such, needs to fine-tune the senses. To do this, she devoted an entire volume to sharpening skills in the habits of observation and interviewing as means of collecting data. She also addressed writing, conceptualizing, and reflecting. I suggest you use some activities from her work in conjunction with activities I include in the modules at the end of each chapter. Gerstl-Pepin and Patrizio (2009) proposed using a reflexive **journal** to record memories and reflections. Such a journal would assist researchers in making their assumptions more explicit.

What I find so interesting are the views put forth by students and how these concepts cause some confusion for many. Below are comments I located in my search of the Internet. Since so much material online is ephemeral, you might discover that these links are no longer available. But I believe you can find similar ones if you conduct a search.

You might find it useful to read comments from a student blogger, Heather Davis (2009), about the PhD journey. Quoting from a book about how to write a dissertation, she commented that it is important to be aware of the researcher's personal and professional concerns as well as assumptions about the world. Earlier, I talked about different kinds of reflexivity and I mentioned an epistemological stance. Davis commented on the same idea.

Ross (2011), a marketing doctoral student, offered his reflections on a course in qualitative methodology. He suggested that he was influenced by a chapter from Schram about clarifying your perspective. He commented that Schram forces the researcher to look more closely at ontological assumptions in QR.

Moore (2008, abstract), a doctoral student in humanities and education from Australia, explored the concept from the viewpoint of a feminist poststructural position. She stated that she constructed many "mes" in order to address both personal values and the expectations of the institution. This research is part of the general issue of researcher identity and research significance that are the focus of a special issue of *eContent Management*. (See also George-Walker & Danaher, 2008.)

At times, you may encounter information on the Internet that you have not seen before. I have to thank the Center for Positive Organizational Scholarship in the Ross School of Business, University of Michigan, for leading me to a book titled *Research Alive: Exploring Generative Moments in Doing Qualitative Research* (Carlsen & Dutton, 2011b). I have been reading and writing about QR for a long time. It was with anticipation that I read in this newsletter post (Carlsen & Dutton, 2011a) that the 40 short stories in this book describe how the researchers feel alive—the stories are personal accounts and far ranging. The new ideas they gleaned from the stories are about seeing with new eyes, daring to engage, reciprocity, and playing with artifacts.

Critical Elements of Qualitative Research

I digressed from my discussion of developing a research question because it is important to understand that the questions you identify and the way you go about answering them are influenced greatly by who you are, what you believe about the world, and how you obtain information. I would like you to revisit the research questions or statements I identified earlier in this chapter. As you begin to think about how you would conduct a study to answer a question in a qualitative manner, you should keep in mind the critical elements associated with QR. Thus, after reviewing how to develop research questions and how your role as researcher influences all aspects of your research, I turn your attention to critical elements of QR.

Purpose Is to Describe, Understand, and Interpret Human Behavior

In general, the main purpose of QR is to provide an in-depth description and understanding of the human experience. It is about humans. The purpose of QR is to describe, understand, and interpret human *phenomena,* human *interaction,* or human *discourse.* When we speak about *phenomena*, we often think of lived experiences of humans. When we speak about human *interaction*, we often think of how humans interact with each other, especially in terms of their culture. When we speak about human *discourse* or *narrative*, we think of humans communicating with each other or communicating ideas. Sometimes phenomena, interaction, and discourse are intertwined.

Qualitative researchers tend to ask *why* questions and questions that lead to a particular meaning (Holloway & Jefferson, 2000). Because qualitative researchers are interested in meaning and interpretation, they typically do not deal with hypotheses. QN is designed to test hypotheses. QR is not designed to test hypotheses or to generalize to other groups. Early efforts at QR were primarily descriptive; however, it is now more generally accepted that QR goes beyond pure description. You may know of some early work that sets forth things that happen to a particular group, group member, or subculture. I remember a piece I read many years ago that gave a detailed account of a principal after following him for a year (Wolcott, 1973). His emphasis was primarily descriptive rather than interpretative.

Many believe that it is the role of the researcher to do more than just describe a situation or person. It is the researcher's role to bring understanding, interpretation, and meaning as they examine data. An example might help you to see this more clearly. Richardson (2008) wrote a humorous ethnographic account of her dinner with Lord Esqy and other prominent figures on the occasion of her giving a lecture at the University of Melbourne. In this account, she moved beyond the simple description that Wolcott offered and led us to greater insight into the culture that was so different from hers.

Some feminist researchers and postmodernists move even further from description and interpretation. They take a political stance and have an agenda that places the researcher in an activist posture, less remote and more action-oriented. These researchers often become quite involved with the individuals they study and try to improve their human condition. So their purpose takes on a social or political posture.

Qualitative Research Is Dynamic

In general, QR is thought to be fluid and ever changing. As such, it doesn't follow one particular way of doing things. Below, I illustrate four ways in which QR is dynamic. First, I talk about how qualitative researchers have changed the way in which they study culture. Next, I describe the dynamic aspects of interviewing. Following that, I address how qualitative researchers work in a fluid rather than fixed environment. I conclude with the idea that qualitative researchers may not necessarily have a detailed, immutable plan for the conduct of the research.

Studying Culture in New Ways

One popular tradition comes from the field of anthropology. A brief history should help you understand the current context. In the past, anthropologists traveled to countries different from their own. They immersed themselves in the culture for an extended period and attempted to understand the culture. One of the best known anthropologists, Margaret Mead (a young anthropologist), traveled to Samoa and immersed herself in the culture over a period of several years. Her book about the culture was widely read (Mead, 1928). In the 1980s, Freeman challenged her findings, thinking she had been duped or fooled. You might gain some insight into doing ethnographic work by reading her work and Freeman's interpretation of what happened. Another important anthropologist was Oscar Lewis (1973), who studied poverty among five families in Mexico in and 1950s. I recall being mesmerized reading his account. These examples are situated in the discipline of anthropology.

Some sociologists also conducted research in a similar manner. In the 1920s and 1930s, as large waves of immigrants moved to the cities, some sociologists, especially those associated with the Chicago school, used the methods of ethnography to study immigrants and their life experiences (e.g., Park, 1950). (As an aside, a movement called ***symbolic interactionism*** emerged after World War II in the same department of sociology. This latter movement involved analysis of communication patterns.) Even today, some sociologists take field trips with their students: Harris (2011) conducted fieldwork with his students in Coastal Ecuador; Blommaert and Jie (2010) described their experience in the field.

Rather than traveling to remote locations, some researchers study virtual cultures on the Internet. For example, Markham (1998) explored themes of life in cyberspace. Fay's (2007) research dealt with cyberethnography. She addressed the issue of mobility and non-fixedness in the group she studied. Nimrod's research illustrates some of the challenges in such online studies (2011). He used data drawn from six online communities that spanned one year and included about 50,000 posts. Labeled *netnography*, the study used an online ethnographic approach. Observations of technologically mediated interactions were used. Four factors distinguished this approach—it was based on published texts, observed behaviors of people (but the individuals themselves are not seen), relied on archival saved communications, and looked at private interactions that take place in a public space. In each of these examples, researchers found themselves moving into uncharted territory in terms of how a study should be conducted. You can see how researchers operated in a dynamic rather than static manner as they pursued the study of culture.

Dynamic Aspects of Interviewing

Why do I say that interviewing is dynamic? Rather than following a predetermined script or set of questions, qualitative researchers often conduct interviews in which the participants tell their stories in their own way. Questions are broad and open rather than structured and rigid. Rubin and Rubin (2005) commented that in qualitative interviewing "you can understand experiences in which you did not participate" (p. 3). Because much of the interviewing is unstructured, they suggested that qualitative interviewers "explore new areas and discover and unravel intriguing puzzles" (p. 4). I know that this dynamic nature of qualitative interviewing is a critical element in the development of a successful qualitative study. Kvale (1996) and Kvale and Brinkmann (2009) also speak of the interview as conversation, suggesting that the interviewer does not have preconceived questions but is open to new and unexpected phenomena. Dundon and Ryan (2009), from the school of business and economics at the National University of Ireland in Galway, illustrate how dynamic interviewing practices in the case study of Waterford Wedgewood Crystal resulted in respondents opening up and revealing important information.

Fluid Environment

Qualitative researchers do not always know what they will study. Qualitative researchers feel free to modify protocols as they progress through the ever-changing landscape of those they study. Brown (n.d.), a professor in the department of sociology at Brown University, speaks of several important components of QR in environmental health. He identifies a flexible study design since

> we don't always know until we're well into the project where we are placing our emphasis. Often we change directions and take new tacks in the midst of the work, due to our own realizations about the material, and in part from the ongoing interaction with people. (p. 11)

Another aspect of fluidity is the identification of participants. Often researchers do not know whom they will study or how many participants there will be. They sometimes rely on some of their participants to identify others who might be studied by using a snowball sampling technique (Noy, 2007), or they might ask key **informants** to nominate others who can be studied.

Plan May Be Modified

Qualitative researchers do not always begin with a detailed and concrete plan for how they will conduct their research. They may find that the questions they investigate evolve as they begin to gather and analyze their data. In keeping with the dynamic nature of QR, you will discover that

> qualitative research characteristically does not use standardized procedures—and this is a main reason for the low reputation of qualitative research in some social disciplinary 'communities.' Doing qualitative research makes the impact of the researcher far more obvious than in its quantitative counterpart. (Breuer et al., 2002, para. 3)

No Single Way of Doing Something

There is not just one way of doing QR. It is informed by many disciplines. It borrows ideas from the social sciences, the natural sciences, philosophy, humanities, and the arts.

I think the fact that there is no specific or best way to conduct QR is one of the reasons students sometimes have difficulty understanding what QR is. They want it to be a single thing. "Tell me how to do it," they say. After all, if I do scientific research and conduct an experiment, I know what makes a true experiment. I know what difficulties there are in conducting an experiment in a real-world setting and how to approximate a true experiment (Cook & Campbell, 1979; Trochim, 2006). I know how to conduct a survey. Why can't I learn the "right" or "best" way to conduct QR? As consumers and conductors of research, we are often wedded to our old paradigms, and we know that old ways are hard to discard.

We are all aware that there is no *one way* to do something; there is no *right way* to do something; there is no *best way* to do something. You might come to appreciate this idea if you move out of the discipline of research and into the field of art. What is the way art should be? The Church used to set the standard for good art. There was only one way. But then some artists tried new ideas. People laughed at Impressionists like Monet, but now, many appreciate their work. People made fun of the Cubists (Picasso and Braque), and yet they are seen as opening the doors to so many other ways of making art. People said modern art was not art, and now, much of it commands millions of dollars. So I urge you to keep your minds open as you explore alternative ways of doing research.

Reality Interpreted by the Researcher

Recall what I said about the researcher as instrument. Can you accept that there is no single reality that exists independent of your interpretation? I am not talking about the philosophical question of whether a branch dropping from a tree in the forest makes a sound. I am talking about social interactions among humans, thoughts individuals have about a topic, or the inner workings of a unit in a small company. There are potentially several ways to interpret what you see or hear. As the researcher, you do the interpretation. Of course, your interpretation will carry more weight if the data you gather, the manner in which you organize the data, and the vehicle you use to present your research supports your findings.

Qualitative Research Is Inductive

A traditional approach to research follows a deductive approach. Deductive reasoning works from the general to the specific. In contrast, QR moves from the specific to the general. You can think of this as going from the bottom up, by using observations to generate hypotheses, if indeed there are any hypotheses. QR moves from the concrete to the abstract. Researchers begin with data and use the data to gain an understanding of phenomena and interactions. They do not test hypotheses (except in the research approach of grounded theory), as is typical in experimental research.

Because QR employs an inductive approach, I have used an inductive way of writing and presenting the material in this book. I suggest that you begin by collecting data for some kind of research project. This inductive approach is the opposite of a deductive approach to doing research. In the latter type, you would do a considerable amount of planning and write a proposal for research prior to gathering data.

You have heard the term *inductive approach* often throughout your school experience. But what does it really mean? When using an inductive approach, one thing leads to another, like scaffolding. You begin by gathering a considerable amount of data. You then go through your data to see whether you can find many examples of a particular thing in order to identify a central issue or idea (a concept or theme). Of course, you might find some statements that do not support the theme. As you simultaneously collect and look at your data, you begin to move to more general statements or ideas, based on the specifics found in your data.

Qualitative Research Deals With the Whole

QR involves the study of a situation or thing in its entirety rather than identification of specific variables. You can think of it this way: Qualitative researchers want to study how something is and understand it. They are not interested in breaking down components into separate variables. Many of you are familiar with the scientific method of research and are used to looking at how one variable is caused by another or how several variables are related to each other. Such an approach is used in order to test hypotheses. But in QR, we are not interested in testing hypotheses. In fact, most QR traditions aim for description, understanding, and interpretation and not examination of cause and effect.

Let's look at an example. Sharon has been working with young females who have returned to complete a high school education after having a baby. She meets with them once a week in the evening at a local high school. Although Sharon feels that she knows something about their basic skills in reading and math, she does not understand other aspects of these students' lives. She decides to try to determine what life is like for these students. She is not interested in looking at various factors that might predict their poor performance; she feels that she knows some of this already. Rather, she wants to know what they are like as individuals. How is their life now, and how do they think it will be when they complete high school? I think this is an ideal situation for doing a qualitative study from a feminist perspective. The students are available, she has access to them, and she hopes to empower them to take charge of their lives in a more meaningful manner.

Qualitative Research Occurs in Natural Settings

QR typically involves studying things as they exist rather than contriving artificial situations or experiments. So a qualitative researcher might be interested in looking at a particular organization as it experiences downsizing. Who are the key decision makers? On what basis are decisions made regarding individuals? What counseling and support services are available for those who leave as well as those who stay? As a researcher, you would need to be especially sensitive to the needs of the organization as well as the needs of individuals. **Gaining access** and getting diverse accounts of the process would prove challenging and illuminating. From a psychological viewpoint, you might be interested in ways organizations provide counseling and support for individuals.

Natural settings are used when talking to people or observing them. Some prefer direct face-to-face contact for interviews. Others have explored interviews through web conferencing. Glassmeyer, professor and qualitative researcher whose work I include in detail in Chapter 7, described a study he conducted using Elluminate (software to facilitate web conferencing).

Other researchers have used technological tools such as Skype or GPS in their work. I describe some of this work in Chapter 8. As technology improves, I believe that we will find increased use of alternative ways to conduct interviews.

Natural settings are also desirable when collecting other types of data, such as photographs, videos, or pictures created by the participants or of the environment in which the participants live or work. I have seen family portraits used as data. I have seen drawings made by children used as data. Notes taken by the researcher, either at the time of an observation or as soon thereafter as possible, are also data.

Role of the Researcher

As I discussed earlier, the researcher plays a pivotal role in the QR process. Data are collected, information is gathered, settings are viewed, and realities are constructed through his or her eyes and ears. Further, the qualitative researcher is responsible for analyzing the data through an iterative process that moves back and forth between data collected and data analyzed. And finally, the qualitative researcher interprets and makes sense of the data. Saldaña (2009) offered a detailed explanation of **coding** and analytic procedures. But it is the researcher who will select and apply a particular procedure. Quantitative researchers are more likely to select a statistic that is appropriate to the hypothesis being tested. Their role in the actual analysis is, therefore, limited. Of course, how they interpret the statistical data and how they organize and report it are critical.

It is important to remember that the researcher is the primary instrument of data collection and analysis. Unlike when doing an experimental study, in which scientific scales or measuring instruments are often used, when doing QR, the researcher decides what information to gather. All information is filtered through the researcher's eyes and ears and is influenced by his or her experience, knowledge, skill, and background. Most qualitative researchers acknowledge the dilemma of trying to be unbiased and objective. In fact, postmodernists, interpretists, constructivists, and feminists acknowledge that the elusive objectivity often sought in traditional or scientific research is inappropriate in the QR arena. They have come to believe that what exists out in the world can be understood as it is mediated through the one doing the observing. I want to be very clear about this idea: There is no getting it right, because there could be many "rights." Descriptions, understandings, and interpretations are based on the data you collect and your ability to organize and integrate them to make a meaningful whole.

A *bias* is a preference that inhibits impartial judgment. Bias and QR are topics that challenge both students and their professors. One view is that bias can be eliminated (or at least controlled) by careful work, triangulation, and multiple sources. I do not believe this is true. Bias is a concept that is related to foundationalist, traditional, or post-positivist thinking. The position I take here is that striving for objectivity by reducing bias is not important for much of QR. I think that some researchers are reluctant to adopt a QR approach because they think the researcher (and by implication, the research) is biased. Well, of course, the researcher has views on the topic. After all, he or she probably would not be investigating a particular topic if he or she had not thought about the topic. There is no single or simple answer to this dilemma. I think the following viewpoint is instructive.

> The (social) sciences usually try to create the impression that the results of their research have *objective* character. In this view, scientific results are—or at least should be—independent from the person who produced the knowledge, e.g., from the single researcher. According to this perspective, objectivity is what makes the difference between valid scientific knowledge and other outcomes of human endeavors and mind. On the one hand, there are many efforts to justify this perspective on epistemological and philosophical grounds. On the other hand, various practices are used to support and produce this idea of objectivity (a rather well-known and mundane example is the rhetorical strategy of avoiding the use of the first-person pronouns in scientific texts). In their everyday scientific life almost all (experienced) researchers nevertheless "know" about the impact of personal and situational influences on their research work and its results. "Officially" and in publications, these influences are usually covered up—they are treated as defaults that are to be avoided. (Breuer et al., 2002, para. 1)

Researchers know that they influence the research and results. But some researchers—those who still hold on to a positivist or post-positivist position about objectivity, maintaining distance, and the need to reduce bias that Breuer and his colleagues (2002) cite—try to identify ways to reduce the subjectivity of the qualitative researcher. There are several stances taken. Some qualitative researchers, those who see themselves as phenomenologists, use a technique they call *bracketing*. I will talk more about this later, but for now, think of *bracketing* as trying to identify your views on the topic and then putting them aside. Other qualitative researchers take the view that they can verify their interpretations by having others look at the data and go through the same process. They refer to this process as *member checks* or *interrater reliability*. Other qualitative researchers take the view that if they collect data from multiple sources, they will have a more accurate picture and thus remain less biased. They refer to this as *triangulation*. For me, these strategies are associated with the viewpoint of a post-positivist. My personal position is more in keeping with that of a postmodernist or an interpretist, and as such, I would not adopt those techniques. At this point, you are probably beginning to question some of your basic assumptions about doing research. Can we really take an objective stance? Should we want to? Why should we want to?

In-Depth Study

Another critical element of QR involves looking deeply at a few things rather than looking at the surface of many things. An important aspect of the investigation is to look at the whole rather than isolate variables in a reductionistic manner. If we want to understand something fully, we need to look at it much more completely. It is like opening up an artichoke and looking at the layers upon layers until you reach the core. There are often gems hidden deep inside, but there is a struggle along the way to get there.

So much of QR involves studying and looking at a few individuals, sometimes just one person. Some researchers study themselves using a technique called *autoethnography*. Kaufmann (2012) explored the relationship between her personal stories and her capacity as a qualitative researcher. Others apply newer techniques. Kang (2010) interrogated a famous Korean drummer and the sociocultural and historical context of his life. Since the drummer had died 20 years previously, he devised a technique using different methods of inquiry. Interestingly, he wrote a series of imaginary email exchanges to present his findings.

Others tend to study small groups as they interact with each other in a particular setting. Some of these groups may be highly structured and others loosely structured. The number of individuals you study is not critical; rather, the nature of the study and the degree to which you explore complex, in-depth phenomena distinguish QR.

Words, Themes, Narratives, and Writing

Words, rather than numbers, characterize QR. Quite often, direct quotes from the participants are included to illustrate a certain point. Details are often included about those studied or the setting in which a study was conducted. Those who studied cultures, the *ethnographers*, took the position that **thick description** (Geertz, 1973) is desirable in order to see underlying meanings and understandings. The idea of thick description has been adopted by many different kinds of qualitative researchers. You will often read details about the setting in which a study was conducted, how the participants looked, or even the respondents' nonverbal gestures.

I suspect that almost any QR study that you read will have used either interviews, observations, or both as a major source of data. But most of you think of data as numbers, not words. As you begin to think about any kind of QR, try to remember that data do not have to be numbers; data can be words and visual representations as well. Here is an example: Diane was studying women managers and how they dealt with issues of power imbalance. She interviewed 10 mid-level managers. She also observed them in their offices, at company meetings, and in informal settings. In addition, she reviewed their written memos to staff. It should be clear that she obtained her data from interviews, from observation, and by reviewing written material. The kind of data she collected were the managers' thoughts about interacting with superiors and subordinates, the observations she made of how the managers interacted with these two groups at meetings, general observations of the physical surroundings in which they worked, and written material provided by the managers. As you read the information in later chapters, you will find some differences in the kind of data that are collected by the various traditions. For example, ethnographers tend to spend more time immersed in the cultural environment, while phenomenologists are more likely to talk at length to participants. Contemporary ethnographers often study online culture, so the data they collect may come from emails or chat rooms.

Concepts and themes are developed from the data. All of the traditions and approaches eventually lead to your taking the large amount of data you collect and making sense of it. Grounded theory uses a structured approach to data analysis and offers specific steps to follow in order to organize and synthesize data. Most of the other approaches are very general in terms of how to make meaning from data. Computer software programs facilitate organizing, searching, combining, processing, and locating data. Unlike a statistical package, however, qualitative software requires your input and decision making.

QR is also characterized by a style of writing that is less technical and formal than is used in more traditional research. Additionally, qualitative researchers often write in the first person or active voice. Such active voice often leads to greater trust and accountability and is more forceful. Intrator (2000) suggested several textual devices that writers can use to get the audience to trust the them and that can show how description and interpretation are intertwined. Colyar (2009) believed that writing should be taught in QR courses. LaRossa (2012) described how writing can vary by latitude (relationship between the humanities and science), longitude (relationship to the number of and length of data excerpts), and altitude (relationship to developing theory).

Rather than writing a report or an account as a vehicle for disseminating information, some avant-garde researchers take the output of QR to a different level. They publish poetry (Weems, 2003) or use participants' words in constructing poems. West (2013) used videos to look at reflexive practices. Some perform a dance (Blumenfeld-Jones, 1995) or write a poem reacting to the dance (Prendergast, 2009). Eryaman (2012) used whirling dervishes—together with photographs—to explain social science inquiry. Sangha and colleagues (2012) used ethnodrama to explain the lived experiences of precarious workers in Canada. Hughes (2011) wrote her dissertation as a magazine. The magazine is called "Phenomenology and the Body." The cover showed a number of young girls. It would certainly grab your attention. Unfortunately, she was not able to submit it to her university in that form. Caulley (2008) urged us to write creative nonfiction using fiction techniques. Jones (2011) developed a documentary film. Using photo-methods, Allen (2011) studied a challenging subject in her research on sexuality and schooling.

Nonlinear

We often think of traditional research as following a certain order. You might begin with a research question, conduct a review of the literature, gather data, do an analysis, and write your conclusions. The order is relatively fixed. In contrast, QR can be viewed as iterative and nonlinear, with multiple beginning points. You could start with an interest in a particular type of individual. You could begin with an observation about how an event affects certain individuals. You could begin with an interest in something you read. In addition, while QN follows the sequence of data collection followed by data analysis, QR takes a somewhat different approach. In QR, the researcher moves back and forth between data gathering/collection and data analysis, rather than in a linear fashion from data collection to data analysis.

Here is an illustration of how Glass (2001) may have progressed through his study of families of autistic children. He identified a number of families who fit the criterion of having an autistic child. He scheduled his first appointment and visited the family in their home for one afternoon. Following his visit, he transcribed the interview he conducted with the mother, recorded his observations of the family, and began his journal. All data were entered into a database or a word processing program. He subsequently imported these files into NVivo (a computer software program for storing, organizing, and managing complex **qualitative data**) and began initial coding. He knew the codes were tentative and served as guidelines. Next, he scheduled a visit with a second family. He refined his questions to these new family members based on his initial coding and his thinking about what he had learned so far. He went back to his journal and his observational record. He also returned to importing his data into the software program, processed the second set of materials, and reviewed everything. This back-and-forth nature of the process is what I mean by iterative and nonlinear.

Challenges of Doing Qualitative Research

I have heard some people say that doing QR is appealing because you don't have to deal with numbers, statistics, and tables. But often, I believe, the lack of rules, the vast amounts of data to process, and the tasks of writing are baffling to some. If you are uncomfortable with ambiguity, have difficulty putting words on paper, and need high levels of structure, you might find QR frustrating.

You no doubt might also find yourself keeping a journal, engaging in self-reflection, writing extensive notes, taking videos or photographs, filling your kitchen table with notecards and colored pencils, learning how to store and retrieve information on your personal computer, learning how to access chat rooms and download conversations, writing drafts of your project, meeting with your faculty advisers, commiserating with fellow students, ignoring your family and social life, feeling the joys and hardships of your participants, and traveling on a journey of growth, frustration, and accomplishment.

CHECK YOURSELF

- Research questions can be developed from different starting points—human interactions, social processes, and phenomena. These could include the following:
  - people—whom you want to study (e.g., aged, managers, bikers, displaced workers)
  - concepts—what you want to study (e.g., power, mental illness, learning to swim)
  - places—where you should do a study (e.g., football field, museum, virtual community)
  - events—special situations (e.g., hurricane, shooting, inauguration)
- What is the role of self—is it reflexive and subjective?
  - Self-awareness and thinking about the self—what you believe, how you come to know things, and your personal views on research—will guide you as you plan your research.
- There are several different types of reflexivity:
  - personal reflexivity—what your values are
  - epistemological reflexivity—your view of how you know the world
  - contextual and ethical reflexivity—the appropriateness of research with some groups and gaining consent to conduct your research
- There have been several points made about subjectivity in this chapter:
  - The researcher is not remote or objective; he or she is part of the system.
  - Subjectivity is connected to reflexivity.
  - Ontology is what you know about the world.
  - Epistemology is how you know about the world.
  - All data are filtered through the senses of the researcher.
- There are eleven critical elements of QR:
  - understanding human behavior
  - dynamic nature
  - more than one way to conduct it
  - researcher interprets reality

- inductive—moving from specific to general
- made up of the whole and not the little parts
- occurs in natural settings
- researcher's role is critical
- looking in-depth
- writing is important
- nonlinear—multidirectional

KEY DISCUSSION ISSUES

1. What are typical research questions that involve human interaction in the natural world?
2. What does it mean to take a reflexive stance? How can you do this?
3. Why should subjectivity be accepted in QR, when I have been taught that objectivity is the watchword of good research?
4. How can I keep straight what the critical elements of QR are? Which ones must I remember?
5. What are aspects of QR that might prove to be a challenge?

MODULE 2

Developing Research Questions and Being Reflexive

Practice developing research questions and being reflexive. Begin by generating at least five questions of interest to you. Write them down. Then try to generate your own reflective ideas about yourself and how they might impact the way you go about answering one of the questions.

Discuss your thinking in a small group. Continue to post on your blog about research questions and self-reflection.

REFERENCES

Allen, L. (2011). "Picture this": Using photo-methods in research on sexualities and schooling. *Qualitative Research, 11*(5), 487–504.

Arber, A. (2006). Reflexivity: A challenge for the researcher as practitioner? *Journal of Research in Nursing, 11*(2), 147–157.

Belousov, K., Horlick-Jones, T., Bloor, M., Gilinsky, Y., Golbert, V., Kostikovsky, Y., . . . Pentsov, D. (2007). Any port in a storm: Fieldwork difficulties in dangerous and crisis-ridden settings. *Qualitative Research, 7*(2), 155–175.

Ben-Ari, A., & Enosh, G. (2011). Processes of reflectivity: Knowledge construction in qualitative research. *Qualitative Social Work, 10*(2), 152–171.

Beneito-Montagut, R. (2011). Ethnography goes online: Towards a user-centered methodology to research interpersonal communication on the Internet. *Qualitative Research, 11*(6), 716–735.

Bishop, E., & Shepherd, M. (2011). Ethical reflections: Examining reflexivity through the narrative paradigm. *Qualitative Health Research, 21*(9), 1283–1294.

Blommaert, J., & Jie, D. (2010). *Ethnographic fieldwork: A beginner's guide.* [Google eBook]. Retrieved from http://books.google.com/books/about/Ethnographic_fieldwork.html?id=5FVIUYvMWm0C

Blumenfeld-Jones, D. (1995). Dance as a mode of research representation. *Qualitative Inquiry, 1*(4), 391–401.

Bosworth, M., Hoyle, C., & Dempsey, M. (2011). Researching trafficked women: On institutional resistance and the limits to feminist reflexivity. *Qualitative Inquiry, 17*(9), 769–779.

Bott, E. (2010). Favourites and others: Reflexivity and the shaping of subjectivities and data in qualitative research. *Qualitative Research, 10*(2), 159–173.

Breuer, F., Mruck, K., & Roth, W-M. (2002). Subjectivity and reflexivity: An introduction [10 paragraphs]. *Forum Qualitative Sozialforschung/Forum: Qualitative Social Research, 3*(3), Art. 9.

Brinkmann, S. (2011). *Current dilemmas in qualitative research.* Keynote address at the 17th Qualitative Health Research Conference, Vancouver, Canada.

Brown, P. (n.d.). *Syllabus, qualitative methods in environmental health research.* Retrieved from http://www.brown.edu/research/research-ethics/sites/brown.edu.research.research-ethics/files/uploads/Qualitative%20Methods%20in%20Env%20Health%20Research%20-%20Brown.pdf

Burnett, E. (2011). Reflexivity in qualitative research: Reflections from a workshop. Retrieved from http://emmaburnettx.wordpress.com/2011/09/29/reflexivity-in-qualitative-research-reflections-from-a-workshop/

Butera, K. (2006). Manhunt. *Qualitative Inquiry, 12*(6), 1262–1282.

Carlsen, A., & Dutton, J. E. (2011a). *Learning from moments of being alive as a qualitative researcher.* [Online newsletter post]. Retrieved from http://www.centerforpos.org/2011/07/learning-from-moments-of-being-alive-as-a-qualitative-researcher/

Carlsen, A., & Dutton, J. E. (Eds.). (2011b). *Research alive: Exploring generative moments in doing qualitative research.* Copenhagen, Denmark: Copenhagen Business School Press.

Carrington, B. (2008). "What's the footballer doing here?" Racialized performativity, reflexivity, and identity. *Cultural Studies, Critical Methodologies, 8*(4), 423–452.

Caulley, D. (2008). Making qualitative research reports less boring: The techniques of writing creative nonfiction. *Qualitative Inquiry, 14*(3), 424–449.

Ceglowski, D., Bacigalupa, C., & Peck, E. (2011). Aced out: Censorship of qualitative research in the age of "scientifically based research." *Qualitative Inquiry, 17*(8), 679–686.

Colyar, J. (2009). Becoming writing, becoming writers. *Qualitative Inquiry 15*(2), 421–436.

Cook, T. D., & Campbell, D. T. (1979). *Quasi-experimentation: Design and analysis for field settings.* Chicago, IL: Rand McNally.

Correll, S. (1995). The ethnography of an electric bar: The lesbian café. *Journal of Contemporary Ethnography, 24*(3), 280–298.

Crawford, P. (2012). Book review: Visual methods in psychology: Using and interpreting images in qualitative research. *Psychology of Women Quarterly, 36*(2), 247–248.

Davis, C. (2012). G.E.D. in 3 voices. *Qualitative Inquiry, 18*(3), 227–234.

Davis, H. (2009, June 5). The concept of "researcher as research instrument" within the hinterlands of research. [Web log post]. *21st Century Leadership Literacies.* Retrieved from http://leadershipliteracies.wordpress.com/2009/05/06/researcher-as-research-instrument/

Doucet, A. (2008). "From her side of the gossamer wall(s)": Reflexivity and relational knowing. *Qualitative Sociology, 31*, 73–87. Retrieved from http://www.andreadoucet.com/wp-content/uploads/2011/02/Doucet-2008-Gossamer-Walls.pdf

Dundon, T., & Ryan, P. (2009). The qualitative research interview: Fashioning respondent affinity. *Journal of Management Research, 1*(1). Retrieved from www.macrothink.org/jmr

Eryaman, M. (2012). From whirling to trembling: A montage of dervishes' performative inquiries. *Qualitative Inquiry, 18*(1), 55–62.

Fay, M. (2007). Mobile subjects, mobile methods: Doing virtual ethnography in a feminist online network [64 paragraphs]. *Forum Qualitative Sozialforschung/Forum: Qualitative Social Research, 8*(3), Art. 14.

Fletcher, R., & St. George, J. (2011). Heading into fatherhood—nervously: Support for fathering from online dads. *Qualitative Health Research, 21*(8), 1101–1114.

Freeman, D. (1983). *Margaret Mead and Samoa.* Cambridge, MA: Harvard University Press.

Galindo, J. (2011). *A plea for reflexivity: The writing of a doctoral dissertation biography.* Retrieved from http://bath.academia.edu/JFernandoGalindo/Papers/437009/A_Plea_for_Reflexivity_The_Writing_of_a_Doctoral_Dissertation_Biography_Draft_Version-January_2011_

Geertz, C. (1973). *The interpretation of culture.* New York, NY: Basic Books.

George-Walker, L., & Danaher, P. (2007). Evaluating value(s): Issues in and implications of research significance and researcher identity. *eContent Management.* Retrieved from http://smtp.smallenterpriseresearch.com/special-issues/333/evaluating-value(s)-issues-in-and-implications

Gerstl-Pepin, C., & Patrizio, K. (2009). Learning from Dumbledore's pensieve: Metaphor as an aid in teaching reflexivity in qualitative research. *Qualitative Research, 9*(3), 299–308.

Gilgun, J. (2010). Reflexivity and qualitative research. *Current Issues in Qualitative Research, 1*(2), 108. Retrieved from http://www.scribd.com/doc/35787948/Reflexivity-and-Qualitative-Research

Gilgun, J. (2011). *Reflexivity and qualitative research.* [E-book]. Retrieved from http://www.smashwords.com/books/view/39985

Glass, P. (2001). *Autism and the family* (Unpublished doctoral dissertation). Virginia Tech, Blacksburg, VA..

Graduate School of Social and Political Science, University of Edinburgh. (2011). *Reflexivity in qualitative research.* Retrieved from http://www.sps.ed.ac.uk/gradschool/research_training_courses/reflexivity_in_qualitative_research

Griffiths, M. (2009). *Critical approaches in qualitative educational research.* Retrieved from http://www.bera.ac.uk/critical-approaches-in-qualitative-educational-research

Harris, M. (2011). *Ethnographic fieldwork in Coastal Ecuador.* Retrieved from http://omniupdate.fau.edu/goabroad/pdf/Anthro_Course_Description.pdf

Holloway, I., & Biley, F. (2011). Being a qualitative researcher. *Qualitative Health Research, 21*(7), 968–975.

Holloway, W., & Jefferson, T. (2000). *Doing qualitative research differently.* London, England: SAGE.

Hughes, H. E. (2011). *Phenomenal bodies, phenomenal girls: How young adolescent girls experience being enough in their bodies* (Doctoral dissertation). University of Georgia, Athens, GA. (Also available in magazine form from the author.)

Intrator, S. (2000). *Eight text devices useful in writing qualitative research.* Paper presented at the American Educational Research Association, New Orleans, LA.

Janesick, V. (2011). *"Stretching" exercises for qualitative researchers* (3rd ed.). Thousand Oaks, CA: SAGE.

Jones, K. (Producer). (2011). *Rufus Stone the movie.* [DVD]. United States: Parkville Pictures. Retrieved from https://www.facebook.com/kipworld

Kang, D. (2010). Creating learning: A Korean drummer's lifelong quest to be the best. *Qualitative Inquiry, 16*(8), 663–673.

Kaufmann, J. (2012). I spit to meet you on a line unfolding. *Qualitative Inquiry, 18*(1), 16–19.

Keefer, J. (2011). *Silence and voice.* [Website]. Retrieved from http://silenceandvoice.com/category/autoethnography-reflective-practice/page/3/

Kvale, S. (1996). *InterViews: An introduction to qualitative research interviewing.* Thousand Oaks, CA: SAGE

Kvale, S., & Brinkmann, S. (2009). *InterView: Learning the craft of qualitative research interviewing.* Los Angeles, CA: SAGE.

Lambe, J. (2011). Developing pre-service teachers' reflective capacity through engagement with classroom-based research. *Reflective Practice, 12*(1), 87–100.

LaRossa, R. (2012). Writing and reviewing manuscripts in the multidimensional world of qualitative research. *Journal of Marriage and Family, 74*(4), 643–659.

Lewis, O. (1973). *Five families: Mexican case studies in the culture of poverty.* New York, NY: Basic Books.

Liebow, E. (1967). *Tally's corner: A study of Negro street corner men.* London, England: Routledge.

Liebow, E. (1993). *Tell them who I am: The lives of homeless women.* London, England: Penguin Books.

Macbeth, D. (2001). On "reflexivity in qualitative research": Two readings and a third. *Qualitative Inquiry, 7*(1), 35–68.

Mackert, M., Love, B., Donovan-Kicken, E., & Uhle, K. (2011). Health literacy as controversy: An online community's discussion of the U.S. Food and Drug Administration Acetaminophen recommendations. *Qualitative Health Research, 21*(12), 1607–1617.

Major, C., & Savin-Baden, M. (2011). Integration of qualitative evidence: Towards construction of academic knowledge in social science and professional fields. *Qualitative Research, 11*(6), 645–663.

Markham, A. (1998). Life online: Researching real experiences in virtual space. In C. Ellis & A. Bochner (Eds.). *Ethnographic alternative book series.* Walnut Creek, CA: Altamira Press.

McCormick, M., Tempel, L., & Probst, B. (2011). *The power of the process: Reflexivity in qualitative research.* Paper presented at the meeting of Society for Social Work and Research, Tampa, FL. Retrieved from http://sswr.confex.com/sswr/2011/webprogram/Session4567.html

Mead, M. (1928). *Coming of age in Samoa.* New York, NY: William Morrow & Company.

Moore, T. (2008). "Me" as the research instrument: Subject positions, feminist values and multiple "mes." *International Journal of Pedagogies and Learning, 4*(1), 31–41. Retrieved from http://jpl.e-contentmanagement.com/archives/vol/4/issue/1/article/2806/

Naidu, T. (2011). Reflective release: Two poems about doing qualitative research with AIDS home-based care volunteers in South Africa. *Qualitative Inquiry, 17*(4), 343–344.

Nimrod, G. (2011). The fun culture in seniors' online communities. *The Gerontologist, 51*(2), 226–237.

Noy, C. (2007). Sampling knowledge: The hermeneutics of snowball sampling. *International Journal of Social Research Methodology, 11*(4), 327–344.

Park, R. (1950). *Race and culture.* Glencoe, IL: Free Press.

Pascal, J., Johnson, N., Dore, C., & Trainor, R. (2011). The lived experience of doing phenomenology: Perspectives from beginning health science postgraduate researchers. *Qualitative Social Work, 10*(2), 172–189.

Peshkin, A. (1988). In search of subjectivity—one's own. *Educational Researcher, 17*(7), 17–21.

Peshkin, A. (2000). The nature of interpretation in qualitative research. *Educational Researcher, 29*(9), 5–9.

Pillow, W. (2010). Confession, catharsis, or cure? Rethinking the uses of reflexivity as methodological power in qualitative research. *International Journal of Qualitative Studies in Education, 16*(2), 175–196. Retrieved from http://www.scribd.com/doc/57491980/Rethinking-the-Uses-of-Reflexivity

Plesner, U. (2011). Studying sideways: Displacing the problem of power in research interviews with sociologists and journalists. *Qualitative Inquiry, 17*(6), 471–482.

Prendergast, M. (2009). The scholar dances. *Qualitative Inquiry, 15*(8), 1373–1375.

Reavy, P. (Ed.). (2011). *Visual methods in psychology: Using and interpreting images in qualitative research.* New York, NY: Routledge.

Reilly, R. (2011). "We knew her . . ." Murder in a small town: A hybrid work in three voices. *Qualitative Inquiry, 17*(7), 599–601.

Repass, M. (2002). *The professional woman's desire to retire: The process of transition.* Unpublished doctoral dissertation. Virginia Tech, Blacksburg, VA.

Richardson, L. (2008). My dinner with Lord Esqy. *Qualitative Inquiry, 14*(1), 13–17.

Ross, S. (2011). *Reflections on a course in qualitative methodology.* [Web log post]. Retrieved from http://www.srossmktg.com/2011/05/11/reflections-on-a-course-in-qualitative-methodology/

Rubin, H., & Rubin, I. (2005). *Qualitative interviewing: The art of hearing data.* Thousand Oaks, CA: SAGE.

Saldaña, J. (2009). *The coding manual for qualitative research.* London, England: SAGE.

Sangha, J., Slade, B., Mirchandani, K., Maitra, S., & Shan, H. (2012). An ethnodrama on work-related learning in precarious jobs: Racialization and resistance. *Qualitative Inquiry, 18*(3), 286–296.

Shaw, R. (2010). Embedding reflexivity within experiential qualitative psychology. *Qualitative Research in Psychology, 7*(3), 233–243.

Smith, S. V. (2006). Encouraging the use of reflexivity in the writing up of qualitative research. *International Journal of Therapy and Rehabilitation, 13*(5), 209–215.

Snyder, W. (2003). *Perceptions on the diffusion and adoption of Skill-soft, an e-learning program: A case study.* Unpublished doctoral dissertation. Virginia Tech, Blacksburg, VA.

Sullivan, G. (2002). Reflexivity and subjectivity in qualitative research: The utility of a Wittgensteinian framework [29 paragraphs]. *Forum Qualitative Sozialforschung/Forum: Qualitative Social Research, 3*(3), Art. 20.

Trochim, W. (2006). *Research methods knowledge base.* [Website]. Retrieved from http://www.socialresearchmethods.net/kb/index.php

Voutier, C. (2011, October 17). CPD23 thing 5—Reflective practice. [Web log post]. *Goings on of a medical librarian . . . it's all about the new.* Retrieved from http://enhancinghealthcare.wordpress.com/2011/10/17/cpd23-thing-5-%E2%80%93-reflective-practice/

Wamsted, J. (2011). Race, school, and *Seinfeld*: Autoethnographic sketching in black and white. *Qualitative Inquiry, 17*(10), 972–981.

Watson, C. (2011). Staking a claim for fictional narratives in social and educational research. *Qualitative Research, 11*(4), 395–408.

Weems, M. (2003). Poetry. *Qualitative Inquiry, 9*(1), 13–14.

West, C. (2013). Developing reflective practitioners: Using video-cases in music teacher education. *Journal of Music Teacher Education, 22*(2), 11–19.

White, N. (2010). Peshkin on interpreting data. *Qualitative inquiry: A blog about teaching and mentoring.* Retrieved from http://qualitativeinquiry.com/?tag=subjectivity

Willig, C. (2001). *Introducing qualitative research in psychology.* Milton Keynes, England: Open University Press.

Wolcott, H. (1973). *The man in the principal's office: An ethnography.* New York, NY: Holt, Rinehart and Winston.

Yüksel, I. (2011). The effects of post-observational reflective feedback modes on teaching beliefs: Peer vs. teacher-mediated feedback. *Turkish Online Journal of Qualitative Inquiry, 2*(1), Art. 4. Retrieved from http://www.tojqi.net/articles/TOJQI_2_1/TOJQI_2_1_Article_4.pdf

Zabrodska, K., Linnell, S., Laws, C., & Davies, B. (2011). Bullying as intra-active process in neoliberal universities. *Qualitative Inquiry, 17*(8), 709–719.

STUDENT STUDY SITE

Visit **http://www.sagepub.com/lichtmanqrss** to access additional study tools, including eFlashcards and links to SAGE journal articles.

CHAPTER 3

Ethical Issues in Qualitative Research

Focus Your Reading

- Definitions of ethical behavior
- Major principles associated with ethical conduct
- Illustrations of misconduct in general and in qualitative research in particular
- Concerns of qualitative researchers; studying vulnerable groups
- Review boards, setting standards, problems with boards

"A well-known psychologist in the Netherlands whose work has been published widely in professional journals falsified data and made up entire experiments, an investigating committee found" (Carey, 2011). Diederik Stapel of Tilburg University committed academic fraud in several dozen published papers. According to *The New York Times,* this was only the latest in "a string of embarrassments in a field that critics and statisticians say badly needs to overhaul how it treats research results" (Carey, 2011). In a wonderful play on words, Achenbach (2011) from *The Washington Post* reported that Stapel was a "lying Dutchman" who had fabricated his raw data. I had not heard of Stapel previously, but according to these articles, he had published about 150 papers. In December 2011, Stapel, a prominent social psychologist, admitted to fabricating results in numerous studies. According to one source (Gonzalez, 2011), his actions are considered to be one of the biggest frauds in scientific history. Also shocking is the report that in a survey of 2,000 American psychologists, some 70% acknowledged "cutting corners in reporting data" (Gonzalez, 2011). I do not mean to suggest that all sociologists or psychologists are unethical. In fact, I don't think these practices are limited to these groups. Peled and Leichtentritt (2002) reviewed published studies of qualitative social work and concluded that as a trend, "ethical considerations are marginal in most phases of the studies" (p. 145).

We have read too many accounts of questionable practices by physicians in the pharmaceutical industry—doctors being on the payrolls of companies or receiving perks such as lavish trips to warm climates—with the implicit understanding that favorable reports will be forthcoming. Whether we are at a crisis regarding **ethical behavior** by researchers is a question that still remains. It is clear to me that there are certainly problems with unethical behavior. I suspect that Stapel was well aware of the expectation not to falsify data; I can only speculate on what motivated him to do so. I recall many years ago when I was in graduate school that a student and graduate assistant—and a very bright student at that—was caught creating data for his dissertation. He was asked to leave the university—I do not know what happened to him.

In this chapter, I identify the central topics related to **ethical conduct** and issues concerning Institutional Review Boards (IRBs), the primary governing bodies and overseers (usually at universities or government agencies) that grant permission for research to be done. Most of the governing bodies are well meaning. In the early days of qualitative research (QR), few had any ideas that there should be a different set of criteria to evaluate QR than there were for quantitative research (QN). In fact, in these early days, qualitative researchers themselves struggled with criteria. But now in the second decade of the 21st century, the field has matured, and many have gone through such experiences. I write about some of them later in the chapter.

A few years ago, I was doing a phenomenological study of teenage girls. I was interested in learning how they coped with conflicting messages about doing well in school and not being seen as "too smart." The school system had approved my proposal, and I had also received permission from the parents of the girls. I promised confidentiality to the girls. My plan called for me to do a minimum of two interviews with each girl. I was well into my second interview with Susan when the tears started to roll slowly down her cheeks. We were talking about how she wanted to do well, but she sensed that the boys might not like her if she was too "brainy." But then she switched topics and really opened up. She started to tell me about how her stepfather was getting too friendly with her and had touched her in those "special places." I knew then that I was on very sensitive ground. Fortunately, or perhaps not so, our scheduled time together was coming to an end. I completed the interview and told her I would be in touch. Now, I was in quite a dilemma. What was I to do? I had promised to keep all information confidential, but if her stepfather was sexually abusing her, was I obligated to report it? And to whom? Was she telling me the truth or just trying to con me? What would you do?

I tell you this story not to shock you but to get you thinking about the kinds of dilemmas in which you might find yourself when doing QR. Even though I had followed all procedures, received permissions, informed my participants, and promised confidentiality, I had learned some information that troubled me. I felt I had a responsibility to Susan not to reveal the confidence. I also felt I had a responsibility to her if she was being abused. However, I really did not know whether the story she told me was true. Because I was not part of the school system and had no supervisor there, I did not know what to do with the information.

This story illustrates a delicate balance you might face between trying to do what is right in terms of maintaining privacy and, at the same time, recognizing that you have received information that might be damaging to the participant. Should you tell someone? If so, who? What about the promise you made to maintain privacy?

You might not have thought about **ethics** while you were planning your research. Yet recently, much has been written on the topic. I want you to think about what kinds of issues you might face and how you would handle them. In this chapter, I introduce you to some of the basic principles associated with ethics and recent controversies concerning universities and monitoring of QR plans. I know you will find the information challenging. I hope it will cause you to think carefully about your research and about the people you study.

The scenario I described with Susan is not something you will encounter on a regular basis. But I began with it to point out that you might find yourself in a situation that is unexpected and that will require you to use judgment and good sense.

You know that much of QR involves interactions with individuals. As a consequence of developing rapport with participants and getting them to trust you, you may find that they open up to you in very personal ways. When this happens, you face an ethical challenge. What should you do with information you obtain that might be damaging to the individual or to others?

You might think that there are clear guidelines available to you as a researcher to assist if you encounter such challenges, but this is not always the case. In your role as a teacher, counselor, administrator, manager, or therapist, you are guided by a code of conduct or set of ethics established by licensing boards or by the organization for which you work. In contrast, researchers do not have a formal licensing body. A number of organizations offer guidelines about ethical standards, but many lack an enforcement mechanism. The Ethical Standards of the American Educational Research Association were adopted in 1992 and revised in 2000 to "evoke voluntary compliance by moral persuasion" (American Educational Research Association, 2005). The British Educational Research Association (2011) issued Ethical Guidelines for Educational Research in 2011. They are available to download or read online. Similarly, the Association of Social Anthropologists of the UK (2011) issued guidelines in 2011. Many universities use review boards to set and enforce standards. Many large school systems have guidelines. Private organizations may or may not have guidelines.

In this chapter, I begin with definitions of ethical behavior. Next, I look at the major principles associated with the ethics of conducting research. I also address problems with the standards. Following that, I review some significant examples of unethical behavior in the general scientific community as well as examine inappropriate behavior in the field of QR. I look next at some special problems faced by qualitative researchers. I conclude with the issues of setting and enforcing standards of behavior.

Ethical Behavior: Definitions and Background

As I begin this chapter, I ask myself, "What is the meaning of ethics and ethical behavior?" They seem straightforward, don't they? In laymen's terms, we all know what we mean when we say *ethics* or *ethical behavior*. I think there are various commonsense responses to the question. It means doing what is right. It means treating people fairly. It means not hurting anyone. The topic is important to many disciplines. *Qualitative Sociology* devoted its September 2011 issue (volume 34, number 3) to the topic of ethics beyond the IRB. Six articles are included. Several were of particular interest to me. Einwohner (2011) addressed the use of archived testimonies in Holocaust research. Her concerns were related to using pseudonyms and identification numbers instead of actual names. Rupp and Taylor (2011) raised an issue I had not previously encountered. They discussed benefits and ethical dilemmas of returning to a group previously studied—in this instance, the group was composed of drag queens whom they had featured in their book. One challenge they faced related to conflicts over royalties they had shared with group members. They concluded that going back to the group contributed to public sociology. Others have also expressed their views on the topic. Schrag (2011a) maintains a blog on the topic of IRB oversight. Denzin and Giardina (2007), in their edited book, highlighted key topics faced by qualitative researchers in a contemporary environment.

Did You Know

It was in 1906, when the Pure Food and Drug Act was enacted, that regulations regarding the use of human subjects in research came into being.

We deal with ethical issues on a daily basis. Should you report someone who cheats on an exam or copies someone else's writing? Should you return that extra dollar given to you by a clerk or keep a wallet found on the street? Should you give children additional time to finish an exam or provide answers to difficult questions on a test?

Here is a general definition: Ethical behavior represents a set of moral principles, rules, or standards governing a person or a profession. We understand that to be *ethical* is to "do good and avoid evil." This general definition is helpful as we try to understand research ethics.

Although research on humans has been conducted since the Middle Ages, codes of conduct regarding appropriate researcher behavior did not emerge until the 20th century. It was not until the 1960s, when U.S. federal government funding became available, that more researchers became interested in school-based research. By the 1980s, qualitative researchers had moved into the educational arena. At first, there were no clear guidelines. But as more QR was conducted, it became necessary for many institutions to establish review boards.

Sociologists, nurse educators, and those in business also became interested in QR. Universities followed suit and set up procedures to review research proposals. In fact, McGinn and Bosacki (2004) and Coupal (2005) recommended that graduate programs include a course in research ethics.

■ Major Principles Associated With Ethical Conduct

Early on, Bannister (1996) made a plea for questioning how we represent others. He concluded that rules for ethical behavior reside in the conscience and the moral codes of individuals. Although noble, most would argue that some guidelines need to be established as a way to protect humans from exploitation and invasion of privacy. The principles of ethical conduct that I identify below represent an amalgam gleaned from many sources.

Do No Harm

Of all the principles associated with research ethics, "do no harm" is at the cornerstone of ethical conduct. There should be a reasonable expectation by those participating in a research study that they will not be involved in any situation in which they might be harmed. Although this is the standard we are most concerned about violating, I think it is fairly safe to assume that the research you plan and conduct will not be harmful to participants. This principle is often applied to studies involving drugs or a treatment that might be harmful to participants. You might have read about mistreatment during experiments. The 1971 Stanford Prison Experiment, in which students played the roles of guards and prisoners, is one example. When it was found that the guards became increasingly sadistic, the study was terminated. Of course, the kind of QR you plan will not be of this nature. We have become well aware of the potential damage caused by such studies. It is still important, however, for you to make explicit any possible adverse effects of your research.

Bottom line: It is best to safeguard against doing anything that will harm the participants in your study. If you begin a study and you find that some of your participants seem to have adverse reactions, it is best to discontinue the study, even if it means forgoing your research plan.

Privacy and Anonymity

Any individual participating in a research study has a reasonable expectation that privacy will be guaranteed. Consequently, no identifying information about the individual should be revealed in written or other communication. Further, any group or organization participating in a research study has a reasonable expectation that its identity will not be revealed. I would like you to think about privacy of two kinds: institutional and individual. If you study an institution, how do you keep the information you learn private? Suppose you take pictures of places in the institution and want to include them in your written product. Suppose the institution you study is sufficiently unusual that it can be identified from a description or from photographs. If you study individuals, you are faced with other challenges. Suppose you have recorded interviews and want to place a hyperlink or a

YouTube interview in your report about the person being interviewed. Will the voice be recognized? Suppose you collaborate with others and maintain files in a database that can be accessed via the Internet or in the Cloud and others gain access. Suppose you use a computer software program that has links to video and audio. How do you guarantee privacy in these cases? Suppose you study individuals of some prominence, and their identities cannot readily be disguised. One idea to consider is to obtain a signed release authorizing you to use such information in your research. Stein (2010) describes her experiences drawn from her engaging book, *The Stranger Next Door.* In this ethnographic account of a small town, the issue of a ballot that divided the town related to gay and lesbian civil rights. The book became very accessible, and although she tried to keep things anonymous, the community was "outed" by a review in a newspaper. She was charged by the right-wing activists with compromising their anonymity. In this article, she reflects on whether anonymity always serves the interest of researchers and those they study.

With the availability of so much information on the Internet (e.g., YouTube, Facebook), you are faced with challenges that were never considered when the original privacy statements were written. Conversely, you might find yourself facing the opposite problem: Your participants may want their identities revealed. They may want to be acknowledged in your written product. Perhaps they see it as their "15 minutes of fame." Can you reveal their identities? In the 21st century, this principle might not be as simple as one would think. Tilley and Woodthorpe (2011) asked us to think about anonymity as it relates to wide dissemination. They raised questions about being accountable to stakeholders and the demands of putting as much information out there as possible, especially on the Internet. Markham (2012) addressed the ethical dilemmas associated with protecting participants in Internet-based social contexts. She posed the use of the term *fabrication*, but not in the sense of fabricating data or results. Rather, she questioned the idea and unspoken assumption that invention represents a lack of integrity. In her words,

> Using the term also helps to highlight the constructive aspects associated with interpretation, a crucial element and strength of qualitative inquiry. My hope in this article is to provide a much-needed framework for qualitative researchers who struggle with the ethical dilemma of adequately anonymizing information while providing accounts that present rich descriptions and important details about the context or people. (abstract)

With the use of face recognition software, other issues of privacy arise. Can a researcher use images captured on the Internet or Facebook and generally available to the public? The individuals are real people, we must remember, but we might not know who they are to seek permission or to assure privacy. Increasingly, we are challenged to consider how to handle these issues. As technology expands in ways we cannot even imagine, we are faced with thorny issues.

Bottom line: Remove identifying information from your records. Seek permission from the participants—if possible—if you wish to make public information that might reveal who they are or what the organization is. Use caution in publishing long, verbatim quotes, especially if they are damaging to the organization or people in it. Often, these quotes can be located on the Internet and traced to the speaker or author.

Confidentiality

Any individual participating in a research study has a reasonable expectation that information provided to the researcher will be treated in a confidential manner. Consequently, the participant is entitled to expect that such information will not be given to anyone else. Think back to the case of Susan that I presented at the beginning of this chapter. Although I had promised her confidentiality and I had gotten her to open up to me, I now had to deal with information that might prove damaging to her or to others. I chose to investigate the situation further to try to determine the truthfulness of her allegations. During your research, you might learn a considerable amount of personal information because many of the interviews you conduct will be open ended and may move in various directions. As a researcher, you are in a situation that you control. If you sense an interview might be moving in a personal direction, you might have to stop the interview and suggest to the participant that she talk to a counselor or other trusted support person. Willis (2012) discussed confidentiality in an online study of lesbian, gay, bisexual, or transgender (LGBT) participants and their sexual practices. He highlighted an issue related to participants using shared computers and email LISTSERVs—he solved the problem by transferring data to a portable drive and deleting relevant personal information.

Bottom line: It is your responsibility to keep the information you learn confidential. If you sense that an individual is in an emergency situation, you might decide that you can waive your promise for the good of the individual or of others. You need to be much more sensitive to information that you obtain from minors and others who might be in a vulnerable position.

Informed Consent

Individuals participating in a research study have a reasonable expectation that they will be informed of the nature of the study and may choose whether or not to participate. They also have a reasonable expectation that they will not be coerced into participation. On the face of it, this might seem to be relatively easy to follow. But if a study is to be done in an organization, individuals within that group (e.g., management, workers) might feel that they cannot refuse when asked. There might be pressure placed on them by peers or by superiors. Although the idea of informed consent appears to be straightforward, there are situations in which informed consent may not be possible. For example, it is more difficult to obtain consent from minors, individuals who do not have a clear understanding of English, or those who are mentally disabled or emotionally fragile. Another issue regarding obtaining informed consent is that your research study—because it is dynamic and subject to twists and turns—might diverge in a direction that causes participants to become uncomfortable or unwilling to continue. Because of this, I believe that the consent people give in advance may not really be "informed." Recently, researchers have expressed concerns about studying people on the Internet. I have read accounts of individuals who became angry that a researcher was using their discussion board or LISTSERV for data collection. Whether you lurk in chat rooms or on LISTSERVs or you enter domains of YouTube or Facebook, you are exploring Internet cultures. There is no general procedure for seeking consent in these arenas. Researchers are now beginning to explore ways of obtaining consent from such groups. Quinnell (2011) raised the question as to whether it is appropriate to lurk as an observer or alleged participant on a publicly owned message board. I think how to handle such behavior is still open for consideration.

Bottom line: Your responsibility is to make sure that participants are informed, to the greatest extent possible, about the nature of your study. Even though it is not always possible to describe the direction your study might take, it is your responsibility to do the best you can to provide complete information. If participants decide to withdraw from the study, they should not feel penalized for so doing. You also need to be aware of special problems that may occur when you study people online. For example, one concern might be the vulnerability of group participants. Another is the level of intrusiveness of the researcher. McCleary (2007) discussed many of these issues from the perspective of social workers; many of these concerns can be transferred to other social science disciplines.

Truthfulness and Accuracy in Reporting Data

The criteria of truthfulness and accuracy in reporting data are assumed in QN. (As I described at the beginning of this chapter, however, this assumption cannot always be supported.) When we have data in the form of numbers and counting, it is incumbent upon the researcher to report accurately what the data say. There are two aspects associated with the criteria. First, we expect that reported data represent the actual values collected or determined. Second, we expect that the data analysis will be appropriate. In the first case, ethical behavior requires that reported values are accurate. This is a given in medical and psychological research. It is more difficult to determine in the latter case, since there is more judgment with respect to appropriate handling of the data. How we deal with these criteria in the case of QR is considerably more difficult because it is through the lens of the researcher that data are collected, analyzed, and reported. There is no single truth that exists independent of the researcher. As such, it is much more difficult to determine the extent to which reporting is reasonable. Some researchers ask several colleagues to review reporting and interpretations. Some researchers use the term **inter-rater reliability** for this procedure. Accuracy also comes into play. Some researchers ask participants to review data analysis to see if what is reported represents what the individual said. Some researchers use the term **member checks**. By no means do all researchers follow this procedure. But these two ideas—using several individuals to verify that data are meaningful interpretations and using participants to verify that data are accurate—are not necessarily the practice of many qualitative researchers.

Bottom line: Ethical practice involves the expectation that the researcher will not create data or fudge data—whether data are in the form of numbers or words. Further, ethical practice in QR dictates that the researcher will provide interpretations based on the reflective nature of the process.

Rapport and Friendship

Once participants agree to be part of a study, the researcher works to develop rapport in order to get them to disclose information. I recall when Alice Lo, a student of mine from China, studied the wives of Chinese graduate students who had relocated to a rural college campus. She found herself getting too close to the women she studied. She was concerned about their language difficulties and the problems they had adjusting to Western society. Yet as she became close to these women, she became sad and frustrated that she couldn't do anything about their situation. She was somewhere between rapport and a faked friendship. Duncombe and Jessop (2005) have brought out issues related to what they call *faking friendship*. From their feminist perspective, they suggest that the interviewer might put herself in the position of being a friend so as to get participants to disclose more information than they really want to (pp. 120–121). I think there is a difference between developing rapport and becoming a friend.

A trend in the medical and health fields is to involve patients in the research process. Schipper and her colleagues (2010) discussed the issue of how equality in such collaborative efforts can be achieved. They identified various tensions. Their article is presented as an ethnodrama, in which the personal narrative of the research partner unfolds.

Bottom line: Researchers should make sure that they provide an environment that is trustworthy. At the same time, they need to be sensitive to the power that they hold over participants. Researchers need to avoid setting up a situation in which participants think they are friends with the researcher.

Intrusiveness

Individuals participating in a research study have a reasonable expectation that the conduct of the researcher will not be excessively intrusive. *Intrusiveness* can refer to intruding on their *time*, intruding on their *space*, and intruding on their *personal lives*. As you design a research study, you ought to be able to make a reasonable estimate of the amount of time participation will take. I remember my student, Mary Repass, conducted research about prominent and busy female executives. She needed to make sure that her study would not intrude on their work lives. She scheduled interviews at their offices and limited her interviews to a maximum of one hour. Intrusion into personal space might be an issue for some individuals; they may not want you in their homes, offices, or classrooms. You might have to negotiate a neutral location for a discussion. Although you may forgo some important information, the trade-off is worthwhile. Invading personal lives is a very real problem when you are studying the lives of others. Sometimes the conversation gets very personal. I recall a class in which we were practicing interviewing techniques—getting participants to open up and talk to each other. One situation became quite sensitive, and one of the class members began to cry. I quickly ended the demonstration, but my eyes were opened as to what can happen when rapport develops quickly and when participants have sensitive issues they wish to discuss.

Bottom line: I don't think there are any easy answers here, either. Experience and caution are the watchwords. You might find it difficult to shift roles to neutral researcher, especially if your field is counseling or a related helping profession.

Inappropriate Behavior

Individuals participating in a research study have a reasonable expectation that the researcher will not engage in conduct of a personal or sexual nature. Here, researchers might find themselves getting too close to the participants and blurring boundaries between themselves and others. We probably all know what we mean by inappropriate behavior. We know it should be avoided. Yet there are documented examples of inappropriate behaviors between teachers and their students, between therapists and their patients, and between researchers and their participants.

Bottom line: If you think you are getting too close to those you are studying, you probably are. Back off and remember that you are a researcher and bound by your code of conduct to treat those you study with respect.

Data Interpretation

A researcher is expected to analyze data in a manner that avoids misstatements, misinterpretations, or fraudulent analysis. The other principles I have discussed involve your interaction with individuals in your study. This principle represents something different. It guides you to use your data to fairly represent what you see and hear. Of course, your own lens will influence you. I am not suggesting that you strive for an objective stance. I think that is more the province of traditional approaches to research. Rather, I am pointing out the potential pitfalls of overinterpreting or misinterpreting the data you collect to present a picture that is not supported by data and evidence.

Bottom line: You have a responsibility to interpret your data and present evidence so that others can decide to what extent your interpretation is believable.

Data Ownership and Rewards

In general, the researcher owns the work generated. Some researchers choose to archive data and make them available through databanks. Questions have been raised as to who actually owns such data. Some have questioned whether the participants should share in the financial rewards of publishing. Several ethnographers have shared a portion of their royalties with participants. Parry and Mauthner (2004) discussed this issue in their article on the practical, legal, and ethical questions surrounding archived data. They suggested that because qualitative data might be a joint construction between researcher and respondent or participant, there are unique issues related to confidentiality, anonymity, and consent.

Bottom line: Most researchers do not benefit financially from their writing. It is rare that your work will turn into a bestseller or even be published outside your university. But if you have a winner on hand, you might think about sharing some of the financial benefits with others.

Inclusion and Social Justice

While researchers are sensitive to keeping information confidential and treating participants in an anonymous fashion, there is also a recognition that we need to "give voice to the voiceless" (Benton, Androff, & Barr, 2012, p. 246). As such, some qualitative researchers take an active role in addressing social problems and social justice. This view is especially prevalent in the field of social work. But I think it takes a sophisticated and special type of researcher to actually move in this direction.

Bottom line: I think a newly trained researcher needs to be careful not to make promises that are difficult to keep.

Other Issues

As you plan your research, you might consider several additional issues. Roth (2004b) discussed the politics of research application approval and how power and control influence those who make judgments about research applications. A **feminist research** perspective is concerned, to a much greater extent, with power, respect, and risk in the research application approval process. Other researchers might take exception to this list. They state that their main concern is the ethics of care for our participants and that these traditional ethical standards may not always be appropriate. Some researchers talk about various types of ethics: procedural or standard (what I have just described), situational (unpredictable moments), or relational (feminist or ethics of care) (Swartz, 2011, pp. 47–48).

Enumerating the list of standards is one thing; monitoring and enforcement is another. Governing bodies purport to be neutral and objective in these latter pursuits. However, some believe that applying criteria to QR is difficult because the standards and criteria were originally developed for scientific research. Universities differ considerably in the extent to which they apply the same criteria to QR that they do for traditional research. Many members of these boards have little or no experience with QR. Cannella and Lincoln (2007) suggested that regulatory boards create "an illusion of the ethical practice of research" (p. 316). They suggested contradictory positions between a regulatory agency on the one hand and a philosophical disposition on the other (p. 317). Their challenging paper introduced various complex issues. It seems clear to me that the more dynamic and fluid the research, the more difficult it is for review boards and committees to determine whether the proposed research will meet the standards.

Here are some questions to consider:

- Can a written QR proposal convey a sense of the research to such an extent that a review panel can determine whether the standards will be met?
- How is a review panel to judge a QR proposal in which the researcher is the instrument of research? In which questioning is fluid and dynamic rather than fixed and static? In which the researcher may modify the plan as he or she proceeds?
- What happens when the standards are violated?
- How does a review panel that represents the dominant culture at a university evaluate a proposal that does not fit the usual mode? Feminist researchers, among others, are particularly sensitive to the politics of the review process.

You need to be aware of these potential pitfalls as you read the standards and think about your own research plans.

It seems obvious that researchers should pay attention to the principles outlined previously. At this point in your reading, I think you will find it helpful to review some of the violations of these principles. First, I look at a few examples of misconduct in the general field of scientific research. Next, I highlight some of the cases in the field of QR.

■ Misconduct in the General Scientific Community

We would like to believe that all people behave in an ethical manner. In practice, we know this is not true. From the politicians who take bribes to the clergy who have inappropriate relationships with their parishioners to the coaches who abuse minors to the teachers who change grades when pressured, there are all too many examples of individuals who have behaved in unethical ways. While it is true that the vast majority of people behave ethically, we are no longer shocked or surprised when instances of unethical or inappropriate behavior occur.

Individuals who work in the research field are no different from those in other fields. Most behave ethically, but some do not. Here is an example of an experiment that went drastically astray. The principle of "do no harm" was ignored, overlooked, or forgotten in the Tuskegee Experiment. In 1972, details of this experiment run by the U.S. Public Health Service became known. The experiment actually began in 1932, when about 400 low-income Black men with syphilis from Tuskegee, Alabama, were identified for a study about the effects of penicillin on the disease. Even when the drug proved to be a cure in the 1940s, treatment was withheld. The experiment continued for 40 years, and not until the NAACP won a lawsuit in 1973 was some restitution paid. President Clinton finally delivered a public apology in 1997. This egregious example, in the name of scientific research, highlights many issues: Individuals without power or status can be mistreated for political or economic reasons; treatment can be withheld, even when it is shown to be efficacious; government safeguards are not always effective. Several factors are especially troubling about this landmark case: The individuals studied were low-income Black men; the study was funded and sanctioned by the government; it took a lawsuit to bring the information to public awareness; the experiment lasted for 40 years; and finally, a public apology to the men in the study and their families was not issued until 65 years later. (For a full account, see National Public Radio's 2002 description of these experiments.)

Another principle of ethical behavior is related to data interpretation. You are probably aware of admonitions to interpret data conservatively and not go beyond what the numbers or facts show. Misleading statements are also to be avoided. But what about the researcher who falsifies or manufactures data? I have already described to you Diederik Stapel and his fabrication of data. What strikes me as so distressing about the following two examples is that the individuals involved were prominent: One was a Nobel Prize winner, and the other was a knighted British psychologist. In his 1992 book, *Impure Science,* Bell (1992) wrote of the competition for research funds from government and industry and how researchers falsified data to obtain or keep funding. The case of David Baltimore is especially interesting. As president of Rockefeller University in the early 1990s, Baltimore, a 1975 Nobel Prize recipient, was accused of research misconduct and cover-up. The allegations were not proven, and Baltimore went on to become president of Cal Tech and the 2007 president of the American Association of the Advancement of Science. His coauthor, Thereza Imanishi-Kari, was accused of fabricating data; the case ultimately went before the U.S. Congress, and Imanishi-Kari was barred from receiving grants for 10 years. In 1996, however, the charges were dismissed. What seems clear to me is that high stakes, power, and influence may lead to corruption or the appearance of corruption. Falsifying data or misrepresenting it may seem minor when so much is at stake. For details about the case, read the compelling account by Kevles (1998).

Another example is that of renowned British psychologist Sir Cyril O. Burt. Born in Stratford-upon-Avon in 1883, Burt attended Oxford, worked on intelligence tests, and was chairman of the Psychology Department at University College in London. He was knighted in 1946. Much of his research involved studies of identical twins, and he rose to prominence for the conclusion that identical twins reared apart were closer in intelligence than nonidentical twins reared together. It was not until after his death that other researchers reviewed his data and concluded that the data were falsified to advance his hypothesis. This case is not completely clear-cut, however, because others examined his diaries and did not find any evidence of misrepresentation. Whether or not Burt falsified his data to support his conclusions is unknown. However, it is clear that temptations are there to manipulate data.

While the examples cited are extreme, I bring them to your attention because the researchers who were involved were considered preeminent in their fields. Rather than serving as role models for those in the ranks, these people were alleged to have violated important ethical principles. What seems clear to me from these examples is that when the stakes are high, our ethical compass sometimes goes off-kilter.

■ Misconduct in the Qualitative Research Arena

Qualitative researchers have their share of unethical conduct. One case that has come to light concerns inappropriate behavior on the part of the researcher. Harry Wolcott, an ethnographer, wrote a case study of a Kwakiutl village and school in 1967. Later, he wrote about a principal he had followed for one year. He also wrote many texts about conducting QR. In 2002, he wrote about Brad, a young man he had studied and befriended. *The Sneaky Kid and Its Aftermath* (2002) chronicles his "intimate and tumultuous" relationship with Brad. We learned from Roth's 2003 review that this book is actually a first-person account of the sexual intimacy between the researcher and the research participant. Subsequently, we learned that the young man beat up the researcher and set fire to his house (see also Plummer's 2004 review). Staller (2011) observed in an editorial about research ethics and cross-cultural ethical issues that Wolcott had not been very sensitive cross-culturally. While she praised his honesty and courage in writing about the affair and acknowledged the political, personal, and professional risks, she concluded, "Nonetheless, if we are to make any advances in our understandings and knowledge, it is more likely they will come when we have the courage to expose, rather than bury, moments of discomfort and embarrassment when cultures collide" (p. 266). That Wolcott continued to make contributions to the field of QR is quite a puzzle to me. While Baltimore and Burt seemed to have weathered the storms surrounding their alleged data falsification, Wolcott himself admitted to the behavior and wrote about it publicly. Wolcott died in 2012.

One of the first cases of misconduct related to QR is that of Laud Humphreys. This case involves the principles of confidentiality and informed consent. During the 1970s, Humphreys acted as a lookout in a study of homosexuals in public places. He took information about them, especially their license plate numbers. Using this information, he later visited these men, saying they were selected for a random survey. While he violated the two principles mentioned above, some believe that the greatest damage had to do with violation of the "do no harm" principle.

Tolich (2002) discussed issues regarding internal confidentiality. In particular, he talked about confidentiality within connected groups. These groups might be families, couples, or mentors and apprentices. When various informants who are members of a particular group become aware of what other insiders are saying, confidentiality might be compromised. Although Tolich himself didn't violate codes of ethical conduct, he argued that institutional committees need to be aware of internal confidentiality to the same extent that they are aware of external confidentiality.

What appears clear is that researchers may find themselves knowingly or unknowingly violating research codes of ethics. In this next section, I discuss special problems associated with QR and ethical conduct.

■ Concerns for the Qualitative Researcher

Principles and theory are good, as far as they go. But it is now time for me to get practical. One issue concerns potential difficulties in maintaining privacy and keeping information confidential. This example comes from a study a student of mine conducted several years ago. Judy and several of her colleagues had taken the initiative to start a preschool in a low-income area in a large city adjacent to the suburb in which they lived. They had worked for several years, raising funds and getting the school operational. Data were gathered, primarily through interviews with the five founders of the organization. They went through the appropriate channels to receive approval. Now, some years later, I think about the potential ethical issues regarding this study. I see a possible dilemma for them. While they had promised the organization privacy, it was common knowledge in Judy's community and the community in which the school existed that they had started this school. When they published their findings, even though they had disguised names and locations, how could it be expected that many would not know which school and which leaders were interviewed? How could they reasonably maintain privacy and confidentiality in this situation? Damianakis and Woodford (2012) described a similar situation when conducting a study with connected communities.

I suspect this might happen fairly often when case studies are conducted. Imagine that you are located in a very remote area. If you study a particular school or business, it might be impossible to disguise the identity of the school or the business enterprise. Is this a serious violation? Perhaps the problem arises only if the results turn out to be negative in some way. If the problem is more prevalent, I think the researcher needs to take extra precautions to try to avoid revealing identifying characteristics about the case.

Nespor and Groenke (2009) examined ethical issues along several dimensions. They identified three important areas: how the questions are asked, the time and space of the study, and the ways in which participants are defined. They concluded that graduate programs do not deal with these issues and called for them to be considered more fully.

Shaw (2008), in his thoughtful article on ethics and the practice of QR, addressed three important topics: how QR design affects informed consent, how fieldwork affects issues of power and reciprocity, and how analysis might affect narrative and utilization of research. His reflections from the viewpoint of social work addressed participatory and emancipatory forms of research that, as he said, "make conventional views of research ethics hard to sustain" (p. 410).

Another student of mine designed a phenomenological study of the lived experiences of families with children who had autism. During the time period of Paul's study, autism was not as well known or publicized as it is now. Estimates on the number of children with autism have risen dramatically. But in 2000, when Paul conceived of this study, autism was not talked about very much. Those who had studied the topic focused on the children, but Paul had another idea in mind. He wanted to study family life. He was the president of a school for children with autism. His research involved studying the lived experiences of the families. His participants were recruited from the school he directed. When he wrote his findings, he needed to disguise identifiable information about the school. In fact, those who knew him were well aware of his role at that school. Paul's study is another example of problems of maintaining privacy. A second issue with his study was how to ensure that participation was voluntary. Finally, because he planned to go into homes, he needed to make sure to avoid being intrusive. I do not think participants were unwilling to be studied, but if they did not want to, I think it might have been difficult for them to deny his request, given his relationship to the school. You can see that because of Paul's position in the organization, families whose children were at the school might have felt that they could not say no. As I remember, however, Paul had quite the opposite situation. Because he was the father of a child with autism, other families felt comfortable opening up to him. Paul was able to avoid ethical dilemmas and instead presented a candid and revealing picture of their lives. I remember Paul sitting in my office in awe of the cooperation he received from these families and the insight he gained into their lives and his own.

These real-life examples should help you see that the divide between what is written on paper and what you encounter is sometimes great. So much of QR evolves as you proceed with data collection and analysis. Plans that you make in your office or at your computer in the quiet of your own space may shift and turn as you proceed in the real world. As you learn about being a qualitative researcher, you might find yourself facing many dilemmas. McGinn and Bosacki (2004) supported the idea of addressing ethical issues in research courses. Clancy (2011) reported on the ethical dilemmas she faced during an observational field study. She spoke of her own uncertainty, discomfort, and responsibility as she moved through the challenges.

How do you balance the need to respect those you study and not see them as just objects or subjects? Much of experimental research talks about drawing random samples of subjects. These nameless and faceless individuals are there only to serve as representatives of larger populations from which you will draw inferences. But QR is not like that. In fact, that is why I keep using the term *participant* rather than *subject.* That is by design. The people you study are real people. Even if you are on the Internet, you might see them on

Facebook or YouTube. You might even take a liking to them. You might see their personal plights, as Alice did when she studied the wives of Chinese students. But you need to be very cautious about getting too close to the people you study. You cannot save them if they are sick. You cannot offer them counseling if they are troubled. You cannot save their jobs if they are being retired involuntarily.

How do you deal with the politics of review boards? Roth (2004a) cited four fictional case studies related to ethics, politics, and power. He argued, in fact, that he couldn't really write about actual case studies because he would need institutional approval. He concluded that ethics and politics are inseparable. You probably never really thought that research and politics were connected. Some conservative political forces argue for use of traditional experimental research that relies heavily on numbers. But QR neither uses traditional approaches nor relies on numbers. I would argue that it is up to the QR community to demonstrate the appropriateness and rigor of QR designs to the larger community.

Most QR involves observing individuals in their natural settings. You can think of these observations as occurring in public spaces. I remember a student of mine who studied architecture and was curious about how students arranged their physical space in a large university library. She was interested in the extent to which they exhibited open tendencies or closed themselves off by surrounding themselves with books, coats, and papers. She did not obtain consent from these individuals because they were in view of everyone. Maybe she was invading their privacy. You can imagine all kinds of public spaces in which you might want to study people: people at sporting events, schoolchildren on a playground, workers interacting at McDonald's or Starbucks. I have spent quite a bit of time observing discipline strategies of young mothers as they interact with their children in various public spaces. I do not think you need to obtain consent in these situations. If you approach the people you are studying, they might think you are crazy.

Today, researchers are likely to study Internet cultures, lurking in cyberspace where their presence is often hidden. I have mentioned special problems in regard to conducting studies on the Internet. We know that some people resent others using their discussion groups or other communities as data to be mined, as though the writers are not really people. Seeking permission is often problematic. Sometimes you don't know who the people are. Other times, people report that they feel violated. I think we are only beginning to address these issues of privacy, confidentiality, and "do no harm."

Technology seems so wonderful. Writing our papers on computers seems to be the desired approach. I can't imagine going back to a typewriter or a pad and pencil or a quill pen. Yet with these technological advances come so many responsibilities. Here are some things to think about when using technology for QR. Many of us use videos, cell phones, or digital cameras to capture the environments we study. But when you publish your study, how do you preserve anonymity when using video? Prettyman and Jackson (2006) highlighted some important ethical questions. For example, how do you guarantee anonymity when using videos and when linking data through a software program that links audio and video in presentations? New technology lets you link quotes directly back to data, which makes it increasingly easy to find out where data come from.

Who owns the data? Who controls it? You collected it. You have it. You might think that it is yours. Parry and Mauthner (2004) asked the provocative question: Whose data are they, anyway? Unlike quantitative data, qualitative data is a joint construction between the researcher and the participant. Their paper raised a number of issues related to confidentiality and treatment of archival data.

You may wonder how you can possibly manage all these issues. In a later section, I provide you with information about how many universities handle the research conducted by faculty and students.

Studying Vulnerable Participants

As qualitative researchers, you might face special problems when studying participants who might be considered vulnerable. Wiles and her colleagues (2007) addressed some of these issues. In this section, I discuss issues with children; persons with limited English; and persons who are intellectually challenged, visually or auditorially challenged, or those with dementia or limited intellectual functioning. Here are the principles again.

1. do no harm
2. privacy and anonymity
3. confidentiality
4. informed consent
5. truthfulness and accuracy in reporting data
6. rapport and friendship
7. intrusiveness
8. inappropriate behavior
9. data interpretation
10. data ownership and rewards
11. inclusion and social justice

Children

Did you know that early in the 20th century, children in an orphanage were fed a diet known to cause scurvy and rickets in order for researchers to study the effects of such a diet? Or that mentally challenged children in a state school in New York were exposed to hepatitis to study the disease? Children are especially vulnerable to such treatment, since they are in positions without power. They often look up to adults and respect them. You might ask yourself some of these questions: How can I obtain informed consent from a child? Can a parent or guardian supply consent? What if a parent agrees but a child does not want to participate? What do I do about privacy and confidentiality? If a child participates in a study, must I keep the information I learn private? Can I keep information from a parent or guardian? In 2006, Powell and Smith provided ethical guidelines for research with children based on a review of documentation in New Zealand. They found inconsistencies in the way in which ethics committees applied standards. Specific issues were found in regard to informed consent and protection. Fargas-Malet and colleagues (2010) addressed key issues when working with children: access and consent, the context in which research is conducted, confidentiality and protection, and debriefing and rewards. Should children receive payment or vouchers for participating? Nutbrown (2011), in her concern for the protection of children, lamented the growing use of pixelated photographs of children, which she sees as a crisis of representation. She spoke of the "rigor, respect, and responsibility" (p. 11) of working with children. Her extensive reference list will guide you to some thought-provoking articles on the general topic.

Power imbalance is another issue that might arise. Mishna, Antle, and Regehr (2004) and Munford and Sanders (2004) reminded us of power differences between adults and children as well as the perceived freedom to refuse to participate. Swartz (2011), reporting on a study with vulnerable youth from South Africa, was concerned with the idea that vulnerable or marginalized youth have a "moral right to own and control information produced about them" (p. 48). She described using an emancipatory framework in which ethical strategies address vulnerability and emancipation, and she spoke about emancipatory ethics or "giving back." In her heartfelt article, you get the sense that she feels for her work and the youth she studies. Her metaphorical explanation may affect you as well:

> Their (ethical guidelines) usefulness lies in their ability to provide novice researchers with goat paths over rocky mountains and hiking pathways through muddy rivers, to show how broad ethical principles may be harnessed together into a coherent strategy and also how they are enacted during the course of a study. Qualitative research, especially ethnographic research, is too fluid to attempt to provide concrete tracks for those who follow. Nevertheless, a series of ethical questions may help researchers, especially those committed to emancipatory research projects, to navigate the many possible pathways available to them. (p. 64)

If your research involves children, you should refer to some of these recent articles as guidelines.

Persons With Limited English or Other Challenges

You might decide to study those for whom English is a second language or limited. Did the individuals really understand the implication of informed consent? Are they able to participate in a meaningful way? In what ways do positions of power imbalance influence their ability to participate or respond meaningfully? Arndt (2011) described her experiences in interviewing sign language students who were "deafblind." She commented particularly about videotaping and transcriptions.

Those with dementia or other limiting mental functions might not be able to make meaningful decisions in terms of participation. Black and her colleagues (2010) addressed issues of how assent and dissent should be defined for participants with dementia. Perry (2011) examined the websites of 32 universities to see how IRBs defined refugee populations and dealt with their limited English. She concluded that "social science IRBs will use language reflective of medical models for research" (p. 899). Her findings suggest that there is still a long way to go in educating members of IRBs to acknowledge differences in standards and guidelines for QR. In an interesting study about conducting QR with vulnerable groups in developing countries, Czymoniewicz-Klippel, Brijnath, and Crockett (2010) offered case examples of difficulties they faced with approval from review boards. Ellis and Earley (2006) described similar situations in dealing with Native Americans. Many suggest greater collaboration between such boards and QR. As I write today, such calls for collaboration are all around us. In the U.S., we see evidence daily of efforts to achieve collaboration among and between Congress and the President. In North Korea, with the recent death of President Kim Jong Il, I doubt whether we will see collaboration between North Koreans and their neighbors to the South. I am sanguine about collaboration between IRBs and the QR community, given the examples among other groups.

Setting and Maintaining Standards

As students, you are bound by the code of conduct and ethical standards imposed by your college or university. Most have established IRBs. An IRB is a committee whose job is to review, approve, and monitor research involving human subjects. It is designed to provide critical oversight. Actually, IRBs are governed by a federal regulation under the Research Act of 1974. All institutions that receive federal funds, whether directly or indirectly, require IRB approval for all research. When the legislation was passed, research was considered to be of a biomedical or laboratory nature. As social science research has moved away from the purely experimental, review boards have tried to adapt criteria to new ways of doing research. You can read examples of such interpretations, as well as some vignettes, at the National Science Foundation's (n.d.) website. IRBs wield considerable power within a university.

Stark's (2012) *Behind Closed Doors* used observations and interviews to explain the how and why of how IRBs function. Smith (2012) interviewed her for *Inside Higher Education*. Stark conducted a qualitative study as she observed IRB meetings. This had not been done before. As you can imagine, gaining access to IRBs was not an easy task. While she did observe and record the workings of three IRBs over a year, she initially was turned down by six. According to Smith, Stark credits a Princeton sociologist, Robert Wuthnow, who suggested that she obtain permission after she had conducted interviews with board chairmen. This approach eventually led to access to the three IRBs she studied.

One important finding in her book is that IRBs operate in both mystery and misconception. Because different IRBs have different experiences and expectations, one lesson she learned was to talk with IRB administrators, explaining her work and the methodology she used. You might get some ideas about how to approach the IRB at your institution based on her report.

Patterson (2008) described how Canadian universities are pressured to capitalize on research that results in supporting one kind of research over another. As you might imagine, QR approaches often suffer under such circumstances. Connolly and Reid (2007) described a tactic that the IRB at Concordia University in Montreal, Canada, took to support a facilitative rather than an audit approach to ethics review. They found that a supportive review board encourages and facilitates qualitative researchers, but review boards differ across institutions and even within an institution from one year to another. After all, a review board consists of a small number of faculty members, each of whom has a particular viewpoint about what constitutes appropriate and good research. You might determine what type of procedures the review board at your university uses. By examining the case studies that Connolly and Reid discussed, you can be guided in ways to negotiate your own personal situation. It will be your responsibility to prepare a research proposal in such a manner that an IRB will be able to determine whether human subjects are protected from many of the violations mentioned earlier. Many have developed comprehensive instructions and procedures for conducting research.

Usually, an IRB will ask you to prepare a research proposal explaining your study. Such a review board would "expect researchers to develop ethical protocols that outline their study aims and activities and to specify the risks and benefits for participants" (Damianakis & Woodford, 2012, p. 709). Sadik and Broyles (2012) offer suggestions for navigating the review process in the field of osteopathic medicine. The areas they recommend to highlight are those I discuss throughout this book: small samples, use of words and images as data, the inductive process, details about observations and interviews, and doing research in natural settings. In addition to preparing a proposal, the board will usually want you to prepare an informed consent letter or form to be signed by all participants. Typically, your research will involve either identifying an organization or group you wish to study or identifying individuals who represent a particular group or have a particular characteristic. In the first case, you might gain approval from the organization. However, you must also obtain approval from individuals within the organization. Individuals should not feel as though they are coerced and must participate in a particular study. This may seem straightforward, but the voluntary nature of participation needs to be stressed by you. On the other hand, you might be studying individuals with certain characteristics or traits. In such cases, you would identify them from various sources and then seek their consent. Bernauer's (2012) tongue-in-cheek account of seeking approval when doing an autobiographical study should provide you some laughs. He asks,

> An interesting aspect of this study surfaced when I described it to our university IRB chairperson. Seeing that this was an autobiographical study and that I, the researcher, was also the informant, created a bit of a dilemma. Should I give permission to myself to conduct the research? Might I harm myself during the study? Should I grant myself permission to withdraw at any time? Fortunately, keeping perspective and common sense at the fore, we agreed that I would simply write a letter to be kept on file by the IRB describing the study and that would be that! (p. 4)

Many IRBs are quite conservative in nature. It is a perplexing contradiction that some boards are becoming more conservative even as QR is becoming broadly adopted. Whiteman (2007) offers another example of problems researchers encountered in regard to seeking informed consent, maintaining confidentiality, and conducting research on the Internet.

Here are two examples that might help you see this more clearly: Let's say that you plan to study educational programs in an adult training facility. You seek approval from the director of the facility. He gives his approval. All participants in the facility are volunteers.

Everyone will have to complete an informed consent letter. Thus even though the organization approved the research, those members of the organization who are involved also need to provide their approval. A second example involves an investigation of teacher interaction within several schools. Although you receive approval from the school district and from the principals of the several schools, you will still need to obtain signed informed consent letters from the individuals at those facilities. If your study involves non-English speakers or those with certain disabilities, a responsible adult would need to sign the consent. But often, these populations might be reluctant to participate yet do not feel comfortable refusing to do so. I am not sure if clearer guidelines would help in these delicate situations.

In some cases, researchers choose an "opt-out" letter rather than an informed consent letter. Such a letter would say something like this: "We plan to conduct research at your school on the topic of forming friendships. Your child might be chosen to participate. The time involved will be less than one hour. If you do not want your child to participate, please sign the attached and return it to the school office." Although this option seems like an easy solution, some decry such a letter and do not think it actually addresses the underlying issues.

You might wonder about studying people in public spaces—at a football game, in a restaurant, on an airplane, in a hospital waiting room. Obviously, such groups would be transient and not particularly useful for an in-depth investigation. However, one arena that has become popular to study is the Internet. Studying individuals on the Internet has been the subject of some discussion. We can think of the Internet as either public or private space. I do not believe that IRBs have come to a clear decision on how to treat this kind of data. Increasingly, qualitative researchers have developed projects that involve studying individuals they encounter on the Internet. They might want to study people on MySpace or YouTube, or they might want to study individuals who participate in chat rooms. Whether this is public or private space is unclear. But when a researcher intrudes into private space, resentment may occur. Eysenbach and Till (2001) raised questions about privacy and informed consent. In discussing informed consent, they talked about both passive and active research strategies. Passive research might involve observing communication patterns. Although obtaining permission does not appear to be needed, I heard another researcher speak during a webinar about his analysis of real-time Twitter interactions; he was advised that he could not do such an analysis. In contrast, active research might involve more direct involvement of the researcher. Eysenbach and Till (2001) commented that those on the Internet do not expect to be participants in research studies and might even resent a researcher lurking in their online community. They offered two suggestions for obtaining informed consent. First, they suggested sending an email to give people the opportunity to withdraw from the list. Alternatively, they talked about asking individuals retroactively if they want to withdraw from the analysis. They did not think obtaining permission from the list owner is adequate. This is similar to getting permission from the head of an organization to have people in the organization participate. Researchers and IRBs must primarily consider whether research is intrusive and has potential for harm, whether the venue is perceived as private or public space, how confidentiality can be protected, and whether and how informed consent should be obtained.

Eysenbach and Till (2001) also raised questions with regard to privacy. Quoting the exact words of a participant in a newsgroup may violate privacy and confidentiality, even if identifying information is removed. You might wonder how this is the case. They suggest that powerful search engines might enable someone to identify the original source, even if the researcher is not able to. It is not so simple to distinguish between public and private space. Guidelines might be clearer now that more than a decade has elapsed since Eysenbach and Till conducted their research.

Problems With Review Boards

It seemed so simple: Universities would establish boards to review research conducted by faculty and students. The boards would develop a set of standards for research. When IRBs came into being in the 1970s, there was general agreement about what constituted solid scientific research, so most boards adopted standards to monitor research of that type. But as I have discussed throughout this book, many types of QR take a philosophically different position from traditional research. Gabb (2010) pointed to increases in ethical regulations by review panels. Many individuals who serve on IRBs are not trained in QR and may feel inadequate to making appropriate judgments, while others have a bias against research of this type. Many IRBs have been slow to change. Hemmings (2006) added the point that there are different ethical frameworks and orientations toward what she calls "ethical principles of respect for persons, beneficence, and justice" (p. 12). Holland (2007) reported problems with review board approval to conduct research on those with mental illness. He called the comments "paternalistic and medically derived concerns" (p. 895). Finally, Cannella (2004) suggested that qualitative researchers should become activists with regard to such boards.

As a professor in a department of history and art history, Schrag (2010, 2011b) takes a strong position against ethics review boards in the social sciences. Presenting a review of review board practices, he concludes against review boards. Here are his primary reasons: Committees often impose silly restrictions; they lack expertise; they apply inappropriate principles; and they often harm the innocent. In response, Bond (2012)—a research ethics officer in a UK university—while agreeing with Schrag that some of his charges against boards have some substance, concludes that the core issues of rigor, respect, and responsibility must be kept in mind. (For other papers on this debate, see *Research Ethics,* 2012, volume 8, number 2.)

Because a QR proposal often lacks specificity with regard to specific questions to be asked or observations to be made, review boards may find it difficult to determine whether violations might occur. There is some controversy in the field as to whether, and in what ways, IRBs can remain objective while at the same time recognizing that QR is, of necessity, fluid and dynamic. Librett and Perrone (2010) provided an interesting example of the trials and tribulations of negotiating with a review board in seeking approval to do an ethnographic study of undercover police officers.

In fact, some researchers lament that IRBs struggle with finding ways to accommodate QR modes while at the same time enforcing what they perceive to be standards of appropriate conduct for all research. How does a student who wants to write a PhD dissertation in an unorthodox manner go about receiving approval? Murray, Pushor, and Renihan (2012) explored such a conflict in their research on how research ethics boards in Canada resisted research that is difficult to explain and difficult to understand. They concluded that change was possible, since one of the authors was invited to serve on the board. In much the same manner that I suggest that we need to modify our evaluation standards, here, too, I suggest that IRBs should find ways to accommodate what Mauthner, Birch, Jessop, & Miller (2005) called "qualitative research that is characterized by fluidity and inductive uncertainty" (p. 2). They continued, "most ethical judgments applied to qualitative research designs are negotiated within an organisation's own internal regulatory body" (p. 4).

How do rules and expectations of IRBs affect the way research is conducted? Nind and colleagues (2012) reported how ethical regulations limited various methodological innovations they tried to develop. Their study involved incorporating different innovations in conducting research—netnography, child-led research, and creative research methods; however, the culture in which they operated limited their ability to implement these innovations. Gibson, Benson, and Brand (2013), in their study about research on suicide, discussed the limits of confidentiality and anonymity. Their larger concern was how ethics committees assess and monitor QR. Lincoln and Tierney (2004) discussed how IRBs can impede the conduct of QR. They suggested that proposals for such studies often have to be revised numerous times to move them in a more conventional direction. They believed this demonstrated either lack of understanding or prejudice toward nontraditional research. Tierney and Corwin (2007) suggested that IRB regulations are becoming stricter as universities anticipate litigation. They believe that these increased restrictions may impinge on the academic freedom of the researcher. Johnson's (2008) personal narrative about her difficulty receiving IRB approval for her dissertation is extremely revealing. She had planned to study the phenomenon of sexual dynamics in the classroom. Of course, she knew this was a sensitive topic, but she had the backing of her committee. She quickly learned that she had "forgotten the necessity of performing docility" (p. 213). I think she felt betrayed by the institution that, she said, "had once set me free" (p. 213). She noted that one reason she faced so much difficulty is that her work did not fit the standard concept of scientific methodology.

Ultimately, we are our own monitors and judges of appropriate behavior. Guidelines are helpful; they remind us of the areas to concentrate on. They pinpoint specific principles we might not have considered. IRBs serve as monitors for universities, but they also are political beings. Requirements set by government agencies, private organizations, or school systems also attempt to keep us on track. As a researcher entering the field, you have an obligation to those who provide the valuable information for your study. It is easy to focus on your study and what you need; those you study are equally important. Koro-Ljungberg, Gemignani, Brodeur, and Kmiec (2007) suggested that "researchers' ethical decision making and freedom of choice need to be separate from discussions related to researchers' compliance, duties, and institutional responsibilities" (abstract). Boman and Jevne (2000), in their narrative about being charged with an ethical violation, offered this suggestion: "The stories about the dilemmas and the conflicts of our research experiences, often left untold, are paramount to advancing our notions about what constitutes ethical and unethical conduct in qualitative research endeavors" (p. 554).

You might be interested to learn what happened to Susan. She contacted me the next time I was at the school and asked to speak to me. She assured me that she was just testing me to see whether I kept my word. After further questioning, I came to believe that she was now telling me the truth. I only wish all dilemmas would end so easily. Of course, I will never really know which version of the truth Susan was telling.

CHECK YOURSELF

- Definitions of ethical behavior represent a set of moral principles, rules, or standards governing a person or a profession. We understand that to be ethical is to "do good and avoid evil."
- There are several major principles associated with ethical conduct. Key ones include "do no harm," "maintain privacy and confidentiality," and "get informed consent."
- Locate some illustrations of misconduct in general and in QR in particular. Fabricating data is one example. What are some others?
- There are many concerns for qualitative researchers, especially when studying vulnerable groups. Because so much QR involves close interaction with humans, researchers need to take special care when studying young people or those with limited ability to understand nuances of the research.
- Review boards, setting standards, and problems with boards were all discussed in this chapter. At times, review boards, while trying to maintain standards, have instituted restrictions that limit the work of qualitative researchers.

KEY DISCUSSION ISSUES

1. Define ethical behavior. Which components do you consider critical in doing QR? Why did you choose the ones you did?
2. Why do you think some principles are violated by researchers?
3. How have researchers dealt with some of the violations? What is a researcher to do? (Looking at my *Bottom Line* comments for each of the principles will give you some suggestions.)
4. IRBs exist in most institutions. What problems are identified? How can they be addressed?
5. What procedures do you think you might have difficulty following as you think about doing QR?
6. As a new researcher, what role would you play in accepting or challenging requirements at your institution?

MODULE 3

Examining the Principles of Ethical Conduct

Choose from one of the following examples.

1. *Dealing with confidentiality.* You conduct a phenomenological study of teenage students from a suburban school system. You conduct an in-depth interview with a teenager to whom you have promised confidentiality. She tells you she is depressed and plans to commit suicide. You believe she means it. Can you break your promise? If so, whom do you tell?

2. *Dealing with anonymity.* You conduct a case study on a small business in a rural location. When you write up the results, it is almost impossible to disguise the business, yet you promised you would treat the data anonymously. How should you deal with this?

3. *Dealing with inappropriate relationships.* You conduct an ethnographic study of senior management in an organization. Your fieldwork takes you to his home, his office, the bars he frequents, his church, and so on. Over time, you become very attracted to him. You find your friendship leads to feelings toward him that you cannot control. You know that getting too close is inappropriate, but you find it difficult to control your feelings. What should you do?

4. *Dealing with informed consent.* Your plan is to study educational practice among a particular tribe of Native Americans. You approach the leader of the school on the reservation. He gives his permission to study students and teachers. However, when you attempt to get the participation of these groups, no one is willing to sign your permission form. They are willing to talk to you, but they do not trust what you might do with the form. Even though you assure them that you will keep the information private, they see you as someone who represents the leadership and thus are mistrustful. What should you do? How do you convince them that they need to sign the form for you to continue?

5. *Dealing with a reluctant IRB.* You attend a university in the Midwest. You have heard that the IRB is quite traditional, and your study is about teenagers and illegal substances. You have access to a number of individuals through a recreational center. You feel sure that you can get participants to be in your study and open up to you, but you do not want to plan a detailed list of questions because you want the conversation to evolve. You receive support from your advisor and encouragement from your committee members. How do you write a proposal that will get approved?

6. *Dealing with privacy.* You interview college students about life on campus. One student tells you that his roommate seems seriously depressed and spends much time on the Internet looking at sites for making bombs. Do you tell someone? What else should you do?

REFERENCES

Achenbach, J. (2011, November 1). Diederik Stapel: The lying Dutchman. Achenblog. *The Washington Post.* Retrieved from http://www.washingtonpost.com/blogs/achenblog/post/diederik-stapel-the-lying-dutchman/2011/11/01/gIQA86XOdM_blog.html

American Educational Research Association. (2005). *Ethical standards.* Retrieved from http://www.aera.net/uploadedfiles/about_aera/ethical_standards/ethicalstandards.pdf

Arndt, K. (2011). Conducting interviews with people who are deafblind: Issues in recording and transcription. *Field Methods, 23*(2), 204–214.

Association of Social Anthropologists of the UK and the Commonwealth. (2011). *Ethical guidelines for good research practice.* Retrieved from www.theasa.org/downloads/ASAethics guidelines 2011.pdf

Bannister, R. (1996). Beyond the ethics committee: Representing others in qualitative research. *Research Studies in Music Education, 6*(1), 50–58.

Bell, R. (1992). *Impure science: Fraud, compromise, and political influence in scientific research.* Somerset, NJ: John Wiley & Sons.

Benton, A., Androff, D., & Barr, B. (2012). Of quant jocks and qual outsiders: Doctoral student narratives on the quest for training in qualitative research. *Qualitative Social Work, 11*(3), 232–248.

Bernauer, J. A. (2012). The unfolding of methodological identity: An autobiographical study using humor, competing voices, and twists. *The Qualitative Report, 17,* 1–18, Art. 69. Retrieved from http://www.nova.edu/ssss/QR/QR17/bernauer.pdf

Black, B., Rabins, P., Sugarman, J., & Karlawish, J. (2010). Seeking assent and respecting dissent in dementia research. *American Journal of Geriatric Psychiatry, 18*(1), 77–85.

Boman, J., & Jevne, R. (2000). Ethical evaluation in qualitative research. *Qualitative Health Research, 10,* 547–554.

Bond, T. (2012). Ethical imperialism or ethical mindfulness? Rethinking ethical review for social sciences. *Research Ethics, 8*(2), 97–112.

British Educational Research Association. (2011). Ethical Guidelines for Educational Research. Retrieved from http://bera.dialsolutions.net/system/files/3/BERA-Ethical-Guidelines-2011.pdf

Cannella, G. S. (2004). Regulatory power: Can a feminist poststructuralist engage in research oversight? *Qualitative Inquiry, 10*(2), 235–245.

Cannella, G. S., & Lincoln, Y. S. (2007). Predatory vs. dialogic ethics: Constructing an illusion or ethical practice as the core of research methods. *Qualitative Inquiry, 13*(3), 315–335.

Carey, B. (2011, November 3). Fraud case seen as a red flag for psychology research: Dutch scholar cited for faking findings. *The New York Times*, p. A3.

Clancy, A. (2011). An embodied response: Ethics and the nurse researcher. *Nursing ethics, 18*(1), 112–121.

Connolly, K., & Reid, A. (2007). Ethics review for qualitative inquiry. *Qualitative Inquiry, 13*(7), 1031–1047. doi:10.1177/1077800407304456

Coupal, L. (2005). Practitioner-research and the regulation of research ethics: The challenge of individual, organizational, and social interests [34 paragraphs]. *Forum Qualitative Sozialforschung/Forum: Qualitative Social Research, 6*(1), Art. 6. Retrieved from http://nbn-resolving.de/urn:nbn:de:0114-fqs050163

Czymoniewicz-Klippel, M., Brijnath, B., & Crockett, B. (2010). Ethics and the promotion of inclusiveness within qualitative research: Case examples from Asia and the Pacific. *Qualitative Inquiry, 16*(5), 332–341.

Damianakis, T., & Woodford, M. (2012). Qualitative research with small connected communities: Generating new knowledge while upholding research ethics. *Qualitative Health Research, 22*(5), 708–718.

Denzin, N., & Giardina, M. (2007). (Eds.). *Ethical futures in qualitative research: Decolonizing the politics of knowledge.* Walnut Creek, CA: Left Coast Press.

Duncombe, J., & Jessop, J. (2005). "Doing rapport" and the ethics of "faking friendship." In M. Mauthner, M. Birch, J. Jessop, & T. Miller (Eds.), *Ethics in qualitative research* (pp. 107–122). London, England: SAGE.

Einwohner, R. (2011). Ethical considerations on the use of archived testimonies in Holocaust research: Beyond the IRB exemption. *Qualitative Sociology, 34*(3), 415–430.

Ellis, J., & Earley, M. (2006). Reciprocity and constructions of informed consent: Researching with indigenous populations. *International Journal of Qualitative Methods, 5*(4). Retrieved from http://ejournals.library.ualberta.ca/index.php/IJQM/article/view/4356/3803

Eysenbach, G., & Till, J. (2001). Ethical issues in qualitative research on Internet communities. *British Medical Journal, 323,* 1103–1105.

Fargas-Malet, M., McSherry, D., Larkin, E., & Robinson, C. (2010). Research with children: Methodological issues and innovative techniques. *Journal of Early Childhood Research, 8*(2), 175–192.

Gabb, J. (2010). Home truths: Ethical issues in family research. *Qualitative Research, 10*(4), 461–478.

Gibson, S., Benson, O., & Brand, S. (2013). Talking about suicide: Confidentiality and anonymity in qualitative research. *Nursing Ethics, 20*(1), 18–29. doi: 10.1177/0969733012452684

Gonzalez, R. T. (December 2011). Scientific fraud Diederik Stapel signs off on his first official retraction. *io9: We come from the future: Pseudoscience.* Retrieved from http://i09.com/5864296/scientific-fraud-diederik-stapel-signs-off-on-his-first-official-retraction

Hemmings, A. (2006). Great ethical divides: Bridging the gap between institutional review boards and researchers. *Educational Researcher, 35*(4), 12–18.

Holland, K. (2007). The epistemological bias of ethics review: Constraining mental health research *Qualitative Inquiry, 13*(6), 895–913.

Johnson, T. S. (2008). Qualitative research in question: A narrative of disciplinary power with/in the IRB. *Qualitative Inquiry, 14*(2), 212–232.

Kevles, D. J. (1998). *The Baltimore case: A trial of politics, science, and character.* New York, NY: W. W. Norton.

Koro-Ljungberg, M., Gemignani, M., Brodeur, C. W., & Kmiec, C. (2007). The technologies of normalization and self: Thinking about IRBs and extrinsic research ethics with Foucault. *Qualitative Inquiry, 13*(8), 1075–1094.

Librett, M., & Perrone, D. (2010). Apples and oranges: Ethnography and the IRB. *Qualitative Research, 10*(6), 729–747.

Lincoln, Y. S., & Tierney, W. (2004). Qualitative research and institutional review boards. *Qualitative Inquiry, 10*(2), 219–234.

Markham, A. (2012). Fabrication as ethical practice: Qualitative inquiry in ambiguous Internet contexts. *Information, Communication, and Society, 15*(3), 334–353. doi: 10.1080/1369118X.2011.641993

Mauthner, M., Birch, M., Jessop, J., & Miller, T. (Eds.). (2005). *Ethics in qualitative research.* London, England: SAGE.

McCleary, R. (2007). Ethical issues in online social work research. *Journal of Social Work Values and Ethics, 4*(1). Retrieved from http://www.socialworker.com/jswve/content/view/46/50/

McGinn, M., & Bosacki, S. (2004). Research ethics and practitioners: Concerns and strategies for novice researchers engaged in graduate education [52 paragraphs]. *Forum Qualitative Sozialforschung/Forum: Qualitative Social Research, 5*(2), Art. 6. Retrieved from http://nbn-resolving.de/urn:nbn:de:0114-fqs040263

Mishna, F., Antle, B. J., & Regehr, C. (2004). Tapping the perspectives of children. *Qualitative Social Work, 3*(4), 449–468.

Munford, R., & Sanders, J. (2004). Recruiting diverse groups of young people to research. *Qualitative Social Work, 3*(4), 469–482.

Murray, L., Pushor, D., & Renihan, P. (2012). Reflections on the ethics-approval process. *Qualitative Inquiry, 18*(1), 43–54.

National Public Radio. (2002). *Remembering Tuskegee.* Retrieved from www.npr.org/programs/morning/features/2002/jul/tuskegee/

National Science Foundation. (n.d.). *Interpreting the common rule for the protection of human subjects for behavioral and social science research.* Retrieved from http://www.nsf.gov/bfa/dias/policy/hsfaqs.jsp

Nespor, J., & Groenke, S. (2009). Ethics, problem framing, and training in qualitative inquiry. *Qualitative Inquiry, 15*(6), 996–1012.

Nind, M., Wiles, R., Bengry-Howell, A., & Crow, G. (2012). Methodological innovation and research ethics: Forces in tension or forces in harmony? *Qualitative Research, 12*(5), 1–18.

Nutbrown, C. (2011). Naked by the pool? Blurring the image? Ethical issues in the portrayal of young children in arts-based educational research. *Qualitative Inquiry, 17*(1), 3–14.

Parry, O., & Mauthner, N. S. (2004). Whose data are they anyway? *Sociology, 38*(1), 139–152.

Patterson, D. (2008). Research ethics boards as spaces of marginalization: A Canadian story. *Qualitative Inquiry, 14(*1), 18–27.

Peled, E., & Leichtentritt, R. (2002). The ethics of qualitative social work research. *Qualitative Social Work, 1*(2), 145–169.

Perry, K. (2011). Ethics, vulnerability, and speakers of other languages: How university IRBs (do not) speak to research involving refugee participants. *Qualitative Inquiry, 17*(10), 899–912.

Plummer, K. (2004). Book review. Sneaky kid and its aftermath. *Qualitative Inquiry, 4*(1), 125–128.

Powell, M., & Smith, A. (2006). Ethical guidelines for research with children: A review of current research ethics documentation in New Zealand. *New Zealand Journal of Social Sciences Online.* Retrieved from http://www.royalsociety.org.nz/publications/journals/nzjs/2006/009/

Prettyman, S., & Jackson, K. (2006). *Ethics, technology, and qualitative research: Thinking through the implications of new technology.* Retrieved from http://www.qual-strategies.org/previous/2006/papers/prettyman/files/Ethics_Technology_and.ppt

Quinnell, S-L. (2011, October 24). Digital research ethics—some considerations. *Social Science Space.* Retrieved from http://www.socialsciencespace.com/2011/10/digital-research-ethics-%E2%80%93-some-considerations/

Roth, W.-M. (2003). Autobiography as scientific text: A dialectical approach to the role of experience. Review essay: Harry F. Wolcott (2002). Sneaky kid and its aftermath [42 paragraphs]. *Forum Qualitative Sozialforschung/Forum: Qualitative Social Research, 5*(1). Retrieved from http://www.qualitative-research.net/index.php/fqs/article/view/635

Roth, W.-M. (2004a). (Un-) political ethics, (un-) ethical politics [49 paragraphs]. *Forum Qualitative Sozialforschung/Forum: Qualitative Social Research, 5*(3). Retrieved from http://www.qualitative-research.net/index.php/fqs/article/view/573

Roth, W-M. (2004b). Qualitative research and ethics [15 paragraphs]. *Forum Qualitative Sozialforschung/Forum: Qualitative Social Research.* Retrieved from http://www.qualitative-research.net/index.php/fqs/article/view/614/1331

Rupp, L., & Taylor, V. (2011). Going back and giving back: The ethics of staying in the field. *Qualitative Sociology, 34*(30), 483–496.

Sadik, A., & Broyles, I. (2012). Qualitative research: A process for understanding phenomena. *International Association of Medical Science Educators.* Retrieved from http://iamse.org/conf/conf16/1ws4.html

Schipper, K., Abma, T. A., van Zadelhoff, E., van de Greindt, J., Nierse, C., & Widdershoven, G. A. M. (2010). What does it mean to be a patient research partner? An ethnodrama. *Qualitative Inquiry, 16*(6), 501–510.

Schrag, Z. (2010). *Ethical imperialism: Institutional review boards and the social sciences, 1965–2009.* Baltimore, MD: Johns Hopkins University Press.

Schrag, Z. (2011a). *Institutional Review Blog.* Retrieved from http://www.institutionalreviewblog.com

Schrag, Z. (2011b). The case against ethics review in the social sciences. *Research Ethics, 7*(4), 120–131.

Shaw, I. (2008). Ethics and the practice of qualitative research. *Qualitative Social Work, 7*(4), 400–414.

Smith, M. (2012). Behind closed doors. *Inside Higher Education* Retrieved from http://www.insidehighered.com/news/2012/02/08/author-provides-inside-look-irbs

Staller, K. (2011). "Sneaky" kids and cross-cultural research. *Qualitative Social Work, 10*(2), 264–273.

Stark, L. (2012). *Behind closed doors.* Chicago, IL: University of Chicago Press.

Stein, A. (2010). Sex, truths, and audiotape: Anonymity and the ethics of exposure in public ethnography. *Journal of Contemporary Ethnography, 39*(5), 554–568.

Swartz, S. (2011). "Going deep" and "giving back": Strategies for exceeding ethical expectations when researching amongst vulnerable youth. *Qualitative Research, 11*(1), 47–68. doi: 10.1177/1468794110385885

Tierney, W. G., & Corwin, Z. B. (2007). The tensions between academic freedom and institutional review boards. *Qualitative Inquiry, 13*(3), 388–398.

Tilley, L., & Woodthorpe, K. (2011). Is it the end for anonymity as we know it? A critical examination of the ethical principle of anonymity in the context of 21st century demands on the qualitative researcher. *Qualitative Research, 11*(2), 197–212. doi:10.1177/1468794110394073

Tolich, M. (2002, October 4). *An ethical iceberg: Do connected persons' confidentiality warrant vulnerable person status?* Paper presented at the joint IIPE/AAPAE Conference, Brisbane, Australia.

Whiteman, E. (2007). "Just chatting": Research ethics and cyberspace. *International Journal of Qualitative methods, 6*(2). Retrieved from http://ejournals.library.ualberta.ca/index.php/IJQM/article/view/543

Wiles, R., Crow, G., Charles, V., & Heath, S. (2007). Informed consent and the research process: Following rules or striking balances? *Sociological Research Online, 12*(2). Retrieved from http://www.socresonline.org.uk/12/2/wiles.html

Willis, P. (2012). Taking sexuality online—technical, methodological and ethical considerations of online research with sexual minority youth. *Qualitative Social Work, 11*(2), 141–155.

Wolcott, H. F. (2002). *The sneaky kid and its aftermath: Ethics and intimacy in fieldwork.* Walnut Creek, CA: AltaMira Press.

STUDENT STUDY SITE

Visit **http://www.sagepub.com/lichtmanqrss** to access additional study tools, including eFlashcards and links to SAGE journal articles.

CHAPTER 4

Conceptualizing Research Approaches

Focus Your Reading

- Thinking about qualitative research
- History of qualitative research approaches
- Generic versus specific
- Mixed methods
- Combined qualitative
- Meta-synthesis

Thinking About Qualitative Research

How does one begin to think about designing a qualitative study? Some scholars focus on the theoretical or philosophical. Others are more interested in the practical. Some focus on a particular aspect of a study—How can I understand online cultures? What explanations can I provide for understanding lived experiences of people with cancer? How is one to plan and conduct a qualitative research (QR) study? The process you use can be spelled out to a greater or lesser extent. Some prefer very detailed and specific sets of procedures and directions; others prefer to have an overall plan but let the process evolve as things progress. Some institutions require that a student describe in great detail how a study will be conducted; others are less restrictive in their requirements. Some advisors expect detailed plans from their students, while others are open to let things play out in a dynamic manner. In this chapter, I focus on the way you can conceptualize a qualitative study.

Before you get bogged down in many explanations, let me say at the outset that I have selected the term *approach* to cover either the philosophical or theoretical view that undergirds the way you conduct research or the general design related to the conduct of research or both. Thus I use *approach* as a broad term that subsumes what you believe about the nature of research and your role in it and how you will actually do the research. You will come across other related terms in your reading. Some of these include *process*, *method*, *tradition*, *strategy of inquiry*, and *design*. Although there are differences in the meaning of these terms, I don't want to focus on that now.

One other distinction seems important here. A *research approach* (or *methodology*) constitutes a general design. The actual details of how you plan to conduct the study are sometimes referred to as *method*. In Chapters 10 (on interviewing), 11 (on observations, using records, etc.), and 12 (on deriving meaning), I discuss method. To reiterate—in this chapter and the two that follow—I consider research approaches. Later, I consider the ways you gather and analyze data (aspects of method). Some research approaches have specific and detailed ways to conduct the research; however, most do not.

Suppose I have identified a research question or problem. What am I to do with it? How can I provide answers to the question I posed? If you review the critical elements of QR I presented in Chapter 2, you might have a general idea but none of the specifics. But how will you actually go about planning a study? Researchers are faced with these questions regularly.

I want you to think about two critical aspects of doing research: the underlying philosophical or theoretical frameworks and the ways you will carry out your research. For some researchers, thinking about the underlying philosophical viewpoint is critical as they plan and conduct their research. Feminist researchers often address philosophical underpinnings of their research. An example might help you see this more clearly: Imagine that you adopt a feminist perspective. Although you learn from Olesen's work (2011) that feminist research is not a single entity, it still emphasizes the philosophical. Much of what she wrote about in this comprehensive and detailed chapter relates to philosophical and theoretical perspectives. Very little is about the details of how to carry out the research. She suggests that the dominant theme in QR is the issue of "knowledges." In her view, feminist research has moved to the recognition that "multiple identities and subjectivities are constructed in particular historical and social contexts" (p. 129–130).

Much earlier, Brayton (1997) wrote about the structure of feminist research in the social sciences. In this earlier time period, there was a great interest in issues of power imbalance. Others were interested in social change and the oppression of women. I hope you can see that one's underlying philosophical viewpoint would have an effect on how the research is planned and conducted.

In conducting your research, you will, no doubt, conduct some interviews, but the way you do those interviews—how you treat the power issue, for example—will reflect your underlying viewpoint. You can draw from this example about the feminist perspective that your perspective will have an influence on the way you carry out research.

Philosophical perspective is also at the forefront for those who describe themselves as postmodernists or critical theorists. But for many researchers the focus is on the practical rather than the theoretical. Thus a researcher who wants to study how a particular organization functions and the role of the decision makers in the organization is more likely to focus on how the research will be conducted rather than its theoretical or philosophical underpinnings. How the organization is selected, how access to records and meetings will be determined, who will be interviewed, and the researcher's role of insider are issues confronting the researcher. Such a researcher might select a case-study research approach. I describe the case-study approach in the following chapter. But here, I point out that Flyvbjerg (2011) addressed misunderstandings of case-study research. He concluded that trends in case-study research lead to more collaborative positions. For him, collaboration and combinations of QR and quantitative research (QN) are desirable goals.

These are two different examples of how researchers conceptualize aspects of the conduct of a study: Olesen asked us to consider philosophical positions; Flyvbjerg dealt with the pragmatic. In today's world, there is space for both viewpoints in the academy. Thus one option for carrying out a QR study is to select a particular research approach and apply it. I will be discussing a number of these QR approaches in detail in Chapters 5 and 6.

Qualitative researchers are creative creatures. So all qualitative researchers do not choose a particular research approach. Instead of choosing a single research approach, some combine two or more qualitative approaches and create a new research approach. I call this *combined qualitative*. Thus you might locate a study that combines case-study approach with ethnography (e.g., Aldred & Jungnickel, 2012; Jackson, 2004). Others modify a particular approach. For example, studying online communities has led to variations of studying communities face-to-face. In both examples, only QR approaches are used to carry out the study.

In response to concerns and criticisms by some in the general research community, researchers have looked for alternatives to using only a qualitative approach. A recent phenomenon is to combine quantitative and qualitative approaches in the same study. The term for doing this is called *mixed methods*. Becoming popular in the last few years, mixed methods serve as a pragmatic means to address concerns from various factions in the general research community about whether a qualitative or a quantitative approach is better.

An alternative researchers have to selecting a particular research approach is to bypass selecting any particular research approach—whether qualitative or quantitative. Instead, they focus on collecting and analyzing data and presenting findings. In such a generic research approach, the researcher does not rely on any single or combined research approach or a particular tradition or philosophical underpinning. Rather, researchers focus on collecting data through interviewing or observation, analyzing data by identifying themes, and presenting information to the reader in a general manner.

I want things to be clear for you as you learn about QR. Let me summarize:

- Some researchers emphasize philosophical or theoretical viewpoints rather than research approaches.
- Some researchers select a particular QR approach.
- Some researchers select a combination of QR approaches.
- Some researchers select a combination of QR and QN approaches.
- Some researchers use a generic approach and do not select any particular research approach. They gather data, look for themes, and include supportive evidence such as quotations.

I think there is still considerable confusion about what is expected when using a particular approach. Some researchers still hold on to the tenets of QN. For example, they want to verify that the way they are coding the data is right. Or they want to make sure that the way they transcribe an interview is an exact replica of what the person said. Another commonly asked question is: How many people should I interview or how many sites should I study? How much data should I actually collect? I believe that those concerns reflect an underlying assumption that "good" research involves large numbers of cases from which generalizations can be made. As you can probably tell by now, I want you to think about QR as being different from QN, which means that underlying assumptions and expectations are different. Researchers do not intend to generalize from the findings obtained using QR approaches. As I have said before, their intention is to describe, interpret, and understand phenomena.

In summary, a research approach is used to address the *purpose* you have in mind when conducting your study. It is most useful in describing the *process* or how you will actually conduct a study to answer your question. Sometimes it focuses on the *underlying philosophical or theoretical assumptions* or worldview of the researcher.

Purpose

- describe a phenomenon
- explain a culture
- explain a case
- search for an emerging theory
- understand a lived experience
- take action to change a system

Process

- describe participants
- explain how data are collected and analyzed
- explain privacy protection
- describe coding
- identify themes
- use a play or poem to convey findings
- address validity concerns

Underlying assumptions

- role of researcher
- philosophical underpinnings
- views about the world
- feminist viewpoint

In QN, the elements of the research approach are usually limited to the overall experimental design, process, and procedure involved in conducting a study (e.g., subjects/participants, data collection, and data analysis). Additionally, a researcher typically addresses ways to strengthen the validity of a study.

QR does not rely on a single **experimental design** or process to conduct the research. Researchers can choose from a variety of different approaches. Some approaches make explicit the various elements stated above. However, others do not. Some are quite vague about how to analyze data, while others have very specific steps to follow. In subsequent chapters, I write about the major research approaches. In this chapter, I address several topics related to research approaches. I begin with a section about the history of QR approaches. Then I contrast generic approaches with specific approaches. I also discuss problems with research approaches. For you to understand something about the issues, I briefly discuss what has been called *the paradigm wars*. I then introduce you to approaches that combine qualitative and quantitative approaches (known as *mixed methods*). Finally, I conclude with **combined qualitative approaches**.

Did You Know

The Qualitative Research Café offers food for thought on interpretive and critical research approaches and is available at http://blogs.ubc.ca/qualresearch/

History of Qualitative Research Approaches

How do we go about the business of conducting QR in the social sciences? This is not an easy question to answer. Prior to the 1970s, two fields in the social sciences used techniques that were the precursors of the qualitative approaches that are prevalent now. Anthropologists relied heavily on field work and often studied remote cultures. Results were usually reported in extensive documentation, oftentimes book length. Many combined field information with statistical data about demographics and health. Some sociologists (especially the Chicago school) relied on fieldwork as well but used statistics and reported results in traditional formats. Although both disciplines relied on interviewing and fieldwork to collect data, analyses tended toward a quantitative nature. During this time period, most other fields in the social sciences (such as psychology, business, and education) adopted a quantitative paradigm to conduct research. In these early days, many researchers advocated the position that the purpose of social inquiry was to look for causal laws (Erickson, 2011, p. 44).

Anthropology and sociology were developed as new disciplines in the late 19th century and began to be accepted as such within many universities in the United States. I think it is important to understand that in these early years, research in both of these disciplines was characterized by positivist traditions. While anthropologists tended to study cultures different from their own and sociologists tended to study less remote cultures, the tendency was to follow a scientific paradigm. Researchers adopted an objective stance. It was believed that the best research approach would yield scientific truths or approximations of truth.

But beginning in the 1970s and taking hold even more in the 1980s and 1990s, there was growing dissatisfaction among various social science disciplines with quantitative, scientific approaches to research. One solution for the field of education was to use ethnographic methods; those trained as anthropologists found themselves entering classrooms and studying schools. Rather than traveling to remote areas of the world or studying indigenous peoples from the United States or Mexico, ethnographers chose to enter the world of education.

What were some of the problems with ethnography? Although ethnographic methods began to be used by some outside of anthropology, some decried the domination of the field by White men. After all, in the early days, men were those who "had the right to watch other people and question them" (Erickson, 2011, p. 46). Others were concerned that those being studied were treated as objects or subjects, not real people with their own thoughts and feelings. Are you as shocked as I am that one hundred years ago, Alfred Kroeber, a professor of anthropology, housed Ishi, a Native American from the Yahi tribe, at the anthropological museum at the University of California, Berkeley so he could be observed and interviewed? (Jon Voight starred as Kroeber in the 1992 film *The Last of His Tribe,* about Ishi. It is available on DVD.)

Even though ethnographers went into the field and gathered data from real people, some scholars began questioning their work. For example, some felt that a feminist viewpoint was critical. In these early days, feminist researchers were concerned with the lack of attention to marginalized women (often nonwhite, homosexual, or disabled) and issues related to power. Some feminists spoke of research as leading to distorted knowledge about the world. Similarly, others cried out for representation by people of color. These groups felt that ethnography as practiced did not address their concerns.

But others in education still believed in quantitative data. (See, for example, *Equality of Educational Opportunity,* the 1966 study by sociologist James Coleman that led to mass busing to correct racial imbalance in schools. This work is considered by some to be the most important piece of educational research in the last century.) My own research training in the 1960s was of a traditional, QN approach. It was not until the mid-1980s that I began to explore alternative ways of doing research, when I became dissatisfied with using statistical analyses to answer questions in the field of family therapy. But that is another story.

In spite of the entrance of ethnographers into education, most research approaches of this time were traditional in nature. Some researchers felt a dissatisfaction with traditional paradigms and the basic assumptions about the world that guided this traditional approach. Still others were dissatisfied with viewing science as an objective and neutral activity. Others were concerned that the findings of research based on traditional methods did not lead to better decision making than no evidence at all. I recall asking superintendents of many school systems how they made decisions for their educational practice. Selecting from a long list of practices (that included research), most superintendents chose research last among many other alternatives (word of mouth, hunches, and publishers of educational materials).

At this time, we could talk about two main camps—the **traditionalists** or post-positivists and the **nontraditionalists** or postmodernists. The traditionalists were (and are) quite conservative in their sensibilities. They strive for structure and specificity and rules. They like organization. The postmodernists are in contrast to this group. They like to be more on the edge, to do things slightly out of the center of things. Of course, these statements are oversimplifications of the differences between the two groups. Later on, we will come to a third category (as I mentioned earlier)—those adopting mixed methods.

So while ethnographic approaches began to be adopted by some in the field of education, for example, they did not address a number of problems that had been raised. Into the mix came several additional research approaches that we include in QR. Phenomenological research (drawn from philosophy) was one approach that led researchers to study lived experiences. The field of nursing was particularly interested in this approach. Grounded theory was another approach identified by those who wanted some structure—a way to approximate traditional quantitative approaches. Symbolic interaction became popular as a way to make sense of the world by using symbols. In these years, you might also have encountered the use of biography (now usually classified as narrative inquiry) as a way "to discover and to describe in narrative reporting what particular people do in their everyday lives and what their actions mean to them" (Erickson, 2011, p. 43).

By the late 1990s and into the first decade of the 21st century, we began to see a proliferation of many new research approaches. Variations on ethnography led to autoethnography and **performance ethnography**. Duoethnography appeared in 2012. Approaches that led to a call to political or social action resulted in some researchers adopting **action research** or **participatory action research (PAR)** models. Freire's (1970) work explored balance of power and the oppressed and helped us see the political nature of education and the need to make changes.

The use of narrative inquiry also became popular (Chase, 2011). Here, the emphasis was on life stories or biography. The use of stories as a way to gather data and represent data became a popular trend. Creative fiction was explored.

Other research approaches that entered the arena relied on the arts and humanities. Finley (2011) advised that these approaches came out of the crisis of representation by qualitative researchers in anthropology and sociology "who struggled with ways to represent new wave research that was local in nature and based in an ethics of care" (p. 436).

The digital age has led researchers to experiment with all sorts of approaches that utilize technology. Many of these are perhaps not research approaches as much as alternative techniques for defining, gathering, and analyzing data.

While you as a reader might quibble about the qualitative approaches I have mentioned here, that is not what is important. I want you to see that since QR as a way to study humans in the social world has come into its own in the social sciences, it has grown and evolved from a few approaches that trace their roots to anthropology and sociology to a multitude of approaches that come from other roots, such as philosophy, the humanities, and the arts. Many have emerged as a reaction to traditional approaches to science. Established scholars have questioned the meaningfulness of answering questions using traditional scientific means (Bertaux, 1981; Bochner, 2012; Denzin & Lincoln, 2011; Wengraf, Chamberlayne, & Bornat, 2002). Writing in 2002, Wengraf et al. commented, "There is also by now a wide recognition that social science in its longues durées of positivism, determinism, and social constructionism has become detached from lived realities" (p. 245).

I will discuss a number of these research approaches in depth in subsequent chapters. What is important for you to understand is that the way we do research in the social sciences has evolved from the early days. There is no single approach that is correct. While there has been a backlash from those who hold on to tradition in the mistaken view that numbers tell a more accurate and truthful story than words, it is clear that the field of QR is not disappearing. We have pioneers in the fields of anthropology and sociology who led the way for researchers to think about a variety of ways to study and interpret the meaning of human behavior.

We need to reflect on Packer's (2011) comment that "a scientific revolution involves several kinds of changes. It involves, of course, a rejection of the dominant conceptual framework and acceptance of a new, incompatible one" (location 738).

Generic Versus Specific Approaches

Even though I talked about two camps into which qualitative researchers might place themselves, this is not always the case for some. They don't have a specific research approach they want to follow. They are more generic in nature. Just when you think you are beginning to grasp the idea that qualitative researchers rely on a specific approach to the conduct of research, I want you to be aware that some qualitative researchers do not do this. Chenail first proposed the idea of a generic model to me in an interview I conducted with him for *Forum: Qualitative Social Research* (Lichtman, 2004). He stated that he was a generic qualitative researcher. This view would contrast with a researcher who selects a specific research approach, such as phenomenology. Since that time, I have investigated what this means. Some of what I found in the literature is discussed below.

What to label these approaches? Thorne (1997) referred to these generic approaches as *interpretive descriptions* or *noncategorical*. Sandelowski (2000) called them *fundamental qualitative descriptions,* and Merriam (1998) used the phrase *basic or generic qualitative research*. Caelli and her colleagues (2003) reported that they observed a growth in the number of studies that do not rely on any particular set of assumptions of research approaches. Among the reasons they offered for why this is true is that the task is less demanding.

Whatever term might be used, the concept is the same. Instead of following a particular research approach, such as ethnography or grounded theory, a researcher designs a study that usually involves the collection of data via interviews and observation and a simple scheme for coding and looking for themes. Cooper and Endacott (2007) reported that all studies published in the *Emergency Medicine Journal* used generic QR designs. Like Caelli et al., they were concerned with the best practices that can be used when using a generic design. Just two years later, Cooper, Endacott, and Chapman (2009) explained that by using a particular research approach, such as phenomenology or grounded theory, a researcher would have a clearer concept of data to collect and how to analyze and interpret these data. In any case, however, they urge that researchers consider and report in a reflexive manner their role in shaping the research process, the data collection, analysis, and interpretation. In 2011, Cooper, Porter, and Endacott discussed the use of mixed-methods approaches to research. You can see that in just four years, this journal moved from publishing generic approaches to specific approaches to mixed methods.

In her discussion of the role of theory in qualitative health research, Kelly (2010) discussed three potential approaches to research, one of which is a generic approach. Like the health field discussed by Cooper and his colleagues (2011), the field of health research falls into the category of *generic*. For Kelly, one characteristic of generic research is that there is little reference to theory in research reports. Quoting Snape and Spencer's work from 2003, Kelly reported that generic QR appears to have been carried out without reference to other QR traditions and where the beliefs of researchers and their relationship to their research are never explicitly discussed.

Caelli and colleagues (2003) were concerned that by not having a particular research approach, researchers would not have any guidance as to how to actually do a study. While they are not against a generic approach, they caution that credibility will be increased if researchers address their own theoretical position, if they establish rigor, and if they address how they engage with the data.

Kent and Taylor (2007) extended the generic approach to international public relations research. They suggested that a generic body of research principles as the starting point for study is not new (p. 11). They continued their essay with a discussion of applications in the field of communications theory; in particular, they describe a study in Bosnia.

Most of the authors I cite are concerned that by using a **generic approach to research**, the research is somewhat limited. Kelly (2010) is concerned about the ability to include theory, while Cooper and colleagues (2011) imply that using a specific approach offers better opportunities for analysis. Criticism for Caelli and her colleagues (2003) is that credibility might be lacking in generic studies.

In contrast to this work, Iosifides (2011) described a generic conceptual model for conducting realist QR. For him, such an approach has advantages. In his work in the Department of Geography at a university in Greece, Iosifides conducted research on migration. His examples included immigrant employment in Athens, social mobility of immigrants, social capital of Albanian immigrants in Athens, and the evolution of a citizenship regime in Greece. He does not agree with much of the current work. In Iosifides's words,

> My point is that social inquiry in general and qualitative research practice in particular are so strongly influenced by anti-realist doctrines that for many researchers, practising qualitative research means a secure road towards notions of 'reality' through various interpretivist, constructionist and relativist lenses. It is my purpose to challenge this conventional wisdom about qualitative methods, and fortunately this wisdom has already and increasingly been challenged in practice by scholars and researchers who employ qualitative methods and use qualitative data within realist, causal-explanatory research endeavours. (p. 8)

It is beyond the scope of this book to develop his argument more fully. What he proposed is a reorientation of qualitative methods to lead to a more intense engagement with social reality. He developed the idea of realist QR that involves connecting rather than conflating (p. 12). Practicing this type of realist QR involves "the investigation of the complex ways that subjective-agential powers interplay with objective ones (ideational and material). It also entails the departure from the sole preoccupation with meaning, interpretation and discourse and focusing on doings, practices and relations as well. For, doings, practices and relations are possible only within certain causally efficacious contexts" (p. 15).

My point here is that some researchers do not choose to use a particular research approach but select a generic one. For some, the use of a generic way of conducting and analyzing data is appropriate or even desirable. For others, using a generic rather than a specific research approach might mean less rigor. I will come back to this point toward the end of this chapter.

Problems With Research Approaches

I have found that using a label doesn't necessarily mean what it says. I have read many articles that claim to use a particular approach, but they do not really use that approach. Either they don't understand the approach, or they just choose a label because they think it is appropriate. Then they conduct some interviews and code the data looking for themes. Norlyk and Harder (2010) support my viewpoint. In their analysis of peer-reviewed empirical nursing studies, they concluded that the analysis "revealed considerable variations, ranging from brief to detailed descriptions of the stated phenomenological approach, and from inconsistencies to methodological clarity and rigor. Variations, apparent inconsistencies, and omissions made it unclear what makes a phenomenological study phenomenological" (p. 420).

In addition to not implementing a research approach appropriately, a problem is that the research approach itself is lacking in specificity. Many writers are silent with respect to how the data should be collected and analyzed. Most speak about interviewing, but few provide any specifics. Some address the role of the researcher, while others do not. To further add to the confusion, some writers describe the elements for a particular approach in different ways. Grounded theory, for example, which had its origin with the publication of *The Discovery of Grounded Theory* by Glaser and Strauss (1967), has diverged, since Glaser and Strauss took different turns about their own theory. Phenomenology, an approach heavily dependent on a philosophical bent, is often difficult to understand. Postmodernism, with its reliance on French philosophical writings of Derrida and Foucault, is another approach that can be difficult to grasp. Some adopt an approach because it appears to be closer to the objective stance of traditional researchers. They like the idea that there are strategies that appear to lend themselves to being more scientific. You can see from these illustrations that even though a researcher purports to use a particular research approach, when applied, it might actually resemble a generic approach.

■ Paradigm Wars

When QR became more prominent in the social sciences in the 1970s and 1980s, those who championed it wanted a new way of doing research. In these early days, those in the qualitative camp were convinced that their assumptions about the way the world is known and how that knowledge is attained were inconsistent with the prevailing viewpoint. Those holding to a traditional viewpoint were known as *positivists*. The new entries into the arena were known variously as *post-positivists*, *interpretists*, or *constructivists*. And on the periphery were those who were more interested in the issues of power and struggles of those who had been excluded from the discussions. These latter groups were called *critical theorists* or *feminists*. Each position seemed incompatible with the others.

Denzin and Lincoln (2011) described three "wars" during this time period. The first occurred between 1970 and 1990 or so, when positivists were decried by the constructivi By 1990, some in various camps began to talk to each other. We began to see an explosion of published work in QR. I recall, during the early 1980s, teaching classes in QR but not having any materials readily available to use for instructional purposes.

The second war occurred between 1990 and 2005 or so. An emerging group took a pragmatic approach—why not combine the best of QN and QR? But again, there were conflicts, as with any war. The purists did not feel that QR and QN could be combined. Others liked the pragmatic view.

We are in the middle of the third war right now. I believe a backlash has occurred. There has been a call in some circles to return to what they call evidence-based research—another name for scientific, objective, or quantitatively based research. Now the war is between this traditional camp and those who support mixed-methods, interpretive, or critical-theory research paradigms. Denzin and Lincoln (2011) offered some disturbing comments: "Positivists further allege that the so-called new experimental qualitative researchers write fiction, not science" and "ethnographic poetry and fiction signal the death of empirical science" (p. 2). Reacting very strongly to this viewpoint are those who write about how colonialism treats indigenous people in a negative light (Smith, 1999). In spite of these wars, it is clear to me that QR has made sufficient inroads in the social sciences that it is here to stay in one form or another.

I think it bears repeating for you to understand that QR is not a unitary thing. The field is no more settled or without controversy than it was when QR slipped into the research field in the late 1970s and exploded in the 1990s. The controversies of today are somewhat different than they were in the early times, but they are still there. Even today, you may encounter some who think QR represents musings, fiction, or something worse. They believe that the only valid evidence is something that can be quantified or presented in tables or graphs or charts. Some qualitative researchers have reacted to these individuals by making their approaches to research more rigorous, objective, or scientific. Others have reacted in just the opposite way. They write more fiction or poetry or even produce films. Jones (2013) has recently illustrated how research can be turned into film using his poignant account of Rufus Stone.

■ Mixed-Methods Approaches

I have presented the idea that a qualitative researcher chooses one of several routes. He or she places himself in one of several camps. One group, more traditional in style, chose a QR approach consistent with that worldview. Another group, more liberal in style, chose a QR approach consistent with a different worldview. A third option was not to choose any specific approach or camp but to use a generic approach. Now, within the last ten years or so, yet another way to conduct QR has been to adopt a mixed-methods approach.

Mixed approaches or *mixed methods* is one way that qualitative researchers have dealt with the debates and wars that I just described. Teddlie and Tashakkori (2011) help us understand current thinking about using both qualitative and quantitative methods in the same study. While some see problems with a mixed-methods approach because assumptions about knowledge of the world are not addressed, many researchers adopt a more pragmatic view. Even Lincoln and colleagues (2011) acknowledge that it is time to be done with the wars and to find ways to accommodate a variety of viewpoints, assumptions aside. Perhaps mixed approaches will become a way to combat the war between the evidenced-based researchers and those who adopt a more liberal viewpoint.

I have reviewed a number of mixed-methods studies. It is my impression that greater weight is given to the quantitative data than to the qualitative data in many studies. Often, those data are presented first in published research. I also find that the qualitative aspects of the research tend to rely on more traditional approaches—those that seem to have clearer ways of analyzing data, for example—than qualitative approaches that are less conservative.

Although I talk about mixed methods in detail in Chapter 6, I examined just a few studies completed in 2012 and published in the *Journal of Mixed Methods Research.* They cover various disciplines. This journal began publishing in January 2007 and appears quarterly. It is described as an innovative, interdisciplinary publication across social, behavioral, health, and human sciences. The range of topics and geographic locations is vast. From China to New Zealand to the United States in locale; from HIV/AIDS to professional development of a mathematics teacher and a program for school principals, it would seem that there is something for many disciplines.

■ Combined Qualitative Approaches

If nothing else, qualitative researchers are creative. In the early days, many qualitative researchers used a generic approach to research. As more researchers learned about QR, some began to select a specific tradition or research approach. As the field progressed, some decided to combine two or more approaches in the same study. So we might find a researcher conducting a study of the lived experiences of individuals with schizophrenia using an ethnographic approach and a case study (Warin, 2000). Or we might encounter the use of a storyline in grounded theory research as Birks, Mills, Francis, and Chapman (2009) did in their study of nurses in Borneo. They suggested that by using a storyline, "the researcher is able to present findings from grounded theory research in a manner that is contextualised, engaging and relevant to nursing" (p. 406).

Still others have combined elements of new technological advances with more familiar qualitative approaches. Murthy (2008) reviewed a variety of digital research methods in combination with ethnography. He included digital video, social networking, and blogs. As a sociologist, he raised the question of attention to ethics and the digital divide.

■ Meta-Synthesis

In the 1980s, quantitative researchers realized that it might be valuable to combine findings from various studies. Statistical procedures were developed that combined data from individual studies. Thus the evidence from several studies appeared to carry more weight than from one study. Such procedures were complex, but some researchers found value in using numerical data drawn from multiple sources to reach conclusions.

Procedures for conducting meta-analyses using numerical data are well defined. But this is not the case with data that take the form of words or visual representations. Some qualitative researchers also became interested in examining multiple studies addressing the same topic. But there are no specific techniques for combining data as there are in quantitative studies. Not surprisingly, qualitative researchers do not agree on the best approach to do this. Wiles, Crow, and Pain (2011) provided a fairly typical example of a kind of **meta-synthesis**. They reviewed 57 papers published over a 10-year period that claimed to be innovative. They describe their methodology as follows: "In this review we used traditional methods of qualitative systematic review for summarizing data as well as qualitative analysis of text to explore the narratives of the claims being made" (p. 589). What they did was to conduct a qualitative analysis of the results.

Major and Savin-Baden (2011) outlined several ways used by qualitative researchers to combine data from individual studies. In their recent study, they analyzed 177 syntheses published in a variety of social science fields. They described a way of categorizing various approaches that have been used to combine evidence taken from original qualitative studies. The conclusion? They suggest a constructionist approach, "which requires respect for epistemological, methodological and contextual integrity, individual identities, variation and difference in categories, and which recognizes that interpretation brings in uncertainty" (p. 660).

McFadden and her colleagues (2012) explored ways to identify relevant research on child protective workers' resilience. They described the process they used. They reviewed 10 databases and several search engines. They concluded that they needed to use a range of databases in order to conduct a comprehensive search. They also commented that the lack of standardized terminology made the search more difficult.

Carroll, Booth, and Lloyd-Jones (2012) explored the issue of the quality of studies included in a synthesis. Although they found that excluding a study from an overall synthesis because of poor quality "had no meaningful effect on the synthesis" (abstract), they proposed that there might be a case for excluding such studies. Frankly, I am puzzled why they reached this conclusion. The examples cited above illustrate different ways qualitative researchers have explored to combine data from several sources.

CHECK YOURSELF

- Think about QR. There are different underlying viewpoints about the world, and these influence how you actually conduct a study. Some researchers focus on these viewpoints, while others do not consider them. While QR represents many things, it is helpful to think about the purpose, the approach, and the underlying assumptions.
- Dissatisfaction with traditional approaches led to the search for alternative ways of conducting research in the social sciences. But different underlying assumptions led to paradigm wars in the 1980s and beyond.
- Some researchers adopted one or more research approaches, while others relied on the generic process of gathering interview or observation data and looking for themes.

- Mixed-methods research has been a popular strategy in combining qualitative and quantitative approaches in the same study.
- Combined QR is a recent movement to combine different qualitative approaches (e.g., case study and grounded theory).
- Meta-synthesis gathers existing data and conducts secondary analysis.

In this chapter, I took you on a journey that covered what is meant by QR approaches, how they developed over the years, the conflicts among researchers as to which approach is better, and some of the problems with these approaches. We looked at the myriad of approaches and ways to think about doing QR. We examined whether emphasis is on philosophy and theory or on the way QR is actually done. Suffice to say, many qualitative researchers do select a particular research approach to serve as a guide as they plan and conduct a study. In the next two chapters, I introduce you to some of those approaches.

KEY DISCUSSION ISSUES

1. What is a QR approach? How does it differ from a QN approach?
2. Should a specific approach be used, or can a researcher use a generic approach? What are some benefits of the latter? What are limitations?
3. How did various approaches arise in the social sciences?
4. In what ways can qualitative approaches be combined with quantitative approaches?
5. In what ways can one type of qualitative approach be combined with another type of qualitative approach?
6. What is meta-synthesis?

MODULE 4

Developing a Personal Viewpoint Regarding How to Conduct Research

In this activity, you are asked to select five key terms or ideas from this chapter. Try to incorporate them into your own lexicon by writing a paragraph for each term. Then add these concepts to your blog and see what reactions you get from others.

REFERENCES

Aldred, R., & Jungnickel, K. (2012). Constructing mobile places between "leisure" and "transport": A case study of two group cycle rides. *Sociology, 46*(3), 523–339.

Bertaux, D. (1981). *Biography and society: The life history approach in the social sciences.* Beverly Hills, CA: SAGE.

Birks, M., Mills, J., Francis, K., & Chapman, Y. (2009). A thousand words paint a picture: The use of storyline in grounded theory research. *Journal of Research in Nursing, 14*(5), 405–417.

Bochner, A. (2012). Between obligation and inspiration: Choosing qualitative inquiry. *Qualitative Inquiry, 18*(7), 535–543.

Brayton, J. (1997). *What makes feminist research feminist? The structure of feminist research within the social sciences.* Retrieved from http://www.unb.ca/PAR-L/win/feminmethod.htm

Caelli, K., Ray, L., & Mill, J. (2003). "Clear as mud": Toward greater clarity in generic qualitative research. *International Journal of Qualitative Methods, 2*(2), Art. 1. Retrieved from http://www.ualberta.ca/~iiqm/backissues/2_2/pdf/caellietal.pdf

Carroll, C., Booth, A., & Lloyd-Jones, M. (2012). Should we exclude inadequately reported studies from qualitative systematic review? An evaluation of sensitivity analyses in two case study reviews. *Qualitative Health Research, 22*(10), 1425–1434.

Chase, S. (2011). Narrative inquiry: Still a field in the making. In N. Denzin & Y. Lincoln (Eds.), *The SAGE handbook of qualitative research* (pp. 421–434). Thousand Oaks, CA: SAGE.

Coleman, J. (1966). *Equality of educational opportunity.* Washington, DC: U.S. Office of Education, National Center for Education Statistics.

Cooper, S., & Endacott, R. (2007). Generic qualitative research: A design for qualitative research in emergency care. *Emergency Medicine Journal, 24,* 816–819. Retrieved from http://emj.bmj.com/content/24/12/816.abstract

Cooper, S., Endacott, R., & Chapman, Y. (2009). Qualitative research: Specific designs for qualitative research in emergency care? *Emergency Medicine Journal, 26,* 773–776. Retrieved from http://emj.bmj.com/content/26/11/773.full

Cooper, S., Porter, J., & Endacott, R. (2011). Mixed methods research: A design for emergency care research? *Emergency Medicine Journal, 28,* 682–685. Retrieved from http://emj.bmj.com/content/28/8/682.abstract

Denzin, N., & Lincoln, Y. (2011). Introduction: Disciplining the practice of qualitative research. In N. Denzin & Y. Lincoln (Eds.), *The SAGE handbook of qualitative research* (pp. 1–15). Thousand Oaks, CA: SAGE.

Erickson, F. (2011). A history of qualitative inquiry in social and educational research. In N. Denzin & Y. Lincoln (Eds.), *The SAGE handbook of qualitative research* (pp. 43–59). Thousand Oaks, CA: SAGE.

Finley, S. (2011). Critical arts-based inquiry: The pedagogy and performance of a radical ethical aesthetic. In N. Denzin & Y. Lincoln (Eds.), *The SAGE handbook of qualitative research* (pp. 435–450). Thousand Oaks, CA: SAGE.

Flyvbjerg, B. (2011). Case study. In N. Denzin & Y. Lincoln (Eds.), *The SAGE handbook of qualitative research* (pp. 301–316). Thousand Oaks, CA: SAGE.

Freire, P. (1970). *Pedagogy of the oppressed.* New York, NY: Continuum.

Glaser, B., & Strauss, A. (1967). *The discovery of grounded theory: Strategies for qualitative research.* Chicago, IL: Aldine.

Iosifides, T. (2011). *A generic conceptual model for conducting realist qualitative research: Examples from migration studies.* Working Papers Series, No. 43. The International Migration Institute (IMI), Oxford Department of International Development (QEH), University of Oxford, 3 Mansfield Road, Oxford OX1 3TB, UK. Retrieved from http://www.imi.ox.ac.uk/pdfs/imi-working-papers/wp-11-43-a-generic-conceptual-model-for-conducting-realist-qualitative-research-examples-from-migration-studies/at_download/file

Jackson, J. (2004). Language and cultural immersion: An ethnographic case study. *RELC Journal, 35*(3), 261–279.

Jones, K. (2013). *Rufus Stone: A film by Josh Appignanesi.* Retrieved from http://blogs.bournemouth.ac.uk/rufus-stone/

Kelly, M. (2010). The role of theory in qualitative health research. *Family Practice, 27*(3), 285–290. Retrieved from http://fampra.oxfordjournals.org/content/27/3/285.full

Kent, M., & Taylor, M. (2007). Beyond excellent: Extending the generic approach to international public relations: The case of Bosnia. *Public Relations Review, 33,* 10–20. Retrieved from http://faculty-staff.ou.edu/K/Michael.L.Kent-1/PDFs/Kent_Taylor_Beyond_Excellence.pdf

Lichtman, M. (2004). "The future is here; it is just not widely distributed yet"—Adapted from William Gibson. Ron Chenail in conversation with Marilyn Lichtman [19 paragraphs]. *Forum Qualitative Sozialforschung/Forum: Qualitative Social Research, 5*(3), Art. 11.

Lincoln, Y., Lynham, S., & Guba, E. (2011). Paradigmatic controversies, contradictions, and emerging confluences, revisited. In N. Denzin & Y. Lincoln (Eds.), *The Sage handbook of qualitative research* (pp. 97–128). Thousand Oaks, CA: SAGE.

Major, C., & Savin-Baden, M. (2011). Integration of qualitative evidence: Towards construction of academic knowledge in social science and professional fields. *Qualitative Research, 11*(6), 645–663.

McFadden, P., Taylor, B., Campbell, A., & McQuilkin, J. (2012). Systematically identifying relevant research: Case study on child protection social workers' resilience. *Research on Social Work Practice, 22*(6), 626–636.

Merriam, S. B. (1998). *Qualitative research and case study applications in education.* San Francisco, CA: Jossey-Bass.

Murthy, D. (2008). Digital ethnography: An examination of the use of new technologies in social research. *Sociology, 42*(5), 837–855.

Norlyk, A., & Harder, I. (2010). What makes a phenomenological study phenomenological? An analysis of peer-reviewed empirical nursing studies *Qualitative Health Research, 20*(3), 420–431.

Olesen, V. (2011). Feminist qualitative research in the millennium's first decade: Developments, challenges, prospects. In N. Denzin & Y. Lincoln (Eds.), The *SAGE handbook of qualitative research* (pp. 129–146). Thousand Oaks, CA: SAGE.

Packer, M. (2011). *The science of qualitative research* [iPad ed.]. Cambridge, England: Cambridge University Press.

Sandelowski, M. (2000). Focus on research methods: Whatever happened to qualitative description? *Research in Nursing & Health, 23,* 334–340.

Smith, L. T. (1999). *Decolonizing methodologies: Research and indigenous peoples.* Dunedin, New Zealand: University of Otago Press.

Teddlie, C., & Tashakkori, A. (2011). Mixed methods research: Contemporary issues in an emerging field. In N. Denzin & Y. Lincoln (Eds.), *The SAGE handbook of qualitative research* (pp. 285–299). Thousand Oaks, CA: SAGE.

Thorne, S. (1997). The art (and science) of critiquing qualitative research. In J. M. Morse (Ed.), *Completing a qualitative project: Details and dialogue* (pp. 117–132). Thousand Oaks, CA: SAGE.

Warin, M. (2000). The glass cage: An ethnography of exposure in Schizophrenia. *Health, 4*(1), 115–133.

Wengraf, T., Chamberlayne, P., & Bornat, J. (2002). A biographical turn in the social sciences? A British-European view. *Cultural Studies, Critical Methodologies, 2*(2), 245–268.

Wiles, R., Crow, G., & Pain, H. (2011). Innovation in qualitative research methods: A narrative review. *Qualitative Inquiry, 11*(6), 587–604.

STUDENT STUDY SITE

Visit **http://www.sagepub.com/lichtmanqrss** to access additional study tools including eFlashcards and links to SAGE journal articles.

CHAPTER 5

A Detailed Examination of Common Approaches

Focus Your Reading

- Revisiting qualitative approaches
- What can a research approach do?
- Five approaches
  - Ethnography
  - Grounded theory
  - Phenomenology
  - Case study
  - Narrative
- For each approach, examine history and meaning, distinguishing features, special issues, examples from the field, blogs and beyond, and words of caution.

Qualitative Research Approaches Revisited

In the previous chapter, I discussed various ideas about how to conceptualize qualitative research (QR) approaches. Some researchers identify a particular research approach to serve as a guide. In contrast, others believe it is not necessary to use a specific research approach; rather, they use a generic approach to designing QR. Then there are those somewhere in the middle. Some combine elements from both QR and quantitative research (QN) approaches. Others adopt the view that several QR approaches can be combined to form a type of hybrid approach. Whichever choice you make, I believe it is important to have a clear understanding of some widely used QR approaches.

In this chapter, I introduce you to QR approaches that I refer to as common. In the next chapter, I cover some additional approaches. It is very easy to get bogged down in your learning. If you are not careful, you could get lost in the forest and not be able to extricate yourself. One reason for this is that many terms are used interchangeably. Further, the details are, at times, overwhelming. I want to stress that your purpose in learning about these approaches is to find both a philosophical and practical guide to help as you plan your research.

One of the first tasks I set for myself is to decide which approach, among many, I should describe in detail. Also, I look at which approaches might be considered popular and which are somewhat tangential. In addition, the issue becomes somewhat more confused because some approaches are described in great detail, while others emphasize theory with little regard to practical aspects. Some are more a philosophical position than an actual approach. What can you, as a student, take from all of this? There is not a hierarchy of research approaches in which one is better than another.

You might find a little history helpful. In the 1960s, Campbell and Stanley (1963) wrote a small paperback text that described experimental research designs in detail. Some of these were considered *true* research designs, while others were called *quasi* research designs. Those considered *true* or *better* involved randomized assignment of subjects to treatments. The *gold standard* experimental research designs were based on these designs, most of which involved analysis of variance (ANOVA) statistical procedures to analyze the quantitative data that were collected.

Did You Know

A 2012 issue of *Theory into Practice* is devoted entirely to qualitative research in the 21st century. Two articles in particular might whet your appetite: "Using Qualitative Research to Bridge Research Policy and Practice" by Margaret W. Sallee and Julee T. Flood and "Teaching Qualitative Research to Practitioner-Researchers" by Rebecca D. Cox.

These research designs laid out specific steps that researchers were to follow as they designed their experiments. If all the steps were followed, it was thought, a specific independent variable or set of independent variables could be seen as a cause that resulted in changes in a dependent variable. The purpose of conducting research, then, was to test hypotheses and look for cause and effect. It is beyond the scope of this book to discuss the nuances of experimental research design. What I want you to know is that these designs served as specific ways researchers could go about conducting their research.

Note that I use the term *research design* to talk about these experimental research designs. You may have come across related terms—*method*, *tradition*, or *approach*. You may also have heard the term *methodology*. Scott-Jones and Watt (2010) stated that *research method* is "a tool to collect data" while *methodology* refers to the "theoretical, ethical, political and philosophical orientations of the researcher" (p. 14). Creswell (2007) used the terms *tradition* and *approach* synonymously. In this text, I use the term *approach* to cover both how to conduct aspects of research (not just data collection) and theoretical orientations.

When QR began to surface as an alternative way of conducting research, many felt that research designs could be developed to guide the researcher as to how a specific piece of research could be conducted. I want you to recognize that there are some critically important differences in the goals of experimental research (or QN) and QR. Here are some differences you might want to keep in mind before you look at the different kinds of QR designs.

- QR is *not* interested in testing hypotheses.
- QR is *not* looking for cause and effect.
- QR is *not* wanting to generalize from a sample to a population.
- QR is *not* wanting to look at specific variables (e.g., independent, dependent, confounding).
- QR is *not* interested in drawing inferences.
- QR is *not* about reliability, validity, and generalizability.
- QR *does* look at human interactions in natural settings.
- QR *does* look at the whole, not isolated variables.
- QR *does* describe and explain the world.
- QR *does* rely heavily on the researcher.

Back to the need for identifying research approaches. How should QR be conducted? Were there some approaches that were considered better than others? Am I really doing research if I don't test hypotheses or look for cause and effect or generalize? How can I satisfy those for whom QR is little known or little understood? Is this really science? These are some questions qualitative researchers faced in the very early days of the field and, I believe, still face today.

So for those of you who want to learn about some of the common approaches, this chapter is for you. In selecting these approaches in the social sciences, I used several texts aimed at qualitative inquiry in general. Five *traditions* were identified by Creswell in 1997. Some ten years later, Creswell (2007) referred to five *approaches* in the 2nd edition of his text. Four traditions/approaches appeared in each: ethnography, grounded theory, phenomenology, and case study. By 2007, *biography* had been renamed and broadened to *narrative inquiry*.

Berg and Lune (2012), in the 8th edition to their text on QR methods, do not specifically speak of research approaches. Rather, they discuss ethnographic field strategies, action research, oral traditions (**life history**), and case studies.

Denzin and Lincoln (2011), in their comprehensive handbook on QR, include eleven chapters in a section called "Strategies of Inquiry." Among the chapters are case study, performance ethnography, narrative ethnography, mixed methods, grounded theory, and participatory action research.

Lichtman (2013), in the 3rd edition of *Qualitative Research in Education*, identified five popular research approaches (ethnography, grounded theory, phenomenology, case study, and narrative) and a number of additional research approaches (mixed methods, autoethnography, feminist research and feminist theory, and postmodern and critical theory). Using these references as guidelines, I focus on the five popular research approaches I selected for my *Qualitative Research in Education* text.

Hsiung's (2012) viewpoint identified a problem with which you may not be familiar. He contends that

> recently, qualitative researchers in the periphery [outside the Anglo-American core] have begun to articulate a collective professional identity in relation to the Anglo-American core by questioning both the dominance of the Anglo-American core and the current divide between QR in the core and the periphery. (abstract)

He proposed that a global QR voice that is reflective of locally situated frameworks be considered. Frankly, I had not considered this issue; but I think, especially in times of global viewpoints, that the social science research community needs to heed his observation.

What Should a Research Approach Be Able to Do?

1. assist as you plan your research
2. define a set of steps or procedures that you should follow in conducting research
3. ground your research in a conceptual or theoretical model

Ideally, a research approach should be able to do the above three things. In practice, this is not always the case. Most research approaches are long on explanations and broad statements and short on practical applications. Some are silent as to what kind of data to collect and how to analyze the data.

For each of the main approaches, I include several parts: history and meaning of the approach, distinguishing features, special issues related to the approach, examples drawn from various social science disciplines, blogs and beyond, and words of caution. I begin with a widely used approach called *ethnography*.

Ethnography—A Study of Cultures or Subcultures

The purpose of ethnography is to describe the culture and social interactions of a particular group or subgroup. Anthropologists adopted ethnography as their central methodological approach. It involves extensive immersion in a setting (e.g., a business, hospital, classroom, nurses' station, or airport). Offshoots of the ethnographic method that you may come across are autoethnography, photo-ethnography, urban ethnography, critical ethnography, feminist ethnography, visual ethnography, online ethnography, rapid/quick ethnography, or micro-ethnography. In some cases, researchers conduct studies that are ethnographic in nature but do not involve extensive interactions or immersion. The ethnographic approach, long a mainstay of anthropologists, has been widely used in many of the social sciences.

History and Meaning

Ethnography is a term associated with the field of anthropology. Anthropology is a social science discipline that involves the study of cultures. Scott-Jones and Watt (2010) used the more general term of *social scientists* (which included social anthropologists, sociologists, and psychologists) in their description of the history of ethnographic methods. *Ethnography* refers to a systematic description of a culture that is based on direct observation of a particular group. Originally, the term was used to refer to descriptive accounts of illiterate peoples (Scott-Jones & Watt, 2010). Such observation usually involves a detailed study of physical characteristics and social customs.

The field of anthropology began at the end of the 19th century. Originally from England and Europe, it was brought to the United States at the beginning of the 20th century. E. B. Taylor (1832–1917) from Britain and the American scientist Lewis Henry Morgan (1818–1881) were considered the founders of the study of cultural or social dimensions. Franz Boas (1858–1942) and Bronislaw Malinowski (1884–1942), together with Ruth Benedict (1887–1948) and Margaret Mead (1901–1978), were identified with anthropology and ethnography in the United States. Boas contributed the idea of cultural relativism to the literature. Boas's approach was to utilize documents and informants, while Malinowski believed that a researcher must become immersed for long periods in the field. He urged ethnographers to live with their informants, learn the language, and participate with members of the culture. From him, we get the idea of interpretive anthropology, since it was the viewpoint of the "native" that was important. This is the origin of fieldwork and field methods.

I think you will find the details of Malinowski's life particularly interesting. During the First World War, he traveled to the Trobriand Islands, located off the eastern coast of New Guinea. He learned the language of the islanders and settled in for long-term fieldwork. Some said that he stayed there so long because of the war. Swartz (2006) blogged about one of Malinowski's works called *The Sexual Life of Savages.* Swartz compared Malinowski's account to contemporary life and might lead you to think about connections between research conducted almost one hundred years ago and our lives today.

Ethnography became popular in the late 19th century as a way for social scientists to study modern society. Initially, those in positions of power (the colonialists, for example) chose to study "primitive cultures." Scott-Jones and Watt (2010) distinguished between the professional social scientists who theorized and interpreted data and the amateurs who only collected data. From the latter part of the 19th century until the 1950s, anthropology was aligned with a strong scientific foundation. As the field developed, one concern was the power relationship between anthropologists and those they studied. As colonialism ended, new ways of conceptualizing anthropology emerged. In the 1960s, the climate shifted toward acknowledging that the scientific study of culture might not be possible. It was acknowledged that change and conflict might be as prevalent as stability and harmony. By the 1970s, postmodernism and feminist anthropology became popular. Today, ethnography and various offshoots are widely used in many social science disciplines.

Distinguishing Features

What distinguishes ethnography from other types of QR? According to Scott-Jones and Watt (2010), ethnographic researchers, even though the details of their practice might differ, have a number of shared or core values. These include

- participant observation,
- immersion in the setting,
- reflection, reflexivity, and representation;
- the use of field notes and a diary; and
- active participation.

While specific details as to how to conduct ethnography are not explicitly spelled out, most anthropologists have gone through extensive training and have conducted ethnographies under supervision.

Special Issues

As ethnography has moved away from the study of remote cultures over extensive periods of time, a number of issues have arisen. I identify several here, but you should be aware that there are others.

Culture

Originally anthropologists studied non-Western cultures or the *other*. This was in keeping with colonialism. Whereas sociologists studied Western cultures (often urban society), anthropologists tended to study the *colonial other*. I think this is important historically, but not in today's world. Today, we see social scientists studying all types of cultures. Today, the *other* might be a subculture different from your culture, or it might be like your culture. It could be the culture of prisoners, of parishioners, or of pediatricians. Girke and Laszczkowski (2012) explored the social formations of transient cultures. Their examples included transient audiences of street art, friendships in air travel, flash mobs, those in homeless shelters, nomad encampments, or tourist groups. Obviously, who we study leads us to a host of other potential issues in conducting the study.

Gaining Access

How do I actually get into the setting that I want to study? Some settings might welcome a researcher with open arms, while others are wary of an outsider entering their setting and disclosing potential secrets or problems. Feldman, Bell, and Berger (2003) provided detailed accounts based on extensive case studies by field workers on this topic. They dealt with what they call the *stages of access*: finding informants, obtaining permission, the initial contact, developing rapport, and exiting.

Johl and Renganathan (2010) described two different means of gaining access (formal and personal) in their paper. For each, gaining access involved two different studies—one in business and one in education. Their interesting comparisons between formal and personal could serve as a reminder of things we might forget. For example, I was surprised that they spoke about whether they dressed formally (the business study) or informally (the education study) or whether they used surnames or first names. I think it is important that you come away with the idea that you need to be familiar with the mores of the organization or culture that you plan to study. For example, when I think of studying Google (an organization known for informality), I would realize that wearing formal clothes might set up an unintended barrier to open communication.

Participant Observation

Participant observation acknowledges that the researcher actively participates in the culture being studied. An overt observer would reveal the reason they are there; however, a covert observer participates but does not inform the members of the group that research is being conducted. Li (2008) described disturbed feelings in her role as a covert observer in a study of female gambling. She concluded, "I contend that in sensitive studies, research ethics must go beyond the simple avoidance of research covertness to a mindful consideration of the well-being of marginalized individuals and communities being studied" (p. 112). Malinowski and others stressed participant observation, but how can you do that with prisoners or teenage gangs or even dementia patients? You could be neither an overt nor covert participant in these situations. For some practical guidance about conducting participant observations, you might use a module that appears in *Qualitative Research Methods: A Data Collector's Field Guide* by Mack and colleagues (2005). Among the topics covered are ethical guidelines, logistics, and steps in participant observation. Or you can watch a brief video on YouTube about participant observation (Virtualethno09, 2009).

Total Immersion

In today's world, who has the financial resources or time for extensive immersion? Is it only the financially secure or privileged who can afford the luxury of extensive immersion? Might not new technologies fundamentally change the way we learn about others and ourselves?

Power

Power disparities were a particular problem in early ethnographies as Europeans studied colonial cultures. Although this is less a problem today, I think researchers need to be aware of how they are perceived by those they study.

Examples From the Field

I could have chosen from a wide variety of examples to illustrate current ethnographic practice. I begin first with some student work. Let me begin with a study that seems incongruous. Allar (2011), a student at Stetson University, conducted an ethnographic study of the Astor/Astor Park Cemetery. How is that possible, you might ask? I thought you had to study people who presumably are alive. Among her data sources, she listed area maps, a study of the headstones, artifacts of cultural history, personal visits to the cemetery, and death records. I found it somewhat interesting, and a little amusing, that she did not have to go before an Institutional Review Board, because all sources of data were public (p. 3). Her article includes photos and maps as well as some more traditional pie charts.

Of course you can also find articles in peer-reviewed journals. The task is overwhelming. I chose three journals and selected articles that reflect different ethnographic practices, varying content, and different styles of writing.

In the journal *Ethnography,* Trimbur (2011) studied how a group of men negotiated the social problems created by hierarchies of race, gender, and class in a postindustrial society. The writing is fluid and thoughtful. The writer, a woman, begins in a very inviting manner:

> Reclining in a plastic chair with his hands folded behind his neck, ankles crossed, and heels propped on a lopsided Formica table, Jerry, a trainer, is beginning to lecture Cedric, a tall, shy, 14-year-old boxer, in the quiet corner of a Brooklyn boxing gym. (p. 334)

In the journal *Qualitative Inquiry,* Noy (2011) described what he called "an ethnomethodologically inspired reflexive account of an ethnographic research I conducted in a tourist heritage site located in Jerusalem" (p. 917). He used visitor inscriptions in a commemorative visitor book. Much in this article is about reflexivity and the reflexive turn. I found the illustrations particularly fascinating. This is a very contemporary view of ethnography but one from which you should learn a considerable amount.

In the *Journal of Business Communication,* Van Praet (2009) collected data at a British embassy, using participant observation, audio recordings of weekly meetings, and interviews. Her analysis focused on the ambassador as the director and central player and conflicting ideologies of shifting roles. She described her method in some detail and used quotes drawn from the audio recordings or interviews.

Blogs and Beyond

I know peer-reviewed journals are important. But you might find out the latest thinking from those learning about a field by reading blogs. I have selected a few you might find informative. Smith (2012) commented on Goldstein's use of performative ethnography to deal with homophobic education. If you follow the link to Goldstein in Smith's blog, you can read about this meaningful work. Some blogs are less personal. See, for example, EMAC (2012). This blog is devoted to public ethnography and originates in Canada. Another is devoted to photo-ethnography (http://www.photoethnography.com/blog/). Schrag (2012), in his blog about institutional review oversight, commented on Perry's article that ethics requirements do not respect ethnographic participants.

Words of Caution

As you can surmise, ethnographic practice has changed dramatically since its inception almost a hundred years ago. From total immersion and participant observer expectations, the field has moved to encompass a wide range of activities. Online ethnographies using a variety of social media have become popular. Issues of privacy and informed consent are especially challenging. Your particular social science discipline may have certain practices that are preferred.

I leave you with these words from Childers (2011). As a feminist who conducted an ethnographic study of an urban school, she wrote thusly:

> When I entered the building of Ohio Public High School (OPHS) in the fall of 2008, I instantly felt like I was back in high school. I was never a troublemaker; I was actually a very diligent student, but the possibility of getting into trouble always loomed in the

> distance. This same anxiety crept back into my body once I crossed the threshold. It didn't matter that I was a 34-year-old contributing member of society with children and adult responsibilities. I looked for a trashcan to spit out my gum, was worried that a teacher would question why I was roaming the halls during class, and headed directly to the office. This was the beginning of a 2-year ethnographic case study of a nationally ranked high-achieving high-poverty urban high school in Ohio. (p. 345)

Childers (2011) offered an alternative explanation for doing fieldwork. She said it became useful for her to think about being "in trouble" rather than trying to establish rapport while observing and interviewing. In her challenging interpretations of the data, she juxtaposes anthropology, policy studies, critical race theorizing, and postcritical theory with each other to explain and interpret the work. I think you will enjoy reading this, even if some of the terms might be a little outside your knowledge base.

As I mentioned at the beginning of this chapter, other research approaches fall under the umbrella term of QR. One that you might not be familiar with is an approach called grounded theory. It is an approach unlike studying a culture, and those who use this methodology are interested in developing theory about a particular concept or construct. In a recently published study, Kirchhoff and Lawrenz (2011) examined career paths of teachers. Why do some choose to work in high-needs and challenging schools? This is quite a different kind of question from those I described earlier. This question asks us to identify individuals who meet certain criteria and then, through in-depth interviews, see if a theory can be developed that explains their behavior. Notice that we do not begin with a theory about why teachers behave this way. Rather, we move inductively from the raw data into the development of a theory.

■ Grounded Theory—Developing Theory From Context

The purpose of grounded theory is to generate theory that is grounded in, or emerges from, the field. Two key ideas relate to grounded theory. One important hallmark is the use of **theoretical sampling** techniques—a concept that involves drawing repeated samples until no new concepts emerge. A second hallmark is the **constant-comparative method** of coding. This approach was developed in the 1960s (Glaser & Strauss, 1967). Many acknowledge that grounded theory is an accepted, standard method of social science research.

History and Meaning

It is important to know the forces that prevailed during the time period when grounded theory originated and why certain research approaches were developed. In the 1960s, positivism dominated the social sciences. Many researchers were drawn to methods that involved hypothesis testing, statistical manipulations, and computer analyses. I think this is because the scientific method was thought to be the sine qua non of methods. Those in the social sciences—whom other disciplines often saw as soft or lesser and who sometimes saw themselves in that vein—either believed that they were practicing true science or thought that they could convince others that they were. They believed that by using statistics and experimental designs, they were exercising rigor and searching for the truth. Like many of my colleagues, I had an educational preparation that emphasized that view. Employing experimental design and statistical analysis was the best way to conduct research, or so I thought. Although some social science researchers were attracted to ethnography or phenomenology, by far, they were in the minority. These approaches did not have the scientific rigor that was thought to be part of positivism and post-positivism. Words like *touchy-feely* and *soft* were bandied about.

But some researchers were drawn to ideas presented by Glaser and Strauss (1967), who wrote *The Discovery of Grounded Theory*. Strauss was involved in studying death and dying and the care of the chronically ill. After earning his PhD from the University of Chicago, he went to San Francisco to head a new sociology department as part of the school of nursing. He did extensive writing prior to his work on grounded theory. I suspect that he found QN lacking in terms of understanding the needs of the physically ill.

What emerged was his seminal work (with Barney Glaser) on grounded theory (Glaser & Strauss, 1967). Initially, it was directed at sociologists, and many accepted it because it offered an element of scientific rigor and intellectual rationale (O'Reilly, 2010). Haig (1995) concurred with this view and suggested that Glaser and Strauss thought the approach met accepted standards for good science. Haig argued that grounded theory "offers us an attractive conception of scientific method." O'Reilly, Paper, and Marx (2012) provided additional information about its historical development. Grounded theory appealed to those in higher education, adult education, and nursing education for these same reasons (Daalen-Smith, 2008; Eich, 2008; Reid & Moore, 2008).

After some time, Glaser and Strauss broke with each other and went in different directions. As its name implies, their book dealt with how theory can emerge from data. The authors presented a case for using data to develop theory rather than using data to test theory. For a contemporary interpretation of grounded theory, you can read Charmaz (2006), who offered an easy-to-read practical guide to grounded theory. She described the role of data in grounded theory: "data form the foundation of our theory and our analysis of these data generates the concepts we construct" (p. 2).

Oktay (2012) provided a description of grounded theory for social workers. She included three examples from the social work field. Topics of these works included mothers' reaction to sexual abuse of daughters by a family members, resistance and resilience of battered women, and cultural tensions in cross-cultural research. The book's historical section helps you see the connection of grounded theory to the Chicago school of sociology.

Distinguishing Features

- theoretical sampling, sensitivity, and saturation
- constant-comparison method
- specific ways of coding (open, axial, selective)

Although I have separated these activities, in fact, they are intended to occur simultaneously in an iterative process. Think about collecting data, coding data, and analyzing data as multidimensional rather than linear. O'Reilly and colleagues (2012) offered an example from the business world of how this can be accomplished.

Theoretical sampling involves an iterative process of selecting a series of samples and analyzing data simultaneously until no new ideas emerge and the sample is said to be *saturated* (Bowen, 2008; Coyne & Cowley, 2006; Draucker, Martsolf, Ross, & Rusk, 2007). Note that the samples are not limited to participants. They can include events, slices of life, or particular time periods. Tummers and Karsten (2012) suggest that using the literature assists in developing **theoretical sensitivity** during the data analysis phase.

What distinguishes Glaser's (1998) view is the constant-comparative method. Its premise is quite simple. This data technique involves comparing data from one interview (or observation) with data from another interview or observation. This iterative process is supposed to lead to adjustment of the tentative theoretical categories as new data are collected. This concept is closely connected to the ideas of theoretical sampling and saturation.

Specific coding techniques include a process involving specific steps. Three terms you often will encounter are open coding, axial coding, and selective coding. Davidson (2002) explains coding as follows:

> There are three distinct yet overlapping processes of analysis involved in grounded theory. . . . These are: open coding, axial coding, and selective coding. Open coding is based on the concept of data being "cracked open" as a means of identifying relevant categories. Axial coding is most often used when categories are in an advanced stage of development; and selective coding is used when the "core category," or central category that correlates all other categories in the theory, is identified and related to other categories. (para. 4)

Imagine that you are studying workers who have lost their jobs. You are interested in investigating how support from the organization eases their departure and provides stability within the organization. As you collect data from employees who have been let go, you would also collect data from employees remaining. So you would have parallel interview data. You collect data from Employee 1 and then Employee 2; you note the issues they present and compare the two interviews. You would then follow with additional interviews and compare what you learned with what you already have. You would also collect data from those who remain within the organization. You would make note of—or insert in your database—some simple codes that express what you think each is saying. This first step is *open coding*. You would then move from these specific codes to more general categories, concepts, or themes. This is the step called *axial coding*. From these themes, you begin to develop a working theory to help explain the **key concepts** of administrative support, teaching, and urban settings. This last step is called *selective coding*.

Now, how does this process lead to theory? I think Dick (n.d.) said it very nicely:

> Code the second interview with the first interview in mind. Code subsequent interviews (or data from other sources) with the emerging theory in mind. That's constant comparison: initially comparing data set to data set; later comparing data set to theory. (sec. 5)

Special Issues

What are the practical issues when conducting a grounded theory? I would ask myself several questions. Why do I want to develop a theory? Southern and Devlin (2010) suggested that the bottom-up or the *inductive approach* of grounded theory is an accessible method for family counselors to bridge the gap between theory and practice. Do I choose this research approach because I have a theory in mind? Perhaps I select it because I am drawn to the structure of the coding scheme. Do I really understand what is meant by *theory development*?

Deciding on Participants

Do you know in advance who the participants will be and the number of participants? According to the details of the research approach, this should remain flexible. But this scheme remains confusing for the novice researcher. I believe you will find yourself wanting to spell out in advance the number of participants you will actually study, or your committee members might ask you to decide the number in advance.

Theoretical Saturation

Theoretical saturation says that you will continue to gather data until the theory you are in the process of developing becomes *saturated*. That is, no new information comes from the field that dispels or contradicts the theory. This means that you will be working on your data analysis while you are gathering data.

Coding

Several writers have offered suggestions on how to actually do the three-part coding that is a key element of grounded theory. Sbaraini, Carter, Evans, and Blinkhorn (2011) describe the process in detail in their study of social processes in private dentistry in Australia. You will need to familiarize yourself with the steps prior to actually conducting a grounded theory study.

Examples From the Field

The use of grounded theory has taken hold in many fields. Andersen, Inoue, and Walsh (2012) acknowledge that grounded theory has made a "major contribution" to the development of nursing knowledge. Timmermans and Tavory (2012), writing in *Sociological Theory,* state that "a critical pathway for conceptual innovation in the social is the construction of theoretical ideas based on empirical data." Tucker-McLaughlin and Campbell (2012), in their study of Hillary Clinton in her public life, commented that

> grounded theory methodology is a qualitative approach that allows researchers to set aside previous research and focus only on the project at hand. The previous research is then used to help give context to the findings. It is gaining use, but is still rare, in journalism and mass communications research (p. 3).

According to Timmermans and Tavory (2012), grounded theory has become a leading approach promising the construction of novel theories. "Yet grounded theory-based theoretical innovation has been scarce, in part because of its commitment to let theories emerge inductively rather than imposing analytic frameworks a priori" (p. 167).

I have selected a variety of examples of grounded theory from various disciplines so that you can see the range of topics covered. I am interested in the topic of Vlachopoulos and Cowan's (2010) study about various approaches moderators choose (e.g., tutoring, managing, or facilitating) in e-moderation. While they described their study as using grounded theory principles, I think the principles related primarily to how data were coded. Kennedy (2011) also selected an interesting topic using grounded theory. She studied student and teacher interactions in middle school students. Parkes and Jones (2011) used grounded theory coding techniques to study students' motivations for studying music as a career path. De Guzman and his colleagues (2013) used grounded theory in their study of Filipino cancer survivorship. O'Reilly (2010) described her grounded theory dissertation study, which explored lasting relationships between customers and companies and their interactions. Cunningham's (2012) dissertation used grounded theory in a study involving primary health care teams.

Starbuck (2003) relied on data from the Internet in her unusual dissertation about art and collage. Here is an example taken from her work. This dramatic and unusual dissertation offers insight into as yet rarely tapped sources.

> You enter an artist's studio outside of Paris to find an animated group of artists. A heated conversation is in full swing. A dramatic French woman looks around the room and passionately exclaims, "Mail art must move, change like the world. Mail art is just at his [*sic*] starting, we have to re-invent it." . . . Message boards are an art supply in the studio of the networking artists. Artists use message boards to achieve a continuation of correspondence art networking goals. However, in many cases, artists feel that the real communication still takes place in the mail. (pp. 27, 34)

Pieters and Dornig (2013) provide a detailed description of their collaborative journey as they pursued their doctorates. Both used grounded theory. I found their comments about feeling confused, inadequate, and isolated as well as the dreaded condition of what they call *analytic paralysis* quite thought-provoking.

Grounded theory has become a popular research approach for many who value structure and order. I believe it is closest to using a quantitative approach of all the research designs. Some students are attracted to it because it offers a logical and coherent, if somewhat cumbersome, method of data analysis. On the other hand, those very characteristics seem to limit its usefulness, in my view. I wonder how much of what is found in the field contributes to theory. (See Corbin & Strauss, 2008, for a basic text on the topic.)

Blogs and Beyond

Brannan (2012) commented about how she was stimulated by a class project on local factors to develop her thesis. I was surprised that the course called Ethnography & Archival Research involved grounded theory. But the blog is interesting. You can watch Urquhart (2012) discuss grounded theory in a YouTube presentation. You can also view an introduction to grounded theory by Tjitra & Associates (2012) on SlideShare.

Words of Caution

O'Reilly, Paper, and Marx (2012) cautioned that grounded theory for business research "remains elusive and misunderstood by many—even those who advocate its use" (p. 247).

Bryant and Charmaz (2010) also commented that one reason for the confusion is that grounded theory is both a method of conducting research and the theory that emerges.

Almost all QR approaches involve collecting data through interviews, observations, or some other way to gather information from and about people—their thoughts, feelings, aspirations, fears, or opinions. Grounded theory is no exception. Some things researchers need to heed are identified here.

Theoretical Sampling

This involves the difference between words on paper and actual practice. I have read many examples of research studies that claim to use grounded theory. Cormier (2012), in her study of using medication with children with ADHD, appears to follow some of the guidelines. She states:

> Initially, purposeful sampling was used to recruit parents who met study criteria and could provide perspective on the phenomenon being studied. To maximize variation in the data, an effort was made to enroll mothers and fathers, parents of male and female children with ADHD, and children on stimulants alone or in combination with other psychotropic medication. As early interviews were analyzed, it was necessary to collect new data and return to previously collected data for comparison data to illuminate emerging conceptual categories. Theoretical sampling then took the form of recruiting new participants on the basis of what they could contribute, looking for comparisons in the data already collected, and second interviews of participants to ask new questions. (p. 347)

The above is an excellent illustration of how to use theoretical sampling. In fact, I have seen few that actually use this type of sampling technique. For example, in a very engaging study using the voices of the participants, Kennedy (2009) described how she drew her sample:

> The grounded theory study examined middle school . . . classrooms in one school district. Of the six total classrooms, only four were available for the project. Consequently, I observed in each of those four classrooms for eight hours during a three-month period. Of the four teachers in those classrooms, only two were willing to participate in interviews. Therefore, the interview data consists of two teachers and eight students, four students from each of the two classrooms. (p. 1418)

You can also read what Abrahams (2009) said about identifying his sample:

> The study included nine undergraduate music education majors in their junior year enrolled in a praxis course designed to prepare them to teach music in secondary schools. . . . Also included were the three in-service teachers who served in the role of cooperating teachers. (p. 83)

I think researchers say they are conducting theoretical sampling but do not always really understand quite what it is.

Determining True Grounded Theory

Many studies I read that claim to be grounded theory actually use a modified version of grounded theory coding. You have to ask yourself: When is grounded theory really grounded theory? Does it matter if the basic principles are not used? I see a parallel to an experimental study in which the researcher claims to use random assignment to experimental or control groups but, in fact, uses intact groups.

Theoretical Saturation

A related idea to theoretical sampling, *saturation*, states that a researcher continues to gather data until no new information is identified in coding. The comments on Jim's (2008) blog say it all: "Theoretical saturation is of great importance. Unless a researcher gathers data until all categories are saturated, the theory will be unevenly developed and lacking density and precision." I see little or no evidence in published research that this is practiced. So be cautious. Question when researchers say they are using theoretical sampling or theoretical saturation. Are they really doing it?

Theories

What do we mean by theory? One definition is that for modern science, a theory is an explanation of empirical phenomena made in a way consistent with the scientific method. Well, herein is a problem. We don't really have scientifically generated data. I think many grounded theory studies conclude with statements, but I wouldn't really elevate them to the level of theory. To me, they seem more like conclusions.

Following the Coding Rubric

Among all the QR approaches, grounded theory is the one that has specific steps for coding and analysis. Saldaña (2012) discussed these in detail in his coding manual. As others have done, he described how the coding process involves cumulative coding cycles that ultimately lead to a development of a theory. He actually extended the grounded theory coding concept and elaborated the process. But I caution you to question to what extent researchers actually go through the iterations he and others have described. There is little evidence in the written work that such meticulous procedures are actually followed.

Now, it is time to turn your attention to another research approach widely used in the qualitative field. Phenomenology, discussed next, is actually not just an approach, but a philosophy as well.

■ Phenomenology—The Study of Lived Experiences

The purpose of phenomenology is to describe and understand the essence of lived experiences of individuals who have experienced a particular phenomenon. This tradition is closely tied to existential philosophy. Hermeneutics is also associated with phenomenology; its purpose is to interpret text, originally the Bible. Initially proposed by Husserl (1917, reprinted 1981) and predominant in Europe in the 1930s, it has been reinterpreted by a variety of writers and extended to the United States. Bracketing is a key concept. In the last few years, phenomenology has become prominent in diverse areas of the world. In the 1990s, nursing researchers and educators were among the first to make use of phenomenological approaches.

History and Meaning

It is generally acknowledged that Edmund Husserl is the father of phenomenology. I found it instructive to read from Husserl's inaugural lecture at Freiburg in Breslau in 1917: "A new fundamental science, pure phenomenology, has developed within philosophy. . . . It is inferior in methodological rigor to none of the modern sciences" (Husserl, 1981, p. 10). Husserl continued somewhat later in his talk to acknowledge that empirical science is not "the only kind of science possible" (p. 14). Husserl, born in Czechoslovakia in 1859, studied mathematics and astronomy in Berlin and Vienna. Brentano, an Austrian philosopher, led him toward philosophy and away from mathematics. In 1917, Husserl gave five lectures on phenomenology. Although he planned to come to California in the mid-1930s, he became ill and died in 1938.

I think the issue of multiple types of science is important, because it highlights the idea that an approach other than a pure science is an acceptable alternative for conducting research. I discussed this idea previously in the section on grounded theory. Husserl's writings on phenomenology served as the impetus as this philosophical movement spread throughout Europe. Heidegger (a German) and Merleau-Ponty (from France) were leading proponents of the philosophical concept of phenomenology. Sartre's writings on existentialism were closely related. Other leaders include Levinas, who studied with Hurrserl and developed a philosophy of ethics, and Derrida, a French philosopher, whose contribution concerns the idea that there is no single meaning to language or text. Derrida suggested that language is constantly shifting. In recent years, the swing has been back to broader theoretical models. Most influential over the past 20 years has been the structural model developed by Lévi-Strauss in 1968, which seeks to look below the surface of culture to identify the mental structures of human thought that underlie all cultures.

Phenomenology in Today's World

You might be wondering why you are reading about a movement that had its origins in Germany around World War I and was not practiced much in the United States. What does this have to do with studying one's lived experiences? What kinds of links can be made to the use of phenomenology in the current climate?

Phenomenology is not an easy concept to understand. My intention here is to first tell you about key elements of phenomenology and then to introduce you to some of the newer thinking. Researchers, philosophers, and writers do not agree on what phenomenology is. So how do you, as a new learner, come to understand this field?

Phenomenology, as an approach, looks at the lived experiences of those who have lived with or experienced a particular phenomenon. Researchers and students grapple with understanding phenomenology. Oberg and Bell (2012), students in the school of business at the University of Wales, wrote about using phenomenology to study the uses of technology to support learning.

I want you to appreciate that phenomenology, as an approach, has taken hold worldwide. From its roots in Europe, it has now spread broadly into the United States, Canada, and parts of Asia. I want to talk about three trends: first, the use of a phenomenological method in a variety of disciplines, including, but not limited to, education, nursing, adult learning, allied health fields, art education, and special education; second, the broadening scope of interest in phenomenology worldwide facilitated, in part, by the Internet and the opening up of travel throughout the world; and, third, the expansion, modification, and (in some instances) reinterpretations of the application of a phenomenological method.

A Variety of Disciplines

The use of a phenomenological research approach has taken hold in many of the social science disciplines. Beginning in the 1990s, phenomenology in education became fairly widespread (Barnacle, 2001; Robinson, 2000; van Manen, 1997, 2011; Vandenberg, 1996). Phenomenology as a philosophy and research approach has also been used in many other social science disciplines. For a more general discussion in clinical psychology, I refer you to a special issue of *Qualitative Research in Psychology* related to Britain, published in 2011 (http://www.tandfonline.com/toc/uqrp20/9/1). In social work, you can look at McCormick's (2011) study reflecting on conducting a phenomenological study of bodies, food, and eating. Or you can read Simonsen's (2013) account of thinking about of the phenomenal lived body and the phenomenological travel along what she calls the anti/posthumanist lane.

With the development of a variety of QR approaches, phenomenology has been adopted by many disciplines as an appropriate way to explore research questions, which leads to a different way to construct knowledge.

Rose (1993), in a book called *Feminism and Geography,* described how she saw feminist studies and phenomenology influencing the discipline of geography. In particular, phenomenology has become a way to research the gaps in the discipline, those areas that previously were not considered important to research because they had little to do with the public and patriarchal world of geography. Nursing education, in recent moves to define itself as a separate and different discipline from the rational, scientific medical model, has adopted phenomenology as a way to research previously uninvestigated areas in order to inform the theory of nursing practice on which nursing education is based.

Growth Worldwide

There has been an enormous resurgence of the study and use of phenomenology worldwide. Embree (2003) spoke about phenomenology in the 21st century. He suggested that the resurgence is due to the collapse of the Soviet Union, increased international travel, and the Internet. It is interesting to see how this resurgence has developed. In an essay published to celebrate that event, Embree (2003) informed us that there are at least 20 countries with traditions of phenomenology and 22 disciplines other than philosophy that have conducted phenomenological investigations.

He offered a number of reasons to explain the worldwide growth. Colleagues with no personal experience of World War II are coming into leadership positions, so phenomenology has been restored since the end of fascism in Germany. You will recall that I said earlier that

Heidegger was a strong proponent of phenomenology, but his fascist persuasion put him in disfavor with many academics. Embree also suggested that while no tradition in philosophy prior to the 1970s was generally receptive to women, there are now many women new to the field. Although the center of the phenomenological movement is still in the West (remember that its center had been in Europe for long periods of time), greater international travel and the Internet and the widespread use of English have led to a greater interconnectedness among countries.

Reinterpretations of Phenomenology

You have read earlier in this section about the burgeoning phenomenological movement worldwide. I imagine that you will not be surprised, then, to discover that there is no one thing that is considered *phenomenology*. Although most acknowledge Husserl and his influence, what you will find in the research and writing today is that many things, many ways, and many approaches take on the label of phenomenology. These approaches range from very strict, conservative, traditional approaches to very broad interpretations and applications to the study of lived experiences, the thread that holds the various applications together. It is unclear how phenomenology evolved from a rigorous science to an antifoundationalist position.

Phenomenology as a Philosophy and as a Method

Dermot (2000) suggested that the phenomenological movement reflects European philosophy in the 20th century. Husserl's idea was that phenomenology was a new way of thinking about philosophy; rather than being esoteric and metaphysical, phenomenology would enable the philosopher (and phenomenologist) to come into contact with the actual lived experiences. It is beyond the scope of this book to get into the philosophical voyage that Dermot takes. These philosophical underpinnings are quite complex and are not necessary for you to understand as you begin to learn the elements of phenomenology as a method.

We can think of phenomenology as a philosophy, and we can think of it as an approach. I don't think you can begin to understand one without the other, which is why I have tried to give you some key elements of the philosophy. Now, we turn to phenomenology as an approach. If the philosophy is about the lived experiences and the essence of these lived experiences, how is it that we should go about doing a phenomenological study? I have gone into the method of phenomenology in some depth because, at times, it is somewhat confusing. You know that it is a study of lived experience. But it is more than that because, ultimately, the researcher's role is to extract the essence of that experience by means of a reductionist process. The following are important questions to address.

1. *What do we mean by the lived experience?* The *lived experience* is a term from Husserl. In its original German, *Lebenswelt,* or the world of lived experience, comes from Husserl's last work. Lived experiences, or life experiences, are those in which we are all involved. Often, a researcher selects a particular experience or event on which to focus. Several of my students did just that. In the adult education field, Repass (2003), a professional woman preparing to retire, did her study on the lived experiences of professional women as they planned for retirement. Glass (2001), himself the parent of an autistic child, studied families of autistic children.

Think of it this way: Every experience has an objective and a subjective component; thus you must understand all aspects of a phenomenon.

2. *What is meant by the essence of the experience?* On a deeper, more philosophical level, we can ask, how does the nature of the experience indicate the nature of the human being's existence? When we consider the essence of the experience, we are moving to a deeper level of understanding. Harper's (n.d.) dissertation explored the essence of experiences of stepfathers. This idea of extracting the essence is a little difficult to understand; it is related to the philosophical underpinnings of phenomenology. You can see that a description of an experience, while interesting, is not the full intent of conducting the research. I believe, however, that you will encounter a number of studies that are phenomenological in intent but do not go to a deeper level of understanding. Perhaps that is because some researchers are reluctant to bring too much interpretation to the data they have. Or perhaps it is because we do not trust ourselves to move to an understanding of the inner self.

3. *What is the reductionist process?* How are bracketing and *epoché* related to it? Phenomenological reduction is the process that is used to facilitate seeking the essence of a phenomenon. It is here that bracketing and epoché (terms often used interchangeably) describe the change in attitude that is necessary for the philosophical reduction. Bracketing involves placing one's own thoughts about the topic in suspense or out of question. Epoché involves the deliberate suspension of judgment. Giorgi (1989) suggested that the researcher should search for all possible meanings of the phenomenon.

Husserl suggested that a researcher could set aside his or her own views about the phenomenon by using a process of bracketing. As a mathematician, he was interested in objective and logical approaches, so he thought that this act of setting aside one's thoughts about the topic would accomplish objectivity. It has been almost 100 years since Husserl gave us this idea of bracketing. Gearing (2004) provided detailed information about six distinct forms of this concept—ideal, descriptive, existential, analytical, reflexive, and pragmatic—as well as a very clear account of phenomenology. I have found in my own experience that it is too simplistic to think that a researcher can set aside his or her own ideas about a phenomenon. I like to think of making explicit one's ideas on the topic. This is accomplished by writing down one's ideas, preferably prior to immersion in the literature on the topic. The mere task of writing puts the researcher in a mind-set that forces him or her to make explicit his or her ideas.

Finlay's (2012) thoughtful contribution about how to conduct an actual phenomenological study is instructive. She identifies five mutually dependent and dynamically iterative processes. They include "(a) embracing the phenomenological attitude, (b) entering the lifeworld (through descriptions of experiences), (c) dwelling with horizons of implicit meanings, (d) explicating the phenomenon holistically, and (e) integrating frames of reference" (abstract). I think if you read her article, you will come to have a clearer understanding of how to actually conduct such a study.

Hermeneutics is a term related to phenomenology. It is generally thought to be the science of interpretation and explanation. In the hermeneutical process, there is an interaction or link between the researcher and what is being interpreted. I don't want to get involved in too much detail, but you should know that hermeneutics was originally associated with interpretation of textual material, especially the Bible. Two assumptions of hermeneutics are that humans use language to experience the world and that we obtain understanding and knowledge through our language. The word derives from the Greek god Hermes, a son of Zeus and the fastest of the gods. Cohen, Kahn, and Steeves's (2000) text, while written for nurses, should be helpful as you try to understand these ideas. (See also McLeod, 2001.)

You have read about the philosophy and methodology of phenomenology. With an almost 100-year history, this tradition has become widely used. Starting in Europe and transported to the United States, it has now become a dominant tradition worldwide. I think you will find yourself very attracted to the elements of the tradition. However, as with many of the other approaches to research, details of how to do a phenomenological study are not readily available. Further, current writers do not agree on what phenomenology is and even how to do it. You would be well advised to read some completed phenomenological studies to decide whether this tradition is right for you.

Distinguishing Features

- essence of lived experiences
- bracketing
- both a philosophy and a method

I have identified three key elements that will help you distinguish phenomenology from other research approaches. Its primary purpose is to get at the essence of the lived experience of individuals who have experienced a particular phenomenon. In order to do this, the researcher is supposed to bracket his or her own views on the topic. A third important idea is that phenomenology is both a philosophy and a method.

Special Issues

Translating Philosophical Ideas into a Research Approach

Of all the research approaches you study in QR, I believe this is the one that is the only one based on philosophical perspectives. When Husserl wrote about phenomenology a hundred years ago, his ideas were challenging. Today, with so many offshoots and interpretations, the challenge is even greater.

Uncommon Terms

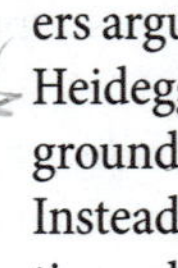

Mentioned earlier, *bracketing* (setting aside your own views about the topic and keeping them out of the system) is a concept with which I disagree. In fact, many modern qualitative researchers argue that since the researcher is the interpreter of the data, the idea is impossible to achieve. Heidegger provided an alternative to bracketing. He acknowledged that our own culture, background, and gender influence our experience. He did not think bracketing was possible. Instead, he talked about *authentic reflection*, which would enable us to know our own assumptions about a phenomenon. Husserl (1981) used the term *epoché*. Tufford and Newman (2012) suggested that there is tension about bracketing. Specifically, they were concerned with who brackets, methods of bracketing, and when it occurs on the research process. Their detailed account of the topic is a must-read if you plan to use phenomenology as a research approach.

Specifics Missing

While a considerable body of literature exists about the philosophy of phenomenology, the practical aspects of actually conducting a study are often left to the researcher. Moving from interviews to the essence is complex, and researchers are challenged.

Complex Ideas

You may come to this field with little background in these philosophers' ideas. I have only touched on some core points, so you will need to delve more deeply into the writings.

Examples From the Field

Phenomenology is a very popular approach in the field of health and nursing. In her article, Salmon (2012) discusses how nurse researchers can use phenomenological designs. I have selected several recent studies that might help you see various ways that researchers approach phenomenology. Hou, Ko, and Shu (2013) interviewed eight women who had suffered intimate partner violence. Participants were recruited from two facilities in Taiwan. The authors present their findings as narratives told by the women. Edmonds (2010) wrote a straightforward description of the lived experiences of nursing students who study abroad. In this research, Edmonds interviewed a group of nurses as well as used their reflective travel journals. She identified four themes. This study is illustrative of many—it uses available participants, gathers data using interviews and supplementary materials, is silent about how the data are analyzed, and presents several themes. Researchers are exploring new ways of conducting phenomenological studies. Ebrahimi and colleagues (2012) studied the experiences of frail elders to gain a deeper understanding of living with diseases and disorders. They interviewed some twenty men and women. They used a semi-structured lifeworld interview for data collection. They included a section on bracketing and reflexivity.

DeLeon and Brunner (2012) addressed the sensitive topic of lesbian and gay educational leaders. In their national study, they were able to recruit seventeen volunteers. Because of the delicate nature of the topic, strategies for providing anonymity were critical. Using what they called a "virtual laboratory," they provided opportunities for participants to interact anonymously. The overwhelming findings led to a "cycles of fear" model. They noted various fear cycles, from movement from silence to voice and then back again. DeLeon received the 2010 AERA award for her dissertation on the study of lesbian and gay educational leaders.

Conklin (2012) investigated the meaning of work that is worth doing. He focused on the question "Does the notion of calling have any relevance as we attempt to make our way in a modern-day economy?" (p. 298). Those he studied worked in the area of the natural environment.

Kingscott and Durant (2010) studied the phenomenon of musical improvisation. In the methodology section, they indicated two experienced improvisers were studied using interviews and observations. The format of the study is fairly typical; however, I am not sure that the work captures the essence of the lived experience of those they studied.

Blogs and Beyond

Look at Skjaerven's (2011) blog about phenomenology and photography. He explored the juxtaposition between Cartier-Bresson's approach to photography and Husserl's phenomenology. Angela (aka "Ajdv660"; 2012) compared ethnographic and phenomenological QR in her blog. I like her attempt to express her own views on the topic but admit that she has a lot to learn. You might feel the same way.

You can read about what a methods chapter in a phenomenological dissertation might look like in another blog, *Phenomenology Blog* (http://phenomenologyblog.com/). In fact, there are many interesting sections to this blog, which has been ongoing for about ten years.

As I mentioned earlier, there has been a considerable amount of interest in phenomenology from the nursing community. A post in Kjellberg's blog in February 2012 compares phenomenology, ground theory, and ethnography in terms of best approaches.

Words of Caution

Phenomenology in Name Only

I commented earlier about authors claiming to use grounded theory when, in fact, they were selecting a coding scheme that drew on constant-comparative methods. Researchers who claim to conduct phenomenological research often do the same thing. Norlyk and Harder (2010) illustrated this practice in their study of published research studies in the field of nursing. In their conclusion, they noted inconsistencies in methodology, clarity, and rigor.

Seems So Easy

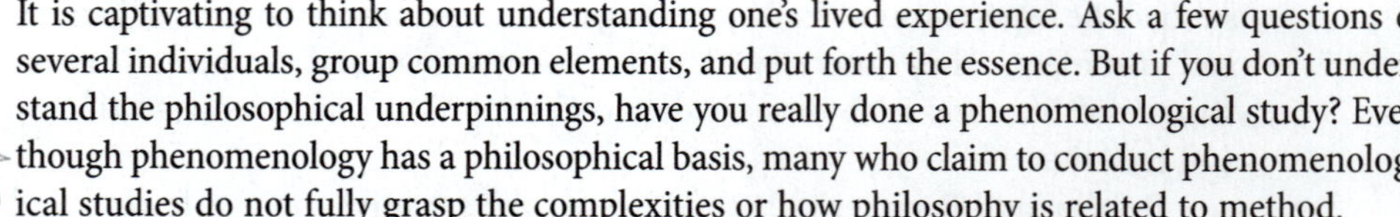

It is captivating to think about understanding one's lived experience. Ask a few questions of several individuals, group common elements, and put forth the essence. But if you don't understand the philosophical underpinnings, have you really done a phenomenological study? Even though phenomenology has a philosophical basis, many who claim to conduct phenomenological studies do not fully grasp the complexities or how philosophy is related to method.

Another research approach that might be accessible to you is that of case study, detailed in the next section. If you are a counselor, you have done case studies of some of your students. If you are a special education teacher, you might have developed a case study about an individual. For these reasons, and perhaps because the approach is quite straightforward, I think it is relatively easy to understand.

■ Case Study—An Examination of a Particular Person, Program, Event, or Concept

A case-study approach is an in-depth examination of a particular case (e.g., individual, program, project, work unit) or several cases. Multiple perspectives related to complexity are sought. You may be familiar with case studies in psychology or counseling; doing case-study research is somewhat similar. But instead of focusing on one individual, a case study often is identified as a particular program, or project, or setting. It is up to the researcher to identify the case and to set limits or boundaries.

History and Meaning

As another approach to QR, case study is without philosophical underpinnings. In many instances, when researchers say they are doing case-study research, they are most likely identifying a single entity to study. The entity could be as small as one individual or as large as an entire business. It is quite common to encounter case-study methods combined with some of the other research approaches I described earlier, so you might come across a phenomenological case study or an ethnographic case study. Runeson and his colleagues (2012) commented that case study is "a commonly used research strategy in areas such as psychology, sociology, political science, social work, business, and community planning" (p. 3). Thomas (2011) supported this position: "Case study research is one of the principal means by which inquiry is conducted in the social sciences" (p. 511). Fridlund (2013) stated that case study research is seldom used in the caring sciences, but he believes it is valuable.

No doubt you have heard of case studies in many disciplines. Business schools use case studies from real life. Psychologists use case studies of individual patients or families. Product designers use case studies to examine new products. Case studies were used fairly often in the early days of sociology, when an interest developed in studying various groups or programs. However, many did not accept case-study research approaches and saw them as less rigorous and not scientific. According to Tellis (1997), the history of case-study research is marked by periods of activity and inertia. He attributed early use in the United States to the Chicago school of sociology. The study of immigrants presented ready-made cases for researchers. However, in a move to make research more scientific, sociologists at Columbia University began to discredit case-study methodology. For many years, the Columbia view was predominant. However, a resurgence of interest in case-study research emerged as qualitative methods began to be accepted in education. You will learn something about the history of this field by reading Yin (2012), Merriam (2002), and Stake (1995).

In spite of the fact that case-study research is so popular, "there is little in the way of organizational structure to guide the intending case inquirer" (Thomas, 2011, p. 511). I know how frustrating this fact is for you as you want to learn more about case study in general and how to conduct a case study in particular. The meaning of case studies actually differs depending on your particular discipline within the social sciences. Some see it from an interpretist frame (e.g., sociology, education, or psychology). If your discipline is in business or politics, you might be drawn to identification of variables. And those in medicine look for unusual phenomena (Thomas, 2011). Chiarello (2013) offers a workshop in case-study research methods through the program in law and public affairs at Princeton University. She covers how researchers define and use case studies and how problems of inference are resolved.

Case study as an approach to QR involves the specific and detailed study of a case or cases. I recall a student of mine who studied the case of the development of a nursery school in an urban neighborhood of Washington, DC. For years, the community was interested in building a school for the neighborhood children, many of whom were non-English speaking. But most people who lived in the immediate area did not have the experience or means to tackle the assignment. It took an outside group of concerned citizens, working together with the clergy and members of the local community, to secure a location, build a staff, and develop a program. My student's research documented this process and the program. Case studies are often of this type.

What is a case? What do we mean when we talk about a case? Here are some ideas that might help you sort through this murky area. A case can be limited to a characteristic, trait, or behavior. You might study a child (or children) with a particular type of learning disability (characteristic). Or you might study a teacher who is outgoing (trait). Or you might study an administrator who exhibits particular behaviors, such as cooperative or collegial interactions (behaviors). The key to this kind of case study is that you identify the characteristic, trait, or behavior in advance and then identify individuals who have or are thought to have the characteristic. This is a somewhat narrow view of case study and might result in missing the very information that would be enriching or informative. More often, a case is limited to a particular entity: for example, Mr. Brown's special education classroom, Ms. Hernandez's honors English class, or an athletic team with the highest win-loss record. By extension, more than one case could be studied. The use of case study in software engineering first appeared in the late 1970s (Runeson et al., 2012). It was not until 1988, however, that a paper included specific information about the methodology of case study.

A case can be limited to one type of situation. These situations are often special or even unique. For example, you might come across a case study of the experience of 9/11. Or you might come across a case study of those who lived in Prince Edward, Virginia, when the public schools closed to avoid integration. Or you might read about a case study of individuals who attend year-round schools. So, we might have cases that are designed to study behaviors, traits, or characteristics. We might have cases that are designed to study a particular program or classroom. Or we might have cases that are designed to study a particular situation. You can see in all of these examples that what is studied is critical to the design, analysis, and interpretation.

Distinguishing Features

- objective is to increase knowledge and bring about change in what is being studied
- empirical inquiry
- contemporary phenomenon
- real-life context

Yin (2012) defined case study as a method that investigates within real-life context. Thomas (2011) suggested two elements: the subject of the case study (the thing being studied) and the object of the study (the theoretical or analytical frame). Neopositivists want to make case studies more objective and generalizable. Ruzzene (2012) addressed the issue in a paper on the topic of external validity.

Special Issues

Selecting Cases

How do you select a case? I propose you consider one of three types of cases: the typical, the exemplary or model, or the unusual or unique. Other kinds of cases you might select could be the constructed or the borderline. One of the most common methods is to select a case that is considered *typical* of others in the same set. For example, if you want to study group homes for the developmentally disabled, you can ask someone knowledgeable in the field to identify such a home in your vicinity. What is typical? It is up to you, the researcher, to think about the criteria you want to use. You might give some guidelines; for example, in my community there are several nonprofit organizations that establish, supervise, and monitor such homes. You could ask someone in such an organization to identify several that are typical. It is usually a good idea to identify more than one case, because it is possible that a particular case does not want to participate, or you may find that you need additional information. Of course, you might have decided to do a multiple-case study, so you would need to have several cases. What I want to stress here is that the case you study is considered *typical.* Since you are not trying to generalize to other group homes, it is not important that you cover the range of all types of homes. Patton (2002) reminded us that we are more interested in the richness of the information we generate from the case than the ability to generalize.

Another approach is to select a case that might be considered *exemplary.* For example, you might want to study the best or the most outstanding mental health care organization in a specific area or system. Again, you would have to rely on nominations from knowledgeable individuals to get the appropriate case. For an exemplary case study, you can read an account of football in Bath, England, in the late Victorian era that was designed to illustrate cultural imperialism (Henson, 2001).

A third type of case you might select is one that is considered *unusual, unique,* or *special* in some way. While this sounds somewhat similar to an exemplary case study, it does not have to be. For example, you might ask for nominations of a home that has instituted special practices or one that has a community outreach program or other aspect that makes a home stand out among the others.

Often, students think they have to identify a case that is representative of all cases of a particular type. This kind of thinking occurs because the novice researcher is thinking about making generalizations to other cases. In QR, this is definitely not so, because you do not have sufficient breadth to make generalizations. So, it is not important to get a case that represents all other cases. Your goal is to get detailed and rich descriptions of the case you select.

We can look at some examples from business as well. If you wanted to study businesses that are small, family-owned enterprises, you might come up with the following:

Typical case: a retail business that operates in a strip mall location and that has average yearly sales of X dollars

Exemplary or model case: a retail business that operates in a multiplex mall with yearly sales far in excess of typical sales of businesses of this type

Unusual or unique case: a retail business that offers a specialized product not normally available in typical stores

Of course, you could select criteria other than yearly sales. There are several important ideas to remember. Your case does not have to be one type or another nor must you include all types of cases. Still another take on selecting cases is one Jensen and Rodgers (2001) offered. They mentioned snapshot case studies, longitudinal case studies, pre–post case studies, patchwork case studies, and comparative case studies.

While most researchers suggest selecting cases using the methods I describe here, Garson (2012) took the position that the selection of a case should be theory driven. This is in keeping with his scientific orientation. His views represent a more scientific, traditionalist view of research. I think you would find that his views are in the minority, however.

What Makes a Case Study

How do you know when you are actually doing a case study? If you have a specific entity, program, individual, or project you are studying and your question is involved with asking what happened when the program was developed or how an individual behaved, then you probably can do a case study.

Defining Limits

An issue you will have to address relates to the limits of the case. You can think of limits in terms of time. Or, you can think of limits in terms of the quantity of data you collect, the number of individuals you interview, or the types of records you examine. As the researcher, you set the limits of your case. Of course, too little information makes for a narrow view of the case, and too much information makes it almost impossible for you to manage.

Going Beyond a Particular Case

Can you have multiple cases? If your question dictates, that is possible. But additional cases require additional data to collect and analyze.

Examples From the Field

There are many different kinds of case studies. Typically, researchers study a program or project on which they have been working. Wingate, Andon, and Cogo (2011) conducted a case study of an academic writing intervention program with students in applied linguistics. O'Brien and Ackroyd (2012) reported on a case study about the recruitment and retention of overseas nurses. Burkett (2011) reported on a case study of professional development for music teachers in rural areas. In the section on method, he reported using a qualitative case study design (p. 4). What makes this a case study is that he concentrated on a particular group of individuals. Zhou and Nunes (2012) used a grounded theory approach to explore knowledge-sharing barriers between traditional and Western medicine practitioners who worked in the Chinese health care organizations. This example illustrates the combination of two QR approaches that I discussed in Chapter 4 under combined approaches.

A researcher might study a larger case. Schelly and her colleagues (2011) studied an entire school district as they explored ways to reduce energy consumption. Or a researcher might study a single individual. Wolcott (1973), in his classic study of a principal, used a microethnographic approach. More than 40 years later, Hoppey and McLeskey (2013) studied a principal during a time of school change. They described their research as a case study. In a section on design of the study, they wrote that the study "combined ethnographic methods with a phenomenological lens to study the lived experience of being a principal" (p. 3). You can see the distinguishing feature of these different case studies is that the researcher or researcher team identified a particular individual, program, school, or school system to study. In all cases, data were gathered with interviews and observations.

From Parsons's (2012) study of two teachers to Morales and colleagues' (2012) research of multiple cases about language in Mexican immigrant families, case-study research covers a large domain of content and process. From case studies of the Temple of Hip Hop in the field of geography (Bazzaroni, 2012) to analyzing the use of various tools in Mongo and MapReduce to analyze a difficult problem involving unauthorized access to a network (Dixon, 2012), case-study research makes an important statement in the 21st century.

Blogs and Beyond

In his blog, Jureidini (2012) reported on a case study of how a drug company manipulated evidence. Greene's blog (2012) reported on mishandling of data related to Head Start. Judith Davidson (2012) posted a blog devoted to QR, and discussed Flyvbjerg's opinion on case studies.

Words of Caution

Utility of Case Studies

Many have suggested that doing case-study research is too particular and that the results cannot be generalized. Flyvbjerg (2006) discussed misunderstandings related to doing case-study research and suggested that conducting case studies is valuable since

> a scientific discipline without a large number of thoroughly executed case studies is a discipline without systematic production of exemplars, and a discipline without exemplars is an ineffective one. Social science may be strengthened by the execution of a greater number of good case studies. (p. 219)

Ruddin (2006) commented that, in some instances, case studies can be generalized (p. 797). He goes on to discuss misunderstandings about the nature of case study research and concludes that "we must find avenues of using the cumulative wisdom of case studies" (p. 807).

Is Case Study a Research Approach?

I have grouped case-study research with other research approaches. Yet I find that details of how to conduct a case study are not spelled out. What makes a piece of research a case study? I think it is when a researcher sets out to investigate a particular person, program, curriculum, or technique. The case can be described in detail, or the researcher can interpret the meaning. Either way is used. So, when you read that a particular piece of research is a case study or uses case-study methodology, you might find a variety of ways of going about gathering data, analyzing data, and writing up the data.

I end this chapter with a discussion of a family of research approaches referred to as *narrative*. Narrative approaches tell a story. In most narratives, the researcher interprets the stories. Some narrative designs involve collaboration between the researcher and the researched in terms of the story and the guiding light or epiphany of the story.

Narrative Inquiry—Focus on Telling a Story

Narrative research inquiry is a group of approaches that rely on the written or spoken words or visual representations of individuals. The distinguishing characteristic of the narrative is that personal **storytelling** is involved. *Narrative analysis* is a general term that incorporates first-person accounts in story form, biography, autobiography, life history, oral history, autoethnography, pathography, **discourse analysis**, or life narratives. These approaches emphasize the lives of individuals as told through stories. According to Clandinin (2007), one of the leading writers in the field, the approach is growing in acceptance. The emphasis in these approaches is on the story and often the epiphany. Narrative can be both a method and the phenomenon under study (Pinnegar & Daynes, 2006). As a method, it uses the told and lived stories people tell. Often, the meaning of the experiences is related in an account.

History and Meaning

Stories. We are all fascinated with them. As individuals, we marvel at accounts of common people who face extraordinary challenges and overcome them. As teachers, we empathize with the child whose family circumstances appear overwhelming, yet he or she comes to school each day. We are amazed to learn of individuals who struggle for democracy in tyrannical countries. We are struck by individual courage to speak out against oppression. All fascinating. But I would suggest that these stories themselves are not research. Research of this type involves a researcher interpreting or making meaning of the told story. There has been increased use of biographical methods and life histories since the late 1980s (Bertaux & Delacroix, 2000; Chamberlayne, Bornat, & Wengraf, 2000; Clandinin, 2007; Creswell, 2007; Denzin, 1989).

There is not a single story of how a narrative tradition made its way into the family of QR approaches. Pinnegar and Daynes (2006) suggested that the use of narrative has evolved due to several factors: the relationship between the researcher and the researched, the move from numbers to words, the move from the general to the specific, and the acceptance of alternative ways of knowing. In fact, these factors help explain why QR approaches in general have become more acceptable in the research community. The relationship between the researcher and those being researched has moved from an objective stance to one that involves an interpretive position. Clandinin (2007) explained, "To enter conversations with the rest of our communities to develop a method—a way of talking and asking and answering and making sense— . . . will allow narrative to flourish in this congenial moment for stories" (p. 1). Clandinin also suggested that the use of narrative is based on Dewey's pragmatic explanation of experience. For a detailed historical account, you can review Clandinin's (2007) *Handbook of Narrative Inquiry.*

Creswell (2007) defined narrative inquiry as a research design that uses an account of an event or series of events connected by chronology. In Creswell's earlier text (1997), he referred to the tradition of *biography* rather than the more general *narrative* term. In their book of readings, Daiute and Lightfoot (2004) suggested that narrative inquiry comes from several traditions: the literary, the cultural and social self, and history.

Life history as a research technique, developed by the Chicago school of sociology, has been popular since the 1920s. But the technique came under fire when the debate between statistics and case studies became more intense and participant observation took on a greater prominence compared to life histories. As I have said throughout this book, QR approaches have been on somewhat of a roller-coaster ride. Riding upward in the 1990s and beyond, they came under question in the first decade of the new millennium, as a conservative movement in education in the United States pushed toward accountability and quantitative data to support student achievement. In spite of this traditional approach, I believe that QR approaches have a place in our understanding of education today. Narrative approaches are one important way of answering questions.

One way to approach an understanding of narrative research is to look at how students learn about it. I draw your attention to an excellent website—Narrative Inquiry in Education—developed by graduate students from University of Western Ontario in Canada (http://www.edu.uwo.ca/Narrative_Inquiry/faq.html). They have developed an excellent resource. If you are more inclined to read what other experts have written, you can go to several sources. I have already mentioned Clandinin's (2007) edited volume or her earlier text (Clandinin & Connelly, 2000). You can also look at other accounts. Denzin (1989) described several steps to conducting a narrative study: collect an objective set of experiences, either chronologically or in life stages; gather actual stories; organize stories into pivotal events or epiphanies; search for meaning in the stories; and look for larger structures to help explain the meaning in the stories. Creswell and Shope (2009) provided key characteristics of narrative designs. They include individual experiences, a chronology, collecting individual stories, restorying, coding, the context, and collaboration.

Visual media have also been used in the construction of narratives. You can read a description of a course on visual narrative and research methods offered by the UC Berkeley School of Information (University of California, Berkeley, 2011).

Distinguishing Features

- reliance on the story aspect of the data
- gathers data in the form of stories
- presents data in the form of stories
- often uses alternative presentation forms

Unlike the other research approaches that I describe in this chapter, narrative relies on a particular story. Researchers gather stories from participants either through interviews, observations, or videos. Often, presentations of results utilize the story form as a vehicle for presentation. I use the term *story* in a general manner, because at times, alternative methods of presentation are utilized. These might include poetry, play, or performance.

Special Issues

Gathering Sufficient Information

As with many qualitative approaches, researchers have a challenge. How much information should they gather? What is relevant? What is important? During data collection, it is almost impossible to determine what to include. I suggest that each story a participant tells is potentially one of importance. But it may not be known until the researcher is organizing the data.

Who Owns the Stories?

You might grapple with this question. If a story is told to you as part of a research project, then you should receive prior approval to use the story in your analysis. Some researchers find themselves working in a collaborative manner with storytellers.

Retelling the Stories

Many who write about doing narrative research recommend that a story might be retold. As the researcher, you act as the reinterpreter of the story.

With multiple stories, what happens when issues are in conflict? I have read a number of studies that involve multiple stories that form an amalgam. This device often works well but might present a challenge for you as a researcher when these multiple stories do not lead to a coherent picture.

Examples from the Field

Rogers (2012) used the technique of public consultative discourse analysis to analyze policy-making processes of an elected school board that permitted immediate connection to the context.

Johnson-Bailey (2002) used a narrative form in her presentation of Cathy's experiences that were affected by race, class, and gender. You should find this type of presentation very interesting to read. Noy (2003) also made use of a narrative style in his reflection about doing a narrative dissertation. This is precisely the article you should read if you think you might use narrative as your research approach. On a less personal note, Sellerberg and Leppänen (2012) developed a typology of narratives in their study of bankrupt entrepreneurs.

Not surprisingly, many examples of published research using narrative inquiry are personal. Hicks (2011) used prose poetry to express a narrative she tells about herself as a female soldier. She begins:

> *I wanted to know,*
>
> *so I checked the speaker phone on my cellular*
>
> *and recorded with a borrowed device*
>
> *and called 4 women to ask. (p. 461)*

I am moved by her account as she grapples with an unconventional topic and an unconventional presentation format. Heydon (2010) explored ethical and methodological issues surrounding the narrative. Ketelle (2011) used photography in a narrative inquiry of school principles. Jones (2012) relied on documentary film to relate the narratives he collected over multiple years. Lieblich (2006) wrote from her perspective as a narrative scholar. In her own story, she wrote of her transformation as she moved from a study of life stories to a book and then a play based on autobiographical narratives of women. Reading about her experiences might assist you as you struggle with understanding QR in general and narrative in particular.

You might find it interesting to read about the lives of the authors White and Dotson (2010) as they moved from traditional narrative research approaches toward a recognition of the positive aspect of subjectivity in their adoption of new assumptions about narrative interviewing.

Blogs and Beyond

McNely (2012), a professor in rhetoric and communication, used his blog to post selections from his readings. A recent post dealt with innovations in QR methods, a narrative review of an article appearing in *Qualitative Research.* In this article, a narrative review is similar to a meta-analysis that I discussed earlier. Donato (2012), a student in elementary education and writing arts, posted her thoughts about Clandinin's *Narrative Inquiry.* She also posted her own thoughts about how she connects with narrative research. I think it is very helpful for you, as a student, to see that others are challenged and excited about this way of answering questions. You can read one more student blog on the narrative posted by Collins (2012).

Words of Caution

More Than a Story

As a beginning qualitative researcher, you might find yourself drawn in by the stories you hear. Yet you might struggle with trying to decide how to move from a story to a "restory" or interpretation of what you hear. When can you put your own voice into what you understand? How is it all right to do so? You might find notions of keeping remote pushing against these new ideas.

Understanding the Context

While you recognize that the participant you study exists within a larger context (familial, social, personal, or political), you may not necessarily have the background to understand the issues involved. I can imagine that gathering narratives of participants who experienced the recent uprisings in the Middle East would be difficult, since the issues are complex and remote.

How to Get Information

In most cases, you would expect to conduct an in-person interview with your participant. However, Holt (2010) asked us to consider using the telephone for narrative interviews. Contrary to the prevailing view that face-to-face interviews are the best, she relayed her experiences using the telephone to interview parents of youth offenders. In particular, she added a component of reflexivity by the participant as well as the researcher. In addition to traditional telephone interviews, contemporary researchers have explored using web conferencing, smartphones, or Skype.

Fact or Fiction

I notice that many researchers are concerned with getting the story *right.* Since all QR is interpreted through the eyes and sensibility of the researcher, there really is no getting it right. In fact, some researchers use creative fiction to tell a story.

Ethics, Anonymity, and Ownership

Much of QR is very personal. This is particularly the case of the data involved in the narrative. How much should be anonymous and how much should be revealed can be negotiated between the researcher and those who are involved as participants in the research. In the use of visuals, achieving anonymity is not possible. In fact, some participants might want to be revealed.

■ Summary of Research Approaches

In this chapter, I present five popular approaches to QR. An *ethnography* describes the culture of a group. *Grounded theory* generates theory that emerges from, or is grounded in, the field. It is characterized by the use of theoretical sampling, the constant-comparative method, and specific coding methods (open, axial, and selective coding). *Phenomenology* is based on description and understanding of the lived experience of one or more individuals who have undergone a particular experience. In this approach, the researcher brackets, or attempts to set

Table 5.1 Comparison of Common Research Approaches

Approach	*Questions/purpose*	*Key elements*	*Process*	*Other issues*
Ethnography	Study of cultures	In-depth; observation in field; symbolic interaction	Emerging in culture; in-depth examination but not necessarily extensive immersion; thick description	Gaining access; spending sufficient time in field
Grounded theory	Theory emerges from data	Theoretical saturation; constant comparative coding	Structured approach to selection of participants; coding data prescribed	Closely aligned with post-positivists and traditional approaches
Phenomenology	Study of lived experiences	Interviews to determine essence of lived experience; philosophical	Bracketing (epoché); in-depth interviews	Understanding philosophical basis
Case study	Study of particulars	A limited and bounded case; key informants	Detailed look at a particular setting	Identifying key players; getting access to documents
Narrative	Study of life history and stories	Individual stories; epiphany	Lives and stories discovered through interviewing	Connections beyond individuals

aside, his or her thoughts on the topic; suspends judgment; and focuses on inductively understanding the meaning of the experience to the one(s) studied. A *case study* is an in-depth investigation of an individual or group with a primary purpose of describing one or more characteristics, behaviors, or traits. *Narrative approaches* rely on the stories of participants to assist in understanding and interpreting the lives of others. For a thought-provoking and stimulating look inside the secret police of East Berlin in 1984, please view the 2006 film *The Lives of Others,* directed by Florian Henckel von Donnersmarck. I lived in Germany during 1985 to 1986; thus, I can share with you how stimulating and frightening this film was to me.

At the end of the next chapter, I present you with a way you can use these approaches to help guide you as you begin to develop your own research.

CHECK YOURSELF

- QR approaches
    - look at human interactions in natural settings
    - look at the whole, not isolated variables
    - describe and explain
    - rely heavily on the researcher
- What can a research approach do?
    - assist as you plan your research
    - define a set of steps or procedures that you should follow in conducting research
    - ground your research in a conceptual or theoretical model
- Five approaches
    - Ethnography—the study of cultures
    - Grounded theory—theory emerging from the data
    - Phenomenology—the examination of lived experiences
    - Case study—a look at the particular
    - Narrative—telling a story
- Details of each approach can be compared by looking at Table 5.1.

KEY DISCUSSION ISSUES

1. There is an abundance of information in this chapter. Select one approach that appeals to you. Identify the key elements. How do you think those elements distinguish that approach from another approach?
2. How can you decide which approach best fits your research question?
3. Is one approach better than another? Does your department prefer one approach to another? If so, why do you think they do?
4. Which approaches seem closer to traditional forms of research? Why?

MODULE 5

Identifying Questions, Selecting an Approach, Planning and Implementing, and Connecting

There are four parts to this activity: identifying questions, selecting a research approach, planning how to implement that approach, and connecting all the components.

Working with two or three others, begin by brainstorming research questions. Generate a list of about 10 questions. Next, select the research approach that seems to be most suitable for answering the questions you have chosen. Then, outline in one paragraph how you would go about conducting the study, using the approach you have selected. Finally, as a total class, discuss how to connect research questions and research approaches, and conduct the research.

REFERENCES

Abrahams, F. (2009). Examining the preservice practicum experience of undergraduate music education majors. Exploring connections and dispositions through multiple perspectives: A critical grounded theory. *Journal of Music Teacher Education, 19*(1), 80–104.

Adjv660. (2012, March 27). Ethnographic and phenomenological qualitative research. *Research Methods in Education*. Retrieved from http://angeladresearch.blogspot.com/2012/03/ethnographic-and-phenomenological.html

Allar, M-L. (2011). An ethnographic study of the Astor/Astor Park Cemetery. *The Journal for Undergraduate Ethnography, 1*. Retrieved from http://undergraduateethnography.org/sites/default/files/papers/JUE%20-%20Mary-Lynn%20Allar_0.pdf

Andersen, P., Inoue, K., & Walsh, K. (2012, June 7). An animated model for facilitating understanding of grounded theory and the processes used to generate theory. *Journal of Research in Nursing*, 1–10. doi: 10.1177/1744987111434188

Barnacle, R. (2001). *Phenomenology and education research*. Paper presented at the Australian Association for Research in Education, Fremantle, Australia.

Bazzaroni, C. (2012). *Spirituality in hip hop: A case study*. Paper presented at the Association of American Geographers Annual Meeting, New York, New York. Retrieved from http://meridian.aag.org/callforpapers/program/AbstractDetail.cfm?AbstractID=47693

Berg, B., & Lune, H. (2012). *Qualitative research methods for the social sciences* (8th ed.). Boston, MA: Pearson.

Bertaux, D., & Delacroix, C. (2000). Case histories of families and social processes. In P. Chamberlayne, J. Bornat, & T. Wengraf (Eds.), *The turn to biographical methods in social sciences. Comparative issues and examples* (pp. 71–89). London, England: Routledge.

Bowen, G. (2008). Naturalistic inquiry and the saturation concept: A research note. *Qualitative Research, 8*(1), 137–152.

Brannan, K. (2012). Visualizing community: Designing & creating queer female space in DC. *Kelsey Brannan: Looking beyond the picture frame*. Retrieved from https://blogs.commons.georgetown.edu/kmb256/tag/grounded-theory/

Bryant, A., & Charmaz, K. (2010). *The SAGE handbook of grounded theory*. London, England: SAGE.

Burkett, E. (2011). A case study of issues concerning professional development for rural instrumental music teachers. *Journal of Music Teacher Education, 21*(1), 1–14.

Campbell, D., & Stanley, J. (1963). *Experimental and quasi-experimental designs for research*. Boston, MA: Houghton Mifflin.

Chamberlayne, P., Bornat, J., & Wengraf, T. (Eds.). (2000). *The turn to biographical methods in social science. Comparative issues and examples*. London, England: Routledge.

Charmaz, K. (2006). *Constructing grounded theory: A practical guide through qualitative analysis*. Thousand Oaks, CA: SAGE.

Chiarello, E. (2013). Workshop series in case study research. *Program in Law and Public Affairs*. Retrieved from http://lapa.princeton.edu/eventdetail.php?ID=1006

Childers, S. M. (2011). Getting in trouble: Feminist postcritical policy ethnography in an urban school. *Qualitative Inquiry, 17*(4), 345–354.

Clandinin, J. (Ed.). (2007). Preface. In J. Clandinin (Ed.), *Handbook of narrative inquiry: Mapping a methodology* (pp. ix–xvii). Thousand Oaks, CA: SAGE.

Clandinin, J., & Connelly, F. (2000). *Narrative inquiry: Experience and story in qualitative research*. San Francisco, CA: Jossey-Bass.

Cohen, M., Kahn, D., & Steeves, R. (2000). *Hermeneutic phenomenological research: A practical guide for nurse researchers*. Thousand Oaks, CA: SAGE.

Collins, K. (2012). Qualitative research and narrative inquiry. *Kate Collins*. Retrieved from http://katie-collins.weebly.com/2/post/2012/03/qualitative-research-and-narrative-inquiry.html

Conklin, T. (2012). Work worth doing: A phenomenological study of the experience of discovering and following one's calling. *Journal of Management Inquiry, 21*(3), 298–317.

Corbin, J., & Strauss, A. (2008). *Basics of qualitative research: Techniques and procedures for developing grounded theory* (3rd ed.). Thousand Oaks, CA: SAGE.

Cormier, E. (2012). How parents make decisions to use medication to treat their child's ADHD: A grounded theory study. *Journal of the American Psychiatric Nurses Association, 18*(6), 345–356.

Coyne, I., & Cowley, S. (2006). Using grounded theory to research parent participation. *Journal of Research in Nursing, 11*, 501–515.

Creswell, J. (1997). *Qualitative inquiry and research design: Choosing among five traditions.* Thousand Oaks, CA: SAGE.

Creswell, J. (2007). *Qualitative inquiry and research design: Choosing among five approaches.* Thousand Oaks, CA: SAGE.

Creswell, J., & Shope, R. (2009). *Educational research: Planning, conducting, and evaluating quantitative and qualitative research, chapter 16 PowerPoint slides.* Retrieved from http://www.authorstream.com/Presentation/rsahragard-267019-narrative-research-education-ppt-powerpoint/

Cunningham, D. (2012). *A grounded theory study of protected learning time.* (PhD thesis, University of Glasgow). Retrieved from http://theses.gla.ac.uk/3329/

Daalen-Smith, C. (2008). Living as a chameleon: Girls, anger, and mental health. *The Journal of School Nursing, 24*(3), 236–264.

Daiute, C., & Lightfoot, C. (Eds.). (2004). *Narrative analysis: Studying the development of individuals in society.* Thousand Oaks, CA: SAGE

Davidson, A. L. (2002). Grounded theory. *Essortment: Your Source for Knowledge.* Retrieved from http://az.essortment.com/groundedtheory_rmnf.htm

Davidson, J. (2012, November 23). Aubrey Rocheleau and qualitative research. *QRfrag.* Retrieved from at http://qrfrag.blogspot.com/2012/11/aubrey-rocheleau-and-qualitative.html

de Guzman, A., Jimenez, B., Jocson, K., Junio, A., Junio, D., Jurado, J., & Justiniano, A. (2013). This too shall pass: A grounded theory study of Filipino cancer survivorship. *Journal of Holistic Nursing, 31*(1), 35–46.

deLeon, M., & Brunner, C. (2012). Cycles of fear: A model of lesbian and gay educational leaders' lived experiences. *Educational Administration Quarterly, 49*(1), 161–203.

Denzin, N. (1989). *Interpretive interactionism.* Newbury Park, CA: SAGE.

Denzin, N., & Lincoln, Y. (Eds.). (2011). *The SAGE handbook of qualitative research* (4th ed.). Thousand Oaks, CA: SAGE.

Dermot, M. (2000). *Introduction to phenomenology.* London, England: Routledge.

Dick, B. (n.d.). *Resource papers in action research.* Retrieved from http://www.aral.com.au/resources/grounded.html

Dixon, B. (2012). *Case study: Using Mongo and MapReduce to analyze a difficult research problem.* Presentation given at the NoSQL Now! 2011 Conference in San Jose, California. Retrieved from http://www.dataversity.net/case-study-using-mongo-and-mapreduce-to-analyze-a-difficult-research-problem/

Donato, L. (2012, March 26). Intro to qualitative research and narrative inquiry. *Lisa Donato.* Retrieved from http://lisadonato.weebly.com/2/post/2012/03/intro-to-qualitative-research-and-narrative-inquiry.html.

Draucker, C., Martsolf, D., Ross, R., & Rusk, T. (2007). Theoretical sampling and category development in grounded theory. *Qualitative Health Research, 17*(8), 1137–1148.

Ebrahimi, Z., Wilhelmson, K., Moore, C., & Jakobsson, A. (2012). Frail elders' experiences with and perceptions of health. *Journal of Health Research, 22*(11), 1513–1523.

Edmonds, M. (2010). The lived experience of nursing students who study abroad: A qualitative inquiry. *Journal of Studies in International Education, 14*(3), 545–568.

Eich, D. (2008). A grounded theory of high-quality leadership programs: Perspectives from student leadership development programs in higher education. *Journal of Leadership & Organizational Studies, 15*, 176–187.

EMAC. (2012). What is public ethnography? *Ethnography. Media. Arts. Culture.* Retrieved from http://publicethnography.net/home

Embree, L. (2003). General impressions of our tradition today. In C. E. Cheung, I. Chvatik, I. Copoeru, L. Embree, J. Iribarne, & H. Sepp (Eds.), *Essays in celebration of the founding of the Organization of Phenomenological Organizations.* (pp.1–4). Retrieved from http://www.o-p-o.net/essays/lesterintroduction.pdf

Feldman, M., Bell, J., & Berger, M. (2003). *Gaining access: A practical and theoretical guide for qualitative researchers.* Walnut Creek, CA: AltaMira Press. (Also available as a Google E-book.)

Finlay, L. (2012, July 21). Unfolding the phenomenological research process: Iterative stages of "seeing afresh." *Journal of Humanistic Psychology.* doi: 10.1177/0022167812453877

Flyvbjerg, B. (2006). Five misunderstandings about case-study research. *Qualitative Inquiry, 12*(2), 210–245.

Fridlund, B. (2013). The case study as a research strategy. *Scandinavian Journal of Caring Sciences, 11*(1), p.3–4. Retrieved from http://onlinelibrary.wiley.com/doi/10.1111/j.1471-6712.1997.tb00423.x/abstract

Garson, G. D. (2012). *Case study research.* [Kindle Edition]. Statistical Associates.

Gearing, R. (2004). Bracketing in research: A typology, *Qualitative Health Research, 14*, 1429–1452.

Giorgi, A. (1989). One type of analysis of descriptive data: Procedures involved in following a scientific phenomenological method. *Methods: A Journal of Human Science, Annual Edition, 1*, 39–61.

Girke, F., & Laszczkowski, M. (2012). Here today, gone tomorrow: Ethnographies of transient social formations. *EASA: European Association of Social Anthropologists.* Retrieved from http://www.nomadit.co.uk/easa/easa2012/panels.php5?PanelID=1319

Glaser, B. (1998). *Doing grounded theory: Issues & discussion.* Mill Valley, CA: Sociology Press.

Glaser, B., & Strauss, A. (1967). *The discovery of grounded theory.* Chicago, IL: Aldine Publishing Co.

Glass, P. (2001). *Autism and the family* (Unpublished doctoral dissertation). Virginia Tech, Blacksburg, VA.

Greene, J. (2012). Head Start, a case study in the unreliability of government research. *Jay P. Greene's blog*. Retrieved from http://jaypgreene.com/2012/03/13/head-start-a-case-study-in-the-unreliability-of-government-research/

Haig, B. (1995). *Grounded theory as scientific method*. Retrieved from http://jan.ucc.nau.edu/~pms/cj355/readings/Haig%20Grounded%20Theory%20as%20Scientific%20Method.pdf

Harper, M. (n.d.). Exploring the essence of lived experiences of stepfathers: A phenomenological study. *Udini*. Retrieved from http://udini.proquest.com/view/exploring-the-essence-of-lived-goid:305150372/

Henson, M. (2001). Cultural imperialism: A case study of football in Bath in the late-Victorian era. *The Sports Historian: The Journal of the British Society of Sports History, 21*(2), 20–34.

Heydon, R. (2010). Knitting teacher: A narrative inquiry of a researcher who has been researched. *Qualitative Inquiry, 16*(2), 130–139.

Hicks, M. (2011). Making my narrative mine: Unconventional articulations of a female soldier. *Qualitative Inquiry, 17*(5), 461–465.

Holt, A. (2010). Using the telephone for narrative interviewing: A research note. *Qualitative Research, 10*(1), 113–121.

Hoppey, D., & McLeskey, J. (2013). A case study of principal leadership in an effective inclusive school. *Journal of Special Education, 46*(4), 245–256.

Hou, W., Ko, N., & Shu, B. (2013). Recovery experiences of Taiwanese women after terminating abusive relationships. *Journal of Interpersonal Violence, 28*(1), 157–175.

Hsiung, P-C. (2012). The globalization of qualitative research: Challenging Anglo-American domination and local hegemonic discourse [27 paragraphs]. *Forum Qualitative Sozialforschung/Forum: Qualitative Social Research, 13*(1), Art. 21.

Husserl, E. (1917/1981). Pure phenomenology, its methods and its field of investigation (R.W. Jordan, Trans.). In P. McCormick & F. Elliston (Eds.), *Husserl: Shorter works* (pp. 9–17). Notre Dame, IN: University of Notre Dame Press.

Jensen, J., & Rodgers, R. (2001). Cumulating the intellectual gold of case study research. *Public Administration Review, 61*(2), 236–246.

Jin. (2008). Theoretical saturation. *Writing with learning and thinking*. Retrieved from http://jin-thoughts.blogspot.com/2008/03/theoretical-saturation.html

Johl, S. K., & Renganathan, S. (2010). Strategies for gaining access in doing fieldwork: Reflection of two researchers. *The Electronic Journal of Business Research Methods, 8*(1), 42–50. Retrieved from http://www.ejbrm.com

Johnson-Bailey, J. (2002). The wrong side of the tank. In S. B. Merriam (Ed.), *Qualitative research in practice: Examples for discussion and analysis* (pp. 314–326). San Francisco, CA: Jossey-Bass.

Jones, K. (2012). Performative social science and narrative research. *Kipworld*. Retrieved from http://www.angelfire.com/zine/kipworld/cprp.index.html

Jureidini, J. (2012, April 5). Insight into how pharma manipulates research evidence: A case study. *The Conversation*. Retrieved from http://theconversation.edu.au/insight-into-how-pharma-manipulates-research-evidence-a-case-study-4071

Kennedy, B. (2009). Infusing participants' voices into grounded theory research. *Qualitative Inquiry 15*(8), 1416–1433.

Kennedy, B. (2011). The importance of student and teacher interactions for disaffected middle school students: A grounded theory study of community day schools. *Urban Education, 46*(1), 4–33.

Ketelle, D. (2011). *The ground they walk on: Photography and narrative inquiry*. Paper presented at the TQR 2nd Annual Conference, Ft. Lauderdale, FL.

Kingscott, J., & Durant, C. (2010). Keyboard improvisation: A phenomenological study. *International Journal of Music Education, 28*(2), 127–144.

Kirchhoff, A., & Lawrenz, F. (2011). The use of grounded theory to investigate the role of teacher education on stem teachers' career paths in high-need schools. *Journal of Teacher Education, 62*(3), 246–259.

Kjellberg. (2012). Phenomenology, grounded theory, or ethnography: Which approach is best? *The Nurse's Wellness Guide*. Retrieved from http://thenurseswellnessguide.blogspot.com/2012/02/phenomenology-grounded-theory-or.html

Li, J. (2008). Ethical challenges in participant observation: A reflection on ethnographic fieldwork. *The Qualitative Report, 13*(1), 100–115. Retrieved from http://www.nova.edu/ssss/QR/QR13-1/li.pdf

Lichtman, M. (2013). *Qualitative research in education* (3rd ed.). Thousand Oaks, CA: SAGE.

Lieblich, A. (2006). Vicissitudes. *Qualitative Inquiry, 12*(1), 60–80.

Mack, N., Woodson, C., MacQueen, K. M., Guest, G., & Namey, E. (2005). *Qualitative research methods: A data collector's field guide*. Research Triangle Park, NC: Family Health International. Retrieved from http://www.nucats.northwestern.edu/community-engaged-research/seminar-series-and-events/pdfs/Family_Health_International_Qualitative_Research_Methods.pdf

McCormick, M. (2011). The lived body. *Qualitative Social Work, 10*(1), 66–85.

McLeod, J. (2001). *Qualitative research in counseling and psychotherapy*. Thousand Oaks, CA: SAGE.

McNely, B. J. (2012, January 10). Annotations: "Innovation in qualitative research methods." *5000*. Retrieved from http://5000.blogspot.com/2012/01/annotations-innovation-in-qualitative.html

Merriam, S. (2002). *Qualitative research in practice: Examples for discussion and analysis*. San Francisco, CA: Jossey-Bass.

Morales, A., Yakushko, O., & Castro, A. (2012). Language brokering among Mexican-immigrant families in the Midwest: A multiple case study. *Counseling Psychologist, 40*(4), 520–553.

Norlyk, A., & Harder, I. (2010). What makes a phenomenological study phenomenological? An analysis of peer-reviewed empirical nursing studies *Qualitative Health Research, 20*(3), 420–431.

Noy, C. (2003). The write of passage: Reflections on writing a dissertation in narrative methodology [54 paragraphs]. *Forum Qualitative Sozialforschung/Forum: Qualitative Social*

Research, 4(2), Art. 39. Retrieved from http://nbn-resolving.de/urn:nbn:de:0114-fqs0302392

Noy, C. (2011). The aesthetics of qualitative (re)search: Performing ethnography at a heritage museum. *Qualitative Inquiry, 17*(10), 919–929.

Oberg, H., & Bell, A. (2012). Exploring phenomenology for researching lived experience in technology enhanced learning. In V. Hodgson, C. Jones, M. de Laat, D. McConnell, T. Ryberg, & P. Sloep (Eds.), *Proceedings of the 8th international conference on networked learning 2012* (pp. 203–210). Retrieved from http://www.networkedlearningconference.org.uk/abstracts/pdf/oberg.pdf

O'Brien, T., & Ackroyd, S. (2012). Understanding the recruitment and retention of overseas nurses: Realist case study research in National Health Service Hospitals in the UK. *Nursing Inquiry, 19,* 3–50.

Oktay, J. (2012). *Grounded theory.* Oxford, England: Oxford University Press.

O'Reilly, K. (2010). *Service undone: A grounded theory of strategically constructed silos and their impact on customer-company interactions from the perspective of retail employees.* (Doctoral dissertation, Utah State University). Retrieved from http://digitalcommons.usu.edu/etd/669

O'Reilly, K., Paper, D., & Marx, S. (2012). Demystifying grounded theory for business research. *Organizational Research Methods, 15*(2), 247–262.

Parkes, K., & Jones, B. (2011). Students' motivations for considering a career in music performance. *Update: Applications of Research in Music Education, 29*(2), 20–28.

Parsons, S. (2012). Adaptive teaching in literacy instruction: Case studies of two teachers. *Journal of Literacy Research, 44*(2), 149–170.

Patton, M. (2002). *Qualitative evaluation and research methods.* London, England: SAGE.

Pieters, H., & Dornig, K. (2013). Collaboration in grounded theory analysis: Reflections and practical suggestions. *Qualitative Social Work, 12*(2), 200–214.

Pinnegar, S., & Daynes, J. (2006). Locating narrative inquiry historically: Thematics in the turn to narrative. *Handbook of Narrative Inquiry.* Retrieved from http://www.sagepub.com/upm-data/13548_Chapter1.pdf

Reid, M., & Moore, J. (2008). College readiness and academic preparation for post-secondary education. *Urban Education, 43*(2), 240–261.

Repass, M. (2003). *The professional woman's desire to retire: The process of transition.* (Unpublished doctoral dissertation). Virginia Tech, Blacksburg, VA.

Robinson, P. (2000). The body matrix: A phenomenological exploration of student bodies on-line. *Educational Technology & Society 3*(3). Retrieved from http://www.ifets.info/journals/3_3/c05.html

Rogers, R. (2012). In the aftermath of a state takeover of a school district: A case study in public consultative discourse analysis. *Urban Education, 47*(5), 910–938.

Rose, G. (1993). *Feminism and geography: The limits of geographical knowledge.* St. Paul, MN: University of Minnesota Press.

Ruddin, L. (2006). You can generalize stupid! Social scientists, Bent Flyvbjerg, and case study methodology, *Qualitative Inquiry, 12*(4), 797–812.

Runeson, P., Höst, M., Rainer, A., & Regnell, B. (2012). *Case study research in software engineering: Guidelines and examples.* Hoboken, NJ: Wiley & Sons. Retrieved from http://my.safaribooksonline.com/book/-/9781118104354

Ruzzene, A. (2012). Drawing lessons from case studies by enhancing comparability. *Philosophy of the Social Sciences, 42*(1), 99–120.

Saldaña, J. (2012). *The coding manual for qualitative researchers.* London: SAGE.

Salmon, J. (2012). The use of phenomenology in nursing research. *Nurse Researcher, 19*(3). Retrieved from http://nurseresearcher.rcnpublishing.co.uk/news-and-opinion/commentary/the-use-of-phenomenology-in-nursing-research

Sbaraini, A., Carter, S., Evans, R., & Blinkhorn, A. (2011). How to do a grounded theory study: A worked example of a study of dental practices. *BMC Medical Research Methodology, 11,* 128. Retrieved from http://www.biomedcentral.com/1471-2288/11/128

Schelly, A., Cross, J., Franzen, W., Hall, P., & Reeve, S. (2011). Reducing energy consumption and creating a conservation culture in organizations: A case study of one public school district. *Environment and Behavior, 43*(3), 316–343.

Schrag, Z. M. (2012, February 1). Educator: Ethics requirements do not respect ethnographic participants. *Institutional Review Blog.* Retrieved from http://www.institutionalreviewblog.com/2012/02/educator-ethics-requirements-do-not.html

Scott-Jones, J., & Watt, S. (2010). *Ethnography in social science practice.* New York, NY: Routledge.

Sellerberg, A-M., & Leppänen, V. (2012). A typology of narratives of social inclusion and exclusion: The case of bankrupt entrepreneurs [75 paragraphs]. *Forum Qualitative Sozialforschung/Forum: Qualitative Social Research, 13*(1), Art. 26. Retrieved from http://nbn-resolving.de/urn:nbn:de:0114-fqs1201260

Simonsen, K. (2013). In quest of a new humanism: Embodiment, experiences and phenomenology as critical geography. *Progress in Human Geography, 37*(1), 10–26.

Skjaerven, K. (2011). *Phenomenology and photography.* Retrieved from http://phenomenologyandphotography.wordpress.com/2011/05/

Smith, A. (2012). Reflection 5: Performed ethnography as an example of critical pedagogy. *Alyson's Sociology of Education Blog.* Retrieved from http://alyson-smith.blogspot.com/2012/03/performed-ethnography-as-example-of.html

Southern, S., & Devlin, J. (2010). Theory development: A bridge between practice and research. *The Family Journal, 18*(1), 84–87.

Stake, R. (1995). *The art of case study research.* Thousand Oaks, CA: SAGE.

Starbuck, H. (2003). *Clashing and converging. Effects of the Internet on the correspondence art network.* Austin: University of Texas. Retrieved from http://www.lib.utexas.edu/etd/d/2003/starbuckmk032/starbuckmk032.pdf

Swartz, A. (2006). The sexual life of savages. *Aaron Swartz' Raw Thought*. Retrieved from http://www.aaronsw.com/weblog/savagesex

Tellis, W. (19997). Introduction to case study [68 paragraphs]. *The Qualitative Report, 3*(2), Retrieved from http://www.nova.edu/ssss/QR/QR3-2/tellis1.html

Thomas, G. (2011). A typology for the case study in social science following a review of definition, discourse, and structure. *Qualitative Inquiry, 17*(6), 511–521.

Timmermans, S., & Tavory, I. (2012). Theory construction in qualitative research: From grounded theory to abductive analysis. *Sociological Theory, 30*(3), 167–186.

Tjitra & Associates. (2012, April 22). *Grounded theory introduction.* Retrieved from http://www.slideshare.net/htjitra/grounded-theory-introduction

Trimbur, L. (2011). "Tough love": Mediation and articulation in the urban boxing gym. *Ethnography, 12(3)*, 334–355. doi:10.1177/1466138110372590

Tucker-McLaughlin, M., & Campbell, K. (2012). A grounded theory analysis: Hillary Clinton represented as innovator and voiceless in TV news. *Electronic News, 6*(1), 3–19.

Tufford, L., & Newman, P. (2012). Bracketing in qualitative research. *Qualitative Social Work, 11*(1), 80–86.

Tummers, L., & Karsten, N. (2012). Reflecting on the role of literature in qualitative public administration research: Learning from grounded theory. *Administration & Society, 44*(1), 64–86.

University of California, Berkeley. (2011). *Visual narrative & research methods sp 2012.* Retrieved from http://blogs.ischool.berkeley.edu/i290-viznarr-s12/

Urquhart, C. (2012, March 20). *Using grounded theory in ICT4D research: A missed opportunity?* [YouTube video]. Retrieved from http://www.youtube.com/watch?v=pIFA75IhRGc

van Manen, M. (1997). *Researching lived experiences: Human science for action-sensitive pedagogy*. Ontario, Canada: Althouse Press.

van Manen, M. (2011). *Phenomenology online*. Retrieved from http://www.phenomenologyonline.com

Van Praet, E. (2009). Staging a team performance. A linguistic ethnographic analysis of weekly meetings at a British embassy. *Journal of Business Communication, 46*(1), 80–99.

Vandenberg, D. (1996). *Phenomenology and educational discourse*. Durban: Heinemann Higher and Further Education.

Vlachopoulos, P., & Cowan, J. (2010). Choices of approaches in e-moderation: Conclusions from a grounded theory study. *Active Learning in Higher Education, 11*(3), 213–224.

Virtualethno09. (2009, August 1). *Internet participant observation.* Retrieved from http://www.youtube.com/watch?v=7EX4F55E9VE

White, A., & Dotson, W. (2010). It takes a village to raise a researcher: Narrative interviewing as intervention, reconciliation, and growth. *Journal of Black Psychology, 36*(1), 75–97.

Wingate, U., Andon, N., & Cogo, A. (2011). Embedding academic writing instruction into subject teaching: A case study. *Active Learning in Higher Education, 12*(1), 69–81.

Wolcott, H. (1973). *The man in the principal's office: An ethnography*. New York: Holt, Rinehart & Winston.

Yin, R. (2012). *Applications of case study research* (3rd ed.). Thousand Oaks, CA: SAGE.

Zhou, L., & Nunes, M. (2012). Identifying knowledge sharing barriers in the collaboration of traditional and Western medicine professionals in Chinese hospitals: A case study. *Journal of Librarianship and Information Science, 44*(4), 238–248.

STUDENT STUDY SITE

Visit **http://www.sagepub.com/lichtmanqrss** to access additional study tools, including eFlashcards and links to SAGE journal articles.

CHAPTER 6

A Review of Additional Research Approaches

Focus Your Reading

- Research approaches are incredibly diverse.
- Action research—a way to address a real problem in an organization or system with a move toward change
- Arts-based research—loosely grouped approaches that use the artistic process and blur lines between science and art
- Autoethnography—exploration of the personal experience of life
- Mixed methods—pragmatic ways of combining information gained in two ways (qualitative and quantitative)
- Selecting a research approach

In the previous chapter, I presented five research approaches. You will recall that ethnographic research designs are useful when you are interested in studying culture. You can use grounded theory when you want to generate an explanatory theory from the data. Phenomenology is suitable when you are interested in studying the essence of lived experiences. Case study approaches address particular programs or practices. And narrative approaches can be used when your questions involve the life stories of individuals.

Choosing a research approach or method is not done by selecting the method or approach you prefer. Rather, it is driven by the topic of interest and the questions you ask. As a student, you should become familiar with a variety of research approaches useful in answering diverse questions. The approaches discussed in this chapter supplement the ones I just described in Chapter 5.

I want to return to the idea that it is important to think about questions and then try to identify an approach suitable for answering that question. Here are some questions that you might ask; let's try to determine which research approach to use: You take a job in a school different from the one where you have worked for more than 10 years. You notice that things seem different in this new school. The facilities are cleaner, there is more order in the public spaces, and teachers express fewer complaints in the lounge. You want to do some research in this new situation. But you are not quite sure how you should go about it. One question you might ask is how teachers feel about working in this school. What have their experiences been? Since you want to study their lived experience, you can use phenomenology to answer this question. Or you wonder if two groups of students you identify—the jocks and the nerds—operate in different ways. What research approach could you use? Ethnography. Look for overt cultural signs (e.g., clothes, hairstyles) or more subtle symbols of behavior. If you wanted to understand this particular school and the details of how it developed, you might want to conduct a case study. These are all approaches I discussed earlier.

Perhaps you have a different kind of question. You notice in your organization that workers appear lackadaisical and are only interested in surfing on the Internet or texting their friends. Even at a time when jobs are difficult to come by, you wonder why they have this attitude and what you can do to change it. One of the research approaches I discuss in this chapter is called *action research* or *participatory action research* (PAR). Perhaps that would work for this problem.

Other questions might also come to mind. What about the self and life experiences? Many researchers are interested in their personal experiences and want to relate those to a variety of issues. Often investigated is how stories of one's ancestors help us understand our own identity. Rath's (2012) account is just such an example. In this chapter, you will read about a research approach called *autoethnography*. That might work for these questions.

■ Interrelatedness of Research Approaches, Research Topics, and Participants

A qualitative research (QR) study has several interrelated components—the individuals studied, the topics under investigation, and the research approach. Figure 6.1 depicts this graphically.

Although I just stated that it is critical to identify your research topic or question first, I find that in reality, some researchers do not really follow this pathway. You might think that the research process follows a logical progression, but that is not always the case. I am reminded of the comment that artist Richard Diebenkorn made when asked about how he develops his paintings. To paraphrase, he stated, I have no plan before I start; I just start working and do it until it looks right. Sometimes I have to do it over again many times. Actually this is very visible in his work, since you can see layer upon layer built up as he worked to get it right.

Figure 6.1 Interrelated Factors in a Qualitative Research Study

You could actually begin research through any of the pathways seen in Figure 6.1. You might think that it is important to identify whom you want to study. I don't mean the actual individuals being studied but the type of person being studied. It might be entry-level workers, seniors planning for retirement, children in math classes, displaced workers, or another category or group of people. As Figure 6.1 illustrates, you could also begin with the research approach, although I don't recommend this for a new researcher. In this chapter and the one preceding, I have given you essential elements and examples of various research approaches.

As I said initially, I think it probably best if you begin with a general topic and develop a research question from that topic. I presented some recent topics in Chapter 2. I located some additional ones in journals that specifically publish QR studies: *Qualitative Inquiry, Qualitative Research, The Qualitative Report, Forum: Qualitative Sociology* (*FQS*) and *Sociological Research Online.* For each topic I present, I include the citation, the method/approach used, and the group that was studied:

- using arts-informed practice to understand, present, and perform research as an aid to understanding the social world (Douglas, 2012; arts-based; seven women professional golfers)
- a family's struggle for meaning (Russell, 2012; autoethnography and narrative; family members)
- knowing the "other" gives voice to people who were previously ignored (Krumer-Nevo & Sidi, 2012; narrative and reflexive; people in marginalized groups)
- exploration of a university queer center (Teman & Lahman, 2012; ethnography; participants at queer center)
- a study of severely disabled youth at a summer camp (Berger & Feucht, 2012; generic and ethnographic; disabled youth and disabled director)
- shadowing a chaplain (Gilliat-Ray, 2011; a [disruptive] technique related to ethnography; one individual)
- power and gender, with females interviewing males on the topic of sexually degrading practices (Gailey & Prohaska, 2011; feminist; males engaging in practices)
- resistance to power: Internet satire and how it contributes to the power relation (Tang & Bhattacharya, 2011; generic; Chinese Internet sites)
- emergence of hospital protocols for perinatal bereavement (Davidson, 2011; feminist, autoethnography, and narrative; hospital-based bereavement protocols)
- social inclusion and exclusion in Sweden (Sellerberg & Leppänen, 2012; generic; bankrupt entrepreneurs)
- experience of labor migration (Thieme, 2012; arts-based film; workers in Kyrgyzstan)

In this chapter, I will introduce you to some alternative approaches that have recently become popular. I want to remind you again that there is not a hierarchy of "preferable" or "better" research approaches. In fact, different social science disciplines may have a preference for one or another approach.

Did You Know

We all need a little humor in our lives. Psychology students and others at the University of Sydney meet regularly and blog sporadically. Recently, they recommended that an Unconference be planned—no pompous plenaries or panels, no prepared talks, and no horrible meals. Some truth in this, I assume! Check out the blog at http://qual-rip.blogspot.com/

As I said previously, a research approach should assist you in planning your research, defining a set of steps you can follow in conducting your research, and grounding your work in a conceptual or philosophical base. Below, I include several research approaches you might find interesting.

Action Research/Participatory Action Research—Solving a Particular Problem

Action research involves identifying a real-world problem in a particular setting, with the researcher and members of the organization or group being studied jointly working together to solve the problem. PAR involves all relevant parties working jointly. It is conducted with the people in a particular community or setting. It involves a reflexive process of problem solving. Emphasis is also on the collaborative and emancipatory nature of the process. Design-based research is a contemporary offshoot.

History and Meaning

There have been several antecedents to action research. Many of those who influenced the field came from a wide range of disciplines. It was Kurt Lewin, a social psychologist and activist at MIT, who first used the term *action research* in 1944. Paulo Freire (1976/2006), a Brazilian educator, strongly influenced the field of education with his Marxist action research about the oppressed. It posed a new relationship between teacher, student, and society. In the field of business, we are indebted to Chris Argyris from the Harvard Business School, who introduced the concept of learning organizations. From a sociological perspective, Abraham and Purkayastha (2012) traced links between research and action, with particular emphasis on action research, participatory research, and feminist research. Their article is an introduction to the special issue of the journal *Current Sociology* (March, 2012) on the topic of action research. Whatever the discipline, these researchers were and are concerned with generating knowledge to solve practical problems—the definition of action research.

A collaboration between researcher and organization has led to a variety of images, some of which you can find by Googling "participatory action research." Some serious, others amusing, these images emphasize the joint nature of the endeavor. I find that the visual presentation says so much.

Unlike other research approaches, action research is designed to address a particular problem and look for a solution to that problem. The emphasis of the research shifts away from gathering data to develop a theory or to describe a particular phenomenon and moves toward seeking to improve a particular condition or group.

In the first decade of this century, design-based research has emerged. Related to action research, design-based research has as its purpose an increase in the impact, transfer, and translation of research into improved practice (Anderson & Shattuck, 2012; Reimann, 2010). In design-based research, interventions are conceptualized and implemented in real-world settings.

Distinguishing Features

- involves participation of all key actors
- relies on collaboration
- identifies a problem and searches for a solution

Special Issues

Getting the Buy-In

Saying it doesn't just make it so. Opening up communication is a topic that is addressed by some (Wicks & Reason, 2009). It is not always so easy to get participants to become involved in designing research for change. Snoeren, Niessen, and Abma (2012) illustrate issues related to getting the primary researcher to become involved. They are concerned with the darker side of involvement and closeness, as researchers become trapped in their own beliefs and prejudices.

Maintaining Academic Integrity

Levin (2012) described the dilemma of potentially conflicting claims for rigor and relevance. He concluded that one way to maintain academic integrity is to support "high rigor in scientific texts for communicating research findings" (p. 133).

Changes over Time

In their thoughtful review of a 23-year project, Sorensen and Lawson (2012) made several observations. The critical role of the key organizer cannot easily be replicated. Technical assistance is dependent on who within a university can provide the actual service. In my own experience, I am aware of the difficulties in getting a university or other institution to commit time and resources as you seek to change an organization within a community.

Examples From the Field

You can locate many examples of this type of research. *Action Research* publishes many such studies. Although the goal of action research is to change an organization, many of the studies I reviewed focused on changing the participants involved in the study. You can see this in the following examples. I found Gordon and Edwards's (2012) description of the use of a virtual participatory project interesting. Students, alumni, and faculty participated in a distance-learning environment. Students gained research experience by participating with faculty and graduates in an action research project. Project was called a success if research skills were increased; this is somewhat different from changing an organization. Rai's (2012) study of improving police effectiveness involved researching how training contributes to creative thinking. The focus in this study was on training rather than changing the organization. James (2008) illustrated complex adaptive issues in a YouTube description. Wöhrer and Höcher (2012) described processes of negotiations between researchers, students, and the teacher in a secondary modern school in Vienna. One observation was that the mixing of roles, tasks, and expectations produced disappointment on the part of students. The March 2012 issue of *Current Sociology* is devoted to linking research and action in practice. *FQS* also has a volume (volume 13, 2012) devoted to participatory QR.

■ Arts-Based Approaches

Arts-based research is an emerging set of extremely diverse methods. One goal is to blur the lines between science and art. Using the artistic process as the primary means of inquiry, this approach emphasizes representation through artistic means.

History and Meaning

I recall reading Elliot Eisner's (1991) treatise connecting research and art more than twenty years ago and also hearing him speak at my daughter's graduation from art school. What he said seemed to resonate with me. He and Sarah Lightfoot are credited by Harvard's School of Education with combining QR with aesthetic concerns and techniques of narrative fiction. They suggest two common forms—poetry-based research, in which data are used for original poetry, and ethnodrama, which combines ethnography with theatrical writing and performance.

Finley (2011) suggested that critical arts-based inquiry

> situates the artists-as-researcher in the new research paradigm of qualitative practitioners committed to democratic, ethical, and just research methodologies . . . a genre of research in which methodologies are emergent and egalitarian, local, and based in communal, reflective dialogue. (p. 435)

This description actually sounds much like the goals of action research that I just discussed.

Recognizing the challenge of combining art and science, the April 2003 issue of *Qualitative Inquiry* considered some of the challenges. It included more than a dozen articles, including a performance ethnography and a poem. Almost a decade later, as I write this book, I observe increasing numbers of poems, ethnodramas, and other artistic expressions. There has certainly been acceptance of some of arts-based inquiry. Seeley (2011) imagined a relationship between the arts and action research, for example.

According to Leavy (2012), artful forms of research have exploded in the last two decades. Further, she suggested that these arts-based types of research are "well accepted in the qualitative research community" (p. 516). (See also Leavy, 2009.) Thieme (2012) commented that since the 1980s, there has been a shift toward the study of visual objects and digital technology. Her literature review provided a number of examples. Barone and Eisner (2012) address major issues surrounding arts-based research, including such areas as whether it is really research and how it can be both political and ethical.

Not all researchers agree, however. Some think that this type of research is not yet widely accepted; they still consider arts-based to be in its developmental stages. "In many ways still in its formative stages, writers in the field of Arts-Based Research have been working to document its diversity and to engage in important questions around methodology and epistemology" (Harvard Graduate School of Education, 2008). What is clear, whichever viewpoint you take, is that there is an increase in the use of visual presentations and representations.

Much of what is written about the field speaks of using arts-based research as an alternative approach to various aspects of the research process. In fact, most of what is available consists of presentations/papers/performances that take on one form or another of artistic expression—whether through film, poetry, creative fiction, or ethnodrama.

Distinguishing Features

- some form of artistic expression used in presentation
- artistic expression also might be used in collection of data
- a search for the artistic nature
- weaving the words of those studied into an artistic presentation
- way to explore dynamic interactions between "power, politics, and poetics" (Madison, 2008, p. 392)

Special Issues

Attaining Legitimacy in a Scientifically Oriented World

It is the special problem of the qualitative researcher who is disposed toward arts-based research modes to justify their use as a legitimate way of conducting research. One thing that we have seen within the last five years or so is an increase in alternative forms of presentation. Perhaps the larger research community will come to embrace something so different from what they have used before. Increasingly, *Qualitative Inquiry* is publishing poetry and dramaturgy.

Seeking Alternative Presentation Forms

We live in the world of words. As researchers and students, we are used to using words to convey meaning. I believe we will see increased use of visual forms that exist without words—painting, drawing, sculpture, multimedia—as a way to present information.

Examples From the Field

Slade (2012) studied immigrants in an adult education employment program. In this study, she combined two qualitative approaches. She combined institutional ethnography and Reader's Theatre in her study of power. Reader's Theatre is an arts-informed research approach that strives to render research into provocative and evocative forms (Knowles & Cole, 2008). Her presentation was in play form. Lapum, Ruttonsha, Church, Yau, and David (2012) studied, interpreted, and exhibited narratives of patients who had experienced open heart surgery. They described their project as an arts-informed narrative study that resulted in an installation of poetry and photography. Writing about it does not do it justice; you need to review the article. Leavy (2012) described the use of fiction in feminist research practice. You might wonder, why fiction? Leavy reflected that fiction provides a different lens into understanding the social experience; it promotes reflection and negotiation and makes social research more accessible to various audiences. I discuss this issue in greater detail in Chapter 14.

Saldaña's (2011) *Ethnotheatre* won the outstanding book award from the SIG Qualitative Research Group of American Educational Research Association. In this work, he outlines the key principles of the approach and includes ethnotheater in the book itself. Jones (2011) produced *Rufus Stone,* a film about love, sexual awakening, and treachery. Both of these works use alternative modes of presenting stories.

Muir and Mason (2012) discussed the use of participant-produced digital footage of family Christmases. The presentation included links to the video clips. Their emphasis was on the study of tradition in families.

■ Autoethnography—Exploring the Experiences of Life

Autoethnography is a QR approach that combines elements of ethnography and elements of the personal narrative. This combination is meant to connect the personal with the cultural by placing an understanding of the self within a social context. Sparkes (2000) said that autoethnographies are highly personalized accounts that draw on the experience of the researcher for sociological understanding. What separates it from a merely personal account is its connection to the cultural.

History and Meaning

For about twenty years, the use of autoethnographies has grown dramatically. Although autoethnography has been around for several decades, it was the work of Carolyn Ellis that brought the practice into the mainstream. During the 1970s and early 1980s, Ellis conducted a typical ethnographic study of two fishing villages. One description of this work is that she found a disconnect between the way she was taught to do ethnography—maintain distance, stay out of the story—and what she was feeling. In 2004, she wrote her story, which essentially explains how the method of autoethnography gained scientific grounding and popularity. While the details of how she began doing ethnography differ, Ellis et al. (2008) explained that she was hurt by some of the ways the information from her study was handled. And she continued,

> This experience did not lead me [Ellis] to do autoethnography—which some think—because I was already doing autoethnography when all this happened. But it did lead me to start thinking about the ethics of research in a whole different way. (p. 272)

Together with Arthur Bochner, they have written extensively and personally in the field, and much of autoethnography's adoption has been due to their efforts. Taber (2010) reminded us that autoethnography is a newly developing field. She provided an excellent review of the field: "My use of autoethnography is my way to 'look up' (and look in) to see what was hidden when I was engaged in the work of being a woman and a mother in the military" (p. 15). The *Journal of Contemporary Ethnography* offers a special issue (August, 2006) on the topic.

One way to learn about autoethnography is to listen to a podcast interview on the "Critical Lede" with Ron Pelias (2011). The "Critical Lede" is described as a resource for keeping plugged in to the qualitative communication research community, and Pelias discussed how these methods can extend to the social sciences as well as to the general state of the research on the topics. Chang, Ngunjiri, and Hernandez (2012) offer a practical guide in conducting a collaborative autoethnography.

Distinguishing Features

- embraces researcher's personal and critical story rather than limiting it
- researcher is the main subject of the study
- response to more traditional, impersonal, and alienating research that claims to seek the truth
- heavy dependence on reflexivity
- evocative autoethnography relates to postmodern views, distinguishing itself from more traditional and analytic ethnography

Special Issues

Little Has Been Written About How to Conduct an Autoethnography

Although there is quite a bit written about autoethnography as a method, it is surprising that little is written about how to do it. Chang's (2008) book offers some suggestions, such as using diaries and awareness of the self. Thus, you have a challenge if you decide to use this research approach. Reading autoethnographies of others will also prove helpful.

Reflexivity Plays an Important Role

Taber (2010) discussed the concept of *a reflexivity of discomfort*. By this, she meant a push toward the unfamiliar and the uncomfortable. These ideas about reflexivity are different from the traditional clarity, honesty, or humility.

Personal Story or Something More

For a beginning researcher, I think it is important to distinguish between telling a personal story or narrative and constructing a story that is connected to the culture. There are no clear guidelines as to how you should do this. You can use your imagination. Also, make sure that you look at alternative means of presentation. I refer you to several examples of videos, poetry, and drama.

Hughes, Pennington, and Makris (2012) attempt to move autoethnography from a purely personal account to a more empirical endeavor. They argue in favor of the approach based on its epistemological and methodological history, using standards for reporting empirical social science research.

Of the various research approaches, this one is very personal. How can you be remote or objective? You would not want to. In many of their writings, Ellis (1995) and Richardson (2002) tell their stories poignantly. You will need considerable skill in determining what information is important, what story to tell, how to connect it to the culture, and how to present it.

Examples From the Field

Harrison (2012) presented an autoethnographic account of his experiences as a teacher of individuals and groups of graduate music students. His work led him to reconceptualize how such education is delivered. Sobre-Denton (2012) intertwined her experience of being bullied with the larger issues of workplace bullying and discrimination. Jewkes (2012) questioned why qualitative researchers need to avoid disclosing emotions to improve acceptance by those who are interested in validity. She argued that it is important to reveal emotions, especially in the area of prison research. It is exciting to see that researchers keep pushing the envelope. Alexander, Moreira, and Kumar (2012) presented a triple autoethnographic text exploring their relationships with their fathers. Their stories press against each other and are an example of both public and private scrutiny.

Cann and DeMeulenaere (2012) constructed a variation on a typical autoethnography. They developed a critical co-constructed autoethnography. From the perspective of a critical theorist, this approach provides a way for activist researchers to reflect on the "tempo, uncertainty, and complexity of research relationships" (p. 146).

Doloriert and Sambrook's (2011) research was based on how a traditional business school accommodates an autoethnographic thesis. Learmonth and Humphreys (2012) also wrote from a business school viewpoint. Their article discussed how contemporary academic identity can help with understanding identity in organizations. Tolich (2010) shared foundational guidelines for autoethnographers. Some of the issues he addressed relate to informed consent by those mentioned in an autoethnography. Even though the work references the self—the author—other individuals are often mentioned directly or by inference. He also addressed ethical rights of strangers (including taking photographs of them), internal confidentiality, and rights of others written into the stories. If you are interested in this field, I suggest you read this article carefully.

For a video autoethnography, treat yourself to a view of learning to play the *guqin*, a seven-string Chinese zither (MusicEduResearch, 2012). It is filmed upside down to illustrate the perspective of the individual learning to play. It has a very unusual tone.

Burns (2012) and I are intrigued by how he began his study on the topic of the autoethnographic approach. What would you expect a student in library and information science do to learn about this topic? He did a Scopus search and retrieved more than 500 documents beginning in 1993 to 2012. He further produced various charts based on the information. Listen to his words:

> Caveat: Aside from it being kind of funny that I'm using basic quantitative bibliometric methods to look at this highly qualitative style of research, this is only a cursory exploration—a way for me to see the whole picture before I dive into the details. To keep this from being a 20 page post, I'm not going to be doing much textual interpretation here. I'll leave that to the reader.

Feminist Research

The purpose of feminist research is to use a feminist perspective in conducting research. Although not exactly a research approach or tradition, feminist theory is a movement that arose in the 1980s. In part, it was a reaction to the disparate power, politics, and equality between those conducting the research (typically White men) and those who were being studied (often women, minorities, or those with disabilities). Feminist theory is also related to postmodernism, postcolonialism, and post-Freudian psychoanalysis. This movement and more contemporary feminist approaches have a stronghold in Canada and Australia as well as in the United States. Geiger (1986) argued that feminism depends on women's point of view, and the meaning of their life experiences and histories provides important insights.

History and Meaning

Feminist research emerged as a reaction to approaches described earlier. As the field of research began to be open to female scholars, there were numerous questions about the appropriateness and adequacy of prevailing approaches. In particular, questions of power disparities were on the minds of many women. This field actually has many principles in common with critical theory, queer theory (which treats sexual and gender identity as social constructs), and postmodernism. But like many of the other approaches I have discussed, there is no general agreement on what is meant by *feminist research*.

Harding (1998) is one of the key figures in this movement. She combined elements of feminist, postmodern, and postcolonial critiques of modern science. You can read an account of an interview with Harding that reflects her thinking (http://www.escholarship.org/uc/item/0cp9z2fk#page-1). Brayton (1997) suggested that what makes feminist research unique are "the motives, concerns, and knowledge" brought to the research process (para. 1). Brayton suggested that it differs from traditional research for three reasons: It removes the imbalance of power (Fine, 1992); it is politically motivated and concerned with social inequality; and it addresses experiences of women. Maguire (1987) defined feminism as

> (a) a belief that women universally face some form of oppression or exploitation; (b) a commitment to uncover and understand what causes and sustains oppression, in all its forms; and (c) a commitment to work individually and collectively in everyday life to end all forms of oppression. (p. 79)

Fine (1992) identified other aspects of feminist research as well. I see many of these as being common to all QR. I wonder whether these principles were identified first by qualitative researchers and then feminist researchers or whether the reverse is true. In any event, Fine identified the unequal power issue and the need to eliminate it. She talked about making research participants true participants by calling them *coresearchers*. Others speak to eliminating the word *subject,* because it is a masculine term. Related to letting participants share in the research is the view that they are experts about their own experiences. Fine also spoke about the researcher taking an active role rather than being a detached and objective observer. Related, then, is the need to address the actual and apparent inequalities between those being studied and those who are doing the study. Research as consciousness raising and transforming is another element. I recall hearing a researcher at a conference speak about sharing the proceeds of her book with the participants. Social change is also important to feminist research. Rosenberg (1999) described how a feminist research circle promotes changing power relationships and contributes to social change. Scheurich (1997) said there are four parts to feminist research. Feminist research aims to create social change; it strives to represent human diversity; it is a perspective, not a research method; and it frequently includes the researcher as a person. Landman (2006) identified several features of feminist research: derived from experience rather than theory; revised continuously based on experience; and reflexive. Gergen (2008) addressed the relationship between qualitative methods and feminist psychology in her detailed chapter in the *SAGE Handbook of Qualitative Research in Psychology.*

Distinguishing Features

- a movement and theory
- stress on issue of power
- political and social agenda

Special Issues

Definition of a Feminist Study

The feminist movement led to feminist theory, which is primarily aimed at inequality in treatment of women. Brayton (1997) wrote about feminist research in the social sciences. She posited that researchers brought motives, concern, and knowledge to the research process. She suggested what she called "distinguishing features" of such research. As with Reinharz (1992) and others, it is feminist theory that is the guiding principle for Brayton. I find it interesting that in 2013, many of these principles (power disparities, role of the researcher, political and social agenda) are those many qualitative researchers adopt, not just those who call themselves feminists. Brayton's (1997) comprehensive bibliography should lead you to many of the writings prior to the year 2000. In 2006, Watts asserted that feminist research practice "is firmly established within the academy" (p. 385). Watts raised an interesting question about how to study women who do not identify with aims of feminism.

No Universal Definition of Feminist Research

By 2010, a number of concerns surfaced. Gringeri, Wahab, and Anderson-Nathe (2010) suggested that research is feminist if it is grounded in feminist theories. In addition, the topics centered on women were concerned with social justice and liberation, focused on gender and gender-related issues, or critically explored or engaged issues of power and praxis (p. 391). However, they also acknowledged that there is not a universal definition or set of rules that make a study feminist. In fact, there seems to be disagreement about some of the key ideas—for example, what the theoretical stance is, how different voices are treated, and the role of policy. Another idea is that feminist research methods might be something to fear. In 2010, Wekker and colleagues offered a course on feminist QR methods entitled "Who Is Afraid of the F-Word?"

Researchers do not always use the same research approach. Allen (2011), in her study of how women respond to partner violence, used a constructivist grounded-theory methodology. She argued that this methodology reflected feminist approaches to research because, she stated, there is no specific feminist research methodology.

Poststructural and Postfeminist Viewpoints

Poststructuralists take the position that in trying to find meaning, they do not approximate the truth or construct the truth. Rather, they take an alternative view. In fact, it might seem a little inconsistent. Rather than looking for similarities, they look for differences. And, rather than looking for the universal, they seek the local.

According to Gill (2007), **postfeminism** is "one of the most important and contested terms in the lexicon of feminist cultural analysis" (p. 147). Of course, like so many other terms I have discussed, there is no agreement as to its meaning. Some see it as a backlash against feminism. Gill described it as a sensibility. While her research is about media culture, you can see that she draws your attention to the preoccupation in the media with the body.

Let me be clear. Feminism and feminists (including men) have made great strides in the field of QR. Researchers today have adopted much of the agenda for which these early feminists fought. Yet postfeminism arose, at least in part, as a response to the feminist viewpoint. Postfeminism dominates contemporary media culture. I don't think it yet dominates QR.

As a philosophical and political stance, feminist research addresses issues of power disparities. I think it is a sensibility and viewpoint rather than a research approach. Feminists use a number of popular research approaches but put their own twist on things. Self-reflection is critical as you go about conducting such a study.

I have heard some ask if you can take a feminist position if you are not female. The answer is yes. But I suspect you are more open to criticism, and it is more difficult. But you men out there, if you are interested, by all means consider thinking and doing research as a feminist.

Examples From the Field

The Druze community is particularly isolated and a minority in Israel. Many of the women wear their faces completely covered when traveling outside the home. I had the opportunity to have lunch at the home of two Druze women on a trip to Israel a few years ago. I was struck by how open they were. The hostess, a married woman of about 50, had learned Hebrew and was about to embark on a study of English.

I was surprised when I came across Weiner-Levy's (2009) study of Druze women. Her focus was on power, alienation, and affinity. She addressed many issues: belonging or not belonging (insider/outsider), the positionality of the researcher (issues of power), shifting social positions, and feelings of alienation. When asked whether the women would like to gather together to hear about the findings, one woman interviewed made the following comments:

> It is as if someone got undressed in front of a dressmaker to have a dress made and she knew she was getting undressed only for this purpose, and suddenly you come and show us forty naked women. (p. 736)

Here are some additional studies you might find interesting. Knowles (2009) used psychogeography (a way to understand how human behavior is shaped by the geographical environment) and its compatibility with feminist research methods. Her audience was the business researcher. Jackson and Weatherall (2010) used a feminist perspective to address feminist sexuality education in New Zealand: "Probing sex education in schools unsettles a turbulent mix of politics and morality" (p. 166). No doubt, you can imagine the challenges they faced in conducting this research. Their perspective is from a feminist viewpoint; however, the method involves observation and recording of sex education classes and follow-up focus groups with those willing to participate. Dealing with a much safer topic, Anderson (2011) reported from a feminist perspective on using portraiture as a research methodology. By *portraiture*, she refers to portraits of educational studies that have helped to develop teaching-led research (p. 114). Lawrence-Lightfoot's (2005) reflections on portraiture are also of note.

Deutsch (2004) reflected on the process of becoming a feminist researcher and writer. I think you will enjoy reading Vargas's (2008) personal account that deals with race, ethnicity, and the power of interpretation. Lather (2007) explored what it means to do feminist poststructural research in her book *Getting Lost: Feminist Efforts Toward a Double(d) Science.* She examined her original study about women living with HIV/AIDS and the way in which she conducted it. As she said, she stumbled and bumbled along the way, making mistakes and getting lost in the name of science. Childers (2008) commented that the book "puts a mark on what it means to practice at this historical moment in feminist research" (p. 301). I recommend you look at these writings as well as Lather's original book, published in 1997. English and Irving (2008) wrote of feminist poststructural issues related to power as they studied gender and learning. Phillips and her colleagues (2009) wrote about their journey in feminist poststructural theory. Jackson (2001) wrote from a feminist poststructural theory of subjectivity. In her article, she presented the story of a young woman who worked with two cooperating teachers with opposing philosophies.

These examples highlight how feminist research topics address social change and power relationships. Feminist research methods and theories acknowledge disparities in power between those who are studied and those who study. They are also interested in issues about women and women's ways of knowing. Like those who have used some of the other new approaches, they are critical of the presumed objectivity and remoteness that characterizes traditional methodologies. They align themselves closely with critical theory and pos ernism. As discussed earlier, new on the horizon are some postfeminist approaches, suggest that there may be a reexamination of the premises of feminist theory.

Mixed-Methods Research

The purpose of a mixed-methods approach is to intertwine both qualitative and quantitative methods into a single study. This method became popular within the last ten to fifteen years. Many students are drawn to mixed methods because they learn that professors prefer the more structured approach of statistics but acknowledge that data from observations or interviews yield rich information.

History and Meaning

Creswell (2009), in his book *Research Design: Qualitative, Quantitative and Mixed Methods Approaches,* provided some details on how to conduct a mixed-methods study. Later, Creswell (2011) discussed various controversies regarding mixed methods. You can also read the Tashakkori and Teddlie (2003) discussion, their later explanation (Teddlie & Tashakkori, 2011) about contemporary issues on the topic, or the work of Johnson and Christensen (2008). Or you can watch Onwuegbuzie (2009) on a video lecture, providing an overview of mixed-methods research.

Bergman (2011) provided a brief history that is instructive. In the first generation of mixed-methods researchers—before the paradigm wars and incompatibility ideas were on anyone's mind—researchers mixed and combined many different types of data. The second generation of researchers, beginning in the 1990s, provided a vocabulary, taxonomy, and process. He credits these with the current success of the field.

Various social science disciplines have accepted, or at least adopted, some form of mixed-methods research. The June 2012 issue of *American Behavioral Scientist,* edited by Burke Johnson, is a special issue devoted to mixed methods. The eight articles in this issue will inform you of the topics currently under consideration. Pearce (2012) concluded that there are challenges to the use of mixed methods in sociology but that the pragmatic nature of mixed methods suggests merit in using the approach. Molina-Azorin's (2012) study of the use of mixed methods in the field of strategic management concluded that mixed-methods studies are cited more frequently than those using a single method. Whether additional citations make for better research is a matter open to discussion, however. Mertens (2012) wrote about the transformative paradigm of mixed-methods research that promotes social justice.

Distinguishing Features

- pragmatic
- combines both quantitative research (QN) and QR approaches
- No clear agreement on what constitutes a common set of principles or whether a set should be delineated now. See, for example, Mertens (2010) and Greene (2007). Teddlie and Tashakkori (2012) commented that in editing their book *Handbook of Mixed Methods in Social and Behavioral Research,* they noted much diversity of opinion on the topic. They identified four characteristics that have evolved as the field grows:

- *Methodological eclecticism.* In other words, researchers can choose from among the qualitative and quantitative field any mix that works to "investigate the phenomena of interest" (p. 776). In the early days, very basic techniques were used, especially within the qualitative domain.
- *Paradigm pluralism.* "A variety of paradigms may serve as the underlying philosophy for the use of mixed methods" (p. 779). They acknowledge arguments against this but still hold to the pragmatic position.
- *Iterative, cyclical approach.* Here, they talk about combining both inductive and deductive approaches in the same study. They also discuss a cyclical approach to research.
- *Set of research designs and analytical processes.* Here, they deal with various research designs and their various nuances (conversion-mixed, sequential-mixed, etc.). They also acknowledge the considerable disagreement in this arena.

Special Issues

Inconsistencies in Terms of Worldviews

Bergman (2011) asserted that mixed methods "deservedly continues its ascent in the social and related sciences" (p. 271). Yet he argued that many consider the approach "insufficiently rigorous," and he agreed with that statement as well. But he urged caution with regard to conceptualization and theorization on the one hand and design on the other. He stated that researchers are not able to bridge the gap about worldviews. Further, with regard to design, there is often a disconnect and a separateness between the qualitative and quantitative approaches. Harrits (2011) also challenged the notion that mixed-methods research represents a coherent paradigm.

Triangulation

The June 2012 special issue of the *Journal of Mixed Methods Research* is devoted to the topic of triangulation (Mertens & Hesse-Biber, 2012). A measurement technique borrowed originally from surveyors and often used in social science research as a way to validate the research, triangulation has not been systematically addressed in this field. I want you to be aware that there are many divergent views on the topic—ranging from Denzin's (2012) view about the incompatibility of using both quantitative and qualitative paradigms in the same study to Howe's (2012) work about causation.

Examples From the Field

I am intrigued with the research of Christensen and her colleagues (2011). Their study involved investigating mobility patterns of children. Combining ethnographic fieldwork, GPS technology, and interactive questionnaires using a mobile phone, they generated understanding about the daily movements of children. While it seems a little intrusive from my viewpoint, perhaps it was thought less so in a suburb of Copenhagen and rural Denmark. What is interesting to me is the heavy use of ethnographic methods. In my experience, many mixed-methods studies emphasize QN and include QR almost as an afterthought. A study by Liu and colleagues (2012) is typical. They were interested in the quality of care provided to patients boarding in the emergency department. The study is described as *exploratory*. It relied on quantitative data from almost 1,500 patient charts. Ten providers were interviewed. Results were described in statistical terms in much of the paper, with a brief mention (one paragraph) of data from the interviews. None of the issues regarding QR (e.g., reflexivity, subjectivity) were addressed, nor was it clear how the data were analyzed. You can locate numerous studies of this type.

I anticipated that the study by Robnett and Leaper (2013) that explored two marriage traditions (marriage proposals and surname changes) would take a different slant; however, upon reading the study, I found that emphasis was on QN. They described their study as *thematic analysis*, yet they studied almost 300 undergraduates using closed and open-ended questions. Analyses were all from a quantitative perspective. I expected something different, however, since part of the title—"Girls Don't Propose! Ew."—hints at something else.

Postmodernism and Critical Theory Research

Postmodernism is another approach that represents more of a philosophy and intellectual movement than a research method or theory. According to Lemke (2003), postmodernism was derived from poststructuralism and deconstructionism, which were initially criticisms of the structuralist movement of the 1960s. Critical theory was derived from neo-Marxism and feminist theory and was extended to include postcolonial theory and queer theory. Bastalich (2009) provided an excellent explanation and commentary regarding the work of Foucault. This is an excellent example that will help you learn more about the topic. One conclusion that Bastalich reached is that there is increased methodological sensitivity to the political dangers of traditional qualitative approaches in the social sciences. The co-construction of conclusions is one area that she recommended.

Perhaps the most characteristic tenet of postmodern critical work is that everything that European philosophy and science has held to be fundamentally true at an abstract or programmatic level is in fact a contingent, historically specific cultural construction, which has often served the covert function of empowering members of a dominant social caste at the expense of others.

Critical QR, or critical theory, is related to postmodern research. Its purpose is to change the social context. Tripp (1992) argued that socially critical research in education is informed by principles of social justice. *Postmodernist* is the term used to refer to sociopolitical analysts known as the Frankfurt school, including Adorno, Marcuse, and Habermas. Freire (2006) has taken the movement into education in his work with oppressed minorities. Tripp (1993) continued, saying,

> It involves strategic pedagogic action on the part of classroom teachers, aimed at emancipation from overt and covert forms of domination. In practical terms, it is not simply a matter of challenging the existing practices of the system, but of seeking to understand what makes the system be the way it is, and challenging that, whilst remaining conscious that one's own sense of justice and equality are themselves open to question. (p. 114)

According to Tripp, there are a number of methodological principles associated with the theory. They include participation by mutually supportive groups, consciousness that influences the way we teach and conduct research, and meaning that suggests that knowledge is not "subjectively neutral objectively verified facts" (p. 114). Rather, knowledge is made up of socially constructed facts that are artificial and held differently by different groups.

Other key concepts associated with critical theory are sexuality and gender. You can see how closely related these ideas are to feminist theory. (See Figure 6.1.)

It is not often that you read a study that involves research of young people by young people. In their interesting paper, McCartan, Schubotz, and Murphy (2012) explored the power relationship from various perspectives: the adult researcher, the young peer researcher, and those being studied. What makes this study postmodern is involving young people as researchers who are involved in constructing knowledge and interpreting power (para. 46).

■ A Summary of Research Approaches

In this chapter, I offer a discussion about additional research approaches. By now, you must be swimming in details, conflicting ideas, and terms that are vague or used in numerous ways. I hope the table below and the one at the end of Chapter 5 will help you as you learn the differences among the various approaches.

■ Selecting a Research Approach

There are various ways researchers plan and execute a study. Earlier, I discussed a number of ways to go about this. You have seen that there are several ways to proceed. In addition to conceptualizing research in ways I discussed previously, I have observed that there are three popular ways researchers often begin to plan a research study: selecting a research approach, deciding whom or what will be studied, and determining what topics to study. I suggested that you could begin at any of the three points.

While logically it makes sense to begin with a research topic and question, in practice, I find that beginning researchers sometimes begin with a group of individuals or a setting they want to study. Thus they might decide to do research on their school or classroom or an individual. They might be interested in their religious group or in sports teams. They haven't quite formulated a research question, but they know whom they want to study. Remember, QR is a dynamic process that does not necessarily move in a linear fashion.

Others might address the problem of planning research by deciding what topic they want to study: how children form friendships, alienation, or living with the threat of teacher reductions. This is closer to thinking about a research question at the beginning, but the limits of the idea are just beginning to emerge.

Still other researchers might begin with thinking that they want to do a certain kind of study. They are interested in doing an autoethnography. They have read about the approach and want to do a study on their own experience and its relationship to their larger cultural group. Or they may want to study lived experiences of individuals who have experienced a particular traumatic event. Or they may be interested in political issues surrounding movements toward democracy in the Middle East.

Here are some ways you might go about putting these ideas into practice. I am going to pose questions around an example in a variety of ways. The way I pose the question will dictate

Table 6.1 Comparison of Research Approaches

Approach	*Purpose*	*Key elements*	*Process*	*Other issues*
Action Research	To take action about a program or political agenda	Work with organization for social change	Co-construction of data; interviews	Getting buy-in from key players
Arts-Based Research	To acknowledge art and humanities as part of research	Use of aesthetics in conducting or presenting information	Sensitivity to nonscientific side of research	Acceptance by traditional research community
Autoethnography	To examine personal accounts	Reflexivity; stories of self; connection to ethnography	Digging deep into self-awareness; biographical	Connections to larger research community
Feminist Research	To account for power issues	Issues of power discrepancies; women's issues	Use of self; sensitivity to issues affecting women	Acceptance by traditional research community
Mixed Methods	To provide a pragmatic combination of QR and QN	Identifying and using two paradigms	Organizing and combining two types of data	Discrepancy between views of world in terms of knowledge
Postmodernism and Critical Theory	To change social context; to examine issues of power	Political and social agenda; philosophical	Details not specific	More a theory than details of how to conduct study

what research approach I will use. At times, it will be obvious what I should do. In other circumstances, you might find it less clear. Let's explore a particular example.

As a parent or an educator, you are especially interested in the topic of bullying in schools. You are aware of devastating outcomes of students who have been bullied. You have seen images of students being bullied. You have read about students committing suicide as a result of being bullied. Recall that QR asks you to refine your questions into *what* and *why*, rather than *who* and *how many*. So, let's try writing some research questions related to the general topic:

Select a research topic and question: Develop a good question, and decide what is important.
Select a research approach: Connect the approach to the question.
Develop a research study: Decide on the details of the study.
Determine your role as a researcher: Clarify your role, being reflexive and creative.

Select a Research Topic and Question

Question 1. What does it feel like to be bullied? How is an individual's life affected?

Question 2. Why do some individuals participate in bullying?

Question 3. Our school has a program to address bullying. How does it work?

Question 4. Regarding bullying mentality, are there disconnects between those who do the bullying and those who are bullied?

I could write numerous questions related to the general topic. What is important for you to recognize is that the way the question is formulated affects the research approach you choose.

Select a Research Approach

What are the possible approaches I can use? Which makes the most sense? What are the differences among the approaches?

Let's look at Question 1. This sounds as if phenomenology might work, since you are interested in studying the lived experiences of individuals being bullied.

For Question 2, you might choose a generic approach. Or you might decide to pursue a narrative approach.

For Question 3, you might choose to conduct a case study and explore a particular program.

For Question 4, you might choose an ethnographic study and explore the bullying culture.

Develop a Research Study

Whom will you study? For each question, you will need to decide whom, what, and how many you will study. Since QR is inductive and iterative, some of these decisions might change as you progress in the study

What data will you gather? For all the questions, you will probably conduct interviews. You might examine comments on social media sites, such as Facebook. Since so much is in the news about the topic of bullying, you might use news articles in your research.

How will data be gathered? For each question, you will need to develop a plan for where and when you will collect data.

What will you do for your analysis? For each question, you will probably have interview data and perhaps some observational data. You might also have visual images. Deciding what you will do with the data is an important component of an overall plan.

How will you present the study? Will you write about the study or develop a poem or a play? Perhaps you will also want to post something on YouTube or Tumblr.

What about informed consent and Institutional Review Boards? You will need to consider how you obtain permission. Special problems relate to consent with minors and consent from public spaces such as Facebook or YouTube.

How do you decide what works for you and your institution? Each institution has a different set of expectations. You will need to learn about those for your institution.

Determine Your Role as a Researcher

Adopt a self-reflexive posture. I strongly urge an open stance. Your own views for yourself as a researcher are important here.

Interpret the data. Recall that you are the interpreter of the data. It is through your eyes and ears that understandings and interpretations occur.

Examine your personal viewpoint (feminist, social activist, etc.). Do you want to take an active role in this important problem? If so, how can you do this?

Use your creative juices to develop novel ways of gathering data or presenting information. Are you up for the challenge? Can you think of novel ways of combining elements from various research approaches?

CHECK YOURSELF

- Research approaches are incredibly diverse.
- Action research leads to seeking solutions to real-world problems.
- Arts-based research uses alternative forms of presentation.
- Autoethnography focuses on the self.
- Mixed methods combines QR and QN.
- There are many things to consider when beginning a research project—identifying a topic, selecting an approach, developing details of the study, and recognizing your role in the research.
- For each approach, you should be aware of the history, distinguishing features, and special issues

KEY DISCUSSION ISSUES

1. From among the many research approaches, try to select a few that seem most relevant to your own interests. Then, make a list of the distinguishing features of each. Are you able to determine how they differ?
2. Much research of an autoethnographic nature has occurred recently. Can you accept that it is research and not just personal musings? What enables you to do this?
3. Mixed-methods research has been seen by some as a pragmatic compromise. Do you think this is true? What compromises does it make?
4. What else do you need to help you figure out how to select a research approach? Return to at least one approach from this chapter or the previous one, and try to see if you can achieve clarity on its central characteristics.

MODULE 6

Read About Mixed-Methods Research or Arts-Based Methods

Look either at mixed-methods or art-based research. Read at least two articles on the topic. If possible, discuss with a faculty member in your discipline to what extent either of the approaches are supported in the field. Then add your thoughts to your blog and discuss some of the controversy surrounding the approach you selected.

REFERENCES

Abraham, M., & Purkayastha, B. (2012). Making a difference: Linking research and action in practice, pedagogy, and policy for social justice: Introduction. *Current Sociology, 60*(2), 123–141.

Alexander, B., Moreira, C., & Kumar, H. (2012). Resisting (resistance) stories: A tri-autoethnographic exploration of father narratives across shades of difference. *Qualitative Inquiry, 18*(2), 121–133.

Allen, M. (2011). Violence and voice: Using a feminist constructivist grounded theory to explore women's resistance to abuse. *Qualitative Research, 11*(1), 23–45.

Anderson, I. (2011). Toward professional integration in the humanities: One teacher-researcher's experience with portraiture. *Arts and Humanities in Higher Education, 10*(1), 103–119.

Anderson, T., & Shattuck, J. (2012). Design-based research: A decade of progress in education research. *Educational Researcher, 41*(1), 16–25.

Barone, T., & Eisner, E. (2012). *Arts based research.* Thousand Oaks, CA: SAGE.

Bastalich, W. (2009). Reading Foucault: Genealogy and social science research methodology and ethics. *Sociological Research Online, 14*(2). Retrieved from http://www.socresonline.org.uk/14/2/3.html

Berger, R., & Feucht, J. (2012). "Thank you for your words": Observations from a disability summer camp. *Qualitative Inquiry, 18*(1), 76–85.

Bergman, M. (2011). The good, the bad, and the ugly in mixed methods research and design. *Journal of Mixed Methods Research, 5*(4), 271–275.

Brayton, J. (1997). *What makes feminist research feminist? The structure of feminist research within the social sciences.* Retrieved from http://www.unb.ca/PAR-L/win/feminmethod.htm

Burns, C. S. (2012, April 5). Bibliometric exploration of autoethnographic research. *Journal of C. Sean Burns.* Retrieved from http://cseanburns.net/2012/04/05/bibliometric-exploration-of-autoethnographic-research/

Cann, C., & DeMeulenaere, E. (2012). Critical co-constructed autoethnography. *Cultural Studies, Critical Methodology, 12*(2), 146–158.

Chang, H. (2008). *Autoethnography as method.* Walnut Creek, CA: Left Coast Press.

Chang, H., Ngunjiri, F., & Hernandez, K. (2012). *Collaborative autoethnography.* Walnut Creek, CA: Left Coast Press.

Childers, S. (2008). Methodology, praxis, and autoethnography: A review of *Getting Lost. Educational Researcher, 37*(5), 298–301.

Christensen, P., Mikkelsen, M., Nielsen, T., & Harder, H. (2011). Children, mobility, and space: Using GPS and mobile phone technologies in ethnographic research. *Journal of Mixed Methods Research, 5*(3), 227–246.

Creswell, J. (2009). *Research design: Qualitative, quantitative, and mixed methods approaches* (3rd ed.). Thousand Oaks, CA: SAGE.

Creswell, J. (2011). Controversies in mixed methods research. In N. Denzin & Y. Lincoln. (Eds.), *The SAGE handbook of qualitative research* (pp. 269–284). Thousand Oaks, CA: SAGE.

Davidson, D. (2011). Reflections on doing research grounded in my experience of perinatal loss: From auto/biography to autoethnography. *Sociological Research Online, 16*(1). Retrieved from http://www.socresonline.org.uk/16/1/6.html

Denzin, N. (2012). Triangulation 2.0. *Journal of Mixed Methods Research, 6*(2), 80–88.

Deutsch, N. (2004). Positionality and the pen: Reflections on the process of becoming a feminist researcher and writer. *Qualitative Inquiry, 10*(6), 885–902.

Doloriert, C., & Sambrook, S. (2011). Accommodating an auto ethnographic PhD: The tale of the thesis, the viva voce, and the traditional business school. *Journal of Contemporary Ethnography, 40*(5), 583–615.

Douglas, K. (2012). Signals and signs. *Qualitative Inquiry, 18*(6), 525–532.

Eisner, E. (1991). *The enlightened eye: Qualitative inquiry and the enhancement of educational practice.* Upper Saddle River, NJ: Prentice-Hall.

Ellis, C. (1995). *Final negotiations: A story of love and chronic illness.* Philadelphia, PA: Temple University Press.

Ellis, C., Bochner, A., Denzin, N., Lincoln, Y., Morse, J., Pelias, R., & Richardson, L. (2008). Talking and thinking about qualitative research. *Qualitative Inquiry, 14*(2), 254–284.

English, I., & Irving, C. (2008). Reflexive texts: Issues of knowledge, power, and discourse in researching gender and learning *Adult Education Quarterly, 58*(4), 267–283.

Fine, M. (1992). *Disruptive voices: The possibilities of feminist research.* Ann Arbor, MI: University of Michigan.

Finley, S. (2011). Critical arts-based inquiry: The pedagogy and performance of a radical ethical aesthetic. In N. Denzin & Y. Lincoln (Eds.), *The SAGE handbook of qualitative research* (pp. 435–451). Thousand Oaks, CA: SAGE.

Freire, P. (2006). *Pedagogy of the oppressed, 30th anniversary ed.* New York, NY: Continuum.

Gailey, J., & Prohaska, A. (2011). Power and gender negotiations during interviews with men about sex and sexually degrading practices. *Qualitative Research, 11*(4), 365–380.

Geiger, S. (1986). Women's life histories: Method and content. *Journal of Women in Culture and Society, 11*, 334–351.

Gergen, M. (2008). Qualitative methods in feminist psychology. In C. Willig & W. Stainton-Rogers (Eds.), *The SAGE handbook of qualitative research.* Thousand Oaks, CA: SAGE.

Gill, R. (2007). Post-feminist media culture: Elements of a sensibility. *European Journal of Cultural Studies, 10*(2), 147–166.

Gilliat-Ray, S. (2011). "Being there" the experience of shadowing a British Muslim chaplain. *Qualitative Research, 11*(5), 469–486.

Gordon, S., & Edwards, J. (2012). Enhancing student research through a virtual participatory action research project: Student benefits and administrative challenges. *Action Research, 10*(2), 205–220.

Greene, J. C. (2007). *Mixing methods in social inquiry.* San Francisco, CA: Jossey-Bass.

Gringeri, C., Wahab, G., & Anderson-Nathe, B. (2010). What makes it feminist? Mapping the landscape of feminist social work research. *Affilia, 25*(4), 390–405.

Harding, S. (1998). *Is science multicultural? Postcolonialisms, feminisms, and epistemologies.* Bloomington, IN: Indiana University Press.

Harrison, S. (2012). "Letting go": An auto-ethnography of higher degree supervision in music. *International Journal of Music Education, 30*(2), 99–110.

Harrits, G. (2011). More than method? A discussion of paradigm differences within mixed methods research. *Journal of Mixed Methods Research, 5*(2), 150–166.

Harvard Graduate School of Education. (2008). *Arts-Based research.* Retrieved from http://isites.harvard.edu/icb/icb.do?keyword=qualitative&pageid=icb.page340895

Howe, K. (2012). Mixed methods, triangulation, and causal explanation. *Journal of Mixed Methods Research, 6*(2), 89–96.

Hughes, S., Pennington, J., & Makris, S. (2012). Translating autoethnography across the AERA standards: Toward understanding autoethnographic scholarship as empirical research. *Educational Researcher, 41*(6), 209–219.

Jackson, A. (2001). Multiple Annies: Feminist poststructural theory and the making of a teacher. *Journal of Teacher Education, 52*(5), 386–397.

Jackson, S., & Weatherall, A. (2010). The (im)possibilities of feminist school based sexuality education. *Feminism & Psychology, 20*(2), 166–185.

James, E. (2008). *Complex adaptive issues: The use of PAR to solve them.* Retrieved from http://www.youtube.com/watch?v=s-SAJPF5xiA

Jewkes, Y. (2012). Autoethnography and emotion as intellectual resources: Doing prison research differently. *Qualitative Inquiry, 18*(1), 63–75.

Johnson, R., & Christensen, I. (2008). *Educational research. Quantitative, qualitative, and mixed approaches* (3rd ed.). Los Angeles, CA: SAGE.

Jones, K. (Producer). (2011). *Rufus Stone the Movie.* [DVD]. United States: Parkville Pictures. Retrieved from http://microsites.bournemouth.ac.uk/rufus-stone/

Kaufmann, J. (2011). Heteronarrative analysis: Examining online photographic narratives. *International Journal of Qualitative Studies in Education, 24*(1), 7–26.

Knowles, D. (2009). Claiming the streets: Feminist implications of psychogeography as a business research method. Retrieved from www.ejbrm.com/issue/download.html?idArticle=201

Knowles, J. G., & Cole, A. L. (Eds.). (2008). *Handbook of the arts in qualitative research: Perspectives, methodologies, examples, and issues.* Thousand Oaks, CA: SAGE.

Krumer-Nevo, M., & Sidi, M. (2012). Writing against othering. *Qualitative Inquiry, 18*(4), 299–309.

Landman, M. (2006). Getting quality in qualitative research: A short introduction to feminist methodology and methods. *Proceedings of the Nutrition Society, 65*, 429–433.

Lapum, J., Ruttonsha, P., Church, K., Yau, T., & David, A. (2012). Employing the arts in research as an analytical tool and dissemination method: Interpreting experience through the aesthetic. *Qualitative Inquiry, 18*(1), 100–115.

Lather, P. (2007). *Getting lost: Feminist efforts toward a double(d) science.* Albany, NY: SUNY Press.

Lawrence-Lightfoot, S. (2005). Reflections on portraiture: A dialogue between art and science. *Qualitative Inquiry, 11*(1), 3–15.

Learmonth, M., & Humphreys, M. (2012). Autoethnography and academic identity: Glimpsing business school doppelgangers. *Organization, 19*(1), 99–117.

Leavy, P. (2009). *Method meets art: Arts-based research practice.* New York, NY: Guilford Press.

Leavy, P. (2012). Fiction and the feminist academic novel. *Qualitative Inquiry, 18*(6), 516–522.

Lemke, J. (1994). Semiotics and the deconstruction of conceptual learning. *Journal of Accelerative Learning and Teaching, 19*(1), 67–110.

Lemke, J. (2003). Analysing verbal data: Principles, methods and problems. In K. Tobin & B. Fraser (Eds.), *International Handbook of Science Education.* (pp. 1175–1189). Dordrecht, The Netherlands: Kluwer. Retrieved from http://academic.brooklyn.cuny.edu/educationa/jlemke/papers/handbook.htm

Levin, M. (2012). Academic integrity in action research. *Action Research, 10*(2), 133–149.

Liu, S., Chang, Y., Camargo, C., Weissman, J., Walsh, K., Schuur, J., . . . Singer, S. (2012). *A mixed-methods study of the quality of care provided to patients boarding in the emergency department: Comparing emergency department and inpatient responsibility models.* Retrieved from http://www.ncbi.nlm.nih.gov/pubmed/22922635

Madison, D. (2008). Narrative poetics and performative interventions. In N. Denzin, Y. Lincoln, & L. Smith (Eds.), *Handbook of critical and indigenous methodologies* (pp. 391–405). Thousand Oaks, CA: SAGE.

Maguire, P. (1987). *Doing participatory research: A feminist approach.* Amherst, MA: University of Massachusetts.

McCartan, C., Schubotz, D., & Murphy, J. (2012). The self-conscious researcher—Post-modern perspectives of participatory research with young people [48 paragraphs]. *Forum Qualitative Sozialforschung/Forum: Qualitative Social Research, 13*(1), Art. 9. Retrieved from http://nbn-resolving.de/urn:nbn:de:0114-fqs120192

Mertens, D. (2010). Divergence and mixed methods. *Journal of Mixed Methods Research, 4*(1), 3–5.

Mertens, D. (2012). Transformative mixed methods: Addressing inequities. *American Behavioral Scientist, 56*(6), 802–813.

Mertens, D., & Hesse-Biber, S. (2012). Triangulation and mixed methods research: Provocative positions. *Journal of Mixed Methods Research, 6*(2), 75–79.

Molina-Azorin, J. (2012). Mixed methods research in strategic management: Impact and applications. *Organizational Research Methods, 15*(1), 33–56.

Muir, S., & Mason, J. (2012). Capturing Christmas: The sensory potential of data from participant produced video. *Sociological Review Online, 17*(1). Retrieved from http://www.socresonline.org.uk/17/1/5.html

MusicEduResearch. (2012). *Autoethnography (study of self): Guqin home practice 3-May-2012*. [YouTube video]. Retrieved from http://www.youtube.com/watch?v=Y8WqsmGQckE

Onwuegbuzie, A. (2009). Mixed methods research. *VideoLectures.net*. Retrieved from http://videoletures.net/ssm109_onwuegbuzie_mmr/

Pearce, L. (2012). Mixed methods inquiry in sociology. *American Behavioral Scientist, 56*(6), 829–848.

Pelias, R. (2011). *057: Interview with Ron Pelias—Author of "Leaning: A poetics of personal relations."* Retrieved from http://thecriticallede.com/057-interview-with-ron-pelias-author-of-leaning-a-poetics-of-personal-relations/

Phillips, D., Harris, G., Larson, M., & higgins, k. (2009). Trying on—being in—becoming: Four women's journey(s) in feminist poststructural theory. *Qualitative Inquiry, 15*(9), 1455–1479.

Rai, R. (2012). A participatory action research training initiative to improve police effectiveness. *Action Research, 10*(3), 225–243.

Rath, J. (2012). Autoethnographic layering: Recollections, family tales, and dreams. *Qualitative Inquiry, 18*(5), 442–448.

Reimann, P. (2010). *Design-based research in the learning sciences*. Retrieved from http://www.slideshare.net/perei/design-based-research-an-introduction

Reinharz, S. (1992). *Feminist methods in social research*. London, England: Oxford University Press.

Richardson, L. (2002). Writing sociology. *Cultural Studies, Critical Methodologies, 2*(3), 414–422.

Robnett, R., & Leaper, C. (2013). "Girls don't propose! Ew.": A mixed-methods examination of marriage traditional preferences and benevolent sexism in emerging adults. *Journal of Adolescent Research, 28*(1), 96–121.

Rosenberg, D. (1999). *Action for prevention: Feminist practices in transformative learning in women's health and the environment*. Retrieved from http://openlibrary.org/works/OL12796569W/Action_for_prevention

Russell, L. (2012). Creating meaning from chaos: Narrative and dialogic encounters in family crisis. *Qualitative Inquiry, 18*(5), 391–400.

Saldaña, J. (2011). *Ethnotheatre: Research from page to stage*. Walnut Creek, CA: Left Coast Press.

Scheurich, J. (1997). *Research method in the postmodern*. London, England: Falmer.

Seeley, C. (2011). Unchartered territory: Imagining a stronger relationship between the arts and action research. *Action Research, 9*(1), 83–99.

Sellerberg, A-M., & Leppänen, V. (2012). A typology of narratives of social inclusion and exclusion: The case of bankrupt entrepreneurs [75 paragraphs]. *Forum Qualitative Sozialforschung/Forum: Qualitative Social Research, 13*(1), Art. 26. Retrieved from http://www.qualitative-research.net/index.php/fqs/article/view/1453

Slade, B. (2012). "From high skill to high school": Illustrating the process of deskilling immigrants through reader's theatre and institutional ethnography. *Qualitative Inquiry, 18*(5), 401–413.

Snoeren, M., Niessen, T., & Abma, T. (2012). Engagement enacted: Essentials of initiating an action research project. *Action Research, 10*(2), 189–204.

Sobre-Denton, M. (2012). Stories from the cage: Autoethnographic sensemaking, workplace bullying, gender discrimination, and White privilege. *Journal of Contemporary Ethnography, 41*(2), 220–250.

Sorensen, J., & Lawson, L. (2012). Evolution in partnership: Lessons from the East St. Louis Action Research Project. *Action Research, 10*(2), 150–169.

Sparkes, A. (2000). Autoethnography and narratives of self: Reflections on criteria in action. *Sociology of Sport Journal, 17,* 21–41.

Taber, N. (2010). Institutional ethnography, autoethnography, and narrative: An argument for incorporating multiple methodologies. *Qualitative Research, 10*(1), 5–25.

Tang, L., & Bhattacharya, S. (2011). Power and resistance: A case study of satire on the Internet. *Sociological Research Online, 16*(2), 11. Retrieved from http://www.socresonline.org.uk/16/2/11.html

Tashakkori, A., & Teddlie, C. (Eds.). (2003). *Handbook of mixed methods in the behavioral and social sciences*. Thousand Oaks, CA: SAGE.

Teddlie, C., & Tashakkori, A. (Eds.). (2010). *Handbook of mixed methods in social and behavioral research* (2nd ed.). Thousand Oaks, CA: SAGE

Teddlie, C., & Tashakkori, A. (2011). Mixed methods research: Contemporary issues in an emerging field. In N. Denzin & Y. Lincoln (Eds.), *The SAGE handbook of qualitative research* (pp. 285–300). Thousand Oaks, CA: SAGE.

Teddlie, C., & Tashakkori, A. (2012). Common "code" characteristics of mixed methods research: A review of critical issues and call for greater convergence. *American Behavioral Scientist, 56*(6), 774–788.

Teman, E., & Lahman, M. (2012). Broom closet or fish bowl? An ethnographic exploration of a university queer center and oneself. *Qualitative Inquiry, 18*(4), 341–354.

Thieme, S. (2012). "Action": Publishing research results in film [46 paragraphs]. *Forum Qualitative Sozialforschung/Forum: Qualitative Social Research, 13*(1), Art. 31. Retrieved from http://www.qualitative-research.net/index.php/fqs/article/view/1671

Tolich, M. (2010). A critique of current practice: Ten foundational guidelines for autoethnographers. *Qualitative Health Research, 20*(12), 1599–1610.

Tripp, D. (1992). Critical theory and educational research. *Issues in Educational Research, 2*(1), 13–23.

Tripp, D. (1993). *Critical incidents in teaching: Developing professional judgment*. London, England: Routledge.

Vargas, Y. (2008). Marco said I look like charcoal: A Puerto Rican's exploration of her ethnic identity. *Qualitative Inquiry, 14*(6), 949–954.

Watts, J. (2006). "The outsider within": Dilemmas of qualitative feminist research within a culture of resistance. *Qualitative Research, 6*(3), 385–402.

Weiner-Levy, N. (2009), When the hegemony studies the minority—An Israeli researcher studies Druze women: Transformations of power, alienation, and affinity in the field. *Qualitative Inquiry, 15*(4), 721–739.

Wekker, G. (2010). *Who is afraid of the F-word? Feminist qualitative research methods.* Retrieved from http://www.intergender.net/?q=courses/doctoral/previous

Wicks, P. G., & Reason, P. (2009). Initiating action research: Challenges and paradoxes of opening communicative space. *Action Research, 7*(3), 243–262.

Wöhrer, V., & Höcher, B. (2012). Tricks of the trade—Negotiations and dealings between researchers, teachers and students [77 paragraphs]. *Forum Qualitative Sozialforschung/Forum: Qualitative Social Research, 13*(1), Art. 16. Retrieved from http://nbn-resolving.de/urn:nbn:de:0114-fqs1201164

STUDENT STUDY SITE

Visit **http://www.sagepub.com/lichtmanqrss** to access additional study tools, including eFlashcards and links to SAGE journal articles.

PART II

The Qualitative Research Process

CHAPTER 7

Planning and Conceptualizing a Qualitative Research Study

Focus Your Reading

- Innovations from the field
- Taking chances in a new venture—painting
- Developing a qualitative research proposal

This chapter addresses planning and conceptualizing a research study and writing a research proposal. You have read about ethical issues in qualitative research (QR). You also read about various QR approaches or designs. Now, it is time to put some of these ideas into practice. To that end, I present a fictionalized research study about baby boomers and social media. I take you through my thought processes as I think about and plan the study. Then I take my ideas and develop them into a mini research proposal. Finally, I ask you to consider some issues about writing QR.

First, in order to get you thinking outside the box, I present you with perspectives from researchers who work in different disciplines and cover a range of locations. I do this for several reasons. I want you to see that there is no single way to do QR or even to conceptualize it. Your own perspective is critical and must be acknowledged. I hope these examples will stimulate you to expand your thinking about what QR is and how you should or could do it. Jim (education) and Christine (transpersonal psychology) represent two very different conceptual frameworks and backgrounds. Jim comes from a quantitative tradition; Christine is from the theater and the arts. David and his colleagues work in the math field, while Laura is in social policy and management with a background in photojournalism. Kip is in QR and performative social sciences. All pieces were specifically written for this text.

Did You Know

Some recent innovations involve online journaling and video diaries. Using online journaling, participants write their own blogs and can include photos or videos. With video diaries, participants speak directly to a webcam connected to their computer, smartphone, or digital video camera. They can then email or upload to an online platform. To learn more, look at http://www.newqualitative.org/qualitative-research/online-journals-and-video-diaries/

Innovations From the Field

I want to share with you contemporary practice from a range of disciplines that cover the U.S. from coast to coast and the UK. I asked several individuals to prepare a contribution specifically for this book. Responses represent a wide range of ideas and styles. I leave them pretty much intact, with the exception of some minor editing for space. A copy of the request is shown in Appendix A. Accompanying references for contributions are also in Appendix A.

I begin with Jim. He shares lessons he learned as he ventured into the qualitative arena. Trained as a quantitative researcher, he writes from a perspective familiar to some of you. James Bernauer is associate professor in the School of Education and Social Sciences at Robert Morris University in Pittsburgh, PA. He holds a doctorate from the University of Pittsburgh. Jim (with Laura O'Dwyer) is currently preparing a book for SAGE about QR for the quantitative researcher.

Traversing the Lonely Road: My First Qualitative Venture, aka Lessons Learned via Pithy Sayings

by James Bernauer

When I got to the point where there was a reasonable expectation that I would graduate from my doctoral program in education, I got the jitters. Because my goal was to teach at a university, I knew that publishing would play a large part in my success. Unfortunately, the recurring image that filled my mind was that of my sitting alone in a barren office thinking to myself over and over, what am I going to write about?

Now let's use one of the many pithy expressions that we come across in life—"hindsight is 20/20." Let's unravel this. You see, I was trained in the quantitative tradition. I was also fortunate enough to have a full-time assistantship and to work under the tutelage of a premier quantitative researcher. I was also quite proud of myself since, although I never considered myself a "math" person, I did quite well in my courses, including that bane of many graduate students—statistics. I also had access to mounds of numerical data that I helped to organize as part of my assistantship and built my dissertation around these data—pretty sweet deal! In addition, I was offered a job following graduation, where even though there was no great pressure to publish, I was made the associate director of a school district assessment project, and my first article was a natural outgrowth of this position. It turned out, however, that the "data" for this article was not numerical but rather in word form (which should have been my first clue about where I was headed and hence the 20/20 analogy). However, our paradigmatic grounding dies hard, so my cultural upbringing in the quantitative tradition continued.

While I could go into great detail about the tortuous path that my career took after this point (and would probably enjoy doing so!), let's interject another expression at this point—"cut to the quick." While I'm not exactly sure what "the quick" initially meant, we can fall back on the old business expression of getting to the "bottom line" as a reasonable facsimile. So, here is the bottom line about hindsight being 20/20—I now teach qualitative research and write and care about looking at things from a qualitative perspective. How is that for the "bottom line"? [Note: One explanation for the "cut to the quick" expression is that *quick* refers to the finger underneath the nail and if you cut your fingernail too short and expose it to the flesh beneath, you have cut it to the quick. Several other explanations all lead to the bottom line that you should penetrate the dead stuff and get to the important parts.]

At issue, however, is that I was given the charge to write about something that graduate students might find useful. Therefore, the first thing that I would like to point out is that the writing style that you are now reading would have never emanated from me during most of my academic career. In fact, I probably would have written something like "based on the data that was presented in Table 1, the most reasonable conclusion is that variables extraneous to those included in this study by the researcher are at least partially responsible for the unexplained variance in predicting the outcome variable." Instead of this declamation, what I now wish to say is that "I am not quite sure why I am where I am nor exactly what I have done to get to this point, but I continue to learn a little bit every day." So now I think it is time to ease into talking a little bit about the title of this article.

As implied above, the switch from quantitative to qualitative researcher happened imperceptibly, beginning with my first published article at my first university. On the other hand, having been given the charge to teach a graduate qualitative research course at my second university, the pace of my "switch" increased dramatically and exposed me as more of a words than a numbers guy. In my field of education, grounding in quantitative methodology at the graduate level has traditionally been taken for granted. A reading of the history of education and educational research (see Lagemann, 2000) shows quite clearly that psychology adopted the "hard" sciences as their model, education adopted psychology, and there you have it. What makes this surprising is that when you really think about what goes on daily in classrooms and schools, it has little to do with numbers and precision and more to do with empathy, conversation, understanding, friendship, maturing, caring, and identity formation. While content is certainly important, when we think about our best teachers, we usually think about those who showed a genuine caring attitude and excited us about learning. I just don't get that same feeling when I think about a scientific approach to learning and teaching.

To continue our discussion and direct it more to the title of this article, let me first define *research*. Research is a systematic process to make things known that are currently unknown by examining phenomena multiple times and in multiple ways. Nice academic definition, I think. So, what does it mean in simple terms? Something like "every day in every way, we can learn a little bit more about our world if we keep our eyes, ears, hearts, and minds open." Some days, the eyes and ears can teach us a lot by what we can see and hear if we are in a receptive state. The heart and mind are really the wild cards in all of this. While these two capacities can trump just about any sensory input, they can also go "hand in glove" with sensory data to interpret and give meaning to experience. OK, so now, having worked through some of this theoretical stuff, let's see how it all played out with the experience that I now describe.

When the mantle of qualitative professor was thrust upon me, my work ethic kicked into high gear and I decided to go full throttle on this new task. Even though my field is education and schooling is my game, I wanted to go beyond the walls of the school building to gather my story (aka, *collecting data*). My initial foray was to tackle an unsuspecting clerk at a beer store who I had previously engaged in a stimulating conversation after an evening graduate class. This guy was very intelligent and asked good questions. I was constantly stimulated to ask questions: Why was he working here? What were his goals? What was going on here? So, in a not very smooth way, I got him to agree to meet for coffee and talk about his take as a high school grad and making it in this life. I now need to use my "to cut to the quick" again—he never showed up.... In fact, I never saw him again. So went my first foray into conducting a qualitative study. I felt that I was alone on an island without either friends or refreshments.

Not long after this first defeat, I developed an interest in the concept of "expertise"—again, cutting to the quick (I think I need to find another expression), it struck me like "a bolt of lightning" (there, the sought-after new expression) that expertise did not reside only at NASA but also in restaurants, auto repair shops, dentist offices, and the like. So I set up interviews and site visits with business people in my neighborhood and began listening to their stories and observing their lives. I found this experience to be both lonely and exhilarating. I was unsure what to ask and how to observe, so I did what my dad advised me when I was growing up and that was "to do *something*, even if it's wrong!" And so I did. My first interview took place with the owner of a small Italian restaurant. My "field notes" consisted of some scribbling on napkins, and my taping was awkward. However, this first tentative concrete step seemed to light up my neural and creative pathways, and so I completed my subsequent site visits, if not with panache, at least with a greater sense of self confidence. While I wish I could say that this adventure resulted in a tome on expertise, it did not. In fact, much of the data remains un-interpreted. [I think here it would be appropriate to officially point out a lesson that qualitative researchers often intone: Qualitative data is a lot easier to collect than to make sense of (aka, *interpret*).] Fortunately, although my data was not "transformed" (Wolcott, 1994) into what I had in mind, I have used parcels of it when writing other things, and so I count my foray into the shops in my neighborhood as quite worthwhile.

Another life experience that helped me to launch this neighborhood foray happened when I worked with another guy to construct a bathroom in the basement of my house. Let me first provide some "thick" description, although here, I find myself again needing to cut to the quick and that is "I hereby proclaim without reservation that we were both basically incompetent when it came to tools and building things." "In a nutshell," here is what happened. We sat and stared for quite a while at the blank area where we were going to construct this bathroom. In fact, we stared at the blank area quite blankly . . . or at least it seemed. However, using our 20/20 lens, I now recognize this semi-coma state as the necessary incubation period that precedes any creative undertaking. After a fairly long period of "incubation" (aka, *staring*), my friend said, "Let's do something" (this reminded me of my dad's advice), so up we got and placed a 2x4 against the blank wall to mark the one perimeter of the bathroom. We then placed and bolted a corresponding "footplate" (I think this is the correct term) on the floor. From there, my memory blurs, because things then started to fall in place, and the bottom line is that we ended up with a bathroom. While this, of course, is a time-lapsed version of what actually happened, this lesson underscores the need to follow up reflection with action—do something, even if it's wrong, because guess what?—we all tend to learn by doing. And that's how I learned and continue to learn about doing qualitative research.

I am very aware of the folksy nature of what I have written. In fact, my meta-cognitive awareness (aka, *reflexivity*) may have peaked as I wrote it. So, perhaps it's time to sum up the lessons that I have learned regarding qualitative research by temporarily resorting back to that favorite among quantitative researchers as well as the anal retentive among us—the numbered list. So, here is what I think I have learned *thus far* and what I offer to those of you who have continued reading to this grand culmination:

1. Each of us has unique and wonderful capacities for understanding and interpreting the world that we live in. (I love ending sentences in a preposition, the so-called "Addisonian Termination.")
2. Hang onto complexity as long as you can; don't rush to simplification (such as a numbered list)—the time will come soon enough when you will need to simplify and "reduce" data.
3. Recognize that trying to make sense of complex data requires that you step out into the unknown—that first step gets things going!
4. "In the final analysis" (trite but true), qualitative data analysis is essentially critical thinking.
5. Conducting qualitative inquiry should be fun—demanding, challenging, exhausting, misunderstood by others . . . but still fun—so do it with delight!

As a professor, I have many more things to say (give a professor an inch and she or he will barrage you with a mile of insight as well as minutia); however, I choose to end this [can't seem to find the right word to describe what *this* is—so, dear reader, insert what you wish] here. Except, I offer this last piece of advice regarding qualitative research—find your passion, and then don't allow others to keep you from it!

Qualitative researchers are doing innovative things with technology. I asked David to describe his work with smartphones and other commonly used technology. His contribution is written as a journal article and begins with an abstract. David Glassmeyer teaches in the School of Mathematical Sciences at the University of Northern Colorado. R. A. Dibbs is a math educator, and Maria Lahman is a qualitative methodologist, both at the University of Northern Colorado.

Transparent Technology: Using Smartphones for Sensitive Interview Topics

by R. A. Dibbs, David Glassmeyer, and Maria Lahman

Abstract: Transparent technology (e.g., cell phone, elevator) is accepted as part of the landscape in society and typically not remarked upon. Researchers now have the capability to record and email interviews, increasing participants' comfort during an interview, but there are also potential ethical dilemmas. Framed by a study on undergraduates' experiences with repeating a course, the authors discuss methodological and ethical concerns relating to the use of transparent technology, including smartphones, smart pens, laptop computers, and digital music players, as a data collection instrument. After providing background on transparent technology, the authors briefly highlight the research conducted and review four potential ways of recording data transparently. They then describe the ethical decisions that occurred due to choices for recording data and the decisions made. Finally, methodological considerations in the areas of cost, ease of use, and ethics are advanced.

Amanda is talking animatedly about a topic that many avoid: repeated failures in the mathematics courses required for her major that she attributes to instructor prejudice and the pressure of being a second generation immigrant. Her body is relaxed; Amanda is animated and making gestures that expand on what she is saying. Since there seems to be no recording device present and indeed, no technology other than a mobile phone on the table, an onlooker would perceive this interaction as a conversation rather than the formal research interview it is. As researchers, we are struck by how the major differences between conversational exchange and an interview may be seen in the explanation of the consent form and the use of a recording device. While the devices have become less intrusive, moving far away from large or clipped-on microphones, the ubiquity of a smartphone, digital music device, smart pen, or computer adds a level of transparency as yet unseen as illustrated by Amanda's research interview. This transparency is also reflected in the scant methodological literature we identified. In the past years, we have seen a rapid proliferation of (mobile) emerging technologies, also referred to as ubiquitous, pervasive, or context-aware applications. Many of these applications are inherently personal in nature; they stay or travel with one person most of the time and are therefore used in various contexts. Evaluating such technologies is challenging (Mulder & Kort, 2008).

In a research study we conducted, little literature was identified regarding the use of smart devices for recording interviews. After taking certain precautions, we used a smartphone as the recording device for interviews and reflexively journaled about the process. These efforts were the basis for this article, through which we provide recommendations that will assist other researchers interested in using transparent technology, specifically smartphones, MP3 players, smart pens, or laptops, to conduct interviews over topics that may be sensitive to the participants. Following a brief literature review on the use of transparent technology as a research tool, we discuss the methodological themes identified in a study where we conducted interviews with undergraduates who were repeating a calculus course. After briefly describing the research design of the study, we present three major methodological areas for consideration with transparent recording technology: practicality, quality of data, and ethics; finally, we will identify directions of future research.

Literature Review

Since the beginning of available interview research, technology and the enactment of the interview have been inextricably entwined (Geist, 2008). Whether the technology was a pencil or pen held by the researcher or an employed stenographer (e.g., Blumer's study of motion pictures), a phonograph, wire recorder, cassette tape, CD, or digital file (Geist, 2008), the interview act cannot be separated from the extant technology relied on. While little research exists on current transparent technology, researchers have used cellular phones for data collection in a number of ways during recent years. Shortly after "smart" phones became available, then called "handheld computers," researchers recognized the potential of such devices for data collection (Greene, 2001). Since the onset of this idea, cellular phones for data collection have been used readily within medicinal and therapeutic research fields; research from Braun et al. (2005) and Cleland, Caldow, and Ryan (2007) demonstrated "that linking mobile phone technology with electronic data collection supports the recording of many patients' information about their status and improves their compliance with the treatment" (Preziosa, Grassi, Gaggioli, & Riva, 2009, p. 317). These researchers advocate the advantages of smartphone data collection, but some controversy surrounding ethical issues in this process remains unanswered and perhaps unanswerable.

Advantages to smartphones as a method for data collection include the ability to hold a large amount of data, portability, accessibility to increased amounts of information, improved data quality, and in most cases, smartphones are more affordable than other technology offering the same benefits, such as a laptop (Greene, 2001; Gorge, 2005; Gravlee, 2002). While research involving smartphones for data recording during interviews is limited, researchers report participants feel more at ease with mobile recording devices than they do with technology such as laptops, especially when discussing sensitive topics (Bosley, Conrad, & Uglow, 1998; Gravlee, 2002). Many researchers advocate potential use of technology such as smartphones for this type of data collection, especially as a new generation of smartphones become more popular; these devices allow voice recording in digital formats to be easily transferred within a user-friendly interface (Cleland, Caldow, & Ryan, 2007; Couper, 2005; Preziosa, Grassi, Gaggioli, & Riva, 2009).

The considerations of using smartphones to record research data have also been made explicit; low levels of public awareness concerning security threats of smartphones should raise caution among researchers collecting data in this manner (Gorge, 2005). Through advanced technology such as Bluetooth, hackers can bug (and have bugged) smartphones, revealed passwords, and distributed/sold sensitive data from the hacked phone. Citing similar threats on a computer, Loo (2009) stated, "The risks of using Bluetooth and smartphones are relatively low compared with those of other technologies, provided that they are used properly" (p. 152). Overall, researchers seem to emphasize both the potential to use transparent technology such as smartphones as an advantageous for data collection and the cautions associated with such technology.

The Research Study We Reflect On

As I, Dibbs, began to think about scheduling students repeating their calculus course to talk about their experience, I grappled with two major issues: I found my own experience of repeating a course deeply embarrassing and worried that the participants would also be uncomfortable and unwilling to share, knowing that their personal failures were being recorded. I didn't have access to a traditional recorder. However, I did have a smartphone that recorded audio files and an MP3 player with similar capabilities. Eventually, after much experimentation I chose to use the phone for all interviews. My hope was that the phone—ubiquitous, transparent technology we take for granted—would help participants become more comfortable and willing to share more of their story.

The Researchers

Dibbs is a mathematics educator whose major focuses are mathematical, motivation/frustration, formative assessment, and precision teaching. Prior to this study, she had five years of undergraduate teaching experience and taught a calculus course twice before. She began working with Glassmeyer and Lahman during the study for peer-checking purposes and to discuss the methodological issues of using transparent technology. Glassmeyer is a mathematics educator familiar with the study who had published research on using technology for research purposes; he had worked with Dibbs to publish the technological and ethical considerations necessary to facilitate interviews involving nontraditional modes of recording (Glassmeyer & Dibbs, 2012). Lahman is a qualitative methodologist expert who became intrigued by the study because of the use of smart technology as a recording device. The benefits and ethical issues involved with this type of recording attracted her to the research team, as she believes researchers need to keep those issues in mind to reflect on the impact of using any technological improvement on research before embracing it wholeheartedly.

The Research Design

This qualitative study, which we refer to as the "repeating calculus study" throughout this article, utilized interviews with students who were currently enrolled in a Calculus I course for at least the second time. Eight students, ranging in age from 18 to 28, participated in conversational interviews conducted in a quiet office that lasted 15 to 45 minutes in length around midterms of the semester (Merriam, 1998). Seven of the participants were Caucasian, and one was Asian American; students were selected for maximum variation of their reasons for repeating calculus, as stated on the initial intake survey sent out with consent letters.

Three participants were reinterviewed during the last week of classes to follow up on their first interviews and ask participants about the smartphone recording of their interviews. The institution this research was conducted at is a midsize doctoral-granting institution in the Rocky Mountain region. The interview questions on the script were asked only if conversation stalled. Typical questions included: As much as you are comfortable, can you share how you came to repeat calculus this semester? Did you have a moment where you knew you would need to repeat calculus? What were you expecting this class to be like? What, if anything, are you doing differently this time? How do you feel the current class is going for you? In the second interview, which was semi-structured, participants were asked specific questions about some of their disclosures, and all participants were asked to describe their experience of being interviewed with a smartphone recorder.

Discussion: Methodological and Ethical Considerations

During the data collection process, memos were taken about how the data collection method could affect the richness of the data, and ethical considerations were noted. Three themes emerged from the use of an alternative recording device: *practicality, quality of data,* and *ethics*. Though these themes are discussed independently below, we acknowledge that that there is significant overlap among them.

Practicality

Since it is unlikely that we or anyone else would buy a smartphone, MP3 player, or laptop with the express purpose of using it as a research tool, the first theme that emerged was how practical a given piece of technology would be for data collection. Three dimensions of practicality were considered when we decided what to use in the repeating calculus study: cost, ease of use, and the likelihood the technology would be on our person for spontaneous data collection.

None of the three technologies had any additional costs associated with their use as data collection instruments. The smartphone used in this study was a current-generation Droid phone. Dibbs already owned the phone and had a data plan that allowed files to be emailed directly from the phone. The laptops all had access that allowed for the recording of sound files directly in Microsoft Word, and the iPod files were easy to export to a computer for further transcription. While there were no additional costs in our case, cost is a factor to consider when using transparent technology; it's not economical to use a smartphone only as a recording device.

Given that the choices were free to convert to recording devices and were already items Dibbs used for another purpose, the next thing she considered was how easy they were to use. She did not want to fumble with technology and make participants even more aware that they were being recorded. The laptop's microphone was highly directional on the model she used; on the playback one could hear only whom the screen was pointed at [an odd social setup], and placing the screen perpendicular to us caused the microphone to pick up a lot of ambient noise. However, this may be a computer-specific problem. The MP3 player and the smartphone were both easy to use and discreetly recorded, but the slightly larger buttons and the placement of the microphone on the smartphone made the phone easier to use as a data collection tool.

The final consideration for practicality was whether the technology was something we carried with us all the time—so it was always available. Finally, it is prudent to purchase an extended battery, if available, to ensure that the smartphone will most likely have power when an opportunity for spontaneous data collection arises. In this study, the availability gave the smartphone an edge over the iPod, though this was wholly a personal decision.

Quality of Data

All three instruments, when correctly set up, eventually recorded data that were audible for later transcription, though the amount of effort to set up for good recording varied by technology. The smartphone needed to be on, recording, and near the participant. The iPod microphone needed to be on a stable surface and between the participant and the interviewer; we found that the microphone, if held, picked up more ambient noise. The laptop recorder required that the laptop be open with the screen facing the participant—we found that the microphone in our laptop recorded the person the screen was facing better than the other one. This created awkward relative positioning of the researcher, participant, and recording device, and for this reason, we never used the laptop as a data collection tool.

When Dibbs reinterviewed three of our participants (Andrew, Amanda, and Elizabeth; these are pseudonyms) about data collection in the repeating calculus study, she showed them the three potential setups and a traditional recorder and asked them how being recorded on these devices would have compared to being recorded by a smartphone. All of the participants preferred the smartphone, as illustrated by Andrew's statement: "Of the choices, the phone is best, I think. It looks the most natural, you know? Like, the laptop and the [MP3 player] are not where I would expect them to be. I think that I wouldn't notice after a bit, but they don't look right on the table."

Amanda, in particular, talked about how she felt comfortable right away in her first interview: "I know that you said you were recording, but I didn't see a microphone anywhere or anything that looked like a recorder, so I forgot about it pretty quickly." Elizabeth and Andrew agreed with Amanda's statement. This led us to reconsider Andrew's transcripts. Dibbs interviewed Andrew for both the repeating calculus study and another mathematics education study that semester, though that study was on an instructional technique, a far less sensitive topic. In that qualitative study, interviews were recorded with a traditional recorder. Upon reanalysis, Dibbs determined Andrew made more significant statements in the first five minutes of the interview recorded with the smartphone; furthermore, he made more significant statements in the smartphone-recorded interview than the traditionally recorded one. However, more research would need to be conducted to see if this was a general trend.

Ethics

There are three ethical issues we consider with a smartphone: spontaneous data collection, data security, and transparency. Since Dibbs always had her smartphone with her, there were times through the data collection period where conversations in the hallway, classroom, or tutor lab could easily be turned into short conversational interviews and recorded. However, since the smartphone was always on her person, it was important for Dibbs to be reflexive about when and how to introduce recording. She explicitly stated that she was going to record with the phone and asked for permission to record every time. This was necessary, because the recording application used made the phone's screen black—while recording, the phone appears to be off. Far more careful consideration needs to be given to data security. It is important to minimize the risks to the participants by taking the same care that their data are as secure as with a traditional recorder. It is of note that Mann and Stewart (2002) wrote, "Working with digital data in a virtual environment, researchers cannot avoid engaging with legal and ethical issues that are still in a state of flux" (p. 609). Clearly, once the sound files are removed from the smartphone and stored securely, there is no longer a particular risk to the data, though we recommend checking how long your email provider stores email files before using an email account for research purposes. By sending the data to a secure server as soon as possible after the interview and then erasing all data from the phone upon confirmation of receipt—including sent email—the data security risks can be minimized. The cell phone provider used for this study, *Verizon Wireless,* stores email on their servers for only 24 hours once the email is moved to the trash folder. We were also able to record files directly from the phone to a secure computer by playing back the interview on the phone and then using *Express Dictate* on the computer, which may be a way to minimize risk of accidental leaks for extremely sensitive data. However, any smartphone used for data collection must have current antivirus software updated and the Bluetooth feature disabled.

Finally, the transparent nature of the smartphone, which puts the participants at ease during a sensitive interview, deserves close ethical reflection. Is it ethical to record someone who has forgotten they are being recorded? While this tension may be seen throughout the history of research, it is not easily resolved and perhaps should not be. We recommend balancing the transparent nature of the interview with a follow-up member check of transcripts. That way, the interview itself does not have to be a stressful experience, yet participants are provided with ample opportunity to reflect on their transcripts later, in private, and may ask for changes or deletions as warranted.

Conclusion

Smartphones may have the potential to be advantageous to researchers investigating sensitive topics that require interviews with the participants, provided the appropriate ethical and technological considerations are made. So if one is smart when using smartphones for interview research, there is great potential for this burgeoning yet transparent technology.

Laura Lorenz is senior research associate and lecturer at the Heller School for Social Policy and Management, Brandeis University, in Massachusetts. Prior to her position at Brandeis, she worked as a photojournalist in Africa, Asia, and Latin America. She and I had a discussion about how she used the technique called **photovoice** *in her qualitative work. A kind of participatory action research, Laura's work reveals the power of using data to spur action in a community.*

Photovoice in Practice: Ensuring Safety and Encouraging Action
by Laura Lorenz

Photovoice (Wang, Burris, & Ping, 1996) is a participatory visual research method that involves visually documenting everyday problems and strengths in photographs, considering possible causes and alternatives for change, and (ideally) taking action to address identified problems and support identified strengths. With photovoice, participants (1) learn about being a researcher in their community; (2) take photographs and discuss them to understand both positive and negative aspects of a situation, community, or health condition; and (3) develop outreach products or activities that use both images and text and are aimed at creating awareness and encouraging action.

I have used photovoice in the United States and South Africa since 2001 with adolescent girls, township youth, and adults living with disabilities after brain injury. For each project, participants took photographs in their homes and communities, selected photos they wanted to discuss with the group, wrote or dictated captions, sorted their photos into themes, and developed a project exhibit to create awareness of their situations, perspectives, and lives. Each project took on a life of its own, became integrated into the activities of the sponsoring organization, and provided opportunities for individuals whose voices are not usually heard to have a say in their communities and beyond.

In this chapter, I share some of my learning related to using photovoice with vulnerable individuals and groups, such as girls and people living with HIV. In my experience, two photovoice facilitation issues that are vital but potentially challenging in practice are how to ensure safety and how to encourage action. I frame this discussion with a drawing and a photograph from two photovoice projects I facilitated in 2001.

Ensuring Safety

Your photovoice participants may face dangerous situations in their communities before you arrive, while you are there, and after you leave. They may want to discuss these situations during project sessions and depict them in photographs. In Mdantsane Township, South Africa, participants wanted to document issues of violence in their community with their photovoice project. But how would they document this common but dangerous topic safely, without putting participants and other community members at risk?

The project was sponsored by the Youth Academy (YA), a youth-run nonprofit organization in Mdantsane Township that provides youth-led opportunities to improve township life, for example, by using training and outreach to encourage household vegetable gardens. For photovoice, YA recruited 16 participants aged 18 to 32 and living in the Township. They included 11 women and 5 men, and all had completed at least 10th grade. Most were unemployed, and nine were living with HIV and recruited through a local organization for people living with HIV/AIDS.

The YA photovoice project was supported with funding from the Equity Project, a partnership of the Department of Health South Africa and the U.S. Agency for International Development to improve the quality and management of health services in South Africa. The photovoice project was intended to increase policymaker awareness of assets and problems in Mdantsane Township, including health services and the HIV/AIDS epidemic, as seen from the perspective of the participating youth. We met three times per week for four weeks. Four youth were coleaders with me, and each led a team of four participants throughout the project as they reviewed and discussed their photographs, selected some for exhibit, wrote captions, and grouped their photos into themes. The final exhibit had 80 photos and captions grouped into six themes: health and welfare, education and training, community vision, economic opportunity, security, and township life.

Before they received their project cameras, participants were asked to draw two pictures, one of a community problem and another of a community asset in Mdantsane Township from their perspectives. For his problem, a 19-year-old participant drew a picture showing a man lying on the ground and bleeding while another man, his face hidden from the viewer, runs away (see Figure 7.1). The participant who drew this picture had been mugged and robbed near his home not long before the project started. As a group, we discussed how he might safely depict what had happened to him. His solution was to take a photo of the street corner where he was attacked; the mild image of a dirt street lined with bushes and tall grass contrasted sharply with his caption: "I got mugged here in October when I was walking home from the store. It was dark. The men beat me and took my wallet, my belt, and my jacket. I thought they were going to kill me. This place is near my home." He grouped his photo under the theme "Security," which had 11 photos and illustrated community problems (such as abandoned buildings, carjackings, and sexual abuse) and community assets (such as policemen, improved roads, and traffic signs).

Figure 7.1 Drawing of a Community Problem

SOURCE: "Speaking with Pictures," Youth Academy Photovoice Project, Mdantsane Township, Eastern Cape Province, South Africa, 2001.

Project participants faced the risk of violence during project implementation as well. Late one afternoon, the youngest project participant, a 16-year-old living with HIV, had gone to the grocery store to buy food for the family dinner. On her way home, she left the main road to take a footpath to save time. She knew that thugs hung out there but thought the path would be safe during daylight. Her project camera was in the plastic bag with the groceries. A man stepped out from behind a bush, said she shouldn't be going that way, and demanded that she give him the bag of groceries. All she could think about was her camera—not her personal safety or the family food. She quickly slipped the camera out of the bag and hid it under her blouse as she handed him the bag. So he got the groceries but not her camera. "I have become very attached to my camera," she explained in a project session the next day. In this instance, her camera could be seen as a metaphor for community voice.

As these examples show, photovoice can provide an important opportunity for participants living in vulnerable circumstances to have a community voice—an opportunity to express their perspectives on their community. Thus an essential photovoice leadership task is to create opportunities for meaningful expression of voice while at the same time ensuring participant safety. One way to learn about potential safety issues is to ask participants to create drawings of problems and assets in their community before they get their project cameras. During project sessions, practice explaining the project and its purpose to others through role-play. Consider providing participants with project identity cards, T-shirts, or handouts that describe the project and its purpose. Include in your exhibit only those photos for which you have a signed permission form from (1) the photographer, (2) any individual who can be recognized in the photograph, and (3) any individuals whose property is shown. And finally, work with your participants and community partners to discuss potential risks, and develop strategies for safety that are appropriate for your context.

Encouraging Action

Photovoice provides practice in working with peers to identify community problems and assets, take photographs and write captions, prepare an exhibit, and have a community voice. The practice of photovoice can lead to feelings of greater self-esteem and empowerment. Accomplishing action, however, is a basic photovoice project purpose and will reinforce participants' practice of community voice.

For my first photovoice project, five girls aged 12 to 16 participated through an afterschool program of Girls Incorporated of Greater Lowell in Lowell, Massachusetts. The American Association of University Women provided funding through a Career Development Grant for my Master of Education studies in Instructional Design at the University of Massachusetts, Boston. I designed the project in the fall of 2000, and we implemented it in 16 weekly hour-long sessions from January through May in 2001. Our photovoice exhibit was posted in the lobby of Lowell City Hall in May, and the exhibit had 40 photos grouped into seven themes: recreation, girls' empowerment, home, neighborhood, trash, school, and friends.

Girls took photographs to answer two questions: What are some things that you like in your community (resources)? What are some things that you do not like in your community (problems)? One participant had been frustrated for several years by a crack in the wooden dance floor at her high school. She decided to highlight this problem in our exhibit (see Figure 7.2).

"This is one of many cracks in our dance floor at my high school. Cracks like this are very unsafe and can cause major injuries. Our dance teacher tells us to be careful so we do not get hurt. One girl was injured earlier this year. Our dance teacher has made numerous complaints to the school about this problem. I hope that including this photo will get the floor fixed and that my dance teacher does not get in trouble, because this was my idea."—Participant, Age 17, Girls Incorporated of Greater Lowell, Lowell, MA, USA, 2001

We invited Lowell's mayor (a woman) to speak at the exhibit opening. After her speech, she walked through the exhibit and spent time speaking with the participant about her photo of the dance floor. At the next city councilors' meeting, the Mayor insisted that the councilors walk down with her to the see the photovoice exhibit in the lobby. She pointed to the photograph and caption of dance floor, said that they were evidence of a problem that needed to be fixed, and urged the Council to do something. That very night, the councilors approved funding to repair the floor, and by fall 2002, it was fixed.

There are no guarantees that your photovoice project will result in action or change. However, photovoice will almost certainly generate enthusiasm among your participants and plant a seed of activism and change. In order to grow, the seed must be nurtured. Direct

Figure 7.2 Our High School Dance Floor Is Broken

SOURCE: "Girls Vision, Girls Voices Photovoice Project," Girls Incorporated of Greater Lowell, Lowell, Massachusetts, 2001.

participants' energy and enthusiasm into positive action by building discussion of possible action into your project design. Examples could include organizing a trash clean-up campaign, lobbying public officials for funding to fix a problem, starting a community newspaper, establishing a student-run "school improvement community," raising money for a local animal shelter, or starting an environmental club. Besides inviting stakeholders, such as elected officials, to your photovoice final exhibit, hold a small practice exhibit for stakeholders, such as teachers, school administrators, health-care workers, and community volunteers and non-profits, to discuss the photos and possible community solutions or supports. Plan for a range of outreach activities to reach different audiences, and provide participants with practice in public. Develop workshops to support participant interests such as photography, business skills, writing, or video. Reach out to local businesses and government to generate internship and volunteer opportunities. And finally, support participant-leaders' efforts to generate action and change.

A Story About How/Why I Developed This Idea

From 1991 to 1997, I worked as a journalist and photojournalist in West Africa and India for United Nations Children's Fund (UNICEF), the U.S. Agency for International Development, World Food Programme, CARE, and other agencies. I had control of the camera, and basically, I told people's stories for them. When I returned to the U.S. in 1997, I got a job developing continuing education materials for health program managers in Africa, Asia, and Latin America. This work was rewarding, but I realized that I needed more contact with people. I enrolled in a Master of Education program in Instructional Design (Adult Education and Training) at the University of Massachusetts, Boston, Graduate School of Education while continuing to work full time. My studies prompted me to wonder whether the camera could be an instructional design tool. A professor agreed to be my advisor for an independent study using photography. However, he did not want me to take the photographs. Rather, he asked me to give cameras to young people to explore their community. At first, I hesitated. I wanted to take the photographs! But upon reflection, I thought I should listen to his advice. A wise decision! In a research methods class in the fall, I read literature on arts, activism, youth, and experiential learning. In November, I found a paper that described a photovoice project in China that included the perspectives of village women in a regional development effort (Wang, Burris, & Ping, 1996). At last, a model for what I wanted to do! At the American Public Health Association meetings in Boston a few days later, I saw a session on photovoice. Four panelists discussed their projects in Detroit, Vietnam, and elsewhere. I based my photovoice project design on the approach of Wang and her colleagues and adapted it to youth, based on the education and arts literature. In Mdantsane Township, I began to incorporate more visual learning, such as the photovoice path into the project design, and my Mdantsane youth coleaders added new ideas, such as putting on a mini-exhibit with invited guests to discuss participants' photos. The experience of these two projects made me want to continue my studies. Photovoice was one of the methods I used in my doctoral dissertation study in social policy at the Heller School for Social Policy and Management at Brandeis University. Once you give the camera to someone else to see through their eyes, you may never go back!

Anything Else Relevant

The use of photovoice and other participatory visual methods, such as digital storytelling, has grown tremendously since the 1990s. Explore the literature on visual methods and adapt the different approaches you find to the needs, goals, and purposes of your participants, community, and project. In other words, learn from those who have used photovoice and make it your own.

My Bio Information

Laura Lorenz is a senior research associate and lecturer at the Heller School for Social Policy and Management at Brandeis University. Before coming to Brandeis, Laura worked in international development as a photojournalist, writer, editor, and educator in Africa, Asia, and Latin America; her assignments often involved encouraging community partnerships, project replication, and behavior change—for example, to improve girls' access to education and prevent transmission of HIV. Since 2001, Laura has used photovoice in the U.S. and South Africa to engage patients, youth, and communities in picturing local problems and strengths and motivating action for change. Much of her work since 2004 has focused on including the perspectives of patients on their health and healthcare experiences in the policy-making process. Laura has presented and published on identity after brain injury, the patient-provider relationship, issues of voice and representation, visual and narrative methods of research and analysis, and communications for policy advocacy. She teaches social policy and qualitative methods. She is author of *Brain Injury Survivors: Narratives of Rehabilitation and Healing* and has published papers in the fields of sociology, health, visual studies, and medicine.

Christine and I had a discussion about quantitative research (QN) and QR and my experience with feeling like an outsider in a research department with a quantitative bent. In this piece, she shares her very different experience of coming at QR from a humanities perspective. Christine Brooks is associate professor and chair of the residential master's and doctoral programs in transpersonal psychology at Sofia University in Palo Alto, CA. Her research focuses on intentional childlessness as a lifepath, expressions of gendered identities, and the interface of transpersonal psychology and transformational educational scholarship.

Life in the Social Sciences—An Alternate View

by Christine Brooks

My life in the social sciences has two distinct parts. As child, I was an outside observer during the heyday of the humanistic turn. The daughter of a therapist with a PhD in public health, I witnessed the rise of psychotherapy as a healing tool for all and not just the wealthy who could afford analysis on the couch. Civil rights and liberation movements of the prior decade had radicalized and politicized psychology. The concepts of unconditional positive regard and respect for the dignity of the client began to upend the top-down, expert status of the clinician. Marriage and family therapy and group process emphasized the value of people's stories. Narrative therapy was, in fact, founded on the ways that people story their reality into being. I learned, from being immersed in my father's world, that telling and revising one's story indeed has the capacity to heal.

In the past decade, I became an inside observer as a later-in-life graduate student in transpersonal psychology and, most recently, as a researcher and educator. Since those early days of childhood and throughout my doctoral education, I have witnessed the increasing biomedical focus of research in psychology: Efficacy studies and generalizability of human factors and qualities drive treatment protocols. Medication and symptom management are the stories we now tell more often than relying on the talking cure to help us make meaning of our experience. While the mainstream discipline of psychology continues to move further away from the philosophical roots of the healing arts toward the scientific management of the human psyche, the field of transpersonal psychology has maintained a stance that individual, subjective accounts of lived experience must be valued in our attempts to understand the human condition. Thus I have had the privilege of working within an academic community that maintains a strong tradition of expertise and excellence in qualitative research.

Nonetheless, working within the field of psychology, I have been dealing mainly with individuals who work in the sciences for much of their careers. As with many aspects of my life, including my passion for qualitative research, my pathway to the social sciences was circuitous and has included experiences in eclectic educational and professional environments that have shaped who I am as a researcher and scholar. A conversation I was having with a colleague at a conference not long ago brought me to the realization that qualitative research is a natural experience for me and that this felt sense differs for those who have been educated solely within the scientific disciplines. My way of working and philosophical view of research in the social sciences was profoundly and unalterably shaped by more than 20 years in the arts and humanities in my early academic and professional work. Early influences on my understanding of the human experience include the works of great acting teachers like Uta Hagen and Sanford Meisner and the dramatic works of artists as varied as Caryl Churchill, Samuel Beckett, and Anna Deveare Smith. I was trained as an actress for two decades and was taught to get inside of the life of a character. Body, psyche, and prior knowledge were brought with me into character development and, ultimately, into performances. The boundaries between self and other are thin when playing a role, most especially when performing on the stage. An actor's performance is an interpretation of a character as perceived by a playwright. Both the performer and the author have specific ideas of who the character will be when brought to life; and each performer brings her *self* to the performance. Thus, there is no mandate for objectivity in the arts. The subject is vital to the success of the very performance itself. The lessons I have learned about human engagement, the importance of storytelling, and the way in which voice is profoundly different as a spoken tone or a written word all come from my early life in the theater. There is expressive and beautiful work being developed related to the utilization of performativity in qualitative research, including the work of Kip Jones, who is also featured in this text.

While the theater shaped my relational style and informed my understanding of the human psyche most profoundly, my education in the humanities as an undergraduate and early graduate student has shaped the philosophical and practical lenses with which I practice the craft of qualitative research. A term such as *craft* may seem demeaning or unscientific to many in the fields of social science, and notably so in my own discipline of psychology. However, I bring from the discipline of acting a long legacy of using the term *craft* to describe the ongoing refinement of one's artistic expression. I also argue for the utility of the term in the context of being a researcher, because the term *craft* suggests a practice involving both skill and art to produce something utilitarian and potentially beautiful. In the humanities, an appreciation of the beauty and power of the written word is inherent to many disciplines, including literary analysis, philosophy, and cultural studies; three disciplines that greatly influenced much of my education and are core tools in my current craft as researcher.

My early adulthood was spent immersed in art and literature, first as an undergraduate theater major who experienced a radicalizing feminist awakening at age nineteen, then as a graduate student studying the works of Gerda Lerner, Gloria Anzaldua, and Judith Butler. I witnessed the rise of the third wave of feminism in the early 1990s. Feminist voices were underscoring the ways that political structures colonized, oppressed, and constricted the lives of women across the globe. Postmodernism was driving the scholarship of many departments in the humanities, and the decentering and destabilizing of personal, sexual, and gender identities were at the fore of the rising tide of queer theory. The fluidity of the self that I had experienced in moving from character to character in performance was now also real and available in my daily life, both in academe and on the streets of New York City, where I lived at the time. My malleable self now had political implications.

The radical and provocative concepts that I had learned in the classroom were then taken to the streets. I woke up to a realization that I, as a woman, experienced governmental circumscription of my rights, most notably relating to reproductive freedoms. In April 1992, at age 21, I stood in Washington, DC, on the Mall with hundreds of thousands of other women, raising our voices in protest. It was my first experience of this kind and afforded me keen awareness of the power of the subjective voice. An image stands out to me so starkly even to this day: In a park near the Mall, where women were gathering to eat lunch and rest before the march, a jungle gym had been covered in wire hangers. It was a grim reminder of the women who had died without appropriate access to care. This public art gave voice to those who were gone and could not speak for themselves. But even more profound were the stories of the women who were there. Earlier that morning, a large coalition from New York University got on a bus and rode to Washington for the march. Some of us knew each other, but most did not. On the bus, the hum of voices slowly began to rise and drown out the whir of the engine and tires. The air became thick with low whispers, punctuated accents, and some tears. Strangers telling strangers tales of times when friends died in alleyways; their own personal stories of making terribly difficult decisions as scared, pregnant teenagers. The shared narrative of this group of women was an instantaneous thematic analysis in real time. The main themes were keeping women safe, shared secrets and shame, social justice, and the power of the collective. Now, exactly 20 years later, I have a student doing qualitative research on stories very similar to the ones that I heard on that bus. Embodied memories I have of that day serve as reminders of the very real high-stakes human experiences that are often at the core of qualitative research endeavors. The postmodern and cultural perspectives afforded me via my humanities educational upbringing serve me well in consistently reminding me that actual people and crucial matters in their lives are at the heart of qualitative data collection. Thus, in my opinion, great care must be taken in engaging with participants and in the analysis and interpretation of their personal narratives.

Feminist research methodologists and psychotherapists have informed the perspective expressed directly above. Shulamit Reinharz and Jennifer Brayton are among the feminist researchers who underscore the political nature of feminist research. While Brayton has argued that there is no one definition that constitutes feminist research as a whole, there are central tenets that are common within the school of thought. The relationship between the researcher and the research participants has been reconsidered. Questioning the naturalness of an assumed hierarchical power dynamic between the researcher and research participants, a feminist researcher takes the approach that she is not the expert in the interview setting; the participant is the expert of her lived experience. An additional tenet of feminist research is that the outcomes of feminist research promote social change and social justice.

In similar sentiment, feminist psychotherapists such as Laura S. Brown and Jean Baker Miller have written extensively on the critical nature of the therapeutic relationship and the healing nature of relationality. Ongoing dialogue in the feminist psychotherapeutic community includes the dismantling of the expert status of the therapist and a nonhierarchical quality to the therapeutic relationship. In addition, questions related to the purpose, appropriateness, and timing of self-disclosure are constant points of debate. While other schools of psychology are founded upon a belief that that self-disclosure is problematic and disruptive to the therapeutic alliance, feminist psychologists actually use self-disclosure as an intervention technique. Even the fact of labeling one's self as a feminist therapist is an act of self-disclosure in that it indicates a political stance related to social justice based upon gender. In addition, self-disclosure may model an ability to claim one's self for the client. In other words, by naming her own experience, when appropriate, a feminist therapist may create a greater therapeutic alliance while also demonstrating an act of self-determination for her client.

In my own doctoral research, which was grounded in postmodern, feminist, and social constructionist philosophies, I experienced a tension in my own dance around relationship with the participants who gave of their time and energy. Having studied clinical psychology and research ethics for years, the ongoing debate about right relationship with research participants was of keen interest to me. The protection and confidentiality of participants is of paramount importance in any research endeavor. A history of unethical behaviors in research are well documented, and even in seemingly benign research, a participant may be triggered in the act of recollection about past or current lived experience. However, as noted above, feminist research methodologists argue that equality, respect, and relatedness are key elements for conducting successful research. Thus, taking a stance on the issues of self-disclosure and the reflexivity, positionality, and subjectivity of the researcher became an important development in my research life.

My dissertation work explored the lived experience of *intentional childlessness*, or the active and lifelong choice to never have a child. As a researcher, I had insider status in the group in that I had recently come to the realization that I did not want to either bear or mother children. We, 31 participants and me, shared a profound link to a decision that a minority of women make in the United States as well as worldwide. I interviewed each woman individually, and it was fascinating to note how many claimed they had never had an opportunity to speak openly about their choice. In their daily lives, if asked at all about their decision, the women reported that they were faced with scrutiny and incredulousness. Many times, the women reported that they were repeatedly reminded that meeting the right man would most certainly result in a change of mind and the production of a child. I had experienced such affronts in my own life as well; and it never ceased to shock me, just as it consistently shocked the participants in my research. In short, their narratives were disbelieved and discredited on an ongoing basis by friends, family, and the cultures in which they lived. My self-disclosure as an insider to their experience created trust in the interview container that I believe enriched the data I was able to gather.

As I conducted this work, I was repeatedly struck by realizations that the only way to truly know the experience of repeatedly having to justify an incredibly private choice was to be in conversation with these women. To learn each individual narrative and have each individual permit me to be in relationship with her and her version of the common story shared by all of us. However, some of the most profound moments of relationship came after the fact of the interview. I developed a process in which I used voice-recognition software (VRS) to transcribe the digitally recorded interviews into written text; a process

I described as *embodied transcription* (ET). The catch with ET is that the researcher, or the individual transcribing the material, must speak the words of the participant in order to capture the data, since VRS only works with one voice at a time. I have suggested elsewhere that the process is akin to simultaneous translation. But the difference is that the translation is not taking place in real time, and thus there is opportunity for the researcher to take time for reflection and noticing of felt senses and intuition. As the field of qualitative research matures and develops, such body-based ways of knowing and the intricate way that the researcher's subjectivity influences the interpretation of data are increasingly acknowledged as valid and, in fact, vital to the research process. Thus, my experience as a researcher circles, once again, back to my training in the arts and humanities.

Within the humanities, there is a long legacy and inherent acceptance of the utility of self-exploration and using the self as the subject of narrative. It is through literary forms such as the roman à clef, philosophical treatises, and autobiography that meaning and understanding are created, both for the author and for the reader. The memoir is a classic form of self-exploration that has at its core not the rigid exposition of the facts of a life but an impressionistic account of the meaning of a life and, by proximity, the lives of others. While maintaining integrity with the facts that a participant shares with the researcher is a benchmark of quality and credibility in qualitative research, nonetheless, the meaning of the expression of those facts is of equal value. In the early days of psychology in the United States, the philosopher psychologist William James argued for radical empiricism, a stance promoting a belief that our interpretation and meaning-making of observed phenomena are of equal value to the objective description of the observation itself. The heart of qualitative research holds these very concepts as central: Narrative, meaning making, and interpretation are human capacities and worthy of equal consideration in any study of the human experience. James paved the way for qualitative research in the social sciences by taking this stance. A need for quantifiable facts (which is, undeniably, a crucial element in the science of psychology) and valuation of the meaning individuals place on their own psychological experience need not be mutually exclusive. My own experience has been that as a qualitative researcher, then, I am both the expositor of fact *and* the interpreter of meaning.

My life in the arts and humanities afforded me a novel view during my education in qualitative research. Because of my background, I felt that the methodology, methods, and epistemologies of qualitative research came immediately and intuitively to me. As noted earlier, there was a naturalness to data analysis that I was not seeing reflected in many of my fellow graduate students' experiences, most notably for those who had come out of undergraduate education in the hard sciences. Decades spent engaged in the hermeneutics of social, political, and creative texts sharpened my ability to construct and also interpret qualitative data. I found the tying together of the constituent parts of the codes, categories, and themes an inverse process to the deconstruction of already-written narratives I had encountered in my prior education. Nonetheless, both processes were in the service of making meaning of human lived experience. The core of my work as a qualitative researcher is thus informed by the texts and ideas I discovered in the humanities: a love of words, a commitment to social justice, and profound respect for the infinite expressions of human experience.

I have followed Kip's work for some time. When I learned of his film, Rufus Stone, *a film about positioning, aging, and gay life in rural England and Wales, I thought it the perfect culminating piece to conclude this section on innovations in the field.*

Turning Research Into Film: Trevor Hearing Speaks With Kip Jones About the Process of Creating the Short, Research-Based Film, *Rufus Stone*

by Kip Jones, With Trevor Hearing

Introduction

Kip Jones is a reader in Qualitative Research and Performative Social Science at Bournemouth University in the UK. He has spent more than ten years developing the use of tools from the arts and humanities to research and/or disseminate social science knowledge or a performative social science. What *performative* refers and relates to is the communicative powers of research and the natural involvement of an "audience," whether that be a group of peers or a group of students, a physical audience, a cyber-audience, or even a solitary reader of a journal or a book. This is good news not only for participants in research studies, who can often be involved in producing subsequent performative outputs, but also for the wider community to whom our findings should be directed.

Trevor Hearing leads television and film production studies at Bournemouth's Media School and has years of experience working in the television industry as a documentary filmmaker. His recently completed PhD examined the possibilities of using media as research tools.

Kip and Trevor have worked on many joint projects, including documenting the filming of *Rufus Stone* and producing a trailer for it.

Background

The short, professionally made film, *Rufus Stone,* is the key output of the three-year "Gay and Pleasant Land?" research project led by Bournemouth University academic, Dr. Kip Jones. This project about positioning, aging, and gay life in rural South West England and Wales was a work package in the UK-wide New Dynamics of Ageing Project, "Grey and Pleasant Land?: An Interdisciplinary Exploration of the Connectivity of Older People in Rural Civic Society." The projects were funded by Research Councils UK. The film was produced by Parkville Pictures, London.

The stories that form the foundation of the script for *Rufus Stone* are entirely based upon research undertaken by Jones and his team from the University's School of Health and Social Care with the assistance of a citizens' advisory committee. The film's "fictional" story was created over time using composite characters and situations, all uncovered in the "Gay and Pleasant Land? Research Project" through in-depth biographic life story interviews, focus groups, and actual site visits to the rural locations where older gay or lesbian citizens were living.

Josh Appignanesi, who also directed the feature film, *The Infidel,* written by David Baddeil, directed *Rufus Stone*. Appignanesi, who also wrote the final script, outlines the plot of *Rufus Stone*:

> The story dramatises the old and continued prejudices of village life from three main perspectives. Chiefly, it is the story of Rufus, an 'out' older gay man who was exiled from the village as a youth and reluctantly returns from London to sell his dead parents' cottage, where he is forced to confront the faces of his estranged past. Of these, Abigail is the tattletale who "outed" Rufus 50 years ago when he spurned her interest. She has become a lonely deluded lush. Flip, the boy Rufus adored, has also stayed in the village: a life wasted in celibacy (occasionally interrupted by anonymous sexual encounters) and denial. [He] is looking after his elderly mother. But Rufus too isn't whole, saddled with an inability to return or forgive.

Jones speaks in his role as executive producer of the film: "Our hope is that the film will dispel many of the myths surrounding aging, being gay and life in British rural settings."

Interview

Trevor: So where did all of this begin, Kip, this turning research into film?

Kip: From the very beginning, from the inception of the idea of a professionally made film to represent in-depth research. The first thing that motivated me is that a lot of research ends up on the shelf—or in journals on the shelf—[so] not many people read it, and it kind of dies a slow death there. In order to have impact in the larger world, I thought it was necessary to move into a field where you could produce something that would be able to be diffused amongst a wider population. So, when I saw a film that Josh (Appignanesi, director of *Rufus Stone*) had done on dementia (*Ex Memoria,* 2006), I thought, "Ah! This is getting close to the way I'd like to work." So that's where we started from, right there—entering into an unknown world, really, and seeing if it would work.

Trevor: And you were using this new approach, as you say, to get into an unknown world, telling a truth that was otherwise hidden by the mythology of the English countryside?

Kip: In terms of the study itself, I knew pretty early on from my own experiences of interfacing with some groups of older people in organisations that particularly represented rural England that there was resistance to our study. I came to realize that there was a great deal of prejudice and a lot of misunderstanding of what being gay or lesbian was even about—an assumption that even talking about being gay or lesbian meant that you were talking about sex. There were a lot of, as you say, myths that needed to be dispelled and a lot of consciousness raising that needed to go on.

Trevor: The film is a culmination of a much deeper level of research, isn't it? Do you think, in a way, that the film distracts from the depth of the research that was done beforehand?

Kip: I'm fond of saying that if performative social science is really working well, the areas where we've cobbled together in-depth research and art—or filmmaking, in this case—should be seamless, that there truly is a fusion of two disparate fields, science and art, really. What I'm hoping is that the audience will almost forget about an academic approach to the material and be reached on what I consider a deeper emotional level. That's not to say that the research wasn't very, very in-depth and well-constructed. Certainly, any project that takes place over three years is almost a gift these days, in terms of an opportunity to carry out substantial research. To be able to do in-depth interviews and follow-up interpretation by citizen panels, then to conduct focus groups and to use theatrical interpretation of some of the data—all this wealth of data added to the richness of the story that we finally were able to present to the filmmaker.

For example, the following text is an exemplar of the type of creative writing using the fictional interspersed with the autobiographical that preceded the development of the film's treatment and the subsequent script:

> The lapping movement of the water's surface with its shiny viscosity created by the light prompt me to recall those moments. I remember more clearly then, what those flashes of innocent intimacy were like.
>
> Memory is not text, not even remembered action, really. The past is re-created by recollections of an atmosphere, a sound, a temperature. Remembering the arrangement of the furniture often reveals more to me about a moment than the people sitting on it. So is the nature of key moments in our story of young Rufus and Flip.
>
> Images such as dappled sunlight are not a routine physical reality. They are as much a precise instance in the life course as a particular sixteenth birthday. Our first experience of mottled sunlight is a rite of passage, a singularly unique occurrence in our young lives.
>
> Roll the film. Capture it.

Perhaps if I explain a bit here: As we observe throughout life, certain cultural images become private and iconic. They twist and turn and eventually morph in various ways to be included as our own graphic memories. (I shall always remember Mary Gergen's recounting of the Midwest grain storage towers from her childhood in my interview with her [http://www.qualitative-research.net/index.php/fqs/article/viewArticle/554]). These images are truly ethnographic. These visual memories become imbued with both intense cultural and personal meaning.

Trevor: Was it a risk, making the film?

Kip: I think so! It was a risk in the sense that it was doing something that hadn't been done at this level before. There certainly have been films made involving social science projects, and they tend to be a film of a theatrical production put on by participants in a project. No one has gone to the next stage, which is, in a sense, fictionalising the research—and that's what we've done here. By using composite characters, we've created a fiction in the end. They're still true to the research, and even lines that they say in the dialogue often are verbatim lines that people said in the interviews. The story, however, is fictional—it didn't really happen exactly as it is told in the film to any one person. Using fiction, we were able to enhance not only the interpretive utility of the research but also the entertainment value, and by *entertainment value,* I mean that in the strictest terms of entertainment as something that makes people really think and makes them think at a very deep level.

Trevor: In terms of the premise behind your film, is it promoting the role of the artist as researcher?

Kip: I like to say, "Who best to translate the excitement of discovery to an audience but an artist? How better to take sometimes dry and tedious data and transform it into story and action?" This is the premise behind our performative efforts.

Trevor: I like the idea that you've mentioned about telling "your story"—that becoming a moment for you. It is very much embodying you as a researcher as well.

Kip: One of the things that I have been exploring in the past five years is autoethnography, which is using your own story to research or to enrich a certain area of concern or interest in an investigation. Again, I return to my example of the autoethnographic/fictional writing upon which the final script was built:

Close your eyes and recollect this patterned lightness on the patchwork English country landscape and you will see young Flip—dark, tan, laughing—happy to be with you. There has been no other instance in your life like it. You wish that this moment will go on forever, but, even in your youth, you know it will not be so. You have been taught this in songs, and they are sad ones.

Your soul has always been an old man's; your cautious, fearful, doubting heart. We are forged as we will be early in life and spend the rest of it unraveling that fact. The child somehow knows that as a man, you will seek to re-create this moment over and over again, and so you prepare yourself for such a journey, even in your youth. Play the Mahler 5th. You understand it intimately.

You and Flip walk over hills towards a wood. This is not a memorised landscape, however. It is a recollection of a three-dimensional physicality consisting of the soil under foot, the sound of the swish of tall grass, and the crunchiness of pebbles mixed with earth. The intensity of the English sky's summer blueness creates a light pressure against your skin. The warm country air is more uncontaminated than any you will ever breathe again. His arm around your neck as you walk is the last uncorrupted act of commitment that you will ever experience. This is the purest state of coupling.

You are in the stream at a point where the water, the great purifier, creates a deep pool. The chilly water laps against your body, as you will lap against his. The surface of the water makes a fluid partition that allows grazing against his body beneath it seem easier, less obvious, but still dangerous. The pretence is played out above the surface, the risk and the release beneath. If he ever objected ... but he never did. The physicality of your relationship remains in its purest state.

You can smell him on his shirt that you have innocently taken home with you. That night in your single bed under the farmhouse's eaves you lay next to this piece of worn cotton clothing and dream of his unpolluted perfect being. The shininess of his young dark skin, his naturally sun-licked hair, his warm arm around your neck, his smile's innocence, laughing, always laughing.

I have realized, somewhat late in life, that the "love-sick" feeling in the pit of our stomachs that we sometimes experience remains the same, whether seventeen or seventy. The only difference now is that I have the visual reference points with which to tell that story again.

I tend to see autoethnography when it's working best as using myself as a conduit to other people and other people's stories and events in their lives. This became quite apparent to me when I was writing the treatment for the film. We knew what the story was, and we knew what the characters were doing, but we needed detail. I realized that I had to rely on my own experience as well.

For instance, I was starting to write about Rufus and his grandfather, and the easiest way for me to do that was, in a sense, to embody the character of Rufus by recalling my own grandfather. My memory at that very moment of writing was sitting on my grandfather's lap and his cheap grandfather clock ticking away in the background. So I wove that into the treatment. In the end, the clock is a very important piece of the story and symbol, representing time passing, our memories of the past, and, in the end, what happens to the clock in the film is very powerful. This was a place whereby reaching into my own story and embodying the character, I was able to really enrich the story of the other person.

Rufus reconsiders the countryside of his youth as he drives.

It is a memory of a five-year-old boy sitting on his grandfather's lap. Granddad's hand, rough and worn from working the land, his thumbnail somehow permanently split, reaches into the pocket of his tattered woolen trousers and magically produces a cellophane-wrapped peppermint sweet for the boy. The tall case clock ticks in the background, the same clock that ended up in Rufus's parents' farmhouse hallway. The sound of this clock has always provided him with comfort in times of crisis. It is recollections of his grandfather that most warmly represent the countryside to Rufus.

Figure 7.3 Cinematographer Annika Summerson behind camera with crew shooting scene with Harry Kershaw (center), who plays young Rufus Stone.

SOURCE: Kip Jones

■ Jumping Outside Your Comfort Zone—Painting 101

Now, it is time to get practical. How do you actually develop a QR proposal? What should you focus on? What are potential pitfalls? Can you really do this? Please use the example below as an illustration. Remember, there is no one way to do QR. Thinking outside the box as our writers and researchers did should help you as you weave together a proposal.

I had been thinking quite a bit about how hard it is to do something that is new to you. Of course, thinking about it is one thing, but doing it is something else. So I decided to take a course in painting. I had looked at thousands of paintings over the years and felt I knew something about painting. I have some artists in my own family. But I had never taken a painting class. Imagine how I felt when I entered the class of a dozen or so other students. As I looked around, I saw that they all had their brushes, tubes of paint, and related materials. Turns out, I had purchased all the wrong things—the wrong type of paint, wrong brushes, not a real canvas. But I was determined to figure out how to learn something new. So I trudged on. Each week, we learned a new skill or concept. Our excellent instructor, Erik (John Erik Swanson, who teaches painting at the Corcoran College of Art and Design in Washington, DC), talked about a specific idea and then demonstrated it. We were left on our own to practice. And Erik came around and made comments and suggestions. How humbling and exhilarating at the same time. Now that my last class is about to happen, I feel that I have just begun to touch the surface. I need lots more practice. But I did make several paintings. I did try something new without knowing quite how to do it. I did find some impediments along the way, but I

Figure 7.4 Still Life 1, My First Painting Ever

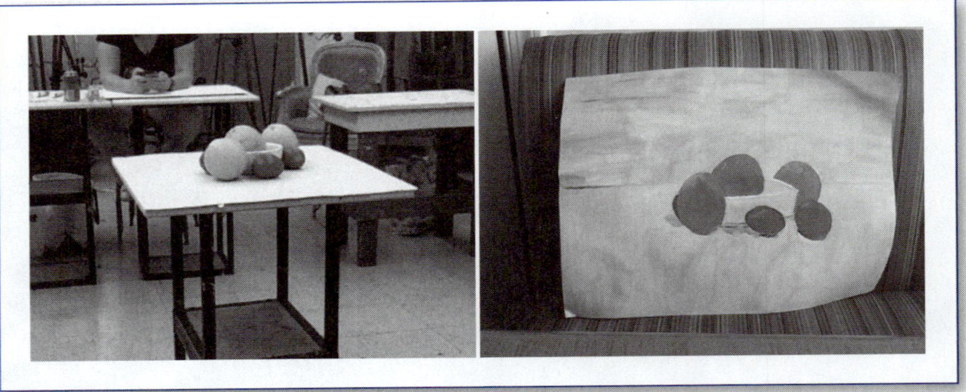

Figure 7.5 Still Life 2, Deconstructed

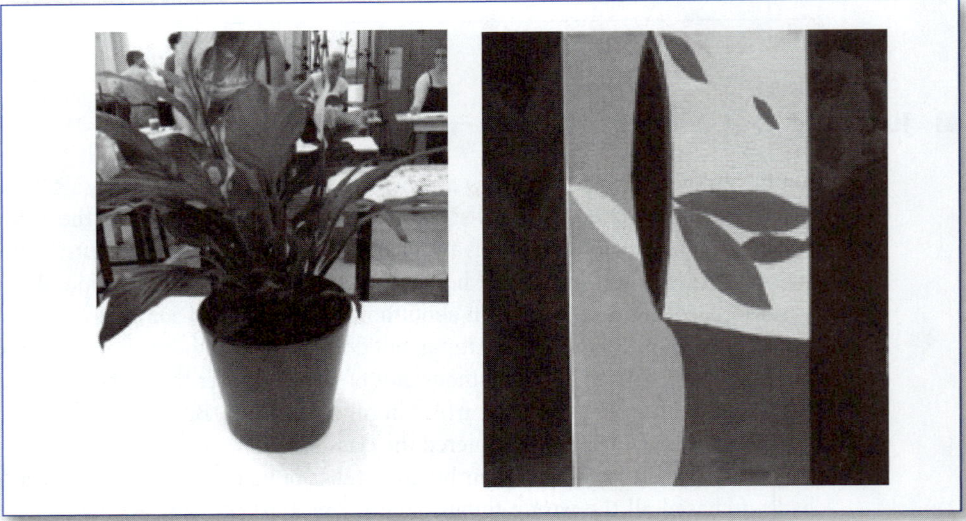

persevered. Take a look at some of my work—from first to last. So too with QR. You can talk about it and read about it, but doing it is something else.

I hope you make the same observations about my paintings that I have. In the first pair (Figure 7.4), I tried to accurately represent what I saw in front of me. I did this because I thought that was what I was supposed to do. In the second pair (Figure 7.5), I had been urged to branch out into something new. I tried deconstructing the flowerpot and making it more abstract. I believe both attempts are representations as seen through my lens. One is not better than the other. They are just different. Now, try to apply these ideas to developing a QR study.

Developing a Qualitative Research Proposal

By using spokes of a wheel, I identify elements included in a research proposal. Although there is no particular order you have to follow—recall that QR is dynamic and inductive—in my illustration, I begin with the purpose.

Purpose

More than any innovation in recent years, the Internet has captured the minds and hearts of people worldwide. Through the power of the Internet and Facebook, we witnessed the Arab uprisings. We saw the new president of North Korea being inaugurated. We learned about media personalities, sports heroes, and illegal or improper Wall Street trading. News is

Figure 7.6 Developing a Qualitative Research Proposal

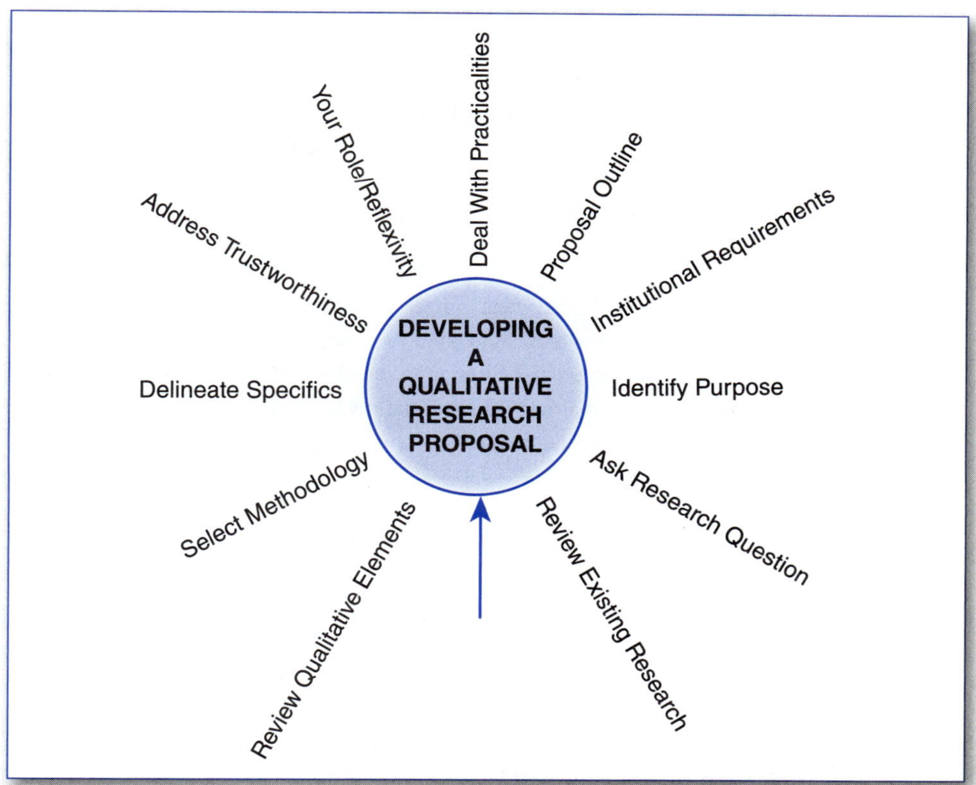

instantaneous. People participate online in groups of all types—user groups, LISTSERVs, chat rooms, and on Facebook. Some groups are open to all; others require permission to join. Some are formed for a brief time; others are lasting. I believe we have just begun to touch the surface of ways we can use the Internet and social media in QR: collecting data, identifying participants, studying subcultures, observing groups, analyzing data, creating and retelling stories, and ways I haven't thought of.

Beneito-Montagut (2011) reminded us that "it is a growing concern of ethnography to incorporate the Internet and social information and communication technologies (SICT) into its realm of research and methodology to achieve a more up-to-date understanding of current social life" (p. 716–717). Her research centered on online communication and how ethnography could be applied to online relationships. Using her research ideas, I find myself drawn to this type of study.

> *My reflections*: This problem is too big. What should I look at? How can I narrow it down? How can I make this manageable? Is this legitimate to study? Will my committee support me? So I decide to narrow down my questions. I know that QR is iterative, so I am not discouraged.

My purpose in this study is to identify a way I can tap into existing social media networks to investigate a particular subculture of users and study them. As baby boomers enter the retirement phase, I think they might be the perfect ones to study. They face many challenges—children in college, aging parents, empty nests, financial hardships, health issues, and so on. These are all external surface questions. Perhaps I can get at some inner, underlying issues as well: feelings of loneliness, self-worth questions (Is this all there is?), family dynamics, and so on. I think this would be a great area to explore.

> *My reflections*: This already feels better. At least I have narrowed down the focus. But it still seems too unwieldy. And I know I will face some challenges. How do I find these baby boomers online? They must be there. Where should I turn? And what do we know about them already? I see what my next steps are. I think it is time to make a first pass at a research question.

Research Question and Conceptual Framework

What are central issues faced by baby boomers? How are these manifested in their online interactions with others?

Adult development issues have been explored by Abraham Maslow and others. Murray Bowen looked at intergenerational issues. What constitutes a baby boomer today? Growing up in such a different culture, I suspect, affects them differently than parent and grandparent generations. Online communities might offer opportunities for interactions and problem solving not available in the past.

> *My reflections*: I hope I am on the right track here. I know I need to dig into the literature, but I don't want to close myself off to other ideas. I need to be cognizant of learning what is out there, on the one hand, and being willing to look for other things. I can see what my next steps are.

Start My Review

Conduct a review of literature using *baby boomers* as a key term. You also might want to include social media, online networks, user groups, and other relevant resources as they emerge. Use existing databases and search engines. Focus on journals, but you may need to look at classic work about adult development. Focus on the last five years. Also, look at dissertations. You will also need to do some basic searching. First, look for a definition: A *baby boomer* was born during the post-World War II baby boom between 1946 and 1964. Sometimes the term is used in a cultural context: Baby boomers grew up at time of dramatic social change. They control over 80% of financial assets. Baby boomers started retiring in 2007 and 2008.

> *My reflections*: I suspect there is so much out there, I will never get done. I am not yet sure what is critical to look at. Should I look only at studies that use qualitative methods? I think I should look at all types. After all, I am interested in baby boomers. But perhaps a way to narrow things down is to look at the joint intersection of baby boomers and social media. Now, I am thinking maybe I want to go in an entirely different direction with my research question. Maybe I should simplify and look at how baby boomers use social media. I need to talk to my adviser here.

Review Qualitative Research Elements

I remind myself of some critical elements of QR practice. It is *inductive,* moving from the concrete to the abstract. So I need to plan to get into the field (whatever that is) to collect my data and study my group. It is *iterative,* not linear. So my planning process does not necessarily move in a straight line. I am free to modify and change as I think and rethink my question and how I will try to answer it. And my purpose must stay in the forefront as well. There is *no one way* to do QR. I remind myself that I am free to explore alternative ways of doing things. It exists in a *natural setting.* This piece is critical for me, since I want to study online groups. I review other aspects of what I know so far about QR.

> *My reflections*: Positive aspects for me include the opportunity to explore something new, exciting, and challenging. Negative aspects for me include questions—Can I really do this? Will I know how to do this? Will I make a mistake? Why aren't there any clear-cut rules? Will I ever graduate and get on with my life?—just the way I felt in my painting class. Don't let it get you down.

Select a Qualitative Research Approach

I review the research approaches I just talked about in Chapters 5 and 6. Two seem to come to mind. If I focus on the experiences of this group of people, I think I want to use phenomenology—a study of lived experiences. However, if I want to study communities of baby boomers on the Internet using social media, maybe I want to do some type of ethnography—a study of culture.

> *My reflections*: I need to nail this down before I actually write a proposal. I am leaning toward ethnography, autoethnography, or online ethnography. As part of the iterative nature of QR, I know I need to go back and refine my original research question. Again, I think I am too ambitious for a first-time study. Maybe I need to carve out just one small niche.

Explain Elements of Approach

Whichever research approach I use, I will need to figure out how to find online groups of baby boomers. The first step is to find them. This might prove easy or impossible or somewhere in between. But I have some ideas to start. If I find them, I need to figure out the following: (a) gaining access, (b) getting permission to capture words and visuals, (c) figuring out what to capture in terms of their interactions, (d) protecting confidentiality, (e) setting parameters on how long I observe, how often, and so on. I also need to decide if I am going to interview some of them separately or in focus groups. How many, how often, on what topic will all be connected to my research question. I know it is not too early to think about what I will do with the data once I get it. With available technology, I hope I can capture interactions via live streaming or something similar. I know others who use a technology that does this. I also want to capture visual images. Do I need more than one group? And how many people should be in the group? My plan is to identify a single group with a nucleus of people to study. I will have a backup group in case something happens with the group I select. I also need to address data analysis; at this point, I anticipate doing some kind of coding looking for themes. I may also need to use qualitative software.

> *My reflections*: I need to make sure I know the key elements of each of these research approaches so I know what I will have to do when I get started. I think a study of the lived experiences might prove easier to accomplish. But should I pick that because it is easier? What will my study add to what we know about baby boomers? If I use that, then all I am really doing with social media is identifying a group of people to study. Does that take me away from my purpose? As I think this through, I lean more toward ethnography. I have just discovered I need to expand my literature review to study ethnography online. Annette Markham has done some interesting things, so I will start with her work. If I can pull this off, I will be so happy. Am I an outsider looking in? Will that be a

problem? I also need to think about permissions. Some members of the group might not be so happy, while others might welcome me. What do I do about that? I also know that I need to find out about software. I have read about NVivo and think I can explore that more fully by using their website (http://www.qsrinternational.com).

Trustworthiness

Participants—how many do I use? How do I pick them? I begin to think about how many people (or how many groups) I should include in my study. How do I answer this question? I know that it depends in part on the research approach I choose. I remind myself that if I am using grounded theory, I need to get sufficient participants until I have reached a saturation point. But since I am thinking about either phenomenology or ethnography, I turn my attention to what is in the literature. I find that there are no specific guidelines. I also think about how I select my participants. I know that I need to find an online group (or groups) to study. Since I will not be using my research to test hypotheses or theory, I believe I am okay on this front.

Triangulation—I have read about this idea. It comes from the concept of locating submarines using three data points. In research, I think it has at least two meanings. One is the idea of using different sources of data to get at the same thing. This would mean using interviews, observations, and visual diaries, for example. It also seems to mean using multiple raters to look at the data and see if they reach the same conclusions. This is also called *inter-rater reliability* or *member checking*. But I remind myself that I am doing a qualitative study, and thus it is the researcher who is the primary source of data; it is through his or her lens that all flows. So I don't think I need to pay attention to this.

Thick description—I recall that ethnography asks for many details. Therefore I might need to expand the time I spend observing my group. I need to incorporate visuals to the extent that I do not violate any privacy issues.

Four parallels to QN that come from Lincoln and Guba's 1985 work seem out-of-date to me. They are *credibility* (internal validity), *transferability* (external validity), *dependability* (reliability), and *confirmability* (objectivity). I decide that I should become familiar with these in case I am asked about them. They keep coming up in the literature, but I know there are some newer ideas out there.

Bias and subjectivity—I also read about this topic. But since I accept the assumption that I, the researcher, will design and conduct all aspects of the study, I need to reframe the idea. I do not want to strive for objectivity, because that is a principle associated with a different kind of research.

My reflections: This area seems confusing to me. One school of thought is that I should strive to make my study conform to certain basic principles that have evolved from QN. There are several areas I am concerned about. Another viewpoint is that QR is fundamentally different from QN. As such, trying to develop parallel criteria is a waste of time. I think perhaps I need to read more about this. I know I can look at Chapter 14 in this text.

Researcher Role

My role will influence everything I do. I begin my reflexive journal on my computer by writing down what I know about baby boomers, naming any baby boomers I know, and so on. I am aware of how the media influence me in my thinking about this group.

> *My reflections*: I need to read more about reflexivity. I need to reread Chapter 2 in this text. Do I have the skills to pull this off? What kind of help can I get with some of the technological aspects of the study?

Practicalities

I address three immediate practicalities: feasibility, time, and cost. But I take them in the reverse order. With accessibility to many networks, I believe I can accomplish a study with little or no cost for studying groups, conducting interviews, and doing an analysis. If I decide to create a visual presentation of results, I might have some small costs. Next, I address time. I will set a defined time to study the group I identify. Once I do some preliminary observations of the group, I will be able to know how much time I need to spend. The biggest problem I face is feasibility. I have to believe there is a suitable group out there, but I haven't begun to look yet. I will need to set some parameters of what constitutes a suitable group.

> *My reflections*: I definitely need to read more about doing online research. I wonder what other things I haven't thought about. I look again at Janet Salmons's book, *Online Interviews in Real Time* (2009).

Qualitative Research Proposal Outline

My proposal will have three parts. In Part 1, I intend to include information about the study—some background, the purpose, the research question(s), and a conceptual model. In Part 2, I will include a brief review of the literature related to baby boomers, online groups, and QR issues. In Part 3, I will include information about how the study will be done. After identifying my research approach, I will discuss how I select the setting and participants and how I gather data (observation, online streaming, interviews with participants, video or stills of some discussions). A preliminary plan to analyze the data will be proposed. I anticipate using a **generic approach to coding** chunks of group discussions as well as interview data. I also intend to include information about the research approach I chose (online ethnography, autoethnography, or phenomenology). I plan to discuss the role of the researcher as well as include some general information about QR. Ethical considerations for participants will be considered. I plan to produce a video for YouTube or Flickr as a final product. I will discuss what influenced me to do this and what is known about this type of research. I plan to reference Kip Jones and Johnny Saldaña, who have done work in this area. With regard to written information, I propose that I will write either a script or ethnographic description. My literature review will be interspersed throughout the proposal rather than appearing at the beginning of the section.

> *My reflections*: I wonder if I am going out on a limb and my department will not be disposed to approve a dissertation like this. I know I will need to inquire and discuss further with my adviser and committee members. I recognize that I might also have to write something to support what my plan is for a visual presentation. Since I am not concerned with validity, I omitted this from my presentation. Validity is a concept related to QN. I decide to review some QR proposals I find online.

Institutional Requirements

I review the requirements for research at my institution. I prepare a research proposal, spelling out as many details as possible. I submit an Institutional Review Board (IRB) form for approval.

> *My reflections*: I have read so many horror stories about how review boards either lack understanding or are negative toward QR. I know one problem is that interviews often lack a specific protocol, and review boards often want to look at a specific questionnaire or set of questions. I try to do my homework. I try to get my adviser and committee members on my side, but I am somewhat apprehensive. I need to determine if my institution will support using visual presentations as part of a dissertation.

Qualitative Research Proposal Elements

For those of you who are new to the field, a typical research proposal often has several parts. Part 1 includes why a study is proposed. Purpose, research questions, and a theoretical framework are often included. Limitations of the study are discussed. A brief background into the issues is normally included. Some include a detailed review of the literature, while others will put a review in a separate section. Heath (1997) advised beginning with something interesting, such as a quote or story. Caulley (2013) bemoans poor writing in QR. His most recent writing explorations are described in his blog. He suggested that the first paragraph is critical because it grabs the reader. Part 2 spells out how the study will be done. Details about research design, selection of sample, how data are collected, and how data are analyzed will be described. Issues related to reliability and validity are addressed. A section on IRB procedures may also be required. Part 3 describes the importance of protecting the human subjects.

1. *Introduction and research problem.* You can think of this first section as addressing such questions as what the issues are, what you hope to focus on, and why it is of value. Your purpose is to convey to the audience the topic of your research, why it is important, and how it fits into our larger understanding of the issues. Headings might include Introduction, Central Research Question, Related Literature, Conceptual Framework, and Potential Significance of your research. I do not think it is important to conduct an extensive review of the related literature; however, introducing key ideas is important. In a sense, this first section will be very similar to a traditional research proposal.

2. *Methodology of the study.* In the second section, you address such issues as the research approach you plan to take, participants, the data you anticipate getting and how you plan to collect it, and the manner in which you anticipate dealing with your data. Headings might include Research Approach, Ways to Collect Data, and Ways to Analyze Data. You will also address issues of the role of the researcher and how to judge value. While the headings for this section are similar to what you might find in a traditional proposal, much of the content will be vastly different.

3. *Protection of human subjects.* You will most likely have to complete an IRB form and submit it to your institution. You should inquire about the process from your advisor. Guidance can also be obtained by reviewing information provided by other universities. Look at the University of Texas at Austin (n.d.) pages on human subjects research or the one provided by Stanford University (n.d.).

QR proposals may follow this general outline but often include other subtopics. Take a look at a proposal presented by Karen Black (2012), MD for a family medicine program. These are the main topics:

- Introduction and definitions—She addresses three important issues: what can be known (*ontology*), what is the relationship between the researcher and what can be known (*epistemology*), and what are the ways to gain knowledge (*methodology*).

- Theoretical and conceptual background—These are informed by knowledge of various theories, such as organizational behavior, learning theory, or critical social theory. The methodology of QR refers to assumptions that you make about QR. The method (I call it *research approach*) refers to how you will collect and analyze data.

- Types of questions—For Black, types of questions include the *what* and *why* questions, not *how many*. I like her examples: "What are the dynamics of team members? Why is there brand loyalty to antibiotics? How does the learner gain confidence?" (p. 8). Questions do not look at cause and effect or differences between groups of individuals. Save those for the quantitative studies.

- Possible approaches—Here, Black discusses those approaches I describe in Chapters 5 and 6.

- Before data collection—She considers gaining permission (including IRB approval) and recommends designing an interview guide, identifying personnel, and considering a budget.

- Methods—Black considers sampling strategies of purposive sampling as well as different ways of collecting data.

- Analysis—Black mentions the methods associated with specific research approaches. For example, constant-comparative analysis is related to grounded theory. She talks about developing coding and developing themes. I write about this in detail in Chapter 13.

- Qualitative software—If you plan to use software, you will need to look at what is out there. Some packages are priced for student use. Most software requires a learning curve that is much more difficult than learning statistical software packages. Some software developers offer training in software use.

- Reflexivity—Black recommends that you include a discussion of this topic in the proposal.

- Ethics submissions—She asks you to consider the issue of confidentiality, especially with regard to stories people tell.

I want you to understand that these outlines provide you only with a general framework for proposal development. Underlying this framework are some issues that you need to consider. The first task you face as you develop your idea is to clarify in your own mind what you plan to do and how you plan to do it. Haverkamp and Young (2007) suggested that a first step is "gaining clarity on one's foundational framework for qualitative research, as reflected in the identification of a philosophy of science paradigm" (p. 266). I recognize that some of the details may not be clear to you, for the research process is inductive and iterative. But to the extent possible, you need to decide what your study is about and how you plan to conduct it. I see this as a process between you and your mentors. Your colleagues can also play an important role in the process. So before you actually write anything, you will need to meet with others to clarify your thinking.

Once you decide on the general topic area and research purpose, these are some of the issues that you need to be thinking about: Will you select one of the approaches I discuss in Chapter 4, 5, or 6? For example, are you interested in the lived experiences of children who have recently immigrated to the United States? If so, you would use a phenomenological approach. Are you interested in exploring ways in which beginning teachers interact with their students? If so, you might want to consider an ethnographic approach. Or would you like to see how a school that is scheduled to close deals with the myriad issues as they plan for the final year? If so, you might want to conduct a case study.

You will also need to consider a section on the role of the researcher. It is critical that you explain how QR requires the researcher to move away from objectivity and take a reflective and subjective stance. I find it helpful to write about this in your research proposal.

Often, sample sizes in QR are small and are purposeful samples or samples of convenience rather than random samples from which you can generalize to a larger population. You will need to defend this approach and speak about the goal of QR being more about description, understanding, and interpretation than hypothesis testing.

Because you will probably not use a formal questionnaire (so there will be nothing that you can submit for approval), you will need to address how you plan to collect data. Most likely, you will use some form of interviewing (see Chapter 10) combined with other ways of collecting data (see Chapter 11).

You will need to explain the process you anticipate using to analyze your data (see Chapter 13). If you plan to use a computer software program, you need to demonstrate either your expertise or how you plan to gain expertise by taking a course, a tutorial, or seeking outside assistance. Because you may choose to write in a less formal style and use the first-person pronoun, you will probably need to address these issues and provide a justification (see Chapter 14).

How should you write your proposal? You can choose to follow the fairly traditional style that I provide earlier in this section. Or you can choose to weave a narrative addressing the topics I present. If you choose the latter, I strongly suggest that you seek approval from your advisor and committee members prior to presenting it to a larger group. You need an advocate on your side, and you need to know that someone at your institution supports what you plan to do. Some recent experiences of alternative styles are documented in the following research. Doloriert and Sambrook (2011), in describing an autoethnographic dissertation written for a traditional business school in the UK, chose to write it chronologically, with a presentation of an authentic journey of discovery and learning. For example, the first chapter deals with methodological choices, and this narrative continues throughout her dissertation. If you are willing to take some chances, then this approach might be for you. You will need the support of a strong advisor to overcome many obstacles you no doubt will face. Ells (2011) presented a Canadian case study based on her experience on IRBs. I am surprised that she said that the major hurdle in conducting QR is to get approval from the IRBs. In my view, the board should be there to provide safeguards for human subjects.

The challenge of writing a research proposal is clear. You are a novice in this arena. The group to whom you are communicating may also be novices, or, worse, they may have preconceived ideas of what a proposal should look like and how a study should be designed. According to Gorman (as cited by Eliot, 2011), one thing that is helpful is to know what the reviewers are thinking as they review your proposal. A number of researchers recount their experiences in dealing with IRBs and the political dynamics of such boards. There is clearly a power struggle here, because a review committee may hold the power to approve or disapprove your research. It is your responsibility to convince yourself first of what you are doing, convince your committee, and finally convince an outside panel to support your idea. You will be extremely well served if you write clearly, are prepared with evidence of what constitutes appropriate or good practices in the arena in which you plan to work, and remain confident that your study is of value and will contribute to a better understanding of education.

Final Considerations in Writing a Proposal

Engage the reader at the outset. It is critical that you draw readers in rather than have them think this is just one more study to put on the shelf. One way to do this is by how you write. You might begin with an interesting story. Or use some other hook to capture the audience. I like to use visuals to stimulate readers.

Establish who you are and how you will present information. It is critical that you establish your voice and point of view. Many qualitative researchers choose to write using the first person. As you know, I use this style. By using this open style, you become less remote and inaccessible—an objective position. Your role is important. Do not distance yourself. You might want to review the presentations from the field that I present at the beginning of this chapter.

Write clearly. Avoid jargon and abstract terms. There is a tendency for academic writing to be dry and remote. I think it is an old prejudice that suggests the more obtuse you are, the better your work will be received. Get rid of that notion. In today's QR world, it is incumbent on you as a writer to communicate clearly and effectively.

Make a case for doing your study: not just that you are interested in the topic because you are either like those being studied or know someone like them. That is an insufficient reason to conduct research, even though it might be what is driving you. See Valery's comment in Appendix A.

Avoid redundancies in your writing. Enough said.

Try to write an abstract of about 150 words that succinctly states what you are studying, why, and how you plan to do it. This will help you avoid getting lost in extraneous details.

CHECK YOURSELF

How well did you grasp key features in this chapter? Focus Your Reading should guide you as you look for critical parts. See how much you agree with me. What else would you add?

- There have been many innovations in the field—moving from QN to QR, using smartphones for sensitive interviews, using photovoice to encourage action, connections between social science and the humanities, and turning research into film
- I discussed ways of putting your ideas into practice.
- I explained my experience of taking chances in a new venture—painting—and how this experience in the new world of painting informed my thinking and actions.
- There are several things to things to keep in mind when developing a QR proposal. Figure 7.6 uses spokes of a wheel to think about proposal development, from purpose to institutional review and approval.

KEY DISCUSSION ISSUES

1. Reflecting on the five innovations discussed in the first part of this chapter, how can you use this information to inform your thinking about planning your own research?

2. In what ways does my section on learning about painting help you to see that you can challenge yourself in a field that is new to you? I intended to be reflexive and reveal some of my shortcomings. Did it work?

3. What about elements of a research proposal? Are you more comfortable with a traditional style, or are you willing to take some chances? How does your own personal sensibility affect the choices you make?

4. Reading about what others have done and thinking through some of the issues should help you on your journey. Are you being helped or bogged down?

MODULE 7

Developing a Mini-IRB Protocol

The purpose of this activity is to practice writing an IRB application specific for your institution. You will need to locate the guidelines for your institution. Your instructor should be able to assist you.

Choose a partner for this activity. Decide on a hypothetical research study and discuss how you might go about conducting it. Choose a specific research approach or a generic one. Identify some activities you might conduct. These should include what or whom you will study, how you will get the information, and what you will do with the information.

Complete an outline that meets the guidelines of your institution. You can find several examples of guidelines on university websites.

At the University of San Diego (2012), these guidelines include (a) the application, (b) a consent form template, and (c) a sample application. This template is specifically designed for qualitative researchers.

At Belmont University (n.d.), there are specific guidelines for qualitative studies.

At the University of Illinois at Chicago (2009), there are some tips when doing some qualitative projects.

REFERENCES

Belmont University. (n.d.). Institutional review board. Retrieved from http://www.belmont.edu/irb/instructions/qualitative.html

Beneito-Montagut, R. (2011). Ethnography goes online: Towards a user-centered methodology to research interpersonal communication on the internet. *Qualitative Research, 11*(6), 716–735.

Black, K. (2012). *Refining a Research Question*. Retrieved from http://research.familymed.ubc.ca/files/2012/03/StudyDesignsIII21715.pdf

Caulley, D. (2013). *Happy new year*. Retrieved from http://darrencaulley.com/blog.php

Doloriert, C., & Sambrook, S. (2011). Accommodating an auto-ethnographic PhD: The tale of the thesis, the viva voce, and the traditional business school. *Journal of Contemporary Ethnography, 40*(5), 582–615.

Eliot, S. (2011). Paul Gorman on qualitative research proposals. *The Listening Resource*. Retrieved from http://www.qualitative-researcher.com/qualitative-research-2/paul-gorman-on-qualitative-research-proposals/

Ells, C. (2011). Communicating qualitative research study designs to research ethics review boards. *The Qualitative Report, 16*(3), 881–891. Retrieved from http://www.nova.edu/ssss/QR/QR16-3/ells.pdf

Heath, A. (1997). The proposal in qualitative research. *The Qualitative Report, 3*(1), Retrieved from http://www.nova.edu/ssss/QR/QR3-1/heath.html

Lincoln, Y., & Guba, E. (1985). *Naturalistic inquiry*. Newbury Park, CA: SAGE.

Merriam, S. B. (1998). *Qualitative research and case study applications in education*. San Francisco, CA: Jossey-Bass Publishers.

Salmons, J. (2009). *Online interviews in real time*. Thousand Oaks, CA: SAGE.

Stanford University. (n.d.). *Human subjects research and the IRB*. Retrieved from http://humansubjects.stanford.edu/

University of Illinois at Chicago. (2009). Tip sheet: IRB review of oral history and other social science projects. Retrieved from http://tigger.uic.edu/depts/ovcr/research/protocolreview/irb/policies/0902.pdf

University of San Diego. (2012). Institutional Review Board. Retrieved from http://www.sandiego.edu/irb/review/app_forms.php

University of Texas at Austin. (n.d.). *Welcome to human subjects research and IRB*. Retrieved from http://www.utexas.edu/research/rsc/humansubjects/

■ References for Individual Contributions

References—Bernauer

Lagemann, E. (2000). *An elusive science: The troubling history of education research*. Chicago, IL: University of Chicago Press.

Wolcott, H. (1994). Transforming qualitative data: Description, analysis, and interpretation. Thousand Oaks, CA: SAGE.

References—Dibbs, Glassmeyer, & Lahman

Bosley, J., Conrad, F. G., & Uglow, D. (1998). Pen CASIC: Design and usability. In M. P. Couper, R. P Baker, J. Bethlehem, C. Z. F. Clark, J. Martin, . . . & J.M. O'Reilly (Eds.), *Computer assisted survey information collection* (pp. 512–541). New York, NY: John Wiley.

Braun, R. P., Vecchietti, J. L., Thomas, L., Prins, C., French, L. E., Gewirtzman, A. J., . . . & Salomon, D. (2005). Telemedical wound care using a new generation of mobile telephones: A feasibility study. *Archives of Dermatology, 141*(2), 252–258.

Cleland, J., Caldow, J., & Ryan, D. (2007). A qualitative study of the attitudes of patients and staff to the use of mobile phone technology for recording and gathering asthma data. *Journal of Telemedicine and Telecare, 13*(2), 85–89.

Couper, M. P. (2005). Technology trend in survey data collection. *Social Science Computer Review, 23*(4), 486–501.

Geist, M. R. (2008). *A methodological examination of a focus group informed Delphi: A mixed methods investigation of female community college science, technology, engineering, and mathematics students.* (Published Doctoral of Philosophy dissertation). University of Northern Colorado, Greeley, CO.

Glassmeyer, D. M., & Dibbs, R. A. (2012). Researching from a distance: Using live web conferencing to mediate data collection. *International Journal of Qualitative Methods, 11*(3), 292–302.

Gorge, M. (2005). USB & other portable storage device usage: Be aware of the risks to your corporate data in order to take pre-emptive and/or corrective action. *Computer Fraud & Security, 8*, 15–17.

Gravlee, C. C. (2002). Mobile computer-assisted personal interviewing with handheld computers: The entryware system 3.0. *Field Methods, 14*(3), 322–336.

Greene, P. D. (2001). Handheld computers as tools for writing and managing field data. *Field Methods, 13*(2), 181–197.

Loo, A. (2009). Security threats of smart phones and Bluetooth. *Communications of the ACM, 52*(3), 150–152.

Mann, C., & Stewart, F. (2002). Internet interviewing. In J. F. Gubrium & J. A. Holstein (Eds.), *Handbook of Interview Research* (pp. 603–627). Thousand Oaks, CA: SAGE.

Merriam, S. (1988). *Case study research in education: A qualitative approach.* San Francisco: Jossey-Bass.

Mulder, I., & Kort, J. (2008). Mixed emotions, mixed methods. The role of emergent technologies in studying user experience in context. In S. N. Hesse-Biber & P. Leavy (Eds.), *Handbook of emergent methods* (pp. 601–612). New York, NY: Guilford Press.

Preziosa, A., Grassi, A., Gaggioli, A., & Riva, G. (2009). Therapeutic applications of the mobile phone. *British Journal of Guidance & Counseling, 37*(3), 313–325.

References and Resources—Lorenz

Castleden, H., Garvin, T., & Nation, H. (2008). Modifying photovoice for community-based participatory indigenous research. *Social Science & Medicine, 66*(6), 1393–1405.

Catalani, C., & Minkler, M. (2010). Photovoice: A review of the literature in health and public health. *Health Education & Behavior, 37*(3), 424–451.

Foster-Fishman, P., Nowell, B., Deacon, Z., Nievar, M. A., & McCann, P. (2005). Using methods that matter: The impact of reflection, dialogue, and voice. *American Journal of Community Psychology, 36*(3–4), 275–291.

Hergenrather, K. C., Rhodes, S. D., Cowan, C. A., Bardoshi, G., & Pula, S. (2009). Photovoice as community-based participatory research: A qualitative review. *American Journal of Health Behavior, 33*(6), 686–698.

Lorenz, L. S. (2010). *Brain injury survivors: Narratives of rehabilitation and healing.* Boulder, CO: Lynne Rienner Publishers.

Lorenz, L. S. (2010). Visual metaphors of living with brain injury: Exploring and communicating lived experience with an invisible injury. *Visual Studies, 25*(3), 210–223.

Lorenz, L. S., & Chilingerian, J. A. (2011). Using visual and narrative methods to achieve fair process in clinical care. *Journal of Visualized Experiments, 48*. Retrieved from http://www.jove.com/details.stp?id=2342

Lorenz, L. S., & Kolb, B. (2009). Involving the public through participatory visual research methods. *Health Expectations, 12,* 262–274.

Lorenz, L. S., & Webster, B. (2009). Doing your own photovoice project: A simple guide for support groups. Retrieved from http://www.brainline.org/multimedia/presentations/photovoice/Photovoice_Facilitators_Guide.pdf (Related photovoice project: "Brain Injury X-Posed: The Survivor's View," Retrieved from http://www.brainline.org/multimedia/photovoice.html)

Lykes, M. B., Blanche, M. T., & Hamber, B. (2003). Narrating survival and change in Guatemala and South Africa: The politics of presentation and a liberatory community psychology. *American Journal of Community Psychology, 31*(1/2), 79–90.

Rhodes, S. D., Hergenrather, K. C., Wilkin, A. M., & Jolly, C. (2007). Visions and voices: Indigent persons living with HIV in the southern United States use photovoice to create knowledge, develop partnerships, and take action. *Health Promotion Practice, 9*(2), 159–169.

Wang C., & Burris, M. A. (1997). Photovoice: Concept, methodology, and use for participatory needs assessment. *Health Education & Behavior, 24*(3), 369–387.

Wang C., Burris, M. A., & Ping, X. Y. (1996). Chinese village women as visual anthropologists: A participatory approach to reaching policymakers. *Social Science & Medicine, 42*(10), 1391–1400.

Wang, C. C., & Redwood-Jones, Y. A. (2001). Photovoice ethics: Perspectives from Flint photovoice. *Health Education & Behavior 28*(5), 560–572.

Wang, C., Yi, W. K., Tao, Z. W., & Carovano, K. (1998). Photovoice as a participatory health promotion strategy. *Health Promotion International, 13*(1), 75–86.

Resources—Jones

Rufus Stone, the movie on the web: background, cast, and crew and updates on screenings and availability of the film:

http://www.rufusstonemovie.com/

http://microsites.bournemouth.ac.uk/rufus-stone/

Trailer for *Rufus Stone*:

https://vimeo.com/43395306

Journal articles:

Connecting participatory methods in a study of older lesbian and gay citizens in rural areas. *International Journal of Qualitative Research, 9(4).* Retrieved from http://ejournals.library.ualberta.ca/index.php/IJQM/article/view/8652

Exploring sexuality, ageing and rurality in a multi-method, performative project. *British Journal of Social Work. Retrieved from http://bjsw.oxfordjournals.org/content/early/2011/05/04/bjsw.bcr058.short?rss=1*

Press comments:

New York Times:

Shunning the journals, scholar brings work on older gays to life in film. Retrieved from http://www.nytimes.com/2011/07/11/world/europe/11iht-educSide11.html?_r=1

Times Higher Education:

Camera turns to capture gay and unpleasant land. Retrieved from http://www.timeshighereducation.co.uk/story.asp?storycode=416473

BBC Radio 4:

Thinking allowed. Laurie Taylor talks with Kip Jones about the research behind *Rufus Stone.* Retrieved from http://www.bbc.co.uk/programmes/b017chq4

STUDENT STUDY SITE

Visit **http://www.sagepub.com/lichtmanqrss** to access additional study tools, including eFlashcards and links to SAGE journal articles.

CHAPTER 8

Social Media, the Internet, and Technology

Focus Your Reading

- There are enormous advances in social media, Internet technology, and hardware.
- Research on and about the Internet
- Privacy, informed consent, and confidentiality are especially critical.
- Examples of how tools are used
- Researchers have demonstrated enormous creativity in the use of technology.

Using technology. The digital age. We are there. Instant news. I am horrified at the events I learn about on the news. Yesterday, December 14, 2012, a gunman shot and killed twenty young school children, the principal, and several other personnel at a school in a small town in Connecticut. When I revised this chapter in September, people around the world commemorated the eleventh anniversary of the 9/11/2001 bombings on American soil. I also learned that Ai Wei Wei, artist and Chinese dissident, was in the hospital, after being beaten by Chinese police. Subsequently, as I wrote this, I learned that the American Ambassador to Libya, J. Christopher Stevens, and three of his staff members, were brutally murdered. Instantaneous news and videos. Horrible. One news account stated that reactions to a YouTube movie posted on the anniversary of 9/11 motivated the mob in Lybia. Beyond our comprehension in a free world. We are witnessing these events before our eyes. How can we use this technology to gain an understanding of the world and perhaps make the world a safer place for all to live in freedom and security?

Whether you like it or not, the way we gain information and transmit information is fundamentally different from the situation of just a few years ago. As researchers, we can embrace this and develop new ways to use these new ideas. How can we possibly keep up with things? I am delighted to find Jeffrey Keefer. He is a doctoral student at Lancaster University in Lancaster, UK. However, he lives and works in New York. Keefer's (2011) blog is Silence and Voice. Keefer posts tweets daily. I follow him and receive an update via email. Read his tweets from May 31, 2011:

> Today's agenda includes (formally) beginning my thesis literature review and prepping for a supervisory meeting tomorrow #phdchat
>
> Awoke in the early am due to very strong thunder and lightning storms. Could not get back to sleep as started thinking about coffee.

Read part of his post from December 18, 2011:

> Have you ever had your work rejected for a conference? Something about that term, REJECTION, when it has to do with our research or professional representation of our work can be difficult to take, and while I cannot pretend it gets easier over time, a tenured professor once said to me that everybody in the room, including all those big-named speakers up there, have had their work rejected at some point.

You can read these and much more on his site.

You may ask why I spend so much time on Keefer. No, I do not know him. But I know so much about him. He is technologically savvy. He is reflexive. He reveals so much about himself. He is thoughtful. He is engaged. He has been posting since December 2006, and not just on Twitter. Keefer also posts images on Flickr. He seems to enjoy life. Even though his recent submission was rejected, I believe he models excellent behaviors that qualitative researchers should address.

In these times of rapidly growing technology, our world, the way we know about things, and how we communicate with each other have made us think about whom we study, what we study, and how we study in vastly different ways. I begin this chapter by talking about social networks and technological advances. I provide definitions and possible uses. I also address the impact of social media and technology. Issues of privacy, informed consent, and confidentiality are on the minds of many as we explore these uncharted territories. I conclude with some examples.

■ What Are Social Media and Social Networking?

You will not be surprised that there is a social media revolution. That is what you can see if you view *Social Media Revolution* 2011, a video by Erik Qualman (2011). The growth of the use of social media is phenomenal. For example, in 2008, 5% of Americans reported being familiar with Twitter. In just two short years, 87% reported familiarity. According to Golijan (n.d.) from NBC, Twitter has 175 million users. I have tried to organize this enormous flow of information to help you make sense of it. I begin with social media.

Definitions

According to boyd and Ellison (2007), social network sites are

> web-based services that allow individuals to (1) construct a public or semi-public profile within a bounded system, (2) articulate a list of other users with whom they share a connection, and (3) view and traverse their list of connections and those made by others within the system. The nature and nomenclature of these connections may vary from site to site. (para. 4)

Kaplan and Haenlein (2010) defined social media as a group of Internet-based applications that build on the foundations of Web 2.0. Social media include online technological tools that permit people to easily communicate with each other. Bradley (2010) blogged that "social media is a set of technologies and channels targeted at forming and enabling a potentially massive community of participants to productively collaborate." The May–June issue (volume 54, issue 3) of *Business Horizons* is a special issue devoted to social media.

Popular Social Networking Sites

I have identified several social networking sites that are currently in use. I am sure you are familiar with each of them. Here are some details about their founding and development. All began in the new millennium. Social networking sites allow people to stay connected with others via the Web.

Facebook (launched in 2004) is a social networking website. Users can create profiles, upload videos and photos, send messages, and keep in touch with friends and family. Currently, it is available in at least 70 languages. It was founded by Mark Zuckerberg and went public in 2012. It had more than 600 million active users at the beginning of 2011. In 2010, the film, *The Social Network,* documented the development and rise of Facebook. More than 40% of the U.S. population had a Facebook account in 2010. According to *The Washington Post* (Kang, 2011), 5 million U.S. Facebook users are younger than age 10 and 2.5 million subscribers are 11- or 12-year-olds. At the other end of the age spectrum, Madden (2010) reported that social networking among users over age 50 has nearly doubled from 22% to 42% in the last year. In fact, she says that "older users have been especially enthusiastic over the past year about embracing new networking tools." Xie (2008) studied older Chinese Internet users' participation in voluntary associations and communities. He studied members of a senior-oriented computer training camp in Shanghai. I was surprised that he concluded that the Internet facilitated civic engagement.

YouTube (launched in 2005) is a video-sharing website. Purchased in 2006 by Google for $1.65 billion, it uses Adobe Flash Video and htm15 technology. Introducing some humor, YouTube features an April Fool's prank on its site: In 2011, it celebrated its "100th anniversary" with silent early films.

Twitter (launched in 2006) is a social networking and microblogging service. Readers send and receive messages called *tweets*. A tweet is a text-based post with a maximum of 140 characters displayed on the user's profile page. Privately owned, Twitter is supported by venture capital. It is estimated to have 200 million users, generating 190 million tweets daily. Users can subscribe to tweets of others by *following* them. Users can also group messages together by topic. The market research community has been blogging about how Twitter offers opportunities as a qualitative research (QR) method. Benefits are that it is free, fast, and natural. However, drawbacks are that it is limited to 140 characters and is somewhat artificial. According to Dugan (2011), Twitter is the most buzzed-about social network, beating out LinkedIn (in second place) and YouTube (the 2010 winner).

LinkedIn (launched in 2003) is a social networking site for business professionals. Users can share work-related information with other users. An initial public offering (IPO) appeared in May 2011. There are more than 100 million users.

Pinterest (launched in 2012) is a photo-sharing website with social networking features. It uses a grid-style layout that arranges images into what is referred to as *virtual pinboards*. Individuals can post images onto a public browsable bulletin board or onto a private board.

Tumblr (launched in 2007) is a network-blogging platform. It is useful for those with little programming experience. Multimedia can be posted to a blog. Users can use blogs of others.

Did You Know

Samuel F. B. Morse patented the telegraph in 1849. William Gibson coined the term *cyberspace* in 1984. Launched in 1997, SixDegrees.com was the first recognizable social networking site. Beginning in 2003, so many new such sites were launched that one commentator coined the term *YASNS*—Yet Another Social Networking Service. The first Twitter message was posted in March 2006 at 9:50 p.m. PST when its founder, Jack Dorsey, wrote "just setting up my twttr."

■ Advances in Technology

Definitions

Internet technology includes tools to assist in using the World Wide Web (WWW). The Web and the Internet are older than you think. It was the space program that influenced President Eisenhower in 1958 to initiate a plan for communication among the military. In 1969, the Advanced Research Projects Agency (ARPA) was created to facilitate networking technologies. The first basic email programs began in 1972. IBM introduced the first personal computer in 1981, followed by the Mac (introduced by Apple) in 1984. Domain name systems such as *.edu* or *.gov* were designed in 1983. In 1990, ARPANET ended, and Tim Berners-Lee created the World Wide Web. Fast-forward to the last five years. Various tools have been developed to assist in using the Web. I describe some of them next. Perhaps by the time you read this, there will be other new ones.

Internet Tools

Browsers

Once the Internet became popular, it was only a matter of time before creative people began to develop various tools to make it more efficient. One of the first tools to be developed enabled users to search the Web in order to locate information on a particular topic. One browser became so popular that it became a verb: All of you have "Googled" something. Initially, browsers were aimed at presenting and retrieving information. Here are some browsers you may have heard of or use: Mozilla Firefox (2002), Internet Explorer (1995), Google Chrome (2008), and Safari (2003). Berners-Lee invented the first browser in 1990.

As the second-generation browser Web 2.0 became viable, designers developed various tools, some of which I describe subsequently. However, it is possible that by the time this book is published, some of these tools will have become obsolete and others developed to replace them.

Although not exactly a tool for using the technology, Web 2.0 allows web applications that facilitate information sharing and collaboration on the Web. Websites built using Web 2.0 facilitate the retrieval of information and also provide the user with additional capabilities such as more storage space and software. Users can interact and collaborate with each other in a social media dialogue. Web 2.0 was first announced in 2004 by Tim O'Reilly. It allowed software developers and end users to use the Web differently than the initial Web environment.

The browser Web 3.0 is currently under development. This version is supposed to make it easier and faster to search for things like movies. It is also envisioned that it will act like a personal assistant. A little scary to some, it is said that the more you use the Web, the more your browser learns about you and is able to be more specific in your search results. Perhaps you have seen some inklings of this with books. I know that Amazon seems to know what types of books I might like to read based on the ones I have already purchased or looked at for purchase. As I write, however, this Web 3.0 version has yet to be perfected.

Application Software (App)

Where do these tools come from? They are developed by a variety of people. Some have an idea but do not have the technical capability to carry out their idea, so they use software developers to assist them. The term they use for all of these is *app*, which stands for application software. An app is software designed to help the user do certain specific tasks. The type and number of apps is increasing at great rates. Apps can be downloaded to a smartphone, a computer, a tablet, or a handheld device.

Since the range of apps is so vast, it is somewhat difficult to organize the apps (tools) in a meaningful way. Some are so new that I have not had a chance to work with them. For the most part, tools are designed to be user friendly, to be free or low cost, and to allow people to interact with each other, share information about each other, or find each other. Thus, all apps would appear to have something that can be used as qualitative researchers venture into new territories.

Cloud Computing

Latest to appear on the scene is cloud computing. Cloud computing (initially started in 2007) allows a user to use a network (*in the cloud*) to conduct common applications such as word processing. The cloud can be accessed via the Internet. This is a type of app. You can obtain a free trial from Google. Also, the cloud (launched 2011) acts as a storage locker or walk-in closet where you can put photos, music, books, and documents from any Apple device. Prior to his death in 2011, Steve Jobs, the chief executive of Apple, moved Apple into a position on the Internet with the adoption of the cloud. This feature enables users to "build Internet-smarts into all of Apple's gadgets" (Manjoo, 2011).

Visual Tools

One group of tools addresses the visual aspect and capability now available on the Web. Where do all the images come from? Some are posted directly on Facebook, while individuals post others using photo-sharing or slide-sharing technologies. Many pictures or videos are posted on YouTube. Here are some examples of visual tools that are used today:

Facial recognition software is an app that automatically identifies an individual from a digital image or video frame. In 2011, Facebook added the software to its platform, leading to a large negative response involving invasion of privacy.

Online photo sharing provides a platform for publishing or sharing digital photos online. Most programs permit public or private sharing. In 2011, common photo-sharing sites included Snapfish, Photobucket, Picasa, Shutterfly, and Flickr.

SlideShare is one of several tools for sharing videos online. You can get suggestions for using the iPad in QR by looking at the Merlien Institute's (2011) SlideShare presentation.

Instagram technology is an app that changes the format of photos. It is a free photo-sharing program. As of September 2012, Instagram had 100 million users.

Location Tools

We might also want to locate each other. Many of you have GPS technology in your car or phone, so you are familiar with this.

Global Positioning System (GPS) is a satellite-based navigation system made up of satellites placed in orbit. Satellites circle the earth regularly. GPS receivers use the information and triangulate to identify precise locations.

Google Maps is an Internet-connected navigation system you can use on a browser or a mobile phone. It lets you track where you are or where you have been as well as plan routes for the future.

Tools for Rapid Communication

We certainly want to talk to each other or write each other. Many of you are familiar with ways to accomplish that.

> Email is ubiquitous. You can get free or low-cost email access from many different providers.
>
> LISTSERVs are a way for individuals to form or join groups with a common interest. Most LISTSERVs have a moderator who monitors for inappropriate postings or inappropriate netiquette (online etiquette). Usually, users post information to the entire group for all to see.
>
> Instant messaging (IM) is a real-time, direct, text-based communication system. Text is typically conveyed over the Internet.
>
> Twitter is a real-time communication system that limits its format to 140 characters. Individuals can have Twitter accounts and can follow others on Twitter.
>
> Texting involves communication between mobile phones using words rather than voice.
>
> Skype, introduced in 2003, allows users to communicate over the Internet. Its free service is widely used by individuals who like to connect faces to voices.
>
> Web logs (blogs) are like diaries, although open for all to see. Typically, a writer makes regular entries and posts them online. Some blogs permit others to make comments. Group blogs, in which a number of individuals post on the same blog, are also becoming popular.

I find blogs especially interesting as a vehicle for individuals to post their thoughts on a particular topic. Many students and faculty have developed blogs on the general topic of QR. I found several course syllabi asking students to create a blog as part of their class assignments; I suspect you might be able to locate student blogs as well. I have read numerous blogs by individuals who are pursuing degrees in QR. I also suggested to you earlier that you start a blog as part of your coursework activities.

Here are excerpts from several blogs related to QR. Schostak (2011), on his QR blog, posted this on April 17, 2011:

> It seems to me that if we are to create real democracies then as I've argued in various articles and books . . . as well as the paper on the middle east and wikileaks mentioned above, there must be a close relationship between education, research and the conditions of freedom with equality necessary for any political, economic, social and cultural organisation through which people meet their needs, their interests, their hopes and their demands.

Parsons (2011) commented about QR in Japan on his blog. Written from a marketing perspective, he cautioned about possible contradictions between fundamental aspects of Japanese culture and QR as conceived from a Western viewpoint. On the other hand,

Kawamura (2011), a professor of sociology at the Fashion Institute of Technology, seems to have tapped into Japanese youth and subcultures in ways Parsons does not consider. Her book on doing QR in the fashion industry challenges our old ways of thinking.

You can learn about Dedoose (2012) by reading their blog. It doesn't quite fit into my organizational structure above. It is described as a QR software program that uses the Internet. Features include the ability to collaborate with others in your research group and "to analyze data intuitively and thoroughly." I have not actually examined this directly, but I think you need to learn more about it.

Mathison (2012) always leads me to something interesting. Her post about Marvin the Martian and how ideas are spread on Facebook is stimulating. Similarly, you might look at Israeli graphic designer Ronny Edry (2012) who shared how he used Facebook to send the message that Israel loves Iran and Iran loves Israel. This poignant account should stimulate you into using Facebook and other sources on the Internet as you explore QR. Michael (2012) suggests that advances in technology and social media will be a game changer for the way QR is conducted online.

Salmons (2012) comments about digging into social media using qualitative methods. She suggests that "qualitative research approaches allow us to dig below the surface to explore how, why or what, and to explore relationships and connections not readily evident in Big Data." She introduces the idea of deep data.

Organizing and Analyzing Information on the Web

Another category of tools is concerned with how the user can utilize technology to organize and make sense of the information available online. Human language tools are available for reviewing large numbers of public documents. Textifier is an example, developed by Shulman (2011). His software supports such tasks as text classification, blog capture, manuscript review management, or qualitative coding.

Users also want to share information. Who would have thought that an encyclopedia could have online, nonexpert-driven technology to share information? The most well-known of this type of encyclopedia is Wikipedia. Wikipedia, a free encyclopedia, is available in many languages, and the topics and material are increasing exponentially. A *wiki* is a collection of web pages designed to let anyone modify the information. The first wiki, WikiWikiWeb, was developed in 1994.

A number of QR classes make use of wiki for communication. See, for example, the Introduction to Qualitative Research Wikibook, created by students at Texas A&M (2010). You can also learn more about wiki development at http://www.wikispaces.com. Or you can look at the information you can find about QR on Wikiversity (n.d.). Castanos and Piercy (2010) comment that wiki is a virtual space for qualitative data collection.

Google Art (googleartproject.com) is a service that has organized masterpieces of art using digitized images from seventeen of the world's major art museums. You can virtually travel to the Freer Gallery of Washington, DC, to the Van Gogh Museum in Amsterdam, and to the Alte Nationalgalerie in Berlin. While I have been to each of these and there is nothing like the real thing, if you are interested in art, check this out. I think all will enjoy the very high quality of the images.

Types of Hardware

In addition to various apps and tools you can use as you navigate the Web, developers have increasingly moved to taking advantage of smaller and smaller computer chips and other technologies that power devices. In today's world, you might be lost without a mobile phone or other device. Even those most averse to using technology recognize its importance. Many of our devices, including smartphones, can be used as we investigate ways to gather and process information for QR.

Definitions

Numerous portable devices permit the user to communicate with others, easily photograph or record people or events, read, or do all of these activities in one device. I do not know the number of users of such devices, and I suspect that the numbers are growing at enormous rates. Apple cannot keep up with the demand for its newest iPad. Mobile phones have replaced landlines in some countries. Cameras using film have become almost obsolete for the casual user. Bookstores are closing or consolidating, and Internet sites have become important places for readers to learn about books. Amazon purchased Goodreads, a social media site used for sharing information about books (Kaufman, 2013).

Popular Devices

Smartphones are usually thought of as cell or mobile phones. Many have picture-taking and texting capabilities. Instantly posting these visual images to Facebook, YouTube, or other social media is common.

Digital cameras are now so small that they fit inside a jacket pocket or small purse. Battery life is long, images are clear, and the point-and-shoot feature makes it easier for both the elderly or the very young. Of course, children and young adults are completely familiar with their use.

E-readers (e.g., Kindle, Nook, etc.) allow the user to download entire books in a few minutes. New technologies make reading easier, and newer versions keep the weight lighter than a traditional book. Most devices permit downloading thousands of books. Books can then be returned to a cloud or location not on a personal device for future reference. These devices have search capabilities that facilitate the location of information. Public libraries in some states provide digital copies of books (e-books) for e-readers. I currently have several books borrowed from my local library and installed on my Kindle app on my iPad2. I need to read them quickly, because I understand they will be automatically deleted when the loan time expires.

Tablets are also increasingly popular. Apple introduced its second-generation iPad in 2011. Weighing about 13 ounces, this device enables one to read email, take pictures, access the Web, take notes, read e-books, and listen to iTunes. Samsung and Toshiba, among others, also offer this technology. With new apps available for free or a small cost, tablets have revolutionized the way we think about the Internet, communication, and social media.

Research Related to the Internet

Instantaneous connections and transmissions among millions of people have resulted in incredible happenings. From the uprisings in the Middle East in 2011 to exposés of politicians and prominent people, social media have made and will continue to make an enormous impact on how information is transmitted and how individuals behave. There is so much to say, but my focus here is to examine several aspects of research and social media.

Social media and education is a topic explored by some researchers. Khang, Ki, and Ye (2012) studied patterns and trends in the use of social media over more than a dozen years. They looked specifically at advertising, communication, marketing, and public relations. They reported that about 15% of the research they reviewed used qualitative methods and another 6% used mixed methods. Wilson, Gosling, and Graham (2012) reviewed more than 400 articles on Facebook research. The types of research were then organized into five categories: descriptive analysis of users, motivations for using Facebook, identity presentation, the role of Facebook in social interaction, and privacy. Read and her colleagues (2012) identified a group of 21 adolescents (what they called "the new millennials") and used grounded theory as a base to conduct interviews about their use of social media, in particular, Facebook. One conclusion was that this group showed a fluid integration of technology and social media. According to the Horizon Project (2011), young children have used social media sites to create virtual pets or to interact with others by blogging or chatting. At the middle and high school grades, students can blog about academics. Kessler (2010) argued the case for social media in the schools. She described how one seventh-grade teacher used a social media forum in a positive way. Reasons for making use of social media include the fact that they are not going away. Also, since it is free, this is of great value when schools are faced with such tight budgets. She also suggested that kids are engaged with social media and therefore learn better. If you look at her website, you will gain ideas of how you might use social media in your school. Or you can get additional ideas by looking at the YouTube video of the positive effects of social media in education (Follett Software, 2011). You will find many accounts of this type or examples of how teachers use social media.

Ignacio (2012) provided a timely summary of current uses of online methods, and I refer you to her numerous citations. In particular, she is interested in examining the benefits and problems with studying diasporic communities. Some benefits include the study of people in diverse locations. One challenge is the location of the researcher and the location of those studied. In particular, reasons for emigration—whether political or economic—need to be considered.

In a mixed-methods study of school principals and social networking, in-depth discussions were held with principals. Responses were analyzed, looking for themes. Among those mentioned were the value of social networking to share professional knowledge, teacher-student contact, and legal concerns related to cyberbullying and inappropriate student posting (edWeb.net, IESD, MCH, & mms/education, 2011, pp. 10–11).

Seale, Charteris-Black, MacFarlane, and McPherson (2009) used keyword analysis of interviews and archived Internet postings involving people with breast and prostate cancer and discussion of sexual health. Researchers dealt with the data in an anonymous context.

Beneito-Montagut (2011), studying interpersonal communications and emotions online, used empirical data generated in a study of everyday life. She explored how people establish relationships on the Internet. Observations of various social media such as Gmail, Google Talk, and Twitter were made. Each user was followed for five weeks. This was a comprehensive study from which readers could gain considerable knowledge.

The variety of ways researchers explore the use of the Internet is evidenced in Chapple and Ziebland's (2011) study of experiences of people who have been bereaved by suicide. Narrative interviews were used to determine how social networking sites were useful in establishing a community.

D'Orazio (2009) presented a thoughtful account of how social media have changed QR. I have highlighted some of his main points for you: He first described a way to think about using social media. Using a creative presentation format, he then addressed a number of questions. What do users want from the Web? He suggested that social media are not a window into someone else's world but a mirror, a projection, or a construction. I agree with him that social media contain rich fields of information that are always current. He suggested that social data can be used in at least three ways: to determine who you are (identity), to determine whom you know (contacts), and to determine what you do (activities).

D'Orazio (2009) continued by describing four ways that have evolved in using social media: netnography, use of research communities, crowdsourcing (assigning a task to a large group or crowd), and cocreation. All of these move toward an active involvement of the user. Started in 1996, netnography studies behaviors in online communities. The focus is on social meanings and activities. The researcher either studies a community or directly participates in it. Do you see a parallel to early days of ethnography? The kind of data used are text, downloaded files of group postings, transcripts of virtual worlds or chat sessions, videos, email exchanges, and so on. In addition to common ways of analyzing the data through discourse or **content analysis**, the researcher can use what D'Orazio has called *social network analysis.* Another way of using social media is through *cocreation,* in which peer-to-peer research is developed and social insights are identified. Also, you might find Boyd's (n.d.) bibliography of research on social network sites helpful.

Innovation in presentation is a hallmark of the D'Orazio (2009) site. I encourage you to examine his format presented on SlideShare site, noted previously. Visuals that accompany the text are humorous and appropriate. The site can easily be emailed, saved as a favorite, downloaded, embedded, or zipcast. It has links to Twitter, Facebook, and other avenues of dissemination. It has a button to indicate whether you like the presentation. On the day I viewed it, there had been 7,399 views. This type of information for the audience and the creator provides instant feedback about usage and, to some extent, about usefulness.

Privacy, Ethics, and Informed Consent

As the variety and range of projects grow, some are concerned with privacy issues. What about privacy? To assist, Boyd and Ellison (2007) summarized some of the research. They dealt with the safety of younger users of social networking sites. One paradox they noted was the disconnect between the desire to protect privacy and the need to study their behavior. According to D'Orazio (2009), certain social media options might be invasive and frightening to some, but social media can also help us determine purchases, reading habits, and personal preferences. Since he is a marketing person, I am not surprised that he emphasizes personal preferences and habits of users.

Madge's (2007) research explored the debate surrounding online research ethics. The author made a plea for reflexive debate among geographers rather than routinely applying standards designed by bureaucratic committees.

A recent discussion on a qualitative LISTSERV highlights some of the issues. Preissle (LISTSERV communication, May 25, 2011) spoke of the differences between public and private access to social networks. She suggested looking at ideas from Zimmer (2008) in particular, as well as other sites. Zimmer (2010) also addressed research ethics in the Facebook era. You can look at several areas that relate to archiving data and releasing data. A discussion ensued in which one commentator suggested that people in a crowd are in a public space, and thus getting permission is not an issue. Collier (LISTSERV communication, May 25, 2011) comments that "the use of social media and digital documents present us with more nuanced ethical dilemmas than other forms of data."

Williams's (2012) thoughtful review of McKee and Porter's book on the ethics of Internet research led me to a new discovery. He describes it as the first text on research ethics and the Internet in five years and states that it is essential reading. One of the topics it deals with is researching social networking sites, an area of investigation that has become increasingly popular. One topic that is new to me is the ethics of intellectual property and copyright in online spaces.

So, the question of privacy has not been resolved. How the issue might affect research using online groups is unclear. Does permission need to be obtained? What if a member does not wish to participate? What if facial recognition software is used and members are concerned about privacy? Would it affect studies of virtual learning and teaching? What about the use of human language analysis tools? Would Shulman's Textifier be invading privacy if information was publicly available?

■ Ways to Use Tools

It seems to me that there are several ways we can think about using these tools. We can study how students learn and how learning is taught online. I call this *virtual learning*. We can also look at how various hardware and software and other tools can be used for data collection and analysis. Bryson (2011), a marketing expert, commented on how to create "hybrid" research by combine quantitative research (QN) and QR. This is what academics have been doing when they use mixed methods. Bryson commented that the field is changing so rapidly that the big question is what will happen next.

Virtual Learning

Teaching and learning in cyberspace is one topic of interest. There are several literature reviews that you can access. Barbour's (2010) blog posts this query: Are you aware of the problems that virtual school leaders face? He advises people to look at the literature. He and his colleagues have written comprehensive reviews. Barbour and Reeves (2009) reviewed the literature on virtual learning (formerly *distance education*). They discussed delivery methods as being synchronous, asynchronous, or independent. One conclusion they offered is that successful students are those who are independent and intrinsically motivated. You can also look at Cavanaugh, Barbour, and Clark (2009), who concluded that researchers need to continue to look for the best online practices. Rice (2006) reviewed distance education. Among other issues, she addressed needs of at-risk learners.

Chapman and Stone (2010) used a case-study approach to investigate the evaluation practices used in studies of the virtual world. Deed and Edwards (2011) looked at unrestricted student blogging in a Web 2.0 environment. Pearson (2010) used blogs with students to improve participation, engagement, and skill building.

Research on Hardware and Tools

Larsson and Moe (2012) used Twitter in a case study of the 2010 Swedish election. An important contribution of this study was examining different user types. Cordelois (2010) used digital technology (Subcam and Webdiver) as part of her ethnographic observation of the experience of coming home. Erickson (2010) described a documentary study using social media and what she calls *locative technology* (using GPS locators). Jones, Drury, and McBeath (2011) described how GPS-enabled mobile computing could be used to augment qualitative interviewing. They called this "sociolocative broadcasting" or sharing georeferenced digital media with others using Facebook or Flickr. The technology they used points to a trend in mediated communication in the future that will continue to emphasize not only the connection between identity and place (e.g., synchronous self-in-place broadcasting) but also create new digital platforms for documenting and archiving history and stories about specific places and for bringing people together and informing them about what is salient in their community or in the world at large (p. 395). In another study, Schwitzer (2011) used mobile ethnography to study a Super Bowl game. Although this study was aimed at market researchers, you might think of ways the technology can be used in a phenomenological or ethnographic investigation to study the lives of adults or children.

Erichsen and Goldenstein (2011) addressed issues of how new technology can be used to assist in collaborative and interdisciplinary research. Humphreys (2010) wrote a case study of how mobile communication and urban public space are negotiated using mobile social networks. He used a Google technology called Dodgeball, which let users inform friends as to whether they are at a particular bar or restaurant by using their mobile phone. Paiewonsky (2011) described a participatory action research (PAR) project in which college students with intellectual disabilities document their experiences using multimedia tools and then share them with a digital storytelling website.

Chenail (2011) wrote about blogging. He described how researchers can use blogs to express their thoughts about doing QR. He included many links to such blogs in this interesting article. Davis (2010) studied the developmental underpinnings of girls' blogs. She interviewed 20 girls who had been blogging for more than three years. Her study led to new understandings about self-expression and peer interaction. Blogs were also of interest to Bjarnason, Gudmundsson, and Olafsson (2011), who studied the social structure of the

Icelandic adolescent blogosphere. While I know Iceland is a small country, I was surprised to learn that almost all adolescents age 15 to 16 in Iceland regularly read blogs, many on a daily basis.

Arceneaux and Weiss (2010) used grounded theory to analyze press coverage of Twitter for a three-year period. They concluded that the public response is similar to that of early communication, such as the telegraph and radio. And Robards and Bennett (2011) used ethnographic data from Australia to study subcultures from Myspace and Facebook.

You can learn more about Web 2.0 by reading Greenhow, Robelia, and Hughes's (2009) informative article on shifts in the nature of the Web and classroom research. For example, Web 2.0 lets learners link and share on a global scale. It also allows for creation of material and remixing of material into new materials. Further, it does not require that users have sophisticated technological expertise to create blogs or wikis and to share videos.

This is just a handful of examples to show how researchers are either using technology for their research or studying how individuals use technology. We see researchers using GPS technology, Web 2.0 technology, or other hardware and software to facilitate their inquiry. Concomitantly, we see evidence of research about the effects of technology on participants and studies about how individuals use technology. I believe that we are at the start of a new revolution for QR. Young children are tech savvy in ways we cannot yet imagine. My ten-year-old granddaughter has her own email account and iPod touch. She has built her own website and is writing an online story. Most college students have personal computers. Most elementary and high schools are equipped with computer labs. Many now have iPads. It is up to you as you join the research community to continue to create ways to effectively use these tools and others not yet invented.

■ Summary

This chapter addresses social media and the various technologies and hardware that have been developed to facilitate using it. I have also addressed issues of privacy. Finally, I concluded with examples of research that has been done either about online groups or using tools and technology or ways to present information. Much remains to be done in this field. Qualitative researchers can make enormous inroads into this dynamic and growing field.

CHECK YOURSELF

There are enormous advances in social media, Internet technology, and hardware. Popular social networking/media sites include Facebook, YouTube, Twitter, LinkedIn, Pinterest, and Myspace. Advances in technology can be grouped into Internet tools (e.g., browsers, apps, and cloud computing), various visual tools, location tools, and tools for rapid communication. There are also new hardware devices (e.g., smartphones and tablets).

- Illustrations of several studies on and about the Internet are offered in this chapter.
- Privacy, informed consent, and confidentiality are especially critical.
- Researchers have demonstrated creativity in the usage of technology.

KEY DISCUSSION ISSUES

1. That social media sites are here to stay, there is no doubt. What are the sites you have used, and what kinds of studies do you imagine you could develop? What issues do you see as potential drawbacks?
2. Advances in technology are amazing. Decreasing sizes of computer chips enable developers to come up with ever-exciting ideas. In what ways can you use these technologies in developing your own research?
3. What about the issue of privacy and informed consent? How will you address this in your own research?

MODULE 8A

Interact in a Virtual Community

Purpose: Interact in a virtual community and comment about QR.

Activity: Ask the group to develop a wiki similar to the one created by students at Texas A&M. Or, alternatively, develop a group blog that is posted.

Evaluation: Explore the extent to which users can master the technology and express their ideas.

MODULE 8B

Combine Visual and Textual Information

Purpose: Combine visual and text information to present new information.

Activity: Work to develop a video-sharing or slide-sharing program. Try it with other class members. Post your results online.

Evaluation: Determine the ease in using technology and how information can be effectively communicated and enhanced with visuals.

REFERENCES

Arceneaux, N., & Weiss, A. (2010). Seems stupid until you try it: Press coverage of Twitter, 2006–9. *New Media & Society, 12*(8), 1262–1279.

Barbour, M. K. (2010). *Virtual school meanderings.* Retrieved from http://virtualschooling.wordpress.com/2010/04/22/dissertation-research-ideas/

Barbour, M. K., & Reeves, T. C. (2009). The reality of virtual schools: A review of the literature. *Computers and Education, 52*(2), 402–416.

Beneito-Montagut, R. (2011). Ethnography goes online: Towards a user-centred methodology to research interpersonal communication on the Internet. *Qualitative Research, 11*(6), 716–735.

Bjarnason, T., Gudmundsson, B., & Olafsson, K. (2011). Towards a digital adolescent society? The social structure of the Icelandic adolescent blogosphere. *New Media & Society, 13*(4), 645–662.

boyd, d. (n.d.). *Bibliography of research on social network sites.* Retrieved from http://www.danah.org/researchBibs/sns.php

boyd, d., & Ellison, N. (2007). Social network sites: Definition, history, and scholarship. *Journal of Computer-Mediated Communication, 13*(1), Art. 11. Retrieved from http://jcmc.indiana.edu/vol13/issue1/boyd.ellison.html

Bradley, A. J. (2010). A new definition of social media. *Gartner* [Web log]. Retrieved from http://blogs.gartner.com/anthony_bradley/2010/01/07/a-new-definition-of-social-media/

Bryson, J. (2011). *Qualblog.* Retrieved from http://www.qualblog.com/

Castanos, C., & Piercy, F. (2010). The wiki as a virtual space for qualitative data collection. *The Qualitative Report, 15*(4), 948–955.

Cavanaugh, C., Barbour, M. K., & Clark, T. (2009). Research and practice in K–12 online learning: A review of literature. *International Review of Research in Open and Distance Learning, 10*(1). Retrieved from http://www.irrodl.org/index.php/irrodl/article/view/607

Chapman, D., & Stone, S. (2010). Measurement of outcomes in virtual environments. *Advances in Developing Human Resources, 12*(6), 665–680.

Chapple, A., & Ziebland, S. (2011). How the Internet is changing the experience of bereavement by suicide: A qualitative study in the UK. *Health: An Interdisciplinary Journal for the Social Study of Health, Illness and Medicine, 15*(2), 73–187.

Chenail, R. J. (2011). Qualitative researchers in the blogosphere: Using blogs as diaries and data. *The Qualitative Report, 16*(1), 249–254. Retrieved from http://www.nova.edu/ssss/QR/QR16-1/blog.pdf

Cordelois, A. (2010). Using digital technology for collective ethnographic observations: An experiment on "coming home." *Social Science Information, 49*(3), 445–463.

Davis, K. (2010). Coming of age online: The developmental underpinnings of girls' blogs. *Journal of Adolescent Research, 25*(1), 145–171.

Dedoose. (2012). *Mixed methods & qualitative research.* Retrieved from http://blog.dedoose.com/2012/09/what-is-qualitative-research/

Deed, C., & Edwards, A. (2011). Unrestricted student blogging: Implications for active learning in a virtual text-based environment. *Active Learning in Higher Education, 12*(1), 11–21.

D'Orazio, F. (2009). *How social media have changed qualitative research.* Retrieved from http://www.slideshare.net/abc3d/introduction-to-social-media-for-qualitative-research

Dugan, L. (2011). Twitter tops list of social network with most buzz in 2011. *All Twitter: The Unofficial Twitter Resource.* Retrieved from http://www.mediabistro.com/alltwitter/twitter-tops-list-of-social-network-with-most-buzz-in-2011_b16820

Edry, R. (2012, December). Israel and Iran: A love story? *TED.* Retrieved from http://www.ted.com/talks/israel_and_iran_a_love_story.html

edWeb.net, IESD, MCH Strategic Data, & mms/education. (2011). *Final report. School principals and social networking in education: Practices, policies, and realities.* Retrieved from http://www.edweb.net/fimages/op/PrincipalsandSocialNetworkingReport.pdf

Erichsen, E., & Goldenstein, C. (2011). Fostering collaborative and interdisciplinary research in adult education. *SAGE Open.* Retrieved from http://sgo.sagepub.com/content/early/2011/04/28/2158244011403804.abstract

Erickson, I. (2010). Documentary with ephemeral media: Curation practices in online social spaces. *Bulletin of Science, Technology & Society, 30*(6), 387–397.

Follett Software. (2011). *Positive effects of social media in education.* [YouTube video]. Retrieved from http://www.youtube.com/watch?v=oq0vrM6P_Is

Golijan, R. (n.d.). Just how many active Twitter users are there? *NBCNews.com.* Retrieved from http://www.nbcnews.com/technology/technolog/just-how-many-active-twitter-users-are-there-124121

Greenhow, C., Robelia, B., & Hughes, J. (2009). Learning, teaching and scholarship in a digital age. *Educational Researcher, 38*(4), 246–259.

Horizon Project. (2011). Overview of social networking's impact on education. *Impact on Education SocialNetworking.* Retrieved from http://horizonproject.wikispaces.com/Impact+on+Education+SocialNetworking

Humphreys, L. (2010). Mobile social networks and urban public space. *New Media & Society, 12*(5), 763–778.

Ignacio, E. (2012). Online methods and analyzing knowledge-production: A cautionary tale. *Qualitative Inquiry, 18*(3), 237–246.

Jones, P., Drury, R., & McBeath, J. (2011). Using GPS-enabled mobile computing to augment qualitative interviewing: Two case studies. *Field Methods, 23*(2), 173–187.

Kang, C. (2011, June 15). Facebook: As rough as recess, but without the monitor. *The Washington Post,* p. G1.

Kaplan, A. M., & Haenlein, M. (2010). Users of the world, unite! The challenges and opportunities of social media. *Business Horizons, 53*(1), 59–68.

Kaufman, L. (2013, March 28). Amazon to buy social site dedicated to sharing books. *New York Times.* Retrieved from http://www.nytimes.com/2013/03/29/business/media/amazon-to-buy-goodreads.html?_r=0

Kawamura, Y. (2011). *Doing research in fashion and dress: An introduction to qualitative methods.* New York, NY: Berg Publishers.

Keefer, J. (2011). *Silence and voice.* [Web log]. Retrieved from http://silenceandvoice.com/

Kessler, S. (2010). The case for social media in schools. *Mashable.* Retrieved from http://mashable.com/2010/09/29/social-media-in-school/

Khang, H., Ki, E., Ye, L. (2012). How scholars have responded to social media phenomena in advertising, communication, marketing and public relations research from 1997–2010. *Association for Education in Journalism and Mass Communication.* Retrieved from http://www.aejmc.org/home/2011/06/mcs-2011-abstracts/

Larsson, A., & Moe, H. (2012). Studying political microblogging: Twitter users in the 2010 Swedish election campaign. *New Media & Society, 14*(5), 729–747.

Madden, M. (2010). Older adults and social media. *Pew Internet & American Life Project.* Retrieved from http://pewresearch.org/pubs/1711/older-adults-social-networking-facebook-twitter and http://pewinternet.org/Reports/2010/Older-Adults-and-Social-Media.aspx

Madge, C. (2007). Developing a geographers' agenda for online research ethics. *Progress in Human Geography, 31*(5), 654–674.

Manjoo, F. (2011, June 13). With iCloud, Jobs reaches for the web. *The Washington Post,* p. G5.

Mathison, S. (2012). Clever visual representation of FB data. *Qualitative Research Café.* Retrieved from http://blogs.ubc.ca/qualresearch/?s=Clever+visual+representation+of+FB+data

Merlien Institute. (2011). *The use of the iPad in and for qualitative research.* Retrieved from www.slideshare.net/merlien/the-use-of-the-i-pad-in-and-for-qualitative-research

Michael, M. (2012). Latest social media research blog from DigitalMR: New online qualitative tools changing the way we conduct research. *Yahoo News.* Retrieved from http://news.yahoo.com/latest-social-media-research-blog-digitalmr-online-qualitative-080908404.html

Paiewonsky, M. (2011). Hitting the reset button on education: Student reports on going to college. *Career Development for Exceptional Individuals, 34*(1), 31–44.

Parsons, J. (2011). Qualitative research in Japan. *Connect.* [Web log]. Retrieved from http://rwconnect.esomar.org/2011/01/20/qualitative-research-in-japan/

Pearson, A. F. (2010). Real problems, virtual solutions: Engaging students online. *Teaching sociology, 38*(3), 207–214.

Qualman, E. (2011). *Social Media Revolution 2011.* [YouTube video]. Retrieved from http://www.youtube.com/watch?v=3SuNx0UrnEo

Read, P., Shah, C., S-O'Brien, L., & Woolcott, J. (2012). "Story of one's life and a tree of friends"—understanding millennials' information behaviour in social networks. *Journal of Information Science, 38*(5), 489–497.

Rice, K. L. (2006). A comprehensive look at distance education in the K–12 context. *Journal of Research on Technology in Education, 38*(4), 425–448.

Robards, B., & Bennett, A. (2011). MyTribe: Post-subcultural manifestations of belonging on social network sites. *Sociology, 45*(2), 303–317.

Salmons, J. (2012). Deep data: Digging into social media with qualitative methods. *Web-Based Communication and Learning Designs.* Retrieved from http://webcommdesigns.com/post/36711648065/deep-data-digging-into-social-media-with-qualitative

Schostak, J. (2011). *Qualitative research blog.* [Web log]. Retrieved from http://methodologyblog.imaginativespaces.net/blog

Schwitzer, K. (2011). 7learnings from the Super Bowl XLV (2011) mobile ethnography. *NewQualitativeResearch.* [Web log]. Retrieved from http://www.newqualitative.org/blog/7-learnings-from-the-super-bowl-xlv-2011-mobile-ethnography/

Seale, C., Charteris-Black, J., MacFarlane, A., & McPherson, A. (2009). Interviews and Internet forums: A comparison of two sources of qualitative data. *Qualitative Research, 20*(5), 595–606.

Shulman, S. (2011). *JITP 2011: The future of computational social science.* Retrieved from http://www.umass.edu/jitp/Shulman.htm

Texas A&M. (2010). *Introduction to qualitative research wikibook.* Retrieved from http://wikis.tamu.edu/display/qualiwiki/Introduction+to+Qualitative+Research+Wikibook

Wikiversity. (n.d.). *Qualitative research.* Retrieved from http://en.wikiversity.org/wiki/Qualitative_research

Williams, M. (2012). Review: Heidi A. McKee and James E. Porter, *The ethics of Internet research: A rhetorical, case-based process. Qualitative Research, 12*(1), 96–97.

Wilson, R., Gosling, S., & Graham, L. (2012). A review of Facebook research in the social sciences. *Perspectives on Psychological Science, 7*(3), 203–220.

Xie, B. (2008). Civic engagement among older Chinese Internet users. *Journal of Applied Gerontology, 27*(4), 424–445.

Zimmer, M. (2008). On the "anonymity" of the Facebook dataset. *Michael Zimmer.org.* Retrieved from http://www.michaelzimmer.org/2008/09/30/on-the-anonymity-of-the-facebook-dataset/

Zimmer, M. (2010). Revisiting research ethics in the Facebook era: Challenges in emerging CSCW research. *Michael Zimmer.org.* Retrieved from http://michaelzimmer.org/2010/02/06/revisiting-research-ethics-in-the-facebook-era-challenges-in-emerging-cscw-research/

STUDENT STUDY SITE

Visit **http://www.sagepub.com/lichtmanqrss** to access additional study tools, including eFlashcards and links to SAGE journal articles.

CHAPTER 9

A Review of Research Literature

Focus Your Reading

- Why we conduct a review of research
- Steps in conducting a review
- Incorporating review into your work

It has long been accepted practice to include a review of related research when conducting quantitative research (QN). How are you to know what else is out there and how your piece of research fits into the overall knowledge base if you don't look at what has already been done? Few would question this notion. Of course, there are differences—some subtle and some not-so-subtle—in how such a review might be done. Here are some questions that are often asked: What studies should be selected for review? Must they appear in a peer-reviewed journal? What constitutes a complete set of studies in terms of content or publication date? How should a review be organized? Should a reviewer limit comments to reporting? Or should a reviewer take a proactive stance and critique other research? How can a researcher build an argument to support the need for a proposed new study? In what ways can a researcher make claims for new information based on the relationship between existing research and new findings?

Just as so many practices once thought to be critical for conducting research have been rethought, abandoned, or dismissed when doing qualitative research (QR), so too has the almost-rote practice of doing a literature review prior to conducting a QR study. In this chapter, I want to look at this topic from several viewpoints. When you complete the chapter, you should be able to make your own decisions.

I will address three topics: why, how, and in what manner the research literature should contribute to your own research.

First is the *why* question:

- Why should I do a review of related literature when conducting QR?
- Why should I omit a review of related literature?
- Is there a middle ground?

Next, I address the *how* question:

- How is the research located?
- What is considered useful research?
- In what ways can research that doesn't meet traditional standards (not peer-reviewed or not in "legitimate" sources) be used?
- What about using QN?
- How do you assess the legitimacy/value/worth of research you find?
- How can it inform your own research?
- What other types of information can be included in a review of research—theoretical presentations, conceptual interpretations, blogs, videos, social media?
- Consider the source. Some of our best ideas come from those who are unknown or who make new discoveries by chance.
- How do you keep track of all the research? There are a myriad of details involved in doing so.

I also discuss how research literature should be integrated into your own thinking and writing:

- How do you write about it in your own work?
- Where do you locate it in your written work?
- How can it be used if your work uses an alternate presentation format, such as poetry, performance, or autoethnography?
- How do you relate your new work to existing work?
- Do you need to relate your work?
- What about other practicalities? Your institution, your discipline, or your adviser may have requirements or expectations. If your goal is to complete a degree, you may have to pick your battleground.

■ Introduction

Today, I saw a clip on television that decried the overreliance by the youth of today on technology, specifically on mobile apps. The commentator spoke about how his daughter ordered food via her smart phone that would be delivered to the house. He was concerned that she didn't understand that money was involved and, in fact, told her father that the food was free. Somehow, she had lost touch with the way things used to be. I am not one to suggest that we return to the days of accessing information as we have done in the past. In fact, I accept technology and am an avid user of it. From smartphones to tablets to laptops, I could not operate without it.

The way we access information has changed much in just a few short years. Ask your parents or grandparents about the *card catalog*. It was a catalog of all books and documents found in a library. The objectives of such a catalog were first stated by Charles Cutter in 1876. Its purpose was to help someone locate a book, to include what the library's holdings were, or to help someone choose a particular book. More than one hundred years later, in 1998, functional requirements for bibliographic records were actually quite similar. There are four goals: find, identify, select, and obtain. For a look at some old card catalogs, go to Wikipedia (2013) or to Flickr (2012), where you can see the card catalog of the Library of Congress in Washington, DC. I was surprised that the public does not get to see the main card catalog except for twice a year, when there is an open house. The main card catalog contains 22,000 drawers and 22 million cards. No cards have been added since 1980!

Today, card catalogs have been replaced by an online public access catalog. Basically, this is an online database of materials held by a library. The first online catalogs were developed by Ohio State University in 1975 and the Dallas Public Library in 1978.

While published books are an important source of information, I suspect that much of the information you need exists in other forms. How do we access other types of information? Later in this chapter, I will discuss two primary ways: the use of online databases that lead you to journals, conference proceedings, or dissertations and the use of a search engine such as Google on the Internet.

We all know that the Internet has transformed our lives. Information is instantaneous, whether it comes from down the street or the other side of the world. You can learn about the Arab Spring as it is happening or about a new discovery in treating cancer as patients are undergoing experimental use of it. Information is exploding at such a pace that it is impossible to keep current with it. There used to be a body of information that all were expected to learn to become an educated person. Now, some of that is irrelevant or in error. Information is ephemeral, sometimes here today and lost the next day. The blog I loved so much is no longer around. The YouTube video I viewed yesterday has been removed from the Internet today.

In this chapter, I will talk about information. Specifically, I will target information that can be classified as research or information of other types that might be related to a particular topic of interest. I will answer three main questions: Do we need a review of related information on a topic, and why? If we do need one, how do we go about obtaining it, and what do we do with it? Finally, how can we use that information and relate it to our own research?

Did You Know

We are a far cry from staid libraries and card catalogs. Today, we might look at a new book, *Popularizing Research* (EMAC, n.d.). If you go to the link, you will find nine sections of the book: film; visual media and graphics; exhibits and installations; audio; periodicals; books and reports; dialogue; performance; and publicity. So keep your mind open as you think about reviewing research.

The Question of Why

Value of a Review

"The issue of when and how to use the literature in qualitative research is relevant to quite a number of social science disciplines" (Tummers & Karsten, 2012, p. 65). As I began my quest to find an answer to the question of whether QR needed to include a literature review, I came across a guide to doing a Review of Literature for a thesis at the University of Missouri (Ludwig, n.d.). The paragraph written by the author—clearly slanted toward QN—has some interesting information.

I think many writers, advisers, students, and colleagues would take the position that you should conduct a literature review prior to actually doing research yourself. Young (n.d.), writing an eHow blog, stated that examining related research is a requirement. Rocco and Plakhotnik (2009) admonished that all methods "must be connected to literature or concepts that support the need for the study" (p. 120). Here are some reasons why. I know of many researchers who begin with a review of a literature on a topic to generate ideas for additional research. Someone might be interested in a study of bullying but not have any specific or clear ideas about what else might be done. Some would say that looking at the available literature could serve as a starting point. Once a specific area has been chosen, it needs refinement or a narrowing. You might want or need to demonstrate your knowledge about a particular topic or field (Randolph, 2009). You can use the literature to provide clarity about a topic or determine a particular focus (Bearfield & Eller, 2007; Havercamp & Young, 2007; McNabb, 2002). Or you might want to become familiar with the key players in the field (Randolph, 2009). You might want to establish a framework for the analysis of topics (Justice, 2007). Or you might use a literature review as a type of expert witness to support or contradict conclusions of your research (Metcalfe, 2003).

Numerous research texts suggest that conducting a literature review helps set the framework and stage for your own research. This is true in many social science disciplines. For example, Tummers and Karsten (2012) cite three methods books in public administration that favor such a use.

As counseling psychologists, Havercamp and Young (2007) addressed the iterative, circular nature of QR. In particular, they were concerned with literature as it relates to a researcher's knowledge of theory and related work and the presentation of literature in a written manuscript.

Lorenc and his colleagues (2012) discussed the role of systematic reviews of QR in evaluating interventions. The purpose of this research was to determine if the use of qualitative information could be helpful in deciding on an intervention related to skin cancer. They concluded,

> We find that qualitative evidence not directly related to interventions is likely to be of value for such reviews, that it is often not possible to construct fully comprehensive search strategies, and that there are diminishing returns to the synthesis, in terms of added value or insight, from the inclusion of large numbers of primary studies. We conclude that there are a number of ways in which systematic reviews of qualitative evidence can be utilised

in conjunction with evidence on intervention effectiveness, without compromising the rigour of the review process. In particular, the use of theory to inform frameworks for synthesis is a promising way to integrate a broader range of qualitative evidence. (p. 1)

Potential Limitations of a Review

Psychologists have written often about the power of suggestion. Educators talk about self-fulfilling prophecy in expectations about student performance. How does this relate to doing research? In the field of public administration, Tummers and Karsten (2012) suggested that there is a fine line between "being theoretically sensitive and imposing preconceived ideas" (p. 64). You might find yourself developing a barrier to new insights. In spite of these cautions, Tummers and Karsten stated clearly that researchers "have to relate their work to the existing literature in their field" (p. 71). They discussed the issue of when to use literature and whether it should be used in the analysis phase of research. For a detailed explanation of the use of literature in research design, data collection, and data analysis phases of research, I refer you to their interesting article.

It is the group associated with the grounded theory approach that is most critical of the use of related research. You will recall that I discussed grounded theory in Chapter 5. Remember that its purpose is to develop theory that is based on the gathered data. This inductive approach is in contrast to testing previously espoused theory. Glaser (1998) admonished against conducting a literature review, and Morse (2002) warned that using a review violated an inductive approach. In fact, Morse suggested that a researcher's dilemma was whether or not to go to the library prior to conducting research. But Havercamp and Young (2007) concluded that such an interpretation is a misunderstanding of the work. While they acknowledged that researchers can be biased, they suggested that an open stance is what is critical.

It is the rare published article that omits any type of literature review. Several researchers have ventured into publications that use poetry or autoethnographic solely (see Bassett, 2012; Ellis & Bochner, 2000; Glesne,1997; Lambert, 2012; Naidu, 2011; Richardson, 1997, 2005.) One example that does include a review is Davis's (2012) presentation of three poems constructed from the words of GED students. Some who publish such pieces include references embedded in portions of the play (Teman & Lahman, 2012).

Although not specifically about the limitations of conducting a review (but rather about the possible limitations of articles that are included in a review), Carroll, Booth, and Lloyd-Jones (2012) questioned whether or not to exclude inadequately reported studies in a systematic review. Using two case studies, they concluded, "We found that in no case did these exclusions appear to affect either the overall conceptual findings of these systematic reviews or the richness of the data underpinning their results" (p. 1432). I think it is conventional wisdom that it is not good to include studies that are not done well. But this study suggests that the overall conclusions are not affected by including some poorly designed studies.

When Should You Conduct a Review?

As I indicated, there is no agreement among the QR community about whether you should conduct a review. But those who are entirely against some type of review are in the small minority. Others take a slightly different position. Some suggest that you should wait until you have completed your research before you look at what others have done. The primary reason for this is to avoid being influenced—knowingly or tacitly—by what you read. Some believe that you should conduct a review concurrently with conducting your research. They hold the position that since QR is iterative and inductive, it would be valuable to conduct a review as you gather data and conduct an analysis. Dunne (2011), reflecting the views of Bryant and Charmaz in the field of grounded theory, commented that "it is not *whether* a literature review should be conduced—there is consensus that it should—but rather *when* it should be conducted" (p. 113)

What Are You to Do?

My recommendation to you is to conduct a review of the literature. I would begin with a brief review prior to planning my study and continue the review process throughout the life of the study. I will discuss later in this chapter what you should do with the review, how to write about it, and integrate it into your own work. But for now, get ready to learn what others have done.

■ The Process of How

Fink's (2010) text on conducting a literature review from Internet to paper includes a number of topics, such as definitions and explanations on what a review is, a section that includes reviews for observational studies (mainly qualitative), and choosing an online database. Below, I identify a number of steps that will assist you to conduct a review of research related to your topic. Following that, I describe some ways in which you can use the review you have conducted.

■ Conducting a Review of Related Research—Critical Steps

Conducting a Review

1. Identify a topic.
2. Determine search terms.
3. Search for information. Access key databases, conduct Internet searches, and include research on qualitative approaches.
4. Select relevant information. Avoid information that is too broad or too narrow.
5. Review critically.
6. Modify your topic, if necessary.
7. Keep track of things.

Identify a Topic of Interest

You might find yourself wondering about a topic you want to study but are not especially clear on details of the topic. Either the topic that is so broad that it would be impossible to learn everything about it, or, conversely, it is so narrow that you will not find anything about the topic. Remember, at this point in your research, your topic is somewhat diffuse. You will work on refining it as you review the research literature.

Determine Search Terms

Even though you have selected a topic of interest, it is not clear what terms you should use for your search. One task you have before you will be to identify key terms. If you do not narrow your search, the output will be enormous. If you narrow your search too much, you might not find anything. You may also want to put limits on your search related to dates. Or you may find it helpful to narrow your search by identifying a critical population (e.g., males, people with HIV/AIDS, teenage girls, displaced workers).

Search for Information

You will need to locate information through various means. No longer will you journey to your library and look in a card catalog. One common way to find information is to search databases that include journals in which you will find research related to your topic. You should be able to get information about which journals are included in databases and how to access them through your library. Below, I list some diverse databases. I also provide ways to access lists of social science databases.

- *Social Science Research Network* (SSRN; http://www.ssrn.com/) is devoted to rapid worldwide dissemination of social science research. It includes an abstract database and an electronic paper collection of downloadable documents. The international scope of this network will lead you to sources not found in the usual databases. The database is extremely easy to use: Enter your search term(s). Choose "title only" or title, abstract, and key words. An abstract will appear. If you want the full article, you can download it to your computer.

- The *Sociosite* database (http://www.sociosite.net/) is designed to provide access to sociologists and others worldwide. Their viewpoint is that the latest sociological research might find its way onto the Internet before it appears in traditional media. As their About page states, "Coming to terms with the Internet and its resources is a most pressing and necessary task for all social scientists." I searched the term *qualitative research* but can't say I found anything particularly useful or recent. Based at the University of Amsterdam, it is comprehensive and easy to use.

- A list of social science databases developed by Langsdale Library at the University of Baltimore (http://langsdale.ubalt.edu/databases/databases-by-subject/social-sciences-databases.cfm) will lead you to some relevant sources. Its organization is helpful. For each database, there are two sections—what you will find and how to search the database. Warning: Some of the databases will need to be accessed through your institution.

- Another list of social science databases can be found through ProQuest (http://www.proquest.com/en-US/products/feature02_subject.shtml). You may need to gain access through your institution, but reviewing the databases should help you narrow down which ones you will want to look at.

- Another source of information is dissertation abstracts. Dissertation Abstracts International (DAI) or ProQuest Dissertations and Theses (PQDT) are bibliographies of dissertations published by University Microfilms International. Section A includes social sciences. For details as to how to access these sites, my recommendation is to check with your institution.

- Accessing data from conferences is another way to locate research that has not yet been published.

Of course, an important source of information is the Internet. You can access topics of interest by using one of any number of search engines. According to Boswell (2012), the top ten search engines for 2012 are

- USA.gov—everything publicly available on the Web, including access to Library of Congress
- Wolfram Alpha—answers fact-based questions. I am interested in their section on cultural events and multimedia as well as people and history.
- DuckDuckGo—keeps your search results private, since it does not track what users are looking for. I have used it to compare with Google and found that it often provides different information.
- Bing—a newer search engine developed by Microsoft
- Google—most popular. It processes millions of searches daily. As you probably know, it is very useful and versatile.

Yes, I included only five here. The others (Pinterest, Twitter, YouTube, Facebook, and LinkedIn) may not be as useful for locating relevant research.

You may want to search journals directly. I have found it particularly useful to search SAGE journals (http://www.sagepub.com/journals.nav). According to its website, SAGE is the world's 5th largest journal publisher. SAGE publishes more than 645 journals in the humanities, social sciences, and science, technology, and medicine. The website is user friendly and includes a number of tools that will facilitate its use. You may be able to gain access to the site through the library at your institution. (Disclosure: SAGE is the publisher of this text and others I have written.)

Some other ways to get relevant research is to use the references gleaned from journal articles you have already located. Often, the references in that article will be related to what you need. You can also join a LISTSERV or user group related to your topic. Some are available through Facebook or Twitter. Attending conferences or reading blogs may also provide you with interesting research. The University of Georgia (n.d.) maintains a

LISTSERV specifically devoted to qualitative issues. It has operated continuously since September 1991.

In reviews of research for QN or survey research, authors assume that readers have a knowledge of research approach and experimental design. This is often not the case when conducting QR. It is to your advantage to conduct a review of the approach you plan to use in conducting your study. I have outlined details of many of the approaches in earlier chapters.

Select Relevant Information

At this point, you will be faced with considerably more information than you can possibly review. There is no good way to decide if what you find will be helpful. I suggest that you start by scanning what you have located. Identify those articles that appear related to your work. Select those and put them in your own database. Your next step is to read the abstract or skim the article. Again, select those that are relevant and create a new database for those.

Begin reading relevant material. As you do so, you will begin to develop an outline with key main threads and subthreads.

Review Critically

As a reviewer, it is up to you to determine whether you find the information useful, credible, and relevant. We know that articles that appear in peer-reviewed journals have been subject to a review by some group. It is conventional wisdom that these articles are more reliable. But I would not ignore or dismiss information that appears in other sources. One of the problems with relying exclusively on peer-reviewed journals is that the length of time for review and publication is at least a year, often longer.

I find myself being challenged by a number of things I read from sources other than traditional journals. This is especially true in regard to articles of a qualitative nature, since only some journals publish those.

Modify Topic If Necessary

Often, a literature review will lead you to modify your own topic. You might change direction or clarify your own research approach.

Keep Track of Things

It is to your advantage to develop a system that makes use of your computer and word processing. I think the best system is the one you develop. But to avoid common problems, I suggest that you stay on the lookout for some issues I identify here.

Avoid Hard Copies and Printing Things

Many references are downloadable in PDF and can be saved to your computer. Others can be marked and identified later, if you need to return to them.

What Do You Write?

Once you have read an article, you may want to make notes about it. Develop a system you are comfortable with. You might want to include authors and dates and then some key points from an article. Or you might want to include a quote for later use. Copying from an article to your own system is easily accomplished with word processing.

Completeness and Accuracy in References

I can't tell you how many hours I have spent trying to get the last detail of a reference. I omitted page numbers, dates were in error, or a name appeared incorrect. Just recently, I ran into an unusual problem: I had multiple entries for the same author. In one case, I had listed the author's first and middle initial. In another case, I did not. So sometimes the name appeared in two different places in a reference list or it was obvious that the same person was listed in two different ways.

Software Programs for References

There are some programs that will permit you to store references and then convert them to the proper form consistent with your particular discipline. I have used EndNotes and Zotero. I experienced some minor problems with both of them. I also found when I tried to merge two different reference lists, I had difficulty with merging and alphabetizing. It is to your advantage to make sure that you are familiar with a particular program or that you find someone who is. NVivo10 (2012) will facilitate your organization and analysis of information you collect.

Using Proper Form for Unusual References

Different disciplines have different expectations for citations. While many in the social sciences use American Psychological Association (APA) Standards, not all do. How to cite things obtained online or through SlideShare or YouTube is not always clear. My advice is to search the Internet for guidelines.

What Do Others Say?

I conducted a review of what others have to say about how to do a literature review. Some of the references below are specific to QR, while others are of a more general nature. For an excellent example of how a team of reviewers implemented these steps, I refer you to Newton and colleagues (2011). After presenting their review, they raised several critical questions. In answer to the question "Are we thinking qualitatively?" they raised four important concerns and suggested several responses. They suggested that researchers stop justifying using qualitative methods but instead explain why the method is appropriate. This article should get you thinking about what QR should and should not try to do.

Some authors outline steps to follow (Creswell, 2012; Pan, 2008). Many are quite similar. You can look in any standard research textbook and find steps that involve identifying research questions and key terms, searching databases, selecting relevant research, evaluating, and presenting it. Other writers offer variations. For example, Cooper (as described in Randolph, 2009) developed a taxonomy of literature reviews organized into several characteristics: focus, goal, perspective, coverage, organization, and audience. For each characteristic, he included several categories.

Writing specifically about QR reviews, Randolph (2009, p. 10) suggested that there are different approaches you might follow when conducting a qualitative literature review. In this case, Randolph dealt with the examination of QR rather than the appropriateness or usefulness of using relevant research in a qualitative study. He provided a specific example related to phenomenology. I found Randolph's steps interesting. He began with bracketing. (I'm not sure how this is part of a review of literature.) Collecting data follows. In this case, a reviewer would read reports of "scientists" who have done research on the phenomenon. (I wonder why he chose the term *scientist*.) Next, he suggested that the reviewer choose meaningful statements and provide meaning. You can choose for yourself if you think this works for conducting a literature review.

Bradshaw, Playford, and Riazi (2012) described the process they followed in conducting a qualitative review of home care. They conducted a search of relevant databases (PsycINFO, Medline, Web of Science, EMBASE, Allied and Complementary Medicine Database, and Cumulative Index to Nursing and Allied Health Literature). Next, they selected relevant papers. They assessed the quality of the methodology using two independent reviews. Finally, they conducted thematic analysis and meta-ethnographic methods to synthesize findings.

Jeon and colleagues (2010) described an approach to conducting a narrative review of the experience of living with chronic heart failure. Just as Bradshaw and colleagues did, they began with a search of electronic databases. They narrowed the search using Boolean methods of three relevant terms (heart failure, congestive heart failure, and chronic heart failure) coupled with qualitative methods and the time period of 1990 to 2008. In case you are not familiar with a Boolean search, in its simplest format, it involves the combination of two terms by a conjunction: *and*, *or*, *not*. So if you want to search for heart failure and its incidence among men, you would search *heart failure* and *men*. George Boole, a British mathematician from the 19th century, developed the logic of this type of search.

Havercamp and Young (2007) differentiated among various research approaches in terms of using a literature review:

> In general, ethnography, critical theory, and consensual qualitative research tend to use extensive initial literature reviews, whereas grounded theory and phenomenology tend to abbreviate this section. Alternately, grounded theory and phenomenology often cite related literature in the discussion section, where it can serve as a form of consensus or triangulation with regard to the conclusions or, more traditionally, as a way to relate the findings to the broader field. (p. 287)

Although not specifically about QR, Machi and McEvoy (2012) described six steps toward a literature review: selecting a topic, searching the literature, developing arguments, surveying the literature, critiquing the literature, and writing the review.

Incorporating Review in Your Work—Critical Steps

Decide on a type of review.

- Contextual—puts your work in big picture
- Historical—development over time
- Theoretical/Conceptual—compares various theories
- Methodological—reviews various research approaches or amplifies specific approach
- Integrative—summarizes what is known and generates new ideas

Decide on a style of review.

- Expository—neutral
- Supporting—positional

Organize your review.

- Themes
- Issues
- Trends

Locate existing research in your own work.

- Initial section
- Throughout paper
- At the end or in the appendix

Relate your research to existing research.

Using the Information

You might be surprised to learn that there is no standardized format for presentation of research reviews. I think this gives you an opportunity to develop your own personal style of presentation. Some of the issues are described below.

Decide on a Type of Review

A challenge you now face is to decide what type of review you are going to write. Since your review is not just a summary of what you found, you need to determine how you plan to present it. Knowing your purpose for the review will help you with this. Several are identified.

Contextual

One of the major reasons researchers conduct a review of related literature is to position their proposed new work in the context of what has gone before. What is known about the topic?

Are there other areas that might be considered? At this point, you might decide to comment on how the research was conducted—QR, QN, or mixed-methods research—or a particular research approach. All are fair game for you to include in a review of literature.

Historical

Another way that you could organize your material is to present it in a chronological manner. I think of how art museums arrange their work. Some choose to present a chronological approach to art, while others organize material around themes or a particular artist. Again, there is no correct way.

Theoretical/Conceptual

Another type of review you might conduct centers on theoretical pieces rather than original work. This is an acceptable form and might be useful in some instances. You need to be mindful of plans you have for your own research, however, and how a review based on theory might prove limiting. An editorial by Reio (2010) stressed the need for this.

Methodological

It is often to your advantage to conduct a review of the particular research approach you plan to use. It can be used to explain and justify what you are doing and why you are doing a particular thing. In addition to research approaches, some writers review the literature on reflexivity, an important component of QR. Newton and his colleagues (2011), following an extensive review on the topic of lower back pain, were surprised that "there was not a single article that we considered an exemplar of reflexive practice" (p. 15).

Integrative

Another type of review is that known as *integrative*. According to Torraco (2005), such a review synthesizes relevant research on a topic in order to develop a new perspective or framework. Torraco suggested that such a review tells a story "by critically analyzing the literature and arriving at specific conclusions about it" (p. 361). Other steps involve synthesizing new knowledge, using logic and reasoning, and writing clearly. Torraco offered an example of such a review in the work of Bailey and Kurland (2002). More recently, Daley and her colleagues (2010) published an integrative literature review on concept mapping in human resource development. This is a comprehensive review—obviously beyond the scope of what an individual can do.

Decide on Style of Review

Just above, I discussed the types of review. The style of review is related to type of review. But here, I am concerned with your own position in using and writing a review. One common way I see reviews presented is one in which the writer takes a neutral stance. He or she presents the review in an expository fashion. This is true if a review is presented in a chronological manner or in a thematic manner. In either case, the reviewer functions as a kind of reporter or conveyer of information. I prefer a more proactive review, in which the reviewer adopts a particular position and then uses a review to support that position. This is akin to an attorney presenting an argument for or against a viewpoint. Your review will have more punch if you adopt this viewpoint.

Organize the Review

Now, you are faced with the task of organizing the information you have collected. You could choose a number of different structures. You might want to write a review based on themes you identify as you review the literature. Or you may choose to identify particular issues. A third structure you use could revolve around trends on the topic. Or you may combine these or other key ideas as well. Whatever you choose, it should help the reader make sense of what you have learned.

Locate Your Own Research

By far, most QR articles include a review of literature at or near the beginning of a paper. One drawback of this style is that the review appears to be just stuck in a location and is rarely used again. Placing a review at the beginning is not always the most desirable location. I have seen a number of effective studies that integrate literature throughout the paper. Finally, some writers, especially those who use alternative presentation modes (e.g., poetry, performance, visuals), either do not have a review or include one in an appendix. Remember, you will have space limitations if you write for a journal. So you will need to pick and choose wisely.

Relate Your Research to Existing Research

I can't tell you how many times I have read the words "further research needs to be done on this topic" or "this research adds to the body of research" at the conclusion of a research study. In other cases, I find that the researcher fails to mention existing research at all. I encourage you to think about why you wrote a literature review in the first place. You had reasons other than your institution's requiring it or your adviser's suggesting it—or it was just something you thought you were supposed to do.

What Do Others Do?

I looked at some recent journals that either publish QR articles exclusively or are open to publishing QR to see how recently published research deals with literature reviews.

The July 2012 issue of *Qualitative Inquiry* includes eight articles. The majority of papers included a review. For example, Stich and colleagues (2012), writing on the topic of conducting ethnographic work, included a review. Mikecz's (2012) work explored the topic of interviewing elites. He included an extensive review. Razon and Ross (2012) also included an extensive review related to the topic of negotiating fluid identities. Although Holliday's (2012) work is based on an interview with a single individual, it included an extensive literature review. Out of necessity, Leavey's (2012) work includes a review (since it is a review of research). Bassett's (2012) very brief poem provides a short review of the use of poetry in QR.

Bai's (2012) article on the topic of love, sex, and marriage in Chinese culture is written as a performance piece and begins with the cast, six scenes, and a coda. Although there is a reference list, none are included in the article. Douglas (2012) used a variety of storytelling and poetry in her account of women golfers. She used literature to support her use of these types of presentation.

The July 2012 issue of *Qualitative Health Research* includes twelve articles. Fairly traditional in style and format, they each include a review of related literature. One is a meta-synthesis of research. The April 2012 issue of *Qualitative Research* includes seven articles. All include literature reviews.

In a thoughtful piece in *The Journal of Applied Behavioral Science,* Huy (2012) explored the topic of improving the odds for publication of qualitative work in "top international journals" (p. 282). The first two tips he offered are relevant here. He recommended that authors "achieve absolute mastery of the relevant literatures" and that they "remain constantly updated on the evolution of the literature" (p. 286).

I also did a Boolean search of articles published by SAGE using *grounded theory* and *qualitative* as search terms for the year 2012. Five hundred and twenty-four articles appeared in various journals. A cursory review of many of the articles revealed that all of them included a review of literature. I also searched recent articles using *poem*, *poetry*, *autoethnography*, or *performance* as search terms. While some poems or autoethnographies stood alone, others included reviews of research in some fashion.

After discussing the merits of conducting a review of research as part of your own research project, I presented you with information about how to conduct such a search, sources of information, and ways in which you can write your review and incorporate it in your own work. Remember, alternatives to traditional QN at times omit such a review, especially when alternative forms of presentation are used (e.g., poetry, ethnotheatre, or dance).

CHECK YOURSELF

- Why do we conduct a review of research? Most researchers see value of review, but some are concerned that a review might limit them.
- I described seven critical steps regarding how to conduct a review.
- I also described the steps you should use to incorporate review into your work.

KEY DISCUSSION ISSUES

1. Many people assume that conducting a literature review prior to doing a research study is necessary. What are some of the reasons offered for not doing such a review in advance?
2. What is the value of using peer-reviewed research? In what ways can other types of research be helpful?
3. What steps in conducting a literature review do you see as critical? Which would you omit? Do you have any to add?
4. What are the different types of literature reviews? Which one seems to fit your own style? Why?

MODULE 9

Conducting a Mini-Literature Review and Writing It Up

Here, you are going to practice narrowing and broadening a research topic. It is best to work with a partner. Identify a research topic. At this point, the nature and style of the topic are open.

Key Term	*Key Term*	*Database*	*Number of Hits*	*Modify*	*Round*
reflexivity	qualitative	SAGE journals			1
reflexivity	qualitative	SAGE journals		Limit to 2012	2
reflexivity	researcher	SAGE journals		Limit to 2011–12	3

Gain access to a database through your institution. Select key terms based on your topic. Search the database with no limitations. Develop a chart similar to the one above, indicating search terms, database used, and number of hits.

Evaluate how many hits you get with each modification. If too many hits, continue to limit. If too few hits, then broaden your search.

REFERENCES

Bai, M. (2012). Love, sex, marriage: A family history on the women's side. *Qualitative Inquiry, 18*(6), 475–481.

Bailey, D. E., & Kurland, N. B. (2002). A review of telework research: Findings, new directions, and lessons for the study of modern work. *Journal of Organizational Behavior, 23,* 383–400.

Bassett, R. (2012). Pensive poetics: Reflections on interprofessional team collaboration. *Qualitative Inquiry, 18*(6), 523–524.

Bearfield, D. A., & Eller, W. S. (2007). Writing a literature review: The art of scientific literature. In K. Yang & G. J. Miller (Eds.), *Handbook of research methods for public administration* (pp. 61–72). New York, NY: CRC Press.

Boswell, W. (2012). *About.com: Web search.* Retrieved from http://websearch.guide.about.com

Bradshaw, S., Playford, E., & Riazi, A. (2012). Living well in care homes: A systematic review of qualitative studies. *Age and Ageing, 41*(4), 429–440. Retrieved from http://ageing.oxfordjournals.org/content/early/2012/06/07/ageing.afs069.short?rss=1

Carroll, C., Booth, A., & Lloyd-Jones, M. (2012). Should we exclude inadequately reported studies from qualitative systematic reviews? An evaluation of sensitivity analyses in two case study reviews. *Qualitative Health Research, 22*(10), 1425–1434.

Creswell, J. (2012). *Qualitative inquiry and research design* (3rd ed.). Thousand Oaks, CA: SAGE.

Daley, B., Conceica, S., Mina, L., Altman, B., Baldor, M., & Brown, J. (2010). Integrative literature review: Concept mapping: A strategy to support the development of practice, research, and theory within human resource development. *Human Resource Development Review, 9*(4), 357–384.

Davis, C. (2012). G.E.D. in 3 voices. *Qualitative Inquiry, 18*(3), 227–234.

Douglas, K. (2012). Signals and signs. *Qualitative Inquiry, 18*(6), 525–532.

Dunne, C. (2011). The place of the literature review in grounded theory research. *International Journal of Social Research Methodology, 14*(2), 111–124. Retrieved from http://staff.neu.edu.tr/~cise.cavusoglu/Documents/Advaced%20Research%20Methods/Qualitative/Dunne%20Place%20of%20Literature%20in%20Grounded%20theory.pdf

Ellis, C., & Bochner, A. (2000). Autoethnography, personal narrative, reflexivity: Researcher as subject. In N. Denzin & Y. Lincoln (Eds.), *Handbook of qualitative research* 2nd ed., pp. 733–768. Thousand Oaks, CA: SAGE.

EMAC. (n.d.). *Popularizing Research.* Retrieved from http://www.popularizingresearch.net/

Fink, A. (2010). *Conducting research literature reviews: From the Internet to paper* (3rd ed.). Thousand Oaks, CA: SAGE.

Flickr. (2012). *Card catalog—Library of Congress, Washington D.C.* Retrieved from http://www.flickr.com/photos/dan-lem 2001/6778397480/

Glaser, B. G. (1998). *Doing grounded theory: Issues and discussions.* Mill Valley, CA: Sociology Press.

Glesne, C. (1997). That rare feeling: Re-presenting research through poetic transcription. *Qualitative Inquiry, 3,* 202–221.

Havercamp, B., & Young, R. (2007). Paradigms, purpose, and the role of the literature: Formulating a rationale for qualitative investigations. *The Counseling Psychologist, 35*(2), 265–294.

Holliday, A. (2012). Interrogating researcher participation in an interview study of intercultural contribution in the workplace. *Qualitative Inquiry, 18*(6), 504–515.

Huy, Q. (2012). Improving the odds of publishing inductive qualitative research in premier academic journals. *Journal of Applied Behavioral Science, 48*(2), 282–287.

Jeon, Y-H, Kraus, S., Jowsey, T, & Glasgow, M. (2010). The experience of living with chronic heart failure: A narrative review of qualitative studies. *BMC Health Services Research, 10*(77). Retrieved from http://www.biomedcentral.com/1472-6963/10/77

Justice, J. B. (2007). Purpose and significance of research design. In K. Yang & G. J. Miller (Eds.), *Handbook of research methods for public administration* (pp. 75–92). New York, NY: CRC Press.

Lambert, K. (2012). The lost boys. *Qualitative Inquiry, 18*(5), 414–417.

Leavey, P. (2012). Fiction and the feminist academic novel. *Qualitative Inquiry 18*(6), 516–522.

Lorenc, T., Pearson, M., Jamal, F., Cooper, C., & Garside, R. (2012). The role of systematic reviews of qualitative evidence in evaluating interventions: A case study. *Research Synthesis Methods, 3*(1), 1–10. Retrieved from http://onlinelibrary.wiley.com/doi/10.1002/jrsm.1036/full

Ludwig, G. (n.d.). *Review of Literature.* Retrieved from http://ludwig.missouri.edu/405/review.html

Machi, L., & McEvoy, B. (2012). *The literature review. Six steps to success* (2nd ed.). Thousand Oaks, CA: Corwin.

McNabb, D. E. (2002). *Research methods in public administration and nonprofit management: Quantitative and qualitative approaches.* Armonk, NY: M. E. Sharpe.

Metcalfe, M. (2003). Author(ity): The literature review as expert witnesses [45 paragraphs]. *Forum Qualitative Sozialforschung/ Forum: Qualitative Social Research, 4*(1), Art. 18. Retrieved from http://nbn-resolving.de/urn:nbn:de:0114-fqs0301187

Mikecz, R. (2012). Interviewing elites: Addressing methodological issues. *Qualitative Inquiry 18*(6), 482–493.

Morse, J. M. (2002). Theory innocent or theory smart? *Qualitative Health Research, 12,* 295–296.

Naidu, T. (2011). Reflective release: Two poems about doing qualitative research with AIDS home-based care volunteers in South Africa. *Qualitative Inquiry, 17*(4), 343–344.

Newton, B., Rothlingova, Z., Gutteridge, R., LeMarchand, K., & Raphael, J. (2011). No room for reflexivity? Critical reflections following a systematic review of qualitative research. *Journal of Health Psychology, 17*(6), 866–885. Retrieved from http://hpq.sagepub.com/content/17/6/866

NVivo10. (2012). *NVivo: QSR international.* Retrieved from http://www.qsrinternational.com/products_nvivo.aspx

Pan, M. (2008). *Preparing literature reviews: Qualitative and quantitative approaches* (3rd ed.). Glendale, CA: Pyrczak Publishing.

Randolph, J. (2009). A guide to writing the dissertation literature review. *Practical Assessment, Research & Evaluation, 14*(13). Retrieved from http://pareonline.net/getvn.asp?v=14&n=13

Razon, N., & Ross, K. (2012). Negotiating fluid identities: Alliance-building in qualitative interviewing. *Qualitative Inquiry, 18*(6), 496–503.

Reio, T. (2010). The ongoing quest for theory-building research methods articles. *Human Resources Development Review, 9*(3), 223–225.

Richardson, L. (1997). *Fields of play: Constructing an academic life.* New Brunswick, NJ: Rutgers University Press.

Richardson, L. (2002). Poetic representation of interviews. In J. Gubrium & J. Holstein (Eds.), *Handbook of interview research, context and method* (pp. 877–891). Thousand Oaks, CA: SAGE.

Rocco, T., & Plakhotnik. (2009). Literature reviews, conceptual frameworks, and theoretical frameworks: Terms, functions and distinction. *Human Resource Development Review, 8*(1), 120–130.

Stich, A., Cipollone, K., Nikischer, A., & Weis, L. (2012). Walking the methodological tightrope: Researcher dilemmas inside an urban school district in times of public disinvestment. *Qualitative Inquiry, 18*(6), 463–474.

Teman, E., & Lahman, M. (2012). Broom closet or fish bowl? An ethnographic exploration of a university queer center and oneself. *Qualitative Inquiry, 18*(4), 341–354.

Torraco, R. (2005). Writing integrative literature reviews: Guidelines and examples. *Human Resource Development Review, 4*(3), 356–367.

Tummers, L., & Karsten, N. (2012). Reflecting on the role of literature in qualitative public administration research: Learning from grounded theory. *Administration & Society, 44*(4), 64–86.

University of Georgia. (n.d.). Archives of QUALRS-L@LISTSERV.UGA.EDU Retrieved from http://listserv.uga.edu/archives/qualrs-l.html

Wikipedia. (2013). *Library catalog.* Retrieved from http://en.wikipedia.org/wiki/Library_catalog

Young, K. (n.d.). *Components of a qualitative research report.* Retrieved from http://www.ehow.com/list_7613569_components-qualitative-research-report.html

STUDENT STUDY SITE

Visit **http://www.sagepub.com/lichtmanqrss** to access additional study tools, including eFlashcards and links to SAGE journal articles.

CHAPTER 10

Interviewing

Focus Your Reading

- Qualitative interviewing is one of the primary techniques researchers use to gather data.
- In-depth interviewing leads to powerful data.
- A number of issues may affect the interview process.
- Interviewing techniques include types of questions asked and strategies for questioning.

There are a variety of methods used by qualitative researchers to gather data. In this chapter, I describe individual interviewing, one of the most powerful tools available to the qualitative researcher. In Chapter 11, I discuss other ways qualitative researchers gather data—focus-group interviewing; online interviewing; observations; using visuals/images; using media and technology; and using written material.

Introduction

First, let me begin with several examples of interviewing. I conducted the following qualitative interview with an eight-year-old girl in her home. The small segment reproduced here occurred after rapport was developed, and the interview continued for about an hour. She was very open and wanted to share everything about her friends.

Interviewer:	How many close friends do you have?
Respondent:	Well, I have three BFFs.
Interviewer:	BFFs? What's that?
Respondent:	Best friends forever. I'll tell you who they are. Stephanie, Samantha, and Anna.
Interviewer:	What do you do with your friends?
Respondent:	Well, we play a lot. We like to play dress-up. And we dance to Michael Jackson numbers. Do you want to see us on video? [She refers me to a short video her mother had on an iPhone camera.]
Interviewer:	Maybe later. Tell me, what makes someone your best friend?
Respondent:	We like to do things together—like play and such. I have known Stephanie for 5 years . . .

This interview represented a very small part of an ongoing discussion with children of this age about how friendships are developed and maintained. I knew her well, so it was not difficult for her to talk to me. She was very open and very talkative. Notice how I tried to keep my questions straightforward and direct. Notice also that I asked one question at a time. And when I was not sure what something meant (e.g., BFF) I followed up with her. Interviewing children, like interviewing adults, requires certain skills from the interviewer. I will review some of these later in this chapter.

The next two interviews were conducted by well-known interviewers with well-known participants. Here is a portion of an interview conducted by Charlie Rose (2012):

Rose:	Warren Buffett is here. As you know, he is perhaps the world's most respected investor. He's also chairman and CEO of Berkshire Hathaway.
Buffett:	Thank you, Charlie. Pleased to be here.
Rose:	Great to see you. It has been, certainly from the middle of 2008 to the middle of 2009, one incredible year.
Buffett:	One incredible year. One to a lifetime, I hope.
Rose:	Yes. Tell me about it for you.
Buffett:	Well, it was—it really was an extraordinary time in this country. We came closer to a financial meltdown than certainly any time I have ever seen, and probably in certain respects even—there was even more panic than the Great Depression, because it came on so fast and so unexpected . . .
Rose:	You made some investments during that period.
Buffett:	Right.
Rose:	General Electric, Goldman Sachs.

Buffett: Goldman Sachs.

Rose: But you just pulled out the big elephant gun.

Buffett: Well, we may have used most of our powder on that one.

[Laughter]

Rose: You said, "I stretched to the last nickel for this one."

Buffett: Yes.

Rose: Why did you do it?

And here is another famous interviewer—Oprah Winfrey (2012)—with another famous person.

Winfrey: So, this is the first time we've met.

Rowling: Yes, it is.

Winfrey: And my producers tell me that your real name is Jo. All this time I thought you were "J. K."

Rowling: [Laughing] Yeah.

Winfrey: J. K. is—?

Rowling: It's just the nom de [plume]—well, it's because my British publisher, when the first book came out, [they] thought, "This is a book that will appeal to boys." But they didn't want the boys to know a woman had written it. So they said to me, "Could we use your initials?" and I said, "Fine." I only have one initial. I don't have a middle name. So I took my favorite grandmother's name, Kathleen.

Winfrey: Kathleen.

Rowling: Kathleen, yeah.

Winfrey: Jo Kathleen.

Rowling: Joanne Kathleen.

Winfrey: And fooled the boys for a while.

Rowling: Yeah, not for too long.

Winfrey: Not for too long.

Rowling: Yeah—because I started getting my picture in the press and no one could pretend I was a man anymore.

Winfrey: Yes—and I don't think the boys have minded.

Rowling: No—it hasn't held me back, has it? Clearly [it has] not held me back.

Winfrey: Not a bit. When we came—just arrived yesterday—it was beautiful. Scotland is beautiful.

Rowling: It's stunning. Yeah, it's stunning.

Winfrey: And the green is greener than anything I've ever seen other than Ireland. [break]

Winfrey: That you thought would be particularly stimulating to your creative process. That's why you wanted to come here? To finish?

Rowling: Well, it turned out to be stimulating. As I was finishing *Deathly Hallows*, there came a day where the window cleaner came, the kids were at home, the dogs were barking, and I could not work and this light bulb went on over my head and I thought, "I can throw money at this problem. I can now solve this problem." For years and years and years I just would go to a café and sit in a different kind of noise and work. I thought "I can go to a quiet place." So I came to this hotel because it's a beautiful hotel, but I didn't intend to stay here. They were so nice to me here—and I think writers can be a little bit superstitious—so the first day's writing went well, so I kept coming back to this hotel, and I ended up finishing the last of the Harry Potter books in this hotel.

Winfrey: We have a lot of things in common.

Rowling: Yeah.

Winfrey: First of all, you know this is the last year that I'm doing the *Oprah* show. I will go on and do other things, but when I came to the end of *Hallows*—"The last trace of steam evaporated in the autumn air. The train rounded a corner. Harry's hand was still raised in farewell. 'He'll be all right,' murmured Ginny. As Harry looked at her, he lowered his hand absentmindedly and touched the lightning scar on his forehead. 'I know he will.' The scar had not pained Harry for nineteen years. All was well." When I came to the end of that, I mourned not only for the end of the series but for you. I cannot imagine what that was like.

Both Rose and Winfrey appear very relaxed, use a conversational style, and are connected to their participant. There is laughter and closeness. Rose uses a technique I really love: He asks his respondent to elaborate on something said. Buffett says it has been "one incredible year." Rose says, "Tell me about it for you." Oprah shares something about herself, another technique designed to have respondents open up and add additional information. Later in this chapter, I will comment on these techniques and others designed to get your participants to talk—whether they are children or adults, well known or the common man. Interviewing elites also presents challenges—especially issues of power differential. In these interviews, however, power issues are not relevant, since the interviewer is also a well-known individual. My intention with these examples is to expose you to different styles and techniques that experienced interviewers use.

Interviews are everywhere—on television, on YouTube, on the Internet, in podcasts, in the print media, and on blogs. Take a look at several interviews I located on YouTube. In describing qualitative interviewing, Marin4F (2011) provides some examples of what to do and what not to do. Like Rose and Winfrey, she includes humor in the presentation. Researchers have demonstrated their ability to use humor in some of these examples.

Packovic (2009a) provides an example of a bad interview. Packovic (2009b) also illustrates these poor techniques with two people. Gibbs (2011) shared two interviews. Qualitative interviewing is used worldwide. If you want a global perspective of how to do such an interview, look at the presentation by Wannheden (2011). You can locate these and other interviews online; they should assist you in studying the interview process. You can also read about qualitative interviews on Driving Wiki (2011). Or you can download a minikit on qualitative interviewing (ebookbrowse, 2011).

No doubt, you have been interviewed yourself. You've been interviewed for a job, or by your physician, or by a coworker. Perhaps you have also conducted interviews. As a counselor, you might have interviewed a client or a parent in a special education planning meeting. As head of the human resources department (HRD), you might have interviewed a prospective employee. It takes considerable planning and skill to conduct a good interview. A master interviewer on public television is Charlie Rose. He has done considerable planning, but he sits at his round oak table without notes. His interview with Warren Buffett (a brief part of which is given above) is one of many that I find fascinating and illustrative of an extremely skillful interviewer.

The examples I just described are not necessarily developed for research purposes. In this chapter, I focus on interviewing as one of the primary ways that qualitative researchers gather data (Brown & Durrheim, 2009; Roulston, 2010). DeLyser and Sui (2013), referring to qualitative scholarship, comment that in spite of recent emphasis away from words (in the field of geography) "current scholarship demonstrates that interviewing remains a vital and vibrant research method" (p. 2). Although the term *interviewing* is used by many, some researchers talk about specific types of interviewing. For example, Rubin and Rubin (2012) emphasized *responsive* interviewing. Fontana and Frey (1994) called interviewing a *social interaction*. In such a technique, the interviewer identifies knowledgeable people, listens to what they have to say about a particular topic, and then asks further questions about that topic. For Fontana and Frey, a *trusting* relationship is critical. I think you can see that trust in Rose's and Winfrey's interviewing styles. Garton and Copland (2010) described interviews as a form of interaction jointly constructed by the interviewer and the person being interviewed. They are especially concerned about the relationship between the two. Berg and Lune (2012) referred to interviewing as a "*performance* [emphasis added] in which the researcher and subject play off of one another toward a common end" (p. 106). They described interviewing as *dramaturgy*, from a symbolic interactionist viewpoint (p. 106–107). Or consider the words of Marmoz (as reported in Deschaux-Beaume, 2012): "The paradox of the research interview is to have the interviewee say and show what he had until then held hidden, voluntarily or not" (p. 17). It is up to you to determine the underlying meaning of what you hear and not just the surface words.

There is so much to tell you about individual interviewing. It seems so easy. "Just a little conversation between two people. I can do that," you say to yourself. In this chapter, I will talk about the following topics:

- the purpose of interviewing
- types of individual interviews

- general issues in interviewing
- a process for in-depth interviewing
- improving interviewing techniques
- questioning strategies to avoid
- how to develop an interview guide
- *dos* and *don'ts* of interviewing

Did You Know

Interviews of many famous people from music, politics, and pop culture have been published by *Rolling Stone* magazine. If you are more interested in literary figures, check out interviews published by *The Paris Review*.

Individual interviewing is a general term used to describe a class of methods that permit you to engage in a dialogue or conversation with a participant. Although it is a conversation, it is orchestrated and directed by you. It can be considered a conversation with a purpose. The interview format can range from highly structured to one with little or no structure. There are several types of individual interviews, including the structured interview, the guided (semi-structured) interview, the in-depth interview, and casual or unplanned interviews.

Purpose of Interviewing

The purpose of conducting an interview is the same whether you use a structured, formal style or select an unstructured, conversational style. You want to gather information from your participant about the topic you are studying. What does she think about the new training program? How does he feel about the new grading policy in the county? What is the culture of the participant's organization, and how does it relate to her individual needs? These are all topics you might study.

Your goal might be to learn what an interviewee thinks or feels about certain things, or your goal might be to explore the shared meanings of people who live or work together (Rubin & Rubin, 1995/2012). In either case, you need to think about an interview in this way. You, as the interviewer and researcher, will set up a situation in which the individual being interviewed will reveal to you his or her feelings, intentions, meanings, subcontexts, or thoughts on a topic, situation, or idea. It is critical to remember that you are not trying to determine these things as if you did not exist or were some kind of fly on the wall that could transmit the ideas directly. In qualitative research (QR), each idea, interpretation, and plan is filtered through your eyes, through your mind, and through your point of view. You are not trying to do away with your role, as you would if you were conducting traditional research. You are not trying to be objective. You adopt the role of constructing and subsequently interpreting the reality of the person being interviewed, but your own lens is critical.

I think the most difficult task a novice researcher faces is what to do about his or her own role. Should she strive to approximate objectivity? Should he gather multiple sources and use triangulation to make sure that what he says is right? Should she get others—especially those with higher status or authority—to verify that what she writes is the way it is? I would answer all these questions with a resounding *no*. I want you to reexamine the assumptions I mentioned earlier in the book. Accept that there is no single objective reality that you strive for. Accept that you, as the researcher, serve as the filter through which information is gathered, processed, and organized.

You may have heard a number of different terms used to describe the individual you interview. In traditional research, the person being studied is usually called the *subject*. In anthropological terms, the person being studied is usually called the *informant*. Ethnographers also use the term *participants*. Feminists tend to use the term *co-researcher*, acknowledging the shared role between interviewer and person being interviewed. I have also heard the terms *interviewee*, *discussant*, *partner*, and *conversational partner*. Rubin and Rubin (2012) talk about people and use *interviewees*, *informants*, and *conversational partners*, depending on the situation. Now, you might ask why it matters what the individuals are called. I think it matters a great deal. In traditional research, the term *subject* is meant to be informative and neutral. Yet some have interpreted this term in a negative manner, suggesting that the relationship between the interviewer and the person being interviewed is hierarchical—I am the king; you are my subject. Feminist research describes a dilemma regarding power and the position of the researcher and deplores the use of *subject*. Although there are many terms used to refer to the person being interviewed, it is interesting to me that I have not read about alternative names for the interviewer.

■ Types of Individual Interviews

Contemporary writers ask us to think about interviews along several dimensions. King and Horrocks (2010) distinguish among three types of interviews: realist, contextual, or constructionist. For each type, they describe underlying assumptions, the knowledge produced, and the role of the researcher. As you might expect, a researcher who conducts a realist interview would strive for objectivity, detachment, and neutrality. As I have said throughout this volume, this perspective is not one that I hold. If you conduct a contextual interview, then it is important to consider the particular time, events, and context in which the interviewee experiences life. The researcher's role in this type is not seen as a bias—in fact, the subjectivity of the researcher is an integral part of the process. King and Horrocks (2010) describe a third type of interview—what they refer to as *constructionist*. The role of the researcher in this type is that of a co-constructionist. Being reflexive is important for the researcher. Whichever of these stances you adopt (you may not be sure at this point in your learning), the way you actually go about conducting an interview is fairly consistent across all types.

The Structured or Standardized Interview

You can conduct a structured or standardized interview in which the questions and format are the same for each individual. Fontana and Prokos (2007) suggest that structured interviews do not include detailed explanations, do not interpret the meaning of a particular question, and do not improvise. This type of interviewing is more often associated with survey research rather than QR. Its strength lies in getting standardized information relatively rapidly as well as being able to use interviewers who have less training in probing and delving into underlying structures. I think most qualitative researchers would not recommend that you use this approach. The purpose of a structured interview is to eliminate the role of the researcher and to introduce objectivity. Novice interviewers are attracted to structured interviews because they are concerned that they might not know what to ask or that there will be dead time, when no one is talking. I am not suggesting that you should not prepare prior to conducting an interview. You need to be prepared. Read further to see how to do this. You will remember that I do not believe that QR is about objectivity and the elimination of bias. I want you to be aware of this type of interviewing technique, but I do not recommend you use it when conducting QR. Rather, other types of interviewing techniques will yield deeper and more meaningful responses.

The Semi-Structured or Guided Interview

Another type of interview is the semi-structured or guided interview. This type of interview involves your developing a general set of questions and format that you follow and use with all participants. Although the general structure is the same for all individuals, the interviewer can vary the questions as the situation demands. I find that some interviewers like this format because they feel uncomfortable with not having a clear set of guidelines to follow. Most novice interviewers seem to like to have something to use for guidance.

The Unstructured or In-Depth Interview

My preference is to use in-depth, unstructured interviewing techniques. I first encountered this kind of interviewing when I read McCracken's (1988) *The Long Interview.* I was greatly drawn to his writing. For once, someone laid out a style of interviewing that did not recommend a specific set of questions. You might think of this type of interview as an informal conversation. Although McCracken suggested that a formal set of biographical questions be used, he recognized that "the first objective of the qualitative interview is to allow respondents to tell their own story in their own terms" (p. 34). He reminded us that the investigator should remain unobtrusive and ask questions in a general and nondirective manner. In their first edition, Rubin and Rubin (1995) spoke to me when they said that qualitative interviewing "is a great adventure . . . [it] brings new information and opens windows into the experiences of the people you meet" (p. 1). Kvale (1996) remarked that qualitative interviewing is a "professional conversation" (p. 5). In keeping with the intent of letting the respondent talk, Boeree (1998) suggested that you should not force the person in any one direction. Fontana and Prokos (2007) stated that in-depth interviews provide greater breadth than other types. They discussed types of in-depth interviews, including oral history, creative interviews, and postmodern interviews. According to them, oral history interviews differed only in purpose but not in method. Creative interviews go beyond the length of a conventional unstructured interview and may take place over some time period. Perhaps most interesting is their description of postmodern interviewing. In an attempt to eliminate the influence of an interviewer, a postmodern approach would provide for different perspectives of various respondents.

You might understand this type of in-depth interviewing more clearly if you considered the underlying assumptions on which it is based. Consider this: Even though you are familiar with a particular topic (and have read related literature), you do not know all the questions to ask. You might consider one topic very important, but your participant or interviewee might have something quite different in mind, something you have not even thought about. If you were using a set of predetermined questions, the topic would never arise. Another assumption you make is that your participants understand the surface and underlying meaning of the words you use. In fact, they might respond in a socially desirable fashion or one they think you wish to hear. In contrast, by using general words and terms, you have placed the participant in a different role. Another consideration is the issue of power. If the interview is structured in such a way that the participant views you as "in charge" or in a "one-up" position, he or she might be intimidated and less likely to respond in a meaningful manner. Feminists address this issue in much of their writing.

Let's look at an example of responses by different participants to the same question.

Interviewer:	I understand you have just been let go from your company. What are your plans?
Participant 1:	I'm going to have a good stiff drink. (frustrated)
Participant 2:	I'm going to go into my boss and tell him what I think. (angry)
Participant 3:	I will redo my résumé and put it online. (seeking to be socially desirable)
Participant 4:	I can't believe this. How did you find out? Please don't tell anyone. (suspicious)

A follow-up question would be different for each participant. We will look at many more examples later in this chapter.

Interviewer to Participant 1:	And then what? (Try to remain neutral and nonjudgmental.)
Interviewer to Participant 2:	How do you think he will react? (This is not a particularly helpful follow-up question, but you might be tempted to ask anyway. Also, in this day of so much violence, you might become concerned about inappropriate behavior.)
Interviewer to Participant 3:	Hmmm. (Maintain a neutral posture rather than be tempted to comment that this is a good idea.)
Interviewer to Participant 4:	I will respect your privacy and keep the information I learned to myself. (Reassure the participant that you will

treat the information in a confidential manner and that he or she had previously agreed to participate and knew the rules. But participant might not have known that you would be told this.)

The Casual or Unplanned Interview

Often, when you are in the field conducting either a case study or ethnography, opportunities arise for you to talk to some of your participants. The data are often useful, but because these interviews are unplanned, I will not discuss them further here.

■ General Issues in Individual Interviewing

Pretto (2011) said it well: "The search for approval, moreover, is a typical feature in any communicative situation and, during the interview, can determine the choice of the interviewee about the events, experiences and feelings that he/she will tell us" (p. 74). Before you actually plan an interview, I urge you to consider some of the issues I identify below.

Identification of Participants

Who should be interviewed, how should they be identified, and how should they be contacted? Typically, the researcher has identified specific characteristics of individuals to study. She might want to study young, pregnant, middle school girls; boys in gangs; students from homes of divorce; displaced workers; first-year teachers; or women managers. After identifying the type of person to be interviewed, the researcher needs to contact individuals who meet the criteria. One method researchers use to identify additional participants is to ask those already contacted to name others with similar characteristics. This technique, called *snowball sampling*, is quite useful when studying hidden or hard-to-reach participants. Atkinson and Flint (2001) provided many examples of the use of the technique. Bunch and Panayotova (2008), in their research on Latinos, used snowball sampling to identify appropriate community college personnel. Baltar and Brunet (2012) used virtual networks to study hard-to-reach populations. In their study of connected personal leisure networks, Kowald and Axhausen (2012) also used snowball sampling.

Snowball sampling is just one way to identify participants. There are a variety of other techniques you can use to identify your participants. Your goal is to identify individuals who meet specific criteria. You can find people in churches, at coffee bars, in schools, or in hospitals. You can locate people online, with advertisements, or through word-of-mouth. All these ways lead you to samples that come under the general heading of purposeful or convenient samples. In contrast to random samples, a purposeful sample is chosen in which participants meet the criteria you have identified as part of your question—pregnant girls, boys in gangs, or displaced workers. You might also select a sample that varies according to demographic criteria (e.g., by age, race, marital status, etc.). However, remember that since you are not planning to generalize from your study to a larger sample, having people with various characteristics is less important.

How Many?

Koerber and McMichael (2008) concluded that "our field [qualitative research] has not yet developed a systematic, transferable vocabulary" for evaluating appropriate samples (p. 458). They suggested that qualitative researchers develop frameworks for sampling that are similar to those in the quantitative domain—in part, I think, for others to evaluate the rigor of the design. It is the realist position (as described by King and Horrocks, 2010) that is concerned with generalizing to other populations. My position, and that of many other qualitative researchers, is not this.

Listen to Mayan (2009) on the topic: "Nothing highlights the difference between quantitative and qualitative methods more explicitly than the logic that underlies sampling" (p. 61). She continued, "Qualitative inquiry depends on samples that are selected purposefully. . . . The researcher chooses individuals and contexts by asking: 'What kind of characteristics of individuals am I looking for?'" (pp. 61–62). You may know that in quantitative research (QN), determining a suitable sample size depends on how much variation there is in the population and how much sampling error you are willing to accept. Because your goal in QR is to describe and interpret rather than to generalize, there are no hard rules about how many participants you should study. Sandelowski (1995) suggested that determining sample size is a matter of judgment. For her, there are times when a sample of 10 might be seen as adequate (p. 179). QR that relies on grounded theory speaks of theoretical saturation as a way to determine sample size (Bojczyk, Lehan, McWey, Melson, & Kaufman, 2011; Lynch, 2012). In other words, when there appears to be sufficient data to understand a concept, then the sample is considered sufficient. It is important to remember, though, that the actual size is not specified. The researcher analyzes data while collecting data. At some point, the researcher decides that there is enough data. In a study of how dentists understand evidence and adopt it in practice, Sbaraini, Carter, and Evans (2012), commented as follows:

> As in all qualitative research, this study was not designed to estimate proportions in a wider population, quantify relationships between pre-determined variables, or provide a representative or average view. Instead, this study intended to explain the variation in participants' practices and understandings. For this reason, we recruited a smaller sample compared to those in quantitative studies, and we recruited informative participants rather than statistically-representative participants. (p. 197)

Most QR studies use a small number of individuals and cover material in depth. It is quite common to see studies with fewer than 10 respondents; sometimes only a single person is studied. I know that the issue of sample size is not fully resolved in the literature. There are those who apologize that the sample is too small and not representative. There are others who do not see this as a problem. Baker and Edwards (n.d.) interviewed 14 prominent qualitative methodologists and five early career academics. Their academic disciplines and styles covered a broad range. The question they asked was: How many qualitative interviews is enough? Their answer? It depends. What does it depend on?

> These include epistemological and methodological questions about the nature and purpose of the research: whether the focus of the objectives and of analysis is on

> commonality or difference or uniqueness or complexity or comparison or instances, Practical issues to take into account include the level of degree, the time available, institutional committee requirements And both philosophically and pragmatically, the judgment of the epistemic community in which a student or researcher wishes to be or is located, is another key consideration. (p. 42)

Mason's (2010) examination of PhD studies using qualitative interviews concluded that the key question to examine is saturation. August (2011) commented that the relatively small sample size limits generalizability (Chambers, Ward, Eccleston, & Brown, 2011). And Saffner, Martyn, and Lori (2011) recommended that their study of sexually active adolescent women be repeated with a larger sample size. Johnson and Christensen (2008), in their recent text on mixed approaches to research, addressed sampling in QR (pp. 243–245), but they did not address sample size.

My sense of the prevailing viewpoint is that those who take a fairly traditional and conservative view of QR would prefer larger and more representative samples. In contrast, those who see QR in a freer fashion are less concerned with the issue of sample size.

Developing Rapport

It is important that you learn to develop rapport in order to conduct an interview that generates meaningful and useful data. Ultimately, you seek the cooperation and participation of the person you are interviewing. I don't think that I can stress too much that you should include time at the beginning of each interview to establish rapport. We all talk about this and assume that we know how to do it. You could probably develop your own list of what you should do: Be relaxed, make the interviewee feel comfortable, be accepting. It is here that I often practice self-disclosure. I may share something about myself that helps the participant connect to me or vice versa. If I am interviewing young women, I might talk about my daughters. If I am interviewing children, I can speak of my grandchildren. If I am interviewing displaced workers, I might comment on a friend I know who lost her job. If I don't have an obvious connection, I might share a story of something that happened to me coming to the interview (e.g., getting caught in traffic, getting lost) or something that happened to me the previous week (e.g., having too much work to do, feeling overloaded). Winfrey (2012) commented to Rowling that she thought her first name was "J. K." and used laughter. These stories help remove the potential power difference between me and the person I am interviewing. In a sense, it is about my being human and approachable, not aloof and on a higher plane.

Selecting a Setting for the Interview

Most interviews you conduct will be in a mutually agreed-on location. It is obvious that the location should be quiet and private, to the extent possible. If you go to the home or office of your participant, you can learn a considerable amount of information. I like to look around and take notes. If it is an office, does the participant display photographs? What other personal items are around? How does the individual office relate to the larger setting in which it is located? If you are in a school, you may have to settle for less-than-ideal circumstances, because there is not usually a private room available for your use.

Observing Surroundings

It is a good idea to pay attention to your physical surroundings and to the person you are interviewing. Keep notes about your observations. If you are in a school, take pictures of the hallway or the classroom or the break room. If you are in an office building, notice the nature of the reception area and other offices vis-à-vis the one in which you conduct the interview. An individual's surroundings reveal so much. What furniture is in the offices, the relationship of furniture, the colors on walls—all provide valuable data for use as you begin data analysis. Take pictures of the person you are interviewing (with permission, of course). Does the person appear comfortable or fidgety? Does he or she look at you? What time constraints exist between your questions and the participant's responses?

Recording the Interview

Since you will be analyzing the data at a later date, most researchers believe that it is critical that you record the interview. Issues related to the type of recording device used, the willingness of participants to speak when being recorded, the protection of privacy, and the quality of transmission need to be addressed. Mechanics of recording also need to be considered. Technology is changing so rapidly that I hesitate to recommend a particular type of device. Smartphones may provide a reasonable solution. Dibbs, Glassmeyer, and Lahman described a recent study using a smartphone for an interview. (See Chapter 7 in this text.) Some interviews have been conducted using Skype (a free program that enables you to see and talk to an individual via a computer). By the time you read this, I suspect other devices will have become available. While unobtrusive, you need to determine that you have the necessary technical skills to conduct such an interview. I believe that new technology will reduce the burden of recording and transcribing that plague so many qualitative researchers today. Voice-recognition software (VRS) is already available, and with each passing day, it becomes easier to use and more reliable.

Transcribing the Interview

A general recommendation is to transcribe interviews. I see many discussions about this topic. Should you, the researcher, do the transcription? What if you do not possess the skills to do so? Should you hire someone else to do this? What if funds are unavailable to you? What might be lost if someone else transcribes? Much new technology can take voice and translate it to text. How accurate must the transcription be?

Some believe that transcription is not necessary. They recommend that data be analyzed directly from the spoken word and the written text phase be omitted, saving time and money while at the same time permitting the researcher to capture nuance in the spoken word. In a recent discussion I had with Bernauer (2012, personal communication), he described a study in which only voice was used for data analysis.

Interviewing Adolescents and Children

I recognize that all interviewing presents special challenges. Conducting interviews with children is an area that has been investigated. Danby, Ewing, and Thorpe (2011) studied how a novice researcher conducted her initial interview with a young child. In particular, they looked at how the researcher provided for the active participation of the child and how artifacts (stickers) promoted interactions. Bassett, Beagan, Ristovski-Slijepcevic, and Chapman (2008), in their study of reflections by interviewers of issues related to interviewing teenagers, suggested that recruiting teens and getting them to discuss complex abstract concepts presented special challenges. Lahman (2008) concluded that children are always viewed as the other or unfamiliar in research. She reminded us that there is little methodology on interviewing children and that the child may say what he or she perceives the researcher wants to hear (p. 294). From my own viewpoint, I suspect that many participants—children or adults—give what they perceive to be the desired or correct response. Alternatively, adolescents might give the shocking response. Of course, you are always the authority figure, due to age differences. Sensitivity and awareness, I think, are critical.

Interviewing Males With Limited Verbal Skills

Affleck, Glass, and Macdonald (2012) point out a possible problem interviewing men with limited verbal communication skills. They comment that in the field of qualitative health research, participants are described as lacking emotional expression when interviewed with traditional open-ended interviews on topics that are sensitive. They recommend using other modes to elicit information, such as photovoice.

Interviewing Elites

At times, you might have the opportunity to interview individuals who can be classified as *elite*, those individuals who have high visibility within society in general or a particular segment of society. Such interviews bring unique challenges for you as the researcher. Mikecz (2012) discussed several methodological issues in his study of political and economic elites in Estonia. He identified three areas of special concern—gaining access, acquiring trust, and establishing rapport. One effective way to establish rapport is for the researcher to become knowledgeable about the life history and background of the participant. By doing this, the researcher will decrease the status imbalance. Harvey (2011) added additional concerns: gauging the tone of the interview, keeping it to an appropriate length, and asking awkward questions. He identified areas that he wished could have been avoided. With the experience of interviewing more than one hundred elites in various economic sectors, his work highlights very specific examples. Some researchers describe their work with particular types of elites. Figenschou (2010) described her experience as a young researcher with media elites in authoritarian societies. Deschaux-Beaume (2012) conducted her research with members of the military in the European Defence and Security Policy. Her position vis-à-vis the military (and particularly language used by the military) caused her to consider reflexivity as an aid in understanding the dynamics of the interview. Piesner's

(2011) research took a somewhat different approach. She examined what she called *studying sideways*. In her project, she interviewed participants who shared professional backgrounds. Here, the issue arose when negotiations replaced a dialogue the researcher had imposed. Her recommendation was to cultivate methods that caused confrontation and disagreement. I don't think you will face this issue of interviewing elites very often, however, since most would not be available to a new researcher.

Power

Feminists have specifically written about the issue of how power dynamics can make a participant feel vulnerable. Razon and Ross (2012) described their struggle to conduct their dissertation research in Israel. Self-described as American-Israeli and Israeli-American Jewish women, they are bilingual and have dual citizenships. With regard to power, they were concerned with who dictates the interview process (p. 501). "Ultimately, the data we collect is contingent on their choices as much as ours, which begs the question, who is really in the position of power?" (p. 502). In my own experience, I have seen this in a focus group study I conducted with parents in a military installation. I was the person from Washington (and the "man" with the money) coming in to judge the effectiveness of a program. I often wonder if I heard what my participants wanted me to hear.

Reflexivity—Researcher as Instrument

I can't say enough about reflexive practice. It is a practice you must follow as you pursue QR. Roulston (2010) made this entirely clear in the last chapter of her book on interviewing. She reminded us that there is no right way to design and conduct an interview. It is a generally accepted principle in QR that the researcher is the instrument through which data are gathered, retrieved, analyzed, and reported. Riessman (1993) acknowledged that the relationship between the researcher and the person being interviewed affects the data. Pezalla, Pettigrew, and Miller-Day (2012) reflected on their own and each other's interviews and characteristics in their article on interviewer self-reflexivity. Its importance when working as a member of a team is discussed. While I have discussed the concept of the researcher as instrument throughout this text, I have not considered the researcher as part of a team. Researchers speak of a conversational space but don't really tell us what that space should be like or feel like. Pezalla and colleagues discussed different types of spaces. For example, they mentioned a Rogerian space, reflecting empathy, transparency, and unconditional positive regard. This type of feminist or poststructuralist space is one way; however, others do not support such an approach, suggesting that it leads to a superficial form of friendship between interviewer and respondent. Again, as in much of QR, you are faced with conflicting descriptions. And there are no right answers. For more about group research, I refer you to this interesting account. Revealing their strengths and shortcomings, they acknowledged that each displayed "classic mistakes of a novice researcher: asking long, complicated questions, posturing closed yes-or-no questions, and leading respondents" (p. 181). I suspect even those of us with long experience as interviewers make these same mistakes and perhaps more than we want to admit.

Interviewer and Participant Gender

Sometimes a problem does not appear to be a problem on the face of it. Researchers have explored issues about women interviewing women, women interviewing men, and men interviewing men. Feminists recognized that women interviewing other women provided a safer environment for females. Gailey and Prohaska (2011) described particular issues that arose when female researchers interviewed males on a sensitive topic, particularly sexual behaviors. They concluded that even when "women researchers interview men about sensitive issues, sexuality still seems out of bounds" (p. 365). They described a situation in which they had to relinquish control to make sure the men would talk. They felt vulnerable and threatened by the interviewees. Earlier, Pini (2005) encountered a situation where she felt treated as a sex object. She interviewed Australian men about the involvement of women in an organization. The men referred to her using the same first name as an Australian Playboy model who had appeared in a centerfold. It happened that they both shared the same last name. Walby (2010) studied men interviewing men, also on the sensitive topic of sex. He reported on his experiences with interviewing internet escorts. For him, the first question was are you gay? His thoughts: "[The] question not only seeks out a singular identity declaration but also flips over established researcher-respondent roles, indicating that the reflexivity of the respondent is as important as the reflexivity of the researcher in shaping the conversation to come" (p. 639).

Emotions and Interviewing

Another issue is concerned with the emotional nature of the interview. After all, you are asking people about themselves. At times, your conversation may take turns that you least expect. I can't offer you any quick fixes here. Awareness and reflection are often helpful. Ezzy (2010) cautions us that we need to be aware of the emotional aspects of interviews (from the perspective both of the interviewer and the interviewee). He reminds us that good interviewing can be facilitated by reflexive awareness and engagement with the emotional side of interviewing. I recall a demonstration of an interview I conducted a few years ago. All students were seated around the periphery of the classroom. The volunteer and I were sitting in the center. I began the demonstration with some general questions—personal background, experience as a student, and so on. But shortly, the volunteer revealed some personal information about himself (I think it was about his homosexuality, but I cannot be sure). What I recall vividly, however, is that all of us were crying and hugging each other and the demonstration had to be stopped. The unexpected emotions this interview generated have stayed with me for many years, long after the content of the interview has drifted into oblivion.

Alternatives to Direct Questioning

A number of variations to direct questioning have been suggested. For example, Jenkins and his colleagues (2010) described a technique of using developmental vignettes for interviewing. One technique involved using a conventional fixed narrative (a hypothetical scenario that unfolds through a series of stages). A second technique involved interactive vignettes created by hyperlinking a series of PowerPoint scenarios and changing the slides based upon responses to previous slide. The way this technique works is that sketches of fictional scenarios are presented to respondents. The respondent has to imagine, based on his or her own experience, how the person in the scenario would behave. Brown and Durrheim (2009) introduced a technique that could be used in special situations. They described what they call *mobile interviews* (interviewing while walking or driving). Ever searching for new ideas, qualitative researchers amaze me. Sutton (2011) used concept cards that serve as tangible objects that help focus the interviewees' attention. This was especially helpful in talking about sensitive topics related to the body. I can imagine that a creative researcher might adapt the technique for use with children in discussing sensitive issues.

Quality of the Interview

Roulston (2010) has asked us to be aware of the quality of an interview. As an experienced teacher of qualitative methods, she is concerned that there is no consistency in judging the quality of qualitative interviews. She asks you to think about interviewing not as a universal technique but one based on a theoretical viewpoint. She suggests that based on one's viewpoint, an interviewer might try to achieve different kinds of goals. In this comprehensive article, she addressed several different conceptions of interviews.

- A *neopositivist* conception of interviewing is the type with which you are most familiar. In this approach, a skillful interviewer asks good questions while minimizing bias and adopting a neutral role. For example, if an interviewer takes a neopositivist conception of the interview process, then an underlying viewpoint is that a sensitive interviewer can reach or discover the authentic self of the person being interviewed.

- Another conception is *decolonizing.* If you are involved in a study of indigenous peoples, you might need to be concerned with a long-term process of bureaucracy and colonial power. An example she cited is negative experiences that those being studied might have had with Whites.

- Another conception of an interview type is what she called *transformative.* In this way of thinking about interviewing, the interviewer might have the intention to challenge and change the understandings of participants and perhaps to change their lives.

- Still another type she called *postmodern.* In this type, the interview is seen as a vehicle to produce performance ethnographies.

- A *romantic* conception acknowledges and actually celebrates the place of the interviewer. A researcher holding this viewpoint would strive for "genuine rapport and trust" (p. 217) between the interviewer and the person being interviewed. This, then, would lead to an intimate and self-revealing conversation.

- A *constructionist* conception of an interview involves a co-construction between the interviewer and the respondent. This is not meant to be a simple idea, but rather how the data are co-constructed is at issue. Brown and Durrheim (2009) see interviewing as a situation in which the interviewer and interviewee actively participate in the live co-construction of the interviewee's stories and subjectivity.

She concluded that since there are different conceptions of the interview, so too will there be different demonstrations of quality.

Collecting Data Using Internet Technologies

I have addressed some of the issues related to using Internet technologies in Chapter 8. According to Hesse-Biber and Griffin (2013),

> The growth of user-generated Internet data has, in turn, challenged the research community to think outside their traditional method practices and research concepts such as the idea of what a field site should look like. Internet-mediated research is already transforming the way researchers practice traditional research methods such as survey research and ethnography as they confront the challenges of taking these traditional methods online. (p. 43–44)

I recognize the importance of this topic, but it is beyond the scope of this text to do more than acknowledge it and speculate that there will be fundamental changes in the ways we think about what questions we can explore using these new technologies.

Interviewing Online

The purpose of any type of interview is to gather information from a participant on a particular topic. I have stressed the idea that the interviewer is the vehicle or conduit through which information is passed. Mann and Stewart (2000) reminded us about what we know so well. A good interviewer begins by building rapport and making a participant feel comfortable. He or she is a careful, nonjudgmental, and perceptive listener. Many interviewers know the importance of nonverbal cues: the wink of an eye or a small smile. Pauses and silent time also appear in face-to-face interviews. But without the face-to-face experience, and perhaps without even being online at the same time as his or her participants, an online interviewer might need to develop a new set of techniques or skills.

Online sampling provides some interesting challenges. If email is used as a means of interviewing, there are no issues regarding traveling, recording, or transcribing. Online sampling also makes it possible to interview people who are geographically dispersed. Mann and Stewart (2000) spoke of "the challenges of presenting self online" (p. 59). The general idea has to do with getting a sense of the other. In theory, this leads participants to trust the interviewer and, hopefully, share their private and social worlds. Online interviewing may present special problems, because none of the usual cues are available. However, there is not general agreement about how and whether online rapport can be established.

Preparing for an Online Interview

I rely heavily on Salmons's (2010) suggestions. She identifies three areas for preparation: the questions or themes to be covered, the technologies, and individual preparation for the interviewer. I see the first step as preparing an interview guide similar to the one I described earlier. She identifies four types of synchronous communications: A text-based type involves communication through typed words, perhaps accompanied by images. Connections can be with a phone, a mobile device or a computer. Another type involves videoconferencing or a video call. A third type utilizes multichannel communications. Lastly, she describes immersive 3-D environments. In each case the interviewer needs to pay attention to the details of time frame and length of the interview. She reminds us that in all cases, an online interview "involves personal, theoretical, and technical steps for the researcher and participant" (p. 135).

One advantage to an online interview is the virtual eye contact. Salmons's images reproduced in her volume give you a sense of how this might work (p. 157). As technology advances and researchers develop better skills, I believe these interviews will run more smoothly.

Issues and Challenges With Online Interviewing

There are both technological and substantive issues connected with online interviewing. Hesse-Biber and Griffin (2013) review various research projects that address the impact of changing the mode of traditional research and going online. They suggest resistance by some researchers to come out of their comfort zone. While this may be true to some extent, I speculate that as new researchers enter the field, such possible barriers will diminish. Technological issues involve such concerns as deciding how the two people should communicate with each other. At the current time, there are several vehicles for online communication. Most are familiar with email, so it is a relatively easy avenue for communication. But other ways of interviewing online are also possible. Some report using Skype to conduct qualitative interviews, although problems with sound quality and transmission have been reported. Schmieder (2011), in his information source for qualitative researchers, reports that everyone is not comfortable talking on Skype. Other issues relate to the quality of data and confidentiality. One advantage is that you can record directly from Skype (with the individual's permission, of course). The use of webinars (a seminar conducted over the Internet) is another vehicle for collecting data online.

Other technological issues might include connection speed (Do the interviewer and participant have access to a high-speed connection?), computer glitches (unexpected disconnects or files being lost), participants' and researchers' lack of skill in typing or spelling (which sometimes leads to reluctance on the part of a participant), wait time (How do you know whether the person is thinking of what to write or does not really get the question?), lack of nonverbal cues (no look of puzzlement, no smiles), sufficient time for an interview (Do you and the participant really have 30 minutes or more of uninterrupted time on the computer?), and difficulties in providing follow-up or probing questions (the interviewer may be unfamiliar with the process and need much more experience).

Substantive issues might also raise a problem. Shepherd (2003) spoke about difficulty establishing rapport and interpreting meaning. She suggested that it is difficult to interpret the emotional tone in which messages are written, for example, when common online abbreviations are used (e.g., LOL). James and Busher (2006) explored issues they faced when using email to conduct online interviews. In particular, they questioned the credibility and trustworthiness of the design and the authenticity of participants' voices. They concluded that asynchronous discussions are valuable. Hamilton and Bowers (2006) also addressed issues regarding email interviewing and recruitment. Suzuki, Ahluwalia, Arora, and Mattis (2007) presented an interesting discussion about observation, interview, and physical data using electronic data from the Internet. They commented that few have written about data collection methods via electronic means. Among the benefits they mentioned are data accuracy, recruiting participants in a variety of remote locations, and potential comfort in discussing various topics because of anonymity. I agree with their concern that visual cues often used to develop rapport are missing. Ethical issues regarding consent and confidentiality are raised by them and by Markham (2005), who questions issues of privacy and informed consent.

Other Technologies

With the new technologies available, researchers are studying a variety of issues as well as technologies available as they conduct QR. Often, it is unplanned, and as such, you will be challenged to think about how you can capture ideas that are available. Here are illustrations of some of the variety of topics researchers are examining. Davis (2010) studied the construction of self and identity through Myspace. Flowers and Moore (2003) provided a detailed account of how to conduct interviews using AOL Instant Messaging. Gratton and O'Donnell (2011) describe a project with remote communities in Canada to obtain health information. Gatson (2011) offers an account of her experiences as a member and participant observer of a community that began with online interactions and moved toward offline interactions as well. Her focus was the movement of ethnography to online textual and graphic communication. She concludes, "They confront the challenges of taking these traditional methods online and offline spaces, multiple online and offline networks, and in doing so, (try to) create a name for themselves" (p. 233). Fielding (2010) also explores issues related to fieldwork in his research on using video teleconferencing to look at various interactional features. These studies should whet your appetite as to what is available in terms of the use of such technologies in QR.

Knowing About Issues

Why have I spelled out these different issues related to interviewing? As a novice interviewer, you probably have not really thought about the assumptions you make regarding your role and how you will conduct an interview. Suffice it to say, becoming aware that underlying assumptions about what an interview is—its purpose, your purpose, and your agenda—should help you as you begin to think about interviewing. Just when you think you have thought enough about other factors that might influence interviewing, I want you to be aware of issues proposed by Carr (2010). Here are some questions she raised: How do the contexts in which people speak influence what they say? How do people build context through linguistic interaction? What are people trying to do by saying particular things? (p.126). I suspect you can identify other issues that might have an effect on interviewing.

The Interview Process for In-Depth Interviewing

As I have said, there are many different kinds of interviews. I prefer in-depth interviews. I feel strongly that in an in-depth interview, you will get information from your participant that is not slanted toward what you want to hear or investigate. I have chosen to talk about what works for me in conducting this type of interview. The purpose in this style of interviewing is to hear what the participant has to say in his or her own words, in his or her voice, with his or her language and narrative. Mindful of the issues that I just raised, I now take you to the intricacies of developing such an interview. Be aware that the following information is useful for face-to-face interviews. Harris and Guillemin (2012) suggest that we should be aware of the senses, especially in the field of health research. Acknowledging the contribution of anthropology, they remind us to be aware of ourselves as well as our participants both during interviews and in the analysis process.

According to Berry (2002), the skill to hear the voice of participants is critical but rarely taught in graduate school. In this section, I provide you with some practical information and skills you need to develop as you prepare to learn how to conduct a qualitative interview.

Advance Planning

Because you will not be using a standardized set of questions, you need to think about what you will be doing prior to the actual interview. Here are some ways to get your thoughts organized. This initial plan will help get you ready to do an in-depth interview. Notice that you do not have a formal set of questions or a structured interview schedule to follow, but you will be well on your way to conducting a successful interview. Of course, practice is critical.

- Identify five to 10 topic areas that you want to make sure you will cover in your interview. I like to put them on a single piece of paper or on an iPad or other type of tablet, keeping space between each one. Remember, these are to be used as guidelines. In fact, you may not actually need all these topics; sometimes, you need only one question and the interview rolls right along.

- Identify the biographic information you think you will need to collect. I am not suggesting that you follow a prescribed format with regard to the information. But if you use a checklist, you can review whether the material is covered incidentally or you need to ask directly. For example, an individual might share with you her marital status, number of children, and so on before you even ask.

- Use your knowledge of the topic and your experience to generate discussion in specific areas. You can look in the literature about the topic, but I believe that it tends to put blinders on you and that it is better to conduct a comprehensive literature review at a later time. Identify some demographic areas that you think you will want to cover with each participant (e.g., for adults, marital status, number of children, or work history; for children, age, grade in school, number of siblings, or favorite activity). Often, these come up in the course of the interview, but you should make them explicit. Of course, the areas to cover are directed by the purpose of your research.

- In the planning stages, think about the questions you might start with and how to phrase them. Inexperienced researchers are often nervous without specific questions to ask.

- Obtain permission to conduct the interview. You might have to obtain a signed permission form or agreement. Different institutions have different requirements; you should determine the requirements of the Institutional Review Board (IRB) at your institution. If you are interviewing children, you will need to get permission from an adult. If you are interviewing a non-English speaker, you might need a translator.

Preliminaries

Before you begin the interview, you should provide some basic information to your respondent: (1) why you are there, (2) your purpose, (3) what you will do with the information, (4) how you will treat the information, (5) how you will protect confidentiality and privacy, and (6) how long the interview will take.

You should ask for permission to use a recording device. Perhaps seek permission to publish the information at a later date.

- Develop rapport by introducing chitchat. While it may seem to you that you are wasting time that you would more profitably use to get at the crux of information, this time is invaluable for getting your respondent to cooperate with you.

- Make the person feel comfortable. You can do this by using laughter, smiles, and nods. You can offer some personal story about yourself (for example, how long it took you to drive to the site, what fun you had at a recent sporting event, or how you get your own children ready for school). I stress that you should try to remain connected to your respondent rather than stay aloof.

- Ask people to say a little bit about themselves. (If they say "Like what?" you can respond with, "Anything you want to share.") Because you have already shared some personal information, they may be more inclined to do so. All these preliminaries are used to help your respondent feel comfortable with you.

The Body of the Interview

You are now ready to continue with your interview. I think it is important to give considerable thought to how you will begin an interview. Your demeanor, dress, and tone will set the stage for what is to come. As mentioned, you have just spent the first few minutes developing rapport and getting the participant to trust you and to open up to you. I often use three kinds of questions to begin:

1. personal questions ("Tell me a little about yourself," or "Would you like to share something?" or "Tell me about your family.")
2. concrete questions ("Tell me something that happened to you last week in the office," or "Tell me your thoughts when you learned last week that you were going to lose your job.")
3. feeling questions ("What is it like to work in a green environment?" or "What are the kids like here?" or "How did you react to having to change schools when the system had a reduction in force?")

Notice that all three questions are personal and immediate. They are not yes or no questions. They usually get the respondent to open up somewhat.

Use your semi-structured or unstructured guidelines to make the interview progress smoother. Remember, you will have a list of five to 10 topic areas that you expect to investigate.

Don't try to take complete notes; it is almost impossible. But do take notes of questions or comments that you want to follow up. Sometimes you will want to probe more fully, but do not interrupt as the interview progresses.

Concentrate on listening to what is said and planning your next questions. Perhaps it is like a game of chess; you have some moves and plans, but your opponent may fool you.

The End of the Interview

Stay aware of the time.

My favorite final question: "Do you have anything you want to add that we have not talked about?" You will be so surprised at what you learn.

Thank them for their participation.

Post-Interview Tasks

Upon completion of interview, take some time to get your materials in order. Mark the tapes or digital recordings, put your notes away, and record the length of the interview or stop time.

Write down your thoughts and reactions in your journal after the interview is over.

Keeping track of things at this point will smooth the way for the work that is to come. If you are conducting multiple interviews in a day, make sure you schedule sufficient time between interviews to finish up before proceeding to the next person.

■ Developing Interviewing Techniques

Conducting in-depth interviews takes a considerable amount of planning and experience. It may look easy, but it really takes quite a bit of forethought. Now that you have considered the main components of an in-depth qualitative interview, I want you to begin to think about the interview questions. I have found that many people focus on the content of the questions. They are inclined to develop a list of questions that they think they want to ask. In my experience, this is a very rigid format and narrows the interview rather than expanding it. Of course, content is important. Your purpose and research question will drive the content. But I would like you to think about questioning in two ways. One way involves the *type of questions* you might ask. The second way is to consider *questioning strategies.* This section concludes with some special areas of concern.

Types of Questions

Below, I describe and provide examples of several different types of questions. Although you can choose the order to follow, I almost always begin either with a grand tour question or a specific or concrete example question.

Five Types of Questions

1. Grand Tour
2. Concrete Questions
3. Comparison/Contrast
4. New Elements/Topics
5. Closing

Grand Tour

This type of question is very general. It is a good way to begin, because it gets the participant talking to you. Your stance should be open and nonjudgmental. The grand tour question comes from Spradley's (1979) work on ethnographic interviewing. Like the grand tour that young men of means took long ago that encompassed an extended tour of continental Europe (or the Grand Tour that I took to Art Basel and the Venice Biennale in 2007), grand tour questions are designed to explain a series of events or describe oneself in detail. A question of this type is meant to be very general and to encourage the respondent to talk at length. It continues to be used in much QR today (Brown & Holloway, 2008; Van Oord, 2008). In their study of Chinese immigrants in the United States, Chen, Kendall, and Shyu (2010) used three grand tour questions and probes:

> [1] Tell me about a time, living in the United States, when you and your family were ill, and how you found the health information you needed . . .
>
> [2] Tell me about your culture and the part it played in seeking health information . . .
>
> [3] Based on your experiences, what makes it easier or harder for you to obtain the health information you need? (pp. 339–340)

Organizational researchers Becker and Burke (2012) recreated a historical event in order to understand organizational phenomena. They used grand tour questions to "gain an initial sense of overall parameters" (p. 322). In a study of intercultural couples, Bustamante and colleagues (2011) used this grand tour question, "Tell me about what you experience being in an intercultural relationship," followed by a probe asking for an example (p. 157). This type of question can take various forms: "Tell me about yourself," "Tell me what being in school is like for you, "or "What can you say about going to the *X* school?" For the adult, you can ask, "What is it like to work at the *X* organization?" I have heard of grand tour questions that ask the participant to draw a map of a dorm room or of a playground. It is important to remember that you want to capture the words and ideas of the person you are interviewing. This will be a rich source of data as you begin your qualitative analysis.

Here are more examples of grand tour questions:

Very general—What is it like to be a graduate student?

More specific—What kinds of stress do you face as a graduate student?

Very general—Tell me about your school.

More specific—What kinds of things does your teacher do that you find helpful?

Very general—What is it like to work in this organization?

More specific—How are minorities treated in this organization?

Very general—Tell me some of the things you feel as a new teacher.

More specific—What are concerns you have as a new teacher in terms of working with parents (or with other staff members or with troubled students)?

Very general—How would you describe a day in the life of a principal (student, retired person)?

More specific—Your challenge as a principal is to modify the discipline at your school. What are some things you have been thinking about along these lines?

Concrete Questions

This type of question gives the participant an opportunity to be concrete and specific and provide relevant information. Gidlöf, Holmberg, and Sandberg (2012), in their study of teenagers' exposure to online advertising, asked "concrete questions about the online advertisements" (p. 335). A concrete example works well, because it is personal and immediate. It is important to ask for a specific story rather than a general statement. It prevents jargon or responses that the participant thinks that you, the researcher, want to hear. People like to talk about their experiences. If you are interviewing students, one way that works well is to have them relate stories about their school experiences. If you are interviewing adults, you might ask them about a recent experience that was meaningful. This use of the concrete guarantees a rich source of data. The less you are involved in abstract concepts, the richer your data will be.

Here are examples of concrete questions:

Tell me something that happened at this school that you think is a direct result of the new Site-Based Management plan.

What was something that happened last week that you think contributes to your stress?

What did you see (or hear) in your office that indicates that there is sexual harassment?

Tell me something that happened to you last month that made you annoyed with your boss.

When your teacher asked you to work with a new student who was transferred, what kinds of things made you happy or sad?

Comparison/Contrast

This type of question challenges the participant to think about other times, situations, places, events, or people and draw comparisons between them. Choose comparisons that are meaningful to the respondent; it helps them put their current situation into a meaningful framework. Contrasts and comparisons provide additional insight and serve to highlight what you are studying. "How did you take care of yourself differently in your own country?" is a contrast question used by D'Alonzo (2012) in her study of immigrant Latinas.

Here are examples of comparison/contrast questions:

How are things at this school now compared to when Mr. *X* was principal?

Remember when you were a child. How do you feel now compared to then, in terms of your ability to accomplish and meet your own standards?

Imagine you could choose to have a work setting any way you want. What would it be like compared to the way it is now?

How does this situation compare with where you worked previously?

In what ways does what you describe differ from your previous experience?

How could you compare what you are doing now to what you did in the past?

Does the situation with Mr. X differ from the situation with Mr. Y? In what ways?

This year you say you are doing (or feeling) ________. How is that like the way you felt last year? How is it different from the way you did it last year?

How do you think things will be in the future regarding ________?

New Elements/Topics

Shifting to a new topic must be done in a very subtle manner. You might feel during an interview that the participant is stuck on a particular thing and keeps repeating information. Here is a chance for you, as interviewer, to introduce a new topic. You are interested in covering areas that may not have been considered in previous questions. (Note: Some qualitative researchers are opposed to this approach and feel that the areas of interest should emerge from the data.) You might draw from the research literature and your own background topics of importance to the problems at hand. You can introduce topics not previously mentioned by the respondent. Avoid leading the respondent to say what you want him to say. Use transition statements to move from one area to another. Use *why* and *how* questions for completeness.

Here are examples of new elements questions:

We've talked for a while about discipline in the schools. Are there other aspects of working in a school you would like to discuss?

You've talked about many challenges you face as a displaced worker. What can you say about having a life coach?

Can you think of some other things about the nature of your work life that you think are important?

We've talked quite a bit about _____________. Are there other issues you would like to discuss?

Let's look at some other areas we haven't yet covered. What do you think about _______?

Our time is somewhat limited, and I want to be sure we've covered everything of interest to you; let's move on to some other areas. I'd like to talk about _____________.

What else is important to you about _____________? Can we talk about some other areas (issues, factors, topics)?

You mentioned _________________ as being an important area for you. What about __________________?

Do you see _____________ as something that you consider important? In what ways?

Why do you think _______________ has an influence in this organization?

How does _____________ work in this school?

Can you clarify what you mean by ____________? How are you thinking of it in this context?

Closing

A closing question provides a chance for the participant to add anything else that has not been mentioned. "Closing questions were asked to understand what students *think* and how they *feel* about the extent to which group assignments contribute to their development of skills and course-related knowledge" (Neu, 2012, p. 69).

Here are examples of closing questions:

Can you think of anything else you would like to say about ________?

Is there anything else you would like to add to what you have already said?

Strategies for Questioning

Questioning Strategies

Elaboration	Expand ideas
Probing	Elicit more info; delve deeper
Using Stimuli	Using external enhancers
Neutrality	Maintain non-directionality
Single Question	Only one
Wait Time	Silence; pauses
Special Areas of Concern	Listen; don't assume

Elaboration

This strategy provides an opportunity for the participant to say more or to clarify and elaborate on his or her responses and allows for additional input by the participant. It may reveal other ideas that the participant has thought about but has not mentioned. Asking respondents to add additional information or say more about a topic will help you in delving deeper into meaning. It is important to avoid glib or superficial responses that respondents often give. Here are some examples you might use:

> You've talked about your frustration in working with your new boss. You mentioned that her age is intimidating. What else can you say about why you feel so frustrated?
>
> You said that you feel so happy working with a new group of classmates. What kinds of things have made you happy?
>
> What else can you tell me about being in the *X* factory?

Probing

This strategy provides the interviewer a chance to try to get the underlying meaning of what is said. Sometimes you think you know what is meant, but it is always better to follow up, because words take on many different meanings. Repeat the words that are said (an *echo probe*), raise an eyebrow (the *silent probe*), or use a noncommittal response, such as "uh-huh." This idea is closely related to elaboration, but here, the emphasis is on digging down deeper into the feelings. Use the person's own words when restating, use nonverbal cues, and provide encouragement.

> Can you tell me some more about that?
>
> What do you mean when you say it is challenging as a teacher?
>
> I see. What do you mean by______________?
>
> Yes. Go on.
>
> Hmm. What else can you say about ________________?
>
> That's good. I'm not sure I understand when you say ______________. Can you explain more fully?
>
> Let's talk about that in more detail.
>
> I'm trying to find out what you think about _____________. Tell me more.
>
> It's not clear to me. Can you give an example of what you mean when you say ___________?

Look at the person, nod your head yes, or use your eyes or eyebrows to indicate that you want the person to continue.

> That's interesting. Give me some additional information.
>
> I have heard you say during this interview that you feel frustrated. Why do you think you feel so frustrated?

Happiness means different things to different people. I want to get at what it means to you. Tell me some more about it.

Using Stimuli

This strategy makes use of external stimuli in conjunction with questioning to improve responses of participants. For example, Smith, Gidlow, and Steel (2012) used photographs to stimulate the conversation with adolescents who participated in an outdoor education experience. Sutton (2011), a sociologist, enhanced her interviews and observations conducted with women from Argentina by using concept cards. The cards covered a range of topics from abortion and menopause to violence and pleasure. Respondents not only could select or delete cards, but they could attach a story to the concept.

Any tangibles, such as photographs or drawings, can serve as stimuli. They can be prepared by the researcher, the participant, or jointly.

Neutrality

This strategy puts the interviewer in a neutral position, neither for nor against something. It is very tricky. Avoid letting your nonverbal and verbal cues lead the participant in a particular direction. We know that how you react has an influence on what the respondent says. Yes, I have talked about things being filtered through the eyes of the researcher. And I still believe that. But asking questions in a non-directional manner is different.

Good: We have talked about being a graduate student. What is the experience like for you?

Avoid: We have talked about being a graduate student. I agree with you that it is frustrating, because you have so little time to do everything.

Good: Being a first-year teacher has challenges and rewards. In what ways have you experienced challenges? What about satisfaction?

Avoid: I remember when I taught first grade—I couldn't wait for the term to be over. Those kids nearly drove me crazy! Have you found the same thing?

Single Question

Ask one question at a time. Stop and give the participant a chance to respond. It is so easy to pack three or four questions together. By the time you have finished with what you have to say, your respondent is lost. It is difficult to keep so many different ideas in one's head at the same time. Limit your questions to one idea. Not giving the respondent time to respond is the biggest mistake I see even experienced interviewers make.

Good: Let's talk about being in graduate school. Tell me about the experience.

Avoid: Let's talk some more about being in graduate school. What courses are you taking? What is your major? Why do you think you decided to return to graduate school?

Wait Time

After you ask a question, be quiet and let the participant think and then talk. Use nonverbal cues. You might look down at your paper or fiddle with your recording device to give the participant a chance to formulate his or her thoughts. If you add something right away, he or she may lose his or her train of thought. Trust me; your participant will talk if you remain quiet.

> Good: Look down at your notes. Do not tap your pen on the table or look at your watch. Try to remain neutral.
>
> Avoid: Jumping in too soon and repeating the question or asking a different question.

Special Areas of Concern

Encourage the respondent to tell her story in her own words. Don't assume that you know what she means when she says something. Be aware of when to cut the respondent off (when he's talking too much) and when not to cut the respondent off (when he is saying something you want to hear).

> Tell me what you think about _____________.
>
> Take some time to tell me in your own words what you think about or how you feel about _________________.
>
> What do you mean when you say *successful*? I'm not sure I understand. Can you tell me some more?
>
> You've said that when your boss does ____________, that creates problems for you. Can you give me an example?
>
> Do you think ____________ is important in this school? If so, in what ways? (Avoid: Don't you think ____________ is important in this school?)
>
> Well, you've given me a lot of examples of ____________. Let's talk about some other areas. What do you think about ____________ ?
>
> That sounds interesting. Keep telling me about it.

Questioning Strategies to Avoid

You might find it helpful to keep in mind types of strategies you should not use. Here are some general categories followed by examples.

Leading Questions

These kinds of questions set the respondent up to answer in a certain way. These kinds of questions are done either by design or lack of knowledge. They are often used on sensitive topics such as abortion, gun control, or the death penalty. In a school setting, they might include budget cuts, evaluation by student test scores, or school closing. A researcher might say something like: "I thought it was terrible when I read in the paper that *School X* was slated to close next week. How do you feel about that?" I think this is somewhat inconsistent with the concept of being open and reflexive. But it is important to remember that you want to learn what the other person thinks—not necessarily that he or she agrees with you.

Complex Questions

These kinds of questions are so convoluted that the person has lost track of what you are asking. Perhaps you have lost track yourself.

Double-Barreled Questions

One statement per question, please.

Questions With Jargon or Technical Language

These kinds of questions involve the use of technical language or abstract concepts. It is best to use terms that have a common meaning. Avoid language that assumes everyone defines a particular term in the same way.

Chattiness

I can't say it better than Mayan (2009) does as she describes her first interview. "Why did I say that? Why did I interrupt participants? Why did I not keep my mouth shut? Why does it sound more like my interview than theirs?" (p. 71).

■ Developing an Interview Guide

Although experienced interviewers make it seem easy and often do not have a specific set of questions in front of them, they have planned in advance. One way you can prepare is to develop an interview guide. An interview guide is just that—a guide. It is not a predetermined list of questions that you follow in a certain order. Rather, it is a rubric you can use as you plan to conduct an interview. Most guides contain several different categories or topics.

1. *Biographical and demographic information about the participant.* If you are interviewing adults, examples of information you can collect are current family and family of origin, educational history, work history. Let me caution you, however. Do not collect information just to collect it. It needs to be related to the research question you are studying. Another word of advice: I would not begin with a long list of personal questions about an individual. Some of this information might come out in the interview itself. But if you sense an individual does not want to share personal information, do not ask it. If you are interviewing children, examples of information include age, siblings, family situation, or school grade. I am very sensitive to asking personal questions. If an individual chooses to share something with you, that is fine. But do not go beyond the information that you need for your study.

2. *Topics to be covered.* This type of information includes the major topics you plan to touch on during the interview. Some people like to include minor topics. Some like to have the questions written in detail, while others are comfortable with some key terms. You will rely on your own knowledge about the topic as well as what is known from the literature about the topic.

3. *Types of questions.*

Knowledge questions. This type of information relates to actual knowledge the individual possesses. For example, you might want to know what they know about rules of conduct or behavior in a school.

Opinion questions. This type of information relates to what they think about the topic.

Feeling questions. This type of information relates to their emotional response to the topic.

Experience questions. This type of information relates to the individual's personal experience with the topic. For example, if you are studying rules of conduct, you might inquire whether the individual has firsthand knowledge of how the rules are applied.

4. *Etched in stone or flexible.* A guide is meant to be general. It is not a specific map to take you somewhere. It is not a GPS. Rather, it is used to assist you as you conduct an interview. I recommend you review the guide after you begin to conduct an interview. You might even try it out on a friend before you begin collecting data. You would look for what you omitted or what topics emerged that you had not previously considered.

You might enjoy looking at tips two instructors published for teaching in-depth interviewing (Healey-Etten & Sharp, 2010). Some of these points you have already heard from me. Others might be new to you:

- probe
- avoid $100 words
- turn a Clark Kent question into a Superman question (use *why* or *how* questions)
- probe (yes, again)
- do a Homer Simpson question (or just play dumb)
- avoid "you know what I mean" (don't let your people get away with saying this)
- pay attention to order
- avoid leading questions
- enjoy the silence
- shut up

I feel that I have said most of these things already, but it is good to see them repeated with a little humor.

Example of an Interview

I have developed this interview guide (Table 10.1) for a study about how rules of behavior and conduct are developed in elementary schools and the effects of such rules on the school culture. My plan is to interview children, parents, teachers, and administrators.

Table 10.1 Interview Guide

Biographical information: age, grade, gender, siblings, home status, etc.

Topics: rules about behavior, missed class, fighting, tardiness, weapons, bullying, name calling

Types of questions:

- Knowledge—Do you know the rules? Who sets them? Do they differ by grade? Can the rules be changed?
- Opinion—What do you think about the rules? Who do they benefit? How do they affect the school's reputation? Why do the rules exist?
- Feeling—How do you feel about attending the school?
- Experience—What specific thing might have happened to you?

Be flexible. You might find that some of the topics need to be changed based on what you learned along the way. You might also believe that you are not really getting at the underlying meaning about the culture in the school as it is affected by the rules. Then you would need to adjust your categories and types of questions accordingly.

Table 10.2 *Dos* and *Don'ts* of In-Depth Interviewing

Now that you have thought about different types of questions and strategies for questioning, I have a few more reminders for you:

Do

develop rapport.

use a recorder, smartphone, or other device and have a note pad to jot down notes.

use a laptop or iPad if you are proficient with it.

make eye contact.

ask open-ended questions.

provide an atmosphere for respondents to tell their own story in their own terms.

remain unobtrusive. Do not put your own thoughts into your questions.

phrase questions in a general and nondirective manner.

use some questioning strategies, such as repeating the last word of the response or lifting an eyebrow.

make sure you get specific and detailed information.

make sure you have enough discussion about the key issues to use later for data analysis.

(Continued)

Table 10.3 (Continued)

Don't
use jargon or questions that are too technical.
use leading questions.
depend on your memory. Write it down or record it.
answer questions for respondents.
ask three or four questions at the same time.
ask a question and then provide the answer ("I agree that *X* is a good thing").
stop the respondent in the middle of a conversation.
allow the respondent to spend too much time on one topic.
act nervous or uninterested.

Qualitative interviewing is challenging. It opens new doors to learn what others think and feel. It does not rely on a single set of questions; rather, it addresses ways to listen to respondents speak in their own words. I recommend two ways of thinking about asking questions: question types and question strategies. Question types are grand tour questions, comparison/contrast questions, and so on. Question strategies are techniques you can use to get your respondents to talk more, answer in greater depth, and ultimately lead you to their underlying meanings. I continue to believe that the best way to learn about how to interview is to practice. Practice with your friends and family. Practice with your classmates. Practice with your coworkers. Listen to yourself on tape and try to determine what strategies you use and what you want to avoid. You should now be well on your way to mastering one of the most important techniques for gathering data in any kind of QR you choose to do.

■ Summary

Interviews may be structured with set questions, semi-structured or guided interviews with a list of topics or question areas, in-depth or unstructured interviews, or even casual or unplanned interviews.

When conducting in-depth interviews, it is important to look at the components of the interview process. I describe and provide examples of different types of questions. I illustrate strategies for asking questions. I also address issues related to conducting focus group interviews and online interviews. Planning and practice are critical elements to consider as you develop skills of successful interviewing.

CHECK YOURSELF

- Qualitative interviewing is one of the primary techniques researchers use to gather data.
- Key elements in chapter are the purpose of interviewing, types of individual interviews, general issues in interviewing, the interview process for in-depth interviewing, improving interviewing techniques, questioning strategies to avoid, how to develop an interview guide, and *dos* and *don'ts* of interviewing.
- In-depth interviewing leads to powerful data.
- A number of issues may affect the interview process.
- Interviewing techniques include types of questions asked and strategies for questioning.

KEY DISCUSSION ISSUES

1. What can you learn about interviewing from examining the styles of Charlie Rose and Oprah Winfrey? Why do you think I included these for you to look at?
2. Why do I recommend individual in-depth interviewing over other types? What are the advantages?
3. What are some issues related to individual interviewing that you need to consider? What about how you select participants? What about how many participants you have?
4. What are the main steps in the interview process?
5. I discuss two important areas related to interview techniques—types of questions to ask and strategies for questioning. What are the important question types? What are the strategies I recommend?
6. How do you develop an interview guide?

MODULE 10

Group and Individual Activities

Group Activity

Purpose: to develop skill in interviewing

Activity: Identify a co-researcher. Select a topic of interest to you. Identify an individual who is willing to be interviewed and who has some knowledge about this topic. Set aside at least 30 minutes at a mutually agreed-on time and place. Practice the mechanics of interviewing. Your co-researcher will serve as an observer. Identify at least three types of questions and three questioning strategies to practice. After you complete the interview, meet with your co-researcher to debrief on the extent to which you were successful in varying your question types and question strategies. Repeat the process with another individual, changing places with your co-researcher.

Evaluation: Determine which areas are comfortable for you and which ones you need to refine.

Individual Activity

Purpose: to become comfortable with online interviewing

Activity: Identify a topic of interest to you. Contact a friend and ask whether he or she is willing to engage in an email interview at a designated time. Practice varying types of questions and questioning strategies via email.

Evaluation: Comment in your blog about your comfort level with interviews that are not face to face.

REFERENCES

Affleck, W., Glass, K., & Macdonald, M. (2012). The limitations of language: Male participants, stoicism, and the qualitative research interview. *American Journal of Men's Health, 7*(2), 155–162. doi: 10.1177/1557988312464038

Atkinson, R., & Flint, J. (2001). Accessing hidden and hard-to-reach populations: Snowball research strategies. *University of Surrey*. Retrieved from http://sru.soc.surrey.ac.uk/SRU33.html

August, R. (2011). Women's later life career development: Looking through the lens of the kaleidoscope career model. *Journal of Career Development, 38*(3), 208–236.

Baker, S., & Edwards, R. (n.d.). How many qualitative interviews is enough? Expert voices and early career reflections on sampling and cases in qualitative research. *National Centre for Research Methods Review Paper*. Retrieved from http://eprints.ncrm.ac.uk/2273/4/how_many_interviews.pdf

Baltar, F., & Brunet, I. (2012). Social research 2.0: Virtual snowball sampling method using Facebook. *Internet Research, 22*(1), 74–75. Retrieved from http://www.websm.org/db/12/15142/Web%20Survey%20Bibliography/Social_research_20_virtual_snowball_sampling_method_using_Facebook/

Bassett, R., Beagan, B., Ristovski-Slijepcevic, S., & Chapman, G. (2008). Tough teens: The methodological challenges of interviewing teenagers as research participants. *Journal of Adolescent Research, 23*(2), 119–131.

Becker, W., & Burke, M. (2012). The staff ride: An approach to qualitative data generation and analysis. *Organizational Research Methods, 15*(2), 316–335.

Berg, B., & Lune, H. (2012). *Qualitative research methods for the social sciences.* Boston, MA: Pearson.

Berry, J. M. (2002). Validity and reliability issues in elite interviewing. *Political Science and Politics, 35,* 679–682.

Boeree, G. (1998). *Qualitative methods workbook.* Retrieved from http://webspace.ship.edu/cgboer/qualmeth.html

Bojczyk, K., Lehan, T., McWey, L., Melson, G., & Kaufman, D. (2011). Mothers' and their adult daughters' perceptions of their relationship. *Journal of Family Issues, 32*(4), 452–481.

Brown, L., & Durrheim, K. (2009). Different kinds of knowing. Generating qualitative data through mobile interviewing. *Qualitative Inquiry, 15*(5), 911–930.

Brown, L., & Holloway, I. (2008). The adjustment journey of international postgraduate students at an English university: An ethnographic study. *Journal of Research in International Education, 7*(2), 232–249.

Bunch, G., & Panayotova, D. (2008). Latinos, language minority students, and the construction of ESL: Language testing and placement from high school to community college. *Journal of Hispanic Higher Education, 7*(1), 6–30.

Bustamante, R., Nelson, J., Henriksen, R., & Monakes, S. (2011). Intercultural couples: Coping with culture-related stressors. *The family journal: Counselling and therapy for couples and families, 19*(2), 154–164.

Carr, E. (2010). Qualifying the qualitative social work interview. *Qualitative Social Work, 10*(1), 123–143.

Chambers, J., Ward, T., Eccleston, L., & Brown, M. (2011). Representation of female offender types within the pathways model of assault. *International Journal of Offender Therapy and Comparative Criminology, 55*(6), 925–948.

Chen, C., Kendall, J., & Shyu, Y. (2010). Grabbing the rice straw: Health information seeking in Chinese immigrants in the United States. *Clinical Nursing Research, 19*(4), 335–353.

D'Alonzo, K. (2012). The influence of *Marianismo* beliefs on physical activity of immigrant Latinas. *Journal of Transcultural Nursing, 23*(2), 124–133.

Danby, S., Ewing, L., & Thorpe, K. (2011). The novice researcher: Interviewing young children. *Qualitative Inquiry, 17*(1), 74–84.

Davis, J. (2010). Architecture of the personal interactive homepage: Constructing the self through Myspace. *New Media & Society, 12*(7), 1103–1119.

DeLyser, D., & Sui, D. (2013). Crossing the qualitative-quantitative chasm III: Enduring methods, open geography, participatory research, and the fourth paradigm. *Progress in Human Geography, 19,* 1–14.

Deschaux-Beaume, D. (2012). Investigating the military field: Qualitative research strategy and interviewing in the defence networks. *Current Sociology, 60*(1), 101–117.

Driving Wiki. (2011). *Chapter 23: The qualitative interview.* Retrieved from http://www.drivingwiki.org/node/24

ebookbrowse. (2011). *Minikit qualitative interviewing pdf.* Retrieved from http://ebookbrowse.com/minikit-qualitative-interviewing-pdf-d107420707

Ezzy, D. (2010). Qualitative interviewing as embodied emotional performance. *Qualitative Inquiry, 16*(3), 163–170.

Fielding, N. (2010). Virtual fieldwork using access grid. *Field Methods, 22*(3), 195–216.

Figenschou, T. (2010). Young, female, Western researcher vs. senior, male, Al Jazeera officials: Critical reflections on accessing and interviewing media elites in authoritarian societies. *Media, Culture & Society, 32*(6), 961–978.

Flowers, I., & Moore, J. (2003). Conducting qualitative research online in student affairs. *Student Affairs On-Line #1.* Retrieved from http://www.studentaffairs.com/ejournal/Winter_2003/research.html

Fontana, A., & Frey J. (1994). Interviewing: The art of science. In N. K. Denzin & Y. S. Lincoln (Eds.), *Handbook of qualitative research* (pp. 361–376). Thousand Oaks, CA: SAGE.

Fontana, A., & Prokos, A. (2007). *The interview: From formal to postmodern.* Walnut Creek, CA: Left Coast Press.

Gailey, J., & Prohaska, A. (2011). Power and gender negotiations during interviews with men about sex and sexually degrading practices. *Qualitative Research, 11*(4), 365–380.

Garton, S., & Copland, F. (2010). "I like this interview; I get cakes and cats!": The effect of prior relationships on interview talk. *Qualitative Research, 10*(5), 533–551.

Gatson, S. (2011). Self-naming practices on the Internet: Identity, authenticity, and community. *Cultural Studies, Critical Methodologies, 11*(3), 224–235.

Gibbs, G. R. (2011, November 30). *How to do a research interview—old version.* [YouTube video]. Retrieved from http://www.youtube.com/watch?v=FGH2tYuXf0s&feature=related

Gidlöf, K., Holmberg, N., & Sandberg, H. (2012). The use of eye-tracking and retrospective interviews to study teenagers' exposure to online advertising. *Visual Communication, 11*(3), 329–345.

Gratton, M., & O'Donnell, S. (2011). Communication technologies for focus groups with remote communities: A case study of research with First Nations in Canada. *Qualitative Research, 11*(2), 159–175.

Hamilton, R., & Bowers, B. (2006). Internet recruitment and e-mail interviews in qualitative studies. *Qualitative Health Research, 16,* 821–835.

Harris, A., & Guillemin, M. (2012). Developing sensory awareness in qualitative interviewing: A portal into the otherwise unexplored. *Qualitative Health Research, 22*(5), 689–699.

Harvey, W. (2011). Strategies for conducting elite interviews. *Qualitative Research, 11*(4), 431–441.

Healey-Etten, V., & Sharp, S. (2010). Teaching beginning undergraduates how to do an in-depth interview. *Teaching Sociology, 38*(2), 157–165.

Hesse-Biber, S., & Griffin, A. (2013). Internet-mediated technologies and mixed methods research: Problems and prospects. *Journal of Mixed Methods Research, 7*(1), 43–61.

James, N., & Busher, H. (2006). Credibility, authenticity, and voice: Dilemmas in online interviewing. *Qualitative Research, 6*(3), 403–420.

Jenkins, N., Bloor, M., Fishcher, J., Berney, L., & Neale, J. (2010). Putting it in context: The use of vignettes in qualitative interviewing. *Qualitative Research, 10*(2), 175–198.

Johnson, B., & Christensen, L. (2008). *Educational research: Quantitative, qualitative, and mixed approaches* (3rd ed.). Los Angeles, CA: SAGE.

King, N., & Horrocks, C. (2010). *Interviews in qualitative research.* London, England: SAGE.

Koerber, A., & McMichael, L. (2008). Qualitative sampling methods: A primer for technical communicators. *Journal of Business and Technical Communication, 22*(4), 454–473.

Kowald, M., & Axhausen, K. (2012). Focusing on connected personal leisure networks: Selected results from a snowball sample. *Environment and Planning, 44*(5), 1085–1100. Retrieved from http://www.envplan.com/abstract.cgi?id=a43458

Kvale, S. (1996). *InterViews: An introduction to qualitative research interviewing.* Thousand Oaks, CA: SAGE.

Lahman, M. (2008). Always othered: Ethical research with children. *Journal of Early Childhood Research,* 6(3), 281–300.

Lynch, M. (2012). From food to fuel: Perceptions of exercise and food in a community of food bloggers. *Health Educational Journal, 71*(1), 72–79.

Mann, C., & Stewart, F. (2000). *Internet communication and qualitative research: A handbook for researching online.* London, England: SAGE.

Marin4F. (2011, April 3). *Qualitative Interviews.* [YouTube video]. Retrieved from http://www.youtube.com/watch?v=eVf-xYt1-JA

Markham, A. (2005). Reconsidering self and others: The methods, politics, and ethics of representation in online ethnography. In N. K. Denzin & Y. S. Lincoln (Eds.), *The handbook of qualitative research* (pp. 793–820). Thousand Oaks, CA: SAGE.

Mason, M. (2010). Sample size and saturation in PhD studies using qualitative interviews [63 paragraphs]. *Forum Qualitative Sozialforschung/Forum: Qualitative Social Research, 11*(3), Art. 8. Retrieved from http://nbn-resolving.de/urn:nbn:de:0114-fqs100387

Mayan, M. (2009). *Essentials of qualitative inquiry.* Walnut Creek, CA: Left Coast Press.

McCracken, G. (1988). *The long interview.* Newbury Park, CA: SAGE.

Mikecz, R. (2012). Interviewing elites: Addressing methodological issues. *Qualitative Inquiry, 18*(6), 482–493.

Neu, W. (2012). Unintended cognitive, affective, and behavioural consequences of group assignments. *Journal of Marketing Education, 34*(1), 67–81.

Packovic. (2009a). *Bad interview of one person.* [YouTube video]. Retrieved from http://www.youtube.com/watch?v=6ECC-SwpO0M

Packovic. (2009b). *Bad interview with two people.* [YouTube video]. Retrieved from http://www.youtube.com/watch?v=8piOSvbTo5s

Pezalla, A., Pettigrew, J., & Miller-Day, M. (2012). Researching the researcher-as-instrument: An exercise in interviewing self-reflexivity. *Qualitative Research, 12*(2), 165–185.

Piesner, U. (2011). Studying sideways: Displacing the problem of power in research interviews with sociologists and journalists. *Qualitative Inquiry, 17*(6), 471–482.

Pini, B. (2005). Interviewing men: Gender and the collection and interpretation of qualitative data. *Journal of Sociology, 41*(2), 201–216.

Pretto, A. (2011). Italian sociologists' approach to qualitative interviews. *Bulletin of Sociological Methodology, 112,* 71–83.

Razon, N., & Ross, K. (2012). Negotiating fluid identities: Alliance-building in qualitative interviewing. *Qualitative Inquiry, 18*(6), 494–503.

Riessman, C. K. (1993). *Narrative analysis.* Newbury Park, CA: SAGE.

Rose, C. (2012). *Interview with Warren Buffett.* Retrieved from http://www.charlierose.com/download/transcript/10711

Roulston, K. (2010). *Reflective interviewing: A guide to theory and practice.* London, England: SAGE.

Rubin, H., & Rubin, I. (1995/2012). *Qualitative interviewing: The art of hearing data.* Thousand Oaks, CA: SAGE.

Saffner, M., Martyn, K., & Lori, J. (2011). Sexually active adolescent women: Assessing family and peer relationships using event history calendars. *The Journal of School Nursing, 27*(3), 225–236.

Salmons, J. (2010). *Online interviews in real time.* Thousand Oaks, CA: SAGE.

Sandelowski, M. (1995). Sample size in qualitative research. *Research in Nursing & Health, 18,* 179–183.

Sbaraini, A., Carter, S., & Evans, R. (2012). How do dentists understand evidence and adopt it in practice? *Health Education Journal, 71*(2), 195–204.

Schmieder, C. (2011). Initial thoughts on interviews via Skype. *squaremethodology.com.* Retrieved from http://squaremethodology.com/2011/01/initial-thoughts-on-interviews-via-skype/

Shepherd, N. (2003, July 17–19). Interviewing online: Qualitative research in the network(ed) society. In *Qualitative research: Creating spaces for understanding,* proceedings from Association of Qualitative Research Conference, Sydney, Australia (pp. 25–26). Retrieved from http://espace.library.uq.edu.au/view/UQ:10232

Smith, E., Gidlow, B., & Steel, G. (2012). Engaging adolescent participants in academic research: The use of photo-elicitation interviews to evaluate school-based outdoor education programmes. *Qualitative Research, 12*(4), 367–387.

Spradley, J. (1979). *The ethnographic interview.* New York, NY: Holt, Rinehart & Winston.

Sutton, B. (2011). Playful cards, serious talk: A qualitative research technique to elicit women's embodied experiences. *Qualitative Research, 11*(2), 177–196.

Suzuki, I., Ahluwalia, M., Arora, A., & Mattis, J. (2007). The pond you fish in determines the fish you catch: Strategies for qualitative data collection. *The Counseling Psychologist, 35*(2), 295–327.

Van Oord, L. (2008). After culture: Intergroup encounters in education. *Journal of Research in International Education, 7*(2), 131–147.

Walby, K. (2010). Interviews as encounters: Issues of sexuality and reflexivity when men interview men about commercial same sex relations. *Qualitative Research, 10*(6), 639–657.

Wannheden, C. (2011). *The qualitative research interview.* Retrieved from https://pingpong.ki.se/public/pp/public_courses/course08452/published/1303828631046/resourceId/4749298/content/The%20qualitative%20research%20interview.pdf

Winfrey, O. (2012). Transcript of Oprah Interview with J. K. Rowling. *Harry Potter's Page.* Retrieved from http://www.harrypotterspage.com/2010/10/03/transcript-of-oprah-interview-with-j-k-rowling/

STUDENT STUDY SITE

Visit **http://www.sagepub.com/lichtmanqrss** to access additional study tools, including eFlashcards and links to SAGE journal articles.

CHAPTER 11

Additional Methods of Gathering Data

Focus Your Reading

- Five methods of gathering data are discussed—observations, focus group interviewing, visuals/images, the written word, and technology.
- Each method has issues that have to be considered by researchers.
- Qualitative researchers have unlimited possibilities to consider as they plan for how to gather data.

Many social science disciplines rely on methods of collecting data that supplement or enhance interviewing. In this chapter, I will discuss several types of methods. That various disciplines are using qualitative methods more frequently is well documented. From the psychiatric discipline, there is evidence that "papers using qualitative methods are increasingly common in psychiatric journals" (Kisely & Kendall, 2011, p. 365). Originally developed as workshops for the conferences of Canadian and Pacific Rim psychiatrists in 2010, this brief article asserted that qualitative methods are on the increase. The authors commented that data sources included observations, interviews and focus groups, and document analysis. Similarly, Watkins (2012), writing for those in the health field, included focus groups, in-depth interviews, uninterrupted observation, participant observation, and document review as methods or techniques of gathering data. In Chapter 10, I described in-depth interviewing for you in detail. In this chapter, I consider other types of data sources.

When I began teaching courses in qualitative research (QR) in the mid-1980s, there was little available in terms of texts or ideas about teaching QR. One thing I knew—I wanted to teach observation skills. An idea I had was for students to observe the same situation. I decided to focus on family interactions at mealtimes. Remember, this time period is before the Internet or television 24/7. I located a number of films that illustrated my point. The television department at my university reproduced selections from several movies (*Haywire*, *Moonstruck*, and *Witness*, among others).

Once the videotapes were compiled, I introduced them as part of a class exercise. I tried several ways for students to begin their observations. Some students were given the assignment to look for different ways in which women were treated; others were asked to look at nonverbal communication; others focused on exploring differences among cultural groups; and a final group had no direction. I thought the activity afforded many opportunities to illustrate points about conducting observations. We could review the films endlessly; I could stop and start the clips in order to become involved in discussion. We could all view the same thing in the same setting. While I knew that the films were exaggerated and somewhat contrived, they served the purpose. I found it very successful in helping students learn about how to conduct observations. Today, of course, with the wonders of television, instant reruns, and all the capabilities of the Internet, including YouTube, this type of activity can be used and adapted to today's world.

Conducting observations is only one of the myriad ways to collect qualitative data. I have chosen to discuss several other techniques of gathering data. I begin first with learning about observations. Next, I explore focus group interviewing. Then, I examine the use of visuals. I continue with the use of the written word. I conclude with a discussion on the use of technologies. Brief summaries and details are provided for each technique. Although I write about these various methods or techniques separately, be aware that many researchers tend to combine several techniques in a single study. A word of caution: When I speak of combining techniques, I mean they tend to use interviews and observations, observations and archival records, or even three or more sources of data in a single study. This is different from studies in which the research approach is called *mixed methods*. In the latter type, researchers collect both qualitative and quantitative data.

Observations. Observations usually occur in natural rather than contrived settings. You can observe naturally occurring groups in many different settings. These can range from formal to informal settings. If you were studying individuals in a work setting, you might look at a formal work setting (such as a scheduled meeting) or an informal group in the employees' lounge. You might study the medical profession formally in a hospital meeting or more casually in the cafeteria. You can also observe individuals in online environments. (Many of the techniques and strategies related to observations originated with those conducting ethnographies.)

Focus Group Interviewing. Focus group interviewing is a technique of data collection that relies on group interaction and discussion. Although originating with sociologists in the 1920s and later, it has been widely used by market researchers. Of late, however, social science disciplines have adopted the technique.

Visuals/Images. The use of images for collecting data is also documented in various social science disciplines. You can use images such as photographs, films, or videotapes. They can be either existing images or ones made specifically for your research. With digital cameras or Smartphones, images are both easy to create and instantly available. You can also use drawings or sketches. Images can be created by you, by the participants, or by both together. Images from YouTube or other Internet sources can also be used.

The Written Word. There are various types of written documents that you can use in QR. Some researchers refer to these types of information as *archival data*. Qualitative researchers often use existing documents to obtain information. These may include official documents such as minutes of meetings or curriculum guides. They can also include newspaper accounts, letters, diaries or journals, and online course descriptions. Participants can create written material in the form of email messages, blogs, responses to questions, or student journals. Finally, you may create written material in the form of field notes, memos, or a researcher journal. In some cases, you will make notes of your observations; in other cases, you will make notes that are self-reflective or introspective.

Technology. With the widespread use of the Internet and associated technologies, researchers have explored ways in which the use of such technologies can be used to gather data directly or to facilitate more traditional means of gathering data. Smartphones, in particular, offer the opportunity for researchers to study participant movement and interaction. Skype offers researchers an easily accessible means of conducting interviews or of interacting with each other and with participants.

Did You Know

The Pew Internet & American Life Project (n.d.) gathers knowledge about the role of emerging technologies and media trends in society. "The project's researchers study the latest ways in which Web usage is changing daily life from cell phone use to broadband and wireless Internet access to forms of online expression such as blogs and podcasts."

■ Observing in Natural Settings

Many of the ideas about observation in QR are drawn from anthropologists who immersed themselves in remote cultures. These anthropologists were called *ethnographers* and practiced what later came to be called *classical ethnography*. Sometimes, they tried to remain unobtrusive; however, they more often became participant observers. They spent months listening to and looking at those around them. They took notes. Critical to their work was the study of the social interaction among groups in their own environment. The anthropologists' goal was to try to gain a deep understanding of the cultures of these groups. Early in the 1900s, it was common to study individuals in cultures that were completely remote and different from our own, so anthropologists traveled to New Guinea, Samoa, Mexico, or other remote locations. Of course, you need to remember that access to these cultures was very limited. There was no television or Internet, and few Americans had actually traveled to such faraway places. These early types of observations were called *nonparticipant observations.* In some cases, observers found themselves interacting with the people, and their roles shifted to *participant observers.* Today, most qualitative researchers acknowledge that observers cannot remain unobtrusive.

It was not until the late 1980s that ethnography began to be used to any extent in other disciplines. Education (LeCompte, 2002) was among the first to apply such methods to the study of schools and education. Researchers immersed themselves in classrooms, conducted extensive observations, and took field notes. As interest in the technique increased, modifications were made to the length of observations, and shorter observation times became more widely used. Beginning in the 21st century, researchers became interested in online cultures and adapted techniques to the study of online chat rooms or other online communities. Mantzoukas (2012) traced the use of ethnographic research in general and specifically in the nursing field. He commented that spending intensive time observing and using thick descriptions is "not the only type of ethnographic research and possibly not the most relevant type of ethnography for nursing" (p. 421). His detailed article will provide you information about various types of ethnographies, including classical, critical, and interpretive ethnography. In fact, ethnography was adopted by a number of disciplines in addition to education. "Hence, ethnographic methodology crossed disciplines and became part of the academic research landscape of disciplines such as linguistics, health professions, education, material culture, journalism, cinematography, business and consumer research" (Mantzoukas, p. 422). Kawulich (2005) also offered an excellent overview of the topic.

In 2006, a special session of seven senior researchers was held at the International Congress of Qualitative Inquiry at the University of Illinois. An assignment for one group of students was to perform an ethnographic study of the conference by conducting informal interviews and observations. Students had to obtain signed consent forms from the participants. What resulted was a publication based on the informal discussions among the researchers and the observations and comments by Carolyn Ellis, the organizer (Ellis et al., 2008). I believe you will enjoy reading about how these researchers travelled on their journey. One thing you will come away with is how open to new ideas these researchers are. I urge you to take a similar open stance as you explore various means of gathering data.

Purpose of Observations

As I mentioned, gathering data through observation has long been associated with ethnographers. Observing humans in natural settings assists our understanding of the complexity of human behavior and interrelationships among groups. When anthropologists visited groups of people in remote lands, their goals were to study the culture of these groups. One definition of culture is that it is a system of shared beliefs, values, customs, and behaviors that individuals use to cope with their world and with each other. In the early years, non-Western people were studied, and their values were often compared to the values of those who were conducting the study. Although not necessarily made explicit, the assumption was that the values of Western culture were somehow better than those of others. This issue, among others, caused some researchers to adopt more democratic and inclusive stances. Feminist perspectives and critical theory were one result.

As I previously mentioned, studying schools became a topic of interest to many ethnographers. Prior to this time, almost all of the research about schools relied on correlational studies relating student test scores with spending or other quantitative measures. Yet little evidence about the culture of schools was available. This interest in the study of schools led to an increase in QR in general and observational work in particular. Some of the observational studies in schools were done to get a sense of what it was like in a classroom. I recall Kidder's 1989 study of a fifth-grade classroom in Massachusetts. He spent nine months with 20 children and their teacher. His moving account includes sections on homework, discipline, and the science fair. I do not believe he knew which topics he would write about prior to his immersion in the class. Although not written as QR per se, this is one of the earliest detailed accounts of a classroom that provides a rich context about the children and their teacher. Geertz (1973) reminded us that a thick description is to be valued in ethnography. I think he would agree that Kidder does just this.

Although observations emanating from an ethnographic tradition have been used in many disciplines, it is instructive to look at how educators applied these techniques to schools and classrooms. As educators began to spend extended time in classrooms, there seemed to be a desire to study groups of children who were quite different from the observers. Because most researchers who do these kinds of studies are highly educated, they usually are members of the middle class. Yet they tended to study children who were not of the middle class. The greater the difference between those observing and those being observed, the more likely it was that ethnocentric ideas came into play. These were some of the same issues I raised earlier regarding studies of remote cultures. So, for example, when middle-class White observers studied working-class Black students, they saw many differences and, I suspect, found themselves making comparisons that were quite judgmental. Frank's (1999) practical observation guide written for student teachers should help you in thinking about studying classrooms. You can also learn more about using ethnographic methods of observation in classrooms by examining the program at California State University–Chico (2011) designed to study new teachers.

But the study of schools was not the only arena into which ethnographers delved. Others also studied groups who were outside the mainstream culture. Pascoe's (2007) book, *Dude, You're a Fag* (winner of the American Education Research Award for 2008), is an account by a female sociologist who spent a year and a half in a high school studying gender, sexuality, inequality, youth, and new media. A major component of her study is the use of observations. She revealed to the students at the end of her research that she is gay. You should be able to get a much clearer understanding of using observations in a variety of settings from this fascinating account. Jordan (2012), in her edited book of ethnography in corporate environments, offers accounts by scholars of how to look at practical realities of doing ethnography in business settings. If you read the anthropological literature, you will see many references to studies of groups that could be seen as outsiders: motorcycle gangs, the homeless, homosexuals, pregnant teenagers, drug addicts, and the like.

Unlike Pascoe, many researchers do not have the luxury or financial wherewithal to immerse themselves in settings for such a long time or in such depth. Given increased violence in the workplace and heightened security, many organizations are reluctant to let outsiders in for extended observations. Some businesses might be reluctant to have observers spend considerable time in their corporate offices, lest they reveal or uncover corporate secrets. And many schools, teachers, parents, and students might be reluctant to give permission for outsiders to come into their settings for an extended time.

As a consequence of these issues, using observation to gather qualitative data has moved away from the kind of immersion practiced by anthropologists and sociologists. The activity has become shorter and less intense. So, now, you have to rethink what is meant by *observing*. In my experience, it is an activity that is much narrower in scope. I recall a student who studied kindergarten classrooms to determine how rules were formed. McIntyre (2002) studied violence in the lives of Northern Irish women. I remember reading a study of teenagers in malls and how groups interacted. In all these examples, the researchers limited themselves to a particular aspect of human interaction. They targeted that information and limited the scope of their observations to a predetermined area. You can also examine a virtual ethnography class on Facebook (UP Virtual Ethnography Class, 2009).

Issues Regarding Observations

Deciding Who Is to Be Studied and in What Situations

Do you want to study displaced workers in new environments? Do you want to study interracial interactions in public places in the American South (Anderson, Austin, Holloway, & Kulkarni, 2012)? Are you interested in mass incarcerations (Earle & Phillips, 2012)? Do you want to study first-year teachers in their classrooms? Do you want to study community engagement in public libraries (Sung, Hepworth, & Ragsdell, 2012)? Do you want to do research on nurses in emergency rooms? Often, qualitative researchers select one or several key demographic characteristics of a group of people and decide to study them by observing them in their natural settings. Often, they first decide on the type of individual to study. Observations then can occur in a number of places. If school children are selected, then the observations might occur inside a classroom, on the playing field, on the bus, in the cafeteria, or in the hallways. Fordham (1988) studied successful inner-city, poor, minority children and observed them at church, at home, and in social situations. Glass (2001) studied families of autistic children and studied them in their homes. Berger (2004) studied wheelchair athletes. Cocks (2008) studied the peer culture of disabled children. Condell (2008) reported on writing field notes while studying collaborative experiences of peers. Low (2010) studied the hip-hop culture in an urban school where she taught.

Types of Groups

You might not have thought about this before, but there are different kinds of groups you can study. A *formal group* is stable, with the same people serving as a nucleus, such as a class, a family, a team, a gang, or a work unit. These same people come together regularly for either work or play. There are usually formal or informal rules and boundaries that are known by all members of the group. *Informal groups,* on the other hand, are in contact with each other, but members may move in and out, and they do not meet regularly. Examples of informal groups are a card-playing group, members of an online chat room, a play group with parents and children, a community action team, or members of a club or a support group. An *occasional group* consists of people who might come together once or a number of times but whose membership is constantly shifting. All types of groups can be observed, but you might look for different things in each. Various types of *online groups* might include chat rooms, LISTSERVs, or online classes.

Gaining Access

Roesch-Marsh, Gadda, and Smith (2012) observe that the "process of gaining research access in the social sciences is becoming increasingly difficult" (p. 249). They speak of a cautionary approach that public service providers take to minimizing risk. Writing from a feminist viewpoint and as students, they discuss the importance of adopting a reflexive approach. They suggest that one important way to gain access was to "develop networks which supported and enabled the process of gaining access" (p. 259–260). If studies are conducted in schools, gaining access is often difficult. In the current climate of violence, many school officials are reluctant to let outsiders enter the schools. Often, researchers have to submit detailed plans outlining what they want to do and how much time they will take doing it. They usually have to obtain approval from parents to study minors. They may be asked to speak of how the research will benefit those studied. Large school systems are very difficult to penetrate and often receive many more requests than they can handle. If studies are to be conducted with specific subgroups of students or teachers, it is often difficult to get access to these groups. If studies are to be conducted in the workplace, gaining access might be easier, but some members of the group may not want to participate for fear of reprisals.

Almost 40 years ago, Liebow (1967) studied Black men on street corners in Washington, DC, and had to overcome the participants' reluctance to let him into their subculture. Gaining access when you are an outsider continues to be challenging, as Berger (2004) remarked about his surprise as he faced difficulties gaining access to observe people with disabilities. As you think about conducting your own observations, sensitivity and awareness of these issues are important considerations.

What to Study

In my experience, what is most difficult about conducting observations is determining what to look at or what to look for. There is so much going on when humans are together. Should you concentrate on a single person? If so, who? If you try to take in the whole setting, it becomes overwhelming. I find that beginning students are more comfortable with some guidelines. In the next section, I offer you some concrete suggestions. Boeree (1998) distinguished between the physical nature of human interaction and the meaning of interactions. As the observer, it is up to you to decide when an interaction is meaningful. In my experience, the distinction begins to emerge as you process the data you have collected. It might not be evident during an observation which interactions are meaningful.

Frequency and Length of Time

Obviously, this varies depending on what you are studying, whom you are studying, and how much time you have available. For a comprehensive ethnography of a situation or setting, you might need to allocate several months or longer. To gather data as part of the total process of collecting information, you might conduct your observations several times and allocate between 30 minutes and an hour for each observation. Some settings are routine and predictable, while others are extremely varied.

Your Role

Observers take on different roles. If you are part of the group you observe, or if you become part of the group, you are a participant observer. If you are not known to those you are studying, you are a surreptitious or unobtrusive observer. If you observe in cyberspace, you might be a completely unknown or unnoticed observer. In postmodern ethnography, the observer's role is an interaction in which his or her voice is made explicit. This contemporary position reflects relatively new thinking about power and privilege and the relationship between those being studied and those doing the studying. Keiding (2010) reaffirms the idea that there is "no such thing as a neutral or objective description" (abstract). In fact, observation is always participation, she says. Using a systems theory perspective, she reminds us that all observations are interpretations of the observed. Lugosi (2006), however, suggests that, in certain situations, the observer might need to remain concealed.

How to Conduct an Observation

Qualitative observations differ tremendously, depending on the concepts and issues to be studied, location of the observation, length of time of each observation, number of observations, and type of group studied. Below are some suggestions as you begin to practice doing observations.

Planning

- Most people prefer to begin observations by deciding on a particular aspect of social interaction to study. It is difficult to just "go in and look" without knowing what you will look at or what is important. I suggest you identify a specific aspect of human interaction to study. Many find it difficult to study culture in general and are better able to identify a particular dimension of human interaction to study. I have looked at interactions of aides with children, families interacting during different occasions (e.g., meals, parties, and leisure time), teachers in faculty meetings, and teacher-parent meetings. I have had students study staking out space in the library, motorcycle gangs in bars, and female athletes in the locker room.

- Identify three to five areas to look at, such as who begins a conversation, reactions of participants to a particular issue, or nonverbal signals shown by participants. This should be seen as freeing, not limiting. Sometimes observers go into a situation with no agenda, and this works well; but other times, students report being overwhelmed and unable to focus on a particular thing because so much is going on.

- Decide whether you will take notes, use videos or digital technology, bring along your laptop or smartphone or iPad, or rely on your memory. If you decide on the latter, then make sure that you allow sufficient time immediately after the observation to record your impressions.

- Decide how much time you will allow for your observation. I suggest at least 30 minutes initially. I would then follow up with a one-hour observation.

- For your initial observations, I suggest that you choose public spaces where individuals interact with each other. This way, you do not need to obtain permission, and you can blend in with those you are studying. I use cafés, fast-food restaurants, playgrounds, shopping malls, airports, religious institutions, or any other place where people congregate.

Conducting the Observations

- Once you arrive at your destination, you need to settle down in a place where you will be able to look and listen. I frequently observe at a fast-food restaurant. I get some coffee and choose a table where I can be comfortable and can see and hear plenty of people. I find it helpful to drink my coffee and survey the space. I need to take notes, so I use an iPad; however, in some situations, you might find this gets in the way, and you will have to rely on your memory.

- I find it very helpful to begin my observations with a look at the surroundings. I often draw a sketch or take a picture as a memory aid. I also use my iPhone or digital camera to take pictures of the surroundings. If I am in a school or office, I note how the furniture is arranged, what kind of art is displayed, the lighting, and the air quality. If I go to the same location regularly, I make note of any changes in the physical space.

- Because your study is about individuals, you may decide you want to describe the main characters in the setting. What are they wearing? Is their speech formal or casual? How well do the players appear to know each other?

- Because your goal is to observe human interaction, you need to decide what to focus on. In some settings, there may be several different things happening at the same time, and you will need to set some priorities. There is no right thing to look at. You just need to decide what is challenging or interesting to study.

Other Issues

- What is your role? Do you want to participate in the interactions, or do you want to remain aloof? Is there a right or best way to behave? Can you behave one way one time and another way another time? I suspect you know that it is up you to choose what you want to do. I have observed in many classrooms where I was silent and sat in the back of the room. I have also found myself helping children who needed help. Should you disclose your role to members of the group or keep it hidden? It depends on the situation.

- Things are not always as they seem. If people know you are observing them, they might want to look good, so you might not be seeing underlying human experience. Or people might decide to behave as they think you want them to behave. If you are in a public setting, this is less likely to occur.

- Should you reveal to people what you are doing and why? Should you keep it quiet? Should you tell a fictitious story? These are decisions you will need to make once you begin an actual research study. For now, because you are practicing and honing your skills, this is less critical.

- Should you have a very narrow focus, or should you look at everything? Here, you need to strike a balance. It should be obvious that you can't look at everything, but you may not know what is important until you have spent some time looking and listening and thinking about the underlying meaning of what you see and hear.

- How much is enough? You can only get a slice of life, so how large a slice should you get? You can answer this question by beginning your data analysis while you are observing. That means you will have to take notes either while you are observing or when you complete an observation. Sometimes circumstances dictate how long you can observe. I recall being at a preschool in Japan for about a week. I studied several classrooms, met with the principal, and observed children on the playground. Although I would have preferred to be there a longer time, it was not possible.

- Can you really get at the essence of the culture of the group? This is a difficult question to answer. I believe you can come to understand how individuals interact with each other and develop new insights through observation. A word of caution, however: As individuals become more sophisticated and worldly, they may learn to mask underlying meanings. Your task is to uncover deep meaning rather than surface structure.

- I am not sure that practice makes perfect, but I believe you can train yourself to be more observant. Exercises that involve observing the same phenomenon—for example, looking at films or videos, discussing what you observed with others, and then looking again at the same videos—will heighten your powers of observation. You can train yourself to focus on details or to look at the whole and ignore the details. You can train yourself to look for the emotional content and meaning expressed in everyday language.

Four Scenarios for Practice

I have found it very effective to practice some ideas in advance before I actually conduct an observation. I think of these as scenarios. Consider each of the following scenarios before you actually begin an observation.

Scenario 1

Topic: Using television families to study power

Your role: Observer

Setting the stage: Select several current television series that concern a family. I suggest you pick several different kinds of programs and that you choose traditional and nontraditional situations. Choose at least three different episodes of the program.

Providing focus for your observation: You are interested in studying power as it manifests in families. Prior to observations, you need to develop a working definition of power from your point of view. As a start, you might ask yourself these kinds of questions: What are the signs of power? How is it manifested? Who exhibits power in a specific family? What are ways in which it is accomplished? Are there power issues that are appropriate (from your perspective) or inappropriate in the families you observe?

Conducting the observation: The first time you watch a specific program, you may just want to get used to looking at different interactions and taking notes. After you feel comfortable, return to your question and try to jot down an example and evidence related to your focus. Continue this process through several episodes of the program.

Making sense of what you found: Because you are only practicing, you cannot conduct more than a tentative analysis. Write down your general thoughts about the topic.

Advantages: By using a television program, you can review your data many times. You can also do this observation in conjunction with other students and compare your comments.

Limitations: Television programs do not really reflect real life; most things are exaggerated. You may not find any evidence related to your topic.

Scenario 2

Topic: Examining the effects of parental cultural expectations on children's behavior

Your role: Unobtrusive observer

Setting the stage: Identify a fast-food restaurant near your home where you might encounter families from many cultural backgrounds. Choose a weekend mealtime for your observation. Go to the restaurant prior to your actual observations to determine whether you can sit and observe. You might want to talk to the manager, who may become suspicious and ask why you are there.

Providing focus for your observation: You are aware that family expectations differ dramatically based on cultural backgrounds. You might look at such things as whether expectations for family members are based on gender. Are the adult men and women behaving in ways that might influence their daughters to be more traditional, to act out, or to be subservient? What kinds of rules do you think girls would learn in different cultural settings? Do parents behave differently toward their male or female children?

Conducting the observation: This is a more difficult than observing a television program. People might wonder why you are looking at them. You might not really be able to take notes while you look. In my experience, however, you should find some interesting things in public places.

Making sense of what you found: You can try your hand at writing some general thoughts about the different styles exhibited by cultural groups as they interact over a family meal. You may also want to restate your question, because you might not be clear about your focus.

Advantages: Understanding different styles among cultural groups is a critical topic, especially as our culture becomes increasingly diverse.

Limitations: Conducting an observation in a public place without drawing suspicion may be a problem, in light of increased concerns about security.

Scenario 3

Topic: Examine the discrepancies between verbal behaviors and nonverbal cues

Your role: Participant observer

Setting the stage: Identify locations where you are able to observe adults interacting with each other. If you choose an office, the people might be more careful of their behavior. If you choose a social situation, you might see different kinds of behaviors.

Providing focus for your observation: You have long had an interest in the relationship between verbal behaviors and nonverbal cues. You've suspected that what one says and what one does may often be at odds. You've noticed that when talking to people (e.g., in your office), you are struck by the abundance of comments that are socially acceptable. Yet when you observe the way people behave, they often act in ways contrary to their words. You decide to observe people interacting in natural settings and look specifically for nonverbal cues, especially those that contradict verbal statements. You might begin by asking yourself, "Do I see discrepancies? What kinds of discrepancies do I observe? Do people misunderstand the meaning of what others say and do?"

Conducting the observation: Your observation can be conducted in any social or work setting. It can be a party, a social gathering, a work environment, or an informal get-together. Your role is participant observer; you are actually part of the setting. Practice before you actually observe by paying special attention to certain words and behaviors. Then, identify several settings where you can see evidence of these behaviors. When you leave the setting, write down your thoughts in your journal, since it would be awkward to do so while attending an event.

Making sense of what you found: Again, you have insufficient data to make any meaningful statements. However, you can try to organize your notes into themes.

Advantages: You have immediate access to a natural setting, because you are part of the group.

Limitations: You might not see what you are looking for, or you might forget what you see because you are not able to take notes while you are interacting.

Scenario 4

Topic: Study gender differences in a math classroom

Your role: Postmodern observer

Setting the stage: Identify a classroom that meets the criteria.

Providing focus for your observation: You are aware of many issues regarding the different behaviors of and expectations for males and females. Rather than identify a particular scenario or area of focus, in this observation, you will gather data to target your observations. You will enter the situation with predetermined ideas about teachers' different expectations of performance. Because you have already adopted a stance, you might find it difficult to keep an open mind as you observe.

Conducting the observation: I usually find, with a general idea such as this, that several observations are in order. Once you select a classroom, you might find yourself moving from unobtrusive observer to one who takes an active role. I have seen observers in such classes help students with homework or explain different ideas. In fact, sometimes, they forget to do their observations. It takes a good deal of skill to focus your attention and not get caught up in a particular situation.

Making sense of what you found: As with the other examples, you might find yourself having difficulty determining what it is you really have gathered.

Advantages: You are not limited to looking at a particular situation and may discover that new insights emerge.

Limitations: By not having a focus, you might find yourself struggling to determine what it is you should look for, or you might discover that you see what you want to see.

These illustrations should give you some ideas of places to observe and ways in which you can engage in observations. Many students who are just beginning their experiences with QR find that targeted practice helps them begin to refine their observation skills.

Astute observing is an excellent way to gather information for your qualitative study. While it is fairly unstructured, it offers endless possibilities for learning how humans interact. You can increase your observational skills through practice, feedback, and discussion with others. Using television and film enables you to look and look again. Today, with sophisticated technology readily available, we find observation taking on entirely new dimensions. For example, we have video ethnography, a technique suggested by Genzuk (2003), who recommends that you begin by watching people at school, work, or leisure. I agree with him. Tutt (2008) provided a fascinating account of a yearlong study of living room interactions using video ethnography. I discuss several other examples of this technique in the section below on Images and Visuals.

The use of observations is a key technique for gathering qualitative data. It is critical when conducting ethnography. It is also valuable in doing case study, phenomenology, or grounded theory. As I have said repeatedly, nothing replaces practice in the real world.

■ Focus Group Interviews

I was in a large, comfortable room, having been invited to participate in a focus group discussion. I wasn't quite sure what was going to happen, but I had agreed to come. I arrived at the scheduled time, got a cup of coffee, and found my name tag. I was not precisely sure what I would be doing, but I had agreed to participate because someone called me, asked if I would, and offered me $100 for my time. I took a place at the table and chatted with others around me. I did not see anyone I knew. Soon an individual entered the room, took a seat, and got the group's attention. She thanked everyone for coming and said that we would begin shortly and that we would spend about an hour in a discussion. After getting our permission to record the session, she began. I should tell you that when I was called, I was told that someone had recommended me because I had had breast cancer. I confirmed the fact with the telephone interviewer, so I knew that we would be talking about that topic. Anticipating the actual meeting, I had been reflecting on my experience. How could I not begin thinking about the topic, especially one so painful and personal?

This is how we began: The moderator said, "I am Mary Jones, and I work for the Cancer Foundation. We are here tonight to listen to your views on a topic you know only too well. I am married, have two children, and have been working with the Cancer Foundation for about five years. We're going to begin this evening by learning a little bit about each of us and then share our own journeys. I was diagnosed with breast cancer eight years ago. I didn't know how I would survive or what my life was going to be like, but here I am to tell the story." Mary paused and looked around the room. "Now, it is your turn to share your stories. Who wants to begin?" Mary turned her attention to some papers in front of her. She did not look at anyone. The assembled body was silent. I wondered who would lead us off. Soon, one of the women sitting across from me began to speak. "I am Ann Spencer. I am not working now, but I used to teach elementary school. My boyfriend and I live together and are trying to decide whether to marry or not." She continued, sharing with us how she discovered that she had a tumor in her breast and the treatment she received. When Ann finished, Dianne spoke up. Mary was listening but not talking. She seemed intent on what we were saying, occasionally taking notes. As Dianne spoke, one of the other women—Kelly—asked Dianne a question. She responded. And then I chimed in as well. All the women in the room shared their stories. Mary listened intently but rarely spoke. Toward the end of the hour, Mary said, "We've talked from our hearts about this experience. Let's finish up by talking about how our lives have changed." There was no holding the group back. After we were well into the second hour, Mary indicated that we had to stop and thanked us all for coming. Some of us left the room. Others lingered, talking about our experiences.

I have told you this story because it illustrates one type of focus group interview. It exemplifies what Morgan (1988) called a "self-managed group." The moderator introduces the topic, often by sharing personal information herself. The group essentially runs itself. When the moderator senses that the group has run out of ideas, she either introduces a new topic or reminds the group to reflect on why they are there. The group interaction is critical. It emerges because individuals who share a common experience stimulate each other to talk. The moderator's role is minimal. She knows that the group will talk and react to each other. For me, this is the best kind of focus group interview to conduct; the data are rich and varied.

A special type of interviewing technique, focus group interviewing had its origins in 1926 when Emory Bogardus used group interviews as he developed a social distance scale. Merton, a social scientist who studied response to wartime propaganda during World War II, is also credited with its development (Merton & Kendall, 1946). It has been widely used as a technique in market research by Lazarsfeld and in gauging political viewpoints (Lewis, 1995). Much of the writing and information about focus groups related to market research—and much still does. "However, the focus group method has now been regaining more popularity among academic researchers in the health and social sciences. Many of these researchers have been developing the method and steering it to suit their research needs" (Liamputtong, 2011, p. 2). Millward (2012) asserted that within psychology, focus group research had gained a substantial foothold in the 21st century (p. 414). It is particularly popular in applied and health psychology and with young people and children.

In addition to bringing together individuals from diverse locations, using focus groups saves on costs and time. Millward's (2012) comments (quoting Hollander and Halkier) are particularly insightful: "appreciating how focus groups can furnish 'tiny glimpses of the world' one might not normally be able to see" (p. 415). She suggested that using focus groups might generate new perspectives not previously considered by the researcher. This is similar to unexpected findings in other types of research that often lead to new ideas or insights.

Just as qualitative interviewing takes many forms, so, too, does focus group interviewing. Some see it as a highly structured activity in which participants and leader follow a predetermined set of questions. Stewart and Shamdasani (1990) took the position that a formal interview guide should be developed, with questions moving from the general to the specific, placing those of greater importance at the beginning. Krueger (1988) suggested the number of questions to be included be no more than 10 and usually about five or six. Other details about the moderator's specific role in the group are part of a structured approach. My preference, however, is not to use such an approach. I believe it limits the nature of the discussion and is used in an attempt to lend a patina of objectivity to the task.

As with individual qualitative interviews, focus groups can be of a semi-structured type. In such an approach, the moderator/interviewer has developed a list of questions and has a preconceived plan for proceeding. Many researchers use such a plan as a guide and are willing to modify it as needed. In my experience, many new researchers find it helpful to have a list of questions or question areas that they wish to follow. They seem to need this almost as a crutch. I think it is important, however, that the group lead the way, to the extent possible. With practice, moderators can move into a less structured, less directive approach to conducting focus groups.

A third type is much less structured. In this type, the leader plays the role of facilitator and lets the group process evolve into questions and responses. As with so much of QR, there is no right way to conduct a focus group.

No matter which level of structure you choose, however, there are common elements to focus group interviewing. All researchers agree that a focus group consists of a set of people (anywhere from six to 12) who come together for approximately one hour. The purpose is to discuss a specific topic. As I mentioned, the leader/facilitator may play a very directive role, by leading the group toward specific ends, or he or she may be very indirect and let the group take the leadership role. It is believed that by participating in a group discussion, members of the group may stimulate others to comment or react in ways that do not occur in individual interviews.

Purpose of Focus Group Interviewing

The purpose of using focus groups is to gather information from participants about the topic of interest. It is the content that results from the group discussion and interaction that is important. Often, this type of information cannot be obtained through a survey or individual interviews. A focus group is a group interview. Kitzinger (1994) refers to an "organized discussion." What is critical about the group involvement is that there is group interaction. What distinguishes focus group interviewing from qualitative interviewing with a single individual is that the group interaction may trigger thoughts and ideas among participants that do not emerge during an individual interview.

Your goal might be to learn how individuals think or feel about a particular topic that is common to each of them. I vividly recall interviewing parents in military schools in Panama who had experienced site-based school management. I asked them what changes they had noticed in their school after site-based management was introduced. They were able to provide specific and concrete examples of changes that they had tried for years to achieve but had not been able to accomplish until management was turned over to the local school. By participating in the group, individuals were stimulated and thought of examples and ideas that might not have emerged during individual interviews.

Sometimes your goal might be to talk to individuals who have a common experience. Morgan (1988) suggested that although not everyone may want to state an opinion about something, most are willing to share their experiences.

Although I think of focus group interviewing as another way to collect data, Millward (2012) offered additional perspectives. Some of the purposes behind focus group interviewing include developing constructs preparatory toward questionnaire development, checking validity of conceptual models, supplementing traditional methods, generating a different perspective, and generating conversation (pp. 416–417). In my mind, these suggestions seem to treat focus groups as almost preliminary or secondary to other forms of data collection. I subscribe to Millward's comment that "focus groups can offer evidence from an alternative and equally valid perspective on a topic than is possible using more traditional methods" (p. 417). In fact, postmodern perspectives make use of the discourse in focus groups for analysis. Halkier (2010) and Farnsworth and Boon (2010) are interested in the social-interaction aspect of focus groups. Despite the interest in studying this interaction, Belzile and Öberg (2012), in their review of focus group literature, noted an absence of interaction data and called for making explicit how such interaction should be handled.

Issues Regarding Focus Groups

Deciding on the Size of the Group

I will start by asking this question: Why do you think the size of the group might be important? You have no doubt heard that it is better to have a larger group than a smaller one. One explanation is technical—if you plan to generalize from a sample to a population, the error rate is reduced as the sample gets larger. But you are not planning to generalize to a larger group. That concept is associated with hypothesis testing and quantitative research (QN). Recall that when doing QR, your goal is to answer *why* and *how* questions. Wolcott (1994) speaks of QR as resulting in description, analysis, and interpretation. So disabuse yourself of the idea of generalization. Some researchers still cling to this concept and apologize or speak of limitations if the sample size is small. Look at some examples of recent publications that offer apologies. Tomlinson, Barker, and Soden (2012), in their study on cancer patients' experiences, not only apologize for the small sample size; they also apologize for a study that is "entirely qualitative" (p. 763). And apologies also come from Ozsivadjian, Knott, and Magiati (2012). They discuss their study's limitations thusly: "One important limitation is the small sample size and representativeness of the participants, who were a self-selected group from a relatively small geographical area" (p. 117). These comments are indicative of what I believe are misunderstandings about the nature of QR in general and the use of focus group interviewing in particular.

Most who write about focus group interviewing recommend a group of six to 12 people. I agree with this. If there are more than 12, the session takes too long, and group interaction becomes more difficult to achieve; if there are fewer than six, there may be insufficient interaction. Nielsen, Brixen, and Huniche (2011), in a study of men with osteoporosis, used small groups of three to five men, citing that they wanted each to have ample opportunity to express his own views. I am struck that they seemed less concerned with the interaction among the men. On a related note, I often schedule more than 12 people, because in my experience, several participants will fail to appear on a given day, even though they have agreed to participate. This is particularly true if you are not compensating the participants. When I conducted focus groups on a military base, some were called away on temporary assignment and had to miss the session. When I conducted focus groups with students, some were not available due to scheduling conflicts or illness.

Deciding on the Number of Groups

Just as you need to consider how many participants should be in a group, you need to think about how many groups you plan to conduct. Because you are not generalizing, it is not important to involve a large number of groups. At the same time, however, researchers often seem to be more comfortable conducting several groups that address the same topic. If you are conducting your own research, you might be limited by time and budget constraints as well as availability of participants. I have heard it said that if, as the moderator, you can anticipate responses and you find yourself being accurate, then you have listened to a sufficient number of groups.

To determine group size, a number of researchers rely on the concept of *saturation*. Recall that this concept is associated with the QR approach called *grounded theory*. Thus some researchers write that they will continue to conduct focus groups until they have reached saturation. But remember, there is no magic number that will lead you to saturation. In practice, I think many researchers in advance decide how many groups they plan to have and proceed from there.

Carlsen and Glenton (2011), writing in the field of medical research methodology, conducted a study to explore sample size reporting in focus group studies. They examined 220 papers published in 117 journals in 2008. Of these, 37 (17%) explained the number of groups used. Most of these (28 of 37) stated that they used enough groups to reach a point of saturation. However, more than 83% of the studies gave no explanation for the number of focus groups used. Carlsen and Glenton also concluded that most of the studies used poor and inconsistent reporting of focus group sample size.

I am struck by the language used by so many in describing saturation. "After four interviews with 16 men, we found that saturation of the data was achieved" (Nielsen et al., 2011, p. 167). Similarly, Baker et al. (2011) stated, "Saturation of responses was reached" (p. 167). Aroian et al. (2012) made a similar statement in their study of hypertension prevention beliefs of Hispanics. In fact, I could not locate research that offered an explanation of what procedures were used to reach saturation or how the researchers knew when saturation occurred. I suggest that making such a blanket statement does not really address the underlying idea about the concept.

Deciding the Composition of Groups

How should you choose who will participate? You will not be choosing a random sample. In most cases, you will select participants who meet your predetermined criteria. If you are studying those who have survived heart attacks, then, of necessity, you will need people who are survivors. If you are considering those who like a particular brand of soup, then you need to choose people who have used that soup, unless you plan to have a taste test during the focus group. In most cases, researchers recruit participants by advertising, word of mouth, or nomination. The key consideration is that the participants have experience or expertise in regard to the topic. Again, because you are not trying to generalize in a traditional sense, it is not necessary to make sure that the group represents the population in terms of gender, race, ethnicity, educational level, or other demographic characteristics. Some researchers believe it is best to have homogeneous groups, while others want a greater mix. Some believe that it is better to have participants who do not know each other; others find that a discussion might go more smoothly if participants do know each other. There is little scientific research that speaks to group size, group number, or group composition.

Focus Groups With Challenging Populations

Kaehne and O'Connell (2010) remind us that there is very little written about conducting focus groups with people with disabilities. They are concerned especially with the effects of intellectual impairment on the ability of participants to reflect on other comments, the role of advocates or facilitators, over-researching existing groups, and the ethical implications of the capacity of research to change lives. Im, Lee, and Chee (2011) used an online forum to investigate Asian American women in menopause. After being recruited through the Internet, the women participated in online discussions. Cabassa et al. (2011) used a fotonovela in their study of depression among Latinos with limited English proficiency. A fotonovela is described as a popular health education tool that uses posed photographs, text bubbles with simple text, and dramatic narratives to engage audiences and raise awareness about the issues.

Deciding the Role of the Moderator

The moderator plays a key role during the actual focus group interview. He or she will be instrumental in deciding what questions will be included; whether there will be high, moderate, or low structure; and how the group will be conducted. I have found it very helpful to have co-moderators because they can help keep the flow going and make sure all group members participate. My husband and I worked as co-moderators when he had groups of both men and women.

Locating Facilities and Arranging for Recording

Ideally, it is best to use a space that is designated as a focus group facility. This type of space usually has oval tables, comfortable furniture, video cameras and recorders, and one-way windows. But most new researchers have to use whatever space they can find. If you plan to conduct focus groups in school settings, you can request a quiet and private space, but there is no guarantee that you will get it. I remember conducting focus groups with middle school students in a library. My colleague and I were studying a federally funded program. One of the tasks was to listen to what students thought about the program, the materials, and the staff. We identified what type of student we needed, and at the assigned time, they were sent to the library. We had no video equipment, although our audio equipment worked reasonably well; we were constantly interrupted with announcements over the loudspeaker system; and others were using the library. But we had a lively discussion, and the children shared their views about the program. Some children might have been concerned that others could overhear what they were saying.

Transcribing

You are used to transcribing when conducting individual interviews. While time consuming, it is a fairly straightforward task. You might even use voice-recognition software (VRS) that will facilitate your transcription. But imagine that you have an audiotape or videotape with about a dozen voices. Some speak at the same time; others interrupt. Others are so quiet that you cannot really hear them. And you do not know the voices well enough to be able to distinguish one from another. I have personally transcribed some of these discussions, and it is daunting. I suspect that most researchers do not make transcriptions of focus groups; rather, they listen and then extract themes.

Online Focus Groups

I have said this repeatedly throughout this text. The Internet is here to stay. And using its strengths in the field of QR is critical, as we are now well into the second decade of the 21st century.

> The turn of the century has seen the popularization of the Internet as a research medium for the collection of primary data. Gaining popularity first in marketing research, and then in the field of communications and media research, Internet-based data collection is now part of the mainstream canon of methodological choices. Illustrative of this

> acceptance is the frequency with which contemporary methods texts in the social sciences now include sections covering the principles of online research. (Stewart & Matthews, 2005, p. 395)

In a study reported in 2001, Franklin and Lowry described a series of synchronous, computer-mediated focus group sessions using a group support system. They continued "the electronic format improved the accuracy of the data collected by capturing every voice and every comment in 'real time'" (p. 169). Written more than a decade ago, this language seems out-of-place today.

Stewart and Matthews (2005) described two very interesting studies in their report. One involved work by Robson from 1999 using an online focus group on the topic of experiences of inflammatory bowel disease. In the Robson study, issues related to asynchronous time, online moderation, and analysis of digital data were considered. In a second study by Williams from 2003, they looked at synchronous time, 3-D graphical environments, and ethical considerations of online work. Markham's (1998) research considered focus groups and other forms of online research in depth. Markham and Baym (2009) address six main topics in their edited volume about Internet research: defining boundaries; making sense of the issues; decisions about privacy; gender and sexuality; meaningfulness across time, space, and culture; and issues of quality.

Lee and Lee (2012), in their decade review of research on sensitive topics, concluded, "One important recent development is that the focus group has moved online" (p. 114). Although no longer able to have face-to-face contact, the benefits of using online groups related to sensitive topics are "anonymity, the ability to record and analyse virtual interactional dynamics, and, once again, the efficiency gains associated with access to machine readable data" (Franklin & Lowry, 2001, p. 114).

Rezabek (2000) used online asynchronous discussions that lasted for more than two months. Sweet (2001) distinguished between virtual focus group rooms and asynchronous online bulletin boards. She reported on studies to evaluate online and offline advertising, evaluate mock websites, critique existing websites, test and evaluate new products (products mailed in advance of the groups), uncover competitive website information, evaluate training programs, explore decision making, uncover imagery, evaluate concepts, evaluate package images, generate ideas, and ascertain customer and employee satisfaction. Sweet identified issues specific to the technical aspect of focus groups. My impression is that little research has been done on the topic, but suggestions come from practical experience. Much of what is written about this topic is related to market research. Some distinct advantages of online focus groups are lower cost, immediate transcription, and global participation. Disadvantages might include difficulties with technology, inexperience of participants with the format, inability of participants to key in entries and to communicate in this manner, and lack of support for the researcher who is working on her or his own.

I believe there is great potential for online focus groups. It is too early to say what methodological issues may arise. For example, what role should the moderator play? Should the moderator submit a list of questions in advance of the online discussion? Must all participants be present at the same time? Can asynchronous focus groups accomplish the same goals as those that meet at the same time? How does the nature of the group interaction change when the group is not present physically or even at the same time? Do we need eye contact, nonverbal cues, and other aspects of face-to-face meetings? Can we begin to think about alternative ways to elicit information? Does online participation limit the type of person who will participate? Are older people less likely to participate? Are those with limited language skills less likely to participate?

Example of a Focus Group Interview

In this section, I describe to you a focus group study I conducted several years ago. The purpose of this focus group was to collect opinions from various constituents about how their school changed as it adopted a new form of management and control. The schools in this district had long operated from a centralized location. Decisions were made at the central office level, and needs and desires of local schools were largely ignored. A new superintendent decided to implement a plan to move the governance, budget, and decision making to the local level. The building principal, while initially somewhat wary about the decision, decided it would be best to implement it. As if he had a choice! Two years after the plan was implemented, an outside team of evaluators was called in to assess the effect on the staff, teachers, and students. This focus group discussion is illustrative of various discussions that were held. I use it to illustrate how focus groups can yield a large volume of data in a relatively short time. Although conducted with Americans, the school system was in Panama, and the focus group was conducted there.

Prior to the appointed day, I asked the principal to identify a dozen or so parents who might have knowledge of how the new plan had affected the school. She nominated parents, and 12 of them agreed to come. We were to meet in the library of the building at approximately 3:30 p.m., after students had been dismissed. I moved some tables together, arranged my equipment, and waited for the parents to arrive.

As parents began to trickle in after 3:00, I asked them to wait until all had assembled. I was not surprised that at 3:30, only eight people were there. I had been through this many times before and knew that other activities or emergencies tended to interfere with schedules. We sat down around the table, and I wrote my name in large letters on a tent card and put it in front of me so that all could see. The others followed my lead without my saying anything.

I reminded them that the principal had nominated them and that we were gathered together to talk about what changes they were aware of that occurred after the new plan had been implemented. I reviewed details such as the amount of time we would spend together, that no names would be used in the reports, and that all reports would be written and distributed to the principal and to them without identifying which individual gave which response. I asked permission to tape-record and all agreed. I tested the tape and made sure it was working. We were ready to go.

I have found it extremely effective to begin with specific and concrete questions. This is similar to what I do when conducting individual in-depth interviews. In this way, you get comments that are authentic. People do not try to impress you with what they know.

Jargon is avoided. So I began with, "I understand that this school has had two years to move from a centralized administrative structure and to implement the plan to turn budget and management over to the school. Can you think of anything that is different about the school since this plan was adopted?" I finished my comment and looked down at my notes. No one said anything. I waited what seemed like an interminable time. Still no one said anything.

Finally, I heard a voice from across the table. "Well, I know that Timmy's teacher says that she finds it much easier to get materials now than before." The woman seemed to pause.

I encouraged her to continue. "What do you mean? Can you give me an example?"

She thought for a moment. "The teacher was planning a special art project, and she needed a certain kind of paper and paint. It was approved almost immediately, and the following week, the students began the project."

"A good example," I commented. "Can you think of other things that have happened?" I said to the group in general.

Two people began to speak at once. One mentioned new equipment for the playground. Another mentioned sending teachers to special training. One parent asked another, "Do you remember when Mr. Miller tried to get approval for his class to travel to an athletic event? Not until last year was he ever able to get the funds in time." The conversation proceeded in this way for about 20 minutes. I really did not introduce new questions at this point. I indirectly led the group by looking at one person or another. I did not specifically call on anyone. I evaluated the comments mentally as they were made.

I determined that it was time to change the direction of the comments and so offered the following question: "We've talked a lot about funds and equipment. Can we shift gears a little and talk about other things that might have been affected by the program?" I waited for people to comment, and they did.

After interjecting several other comments that changed the direction of the conversation, I determined that our time was up. I then went around the table and asked if anyone had anything else to add to the conversation. I was quite surprised when one very quiet man chimed in. He had said virtually nothing throughout the past hour, but here was his chance. He expressed some concern about the time that it took and about the many meetings that were held when he thought someone should just make a decision. I suspect participatory management was not his preference. Finally, I thanked everyone for participating, gathered my materials, and took a much-needed break before my next group came in.

With this somewhat long account, I hope to illustrate that a lively conversation can occur when people have some experience and thoughts about a particular topic. You do not have to have a predetermined set of questions to get people to talk. I used a general question to begin the conversation, added a comparison question to change the nature of the discussion, and offered opportunities for all to speak.

What critical elements can you extract from this account? Let's look at what Millward (2012) has to say about listening and questioning skills. She suggested that the style of the facilitator in regard to listening and questioning is critical. The same skills described in Chapter 10 in regard to questioning strategies and types can be applied here: asking for elaboration, accepting what individuals have to say, and remaining neutral.

Images and Visuals

I have emphasized throughout that QR relies on the written word; it is the written word that forms the basis of much data. But I also suggest to you that visual information is very powerful. In fact, Prosser (2008) commented that collecting and analyzing visual data in QR is no longer considered a minority field. Crawford's (2012) review of Reavey's book, *Visual Methods in Psychology,* reiterates this position that in the past, the use of visuals in psychology has taken a back seat to methods using language. Demant and Ravn (2013) assert that "one of the central frontiers in the further development of qualitative method focuses on the involvement of visual methods and materials in qualitative research designs." Ray and Smith (2012), in their review of the history of the use of photographic research methods in various disciplines, highlight two important aspects of conducting photographic research: a philosophical stance using photographs in an interpretive fashion and the level of analysis. Just as with written information, visual information can come in various forms: that which exists already (found images), that which you ask participants to create, the images that you create, or the images created by groups of people either acting together or responding to each other. There are several types of images that can be used to collect data. Some are static, such as photographs, fine art, drawings, diagrams, or illustrations. Others are dynamic, such as those produced by Smartphones, camcorders, videos, or film. Some are produced or selected by the researcher; others come directly from participants. Use of video diaries is one example. Obviously, the Internet represents a vast array of sources. I can imagine selecting both dynamic and static visuals from YouTube, Pinterest, or Flickr.

That the use of visual methods has become popular can be seen in several journals. The June 2012 special issue of *Qualitative Research* is devoted to video analysis and videography. Knoblauch (2012) describes an ethnographic means of video recording called *videography*. Knoblauch commented that camcorders not only can be used in data collection and analysis; he suggested that the data they provide for sociology (and related disciplines) was not previously available. He described this methodology and, in particular, the recordings and interpretation of social interaction in natural settings as video analysis. I can only second Knoblauch's assertion about the urgency of using such a method, as there has been an explosion of videos. Videos may offer the researcher a way to study social interaction. Fiele (2012) described a study of the interaction between a call taker and a dispatcher while handling an emergency call. The numerous images reproduced in Fiele's article help bring to life what the author wrote about.

Somewhat earlier, *Forum: Qualitative Social Research* devoted a 2008 issue (volume 9, number 3) to the use of visuals. It covered a broad spectrum, from new developments in the analysis of video and photography to digital memory to a study of math practices using visual analysis. I can't begin to include the myriad of suggestions offered by the authors in this issue. Suffice to say, there is a wealth of information that you can access by going to these thematic issues.

Found images can serve several purposes. They document aspects of social interaction, they can be used as stimuli for interviews, and they can be used in presentations. Images are widely available and easy for you or others to create and display online. A digital camera or video camera can be used to transfer information in fractions of seconds. You can display visual information in your written reports and use hyperlinks to take your reader to photos, videos, or art. You are only limited by your imagination.

If you become interested in this topic, you may want to read about the hermeneutics of seeing. Davey (1999) suggested that hermeneutics can embrace visual phenomena as well as the written word. Knoblauch and Schnettler (2012) described how the analysis of video data is a hermeneutic endeavor.

Purpose of Images

Lester (n.d.) reminded us,

> With digital hegemony, visual messages have reasserted their position as an important communication medium, but at the cost of not recognizing the combination of words and pictures as vital in communication. With the correct interpretation of the proverb, words and pictures live in harmony as they are both used equally in order to understand the meaning of any work that uses them both. (para. 4)

I believe images enhance, embellish, and make alive the words we use to express our thoughts. Whether the images are created by us, our participants, or others, they send powerful messages.

Visual images are central to our culture and our communication. They provide another avenue of meaning. They represent a kind of reality captured by the researcher. However, I think that you need to remember that images, while an apparent representation of reality, are actually created or used by the researcher to reflect a particular stance or point of view. Nevertheless, the power and seductive nature of images cannot be ignored.

Issues Regarding Images/Video

Privacy and Facial Recognition Software

I suspect that researchers are beginning to explore ways to use facial recognition in QR. However, I was not able to locate any reports or published studies of such research. When such studies begin to enter the field, there will be issues regarding privacy. I experienced such an issue recently. While traveling in Israel, I had an opportunity to visit a family of Druze women. I asked if I could take their pictures, and they willingly agreed (through an interpreter). Unfortunately, I did not think about getting a signed release from them so that I could use their images in my work. Yet this family has participated with a particular travel company, and such images are used in promotional literature. Of course, I recognized the two women. Given the development of sophisticated facial recognition software, I believe that privacy issues will emerge as researchers want to display such visual images. In their comprehensive review of research using Facebook, Wilson, Gosling, and Graham (2012), addressed privacy issues. Of the 412 articles they reviewed, 75 (18%) related to privacy and information disclosure. One issue concerns Facebook's policy about privacy. Citing research by Anthonysamy, Rashid, and Greenwood in 2011, Wilson, Gosling, and Graham (2012) highlight the almost-contradictory policies of privacy protection on the one hand and significant privacy problems on the other.

Quality of the Image

One important issue to consider is the quality of the visual representation. If you are going to use an image as part of your document, then how it looks becomes important. Of course, software to enhance or modify images is readily available and fairly easy for even the novice to use. Today, digital cameras and cell phones take high-quality images and can be saved and transmitted almost instantaneously.

Manipulation of the Image

Most people used to believe an image was a literal representation of an event or a person. But whether you choose to manipulate an image with a computer program or to present an image to highlight a particular aspect of it, what you, as a researcher, see and subsequently represent visually is your interpretation of what you study.

Relationship of the Image to Words

I think it is important that your choice of images and words enhance each other. A photograph must have a purpose in the same way that a quotation from a participant must have a purpose.

Selecting Framing for Recordings

Selecting a camera angle uncovers methodological concerns. These concerns reveal the particular demands that video places on researchers (Luff & Heath, 2012).

Examples of Image Usage

Holmes (2012) relied on a variety of art images in her intriguing work on how children develop a reputation for being "naughty" in their early years. She utilizes an image of a line that "denotes space, gestures of containment, impulses to represent and make visible what might otherwise remain invisible" (p. 544). Reproductions of work by Sandback (*ordered chaos,* she calls it), which depicts a simple line, becomes a sculpture aid in understanding Holmes's (2012) research. Personally, I connected with this article and the powerful visual images. Using photo-methods in research on sexuality in secondary schools in New Zealand was the challenging investigation by Allen (2011). Smith, Gidlow, and Steel (2012) used the photo-elicitation method to study outdoor education programs. Chappell, Chappell, and Margolis (2011) used historical photos of school rituals and ceremonies as they tried to understand identity negotiation of young people. They illustrated their article with wonderful archival photos. Bartlett (2013) used cartoons as a way to process and transmit the findings of QR. She cautions, however, that cartoons should be used judiciously, since they may be seen as contrived or might alienate some. Aston (2010) comments on the renewed interest in the role of the senses within anthropology and suggests that digital technologies offer new opportunities and possibilities in the field of visual analysis. She suggests a new technique of split-screen cinema to include interactive montages in which the user has to physically interact with the moving image clips.

Created images have gained in popularity. Allen (2012) described using photographs as visual documentation of social landscapes. Reflecting on these images was a part of his study. In studying the home life of children, Jorgenson and Sullivan (2010) found it helpful to use participatory photo interviewing or photo-elicitation interviewing. In this method, participants take photographs dealing with various aspects of their lives. Then the photos are used as part of the interview process to explore the subjective meanings of the images. Just when I think that I have closed the space on images, I come across the work of de Freitas (2012). She proposed that we rethink our traditional type of diagrams and create a *rhizome* or *knotted image*. I had not heard of these terms before. A *rhizome* is a nonhierarchical network of knotted loops that fold and grow through different entry and exit sites. Deleuze, a philosopher, writes about studying social interactions as complex rhizomatic processes. De Freitas applies this idea to shed light on classroom interaction. You can see numerous illustrations of these rhizomes or knotted images in this article.

Some researchers ask participants to re-create scenes from their earlier life. Kelly and Kerner (2004) described how they used the photographic exhibition, *Positive Lives,* and personal snapshots to document the death of a loved one from HIV/AIDS. Kearney and Hyle (2004) discussed how they used drawings by participants to examine the emotional impact of change. La Jevic and Springgay (2008) used visual journals in a preservice education course. I use an exercise in which students are asked to represent themselves by drawing images on a large piece of paper. Some choose to be literal and often draw a timeline of significant events in their lives; others choose more abstract and metaphorical representations. A number of research projects involve giving participants disposable cameras and asking them to photograph a day in their lives. I have asked participants to bring in photographs of their families and to use these as a jumping off point to initiate interviews. Online images can be created and expanded and disseminated to serve as discussion points for online chats. You only need your imagination to think of how images can be used.

Friend (2010) juxtaposes images of landscapes and interiors (excluding people) with a soundtrack of oral testimonies in her study of immigration detainees. Issues of power discrepancies between the photographer/artist and those studied are also discussed. This very powerful piece includes soundtracks to accompany the images.

Ray and Smith (2012) described a study in which photographs were used in the field of organizational research. Within organizations, they consider several categories of photographs: produced by researcher only, produced by participant only, and gleaned from archives. They describe the details of how to use photo-elicitation in organizations. The accompanying visuals help in understanding the technique of analysis. You will recall reading Lorenz's description of her work with photovoice in Chapter 7.

Mapping

One of the earliest uses of maps and mapmaking in QR can be attributed to a study of London's urban environment in the 1880s. Subsequently adopted as part of social surveys, maps were used to study the Black population of Philadelphia and to study segregation by the Chicago School of sociology in the 1930s (Ball & Petsimeris, 2010). In commenting on the use of maps in such situations, Michel (2010) suggests that maps can be seen as powerful actors in the social construction of reality.

Powell (2010) argues for mapping as a multisensory research method. Powell makes clear that she is not talking about maps as a directional tool. She speaks of several types of mapping, such as social mapping (a method that enables us to study the nature of relationships between people and their social networks), mind or concept mapping (used to develop student thinking about particular concepts), and cognitive mapping (used to help understand spatial literacy and sense of place). She suggests that maps cross disciplinary boundaries of art, creative writing, geography, and cartography as they link with larger issues. Powell reflects on Hill's work that suggests that visual methods are combined with the written word in academia rather than as stand-alone images. It is ironic that in spite of the idea of a picture being worth a thousand words, we still feel the need to use words to explain pictures. She presents data and results documenting the lived experiences of her participants. What a wonderful idea.

Den Besten (2010) describes a study of children's afterschool activities in which children use cognitive or mental maps. For this study, making maps was especially useful, as the immigrant children had limited use of the language in the host country. The author further describes how data analysis was accomplished using the maps. I loved looking at the maps reproduced in the article.

Caquard's (2013) research addresses the relationship between maps and narratives. Of special interest is the state of what he calls the Geoweb era. He reviews issues related to the extensive use of online mapping services such as Google maps to convey stories and to produce new stories. We have only just begun to explore the uses of mapping in this new era.

■ The Written Word

In addition to gathering data using interviews, observations, and focus groups, you can use various other excellent sources of qualitative information. I am referring here to the written word. Some of this information exists, and you have to identify it and gain access to it. We can think of it as *archival information*—records, news accounts, emails, or management reports. Other information comes from participants. We can think of it as *participant product*—blogs, reports, emails, or diaries. Written material created by participants—either in direct response to your requests or created for other purposes—captures the thoughts, ideas, and meanings of participants. Consequently, such material provides a window into the human mind

A third type is *material you create*—a journal, a diary, field notes, or a poem—that provides insight into your thinking, your reactions to what you are studying, and its effect on you and others.

Finally, there is *material that is co-constructed by you and your participants*. All types are legitimate and useful as you gather data for your qualitative study.

Documentation is one of the watchwords of historical research. Whether it is a primary source (such as the Declaration of Independence) or a secondary source (such as a biography of Benjamin Franklin), documents teach us about history. They are evidence of what people did and said and what they thought.

I cannot stress how important such written material is to a study. Of course, one enormous advantage is that its form permits easy storage in a computer and easy use in data analysis.

Issues Regarding Written Material

What material should you use? How do you find it? What might be valuable, and what might be trivial? The first type of material I want you to think about is written material already in existence. I suspect that there is no written material that you should reject without looking at it, but it is likely that some sources, more than others, might prove relevant to your topic. If you were studying teenage pregnant girls, you might find their diaries of interest. Getting access to these is unlikely, however. If you were interested in teachers serving as mentors, teachers' training documents prepared by a school system might be valuable. If you were interested in how parents and children interact with each other around homework, you might find the homework itself of interest, or you might find directions for homework given by the teacher to be valuable. Obviously, your question is critical, but here are some other examples of written information that you might find useful: documents provided by schools, including school newsletters, school board meeting minutes, curriculum guides, teacher lesson plans, email messages, school websites, or notes of observations by principals; documents in the public domain, including newspaper accounts or editorials; documents provided in a work setting, including interoffice memos, reports, or performance evaluations; and documents provided by individuals, including letters, diaries, or stories.

Written material you ask participants to create might include email responses to your questions. In a study of beginning teachers, I have used a weekly email format with three simple questions: How was your week? What problem did you face? How did you solve it? By keeping the format consistent, I minimized the time it took for participants to respond, and I was able to capture many responses over time. The information was already on my computer, so I had little to do before data analysis. You might ask students to keep a journal of their thoughts about being in Mr. Smith's class or about learning a challenging subject. You might ask superintendents to dictate their ideas about school violence into VRS that transfers the material to the computer. Kenten (2010) reviews various kinds of diaries, including researcher-driven diaries, solicited diaries, or diary interviews. Harvey (2011) used private diaries and field notes to explore negotiating use of condoms.

Written material you create might include field notes in connection with your observations, your online journal, memos regarding your thoughts about the qualitative data you collect, field notes that you develop after an extensive observation, a blog about teaching QR, or a poem you write to express your thoughts on a particularly challenging aspect of learning to become a qualitative researcher. You should not ignore class work or papers you create for a class in QR.

Extracting the Essence

Just like any other data you collect, written material challenges you to find underlying meaning in the words of others and in your own words. Reacting to metaphors is especially exciting because they reveal what is beneath the surface meaning of the words you read. I recall asking students to write a short paper describing one of their parents by using metaphors. One student referred to her father as Santa Claus. She wrote, "In my family, we had a wonderful Christmas tradition. Sometime during the month of December, Santa would come in the night and decorate our Christmas tree and fill our stockings. One such night was to be very different, for on one of those nights, Santa kissed me good-night."

Another woman wrote about her father in a poem titled *The Perfect Southern Gent—My Daddy.* She described "his color of rich mocha chocolate with a hint of cream." Another student described his father as "a horse that wears blinders." And another student wrote,

> Boy, write about your parents using metaphors she says. This sounds simple enough, but for the last 24 hours I've agonized over doing it. Seems this assignment has forced me to think about my Mom and Dad in ways that I haven't (or have avoided) during the last 10 years or so. Forgive me as my submission will probably resemble some postmodern stream of consciousness, but that's how things are bubbling up.

And finally, from one of my Middle Eastern students, "My father is the ocean who gives a life to the sand and the rocks that surround him and then retreats to let them nourish with what he gave." We used these submissions as we began our exploration of the meaning given by metaphors. Things are not always as they seem, we began to learn.

Collecting written data is a challenge. Deciding what to collect, what to do with it, and how to use these raw data to answer your research questions is the challenge of doing QR. The final type of data I talk about in this chapter is of a different nature. It does not involve words. It relies on technology. There is a great deal of interest in collecting data of this kind.

■ Technology

Smartphones

Almost everyone I know has a Smartphone—from preteens to the elderly. Most use them for calling, texting, and sending and receiving email. But the small computer chip has moved such devices from being "phone-centric" to "data-centric" to borrow Miller's (2012) terms. A smartphone has its own operating system that can run various software applications (apps) created by software developers. Further, smartphone "technology is the fastest changing sector of consumer products" (Miller, 2012, p. 224).

> By 2025, when most of today's psychology undergraduates will be in their mid-30s, more than 5 billion people on our planet will be using ultra-broadband, sensor-rich smartphones far beyond the abilities of today's iPhones, Androids, and Blackberries. Although smartphones were not designed for psychological research, they can collect vast amounts of ecologically valid data, easily and quickly, from large global samples. If participants

> download the right "psych apps," smartphones can record where they are, what they are doing, and what they can see and hear and can run interactive surveys, tests, and experiments through touch screens and wireless connections to nearby screens, headsets, biosensors, and other peripherals. (Miller, 2012, p. 221)

If Miller's assertion is correct, then it is important to examine research that has been conducted on this topic.

I have to admit, I was surprised that research on the topic has been conducted for 20 years. Miller described four types of studies. In the first type, researchers have persuaded service providers to share aggregated call-routing records. Miller cited some of the studies that allowed for tracking movements and social connections of users. In the second and third group of studies that Miller described, researchers distributed devices to gather certain types of behavioral data. The focus, however, was on developing software rather than on studying behavior. It is the fourth type of study that is most relevant to QR. Miller described these types of studies—apps that participants can download remotely. This is what such an app can do: manage the study autonomously, gain consent, gather data, upload data, debrief the participant, and provide payment.

GPS Technology

Many individuals have Global Positioning System (GPS) technology—either related to their cars or connected to their smartphones. GPS technology relies on cell phone towers. It can be used to locate people or things in space. Researchers have begun to explore its use in mapping locations, looking at social groups, and the like.

Skype

Skype is a form of technology that permits discussions via the Internet. The transmission of picture as well as voice allows for interaction parallel to direct face-to-face contact. Because it is free and relatively easy to use, many are conversant in its use and have the technology available to them. Skype users can be located in geographic locations distant from the interviewer.

Google Products

At this writing, Google has developed a number of sites that enable researchers to readily identify and locate certain things. For example, Google Maps has mapped the entire world. It can identify and provide a visual image of your location in an instant. Google Voice allows for voicemail transcription. Google Images enables you to search by visual images, omitting words. New products are being developed on a rapid and regular basis.

Issues Regarding the Use of Technology

In this section, I rely heavily on Miller's (2012) excellent discussion regarding issues related to using technology.

Technical Limitations

Memory loss and limited battery power are among some limitations. Integration of various apps, unreliability of technology, and untested apps may affect the use of technology.

Recruiting Participants

The pool of participants may be restricted—after all, you can't participate in such a study unless you have a particular technology or it is provided for you.

Participant Behaviors

Limitations of users, especially the elderly or those with little experience with the technology, may restrict the groups that can be studied. Phones can be misplaced or lost. Or users may forget to charge their phones.

Programming Apps

There may be a mismatch between those who have experience and training in developing apps and researchers who need to use them. Further, there may not be commercial advantages to developing apps that can be used for research, which may limit the market.

Managing and Analyzing Data

Smartphones generate an enormous amount of data. How researchers can manage and analyze such data are challenges yet to be addressed.

Institutional Review Board Approvals With Human Subjects

Miller suggests that smartphone research will either make current Institutional Review Board (IRB) approval systems obsolete or the need for IRBs may stifle smartphone research. Conducting research in countries such as China may not be possible in the current climate of suspicion. Getting true informed consent is problematic.

Challenges for Researchers

I am not sure how close we are to implementing some of the ideas about using technology. Apps for using smartphones still need to be developed and tested. Ethical challenges still exist.

Examples of Technology Use

Several studies using smartphones deal with general issues and are not specifically qualitative in design. For example, Dufau et al. (2011) concluded that the coordinated use of smartphones creates a novel instrument to test theories of cognition. Oliver (2010) conducted a large-scale study of smartphone users to see how they interact with energy and consume energy. Although not qualitative in nature, Hallo and his colleagues (2012) used GPS technology to track tourists. Wang, Park, and Fesenmaier (2012) studied stories travelers told regarding their use of smartphones and related apps for travel purposes.

In a novel study, researchers at The London School of Economics and Political Science (2012) have developed an app to track your happiness (http://www.mappiness.org.uk/). It is free for your iPhone and can be obtained from the App Store. One interest is to see how people's happiness is affected by their local environment.

Salmons (2010) discussed experiences with Skype in her book, *Online Interviews.* Christensen and colleagues (2011) studied the everyday movements of children in Denmark. They used GPS technology and mobile phones. Children carried GPS technology for a week to trace their movements. They used mobile phones as a travel diary of their current activities. Spatial analysis can be performed by using GPS tracking technologies interacting with mobile devices. Jones, Drury, and McBeath (2011) describe their studies, one related to fear of crime and the other to the concentration of students in certain areas of cities and towns. Hanna (2012) conducted interviews, allowing participants to select which type of medium they preferred, including Skype. One advantage to using Skype is that participants can preserve flexibility and private space elements. In their co-constructed autoethnography, Cann and DeMeulenaere (2012) described a way for collaborating activist researchers to reflect on the tempo, uncertainty, and complexity of their relationships. Skype was one of the primary tools used for this engagement.

The field of technology and QR is changing, even as I write. New apps will no doubt offer opportunities to facilitate and collect data not yet imagined by researchers.

CHECK YOURSELF

- Five methods of gathering data are discussed—observations, focus-group interviewing, images and visuals, the written word, and technology. Some issues regarding observations include deciding on the group, gaining access, deciding what to look for, and deciding how long the observation should be. Return to the other methods for data gathering and identify the key elements.
- Each method has issues that have to be considered by researchers.
- Qualitative researchers have unlimited possibilities to consider as they plan for how to gather data.

KEY DISCUSSION ISSUES

1. What are the five ways I discuss in this chapter to gather data? Which way seems to fit the research question you have been contemplating?
2. I have discussed various issues associated with the different ways to gather data. What are some of them? Which do you think will be most difficult to overcome?
3. Have you participated in a focus group? How do you see yourself leading such a group? What challenges do you think you might face?
4. Technology is here to stay. What skills would you like to develop to assist you with using technology for research?
5. Using visuals is fairly new to the field of QR. What do you know so far about their use? What do you need to learn?
6. How do you decide which of the various techniques or methods for gathering data make the most sense in terms of the research question you have and the research approach you hope to use?

MODULE 11

Use of Apps for Gathering Data

Objective: Exploring how to use GPS for mapping movement

Activity: Use your classmates for this activity. Work in a team of three people to develop a simple data collection strategy to answer a question about location.

Evaluation: Discuss data that are collected and how they can be used in a research study.

REFERENCES

Allen, L. (2011). "Picture this": Using photo-methods in research on sexualities and schooling. *Qualitative Research, 11*(5), 487–504.

Allen, Q. (2012). Photographs and stories: Ethics, benefits and dilemmas of using participant photography with Black middle-class male youth. *Qualitative Research, 12*(4), 443–458.

Anderson, E., Austin, D., Holloway, C., & Kulkarni, V. (2012). The legacy of racial caste: An exploratory ethnography. *The Annals of the American Academy of Political and Social Science, 642*(1), 25–42.

Aroian, K., Peters, R., Rudner, N., & Waser, L. (2012). Hypertension prevention beliefs of Hispanics. *Journal of Transcultural Nursing, 23*(2), 134–142.

Aston, J. (2010). Spatial montage and multimedia ethnography: Using computers to visualise aspects of migration and social division among a displaced community [23 paragraphs]. *Forum Qualitative Sozialforschung/Forum: Qualitative Social Research, 11*(2), Art. 36. Retrieved from http://nbn-resolving.de/ urn:nbn:de:0114-fqs1002361

Baker, C., Fortney, C., Wewers, E., & Ahijevych, K. (2011). The cultural context of smoking among immigrants from the former Soviet Union. *Journal of Transcultural Nursing, 22*(2), 166–173.

Ball, S., & Petsimeris, P. (2010). Mapping urban social divisions [42 paragraphs]. *Forum Qualitative Sozialforschung/Forum: Qualitative Social Research*, 11(2), Art. 37. Retrieved from http://nbn-resolving.de/urn:nbn:de:0114-fqs1002372

Bartlett, R. (2013). Playing with meaning: Using cartoons to disseminate research findings. *Qualitative Research, 13*(2), 214–227.

Belzile, J., & Öberg, G. (2012). What to begin? Grappling with how to use participant interaction in focus group design. *Qualitative Research, 12*(4), 459–472.

Berger, R. (2004). Pushing forward: Disability, basketball, and me. *Qualitative Inquiry, 10*(5), 794–810.

Boeree, G. (1998). *Qualitative methods, part three.* Retrieved from http://webspace.ship.edu/cgboer/qualmeththree.html

Cabassa, L., Contreras, S., Aragón, R., Molina, G., & Baron, M. (2011). Focus group evaluation of "secret feelings." A depression fotonovela for Latinos with limited English proficiency. *Health Promotion Practice, 12*(6), 840–847.

California State University–Chico. (2011). Research focused on first-year students: Classroom ethnographies. *First-Year Experience.* Retrieved from http://www.csuchico.edu/fye/classroom_ethnographies.shtml

Cann, C., & DeMeulenaere, E. (2012). Critical co-constructed autoethnography. *Cultural Studies, Critical Methodologies, 12*(2), 146–158.

Caquard, S. (2013). Cartography I: Mapping narrative cartography. *Progress in Human Geography, 37*(1), 135–144.

Carlsen, B., & Glenton, C. (2011). What about N? A methodological study of sample-size reporting in focus group studies. *BMC Medical Research Methodology, 11,* 26. Retrieved from http://www.biomedcentral.com/1471–2288/11/26#B7

Chappell, D., Chappell, S., & Margolis, E. (2011). School as ceremony and ritual: How photography illuminates performances of ideological transfer. *Qualitative Inquiry, 17*(1), 56–73.

Christensen, P., Mikkelsen, M., Nielsen, T., & Jardern, H. (2011). Children, mobility, and space: Using GPS and mobile phone technologies in ethnographic research. *Journal of Mixed Methods Research, 5*(3), 227–246.

Cocks, A. (2008). Researching the lives of disabled children: The process of participant observation in seeking inclusivity. *Qualitative Social Work, 7*(2), 163–180.

Condell, S. (2008). Writing field notes in an ethnographic study of peers—Collaborative experiences from the field. *Journal of Research in Nursing, 13*(4), 325–335.

Crawford, M. (2012). Review: Visual methods in psychology. *Psychology of Women Quarterly, 36*(2), 247–248.

Davey, N. (1999). The hermeneutics of seeing. In I. Heywood & B. Sandywell (Eds.), *Interpreting visual culture: Explorations in the hermeneutics of the visual* (pp. 3–29). London, England: Routledge.

de Freitas, E. (2012). The classroom as rhizome: New strategies for diagramming knotted interactions. *Qualitative Inquiry, 18*(7), 557–570.

Demant, J., & Ravn, S. (2013). Visual methods and data-materials in qualitative studies: How and why? Retrieved from http://sociologikongres.au.dk/en/workshop-sessions/visual-methods-and-data-materials-in-qualitative-studies-how-and-why/

den Besten, O. (2010). Visualising social divisions in Berlin: Children's after-school activities in two contrasted city neighbourhoods [30 paragraphs]. *Forum Qualitative Sozialforschung/Forum: Qualitative Social Research, 11*(2), Art. 35. Retrieved from http://nbn-resolving.de/urn:nbn:de:0114-fqs1002353

Dufau, S., Dunabeitia, J. A., Moret-Tatay, C., McGonigal, A., Peeters, D., Alario, X., . . . Grainger, J. (2011). Smart phone, smart science: How the use of smartphones can revolutionize research in cognitive science. *PLoS ONE, 6, e24974.* Retrieved from http://www.mpi.nl/publications/escidoc-1137686/@@popup

Earle, R., & Phillips, C. (2012). Digesting men? Ethnicity, gender and food: Perspectives from a "prison ethnography." *Theoretical Criminology, 16*(2), 141–156.

Ellis, C., Bochner, A., Denzin, N., Lincoln, Y., Morse, J., Pelias, R., & Richardson, L. (2008). Talking and thinking about qualitative research. *Qualitative Inquiry, 14*(2), 254–284.

Farnsworth, J., & Boon, B. (2010). Analysing group dynamics within the focus group. *Qualitative Research, 10*(5), 605–624.

Fiele, G. (2012). The use of video to document tacit participation in an emergency operations centre. *Qualitative Research, 12*(3), 280–302.

Fordham, S. (1988). Racelessness as a factor in Black student school success: Pragmatic strategy or Pyrrhic victory? *Harvard Educational Review, 58*(1), 54–84.

Frank, C. (1999). *Ethnographic eyes: A teacher's guide to classroom observation.* Portsmouth, NH: Heinemann.

Franklin, K., & Lowry, C. (2001). Computer-mediated focus group sessions: Naturalistic inquiry in a networked environment. *Qualitative Research, 1*(2), 169–184.

Friend, M. (2010). Representing immigration detainees: The juxtaposition of image and sound in "Border Country" [69 paragraphs]. *Forum Qualitative Sozialforschung/Forum: Qualitative Social Research, 11*(2), Art. 33. Retrieved from http://nbn-resolving.de/urn:nbn:de:0114-fqs1002334

Geertz, C. (1973). *The interpretation of cultures.* New York, NY: Basic Books.

Genzuk, M. (2003). *A synthesis of ethnographic research.* Retrieved from http://www-rcf.usc.edu/~genzuk/ Ethnographic_Research.html

Glass, P. (2001). *Autism and the family.* (Unpublished doctoral dissertation). Virginia Polytechnic Institute and State University, Falls Church, Virginia.

Halkier, B. (2010). Focus groups as social enactments: Integrating interaction and content in the analysis of focus group data. *Qualitative Research, 10*(1), 71–89.

Hallo, J., Beeco, J., Goetcheus, C., McGee, J., McGehee, N., & Norman, W. (2012). GPS as a method for assessing spatial and temporal use distributions of nature-based tourists. *Journal of Travel Research, 51*(5), 591–606.

Hanna, P. (2012). Using Internet technologies (such as Skype) as a research medium: A research note. *Qualitative Research, 12*(2), 239–242.

Harvey, L. (2011). Intimate reflections: Private diaries in qualitative research. *Qualitative Research, 11*(6), 664–682.

Holmes, R. (2012). A fantastic decomposition: Unsettling the fury of having to wait. *Qualitative Inquiry, 18*(7), 544–556.

Im, E., Lee, S., & Chee, W. (2011). "Being conditioned, yet becoming strong": Asian American women in menopausal transition. *Journal of Transcultural Nursing, 22*(3), 290–299.

Jones, P., Drury, R., & McBeath, J. (2011). Using GPS-enabled mobile computing to augment qualitative interviewing: Two case studies. *Field Methods, 23*(2), 173–187.

Jordan, B. (Ed.). (2012). *Advanced ethnography in corporate environments.* Walnut Creek, CA: Left Coast Press.

Jorgenson, J., & Sullivan, T. (2009). Accessing children's perspectives through participatory photo interviews [43 paragraphs]. *Forum Qualitative Sozialforschung/Forum: Qualitative Social Research, 11*(1), Art. 8. Retrieved from http://nbn-resolving.de/ urn:nbn:de:0114-fqs100189

Kaehne, A., & O'Connell, C. (2010). Focus groups with people with learning disabilities. *Journal of Intellectual Disabilities, 14*(2), 135–145.

Kawulich, B. (2005). Participant observation as a data collection method [81 paragraphs]. *Forum Qualitative Sozialforschung/Forum: Qualitative Social Research, 6*(2), Art. 43. Retrieved from http://www.qualitative-research.net/index.php/fqs/article/view/466

Kearney, K., & Hyle, A. (2004). Drawing out emotions: The use of participant-produced drawings in qualitative inquiry. *Qualitative Research, 4,* 361–382.

Keiding, T. (2010). Observing participating observation—A re-description based on systems theory [81 paragraphs]. *Forum Qualitative Sozialforschung/Forum: Qualitative Social Research, 11*(3), Art. 11. Retrieved from http://nbn-resolving.de/urn:nbn:de:0114-fqs1003119

Kelly, A., & Kerner, A. (2004). The scent of positive lives: (Re) memorializing our loved ones. *Qualitative Inquiry, 10*(5), 767–787.

Kenten, C. (2010). Narrating oneself: Reflections on the use of solicited diaries with diary interviews [41 paragraphs]. *Forum Qualitative Sozialforschung/Forum: Qualitative Social Research, 11*(2), Art. 16. Retrieved from http://www.qualitative-research.net/index.php/fqs/article/view/1314/2989

Kidder, T. (1989). *Among schoolchildren.* New York, NY: Avon Books.

Kisely, S., & Kendall, E. (2011). Critically appraising qualitative research: A guide for clinicians more familiar with quantitative techniques. *Australasian Psychiatry, 19*(4), 364–367.

Kitzinger, J. (1994). The methodology of focus groups: The importance of interaction between research participants. *Sociology of Health, 16*(1), 103–121.

Knoblauch, H. (2012). Introduction to the special issue of *Qualitative Research:* Video-analysis and videography. *Qualitative Research, 12*(3), 251–254.

Knoblauch, H., & Schnettler, B. (2012). Videography: Analyzing video data as a "focused" ethnographic and hermeneutical exercise. *Qualitative Research, 12*(3), 334–356.

Krueger, R. (1988). *Focus groups: A practical guide for applied research.* London, England: SAGE.

La Jevic, L., & Springgay, S. (2008). A/r/tography as an ethics of embodiment. *Qualitative Inquiry, 14*(1), 67–89.

LeCompte, M. (2002). The transformation of ethnographic practices. *Qualitative Research, 2*(3), 283–299.

Lee, Y., & Lee, R. (2012). Methodological research on "sensitive" topics: A decade review. *Bulletin of Sociological Methodology, 114*(1), 35–49.

Lester, P. (n.d.). *A picture's worth a thousand words.* Retrieved from http://commfaculty.fullerton.edu/lester/writings/letters.html

Lewis, M. (1995). *Focus group interviews in qualitative research: A review of the literature.* Retrieved from http://www.scu.edu.au/schools/gcm/ar/arr/arow/rlewis.html

Liamputtong, P. (2011). Chapter 1: Focus group methodology: Introduction and history. *Focus group methodology* (pp. 1–15). Thousand Oaks, CA: SAGE. Retrieved from http://www.sagepub.com/upm-data/39360_978_1_84787_909_7.pdf

Liebow, E. (1967). *Tally's corner: A study of Negro streetcorner men.* London, England: Routledge.

The London School of Economics and Political Science. (2012). *Mapping happiness? There's an app for that.* Retrieved from http://www2.lse.ac.uk/newsAndMedia/news/archives/2010/08/mappiness.aspx

Low, B. E. (2010). The tale of the talent night rap: Hip-hop culture in schools and the challenge of interpretation. *Urban Education, 45*(2), 194–220.

Luff, P., & Heath, C. (2012). Some "technical challenges" of video analysis: Social actions, objects, material realities and the problems of perspective. *Qualitative Research, 12*(3), 255–279.

Lugosi, P. (2006). Between overt and covert research: Concealment and disclosure in an ethnographic study of commercial hospitality. *Qualitative Inquiry, 12*(3), 541–561.

Mantzoukas, S. (2012). Exploring ethnographic genres and developing validity appraisal tools. *Journal of Research in Nursing, 17*(5), 420–435.

Markham, A. (1998). *Life online: Researching real experience in virtual space.* Walnut Creek, CA: AltaMira Press.

Markham, A., & Baym, N. (Eds.). (2009). *Internet inquiry: Conversations about method.* Thousand Oaks, CA: SAGE.

McIntyre, A. (2002). Women researching their lives: Exploring violence and identity in Belfast, the north of Ireland. *Qualitative Research, 2*(3), 387–409.

Merton, R., & Kendall, P. (1946). The focused interview. *American Journal of Sociology, 51,* 541–557.

Michel, B. (2010). Towards a poststructuralist perspective on the making and the power of maps. A response to Ball and Petsimeris [39 paragraphs]. *Forum Qualitative Sozialforschung/Forum: Qualitative Social Research, 11*(3), Art. 28. Retrieved from http://nbn-resolving.de/urn:nbn:de:0114-fqs1003281

Miller, G. (2012). The Smartphone psychology manifesto. *Perspectives on Psychological Science, 7*(3), 221–237.

Millward, L. (2012). Chapter 17. Focus group. In G. Breakwell, J. Smith, & D. Wright (Eds.), *Research methods in psychology.* Thousand Oaks, CA: SAGE. Retrieved from http://www.sagepub.com/upm-data/46878_Breakwell_Ch17.pdf

Morgan, D. (1988). *Focus groups as qualitative research.* Newbury Park, CA: SAGE.

Nielsen, D., Brixen, K., & Huniche, L. (2011). Men's experiences of living with osteoporosis: Focus group interviews. *American Journal of Men's Health, 5*(2), 166–176.

Oliver, E. (2010). *The challenges of large-scale smartphone user studies.* New York, NY: ACM. Retrieved from http://blizzard.cs.uwaterloo.ca/eaoliver/papers/2010/a5-oliver.pdf

Ozsivadjian, A., Knott, F., & Magiati, I. (2012). Parent and child perspectives on the nature of anxiety in children and young people with autism spectrum disorders: A focus group study. *Autism, 16*(2), 107–121.

Pascoe, J. (2007). *Dude, you're a fag.* Berkeley, CA: University of California Press.

Pew Internet & American Life Project. (n.d.). *Technology and media use.* Retrieved from http://www.pewtrusts.org/our_work_detail.aspx?id=56

Powell, K. (2010). Making sense of place: Mapping as a multisensory research method. *Qualitative Inquiry, 16*(7), 539–555.

Prosser, J. (2008). *Doing visual ethnography: Images, media and representation in research* (2nd ed.). Thousand Oaks, CA: SAGE.

Ray, J., & Smith, A. (2012). Using photographs to research organizations: Evidence, considerations and application in a field study. *Organizational Research Methods, 15*(2), 288–315.

Rezabek, R. (2000). Online focus groups: Electronic discussions for research [67 paragraphs]. *Forum Qualitative Sozialforschung/Forum: Qualitative Social Research 1*(1), Art. 11. Retrieved from http://www.qualitative-research.net/index.php/fqs/article/view/1128/2509

Roesch-Marsh, A., Gadda, A., & Smith, D. (2012). "It's a tricky business!" The impact of identity work in negotiating research access, *Qualitative Social Work, 11*(3), 249–265.

Salmons, J. (2010). *Online interviews in real time.* Thousand Oaks, CA: SAGE.

Smith, E., Gidlow, B., & Steel, G. (2012). Engaging adolescent participants in academic research: The use of photo-elicitation interviews to evaluate school-based outdoor education programmes. *Qualitative Research, 12*(4), 367–387.

Stewart, K., & Matthews, W. (2005). Researching online populations: The use of online focus groups for social research. *Qualitative Research,* 5(4), 395–416.

Stewart, D., & Shamdasani, P. (1990). *Focus groups: Theory and practice.* London, England: SAGE.

Sung, H., Hepworth, M., & Ragsdell, G. (2012). Investigating essential elements of community engagement in public libraries: An exploratory qualitative study. *Journal of Librarianship and Information Science,* 1–13. doi: 10.1177/0961000612448205

Sweet, C. (2001). Designing and conducting virtual focus groups. *Qualitative Market Research, 4*(3), 130–135.

Tomlinson, K., Barker, S., & Soden, S. (2012). What are cancer patients' experiences and preferences for the provision of written information in the palliative care setting? A focus group study. *Palliative Medicine, 26*(5), 760–765.

Tutt, D. (2008). Where the interaction is: Collisions of the situated and mediated in living room interactions. *Qualitative Inquiry, 14*(7), 1157–1179.

UP Virtual Ethnography Class '09. (2009). *Facebook.* [Group page]. Retrieved from http://www.facebook.com/pages/UP-Virtual-Ethnography-Class-09/105298383074

Wang, D., Park, S., & Fesenmaier, D. (2012). The role of smartphones in mediating the touristic experience. *Journal of Travel Research, 51*(4), 371–387.

Watkins, D. (2012). Qualitative research: The importance of conducting research that doesn't "count." *Health Promotion Practice, 13*(2), 153–158.

Wilson, R., Gosling, S., & Graham, L. (2012). A review of Facebook research in the social sciences. *Perspectives on Psychological Science, 7*(3), 203–220.

Wolcott, H. (1994). *Transforming qualitative data: Description, analysis and interpretation.* Thousand Oaks, CA: SAGE.

STUDENT STUDY SITE

Visit **http://www.sagepub.com/lichtmanqrss** to access additional study tools, including eFlashcards and links to SAGE journal articles.

PART III

The Final Product

CHAPTER 12

Drawing Meaning From the Data

Focus Your Reading

- In general, qualitative data analysis involves one of two approaches—coding data and looking for concepts/themes or developing narratives.
- When using the concept approach, there are three main steps in analysis—coding, categorizing, and conceptualizing.
- When using the narrative approach, the coding process is more general, and often details are not made explicit.
- Some analyses approaches are specific, while others more general.

At this point in your study of qualitative research (QR), you have had experience with conducting interviews, making observations, and writing reflexive journals. You realize that the type and quantity of the information you will gather (or have gathered) can be vast. But what are you to do with it? What does it all mean? How can you make sense of what you have learned? For unless you do something with all the information you have collected, you have not completed your research. It is now that you begin to consider more carefully what you will do with it. That the details about the process remain vague and lack consensus might not surprise you. In fact, of all the aspects of doing and understanding the QR process, it is data analysis procedures that are less transparent then all others. Hannes and Macaitis (2012), in reviewing numerous reports published between 2005 and 2008, concluded, "A black box remains between what people claim to use as a synthesis approach and what is actually done in practice" (p. 402).

James (2012) offers a somewhat novel recommendation: Use "analytic imagination" as part of the process. For her, it is the *process* of interpretation that is important. I agree completely. She acknowledged Geertz's 1973 admonition concerning the use of scientific imagination. Although numerous attempts to make the process more scientific have emerged since Geertz's comments—including various sophisticated software programs—I believe it is the imagination and creativity of the researcher that moves us from the design, collection, and processing of data to the act of making meaning.

Concomitant with this imaginative and analytic imagination to be used in data analysis, many writers remind us of using the process of reflexivity. Fielding (2004) believes that the process of data analysis *always* involves reflexivity. I concur. Continued immersion in the data is critical for analysis.

These abstract thoughts aside, you still face the task of trying to do something with the data. As a start, I want you to look at some actual interview information. The following comments are taken from an interview with Neil Armstrong as part of the NASA Johnson Space Center Oral History Project. Stephen Ambrose and Douglas Brinkley conducted the interviews in 2001. The entire transcript covers more than 100 pages. As a reminder, Neil Armstrong was the first American to set foot on the moon. He was born in 1930 in Ohio. He died August 25, 2012. This portion of the dialogue includes several responses to questions posed by the interviewer. Questions from interviewer have been omitted.

Box 12.1 Data From the Armstrong Transcript

Armstrong: I began to focus on aviation probably at age eight or nine, and inspired by what I'd read and seen about aviation and building model aircraft, why, I determined at an early age—and I don't know exactly what age, while I was still in elementary school—that that was the field I wanted to go into, although my intention was to be—or hope was to be an aircraft designer. I later went into piloting because I thought a good designer ought to know the operational aspects of an airplane. (p. 3)

Let us think about this. These brief selections and the remainder of the interview are your data. As a qualitative researcher, your task is to organize and make sense of these data. One way to do this is to see if you can identify key concepts that come out of the data. An alternative way to do this is to see if you can develop a story or narrative from the data. Whether key concepts or a story, both are legitimate ways of dealing with the data and making sense of it. There are a number of steps to follow that take you from the actual data that you have at the start to identifying key concepts or stories.

First, let me provide some definitions. *Data* are the information you collect as part of your research study. In QR, data usually take the form of words or pictures. (In quantitative research [QN], they take the form of numbers.) Key concepts are derived from the data through a process of coding, sifting, sorting, and identifying themes. Storytelling or narrative is an alternate way of making sense of the data. As you can imagine, there are numerous steps along the way to move from the actual data you collected to either of these two ways—concepts or narratives—of making sense of the data.

One of the first ways in which you manipulate the data is to assign codes to portions of the data. As a novice researcher, you will find it helpful to identify important portions of the text and choose several words to mark the data. We are going to try this now. Let's return to our original data (Box 12.1).

I want you to try some initial coding. Look at Armstrong's comments. How would you code his response? One choice might be *early interest in aviation*. Another might be *choosing career*. Your knowledge of Armstrong's background might come into play here as you proceed through the transcript. Let's try another bit of data.

Box 12.2 Additional Data From the Armstrong Transcript

Armstrong: Well, my knowledge of aerodynamics was not good enough to match the quality of the Wright Brothers' tunnel, and at that point I suppose I was equally educated to them. But it was a fun project. Blew out a lot of fuses in my home. [Chuckles] Because I tried to build a rheostat which would allow the electric motor to change speed and then get various air flows through the tunnel, not altogether successfully. (p. 4)

How might you code this bit of the Armstrong interview data? *Sense of humor* might be used. Or you could tag *interest in aviation*. Notice that most of the codes are concerned with the topic or content of the response. One is concerned with the emotion shown by the respondent. Both are legitimate types of codes. Saldaña (2009) takes us even further in talking about coding attributes.

I hope you get the idea. You are beginning to move from the data in the raw transcript toward developing key concepts. You are at the very first stages—what Saldaña called "preliminary codes" or "jottings" (p. 17).

Here is another selection from the interview. Try your hand at coding.

Box 12.3 Further Data From the Armstrong Transcript

Ambrose: The assumption among young men at that time was, "As soon as I graduate or as soon as I get to be eighteen, I'm going into the service." But then the war ended when you were fifteen. So you completed the high school without any "I'm going to enlist" kind of feeling.

Armstrong: That's correct. We had a few people in my school who had either lied about their age or were a little older than the class, who had gone into the service, and came back and finished high school after the war was over. We had several of those fellows in our school, but the youngest of those would probably be two years older than I was. (p. 6)

Armstrong: Well, I always felt that the risks that we had in the space side of the program were probably less than we [had] back in flying at Edwards or the general flight-test

(Continued)

(Continued)

community. The reason is that when we were out exploring the frontiers, we were out at the edges of the flight envelope all the time, testing limits. Our knowledge base was probably not as good as it was in the space program. We had less technical insurance, less minds looking, less backup programs, less other analysis going on. That isn't to say that we didn't expect risks in the space program; we certainly expected they would be there, were guaranteed that they would be there. But we felt pretty comfortable because we had so much technical backup and we didn't go nearly close to the limits as much as we did back in the old flight-test days. (p. 33)

Ambrose's comments might be coded *importance of service* or *caring about country* or *making career decisions*. You might find other terms to use to code his questions. Armstrong's comment could be coded *career choices* or *young age and career*. You can continue to practice coding this very interesting interview by downloading it from the website listed by Ambrose and Brinkley (2001). I hope you see that preliminary coding involves moving from the raw data into identifying important elements. It is an iterative process and continuously shifts as you practice and become more familiar with your data.

I have just taken you through the very beginnings of qualitative data analysis (QDA) toward the pathway of developing themes and then key concepts. Later in this chapter, I will take you through six steps to move from raw data into key concepts. Bazeley (2009) supports my view that analyzing qualitative data is more than just looking for themes that are supported by quotes drawn from the raw data. She thinks that much deeper analysis should be involved, which might include interpreting and naming categories or looking at pattern analysis. Later, I introduce you to the idea of *narrative analysis* in contrast to concept/*thematic analysis*. I begin by asking you to think about what qualitative data are. Then, I ask you to consider whether your analysis will involve looking for themes and key concepts or telling stories. Although many researchers have chosen to write about themes and concepts derived from the data, others use stories to discern and convey meaning.

Next, I introduce the idea of data analysis as a process. What constitutes data? When should you do your analysis? How should you get started? What about coding and themes, or would you prefer to focus on the stories and narratives of those you study? How do you know when you are finished? Are you ever finished? I suspect that you will find those questions in any discussion of qualitative analysis.

QR uses an inductive strategy. Its purpose is to examine the whole in a natural setting to get the ideas and feelings of those being interviewed or observed. As a consequence, data analysis in QR is also inductive and iterative. Some people like to collect data and analyze it simultaneously; the analysis can then lead to further areas that could be investigated as the study continues. Others begin with the analysis; while this is not advised, it often happens. You can make the process iterative by proceeding through the six steps that follow with some of your data and then testing it on additional data.

I see data analysis as being about process and interpretation. Whether you analyze your data using statistics or choose some other method, there is a process you follow and interpretations to be made from that process. The process in QN is straightforward—at least, once you determine what statistics to run. When I was in graduate school, the process was very difficult.

You entered your data on 80-column cards and sorted the cards in the appropriate order. You wrote a program or selected a program to run your data, and you had your university run the program on a behemoth of a computer. How you interpreted the data you ran was also straightforward; it was primarily a matter of testing hypotheses and rejecting (or confirming) them. When personal computers replaced large mainframe computers, data analysis also changed. Several statistical programs (e.g., Statistical Packages for the Social Sciences and Statistical Analysis System) became available to analyze data. These and others are still in wide use today. The major issue for analyzing numerical data is to determine the appropriate statistics. Programs produce statistical output that can be used to test hypotheses. While you may not be entirely clear about which statistical approach to use or precisely how to enter your data or even how to make meaning from your data once it is run, you might feel comfortable that the results you obtain are objective and scientific. You also expect that those who read your research will be comfortable with your results and find them objective and believable.

I suspect, however, that you are left somewhat dissatisfied when you try to organize your thoughts and put words to paper. What do those numbers really mean? Why are you rejecting the null hypothesis? Can you even be sure that you understand the null hypothesis? What does it mean to test at the .05 level of significance? To assist, you are usually able to obtain guidance from a professor or tutor who can help you interpret what you did.

Using computer software for qualitative analysis, however, is not comparable to that available in the quantitative domain. In the example I provided about coding Armstrong's interview data, computer programs would not be helpful in terms of identifying elements in the data that *you* deem important. Be aware, though, that there are several software programs available that will facilitate your analysis. It is beyond the scope of this text to review these programs.

Analyzing qualitative data is an entirely different matter. The data are not numerical. There are no agreed-upon ways of analyzing the data you have. Whether you have a theoretical component to your research or not, you have the practical dilemma of how to analyze the data. Most qualitative approaches provide very general information about how to do this. With the exception of grounded theory, you are pretty much left on your own. Thorne (2000) has reminded us that "qualitative data analysis is the most complex and mysterious of all of the phases of a qualitative project, and the one that receives the least thoughtful discussion in the literature" (p. 68). There is a lack of standardization and few universal rules. Basit (2003) commented that QDA is the most difficult and most crucial aspect of QR (p. 143). In 1994, Morse suggested that the actual process of analysis remains mysterious. Morse (2008) considered the issues of collaboration in qualitative inquiry and specifically commented that the researcher must "get inside the data," which makes collaboration somewhat problematic.

At times, investigators analyze the data using more than one method of analysis. Simons, Lathlean, and Squire (2008) described a study in which they used the same data set but two different analysis protocols. First, they tried a thematic content analysis, in which they looked for themes across the data set based on content. Then, with the same data, they applied a narrative analysis. They described a technique developed by Riessman in which the analyst was considered to have the social position of the narrator. Their conclusion was that using iterative and sequential methods revealed a greater depth of understanding than they would have found with only one method. Also, to take experimentation even further, Frost and his colleagues (2010) took the same interview transcript and conducted an analysis using four different analytic approaches: (1) grounded theory, (2) Foucauldian discourse analysis, (3) interpretative phenomenological analysis, and (4) narrative analysis. Kaufmann (2011) has described a poststructural analytic approach in which new meaning is created by looking for differences rather than similarities, by looking for absence rather than presence, and by looking at local rather than universal. Li and Seale (2007) reported on a project involving teaching and supervising their students in conducting qualitative analyses. Their students had difficulty knowing where to start coding, and the students faced problems with ambiguities in definitions of codes, inaccuracies in reporting, and overinterpretation of the evidence. As my extensive experience and these studies suggest, how to analyze qualitative data is an area that remains conflicting or, more likely, somewhat vague. I have thrown many terms at you without any definitions or explanations. Now, I want to bring you back to reality. We will look at some ways you can make sense of the data you collect.

If your analysis is one that involves coding and looking for concepts/themes, there are several ways you can proceed. Whether you approach data analysis via a generic coding strategy or select one of several specific strategies—some of which I mention subsequently—and whether you use computer software or not, I believe you will have the most success with a systematic approach. A systematic approach to analysis and interpretation brings order and understanding to your QR project. You will also need creativity and discipline as you embark on your data analysis. The challenge is that the way you do this is flexible and open to discussion and interpretation.

I also discuss clarification of your philosophical stance. What do you believe QR can do with and for data? What is your belief regarding what I call "who is right"? Do you need to verify what you have done with an expert? After all, who is an expert? Should you connect to theory?

I introduce a concrete example of what I refer to as the three *C*s of analysis and give you a six-step approach that should provide you with enough detail to start your own analysis.

Another topic I cover is whether and in what ways you should make use of computer software to analyze your data. Although most of you will have your data on your laptop computer, this is different from using analytical software. If you choose to use software, which program should you choose? How do you learn the software? Many faculty members are not qualified to assist you. Many of the instructional manuals cannot be used without additional workshops or tutoring. I conclude with new trends, especially in the area of secondary analysis.

Did You Know

Steven Johnson (2004), in *Mind Wide Open,* helped us understand our inner workings and psyches in his fascinating book about the brain and the neuroscience of everyday life. By now, I shouldn't have to remind you that I want you to keep your mind wide open!

Most would agree that qualitative data generally take the form of words, not numbers. Modern writers include visual, audio, or graphic data in the definition as well as verbal or textual data. While some argue that qualitative data can be transformed into quantitative data, I think it is those who practice a traditional or fundamentalist paradigm who take this position. If you support a more inclusive position, then almost any data you gather from, by, or about your study can be seen as qualitative data.

Suppose you are interested in studying single-sex classrooms. Some schools have adopted the practice of organizing classrooms by gender. There are merits and disadvantages on both sides. In a study involving British people born in 1958, Sullivan and her colleagues (2010) found this type of schooling positive for girls but neutral for boys. The American Civil Liberties Union opposes the idea, but advocates see that teaching can be targeted and distractions reduced.

You are interested in going beyond the statistical data. Let's look at the kind of qualitative data you might collect: interview data with students, teachers, and parents; observational data recorded in note form of classroom practices and student behaviors; documents related to the issues; shadowing of selected students; photographs or videos of students interacting; your notes regarding your thoughts about the practice; student work products, either on the computer or in hard copy; student chat room comments regarding their feelings about participating in this type of class; and your observations about the classroom's physical appearance and the appearance of the students. All are legitimate types of data. No one form of data is better or more legitimate or more meaningful than another type. You are limited only by your creativity and the available technology.

As you can imagine, you will have an enormous quantity of data in somewhat different forms. You will most likely transcribe your interviews and observational notes into a word processing program. You may have some data already on your computer, taken from chat room discussions or student work products. All your verbal data can be organized in a word processing program; you will have to devise a way to organize your visual or graphic data. Some qualitative software programs incorporate visual and audio data and provide ways to analyze them.

I want to stress that the data will be collected not at one time but at several times across the life of your research project. In the same way, your analysis should cover the life of the project and should begin as you begin collecting your data. Planning how you will do your analysis should precede actual data collection. Let me emphasize that your plan should represent a general guide and may be modified as necessary, depending on the data you collect and the available tools for analysis.

■ When to Do Your Analysis

I see analysis as an ongoing process throughout the life of a project; however, we write about it in a linear fashion, and often, researchers get so involved in data collection that they do not begin any serious analysis until all data are collected. It would be ideal if researchers could follow a circular model of gathering and analyzing data. Often, a researcher will enter data into a computer program—a word processing program or qualitative software program—in concert with collecting additional data. Even when a researcher makes a decision not to conduct analyses using a computer, he or she organizes the data on the computer. Having entered the first piece of data—an interview, some field notes, or the current teaching unit—a researcher begins the process of analysis. Some do this informally, while others proceed in a more formal manner.

■ Gaining Meaning: Themes/Concepts or Narratives

Looking at Themes/Concepts

In many research approaches, there appears to be general agreement that the goal of analyzing the text and words collected is to arrive at common themes or concepts. Most procedures involve a process in which the researcher chooses to code words, phrases, segments, or other portions of text. Some people believe that the codes should be determined a priori. However, most take the position that the codes emerge from the data via a process of reading and thinking about the text material. Aside from a specific process identified with grounded theory, coding is usually done through a careful reading of the text. I have seen some people read the text and mark large chunks of material with codes. Others work from a micro level and code text chunks or segments. Whatever the process, and I believe it varies by individual and perhaps even by type of data, the initial goal is to arrive at a manageable number of codes.

I see the process as one of organizing and categorizing. You begin with a large amount of material, for example, the text of an interview. That material is dissected and categorized into codes. Next, you proceed to a second interview. Again, dissect and categorize the data into codes; you can use the previous codes or add new codes. This iterative process continues until you have coded all your interviews. By this time, you have reviewed many interviews and coded them. You can now review your codes and look for ones that overlap or are redundant. You might find that you will rename some of your codes. You will likely generate many codes. These codes can then be organized into hierarchical categories, in which some codes will be subsets of larger categories. You might have 80 to 100 codes that you then organize into 15 to 20 categories and subcategories. These categories can then be organized into five to seven concepts. As a general rule, even large data sets do not reveal more than this small number of central and meaningful concepts about the topic of interest.

I see this as a process of sorting and sifting. Imagine that you have a large sieve. But it doesn't look like a traditional sieve. Some holes are square, some round, and some irregularly shaped. You put into the sieve a number of objects—some round, some square, and some irregularly shaped. You shake the sieve. The round ones drop through the round holes. The square ones drop through the square holes. Some of those irregularly shaped drop through the odd-shaped holes, while others stay in the sieve. You have sorted your objects based on a system. Some fit well while others do not. Or think of how you could take items from the pockets of a group of children and put them into a large bin. Your assignment is to organize the items into three piles. Well, you might place edibles in one stack, games or toys into another, and items related to school into a third. Or, shifting your thinking entirely, you might place disposables into one pile and those that are permanent into another. So there is no right way to do this. And you are no more or less expert at doing the task than the next person. Organizing the data you collect takes on the same kind of challenge. There are no clear rules, nor is it obvious how you should begin. As a beginning researcher, I suggest you begin by practicing. By following a process of coding and looking for themes, you can begin to make sense of your data.

Looking at Narratives

One limitation of the type of analysis I just described is that it operates from a reductionist perspective. Do we really believe that we can capture so much of what a person thinks and feels and portray it in five or six basic themes? Some would argue that by doing this, we are trying to move into an analytic mode that is more closely allied to principles of quantitative paradigms. An alternative approach to an analysis that identifies themes and concepts is the emphasis on finding the narrative or telling stories (Coffey & Atkinson, 1996). The intention is to examine how such stories can be used as structured or formal ways to transmit information. (You can read in greater detail Denzin's 1989 account of interpretive biography.) Connelly and Clandinin (1990) have written extensively on the topic. Baumgartner (2000), in her study of HIV-positive adults, shed light on exploring how stories can be used as a source of data. Although Richmond (2002) proposed some specific guidelines for a narrative analysis, most researchers follow their own plan and often do not describe details in their published work. Guy and Montague (2008) analyzed the personal narratives about men's friendships. Zilber, Tuval-Mashiach, and Lieblich (2008) stressed the importance of context in the construction and understanding of life stories. I particularly like Coffey and Atkinson's (1996) admonition:

> There are no formulae or recipes for the "best" way to analyze the stories we elicit and collect. . . . Such approaches also enable us to think beyond our data to the ways in which accounts and stories are socially and culturally managed and constructed. That is, the analysis of narratives can provide a critical way of examining not only key actors and events but also cultural conventions and social norms. (p. 80)

Some researchers have experimented with visual narratives. Researchers might rely on narratives generated by participants or on those the researchers themselves generate. For details using this approach, you can examine a Visual Research Methods course taught at the University of California, Berkeley, during the spring of 2011. Others combine multiple types of data (visual, written, and spoken). Keats's (2009) point is well taken: "Studying narrative texts aids the researcher in understanding how participants experience, live, and tell about their world" (p. 181). Li and her colleagues (2011) have provided an excellent example of visual narrative combined with text.

I am suggesting that you can either conduct an analysis in which your goal is to identify themes/concepts or conduct an analysis in which your goal is to provide an interpretation of the data by telling or retelling a story. Neither way is right. The process you follow to get to the end depends on your goal.

Moving Ahead

Writing about the analysis process is linear; in contrast, actually doing an analysis is anything but. You will be faced with many questions you need to answer and decisions to make. It is often the case that you know in advance the main types of data you will collect. However, as your project develops, you might discover that additional data become available. You may decide in advance that you will use a computer software program to analyze your data. However, the program you want may not be readily available, or you may think you can learn how to run a program that turns out to be much more complicated than you anticipated. You may decide that you are going to concentrate on one aspect of a problem and then find that the data you collect lend themselves to exploring totally different arenas. You may decide to incorporate images in your data, but you are not really able to determine how best to include the visual data and how to incorporate them into an analysis. The process may appear to be relatively clear and systematic; however, in reality, you might find yourself getting bogged down in details you did not expect. You might find that you want to capture information from the Internet (e.g., chat room discussions, LISTSERV comments, the blogs, YouTube videos), but you do not know enough about the logistics to do this effectively. Shulman (2011) has developed Discover Text, which enables the researcher to capture data from Facebook or Twitter in real time and apply preliminary codes.

Conducting an Analysis for Themes/Concepts

The goal of qualitative analysis is to take a large amount of data that may be cumbersome and without any clear meaning and interact with it in such a manner that you can make sense of what you gathered. Again, you should not be surprised that there is no right way to do this. In fact, there is less written about the mechanics of doing such analysis than about any other topic in QR. When authors do write about the process, they are quite vague. I propose here a process that I have used over many years. I suggest you think about it as a starting point rather than a prescription. I hope you will find the ideas useful.

Getting Started

QR is usually a solo activity. You collect data on your own, analyze it on your own, write it on your own, and are responsible for what you say. But we know that much research benefits from interacting with others, trying your ideas out on others, and learning about the reaction of others to your ideas.

I know that students learn by doing and practicing. I encourage you to work with small groups of students as you embark on looking for meaning in what you have gathered Here is an exercise from Barbara Kawulich (personal communication, 2008; exercise used with permission of Barbara Kawulich) that she calls "Hot Monkey Sex": Students are given three Post-it Notes each. On the first, they write their answer to the question "Given all the money you need, where in the world would you like to go for a month's vacation?" On the second, they write down whom they want to go with. On the third Post-it Note, they indicate what they want to do on the vacation. Students work in pairs to analyze the data by organizing the Post-it Notes in various ways to tell a story the responses generate. Kawulich chose the title for the exercise while working with a class consisting of several young teachers and one older, quiet teacher who typically did not get involved in the class. This activity really got the quiet teacher involved: Her Post-it Notes revealed that she wanted to go to Hawaii with Brad Pitt and have hot monkey sex. "The younger teachers roared with laughter, loving her openness and appreciating the fun-loving side we had never before seen." Kawulich reported that once she renamed the exercise, students would bring cameras to class because their friends wanted to see what "Hot Monkey Sex" looked like. Exercises like this can help you see how the codes emerge from the data and how no single scheme is better than another.

I haven't tried the next technique, but Waite (2011) describes it in a recent article. Here is a summary of Waite's illustration:

Each student receives a deck of cards (including any extra cards) that have been shuffled and placed in a box.

Step 1: Students are asked to sort the cards independently—no questions, no talking. Outcome: Most students sort the cards by suit; some also arrange in numerical sequence.

Step 2: Students are asked to sort the cards, but now in a different way. Outcome: This is less predictable; some sort by arranging all cards of same numerical value together and then arrange in ascending or descending order. What is important about the activity is the question then asked: Why did they sort in a particular way?

Borrowing from LeComte's work, Waite suggests using either tacit or explicit theory for their sort. Waite also gets involved with the other types of cards in the deck—the discrepant cards (jokers, scoring, etc.). Discussion ensues about what to do about data that don't fit into the neat categories.

Another technique involves using Pinterest. Pinterest is a virtual pinboard. It allows you to share many things you find on the Web. A *pin* is an image that you can either upload from your computer or select from the Web. A *board* is a set of pins that you or others create. These pinboards are created in real time. For the activity, select a group of 30 to 40 images. You can sort several times. There are no specific rules for sorting, but you will find that some organizations make more sense or represent the data (pins) you have better than others. What is exciting about using Pinterest is that a vast variety of images are available instantly. Working alone or with others, you will develop your skill in making sense of a vast amount of data—in this case, the data take the form of visual images rather than words.

Extending these examples to the sorting of words or visual images is a way to come to understand that sorting groups of things into categories can be done in several ways; one way is not necessarily better than another.

Preparing and Organizing Your Data

Once you have gathered some data, you need to put it into a format that is useful for analysis. In most cases, you will find a way to transcribe interviews, capture online discussions, or otherwise put words and text in a useful format. You should also think about visual or audio data that are not transcribed. I recommend that you place each item in a separate file, using a word processing package. It is helpful to insert your comments in brackets and in a different font or color.

Make a folder and label it, for example, "My Qualitative Research Project." You will place several files in this folder, depending on how much data you have collected. These files can be individual interviews and/or your observation notes or your researcher journal. At the very least, you will place your data and your journal files in the folder. It is helpful if you label each file in a systematic manner. For example, suppose you have four interviews: two with the same person and two additional ones. You would create the following four files: DonaldInt1, DonaldInt2, DavidInt1, DanielInt1. In a large project, you might have observation data as well: DonaldObs1, DavidObs1, and so on. Of course, your choice of file names depends on the type of data you collect. Some researchers like to incorporate a date in the file name.

In addition to these data files, you will want to create your researcher journal or blog. Make another file and label it "Researcher Journal." Some people also put information collected from a literature review in this folder. This folder should be created when you begin your research, not when you finish it. You should plan to keep adding to it as you move along.

Make sure you save a copy of this folder in a location other than your hard drive. In today's computer world, keeping copies of your files is somewhat easier than in times past. But I encountered a serious problem and lost an entire book chapter recently when my file became corrupted and I could no longer save it. An external hard drive or one in the Cloud became the savior.

Reviewing and Recording Your Thoughts

Most people find it helpful to read through all the material in their folders. In keeping with the iterative nature of the process, you can begin by reading a transcript. Add your thoughts and comments to your Researcher Journal file. It is okay to use informal writing here. Remember to date your notes. Your comments might look something like this:

> 9/15/2012. Read through the transcript of DanielInt1. Daniel certainly had a lot to say. I wish I had asked him more about why he decided to leave the field of teaching. I will need to remember to do that in my next interview and if I go back with him as well.
>
> 9/20/2012. Finished my second interview with Daniel. Glad he clarified his thoughts on this topic. Not sure I would have picked this up unless I had read what he said.

Looking for Concepts/Themes—The Three Cs: Coding, Categorizing, and Concepts

You are now at a point where you can see how to move from raw data to meaningful concepts or themes. I call this the three *C*s of analysis: from coding to categorizing to concepts.

Coding interview data, observational notes, and text into meaningful chunks is a challenging task. Whether you work with a word processing program or with other software, it is your responsibility to generate the codes. Do not expect that a computer program will generate codes or organize them; rather, you will need to provide the input. I have broken down this process into six steps (see Figure 12.1).

Figure 12.1 The Three Cs of Data Analysis: Codes, Categories, Concepts

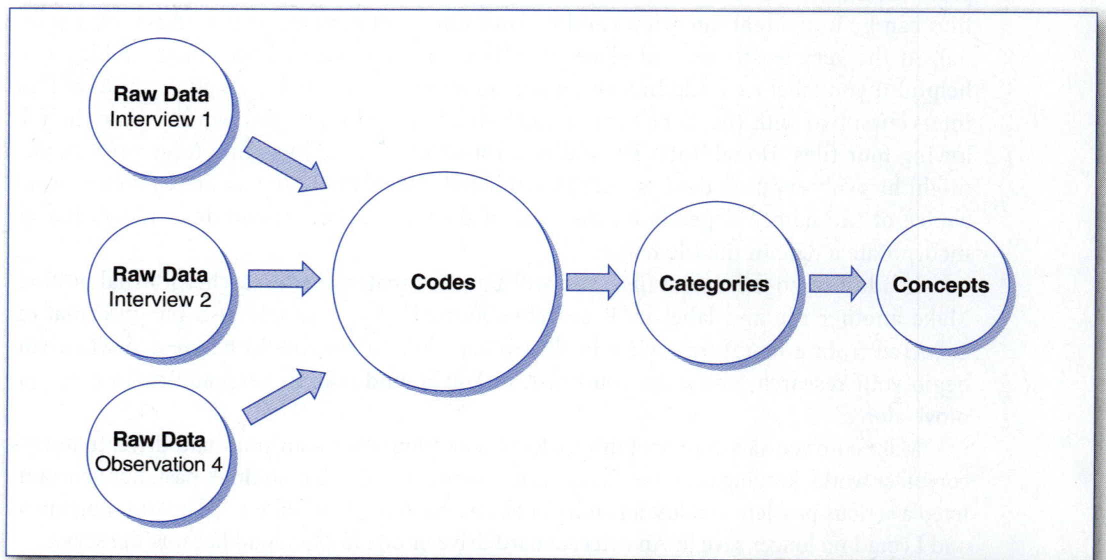

Six Steps in Coding

The six steps are as follows and are subsequently explained in detail:

Step 1. Initial coding. Going from responses to summary ideas of the responses

Step 2. Revisiting initial coding

Step 3. Developing an initial list of categories

Step 4. Modifying your initial list based on additional rereading

Step 5. Revisiting your categories and subcategories

Step 6. Moving from categories to concepts

Step 1. Initial coding. An initial code can be a word, a phrase, or the respondent's own words. You come to it by a careful reading of the text. In my coding of the Armstrong interview, I used brief phrases for my coding. Even if you have collected only a small amount of data, it is not too early to begin coding. Select any transcript. Read the initial page or two. Use the "Comment" function in your word processing program to insert your initial codes (in Microsoft Word 2010, you will find the function on the "Review" tab). Enter your initial codes. Continue reading the transcript while entering different codes. Upon completion of initial coding with one transcript, select another transcript and continue the same process. Box 12.4 is an example that might help you see this more clearly. The researcher's codes are in brackets.

Box 12.4 Examples of Initial Coding

Transcript 1. Partial Interview: Cross-Gender Friendship

It was sophomore year in college. We knew each other—or at least who each other were—from freshman year. Sophomore year on the first day of classes, we met during some orientation. She was orientating freshmen. I was probably hanging around, looking for something or other to get into around campus. About four months after that we started hanging out constantly. [maintenance as friendship only]

We just—or at least I tried to—stay out of situations where it could have turned, become physical. [physical attraction] And we tried not to talk about it—those kind of things. [evolution into something more] After about eight months or so, things shifted. We both realized our feelings had changed. We tried to hold off as long as we could and keep the friendship as long as we could. But we started going to the next step. [potential problems]

One of the main things is that since I'm not actively seeing another person or actively engaged, is that when I meet a girl, any girl, is potentially more than a friend. [tensions/barriers]

(Continued)

(Continued)

Transcript 2. Partial Interview: Cross-Gender Friendship

Someone that I can talk to intimately. Someone that I can tell just about anything. [intimacy, talk to] . . . It's just a spark similar to physical attraction [physical attraction] but it's different. You know, when you talk to them that, you know, you may not agree on things necessarily, but you can understand each other. . . . natural progression. [something more]

Step 2. Revisiting initial coding. By now, you will have developed a large number of codes. Some of them will be redundant, and you will need to collapse them and rename the codes. I have observed that some people tend to code almost every phrase or sentence, while others code larger chunks of information. You need to choose whatever works best. You may want to modify your codes based on an examination of what you have already collected and new raw data. The brief transcript I provide does not give you a chance to show how you might rename your codes. But you should focus on removing redundancies, renaming synonyms, or clarifying terms. If you coded attributes, you should make them consistent (for example: men, boys, teenage boys). Choose one term to describe the attribute.

Step 3. Initial listing of categories. Now that you have modified your codes, it is time to organize them into categories. I have found that certain codes become major topics, while others can be grouped under a major topic and become subsets of that topic. In essence, you have moved from one long list of codes into several lists of categories, with related codes as subsets of the categories (see Box 12.5).

Box 12.5 Example of Initial Categories

(Subcategories have been omitted.)

- Maintenance
- Physical attraction
- Intimacy
- Tensions/barriers
- Problems
- Issues with boyfriend/girlfriend
- Meaning of friendship
- Issues of homosexuality

Step 4. Modifying the initial list. At this point, you will need to continue the iterative process. You may decide that some of your categories are less important than others, or you may see that two categories can be combined. Remember that your goal in the three *C*s analysis is to move from coding initial data through identification of categories to the recognition of important concepts or themes.

Step 5. Revisiting categories. I suggest that at this point, you revisit your list of categories and see whether you can remove redundancies and identify critical elements. In my experience, most novice researchers tend to see everything as important. They appear reluctant to say that one area might reveal more interesting ideas than another. This is where you can exercise your judgment about what is important and what is not.

Here is an example taken from an entirely different context. Suppose you have 100 books, and you want to arrange them into five piles. Well, there are a number of ways you can do this. You can sort by color—all blue-covered books together, all green-covered books together, and so on. You can sort by size—grouping all oversized books together. You can sort by topic—all books on science together, all books on humor together, and so on. Or you can sort by author—all books by Roth together, all books by Faulkner together, and so on. You could arrange by publication date—all books published after 2000 together, all from 1990 to 2000 together, and so on. Obviously, some categories make more sense than others, depending on your purpose. Further, you could place the books in subsets within each of the major categories. To continue with my example, you could place light blue books together, navy blue together, and so on. If you arranged by author, you could put major works together and minor works together.

Step 6. From categories to concepts. The final step in the process is to identify key concepts that reflect the meaning you attach to the data you collect. While there are no definitive rules for the number of concepts you might identify, I believe very strongly that a smaller number of well-developed and supported concepts make for a much richer analysis than many loosely framed ideas. As you read and reread your data, you will see that some ideas appear richer and more powerful than others. It is up to you to determine that. I would suggest, as a rule of thumb, that five to seven concepts should be the maximum number that you find in a set of data. You might consider even fewer concepts as you become more sophisticated in conducting analyses. Obviously, this number depends on the amount of data and the range of the interview. Some information is unimportant even though it is there.

When organizing your codes into concepts, it is your task to decide the most informative or logical manner of sorting. You need to determine what meaning you think can be found from the data. Sometimes your initial thoughts are quite superficial. You will find that reorganizing, rewriting, and rethinking often lead to more powerful ideas. At this point, some writers like to weave information from the available literature together with their new data.

Strengthening the Process

By now, you will have completed the six steps in the movement from codes through categories to concepts. To add texture and depth to your analysis, you may want to return to your documents to look for other things that will enhance your interpretation. One promising area to explore is the use of metaphors. Our language is rich with metaphorical allusions, and they often reveal much about what others mean. To what extent were metaphors used? Are there sufficient metaphors to incorporate as part of your written paper? If so, can you code them according to certain criteria that may emerge? You might look for type of language, metaphor chosen, or gender-related metaphors.

You could also explore the use of stories. To what extent were stories used? Are there stories that might lead to epiphanies? Are some better than others? Other kinds of things to look for in your data are the richness of detail, conflicting ideas from the same respondent, unusual or unique experiences, or ideas that contradict current thinking on the topic.

I want to reemphasize that making meaning from qualitative data is a process that moves between questions, data, and meaning. Figure 12.2 provides a summary of the data analysis process when looking for themes or concepts. Key elements in the model are that it is iterative, circular, and can be entered at any point. You need to try to think of your own work in this way as well.

Figure 12.2 Relationship Between Questions, Data, and Meaning

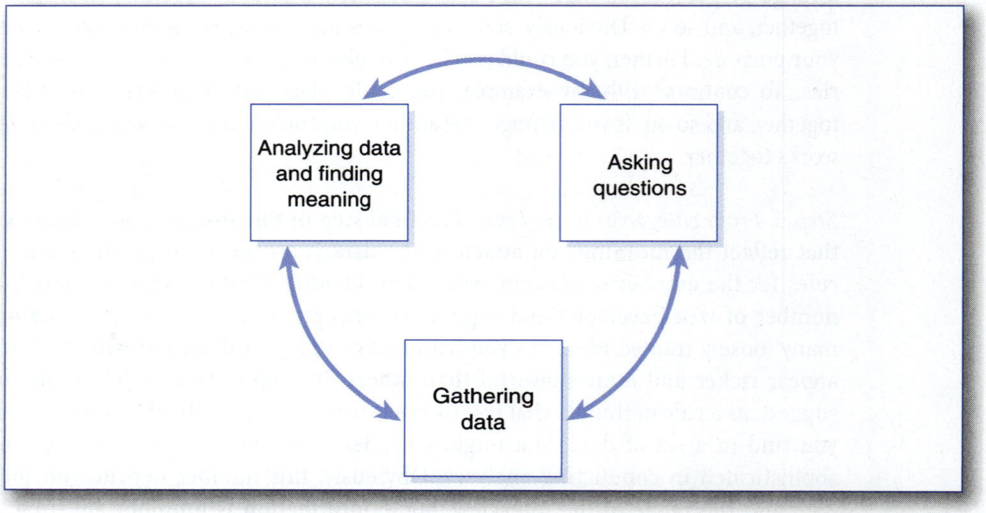

■ Looking for Narratives or Stories

As I said at the outset, a researcher might choose among two basic goals for an analysis. One involves the identification of concepts or themes. I just described the main process of three *C*s—coding, categorizing, and concepts and the details involved in it. An alternative goal might be to look for or analyze the data for narratives or stories. In this section, I describe a way toward that goal.

Before I discuss some of the details, however, I want you to think about a frustrating problem that might cause you some difficulty. In QR, some terms seemed to be used in more than one way. I ask—Is narrative a type of research approach, a way to analyze data, or a way to present data? It is actually all of these. In Chapter 5, I discuss a narrative approach to research. Actually, this term replaced *biography* or *life story* as a way to talk about research approaches. So one meaning of narrative is a research approach as described in Chapter 5. A second meaning of narrative is concerned with how data are analyzed. That is the subject of this chapter. Closely associated with that idea is how data are presented once they are analyzed. Jones and his colleagues (2013) use narrative in the visual story about Rufus Stone that is discussed in detail in Chapter 7. Those who adopt an autoethnographic research approach usually present their information in narrative form, and several examples are provided in the following chapter. Even though I talk about these separately, the ideas are intertwined. So narrative is a research approach, a way to analyze data, and a way to present data.

As I just said, you can also think about narratives in terms of how data are analyzed. Rather than following the three-step coding concepts method I just discussed, you could search for the story that comes from the data. Thus far, I have described a process you can follow if you are analyzing your data by coding and looking for central concepts or themes. But some writers and researchers prefer an analytic procedure that focuses on stories and the narrative. Edwards and Weller (2012) speak of qualitative analysis methods as "concerned with transforming and interpreting data to capture and understand the complexities of the social world" (p. 202). In their work, they use what they call *I-poems* (how participants present themselves in regard to first-person statements). They compare the use of I-poems with a thematic analysis. Bosk (2011), in her review of Wells's work on narrative analysis, comments that Wells's task in her book "is to suggest that narrative analysis is an important research method that is particularly appropriate for social work researchers" (p. 540). Bosk continues, "Analysis of the language of narratives allows us to make sense of stories as something in and of themselves" (p. 541). Riessman (2008) wrote about narratives as telling, transcribing, and analyzing. She includes four analytic approaches: thematic analysis, structural analysis, dialogic/performance analysis, and visual analysis. According to Q: Foundations of Qualitative Research in Education (n.d.), a site developed for students at the Harvard Graduate School of Education:

> Thematic analysis relies on categorizing accounts or aspects of accounts that are being told. Structural analysis looks into the ways in which the narratives are structured and what the language in the stories does both on the textual as well as the cultural level. Dialogic/performance analysis focuses on the difficulty in analyzing accounts that are co-constructed or performed. Lastly, visual analysis focuses on the analysis of all visual media including art, video, and digital media. (para. 3)

Langellier (1989) has added two additional categories: resolution (what finally happened) and coda (return back to the present). Richmond (2002) argued for the importance of studying stories. She studied adult learners by using a story map. You might find her four-step process helpful. The structure you use would include (1) an orientation (setting and characters), (2) an abstract (a summary of the events or incidents important in the story), (3) complicating action (your evaluative comments on events or conflicts or themes), and (4) resolution (the story outcomes). Charmaz (2002) referenced renewed attention to stories told by research participants and the ways in which researchers tell them. In this work, she addresses stories and silences of the chronically ill. Paulson (2011) explained how she used open and focused coding in conjunction with two types of data (ethnographic and narrative interviews) in her study about dance. For me, this is an example of blurred lines. While it is a study based on narrative, she follows quite explicit and detailed coding procedures.

Based on the idea that people use stories to make sense of themselves, narrative analysis explores the data specifically looking for stories. While early narrative analysis relied on Labov's (1972; Labov & Waletzky, 1967) writing, Cortazzi (2002) developed later work in education. Spector-Mersel (2011) has helped us understand ways in which narratives can be interpreted. Her model relies on the idea that identities can be claimed via stories. Her article used life stories of senior officers who come from the generation of those who founded Israel in the 1940s. Banyai and Glover (2012) reviewed the current research on travel blogs. They found that content analysis and narrative analysis were the two most popular methods for data analysis. How did they obtain the information? They searched Google Scholar with the term "tourism travel blogs." You might get an idea of how this can be done by looking at their paper.

My original task was to instruct you, in detail, on how to analyze your data so that you could develop and write in a narrative, storytelling manner. Saldaña (2009) has offered an example of narrative coding. He spoke of how narrative coding emerged after looking at the structures and properties of an interview (p. 110). While helpful, the specific details of how one moves from the raw data into a narrative or story mode is based more on the whole of the data rather than isolation of each part into specific codes. In a sense, the process is about the whole rather than a focus on the details. That is not to make a judgment about the value of this approach. There is an increase in presentations that are based on autoethnography, poetry, performances, and storytelling. You will find many such examples in the journal *Qualitative Inquiry*. The June 2011 issue, for example, includes 10 articles featuring plays, poetry, autoethnography, and performance text. One article includes visuals. None are written in the more familiar style. The April 2011 issue follows a similar pattern.

While there is some writing about narrative analysis, very little of it addresses any specifics on how to do it. Bronken, Kirkevold, Martinsen, and Kvigne (2012) describe how stories are co-constructed between a young woman with aphasia and a trained nurse. In fact, Griffin (2011), in a review of Goodall's volume on writing qualitative inquiry and storytelling, commented "but though it is a rapidly growing area, there is a dearth of practical advice regarding personal narrative as a method of inquiry" (p. 219).

So much of the research we read is written in a bland and neutral manner. In order to create an emotional response and to touch the reader, Ward (2011) used a poetic representation to represent the friendships and social relationships of four severely disabled students in New Zealand. She describes this type of re-presentation as a form of evocative text. Without getting too technical, *evocative text* uses certain literary devices to re-create lived experiences and evoke emotional responses. Other types of evocative texts include stories and autoethnography. Her detailed explanation as well as numerous references will help you if you decide you want to try this method.

In summary, I presented two types of analysis: concept/theme analysis and narrative analysis. In the section on concept/theme analysis, I first spoke about the three *C*s and then provided you with a six-step process to move from raw data to concepts/themes. This process is generic in nature and not associated with any one research approach that I discussed in Chapters 5 and 6. It incorporates ideas from many different research approaches and analysis ideas. I also discussed the idea of analyzing based on narrative or storytelling. What follows are two sections. In the first, I talk about the various QR approaches I described in Chapters 5 and 6 and the procedures associated with analyzing data. In the second, I discuss various analytic techniques that sometimes are used but are not specifically associated with any single research approach.

Qualitative Research Approaches and Data Analysis

I find it very frustrating to try to describe specifically how to conduct analyses. On the one hand, I presented you with a number of major QR approaches earlier in this book. Most of these do not focus on the analysis of the data. Almost all of the material you read will leave you with more questions than answers. It would be very nice if each research approach had a specific data analysis technique associated with it. But that is not the case. It is almost as though qualitative analysis techniques came about independent of research approaches. With the exception of grounded theory, most of the other research approaches are vague with respect to analysis. But to try to help you get a better understanding of the connection between research approach and analytic technique, I want to comment briefly on how the various research approaches you learned about in Chapters 5 and 6 connect with different types of data analysis techniques.

If you were following an ethnographic approach, no specific guideposts are suggested, but you would focus on an understanding of the culture. Often, your data include field notes based on observations. You might also have data from informal interviews. You probably will have visual data as well. Your analysis will typically involve coding and looking for themes. The multistep process I described earlier can be used if you were doing ethnography.

If you were following a grounded theory approach, you would adopt a very specific three-part coding approach: open coding, axial coding, and selective coding. This is also referred to as the *constant-comparative method*. If you choose this approach, it would be helpful to review Strauss and Corbin's (1990) detailed explanation for this multistep coding process. You could also look closely at Charmaz's (2006) text. See also the discussion below under constant-comparative method.

If you were following a phenomenological tradition, you would be interested in the lived experiences of the individuals. You will need to explore some of the philosophical underpinnings of phenomenology, and your data analysis would be facilitated if you bracketed your views. You might choose to conduct either narrative analysis or thematic analysis.

If you were following a case study approach, you might use single cases and then multiple cases, treating each case separately and then comparing cases. Some analysts use cross-case comparisons. How you analyze the data is left unstated in written material about this approach.

If you were following a feminist tradition, you would concentrate on examining power disparities.

If you were following a generic approach, you would look for general themes or use narratives.

If you were following narrative analysis, or biographical, autobiographical, or life history traditions, you might concentrate on the gathered stories and narratives and look for epiphanies. You might choose narrative, content, conversation, or discourse analysis.

If you were following a postmodernist or critical theoretical approach, you might look at issues of sexuality and gender. Because these approaches are more theoretical than practical, analyses are very general.

If you were using mixed methods, you would tend to organize your data and construct tables as well as look for themes. You might also connect data from the two approaches.

Perhaps the preceding discussion simply highlights the lack of clarity between QR approaches and how to conduct an analysis. At times, you will see references to very specific qualitative analytic techniques. Below I list and give examples of some of the major ones.

Additional Qualitative Analysis Techniques or Procedures

Just as various disciplines have influenced the approaches qualitative researchers take in designing their research and gathering data, so too have a variety of disciplines influenced ways in which researchers deal with their data. Saldaña (2009) has taken a somewhat different approach. His work provides very detailed information about all types of coding. He suggested that there are first- and second-cycle coding methods. First-cycle methods include a number of subcategories (e.g., grammatical, affective, and exploratory). Second-cycle methods are concerned with classifying, integrating, and conceptualizing data. His very detailed manual provides numerous specific examples for coding using various kinds of methods. Here are just a few examples drawn from his text. Most of us think about coding for a particular topic or content. Saldaña calls this *descriptive coding*. But you might also code for attributes, where you identify age, gender, or marital status. What Saldaña allows us to see is that first-level coding can be along a number of dimensions—not just content or topic. I find this helpful as I explore coding steps. As I just mentioned, few research designs provide specifics about analysis procedures, while others are either silent or very general. Next, I list some of the major analytic techniques.

Generic Approach

Although there are a number of specific analytic techniques associated with various research approaches, many qualitative researchers use a generic approach to coding. The procedure I outlined previously is a generic style. Creswell (2009) has stated this cogently: "Often we see qualitative data analysis reported in journal articles or books that is a generic form of analysis. In this approach, the researcher collects qualitative data, analyzes it for themes or perspectives, and reports 4–5 themes" (p. 184). For Saldaña (2009), generic coding (both first- and second-cycle coding methods) includes attribute coding and descriptive coding as well as coding for patterns. I reviewed a number of QR studies to determine the approach used. Many discussed coding and looking for themes but did not discuss details of how the coding was accomplished or how the themes were derived from the codes.

Constant-Comparative Method

The constant-comparative method is an analytic procedure closely associated with grounded theory. Its steps involve open coding, axial coding, and selective coding. Open coding is the first step—raw data are examined to begin to develop names and categories. Axial coding is the second step of the constant-comparative method. Moving from the open codes, the researcher relates the initial codes to one another. Finally, the researcher applies selective coding in which choices are made regarding the most important codes. A hierarchy is developed, and one or a small number of codes are chosen to represent the key concepts drawn from the raw data. Ultimately, theory is derived from the concepts. Strauss and Corbin (1990) have provided specific examples of how to use this procedure. Charmaz (2006) also takes you through some of the details. Kirchhoff and Lawrenz (2011), in their study of teacher education, provided an excellent and detailed explanation of how to do such coding. Allen (2011) applied the method in her feminist approach to grounded theory. This detailed procedure involves line-by-line coding from which concepts appear. Her article offers examples of the raw data, the initial codes, and the focused codes. Eich (2008) provided more details of how to use this method in his grounded-theory study of student leadership development programs. Connolly (2003) has adapted and simplified this method, which she refers to in general terms as *qualitative data analysis*. She identifies three phases: generative, interpretive, and theorizing.

Content (Textual) Analysis

Content analysis has been around since Lasswell introduced the idea of studying the content of communication. Krippendorff wrote about it in 1980 (see also Krippendorff, 2004.) Some qualitative researchers are drawn to it, I suspect, because it has a structure and is more in keeping with the position of looking for rigor and acceptance. Hsieh and Shannon (2005) identified three approaches to content analysis. In what they called a *conventional content analysis*, coding categories were derived directly from text. In a *direct approach to content analysis*, a theory or prior research is used to guide the analysis in the initial coding. A third type is *summative analysis*; in this latter approach, counting categories precedes the interpretation. It seems to me that these three approaches are a continuum, from less to more conservative. Denny (2011) used content analysis to explore gender differences in the messages of handbooks and other material from boy and girl scouts. She was interested in the content, the context, and the approach. I found the variety of information she coded fascinating. For example, she looked at badges and badge activities for boys and girls. I was surprised to learn that there were 20 badges and 323 activities for boys and 104 badges and 1440 badge activities for girls. So, you can see the process was very detailed and tedious. Sonpar and Golden-Biddle (2008) used content analysis of qualitative archival data to elaborate on theories of adolescence.

Conversation Analysis

As its name implies, conversation analysis is a detailed analysis of the talk between two or more individuals. Coming from the field of sociolinguistics, the careful study of talk was originally started by Sacks. It is available to view as an online tutorial (Antaki, n.d.). You might also find Belouin's (2010) blog helpful in understanding this approach.

Discourse Analysis

Discourse analysis is a technique with several interpretations. It was originally interpreted as analyzing structure of text content in terms of syntax and semantics. When influenced by poststructural or postmodern views of the world, this procedure "is concerned with the way in which texts themselves have been constructed in terms of their social and historical 'situatedness'" (Cheek, 2004, p. 1144). Prins and Toso (2008) employed discourse analysis in their analysis of a widely used parent profile instrument. Freshwater and her colleagues (2010), writing in the field of nursing, were concerned with QR as evidence and presented clear discussions about ways in which discourse analysis coupled with autoethnography can be seen to have suitable rigor and relevance. Foucauldian discourse analysis emphasizes power relationships and subjectivity. Garrity (2010) discussed the complexity of some of these issues and urged considering some of the complexities of the theory. Fear (2012) distinguishes between Foucauldian discourse analysis and critical discourse analysis; he concludes that these two types can be complementary.

Interpretative Phenomenological Analysis

This analytic approach involves the detailed examination of the lived experience of individuals. It is influenced by hermeneutics. Owens and her colleagues (2011) applied the approach in a study of urban African American males' perceptions of school counseling services.

Qualitative Comparative Analysis

Ragin (1987) developed **qualitative comparative analysis** (QCA) when dealing with comparison across cases. According to Greckhamer, Misangyi, Elms, and Lacey (2008), its purpose is to preserve the complexity of a single case while making comparisons across cases. It has primarily been used in sociology and political science and is more closely associated with conservative or traditional approaches to qualitative analysis.

I believe that many of these analytic approaches were developed to systematize the analysis of qualitative data. All assume that the data are represented by words. They are not as well established as quantitative procedures, and, as you can see, current researchers are still modifying many of the techniques. My philosophy is that, unless you are following a grounded theory approach, you will be best served by using a generic approach and following the steps I outlined earlier in the chapter. This will lead you to a concept/theme presentation. However, if you are interested in using a narrative analysis, then a more global strategy will enable you to weave together a narrative based on your data. Perhaps the last word on coding comes from Woodby and her colleagues (2011), who wrote about the emotional stress of coding on the researchers as they worked with after-death interviews of family members. This led them to write about how qualitative inquiry can impact the emotional well-being of researchers. This may seem a little extreme, but then again, I didn't do the type of coding they did.

Whatever analysis process you choose, there are a number of issues that arise regarding analysis.

Issues in Analysis

What About Transcribing?

There is considerable discussion in the literature, on LISTSERVs, and on the Internet about transcribing interviews. Some want to know whether they need to transcribe their interviews. In one such interchange in May 2011, a user asks whether the audio can be used directly. Several respondents assure him that QDA packages are available, and audio and transcript information can be synched. Most researchers agree that interviews need to be transcribed. Davidson (2010), in a study of the conversation of young children, wrote in detail about the need for transcription, especially since she was conducting a conversation analysis. Some think the researcher needs to do it directly; others concede that someone else might perform the task. In either case, it is generally recommended that the actual words should be used. For some analyses, it is critical. Hammersley (2010) raised a different point. He suggested that using actual transcriptions is a more rigorous type of evidence than field notes, because it offers a more accurate representation of what happened. He is also interested in capturing a description of behaviors.

Some equipment on the market that transcribes audiotapes is not yet perfected. (See Johnson, 2011, for his comparison of voice-recognition software [VRS] with a listen-and-type method. His conclusion is that the latter method takes less time and is more accurate.) Perhaps, by the time you begin your research, better equipment will be available. But for now, you will need to transcribe your interview data—not write a summary. This is, of course, time consuming and quite difficult, especially if you have focus group data. Some will hire a person to transcribe their data, but, in my view, it is worth the effort to do it on your own. Bailey (2008) argued that because transcribing is not just a straightforward and simple task but involves judgment questions about the level of detail to include, the researcher should do the work.

In contrast to the process described earlier, some researchers believe that the analysis process involves identifying salient stories that either emerge from the data or are constructed as composites from bits and pieces of several data sources. For them, the meaning is in the story and in the researcher's interpretation of the story. This process works best if you have interview data from a number of individuals, although I have also used it with detailed and extensive interviews from one or two individuals. Those who adopt this stance take the position that coding raw data into concepts is a reductionistic practice and detracts from the meaning of what is said. (See Chase, 2005, and Riessman, 2005, for additional details about the process.)

How to Know When You Are Finished

Unlike statistical analysis, qualitative analysis has no defined end. You do not create statistical tables or statements about hypotheses. Rather, the process you follow seems to reach a logical saturation point. You collect your data and analyze your data at the same time. At some point, you complete collecting data. That point is often dictated by time or availability of people to interview or scenes to observe. I believe that you will know when you have sufficient data. Glaser (1978) referred to this as "theoretical saturation"; you find that you are not learning anything new. Your analysis follows the same idea. You read through your text. You code chunks, whether large or small. You reread your data. You change your codes. You combine your codes. You add codes. You delete codes. You combine your codes into categories. Your concepts come out of the categories. You reread your data. You look at new data. And so it goes.

Now, it is time to combine these codes into categories and then into concepts. You begin your sifting and sorting process anew, but you are working from the codes, not the raw data. You look to see whether the codes can be combined into categories. You try to winnow the number of codes down to a manageable number of categories. You restructure your codes into major categories and subcategories. Again, you work through a distillation from which concepts emerge from your categories.

Your final step is to select supporting evidence for the concepts you have developed. This evidence is often in the form of quotations from the raw data. Once done, you are ready to write.

Again, if your goal is to use narratives, this detailed analysis might not be used.

Philosophical Stance

I agree with many writers who say that qualitative analysis is the least understood and most complex of all aspects of conducting QR. I think it is important for you to clarify your views about the process of analysis, but first, I want to reveal mine.

As the researcher, you are the best equipped to make sense of the data. Using others to verify your interpretations assumes that there are right concepts to find or that some findings are better than others. Get rid of that notion. Unlike in statistical analysis, in QR analysis there is nothing that says that one set of interpretations is better than another. Now, that does not mean that you might not make a case for one set of interpretations over another, based on your raw data, but "experts" are not needed here. You should be closer to your data than anyone else.

Using computer software makes the process easier; it does not give more reliable or believable results. The hard work of sifting, sorting, coding, organizing, and extracting remains yours.

The analysis is an integral part of the process of QR. As such, it must begin early in your project. You should not wait until all your data are collected before you begin to think about your analysis. There are various procedures that you can choose to follow; whichever you choose, you need to document how you carried out your analysis.

It is important not to get to the end too quickly. The data need to be looked at several times. Don't jump to conclusions and concepts too quickly. That often leads to superficial analyses that don't really add much new information to the literature.

What about the role of theory? Although there is not agreement that theory building is part of QR, some writers support the idea, especially when using grounded theory. And you should be aware of this. Wright (2007) described how she connects data analysis to theory building for her students studying public health. I like her suggestion of using a photograph of a coal mining child to evoke issues of public health. The students were asked to write a story about the child from the photograph. That was their first attempt at coding. After practicing coding, they then practiced reducing the data. They then moved into theory building by looking at how creative and imaginative explorations can enhance systematized mechanical coding. I am particularly drawn to the visual display of data, which you can see in her interesting article.

Data Analysis With Computer Software

By now, you are probably asking yourself, how you will manage all of this? I remember one student telling me that she made 3×5 cards with codes and hung them on the wall in her basement. She placed some codes under others, thereby creating categories with subcategories. She could move these around and regroup in order to organize them into concepts. Another way to organize into categories is to use markers or pencils of different colors and to sort like colors together. If you have a small amount of data, this works pretty well. But even with a small amount of data, you lose the links between the raw data you have coded, the codes and categories you have developed, and your concepts. And what happens if you have a large amount of data? This is where computer programs enter the arena.

As I said earlier, I expect that you will have entered your data into a word processing program. This is, of course, valid for data that are in words. At a basic level, you can use a word processing program to find a given word or phrase in the text. For example, Microsoft Word has a "Find" feature that searches text and indicates each instance of a particular word or phrase. You could begin to code your raw data by asking the program to find a given phrase, then highlighting it, and changing the text color. Next, you could give each of those phrases the same code. You could do this for each set of raw data you have. Of course, you would have to keep track of the color and coding scheme that you have developed. There are several advantages to this simple process: (1) the ability to locate terms in text quickly, (2) the ability to identify text associated with the terms, and (3) the ease of storing and accessing information in comparison to the old way of color coding or sorting on the dining room table.

When I began teaching QR, I was very reluctant to use computers. It seemed to me that by using computers, I was buying into a paradigm that valued numbers, tables, and precision, yet I recognized that most QR took a different approach. What was I to do? I thought a qualitative software program might be too structured; in fact, I was not even sure what these programs did. We are a far cry from note cards and search-and-find features of basic word processing programs. There are now a fairly substantial number of sophisticated computer programs that permit a more elaborate system of coding, searching, and retrieval of information.

About a dozen years ago I traveled to London to learn about using NUD*IST, the predecessor of NVivo. I worked directly with Silvana di Gregorio, at that time, the main expert in the software. We worked for a week on details of the software, applying techniques to our own data. A year or so later, I again traveled to London to give a presentation demonstrating the use of the software. I heard Lyn Richards discuss the work. My review (Lichtman, 2005) of Heaton's book on reworking qualitative data appeared in *Forum: Qualitative Social Research* (*FQS*). Subsequently, I taught courses to graduate students using this software. In my experience, the software has powerful capabilities, with more being developed. There is a long learning curve for this software, but with seminars now offered in the United States in various locations as well as online, students might find this software more user friendly. Bernauer, Jacobs, and I presented a paper at TQR in Florida in January 2013 illustrating the use of NVivo in generic analysis. (See http://qsrinternational.com for details about the latest version of the software.)

Often known as QDA software or as Computer Assisted/Aided Qualitative Data AnalysiS (CAQDAS), as a number of software programs have been developed. Four are thoroughly described in di Gregorio and Davidson's (2008) comprehensive text: ATLAS.ti, MAXqda, NVivo, and XSight.

For a detailed discussion on QDA software, I recommend you read the special issue of *FQS* (2011, volume 12, issue 1). Here is a brief summary: The KWALON experiment involved five developers of QDA software in the analysis of a data set regarding the financial crisis in Europe during 2008–2009. Although not dealing with qualitative data per se, you can get a taste of the many issues surrounding its use (Evers, Silver, Mruck, & Peeters, 2011).

QSR International has been one of the leaders in the field. You can read about their programs on the website (http://www.qsrinternational.com/). I am most familiar with the software this company offers. NVivo will allow you to perform a number of functions that I will describe subsequently. I suspect other software products will allow you to perform similar functions. NVivo has additional functions not described below.

Importing files into a project. You can import any text material into the program directly from your word processing program. You can bring in one or many files at the same time. This saves an incredible amount of time. You can also link any other material that is nontextual through a process of external links. Thus, if you have photographs or audio material that you do not want to lose, you can make links directly to your master file. New material can easily be added. You can also bring in results of your literature review. Thus, all of your data—whether interview data, photographs, references, or notes—can be organized and placed in the same project. This is a tremendous advantage, even if the program does nothing else for you. The latest versions of NVivo have the capacity to handle videos and audio. It is also available in Chinese and Spanish.

Coding information in your project. You can begin coding the various files you have in your project. Some simple keystrokes will enable you to mark a word, line, sentence, or section and code for that piece of data with whatever term you want. The program makes a list of the various codes you have chosen. As your coding progresses, you might find that you have used terms that are similar. The program will let you combine several codes if you wish. New codes can always be added and others deleted. You can also code demographic information and develop tables and charts. If desired, the data can be exported into SPSS Statistical Package for the Social Sciences (SPSS; a software package) or a spreadsheet for display or analysis.

Organizing codes in your project. You can begin organizing the various codes you have developed into a series of nodes with branches. This is similar to putting codes into categories and subsets. In a way, this is how you begin to take your raw data, code them, and develop concepts. The program has enormous flexibility with these nodes.

Searching in your project. One of the great strengths of this program is that you can conduct complex searches once you have coded your data. There are more than a dozen types of searches that you can conduct. Once you decide what you want to do, the program will locate information from any of your files and bring it into a new file and provide ready access.

Building models. You can develop models representing your theoretical position, either prior to your analysis or subsequent to it. Attractive graphics facilitate this task.

Other capabilities. You can create a file for your personal memos or self-reflections and add these to your project at any time. You can manage an enormous amount of data in a single project. You can work on your project with others and share your ideas. QSR training has now reached the United States; the developers are readily available to answer your questions. The website is very accessible. Although based in Australia, they often are in England at workshops and presentations. QSR provides online support and runs a LISTSERV, where most of your questions can be answered.

Limitations. As you can tell, I really like this program. But I will be the first to admit that it is very difficult to learn. I don't think you can learn it on your own, so you need to decide whether it is worth the effort. A student version is available at a reduced cost. If you get it and use it, I believe it will open up many ideas to you that you have not thought of before.

You can read about other computer software programs such as Ethnograph, ATLAS.ti, and so on. I write about QSR International products to illustrate the best of what is out there. However, if you have a small amount of data and a small budget, go for the old-fashioned method. Make use of your computer word processing programs as best as you can.

Shulman (2011) has developed Textifier, mentioned in Chapter 6, a program that captures live data from social media such as Facebook or Twitter and enables basic coding of text. I participated in a webinar that demonstrated the ease with which the system works. One caveat is in order: As of Spring 2011, the coding was limited to basic two or three levels of response (e.g., positive, neutral, or negative).

At a 2010 conference comparing five software packages, Woods and Dempster (2011) described Transana (http://www.transana.org/), a qualitative analytic software that can examine multiple simultaneous video streams.

Most important to remember is that using qualitative software does not increase the type or level of analysis of your data. You are still the medium through which codes are established and data are organized and integrated. The software makes the management of the data easier, but you will need to weigh the value of its use against its cost and time to learn the intricacies of how to use it. A number of discussions appear on LISTSERVs as to which software is better, which is more cost-effective, and so on. As you can guess, there is no general agreement on this.

Other Issues

In what ways can cloud computing be affected by and affect QR? While not technically a software program, cloud computing (introduced in Chapter 8) enables computational resources on demand by using a computer network. Such a paradigm enables users—whether or not they have a particular piece of software—to access the software on demand and pay accordingly. Since it exists in a virtual environment, it is basically in the clouds. Mei, Chan, and Tse (2008) have referred to this paradigm as a way to share data, calculations, and services transparently among many users on a massive grid. Oza, Karppinen, and Savola (2010) reported on a qualitative study of expert users from the Finnish Cloud Software Program Consortium.

How can Web 2.0 be useful in qualitative analysis? Also discussed in Chapter 8, Web 2.0 is associated initially with Darcy NiNucci, who coined the term in 1999. O'Reilly Media ran a Web 2.0 conference in 2004. Today, it is associated with web applications that facilitate information sharing and collaboration on the Web. It has been described as a revolutionary way to create, collaborate, edit, and share user-generated content online—what a great arena for qualitative researchers. Duffy (2008) described a number of QR groups on Web 2.0 social networking sites. She sees their value as incubators for innovation. But I think Europe and the Far East are ahead of the United States on this topic. A conference on QR in social media and Web 2.0 was held in Macau in 2011. The 4th European Conference on Computer-Aided Qualitative Research was scheduled for September 2011 in Switzerland. The latest technologies to be discussed are desktop software, mobile computing, and Web 2.0 platforms.

Secondary analysis of qualitative data is a fairly new idea. Heaton's thoughtful book on reworking qualitative data highlights some important issues (Lichtman, 2005). Corti (2007) has provided information about a project conducted in Finland dealing with archived qualitative data. Mruck (2005) commented on this and issues of data archiving and data protection in her editorial in a special issue of *FQS* on qualitative secondary data analysis.

A number of issues have surfaced recently regarding the use of the Internet and qualitative data. Can you use qualitative data that is found on the Internet for your study? Shulman recently posted in an email that he had captured a large number of tweets related to Bin Laden. He made them available to his research community, but within a day, he was asked not to do so. They have been removed from his site. How can you organize and process data you collect on the Internet? Are there available tools to facilitate this process?

A number of online journals make qualitative data available to the marketplace. How can you gain access? How useful is it? Is secondary analysis of qualitative data legitimate?

Should data be archived? What about the quality of the data? Who should have access? Who should maintain the files? The Irish Qualitative Data Archive (2013) is an example of large efforts made in this arena. Available currently are the following: data sets representing oral history about the relationship between Catholic and Protestants, containing over a hundred interviews; other oral history archives—one involving children traced over a five-year time period; and a photographic archive of more than 30,000 photographs, covering the time period from the 1970s and onward. The university offers a number of courses that provide instruction on key areas of social change in Ireland. SlideShare serves as a teaching resource. This comprehensive effort can be a valuable source for researchers. Gray's (2012) presentation addresses such issues as ownership, accessibility, and keeping anonymity.

■ Summary

Unlike QN, QR—with the exception of grounded theory—lacks prescriptive guides to data analysis, although several approaches are suggested: constant-comparative method, content analysis, discourse analysis, and QCA. Most approaches are based on identifying concepts or telling stories. Regardless of which approach you use, you are a key tool in the analysis process, and you need to document your process.

The three *C*s of data analysis are coding, categorizing, and concepts. I suggest a six-step process: (1) initial coding, (2) revisiting initial coding, (3) developing an initial list of categories or central ideas, (4) modifying your initial list based on additional rereading, (5) revisiting categories and subcategories, and (6) moving from categories to concepts.

For larger data sets, computer programs such as NVivo or other QDA software programs can increase efficiency.

CHECK YOURSELF

- In general, QDA involves one of two approaches—coding data and looking for concepts/themes or developing narratives. Thematic analysis involves detailed examination of verbal data with the ultimate purpose of identifying the key ideas in the data. Narrative analysis involves looking for the central story in the data.
- When using the concept approach, there are three main steps in analysis—coding, categorizing, and concepts. These steps can further be broken down into six phases.

- When using the narrative approach, the coding process is more general, and often, details are not made explicit. The details of how to conduct a narrative analysis or often not specified
- Some analysis approaches are specific, while others more general. There are many different approaches that are too specific to learn about in this overview.

KEY DISCUSSION ISSUES

1. I have described two ways to analyze your data. One involves looking for themes or concepts. The other involves using narratives. What are the differences between the two? Is one better than the other?
2. In conducting an analysis for themes/concepts, I describe six steps. What are they? What is the value of all this detailed work?
3. What is meant by doing narrative analysis? Does this make sense to you?
4. Are there different analysis strategies associated with the different research approaches you learned about? What are they?
5. What about all the different analysis techniques? Which ones are important to learn?
6. Should you use computer software? What are the issues if you do choose to use it?

MODULE 12A

From Coding to Concepts

Group Activity

Purpose: Move from coding to concept development

Activity: Select a piece of writing from the Internet. You can use a blog, a newspaper article, or other current topic. Have each class member provide codes of the text. Form small groups to review the codes together and categorize the codes into concepts. Compare concepts from different small groups.

Evaluation: Explore the extent to which individuals are able to move from codes to concepts.

MODULE 12B

Narrative Analysis

Individual Activity

Purpose: Practice narrative analysis

Activity: Write a short paper using metaphors to describe an important event in your life. Share your paper with class members. Compare analyses using coding and concepts with analyses using narratives.

Evaluation: Determine in what ways class members are able to make meaning from each method of analysis.

REFERENCES

Allen, M. (2011). Violence and voice: Using a feminist constructivist grounded theory to explore women's resistance to abuse. *Qualitative Research, 11*(1), 23–45.

Ambrose, S., & Brinkley, D. (2001). *Johnson Space Center oral history project*. Retrieved from http://www.nasa.gov/pdf/62281main_ armstrong_oralhistory.pdf

Antaki, C. (n.d.). *An introductory tutorial in conversational analysis*. Retrieved from http://homepages.lboro.ac.uk/~ssca1/intro1.htm

Bailey, J. (2008). First steps in qualitative data analysis: Transcribing. *Family Practice, 25*(2), 127–131.

Banyai, M., & Glover, T. (2012). Evaluating research methods on travel blogs. *Journal of Travel Research, 51*(3), 267–277.

Basit, T. (2003, Summer). Manual or electronic? The role of coding in qualitative data analysis. *Educational Researcher, 45*(2), 143–154.

Baumgartner, L. (2000). *Narrative analysis: Uncovering the truth of stories*. Retrieved from http://www.adulterc.org/Proceedings/2000/baumgartner11-final.PDF

Bazeley, P. (2009). Analysing qualitative data: More than "identifying themes." *Malaysian Journal of Qualitative Research, 2*, 6–22. Retrieved from http://www.researchsupport.com.au/More_ than_themes.pdf

Belouin. (2010). *Mixing social science and software design*. [Web log]. Retrieved from http://www.belouin.com/blog/2010/03/conversation-analysis-a-practical-example-of-application/

Bernauer, J., Jacobs, C., & Lichtman, M. (2013). Using NVivo to analyze data based on a generic approach. Retrieved from http://www.nova.edu/ssss/QR/TQR2013/program.pdf

Bosk, E. (2011). Review of Wells's *Narrative Inquiry*. *Qualitative Social Work, 10*(4), 537–554.

Bronken, B., Kirkevold, M., Martinsen, R., & Kvigne, K. (2012). The aphasic storyteller: Co-constructing stories to promote psychosocial well-being after stroke. *Qualitative Health Research, 22*(10), 1303–1316.

Charmaz, K. (2002). Stories and silences: Disclosures and self in chronic illness. *Qualitative Inquiry, 8*(3), 302–328.

Charmaz. K. (2006). *Constructing grounded theory: A practical guide through qualitative analysis*. Thousand Oaks, CA: SAGE.

Chase, S. (2005). Narrative inquiry: Multiple lenses, approaches, voices. In N. K. Denzin & Y. S. Lincoln (Eds.), *The SAGE handbook of qualitative research* (3rd ed., pp. 651–679). Thousand Oaks, CA: SAGE.

Cheek, J. (2004). At the margins? Discourse analysis and qualitative research. *Qualitative Health Research, 14*(8), 1140–1150.

Coffey, A., & Atkinson, P. (1996). *Making sense of qualitative data: Complementary research strategies*. Thousand Oaks, CA: SAGE.

Connelly, F. M., & Clandinin, D. J. (1990). Stories of experience and narrative inquiry. *Educational Researcher, 19*(5), 5.

Connolly, M. (2003). Qualitative analysis: A teaching tool for social work research. *Qualitative Social Work, 2*(1), 103–112.

Cortazzi, M. (2002). *Narrative analysis: Falmer social research and educational studies series, no. 12*. London, England: Falmer Press/Routledge.

Corti, L. (2007). Re-using archived qualitative data—where, how, why? *Archival Science, 7*(1), 37–54.

Creswell, J. (2009). *Research design: Qualitative, quantitative, and mixed methods approaches* (3rd ed.). Thousand Oaks, CA: SAGE.

Davidson, C. (2010). Transcription matters. *Journal of Early Childhood Research, 8*(2), 115–131.

Denny, K. E. (2011). Gender in context, content, and approach. *Gender & Society, 25*(1), 27–47.

Denzin, N. (1989). *Interpretive interactionism*. Newbury Park, CA: SAGE.

di Gregorio, S., & Davidson, J. (2008). *Qualitative research design for software users*. Maidenhead, UK: Open University Press.

Duffy, M. (2008). A review of qualitative research groups in Web 2.0 social networking communities: Prepare to be amused, inspired, and even blown away. *The Weekly Qualitative Report, 1*(5), 25–30. Retrieved from http://www.nova.edu/ssss/QR/WQR/facebook.pdf

Edwards, R., & Weller, S. (2012). Shifting analytic ontology: Using I-poems in qualitative longitudinal research. *Qualitative Research, 12*(2), 202–217.

Eich, D. (2008). A grounded theory of high-quality leadership programs: Perspectives from student leadership development programs in higher education. *Journal of Leadership & Organizational Studies, 15*, 176–187.

Evers, J. C., Silver, C., Mruck, K., & Peeters, B. (2011). Introduction to the KWALON experiment: Discussions on qualitative data analysis software by developers and users [28 paragraphs]. *Forum Qualitative Sozialforschung/Forum: Qualitative Social Research, 12*(1), Art. 40. Retrieved from http://nbn-http://www.qualitative-research.net/index.php/fqs/issue/view/36

Fear, W. (2012). Discursive activity in the boardroom: The role of the minutes in the construction of social realities. *Group & Organization Management, 37*(4), 486–520.

Fielding, N. (2004). Getting the most from archived qualitative data: Epistemological, practical and professional obstacles. *International Journal of Social Research Methodology, 7*(1), 97–104.

Freshwater, D., Cahill, J., Walsh, E., & Muncey, T. (2010). Qualitative research as evidence: Criteria for rigour and relevance. *Journal of Research in Nursing, 15*(6), 497–508.

Frost, N., Nolas, S. M., Brooks-Gordon, B., Esin, C., Holt, A., Mehdizadeh, L., & Shinebourne, P. (2010). Pluralism in qualitative research: The impact of different researchers and qualitative approaches on the analysis of qualitative data. *Qualitative Research, 10*(4), 441–460.

Garrity, Z. (2010). Discourse analysis, Foucault and social work research. *Journal of Social Work, 10*(2), 193–210.

Glaser, B. G. (1978). *Theoretical sensitivity: Advances in the methodology of grounded theory*. Mill Valley, CA: Sociology Press.

Gray, J. (2012). *Sharing and re-using qualitative data in Ireland*. Retrieved from http://www.iqda.ie/sites/default/files/Sharing%20and%20re-using%20qualitative%20data%20in%20Ireland_upload.pdf

Greckhamer, T., Misangyi, V., Elms, H., & Lacey, R. (2008). Using qualitative comparative analysis in strategic management research. *Organizational Research Methods, 11*, 695–726.

Griffin, M. (2011). Book review: H. L. Goodall Jr., *Writing qualitative inquiry: Self, stories, and academic life. Qualitative Research, 11*(2), 219–220.

Guy, L., & Montague, J. (2008). Analysing men's written friendship narratives. *Qualitative Research, 8*(3), 389–397.

Hammersley, M. (2010). Reproducing or constructing? Some questions about transcription in social research. *Qualitative Research, 10*(5), 553–569.

Hannes, K., & Macaitis, K. (2012). A move to more systematic and transparent approaches in qualitative evidence synthesis: Update on a review of published papers. *Qualitative Research, 12*(4), 402–442.

Hsieh, H., & Shannon, S. (2005). Three approaches to qualitative content analysis. *Qualitative Health Research, 15*(9), 1277–1288.

Irish Qualitative Data Archive. (2013). *IQDA* Retrieved from http://www.iqda.ie/content/teaching-qualitative-research

James, A. (2012, June). Seeking the analytic imagination: Reflections on the process of interpreting qualitative data. *Qualitative Research*, 1–16.

Johnson, B. E. (2011). The speed and accuracy of voice recognition software-assisted transcription versus the listen-and-type method: A research note. *Qualitative Research, 11*(1), 91–97.

Johnson, S. (2004). *Mind wide open: Your brain and the neuroscience of everyday life*. New York, NY: Scribner.

Kaufmann, J. (2011). Poststructural analysis: Analyzing empirical matter for new meanings. *Qualitative Inquiry, 17*(2), 148–154.

Keats, P. A. (2009). Multiple text analysis in narrative research: Visual, written, and spoken stories of experience. *Qualitative Research, 9*(2), 181–195.

Kirchhoff, A., & Lawrenz, F. (2011). The use of grounded theory to investigate the role of teacher education on STEM teachers' career paths in high-need schools. *Journal of Teacher Education, 62*(3), 246–259.

Krippendorff, K. (2004). *Content analysis: An introduction to its method*. London, England: SAGE.

Labov, W. (1972). *Language in the inner city: Studies in the Black English vernacular*. Philadelphia, PA: University of Pennsylvania Press.

Labov, W., & Waletzky, J. (1967). Narrative analysis: Oral versions of personal experience. In J. Helms (Ed.), *Essays on the verbal and visual arts* (pp. 12–44). Seattle, WA: American Ethnological Society/University of Washington Press.

Langellier, K. M. (1989). Personal narratives: Perspectives on theory and research. *Text and Performance Quarterly, 9*, 243–276.

Li, W., Hodgetts, D., & Stolte, O. (2011). *The use of visual narratives in research with older Chinese immigration*. Retrieved from http://www.slideshare.net/NZPSSconf/the-use-of-visual-narrative-wendy-li

Li, S., & Seale, C. (2007). Learning to do qualitative data analysis: An observational study of doctoral work. *Qualitative Health Research, 17*(10), 1442–1452.

Lichtman, M. (2005). Review: Janet Heaton (2004). Reworking qualitative data [25 paragraphs]. *Forum Qualitative Sozialforschung/Forum: Qualitative Social Research, 6*(3), Art 15. Retrieved from http://nbn-resolving.de/urn:nbn:de:0114-fqs0503150

Mei, L., Chan, W., & Tse, T. (2008). *A tale of clouds: Paradigm comparisons and some thoughts on research issues*. 2008 IEEE Asia-Pacific Services Computing Conference. Retrieved from http://ieeexplore.ieee.org/xpl/login.jsp?tp=&arnumber=4780718&url=http%3A%2F%2Fieeexplore.ieee.org%2Fxpls%2Fabs_all.jsp%3Farnumber%3D4780718

Morse, J. M. (1994). "Emerging from the data": The cognitive processes of analysis in qualitative inquiry. In J. M. Morse (Ed.), *Critical issues in qualitative research methods* (pp. 23–43). Thousand Oaks, CA: SAGE.

Morse, J. M. (2008). Styles of collaboration in qualitative inquiry. *Qualitative Health Research, 18*(1), 3–4.

Mruck, K. (2005). Editorial: The *FQS* issue on "secondary analysis of qualitative data" [6 paragraphs]. *Forum Qualitative Sozialforschung/Forum: Qualitative Social Research, 6*(1). Retrieved from http://www.qualitative-research.net/index.php/fqs/article/view/497/1066

Owens, D., Simmons, R. W., Bryant, R. M., & Henfield, M. (2011). Urban African American males' perceptions of school counseling services. *Urban Education, 46*(2), 165–177.

Oza, N., Karppinen, K., & Savola, R. (2010). *User experience and security in the cloud: An empirical study in the Finnish Cloud Consortium, Cloud Computing Technology and Science*. 2010 IEEE Second International Conference on Cloud Computing. Retrieved from http://ieeexplore.ieee.org/xpl/login.jsp?tp=&arnumber=5708510&url=http%3A%2F%2Fieeexplore.ieee.org%2Fxpls%2Fabs_all.jsp%3Farnumber%3D5708510

Paulson, S. (2011). The use of ethnography and narrative interviews in a study of "cultures of dance." *Journal of Health Psychology, 16*(1), 148–157. doi:10.1177/1359105310370500

Prins, E., & Toso, B. (2008). Defining and measuring parenting for educational success: A critical discourse analysis of the Parent Education Profile. *American Educational Research Journal, 45*(3), 555–596.

Q: Foundations of Qualitative Research in Education. (n.d.). *Narrative analysis*. Retrieved from http://isites.harvard.edu/icb/icb.do?keyword=qualitative&pageid=icb.page340896

Ragin, C. C. (1987). *The comparative method: Moving beyond qualitative and quantitative strategies*. Berkeley, CA: University of California Press.

Richmond, H. J. (2002, September). Learners' lives: A narrative analysis. *The Qualitative Report, 7*(3). Retrieved from http://www.nova.edu/ssss/QR/QR7-3/richmond.html

Riessman, C. K. (2005). Narrative in social work: A critical review. *Qualitative Social Work, 4*(4), 383–404.

Riessman, C. K. (2008). *Narrative methods for the human sciences.* Thousand Oaks, CA: SAGE.

Saldaña, J. (2009). *The coding manual for qualitative researchers.* London, England: SAGE.

Shulman, S. (2011). *Data mining research interview.* Retrieved from http://www.dataminingblog.com/data-mining-research-interview-stuart-shulman/

Simons, L., Lathlean, J., & Squire, C. (2008). Shifting the focus: Sequential methods of analysis with qualitative data. *Qualitative Health Research, 18*(1), 120–132.

Sonpar, K., & Golden-Biddle, K. (2008). Using content analysis to elaborate adolescent theories of organization. *Organizational Research Methods, 11*(4), 795–814.

Spector-Mersel, G. (2011). Mechanisms of selection in claiming narrative identities: A model for interpreting narratives. *Qualitative Inquiry, 17*(2), 172–185. doi:10.1177/1077800410393885

Strauss, A., & Corbin, J. (1990). *Basics of qualitative research: Grounded theory procedures and techniques* (2nd ed.). Newbury Park, CA: SAGE.

Sullivan, A., Joshi, H., & Leonard, D. (2010). Single-sex schooling and academic attainment at school and through the life-course. *American Educational Research Journal, 47*(1), 6–36.

Thorne, S. (2000). Data analysis in qualitative research. *Evidence-Based Nursing, 3,* 68–70.

University of California, Berkeley. (2011). *Visual research methods: Creating visual narratives.* [Web log]. Retrieved from http://blogs.ischool.berkeley.edu/VizNarrative/potential-readings/

Waite, D. (2011). A simple card trick: Teaching qualitative data analysis using a deck of playing cards. *Qualitative Inquiry, 17*(10), 982–985.

Ward, A. (2011). "Bringing the message forward": Using poetic re-presentation to solve research dilemmas. *Qualitative Inquiry, 17*(4), 355–363.

Woodby, L. L., Williams, B. R., Wittich, A. R., & Burgio, K. L. (2011). Expanding the notion of researcher distress: The cumulative effects of coding. *Qualitative Health Research, 21*(6), 830–838. doi:10.1177/1049732311402095

Woods, D., & Dempster, P. (2011). Tales from the bleeding edge: The qualitative analysis of complex video data using Transana [57 paragraphs]. *Forum Qualitative Sozialforschung/Forum: Qualitative Social Research, 12*(1), Art. 17. Retrieved from http://www.qualitative-research.net/index.php/fqs/article/view/1516

Wright, M. C. (2007). Making sense of data: How public health graduate students build theory through qualitative research techniques. *Qualitative Health Research, 17*(1), 94–101. doi:10.1177/10497 32306294296

Zilber, T., Tuval-Mashiach, R., & Lieblich, A. (2008). The embedded narrative: Navigating through multiple contexts. *Qualitative Inquiry, 14*(6), 1047–1069.

STUDENT STUDY SITE

Visit **http://www.sagepub.com/lichtmanqrss** to access additional study tools, including eFlashcards and links to SAGE journal articles.

CHAPTER 13

Communicating Your Ideas

Focus Your Reading

- Communicating your ideas in qualitative research is demanding and exciting.
- Writing that captures the reader's attention is extremely important.
- It is important to resist the temptation to write in a stilted fashion.

I am not a poet. I wish I was. I am not a writer of fiction. I wish I was. Nor do I write biography or memoirs. Qualitative writing and writers can be informed from these genres. A successful writer captures the audience—and the audience hankers for more. I do know this: When a writer engages a reader, it is something special. The reader stays with it—even into the wee hours of the night. It is more than just the story that grabs the reader. It is the way the story is told. Qualitative researchers have been experimenting with alternative ways of presenting information. Saldaña, Leavy, and Beretvas (2011) discussed eight types of qualitative writing. Caulley (2008) has urged us to make qualitative research (QR) reports less boring. Tierney and Hallett (2010) have asked us to look at the technique of scaffolding for effective writing and to find ways for scholars to develop their voices (p. 683). Norris's (2009) award-winning *Playbuilding as Qualitative Research* explores the theatrical genre known as collective creation, a Canadian technique of collaborative play development. I urge you to think about what you write, how you write, and how to engage the reader. For me, the personal is particularly important.

In this chapter, I discuss ways to write your QR final reports. I talk about several topics: structure of qualitative writing; the use of first person; integrating literature reviews into your writing; acknowledging the voice of informants; the value of the data; truth and fiction in writing; and alternative forms of presentation such as poetry, theater, blogs, videos, and audio. I also present an illustrative outline and samples from student work.

As a student in college or graduate school, you have been taught a number of characteristics of technical writing. It should be objective. It should be formal. You should not use first-person voice; third-person voice is preferred. It should be passive. It should be nonjudgmental. You should just report the facts. If you have an opportunity to look at a dissertation or a thesis, you will likely see a five-chapter account that includes the research problem, the related literature, methods, results, and conclusions or interpretations. Most traditional dissertations will have statistical tables and charts and graphs as well; few will have photographs or other images. With the widespread availability of computers, there is some tendency in the United States to present these works in online formats. Such formats enable the writer to use hyperlinks and other online tools. For the most part, however, the style is formal, cool, and crisp. This style is in keeping with a foundationalist or traditional view of research.

In this book, I present arguments for alternative research approaches. These alternative approaches often use alternative styles of presentation. You may encounter writing that is personal, involves the researcher, and makes use of first person. It is likely to be less formal; a traditional five-chapter account is often abandoned, and many structures and formats can be found. Headings may be derived from the voices of the informants. Many readers of this type of writing report being drawn to the accounts they read. Those studied take on a life of their own and are not just subjects in a research study. But unlike with traditional research, there is no standard form for writing QR.

Chenail (1995) asked us to consider several ideas when writing. Openness is critical because it builds trust between the reader and the researcher. Consequently, the writer should include information that is self-disclosing. I agree with him and recommend a section that I call "Self-Reflection." Chenail suggested focusing on the richness and depth of the data. He commented that a detailed and tight description should precede any generalizations. He introduced the idea of juxtaposing the data you collect with your explanations, analysis, and commentaries. I believe that the strength of what you write is revealed in your ability to convince the reader that your interpretations are reasonable and supported by the data. Whether your writing is accepted depends, in part, on how you weave your data into concepts. Van Maanen (1988), talking specifically about writing about cultures, suggested that the writer reconstruct in dramatic form an impressionistic tale as a way to crack "open the culture and the fieldworker's way of knowing it" (p. 102). He saw this as a way to "braid" the knower with the known (p. 102). In their award-winning study, Ewick and Silbey (2003) used stories of citizen resistance to authority. In particular, they were interested in how people in less powerful roles resist the law by small acts of defiance. From a sociological perspective, Ewick and Silbey looked at how these narratives about resistance can have more power than the resistance itself. Lockford (2013) discusses ways the writer can assert subjectivity in a postmodern text. She presents a personal account of taking her mother to a nursing home, commenting that "qualitative work allows me to account for the difficult and impossible journeys made in this passage from birth to death" (p. 163).

■ First Steps

Your task as a writer of QR, as Liu (2000) suggested, is to transform collected words into a piece of writing. Writing is not just putting down the words; it is making meaning of those words (Coffey & Atkinson, 1996; Liu, 2000). It would be a fairly simple task if you just needed to put down the words.

I want you to think about this idea carefully. How do you make meaning from the information (words or pictures) you have collected? The writing act is inextricably woven with the task of organizing and making sense of your data. I wrote about that extensively in Chapter 12. Here, we focus on the representation or presentation based on your analysis.

Let's first examine the structure of what you write. I suggest that there should be a structure in what you write, but there is no single or correct structure. So you are obliged to develop a structure that fits the data you have collected, the ideas you are trying to convey, and your personal style. It might be easier for me to explain this by telling you what it is not. First, there are no agreed-upon guidelines for the organization or format of what you write. You would know just how to proceed if you were writing a quantitative research (QN) article to be published in a journal or if you were writing a traditional master's thesis or doctoral dissertation or if you were writing a paper for a research class and the information you were presenting was based on a quantitative or experimental study. A journal would typically expect you to have headings such as Purpose, Related Literature, Methods, Results, and Discussion. A thesis or dissertation would usually follow a five-chapter format. A class research paper would generally use similar headings. You would usually include some tables summarizing your statistics. You would write in a third-person, objective fashion.

I want you to take yourself out of that mind-set now and imagine that you are free to develop your own structure and style. You ask yourself, how should I do that? What should I include? How much of myself can or should I include? How much of my participants' voices should be heard? Must my writing be dry and factual? Can I use metaphors and other rhetorical devices? Can I incorporate visuals in some manner? Can I include hyperlinks to information on the Internet? How long should it be? How can I justify my interpretation of what I learned? Will my work be judged acceptable? Are there clear lines between fact and fiction? Should there be?

Did You Know

To give prominence to particular ideas, you can create a word cloud using Wordle (http://www.wordle.net). A word cloud using Chorba's (2011) work provides an excellent example.

Before I ask you to suspend your current mind-set, let me tell you about what is out there. Schwandt's (2007) *SAGE Dictionary of Qualitative Inquiry* noted alternative means of communicating through poetry, film, drama, and dance. Ethnotheatre is an art form that uses theatrical techniques to present real research findings. Curtis (2008) described his use of verbatim theater (somewhat different from ethnotheatre) as an alternative form of qualitative presentation. Hill (2005) explored context and voice through poetry. Butler-Kisber (2002) also used poetry. Robertson (2006) presented the results of her research as a panel discussion. Lewis (2008) presented a documentary film using digital video and computer software in his research on a good teacher.

I have seen a great deal of interest in autoethnography (writing emotionally about the self, discussed in Chapter 6), in which the method and writing are intertwined (Bochner & Ellis, 2002; Holt, 2003). Bochner and Ellis (2002) have written extensively on the topic, and you can read many of their accounts in their edited volumes on alternative narratives. Ellis et al. (2008) are considered the driving force in what is called the *alternative ethnography movement*. I encourage you to explore their ideas; you will certainly read material that is stimulating. Adams (2012) writing reflects this so movingly.

I have seen QR presented as Greek theater (Speedy, 2011), as theater (Bagley, 2008; Garcia, 2008; Parry & Glover, 2011), as art (Hatch & Yanow, 2008), as metaphor (Denton, 2011), as poetry (Owton, 2011; Ward, 2011), as film or video (Downing, 2008; Woo, 2008), as dance (Fraser, 2008), as blogs (Mathison, 2011a, 2011b), or as digital ethnography (Hookway, 2008; Murthy, 2008). Of course, these approaches are quite extreme for someone just beginning, but you need to know they are out there.

I have seen all manner of written work varying by length, by format, by font, and so on. Variation by content is all too common. I suspect this is somewhat more than the mind can tolerate. People tend to want guidelines; they want some structure; they want authorities to suggest how to do things. With that in mind, accept my guidelines and admonitions. They are meant to serve as guidelines only—they should not be seen as rigid. You are to make the decisions.

■ Guidelines for Writing and Presenting Qualitative Research

Your Audience: What Does It Expect?

One of the first things you need to think about as you begin to write your research is the audience you are addressing. It might be your professor in a class you are taking. It might be the editors of a journal. It might be the readers of an online journal. It might be your thesis or dissertation committee. It might be a funding agency or the administration of a school system reading a project you completed. Academic journals seem to have the greatest number of rules and regulations and expectations. The best way to determine what they require is to read the guidelines for authors and to examine articles in current issues. For example, *Qualitative Inquiry* accepts papers from an interdisciplinary perspective. According to its guidelines, it publishes "research articles that experiment with manuscript form and content, and focus on methodological issues raised by qualitative research rather than the content or results of the research." If you want to experiment, this is the journal from which you can get a wealth of ideas. *The Qualitative Report* is an online journal. According to its editorial statement (*The Qualitative Report*, 2013), it is open to a variety of forms, including scholarly activity and debates. It also is open to journalistic and literary shapes that may pique the interest of readers. Both of these journals are based in the United States. For journalistic efforts in the United Kingdom, you can look at the *International Journal of Qualitative Studies in Education* or *Qualitative Research*. For a European perspective, I suggest you look at *Forum: Qualitative Social Research* (*FQS*), based in Berlin.

Sandelowski and Leeman (2012) claim that findings in qualitative health research are too often hard to understand. They recommend translating findings into thematic statements, which then can lead to intervention and implementation.

Different audiences and venues also have different expectations in terms of length. Journal articles might be limited to a dozen pages or less. A final paper for a class might be limited to 25 to 30 pages. A thesis might be about 100 pages, and a dissertation may be even longer.

What Are You Trying to Say?

Do you want to tell a story? Perhaps you are writing a biography or autoethnography. Your goal is to share the life of someone and describe the epiphanies in that life. Maybe you want to describe the lived experiences of individuals who have transferred to a new school. In such a phenomenological study, you might intend to identify a half dozen or so key ideas regarding such experiences as they make themselves known to you through the details of the many experiences. Maybe you take a feminist perspective, and your agenda is to give voice to girls in the sciences. It is up to you to decide, and you are the person who knows best. You need to trust yourself and not rely on others to tell you. Other students and professors can help you clarify your thoughts, even make suggestions, but you need to make the final decisions. Working in collaboration with others may be helpful as well. Gale, Speedy, and Wyatt (2010) wrote a play about their joint writing experiences.

So spend some time getting your thoughts together. What is important about what you learned? What adds new insights or clarifies previously poorly understood concepts? What messages are important to share? You need to go beyond description. To repeat what people have said is interesting, but I don't think it represents research. Research takes you beyond what you heard and involves your interpreting the meaning of what you heard. It is necessary, but not sufficient, to describe; you need to go beyond description to give meaning. And you need to think about how what you learned informs us on the issues and takes us further than the prevailing wisdom or research. You may even have a social or political agenda that you wish to address.

Against the Simplified and Mechanical

Koro-Ljungberg (2012) suggests that researchers have a choice in conducting and presenting QR. She argues against a traditional ordered narrative. In her article, she includes "voids, intervals (reflections, disclosures, images), and examples from other researchers" (p. 809). The use of visuals further enhances her argument.

The First Person

I urge you to adopt a style of writing that uses the first person. I have written this book with that in mind. First-person writing is engaging, it brings the reader into the story, and it acknowledges your role in doing the research. It makes your writing more personal. It takes the reader on a journey, and even the most conservative of writers today generally accept it. In a blog about the American Psychological Association (APA) style, McAdoo (2009) happily reported that APA style recommends using first person to avoid ambiguity.

The notion that writing in third person gives what is written greater weight and is more authoritative is an old one and very difficult to overcome. A conservative viewpoint is that keeping the self outside what is being studied makes representations more believable. Atkinson posited the idea that a rhetorical device—not using first person in written presentations—would suggest that knowledge claims have greater authority (Amir, 2005).

Another reason often cited for not using first-person voice in writing is that third-person writing ensures the material is seen as objective and scientific. In other words, the researcher has removed the self from the message. But we have already acknowledged that in most forms of QR, that idea is inconsistent with the fundamental assumptions of a nonfoundationalist or interpretist movement.

Some words of caution are in order: Many of you will be working with advisors and faculty who were trained in traditional methods and writing styles. They will question some of your new ideas. I suggest that rather than becoming combative, you arm yourself with resources and references.

So, to get back to it, use *I*. You and your readers will be more attentive and more accepting of what you have to say.

General Guidelines for Writing

The APA style publication manual is considered the bible of technical writing in the social sciences. It is now in its 6th edition. You can access detailed information online (http://www.apastyle.org/). There is also a blog about using the APA manual (http://blog.apastyle.org/apastyle/). One interesting entry I found here is for electronic writing. If you are tech savvy and using a Kindle, you can learn how to include citations (Lee, 2009). I have also found the Purdue University (2011) Online Writing Lab (OWL) very helpful.

The Voices of Others

We all agree that we want to hear the voices of others. As technology develops, we are now able to hear or see others, but for most of us, the way we represent the voices of others is through the written word. The people we study are real people. In contrast to traditional experimental research that studies subjects or samples (nameless, faceless individuals who represent a particular category or type), our participants interact with us, and often their stories, thoughts, and feelings capture us in more ways than we can imagine.

I remember a number of years ago sitting in my office in Blacksburg, Virginia. Alice Weiping Lo, a student of mine from Hong Kong, entered my office in tears. "What is wrong?" I asked her. She proceeded to tell me about her encounter with the wives of Mainland Chinese graduate students and the difficulties they faced. She remarked that she felt guilty that life had so many hardships for these women and that she was powerless to do anything about it. She had taken on their struggles as part of her doctoral interviews. It became clear that these encounters were more than just data gathering. I encouraged her to consider working with these women after she completed her own doctoral work. I understand that she has remained in Blacksburg and provides a support network for what is now a large Asian population in the town (Lo, 1993).

I relate this example at length because it gives insight into the way in which the lives of a researcher and the people who are studied can become intertwined. Traditionalists would say this is bad and that it brings bias to the study. I need to remind you that you are not conducting traditional research on subjects. You are learning about the lives of individuals—what they think, how they feel, what motivates them, what challenges they face. It is the goal of QR to acknowledge the individuals studied and to reflect their voices. A parallel goal is to acknowledge that the writer/researcher has a voice that is tied intimately to what and who is studied and the interpretations drawn. Rather than keeping the voice in the distance or hidden, much of QR anticipates and celebrates the voice.

Thus, there are dual voices: the voice of the writer and the voice of those studied. What is the relationship between the researcher and those studied? What should it be? Holliday (2001) suggested that this interaction creates a third culture: the interaction between the researcher and the participant. Holliday spoke of personal authorship by using first person to relate experience or to explain the author's perspective. This use of the personal reflects the role of the writer in the research. The writer's voice is revealed. This type of writing is associated with postmodern and critical thinking. Gilgun (2005) argued strongly that we need to give voice to informants.

By now, you understand that I want you to give voice to those you study. How you do that, how much you say, and how open you are is a matter of some debate. We are used to anonymity in QN. This is not always the case in QR. I can only say it depends. If you interview a public figure or one who chooses to keep his name confidential, that is understandable. But in my experience, many individuals you study like to have their names revealed. That is up for discussion between you and those you study.

I find that using direct quotes is a generally accepted practice. I encourage you to do so. I recommend that you leave the language as it is given to you. You should not try to edit it or make it grammatically correct. After all, you are telling a story in the voices of those you studied. Let the voices be their own.

Writing With Others

Collaborative research and writing are ways the QR community engage with each other. Speedy and her colleagues (2010) have shared stories about the process of writing with others. While you may have experienced the joys and frustrations of writing with others, I doubt that you met every day (either online or offline) as this group did. They spoke about moving beyond, in, out of, and through their individual and collective selves. I think a number of them were personally transformed as a result. Wyatt and Gale have written extensively about collaborative writing. In fact, they completed a joint doctoral dissertation in 2008 and published their results in play form (Wyatt, Gale, Gannon, & Davies, 2010). I recall that many years earlier, I had two students who wanted to complete a joint dissertation. My university could not support the idea in the 1990s. I do not know whether it would be viable in the second decade of this new millennium either.

I want you to think about working with another person or a small group as you embark on writing. I believe you will find it stimulating, challenging, frustrating, and thought provoking.

The Use of Metaphors

One way to enhance your writing is through the use of metaphors. Perhaps this is a way you can avoid the admonition to remove boredom from our writing. With Lakoff and Johnson's (1980) seminal work in the field in mind, we use metaphors because they often reveal much about us as writers and our participants as speakers. We use our metaphors and theirs as well. That is why it is so critical that we capture precise words and language from those we study. What is a metaphor? A metaphor is the use of one idea or term to represent another. It is used to assist with expression and understanding. We can trace the use of metaphors to very early language. Some have said that the stylized cave paintings in southern France are metaphors. I visited six of these caves a few years ago. The seemingly simple paintings took on various meanings to members of our group. One began chanting while the others were buried deep in their thoughts.

Figure 13.1 Photograph of Cave Painting

You can read extensively about different kinds of metaphors, including mixed metaphors, dead metaphors, or extended metaphors. Using metaphors adds variety, clarity, and illumination to your writing. And if you use metaphors spoken by your participants, you will extend your understanding of them and, by implication, our understanding of them.

Imagine how excited I was to have stumbled across Hatch and Yanow's (2008) article on ways of seeing in painting and research. In their study, they used contrasts between Rembrandt and Pollock, among others, as metaphors for seeing differences between realists and interpretists. For them, metaphors are necessary and not just nice, decorative parts of speech. I find their comparisons between painting and research intriguing, in that they talk about seeing social realities through two modes of painting.

Patchen and Crawford (2011) used teacher-generated metaphors to examine whether education is moving from a traditional acquisition-based model toward a model that is based on participation. Their conclusion is that

> most of these same teachers (65%) also expressed little surprise that the metaphor analysis illuminated acquisition-based practices, as illustrated by the response of the teacher [Denise] who said that the "analysis does reflect how I feel, especially where you found that [student-oriented] teachers have an underlying level of acquisition-based teaching processes." For many teachers, this revelation brought to the surface the epistemological struggle they face in classrooms—holding constructivist views yet feeling the pressure to substitute (not integrate) practices contrary to these views in an effort to meet educational demands (e.g., "NCLB mandates," "pass state tests"). (p. 294)

In this example, Denise's metaphorical description moves her from being a gardener who watched growth to becoming a tour guide, taking students from Point A to Point B. I think this says it only too well. You can get a sense of how Barner (2011) used visual metaphors if you look at his case study in career counseling. Koro-Ljungberg (2001) discussed metaphors and how they connect different layers of text, even by telling different stories using different fonts. For a detailed analysis of metaphorical analysis from a poststructural view, read Koro-Ljungberg (2004). To gain a deeper understanding of the poststructuralist viewpoint, you can also study the philosophical positions of Foucault (1972, 1980) and Derrida (1982), among others. Neither is easy reading.

Southall (2013) reviewed the literature related to metaphorical ways in which patients speak of their condition. Southhall's work noted that using metaphors enabled them to create new ways to view their situation and ways to cope with serious illness.

Koro-Ljungberg (2001) used metaphorical data from interviews with successful international scientists. One conclusion is that the epistemology of a researcher, or his or her assumptions about knowledge, changes data and possible interpretations. In describing QR, Shank (2002) stated that using metaphors is a powerful tool that can change the way we understand things. Shank used three metaphors in exploring the reasoning process in research. First, he used the metaphor of the mirror through which one can see sharply and reflectively. Then, he saw the window as a metaphor for what is simple and elegant. Finally, he used the metaphor of a lantern, which is flexible and creative (p. 125).

I have spoken at length about using your voice and giving the voices of others a dominant place in your writing. In the next sections, I address some of the organizational and stylistic issues that you will face.

Creative Nonfiction

Here is a problem: Research writing is basically cold, detached, scientific, and remote. I had always known that quantitative reports were this way—so many tables and charts. I couldn't understand them anyway. In the early days of qualitative writing, researchers found themselves emulating these boring quantitative reports. They thought, I suspect, that their writing would be seen as more credible, more scientific, and more acceptable if they did so. In contrast to this kind of writing, two books made a deep impression on me. Elliot Liebow published *Tally's Corner: A Study of Negro Streetcorner Men* in 1967. Originally, it was his dissertation from the Catholic University of America. As an anthropologist, he used extensive field methods to study these men. Here is a portion of the opening paragraph of Chapter 2:

> A pickup truck drives slowly down the street. The truck stops as it comes abreast of a man sitting on a cast iron porch and the white driver calls out, asking if the man wants a day's work. The man shakes his head and the truck moves on up the block, stopping again whenever idling men come within calling distance of the driver. At the Carry-out corner, five men debate the question briefly and shake their heads no to the truck. The truck turns the corner and repeats the same performance up the next street. In the distance, one can see one man, then another, climb into the back of the truck and sit down. In starts and stops, the truck finally disappears. (p. 29)

Liebow's (1967) writing vividly illustrates Caulley's (2008) principles. He immediately draws you into the narrative with concrete events. Although you don't know precisely what the White driver wants from the men, you know they don't want any part of it. You find yourself thinking about the men and why they are idling. I remember when I first read this; I was surprised that it was based on his dissertation. It certainly was nothing like the dissertations I had read. My copy of the book is brown with age and shows a price of $3.95.

Equally forceful is Tracy Kidder's (1989) *Among Schoolchildren*. It opens thusly:

> Mrs. Zajac wasn't born yesterday. She knows you didn't do your best work on this paper, Clarence. Don't you remember Mrs. Zajac saying that if you didn't do your best, she'd make you do it over? As for you, Claude, God forbid that you should ever need brain surgery. But Mrs. Zajac hopes that if you do, the doctor won't open up your head and walk off saying he's almost done, as you just said when Mrs. Zajac asked you for your penmanship, which, by the way, looks like you did it and ran. (p. 3)

Like Liebow's (1967) book, Kidder's (1989) narrative opens with information about those in the book. Liebow did not name his people initially but does so as his story continues.

Kidder, on the other hand, draws you in immediately with an interesting device: He uses the voice of Clarence, the presumed narrator. Although Kidder's work is not academic and is part of popular literature, the year he spent in Holyoke, Massachusetts, living among these 20 children lends an air of verisimilitude to the writing.

Oliver Sacks (1985) knows how to draw you in as well. How could *The Man Who Mistook His Wife for a Hat*, his book of essays describing his work with neurological patients, be anything but fascinating? Here is a portion of the first essay:

> Dr. P. was a musician of distinction, well-known for many years as a singer, and then, at the local School of Music, as a teacher. It was here, in relation to his students, that certain strange problems were first observed. Sometimes a student would present himself, and Dr. P. would not recognise him; or, specifically would not recognise his face. The moment the student spoke, he would be recognised by his voice. (p. 7)

A little more formal, but nonetheless compelling, Sacks (1985) is particularly effective in providing immediate, detailed, and engrossing accounts of various cases he has investigated. He is able to take complex information—potentially dry and technical—and write about it in such a way that the reader can't put the essay down. One hallmark of Sacks's writing is the titles of his essays are humorous and nontechnical.

All the authors described here write their accounts in a way that draws you in, captures you, and makes you continue reading. They are certainly not boring. Flash forward to 2008: Caulley quoted Richardson's statement that so much QR she reads is just boring. How have we come to this, and what can we do about it?

Caulley has made a compelling case for using techniques associated with creative nonfiction (nonfiction that uses fiction techniques). According to Caulley, the idea originated in the 1960s with *The New Journalism* (2008, p. 424). *The New Journalism*, edited by Tom Wolfe and W. E. Johnson, used unconventional literary techniques when writing about news. They published a collection of such articles by Truman Capote, Norman Mailer, and Joan Didion, among others. This type of writing appeared most often in news magazines such as the *New Yorker*, *Rolling Stone*, or *Esquire*.

Caulley included many techniques and examples in his very interesting article and provided a clear discussion of the controversy surrounding this approach. He suggested that written work should begin with a section that is "vivid and vital" (p. 424). I see the introduction as a hook to get the reader involved, interested, and anxious to read more. You can imagine that this type of opening is not really possible if you are writing formal, objective, third-person text. Another way to get the reader involved and anxious to continue reading is to begin with an arrival or departure. Liebow (1967) and Kidder (1989) do this very well.

Caulley (2008) offered additional suggestions that you will find useful:

- *Dramatic or summary methods*. Caulley has identified two basic methods of writing: dramatic and summary. He prefers the dramatic (or scenic) method of writing to the summary method. Rather than provide a summary of what happened, Caulley suggested that you provide a specific account or slice of life.

- *Scene-by-scene writing.* Many writers of QR offer several quotes, one after another. Caulley argued against this approach; rather, he prefers using a narrative of various scenes. In this way, readers get the sense that the action is unfolding in front of them. Of course, Caulley would not discourage the judicious use of quotes.

- *Use of realistic details.* Many writers speak of the use of realistic details. I suggest that you take extensive notes as you collect data. You may also use a digital camera to capture details that you then incorporate into your text.

- *Show, don't tell.* It is important to remember that what you write should incorporate an active voice and avoid abstract concepts.

- *The active voice.* In active voice, the subject of a sentence performs the action described by the verb. Caulley has provided excellent examples from Cheney: "He was enticed by her black hair" becomes "Her black hair knocked him for a loop." "She was embraced by the clown" becomes "The clown grabbed her and hugged her" (p. 434).

- *Captured conversation.* Many qualitative writers use the words of participants. In my experience, however, novice writers tend to use participants' words to excess. A more effective way of using the voices of others is to interweave quotes with points that the writer wishes to emphasize.

Caulley suggested that you put some of these ideas into practice. I concur. I am indebted to Caulley for organizing and presenting this information in such an exciting manner. He has also led me to read Cheney's (2001) book on writing creative nonfiction. Now, we wait to see whether our writing will be less boring. Goodall (2008) provided examples of creative nonfiction in his book on the personal narrative and political consequences for the ethnographer. Norris's (2009) book, based on the theatrical genre of collective creation, reflects this type of writing. In a recent piece, Tamas (a postdoctoral fellow in emotional geography at Queen's University in Ontario, Canada) and Wyatt (a research fellow and head of professional development at The University of Oxford, UK) write about "the process of narrating yourself before a witness" (Wyatt & Tamas, 2013, p. 60). Here is a short excerpt:

Dr. Wyatt: What do you write about?

Sophie: Cheery things. Trauma, abuse, loss, problems in how we produce knowledge. Personal stories.

Dr. Wyatt: I see.

Sophie: It's my masochistic circus freak career.

Dr. Wyatt: Really?

Sophie: [sarcastic] No, no. It's producing useful knowledge.

Dr. Wyatt: Useful how?

Sophie:	Well, that's the problem, isn't it?
Dr. Wyatt:	What do you think?
Sophie:	It's supposed to be therapeutic.
Dr. Wyatt:	Writing instead of acting out?
Sophie:	But I pretend its scholarship. Helping others, when really it's just picking a scab.
Dr. Wyatt:	You're harsh.
Sophie:	And it's romantic, isn't it? Edgy. As if anything truly dangerous is ever going to happen in a scholarly journal.
Dr. Wyatt:	Why not? (p. 61)

I choose to leave Wyatt's question unanswered. But you can find it in the remainder of the dialogue.

■ Fiction

When is it fact and when is it fiction? Is it both? We find much discussion about using narrative to present qualitative information. Richardson's (2011) personal story about the death of her sister intermingles ethnography and literary techniques. She began *Hospice 101* as follows:

> I was scared. I hadn't applied for a job in over forty years, and I'd never applied for a volunteer position. I feared being rejected. I signed the form giving Ohio Hospice-Ellis House the right to check my criminal, financial, and health records. Where the form asked for three references, I gave six—just to be sure; where the form asked for "special skills," I wrote "none." (p. 158)

As part of her journey in qualitative writing, Richardson brought a particular personal note to this piece. Vickers (2010) has challenged us with her title: *The Creation of Fiction to Share Other Truths and Different Viewpoints*. She illustrated how fiction can be useful to show truths and other viewpoints. She described in detail her journey from a review of nonfiction texts and poetry to the creation of a fictional character and ultimately fictional poetry. You might be surprised to learn that she is a professor of management in a school of business.

LaPoe and Reynolds (2013), in their qualitative analysis, describe how journalists use storytelling to craft resonance. They suggest that it is important to use resonance in their storytelling. By using an example of writing—in this instance the story of the hoax of the balloon boy—they illustrate details about using resonance. I am not sure if I should call this fiction, but I think the point is well-taken that the use of the resonance construct might be useful in qualitative writing.

■ Structure—A Good Thing

I don't mean to imply that structure is bad. In fact, I think it is critical for a good piece of writing; it gives order and unity to what you write. I suggest that the structure you choose should be one you impose and develop based on the data you have, the audience you plan to address, and the meaning you want to convey. Chenail (1995) offered several alternative structures or formats for writing, including "natural, simple to complex, first discovered, theory guided, narrative logic, most to least important, dramatic presentation, no special order" (Ahmad, 2006). Whatever structure you choose, most pieces of QR include the following sections.

Opening Section

The opening section of your report should draw the reader in and set the stage. Traditional research writing often begins with a background, a statement of the problem, and research questions. I think it is a good idea to include such topics near the beginning of what you write. You could include an opening paragraph that is personal and tells a little bit about who was studied or the data collected, or you could relay something one of your participants said. Because much of QR follows an inductive approach, writing from the particular to the more general is consistent with that format.

One exercise I often give my students is to ask them to reflect on their life as a graduate student. In this way, I collected data directly and the students have an opportunity to write about their own views. Here is an example of an opening section. It begins with personal information she provided in her diary:

> Sure there will be times when I wondering why I am in the program at all. It is too easy to find myself feeling overwhelmed by the all the coursework. I feel as though I am on information overload. Still, working on my degree has proven an experience beyond my wildest imagination. The personal and professional growth alone is amazing. I am actually learning to be open to opportunities and let the pathway take me to it. In all honesty and seriousness, I would not change a thing.

In many respects, this journal entry is a tribute to the graduate student journey. Students were asked to write about their own experience as graduate students. This example shared the cultural behaviors and language of that graduate experience. I like the simple perspective drawn from her personal life and feelings. While there are also admitted limitations in the variety of data sources since the data are drawn from students who are studying, the nature of the research question that had to do with the lived experience of being a graduate student provides an opportunity to explore a phenomenological question. Fully realizing that this qualitative effort may not generalize to the larger population, I used the opportunity to capture a glimpse of this world.

Methods and Procedures

While traditional research writing often expects such a section to follow next, I have seen authors choose to include such information in an appendix or at the end of what they write. I believe they do this because they do not want to detract from the personal nature and deep description about the topic. In writing that is of a narrative nature, such as an autoethnographic account, a poem, or a performance piece, methods are not usually discussed. Some other types of qualitative writing are silent about methods and procedures as well.

Profiles of Participants

Much of QR involves the study of individuals. I often see a description of each participant, including demographic characteristics. These are usually introduced with fictitious names. Sparkes and Smith (2003) introduced one of the three men in their study as follows:

> David is 28 years old and a teaching assistant, living in a large city in Northern England. His father, a headmaster at the local school, was the chairman of the local rugby club, and his mother was involved in the general catering for the club. (p. 302)

Harding (2005) introduced the city girl in her study with the following description:

> The 30-year-old national board certified teacher is 5 feet 6 inches tall with a medium build. She has long, red hair that she keeps pulled back in a ponytail meant to harness her curls. She wears glasses when she teaches, and they add to her overall seriousness. She is not a person who starts out smiling—I get the sense that her laughter will have to be earned. Her speech is punctuated with "Ya know what I mean?" I am never sure if she is asking this question of herself or of me. (p. 55)

Concepts and Supporting Evidence

You may see researchers include a section that identifies the major concepts that emerged from the study. Usually, several short quotations that come directly from the data are used to support the concepts. The concept headings are often quotes taken directly from the participants.

Self-Reflection

You will often see self-disclosure in the writing. Here are some examples.

> While I have attempted qualitative research before, I have never felt myself being drawn into the data as I have with these interviews. The students became very real to me and I visualized them as I delved into the transitions that they experienced in their various graduate programs. Breuer, Mruck, & Roth (2002) commented "that doing qualitative research makes the impact of the researcher far more obvious than in its quantitative [counterpart] . . . the interactional and constructional nature of epistemological processes become more than elsewhere evident and can be experienced in existential ways." As a student in adult learning, adult development and individual change are the lenses I use when examining data. As I reviewed the data, it helped me study individual transitions from a new perspective.

> I am feeling very anxious about doing the interview this afternoon. I feel like I have a good relationship with the participant. In some ways this causes more stress because I feel like I have to be very "formal" during this process and this is very different from our usual interactions. Also, I am worried about not having a "pre-set" list of questions. What will happen if I run out of things to ask or if she doesn't respond to the questions? For this reason, I have come up with several questions that I would like to ask her. I feel like at this point I am too inexperienced to "wing it." (anonymous student)
>
> Conducting this study has allowed me to look back on my life as a graduate student. While working a full-time job, being a wife, mother, daughter, sister, friend, and trying to balance the demands of school are difficult tasks. I have missed, and will miss, many family gatherings and outings with friends. Sometimes it is a lonely experience, one that only another graduate student can relate, but the reward is going to be wonderful! (anonymous student)

Research Literature

Very often, the related research is integrated in the paper and not provided as a separate section. For more information about writing reviews of literature, refer to Chapter 9.

■ Alternative Presentation Formats

Social Sciences and the Arts

Davidson (2012a, 2012b) created a very personal account. She began by analyzing an 18-month period of notes from her personal journals. She organized the 303 entries using what she called standard QR methods and used NVivo. What distinguishes this analysis is her use of fiber-arts work to deepen her understanding of the findings. An exhibit of her work was presented at the 2011 annual conference of the International Congress on Qualitative Inquiry. Her article includes numerous visuals depicting her work. You will recall my own presentation in Chapter 7 of my experiences with painting and representation. Lapum and colleagues (2012) developed a project called the "7,024th Patient." It consists of an installation that takes up 1,739 square feet and is 9 feet in height. The installation is a combination of poetry and photography in a path like a labyrinth. Everyone who contributed work had experienced open heart surgery and recovery. Poems and illustrations are included as well as metaphorical sketches. I think I was most moved by the photographs of feet—symbolic representations of being a patient. Gergen and Gergen (2012) offer a range of formats, including collaged voices, photographic playtime, and cartooning, in their efforts to make social science more accessible.

Ethnographic and Autoethnographic Narratives

Adams's (2011) *Narrating the Closet: An Autoethnography of Same-Sex Attraction* won two awards: It received the 2012 National Communication Association Ethnography Division Best

Book Award and the 2012 Organization for the Study of Communication, Language, and Gender Outstanding Book Award. It is described as both scholarly and an excellent account of storytelling. In a description of the book, Adams is said to have been motivated by the death of his partner to redefine the closet as a relational construct.

Photography

Mey (2012, personal communication) used photography in various aspects of his work. In one study, he used photography to represent the old and young. This piece is illustrative of the many photos in the study. The use of public photographs has a long tradition in documentary photography. (See Eugene Atget, considered the father of this genre.) Mathison (2013), commenting in her blog, states that photo essays can be used to illustrate something that words cannot accomplish—in particular, generating an emotional response.

Ethnodrama

Saldaña's (2011) book, *Ethnotheatre: From Page to Stage,* won the Qualitative Research SIG AERA book of the year award. Saldaña includes the key principles of this technique as well as actual contemporary ethnodramas. An ethnodrama can be many things. Its general meaning is to translate data into some type of performance. It can include film, plays, dialogues, or improvised performance art. According to Cannon (2012), a "growing group of qualitative researchers . . . celebrate this narrative (or performative) turn in the analysis and writing of qualitative research" (p. 583). Why must QR be so boring and tedious? I think this is a reaction to the dreaded final paper or report. After first coding through categories and then themes (see Chapter 13 for details on how to do this), Cannon (2012) presents an ethnodrama to show the results. She describes her work with a newly arrived immigrant from Togo. The play speaks for itself.

Poetry

In this interesting paper, Lahman and her colleagues (2011) use three poem types—free form, elegy, and haiku—to represent international doctoral student experience. (Note that Lahman was part of the team that reported on ethics of using smartphones for interviewing, discussed in Chapter 7.) Data are based on interviews with 50 students. In addition to preparing a traditional article and conference presentation, they developed various poetic forms. Here is a small portion:

> The Monster in the Closet: International Students' Graduate School Experiences
>
> *Graduate school is swimming.*
>
> *We have to put our heads in the water and*
>
> *swim hard towards the*
>
> *end of the pool.*
>
> *We work so hard that sometimes we almost*

can't breathe.
If we know how to push our heads out of the water
to breathe,
we won't die
and we can go on.
Learning is rowing a boat up the source of the river.
If you don't row, you will go backwards and
never get to the source. (p. 890)

Magazine

Hughes (2012, personal communication), in her study of adolescent girls and their experience in their bodies, wanted to submit her dissertation as a magazine. Her institution would not accept the format, and she submitted it in a traditional format. However, she did catalog it with the Library of Congress as a magazine. I have looked at the magazine—it will certainly capture your attention. Her dissertation won the 2012 Illinois Distinguished Qualitative Dissertation Award at the 8th International Congress.

Subjective Maps and Children's Drawings

Besten's (2010) study involves the interconnectedness of social and spatial divisions, in particular, urban segregation. It contrasts two neighborhoods in Berlin through maps drawn by the children. Recall that prior to 1989, the Berlin wall divided the city in two. Fragmentation still occurs and is illustrated in this study. Here is a small section from the work using subjective maps:

This drawing illustrates a friend's house drawn by a girl from a bilingual school.

The authors come to the conclusion that belonging and emotional attitudes toward neighborhoods are interconnected.

Performance Film

Kip Jones developed *Rufus Stone*, a film. Details of this film can be found in Chapter 7. Figure 13.3 shows a still from the film.

Alternative Writing Presentations

Phillip Vannini, chair of the School of Communication and Culture at Royal Roads University in Canada, published *Popularizing Research: Engaging New Genres, Media, and Audiences*. As reported by Reisz (2012), "An academic has called on fellow scholars who feel 'alienated from the drudgery of academic writing and inauthentic about producing more of the same drivel' to embrace every possible means of popularising their research." Reisz continues,

Figure 13.2 A Map of Her "Subjective Territory" by a 13-Year-Old German-American Girl From the School in Zehlendorf

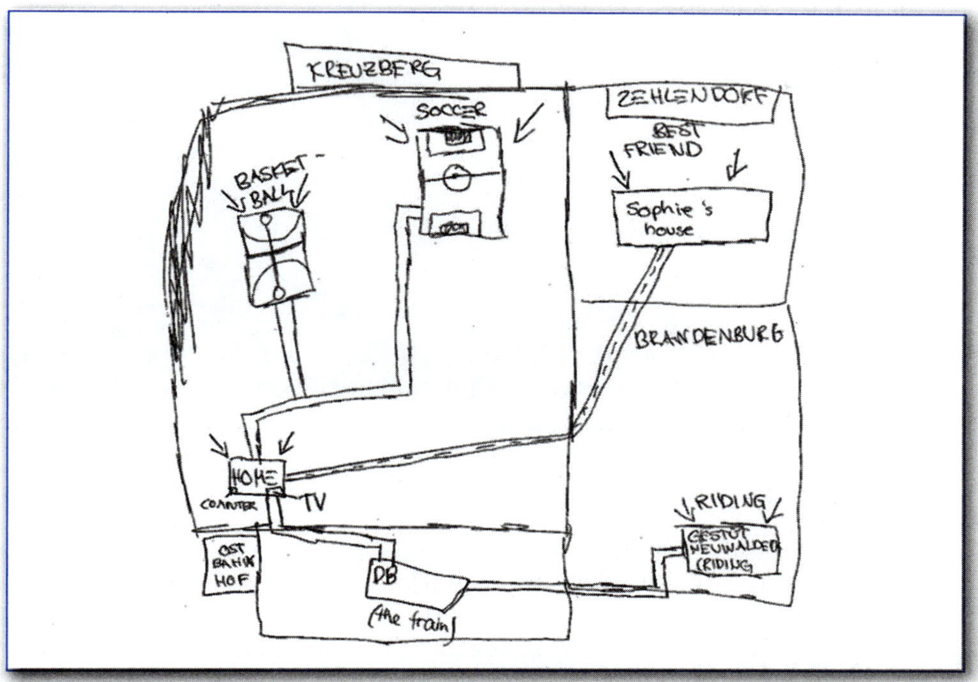

SOURCE: Besten (2010).

The book brings together contributors from more than two dozen countries in disciplines ranging from education and communications to sociology and anthropology. All have found ways to make their work more relevant and accessible through cartoons, performance, exhibitions and films. Others have embraced the myriad possibilities opened up by the internet. *Popularizing Research* has itself been released with a website designed to complement its arguments with "a web-based directory of popularized research."

■ Students' Examples of Qualitative Writing

I want to leave you with some examples written by students. This first excerpt is from a paper prepared by Donna (personal communication, 2002), who was taking an introductory course in QR. Notice how she uses a first-person, direct style. When she actually begins her story, she writes as a fictionalized journal:

Figure 13.3 A Still from *Rufus Stone*

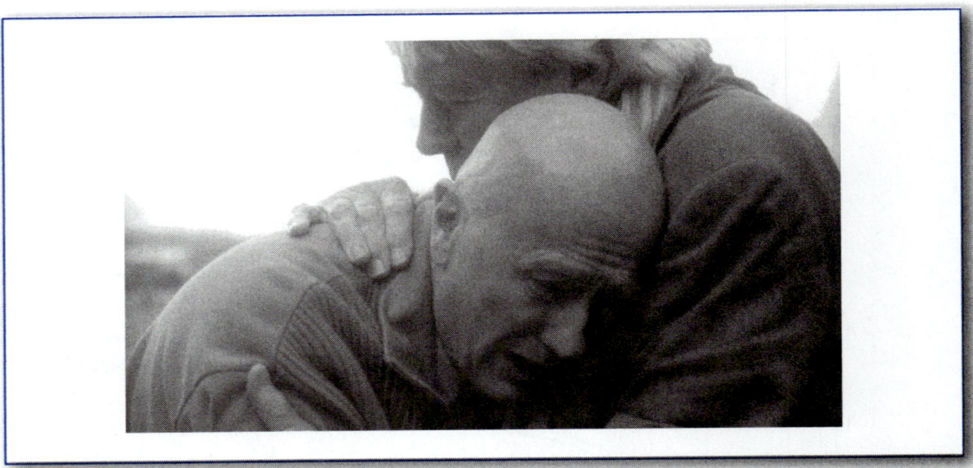

SOURCE: Kip Jones

> January 15. It's time. Applications are due in a couple of months and if I'm going to go back to school, now is the time. Children are still a few years away. I can't even imagine how I could possibly balance young kids and an advanced degree program, although I'm sure some people do so successfully. And I don't want to wait the additional years until I actually have kids and then they reach school age. I've waited long enough. I mean seriously, how long can I drive around with "PRE PHD" on my license plate before actually taking action to make that a reality?
>
> Do I consider relocating or are there viable options close to home? How to choose? I guess I need to get serious and go to the library (maybe online?) and start to weigh this out.
>
> January 19. Just to make sure I am making an informed decision, I looked at everything—every school where my program is offered. There are very viable options locally, so I will continue to focus on these. Staying here rather than relocating is more attractive to me. Beyond cost and the application logistics of degree type (PhD or EdD), fees, requisites, prerequisites, and program size, what else do I consider? What else is important to consider? The basic logistics in the Peterson's guide seem somewhat sterile—no real feel of what this will really be like. Maybe the websites offer more.

The following comments were prepared by Leanne (2002), another student.

> December 3. I need help! I can't do this alone. I need additional strategies next semester. Have to make time to reflect on this—after my papers are done! Why am I even stopping to comment in this journal?!?!
>
> December 13. Ta da! Completion and success. Now can I sleep and de-stress??? YES!!!

> December 20. Met up with a few folks from my class for coffee and tea. All are weary and we look it. But no pity or despair! We are also amazingly resilient and energized by our efforts. One person, a neophyte like me, commented that she had "rediscovered learning is very energizing to [her] and exciting." What an amazing testimony. I love it! I too love "to learn and have gotten a lot of enjoyment out of the people interaction in the . . . program . . . [and] the relationships with classmates—many of them have turned into friends and that's really enriched my life."
>
> January 1. Ever a day of reflection and planning, at least for me. Here goes.
>
> What worked? I continue to rely on my tried-and-true internal standards of commitment, perseverance, and time management (e.g., prioritization, organization). I expect I will continue to tap these in the many semesters ahead. (C. L. Wells, personal communication, 2002)

I chose this next excerpt to reveal how another student, Talisha, described in detail her approach to data analysis. She also used color and inserts to highlight the points she was trying to illustrate. Notice the use of self-reflection.

> There was a lot of information collected in each person's interview that [*sic*] I was not quite sure how to tackle everyone's interview. I decided to begin data analysis by thoroughly reading everyone's interview and jotting notes in the margins about statements that I found surprising, interesting, or themes that were common in everyone's interview. After finding these things, I used Microsoft Excel to create a list for everyone in the class and their interview. The list was titled according to the person who conducted the interview and then interesting and similar statements were listed under the title.
>
> I also color-coded similar themes in everyone's interviews. If a participant mentioned something about self-discovery or self-awareness, the statement would be colored green as in the above example of Heather's interview. Or if someone mentioned the support of family, a spouse, professors, or students, the statement would be colored yellow. Or if someone mentioned something about having to balance work and school, or organize or structure in order to participate in a graduate program, the statement would be colored red. Coding is a technique used in grounded theory's open coding. It allowed me to identify similarities and differences in the interviews. This project could be related to a grounded theory approach because, in the end, a theory could be derived regarding graduate student life from the data.

■ Disseminating Your Ideas and Learning From Others

As I write this section, I am aware that I may be leaving out some of your favorite resources. I apologize in advance. I welcome additions or corrections to the list below. You can communicate with me directly through my email (MarilynLichtman09@gmail.com) or through SAGE.

Selected Journals

How can you let others know about your work? I have identified some sources of publication that are supportive of work in the qualitative arena. Some are general, while others are specific to certain disciplines. Although various journals accept articles that employ QR, some journals are specifically aimed at publishing QR. A few are generic, while others are specific to a discipline. This list is not inclusive; new journals are emerging. You can use this as a starting point to locate articles.

Online Open Access Journals—General and Specific

The Qualitative Report (*TQR*). (http://www.nova.edu/ssss/QR/aindex.html) Organized by the TQR community of NOVA Southeastern University in Ft. Lauderdale, FL, this is a peer-reviewed, weekly, free, online journal. Its first issue appeared in Summer 1990.

Forum: Qualitative Social Research (*FQS*). (http://www.qualitative-research.net/index.php/fqs/index) Based in Berlin, *FQS* was established in 1999. It is a peer-reviewed, open access, multilingual online journal for QR. All abstracts are in English, and most articles are as well. Thematic issues are published triannually.

International Journal of Qualitative Methods (*IJQM*). (http://ejournals.library.ualberta.ca/index.php/IJQM/issue/archive) This web-based journal by the International Institute for Qualitative Methods at the University of Alberta, Canada, is peer-reviewed, published quarterly, and free. The goal is to advance the development of qualitative methods; the first issue appeared in 2002.

Qualitative Sociology Review. (http://qualitativesociologyreview.org/ENG/index_eng.php) Based in Poland, its aim is to create an open-access, online, international scientific journal. It appears three times a year, and the first issue appeared August of 2005. The review process is described as double blind.

International Journal of Qualitative Studies on Health and Well-Being (*QHW*). (http://www.ijqhw.net/index.php/qhw) This is a peer-reviewed, open access publication aimed at the international and interdisciplinary nature of health-related issues. The editor and many of the staff members are based in Sweden. Its aim is to support the emerging field of qualitative studies. It specifically mentions phenomenological, ethnographic, and grounded-theory studies. Publishing quarterly, its first issue appeared in 2006.

Kaleidoscope: A Graduate Journal of Qualitative Communication Research. (http://opensiuc.lib.siu.edu/kaleidoscope/) Published annually, this journal is devoted to communication research at the intersections of philosophy, theory, and practice in qualitative, interpretive, and critical communication research. It is published through the Department of Speech Communication at Southern Illinois University in Carbondale, Illinois.

Online Subscription Journals—General and Specific

Qualitative Inquiry. This journal provides an interdisciplinary forum for qualitative methodology in the human sciences from an interdisciplinary perspective. Refereed articles experiment with form and content. The first issue was in March 1995. The editors are Denzin (University of Illinois) and Lincoln (Texas A&M University). This journal is published by SAGE and is available online and in print.

Qualitative Research. This peer-reviewed international journal publishes original research and reviews articles with a focus in the social sciences. It publishes bimonthly; the first issue was published in April 2001. Its editors are Atkinson and Delamont (Cardiff University). This journal is published by SAGE and is available online and in print.

Qualitative Health Research. This peer-reviewed monthly journal provides an international, interdisciplinary forum to enhance health care. Jan Morse (University of Utah) is the editor. This journal is published by SAGE and is available online and in print.

Qualitative Social Work. This journal provides a forum for those interested in QR. It is open to new voices and welcomes articles from practitioners and others interested in creative ways to work with and write about QR. It accepts supplementary materials (e.g., audio/video files, images, etc.). It was first published in March 2002. Incoming editors are Krumer-Nevo (Ben-Gurion University of the Negev, Israel) and Staller (University of Michigan). This journal is published by SAGE and is available online and in print.

International Journal of Qualitative Studies in Education (*QSE*). This journal is published by Taylor and Francis. In 2012, plans are to publish eight issues annually. The first issue was published in 1988.

Other Avenues of Distribution

LISTSERVs—QUALRS-L began their LISTSERV in the 1990s. It is open to all and accepts comments and questions from students. Begun by Judith Preissle from the University of Georgia in the 1990s, it is a must for you to join. There are other LISTSERVs connected particularly with qualitative software or specific disciplines.

Blogs—There are many blogs associated with QR. Many are targeted to market research, so unless you are interested in that area, pick and choose wisely.

Conferences—Through the efforts of Ron Chenail, founder and editor-in-chief of *TQR*, Nova Southeastern University in Florida sponsors an annual conference in January of each year. It replaced the annual conference held previously at The University of Georgia. The International Congress of Qualitative Inquiry at The University of Illinois holds an annual conference in Champaign, Illinois. Of course, there are many other conferences—some global, some specific to a particular discipline. Annual meetings of many professional associations in various social science disciplines offer opportunities for new scholars. Some have special interest groups in QR.

Publishers

SAGE Publications, with locations worldwide, is an independent publisher of journals, books, and electronic media. It was founded in 1965 by Sara Miller McCune. SAGE's online links to journals and other reference materials is outstanding. As a writer with SAGE for more than ten years, I can only say that they have been phenomenal to work with.

Left Coast Press, based in northern California, publishes academic and professional materials in social sciences and, specifically, QR. Launched in 2005 by Mitch Allen, formerly the founder of AltaMira Press and executive editor of SAGE, they have 350 book titles and more than a dozen scholarly journals. Materials are available in print and electronic formats.

Many university presses have also published work of a qualitative nature.

■ Summary

You might design a wonderful study and collect important data; however, if the way in which you present your findings is unclear, abstract, or boring, you have been unsuccessful. It is critical that you present your study in such a way as to draw in your audience and actively engage them in the process. In most cases, communication is written, although alternatives to the written word have occasionally been used. I recommend that you write in a direct style, using an active voice. Weaving quotes from participants into the fabric of your writing provides support for your interpretations.

I recommend that you use some stylistic techniques drawn from *The New Journalism* and creative nonfiction. Caulley (2008) suggested some tools such as starting with a story, writing scene by scene, and including dramatic details.

Unlike in traditional research, in QR, the writer is free to select from among a variety of presentation styles. For beginning researchers, I suggest including four basic elements: (1) what your study is about, (2) a profile of participants, (3) ways you gathered and analyzed data, and (4) major findings. An open style that communicates the role you played is also valuable.

CHECK YOURSELF

Communicating your ideas in QR is demanding and exciting. You are free to expand your horizons. The message in this chapter is that researchers are exploring alternative ways to communicate their ideas, lest they be put on the shelf and gather dust. A variety of examples are offered. At the same time, it is clear that there is resistance to alternative forms of communication. Whether you, as a student, can be a leader in this movement is unclear. Some of the ways in which you can take steps forward are offered.

- Writing that captures the reader's attention is extremely important. If you choose to present your findings in a traditional written fashion, I urge you to think about capturing your audience through your writing. Various techniques are offered to move forward.

- It is important to resist the temptation to write in a stilted fashion. Traditional academic writing is aloof, objective, and remote. It is not a sign of quality, even though some may think so. I ask you to reflect on how you choose to tell others the stories that you learn and the information that you obtain. I do not think it is necessarily easy to do. But easy is not the only road to take.

KEY DISCUSSION ISSUES

1. How do you move from the data you have to presenting the information? What are some considerations?
2. In thinking about your audience, what should you pay attention to? Why is this important?
3. Academic writing has traditionally avoided the use of first-person voice. What arguments do I make for using first-person voice? How do you counter someone who is against its use?
4. Creative nonfiction and fiction—Do these terms seem to belong in academic writing? What suggestions do I make for their use?
5. If you decide to use the written form for a presentation, what sections do I recommend? What would you add or omit?
6. Are you ready to try something innovative? What would you like to do? How can you convince yourself and others that an alternative form is okay?

MODULE 13A

Simple Writing Task

Purpose: Practice a simple writing task using qualitative data to learn about sharing with others and revealing about the self.

Activities: Combine a group observation with a simple writing exercise. During a break between classes, choose a location where you will meet or see other students. This could be in a cafeteria, bookstore, lounge, or hallway. Take about 30 minutes. You will be focusing on interactions among students. You can choose any aspect of interaction of interest. You will not be taking notes but rather making mental images and practicing your ability to look and listen. Immediately upon returning to class, write three paragraphs. One paragraph will focus on your observation. What did you see? What do you think it means? What insights do you have about this human encounter? The second paragraph will describe your self-reflections. How did you feel? What did you understand about the task and about yourself? The last paragraph will be about the method you used. All writing should be in first person. If possible, you should write on your computer. The final part of this task is sharing and getting insights from others. Depending on the size of your class, you can either share with the entire group or split into smaller groups.

Evaluation: Determine the ease with which you can communicate some ideas to others, and note how others attend to this observation and writing experience.

MODULE 13B

Reinforcing Writing Ideas

Purpose: Reinforce writing ideas by using what you wrote in the group experience and modifying it based on what others did and what you learned about yourself.

Activity: Take the writing assignment that you produced in the preceding Group Activity and rework it. Work on your writing style, your ability to communicate, and your ability to set the tone of what you are trying to say. Send it as an attachment to other class members. Choose one or two other examples you receive and examine how they have been changed. Begin to build a portfolio of your writing.

Evaluation: Continue to assess your ability to communicate. Judge what other information you need in order to move forward with your writing.

REFERENCES

Adams, T. (2011). *Narrating the closet: An autoethnography of same-sex attraction*. Walnut Creek, CA: Left Coast Press.

Adams, T. (2012). Missing each other. *Qualitative Inquiry, 18*(2), 193–196.

Ahmad, S. (2006). *Reporting and presenting qualitative data*. Retrieved from http://www.slidefinder.net/w/week14-data presentationandreporting/32091933

Amir, D. (2005). The use of "first person" writing style in academic writing. An open letter to journals, reviewers, and readers. *Voices: A World Forum for Music Therapy*. Retrieved from http://www.voices.no/?q=fortnightly-columns/2005-use-first-person-writing-style-academic-writing-open-letter-journal-editors

Bagley, C. (2008). Educational ethnography as performance art: Towards a sensuous feeling and knowing. *Qualitative Research, 8*(1), 53–72.

Barner, R. W. (2011). Applying visual metaphors to career transitions. *Journal of Career Development, 38*(1), 89–106.

Besten, O. (2010). Local belonging and 'geographies of emotions'" Immigrant children's experience of their neighbourhoods in Paris and Berlin, *Childhood*, 17(2), 181–195.

Bochner, A., & Ellis, C. (Eds.). (2002). *Ethnographically speaking: Autoethnography, literature, and aesthetics*. Walnut Creek, CA: AltaMira Press.

Breuer, F., Mruck, K., & Roth, W-M. (2002). Subjectivity and reflexivity: An introduction [10 paragraphs]. *Forum Qualitative Sozialforschung/Forum: Qualitative Social Research, 3*(3). Retrieved from http://www.qualitative-research.net/index.php/fqs/article/view/822/1784

Butler-Kisber, L. (2002). Artful portrayals in qualitative research: The road to found poetry and beyond. *The Alberta Journal of Educational Research, XLVIII*(3), 229–239.288.

Cannon, A. (2012). Making the data perform: An ethnodramatic analysis. *Qualitative Inquiry, 18*(7), 583–594.

Caulley, D. (2008). Making qualitative research reports less boring: The techniques of writing creative nonfiction. *Qualitative Inquiry, 14*(3), 424–449.

Chenail, R. (1995). Presenting qualitative data. *The Qualitative Report, 2*(3). Retrieved from http://www.nova.edu/ssss/QR/QR2-3/presenting.html

Cheney, T. (2001). *Writing creative nonfiction: Fiction techniques for crafting great nonfiction*. Berkeley, CA: Ten Speed Press.

Chorba, K. (2011). Book review: *Qualitative research: Studying how things work*, by R. E. Stake. *The Qualitative Report, 16*(4), 1136–1140. Retrieved from http://www.nova.edu/ssss/QR/QR16-4/chorba.pdf

Coffey, A., & Atkinson, P. (1996). *Making sense of qualitative data: Complementary research strategies*. Thousand Oaks, CA: SAGE.

Curtis, A. (2008). How dramatic techniques can aid the presentation of qualitative research. *Qualitative Researcher, 8*, 8–10. Retrieved from http://www.cardiff.ac.uk/socsi/qualiti/QualitativeResearcher/QR_Issue8_Jun08.pdf

Davidson, J. (2012a). The Journal Project: Qualitative computing and the technology/aesthetics divide in qualitative research [80 paragraphs]. *Forum Qualitative Sozialforschung/Forum: Qualitative Social Research, 13*(2), Art. 15. Retrieved from http://nbn-resolving.de/urn:nbn:de:0114-fqs1202152

Davidson, J. (2012b). The Journal Project: Research at the boundaries between social sciences and the arts. *Qualitative Inquiry, 18*(1), 86–99.

Denton, D. (2011). Betrayals of gravity: The flight of the phoenix. *Qualitative Inquiry, 17*(1), 85–92.

Derrida, J. (1982). *Margins of philosophy* (A. Bass, Trans.). Chicago, IL: The University of Chicago Press.

Downing, M. (2008). Why video? How technology advances method. *The Qualitative Report, 13*(2), 173–177.

Ellis, C., Bochner, A., Denzin, N., Lincoln, Y., Morse, J., Pelias, R., & Richardson, L. (2008). Talking and thinking about qualitative research. *Qualitative Inquiry, 14*(2), 254–284.

Ewick, P., & Silbey, S. (2003). Narrating social structures: Stories of resistance to legal authority. *American Journal of Sociology, 108*(6), 1328–1372.

Foucault, M. (1972). *The archeology of knowledge* (A. M. Sheridan-Smith, Trans.). London, England: Tavistock.

Foucault, M. (1980). *Power/knowledge: Selected interviews and other writings, 1972–1977* (C. Cordon, Ed.; C. Cordon, L. Marshall, J. Mepham, & K. Soper, Trans.). New York, NY: Pantheon Books.

Fraser, J. (2008). Dancing with research. *Canadian Medical Association Journal, 179*(5), 450–451.

Gale, K., Speedy, J., & Wyatt, J. (2010). Gatecrashing the oasis? A joint doctoral dissertation play. *Qualitative Inquiry, 16*(1), 21–28.

Garcia, D. (2008). Culture clash invades Miami: Oral histories and ethnography center stage. *Qualitative Inquiry, 14*(6), 865–895.

Gergen, M., & Gergen, K. (2012). *Playing with purpose: Adventures in performative social science.* Walnut Creek, CA: Left Coast Press.

Gilgun, J. (2005). "Grab" and good science: Writing up the results of qualitative research. *Qualitative Health Research, 15*, 256–262.

Goodall, H. (2008). *Writing qualitative inquiry: Self, stories, and academic life.* San Francisco, CA: Left Coast Press.

Harding, S. (2005). *Science and social inequality: Feminist and postcolonial issues.* Champaign, IL: University of Illinois Press.

Hatch, M., & Yanow, D. (2008). Methodology by metaphor: Ways of seeing in painting and research. *Organizational Studies, 29*(1), 23–44.

Hill, D. (2005). The poetry in portraiture: Seeing subjects, hearing voices, and feeling contexts. *Qualitative Inquiry*, 11(1), 95–105.

Holliday, A. (2001). *Doing and writing qualitative research* (2nd ed.). Thousand Oaks, CA: SAGE.

Holt, N. L. (2003). Representation, legitimation, and autoethnography: An autoethnographic writing story. *International Journal of Qualitative Methods, 2*(1). Retrieved from http://www.ualberta.ca/~iiqm/backissues/2_1/html/holt.html

Hookway, N. (2008). Entering the blogosphere: Some strategies for using blogs in social research. *Qualitative Research, 8*(1), 91–113.

Kidder, T. (1989). *Among schoolchildren.* New York, NY: Avon Books.

Koro-Ljungberg, M. (2001). Metaphors as a way to explore qualitative data. *International Journal of Qualitative Studies in Education, 14*(3), 367–379.

Koro-Ljungberg, M. (2004). Displacing metaphorical analysis: Reading with and against metaphors. *Qualitative Research, 4*(3), 339–360.

Koro-Ljungberg, M. (2012). Researchers of the world, create! *Qualitative Inquiry*, 18(9), 808–818.

Lahman, M., Rodriguez, K., Richard, V., Geist, M., Schendel, R., & Graglia, P. (2011). (Re)Forming research poetry. *Qualitative Inquiry, 17*(9), 887–896.

Lakoff, G., & Johnson, M. (1980). *Metaphors we live by.* Chicago: University of Chicago Press.

LaPoe, V., & Reynolds, A. (2013). From breaking news to the traditional news cycle: A qualitative analysis of how journalists craft resonance through storytelling. *Electronic News, 7*(1), 3–21.

Lapum, J., Ruttonsha, P., Church, K., Yau, T., & David, A. (2012). Employing the arts in research as an analytical tool and dissemination method: Interpreting experience through the aesthetic. *Qualitative Inquiry, 18*(1), 100–115.

Lee, C. (2009). How do I cite a Kindle? *APA style* [Web log]. Retrieved from http://blog.apastyle.org/apastyle/2009/09/how-do-i-cite-a-kindle.html

Left Coast Press. (2013). *About Left Coast Press, Inc.* Retrieved from http://www.lcoastpress.com/about_us.php

Lewis, P. J. (2008). A good teacher [18 paragraphs]. *Forum Qualitative Sozialforschung/Forum: Qualitative Social Research, 9*(2), Art. 41. Retrieved from http://www.qualitative-research.net/index.php/fqs/article/view/399

Liebow, E. (1967). *Tally's corner: A study of Negro streetcorner men.* London, England: Routledge.

Liu, Y. (2000). How to write qualitative research? A book review. *The Qualitative Report, 5*(1/2). Retrieved from http://www.nova.edu/ssss/QR/QR5-1/liu.html

Lo, A. (1993). *Sojourner adjustment: The experience of wives of mainland Chinese graduate students.* (Unpublished doctoral dissertation). Virginia Polytechnic Institute and State University, Blacksburg, Virginia.

Lockford, L. (2013). Writing qualitative inquiry and other impossible journeys. *Qualitative Inquiry, 19*(3), 163–166.

Mathison, S. (2011a). *Evaluation: Constructing a good life through the exploration of value and valuing.* Retrieved from http://blogs.ubc.ca/evaluation/author/mathison/

Mathison, S. (2011b). *Qualitative research café.* Retrieved from http://blogs.ubc.ca/qualresearch/

Mathison, S. (2013). Photo essays. *Qualitative research café.* Retrieved from http://blogs.ubc.ca/qualresearch/

McAdoo, T. (2009). Use of first person in APA style. *APA style* [Web log]. Retrieved from http://blog.apastyle.org/apastyle/2009/09/use-of-first-person-in-apa-style.html

Murthy, D. (2008). Digital ethnography: An examination of the use of new technologies for social research. Sociology, 42(5), 837–855.

Norris, J. (2009). *Playbuilding as qualitative research: A participatory arts–based approach.* Walnut Creek, CA: Left Coast Press.

Owton, H. (2011). Granny's memoirs. *Qualitative Inquiry, 17*(5), 459–460.

Parry, D. C., & Glover, T. D. (2011). Living with cancer? Come as you are. *Qualitative Inquiry, 17*(5), 395–403.

Patchen, T., & Crawford, T. (2011). From gardeners to tour guides: The epistemological struggle revealed in teacher-generated metaphors of teaching. *Journal of Teacher Education, 62*(3), 286–298.

Purdue University. (2011). *Purdue online writing lab.* Retrieved from http://owl.english.purdue.edu/owl/resource/560/15/

Qualitative Inquiry. (2013). *Qualitative Inquiry: SAGE Journals.* Retrieved from http://qix.sagepub.com

The Qualitative Report. (2013). *Editorial statement*. Retrieved from http://www.nova.edu/ssss/QR/Editorial/editstm.html

Reisz, M. (2012). Sing another tune to make pop music for the masses. *The Higher Education*. Retrieved from http://www.timeshighereducation.co.uk/420501.article

Richardson, L. (2011). Hospice 101. *Qualitative Inquiry, 17*(2), 158–165.

Robertson, J. (2006). "If you know our names it helps!" Students' perspectives about "good" teaching. *Qualitative Inquiry, 12*(4), 756–768.

Sacks, O. (1985). *The man who mistook his wife for a hat*. New York, NY: Summit Books.

Sage Publications. (2013). *SAGE publications/the company*. Retrieved from http://www.sagepub.com/aboutCompany.nav

Saldaña, J. (2011). *Ethnotheatre: Research from page to stage*. Walnut Creek, CA: Left Coast Press.

Saldaña, J., Leavy, P., & Beretvas, N. (2011). *Fundamentals of qualitative research*. London, England: Oxford University Press.

Sandelowski, M., & Leeman, J. (2012). Writing usable qualitative health research findings. *Qualitative Health Research, 22*(10), 1404–1413.

Schwandt, T. (2007). *The SAGE dictionary of qualitative inquiry* (3rd ed.). Los Angeles, CA: SAGE.

Shank, G. (2002). *Qualitative research: A personal skills approach*. Columbus, OH: Merrill Prentice Hall.

Southall, D.(2013). The patient's use of metaphor within a palliative care setting: Theory function and efficacy. A narrative literature review. *Palliative Medicine, 27*(4), 304–313.

Sparkes, A., & Smith, B. (2003). Men, sport, spinal cord injury and narrative time. *Qualitative Research, 3*(3), 295–320.

Speedy, J. (2011). "All Googled out on suicide": Making collective biographies out of silent fragments with "the unassuming geeks." *Qualitative Inquiry, 17*(2), 134–143.

Speedy, J., Bainton, D., Bridges, N., Brown, T., Brown, L., Martin, V., Sakellariadis, A., et al. (2010). Encountering "Gerald": Experiments with meandering methodologies and experiences beyond our "selves" in a collaborative writing group. *Qualitative Inquiry, 16*(10), 894–901. doi:-10.1177/1077800410383130

Tierney, W. G., & Hallett, R. E. (2010). In treatment: Writing beneath the surface. *Qualitative Inquiry, 16*(8), 674–684.

van Maanen, J. (1988). *Tales of the field: On writing ethnography*. Chicago, IL: University of Chicago Press.

Vickers, M. H. (2010). The creation of fiction to share other truths and different viewpoints: A creative journey and an interpretive process. *Qualitative Inquiry, 16*(7), 556–565.

Ward, A. (2011). "Bringing the message forward": Using poetic re-presentation to solve research dilemmas. *Qualitative Inquiry, 17*(4), 355–363.

Woo, U. (2008). Engaging new audiences: Translating research into popular media. *Educational Researcher, 37*(6), 321–329.

Wyatt, J., Gale, K., Gannon, S., & Davies, B. (2010). Deleuzian thought and collaborative writing: A play in four acts. *Qualitative Inquiry, 16*(9), 730–741.

Wyatt, J., & Tamas, S. (2013). Telling, *Qualitative Inquiry, 19*(1), 60–66.

STUDENT STUDY SITE

Visit **http://www.sagepub.com/lichtmanqrss** to access additional study tools, including eFlashcards and links to SAGE journal articles.

CHAPTER 14

Judging the Research Process and Product

Focus Your Reading

- Criteria for judging qualitative research continue to expand as the field evolves.
- Increasingly, review boards and journal editors recognize that standard criteria suitable for quantitative research may not apply.
- A backlash reflected in a conservative movement in the United States and other European countries has led some researchers, publishers, and universities to require more scientific approaches.

A number of years ago, I wrote an article with some colleagues about the process of supervision for family therapists (Keller, Protinsky, Lichtman, & Allen, 1996). At the time, I believed we used a novel approach. We videotaped several supervisors and students. We then assigned four pairs (composed of a supervisor and a student) to observe each videotape and develop themes independently of each other. The various iterations resulted in common themes based on our individual and joint observations. To our chagrin, the editors of a respectable journal in the field said that although they liked the article, it resembled our own reflections and was not sufficiently scholarly or scientific. We subsequently rewrote the article in light of the criticisms. But I believe the reason it was not accepted was that the reviewers were still developing their own criteria for judging research that did not fit traditional modes. Today, editors of some journals, while still differing on what constitutes acceptable qualitative research (QR), are more open to alternative methods and approaches.

What should we believe about these alternative methods? Phillips and Carr (2009) asked this question in their action-research study of preservice teachers. The authors are teacher educators of preservice students. They began thus: "During a conversation among fellow teacher educators, one colleague suggested that preservice teachers' action research 'didn't really count'" (p. 208). They were challenged by this comment and decided to conduct a study of their own. They acknowledged that the *trustworthiness* of action research is questionable. Their explanation of the term *trustworthiness* in action research includes transparency of the process, the gathering of data for a purpose, a search for multiple perspectives, change in the researcher and in practice, and results that matter. What they did was to reinterpret *trustworthiness* through the lens of a preservice teacher. They illustrated each of the elements of trustworthiness with examples from the preservice teachers. They spoke about valuing those preservice teachers who are powerless. I find this account particularly refreshing. The authors justified a way of evaluating those whose voices are not often acknowledged as having worth. Perhaps you feel that way at times as a student.

As you read this chapter, you will become aware that one of the most controversial areas surrounding QR is how to evaluate what you read. There are currently several schools of thought regarding how QR should be judged, what criteria should be used, and who should determine the criteria. One viewpoint is that criteria for evaluation should be parallel to those used in evaluating quantitative research (QN). Another viewpoint is that it is inappropriate to develop parallel criteria, because the goal of QR is often different from that of QN. Those in this camp believe that a different set of criteria can be developed. Although a small minority viewpoint says that there cannot really be general criteria, today, many scholars accept the idea that some criteria should be developed. But what criteria and who should determine them are still in question.

I see these issues along a continuum. In Figure 14.1, conservative, more traditional views, especially those that emerged prior to 1990, are represented at the right. This view holds that the same criteria used for traditional QN methods should be used for QR. In the early 2000s, other voices were heard, stating that alternative criteria could be developed.

Figure 14.1 Key Issues Associated With Evaluating Qualitative Research

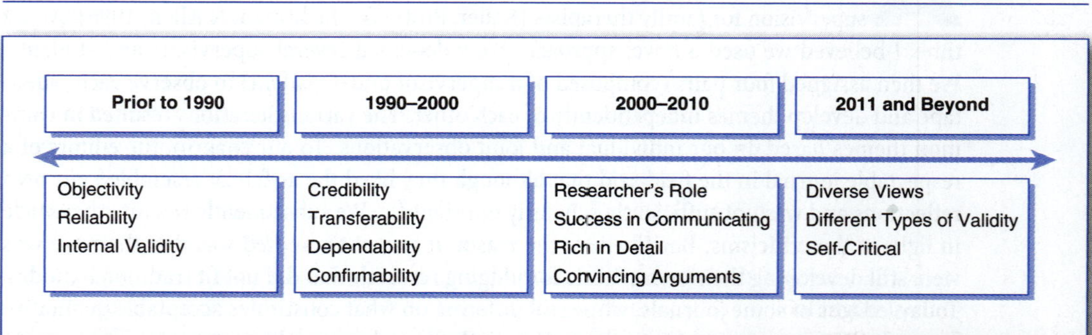

However, there has been a resurgence of interest in this traditional view and in adopting research designs that are quantitative and scientific in nature. This appears to be fueled, at least in part, by the political fervor of the No Child Left Behind Act of 2001 (NCLB; 2001), which requires "scientifically based research." The nursing profession has also felt the impact of the gold standard framework.

In November 2010, the National Institutes of Health, Office of Behavioral and Social Science Research issued best practices for mixed-methods research in the health sciences. Two key figures who developed these standards were Creswell and Plano, the authors of a text on mixed-methods research. The section on the nature of QR states the following:

> A salient strength of qualitative research is its focus on the contexts and meaning of human lives and experiences for the purpose of inductive or theory-development driven research. It is a systematic and rigorous form of inquiry that uses methods of data collection such as in-depth interviews, ethnographic observation, and review of documents. Qualitative data help researchers understand processes, especially those that emerge over time, provide detailed information about setting or context, and emphasize the voices of participants through quotes. Qualitative methods facilitate the collection of data when measures do not exist and provide a depth of understanding of concepts. Typical qualitative approaches used in health research are case studies, grounded theory, ethnography, and phenomenology.

These standards seem to imply that support will be given to studies of this type. In other documents issued by this office, you can find descriptions of community-based participatory research.

Moving along the continuum, there are those who want to make sure that QR remains scientific. They adopt concepts supposedly parallel to those of the traditionalists. For example, to demonstrate reliability, they suggest *triangulation*, a concept that uses several methods or strategies of gathering data as a means of validation. This faction adopts a post-positivist position, in which the researcher strives for an objective stance. But this point of view, too, is not necessarily one many qualitative researchers in the new millennium adopt. Another view is one in which such terms as *trustworthiness*, discussed earlier, and *verifiability* come into play. Criteria developed in the 21st century represent differing points of view. These criteria tend to emphasize the role of the researcher, for example. I find the criteria very much influenced by some of the newer ideas of poststructuralism, feminism, and postmodernism. Politics and power also play a critical role here.

I have identified a number of important issues. What should the criteria be to decide whether a piece of qualitative work is good, appropriate, or suitable? Who should determine these criteria? How do the criteria become modified as time and views change? Should there be a single set of criteria, or are several sets suitable, depending on the type of QR conducted? Or should the criteria be continuously evolving to represent the dynamic nature of the field? In what ways do alternative modes of dissemination, such as the poetry or performance pieces, affect the criteria? Differing audiences may expect different things, so a conservative academic journal might look for one thing, while a more avant-garde source may expect something else. There is the community of those being studied, the academic community, the government community, the educational community, the publishing community, and the general public. At times, they overlap, but not always. Should criteria be published? How specific should they be?

You might understand some of these issues more clearly if you look outside your own field and into the world of art. You may know of Édouard Manet (born 1832), a great painter and one of the precursors of the Impressionists. But if not, I suspect that many of you have heard of Claude Monet (born 1840) and Edgar Degas (born 1834). These artists are considered preeminent in their field of Impressionism. The Impressionist movement was popular in the mid- to late 1800s. It is generally considered one of the most popular and well-received artistic movements today. However, these artists were originally seen as outsiders. They departed from their predecessors by using light and color to depict visual reality. They worked outdoors (*en plein air*) and tried to capture how the light influenced what they saw.

But these artists were not always so well received. In fact, in order to show their art, artists' work had to be accepted in the Paris Salon. This Salon began in 1791 and eventually became a small group of people who determined the criteria for what was good and desirable in art. In 1863, the Salon refused a very important work that Manet had painted: *Déjeuner sur l'herbe* (*The Picnic*). The artistic community of France, supported by Napoleon III, formed an alternative to the traditional Paris Salon and called it the Salon des Refusés (Salon of the Rejected). Manet's painting created quite a scandal. Why? Because it didn't meet the criteria that were acceptable to those who ran the traditional salons. One reason for the scandal was the content of the painting. Manet juxtaposed a female nude with males in modern dress as a gesture of provocation. Further, Manet's painting of Olympia (a nude courtesan) also shocked the viewers at the 1865 Salon. People jeered it. In fact, the first Impressionist exhibition was not held until 1874, although by this time, Manet was no longer involved. By 1886, the 8th and last Impressionist exhibition was held, showing the work of seventeen artists. Subsequently, the Impressionist movement fell into a sharp decline. Those who were judging realized that they had to expand their expectations of what was good and beautiful. Of course, this led to many other breaks with artistic tradition, such as Cubism in the early 1900s, Surrealism some years later, and Abstract Expressionism in post–World War II New York. (In 2013, Ronald Lauder donated his collection of cubist art valued at one billion dollars to the Metropolitan Museum of Art. Some one hundred years after Picasso painted his major cubist painting, *Les Demoiselles d'Avignon*, Cubism is now seen as one of the major contributions to the art world.) By the next century, the artistic world had been knocked completely off its feet, and room was made for a vast range of work ranging from video installations to performance art to ready-mades. (A *ready-made* involves elevating a common object to the status of high art, such as the urinal that Duchamp called *Fountain* in 1917.) No longer is it clear what art is, how to judge it, or what it should look like. What is clear is that the world has opened up to new ideas, to new expressions, and to new people who were not previously in the field.

I have gone into detail about the artistic community because I want you to understand that the issues the Impressionists faced are not so different from what you face. Just as "What is good art?" is a question that cannot easily be answered, "What is good research?" is a question that we consider now. With these ideas in mind, I want to begin with my personal criteria. I stress *personal* and yet want to make clear that the criteria are not presented without considerable thought, reading, and experience.

■ Personal Criteria

You can find many lists of what should be included in a good piece of QR. However, you will find little or no evidence that these criteria are anything more than criteria generated by people who have worked in the field or who have read about the field. They seem to be based implicitly on the philosophy and assumptions made by the writers. Throughout this book, I have chosen to make my personal philosophy explicit.

Did You Know

As I conclude my discussion of QR, I think it is time for you to provide a Did You Know for me. What fact, isolated or general, should I add here? It is your chance to make a contribution. I welcome your comments at MarilynLichtman09@gmail.com

This is important as you begin to understand personal criteria. I will talk about three intertwined concepts: the self, the other, and the interaction of the self with the other. Next, I discuss the importance of positioning what was studied and what was found in a larger context. How convincing is the researcher in arguing a case? A third issue is to make explicit the manner in which the study was done. Does the writer include rich detail and explanation so that others may decide its worth? Finally, I look at success in communication.

Researcher's Role: Revealing the Self-and-Other Connection

Why is the self so important? Shouldn't the self remain outside the research? If the self is involved, can you trust what you read? I believe strongly that the role of the researcher is critical to the work. Researchers should not try to remain outside the system. They need not try to achieve objectivity, because that is an assumption of QN and not of QR. Researchers need not try to get experts to approve of what they write, because the researchers themselves are the experts in the situation. Researchers need to reveal themselves through a process of self-reflexivity. (See Chapter 2 for details on the topic.)

In addition to revealing the self, researchers should reveal what they learn about the other. By *the other*, I mean those who are studied. Unlike in QN, where those who are studied are the *subjects* or the *sample*—nameless and faceless individuals who have been chosen at random to represent others with similar characteristics—those studied in QR are real people with real needs, ambitions, fears, and desires. Their stories touch the researcher and touch the readers. I believe that is why we are so captivated and energized by them. I argue here that an understanding of the other does not come about without an understanding of the self and how the self and the other connect. I believe each is transformed through this research process.

I have chosen to divide my personal criteria along several dimensions: What was studied? What was found? How was the study done? How does the writer communicate?

Convincing Arguments

What Was Studied

I see this concept as critical in an assessment of the worth of a piece of QR, yet it is very difficult to get at its essence. What is important to one person may have no relevance to someone else. Yet if the researcher does a good job, he or she convinces the reader that the topic is an important one to consider and fits into a larger context. You can assume that the topic that is studied is important to the researcher. Otherwise, why would he or she choose to write about it?

I thought it might be helpful to explore what others who have published in qualitative journals are doing. I examined those most current at the time of this writing (April 2013). I did not look at all journals that are known to publish qualitative pieces. The articles I selected are those of interest to me. Here are some things I found:

I looked at articles in the April 2013 (volume 19, number 4) issue of *Qualitative Inquiry.* Eight articles include such topics as critical reflections on embodiments; performing reflexivity; examining the emergence of the first vegetarian organization; and a graduate student enters the field. In the last-named article, Tieken (2013) writes about the first stage of entering the field using portraiture to describe her journey. I know you will be able to connect with her experiences.

I also looked at articles in the April 2013 (volume 13, number 2) issue of *Qualitative Research.* The issue includes both original research and book reviews. Included are seven articles, one review article, and nine book reviews. The articles are very diverse: digital storytelling as a narrative method; a critical examination of saturated sample size in QR; using cartoons to disseminate research findings; and benefits of spontaneous innovation in recruiting participants.

I reviewed articles in the May 2013 (volume 23, number 5) issue of *Qualitative Health Research.* The issue contained 10 articles based on original research, one article about qualitative methods, a letter to the editor and a response, and one book review. All are in the health field; they ranged from a study about malaria in Afghanistan to the counseling and experiences of cancer patients to an illustration of the use of photovoice in mental illness and experiences of breastfeeding.

I explored articles in the March 2013 (volume 12, number 2) issue of *Qualitative Social Work.* In addition to an editorial and one book review, there were eight articles. Topics included a narrative approach to intercultural care; prospective narratives among people in residential care; making meaning and avoidance in parenting; and collaboration in grounded theory analysis. I was intrigued with Taiwo's (2013) use of relational poetry to co-construct reality. The author concluded:

> In keeping with the spirit of the relational form, I have offered my subjectivity to Kumsa's work, even as my plural identities intersect with some of hers. My purpose is to reel in the reader into the process of making meaning and recognizing alternative epistemologies. After all, we are all in our subjectivities. (p. 227)

I looked at *The Qualitative Report* for several weeks in 2013. (This online journal now appears weekly.) Topics included exploration of positive identity development for women living with chronic pain, use of poetry to promote learning and as an alternative to using member checking, ethnodrama of a Latina's learning, queering methodologies and challenge to scientific constraints, and recruiting ethnically diverse participants into qualitative health research.

I reviewed articles in *The International Journal of Qualitative Methods* from the University of Alberta, Canada. (Formerly a quarterly publication, this is now an annual journal that is web based.) Volume 12 (2013) included eight articles. I noticed that contributors come from many places around the world and only one from the United States. One article that piqued my interest was about using drawings that privilege younger children's voices in research (Tay-Lim & Lim, 2013). The authors concluded that the voices of young children could be heard through what they call *in-depth draw and talk methods*. It's an intriguing idea. Several other articles in this issue include participatory drawing as a visual research method, hermeneutics and human interplay, and negotiating with gatekeepers for researching minority communities.

I looked at the April 15, 2013, online releases from the *International Journal of Qualitative Studies in Education* (*QSE*) (volume 6, issue 4). Topics include a longitudinal study of two preservice teachers, ethnocinema (an emerging methodology) and changing culture, and the use of narrative interviews to explore perspectives of teachers learning to learn.

Of course, I did not look at all journals that publish works of a qualitative nature. There are quite a few and in many disciplines. Cardiff University (n.d.) publishes a list of qualitative methods journals in the social sciences. It includes, among others, *Cultural Studies, Critical Methodologies*; *Field Methods*; *Forum: Qualitative Social Research* (*FQS*); *International Journal of Research and Method in Education*; and *Organizational Research Methods*.

What do I take away from this brief exercise about the topics of today? I am struck that they are so diverse. There is not a common theme, although many addressed narrative in one way or another. Personal interests and agendas often drive researchers. Whether these topics are useful or of value to you as a reader is up to you. Are they of value to the larger educational community? We cannot know for sure.

I return to my original position. It is up to the writer to make a convincing argument that the topic is important and may be one from which we can learn about our situation. I am not speaking about generalizing to other situations; that is not something qualitative researchers claim to do.

What Was Found

The reported findings should be directly connected to the questions asked; if the questions are unclear or of little value, then the findings are of little use. "Lies, damned lies, and statistics," said Benjamin Disraeli and Mark Twain when speaking of using statistics and numbers to support weaker arguments. I would suggest that findings or interpretations tied to questionable topics are no better than using statistics to bolster questionable arguments. A personal annoyance of mine is studies that end with a recommendation that further research needs to be done on the topic. I have read so many like this. I would suggest leaving the recommendation out.

So my personal criteria include addressing the two elements: what was studied and what was found. How does your research connect to the larger body of research? After all, your study does not exist in a vacuum.

Rich in Detail: How the Study Was Done

You can judge what you read by the information provided about how it was done. Can you determine what the researcher did, how it was done, and why it was done? Can you follow a path to how interviews were done or how those studied were selected? Can you determine why the researcher chose to conduct a phenomenology or ethnography? Does the researcher provide enough explanation? Does the researcher provide explanations for concepts that are often associated with QR? For example, is the role of the researcher addressed? What about power? If the researcher chooses an approach to research that is not widely understood, is that approach and rationale explained? I think it is important that you be provided sufficient information to determine what was done. I am mindful, however, of the position that some writers take. They omit details about how a study was done or speak only in very general terms.

Although many of the studies that I cite provide detailed descriptions of how the study was done, others do not. I would not be too critical of those that omit this information. Often, but not always, when a new concept or idea is introduced, the researchers provide clear explanations. Adding clear explanations and specific details about methodology helps the reader understand and make critical judgments about suitability and appropriateness.

Communication: How Convincing Is the Presentation?

Finally, we can judge the worth of research only by what we read or hear or see. You need to decide to what extent the writer reaches you by the presentation. Do the words convey a story? Does the play provide insight and meaning? Does the video clip provide a window into understanding a particular issue? Most of what you will encounter is the written word, so I want to say a few more things about what to look for:

Opening. Are you drawn into the context or story immediately? Because QR tends to be inductive in nature, I find that manuscripts that draw me in and take me on a personal journey are those that are most effective. I want to be grabbed when I begin to read. This is not to say that you are just reading a story, but a story is an excellent way to begin.

Engaging style. Does the writer use a style that is open and engaging while at the same time reflecting thoughtfulness and scholarship?

Reflections. Does the writer incorporate personal reflections and insights, thereby drawing the self into the writing?

Integration. Does the writer clarify and draw connections between the extant research, what has been learned on the journey, and his or her own insights?

Rich detail. Does the writer provide sufficient detail regarding methods and findings so the reader can understand the message?

Voices of others. Does the writer use the voices of others to reach new insights and interpretations?

Justification. If the researcher uses a particular approach, does he or she provide ample explanation?

New meanings. Does the writer offer new connections, interpretations, or insights based on his or her research?

These criteria are meant as a starting point for you as you begin to read what others have written and plan your own research. You might find that you will want to add to or modify what I have written; I hope you will. You should also find it helpful to examine criteria as currently delineated and those that have evolved over the past 25 years or so. In the next section, I offer a brief history so you can understand the context of the development of criteria.

■ What Others Have to Say

Although I have offered my criteria for evaluating QR, I think it is helpful for you to understand the larger field and what has come before. I begin this discussion with what is known already.

Criteria for Reviewing Traditional Quantitative Research Approaches

Most would agree that they are *internal validity* (in experimental studies, the degree to which the independent variable has an effect on the dependent variable), *external validity* (the degree to which the findings can be generalized), *reliability* (the degree to which the findings can be replicated), and *objectivity* (the degree to which the findings are free from bias). These are critical and expected of those conducting research based on positivist or post-positivist positions. I want you to remember these as you begin your journey to establish new criteria. A quantitative study that uses a randomized control group design is said to be the gold standard of experimental research. It is the gold standard because it satisfied the four criteria I mentioned above. The study addresses internal validity by using experimental and control groups in a randomized fashion. Subjects are assigned to groups at random, and the experimental condition is also assigned at random. The design addresses the concern for external validity of subjects, who are drawn at random from a larger population. It also ensures the reliability of findings, which can be demonstrated in more than one study. The design also addresses objectivity by keeping the researcher outside of the system (the researcher remains objective).

I am going to remind you again of some of the underlying assumptions on which these criteria are based. One assumption is that methods associated with the natural sciences are the best and can be used in the social sciences. Second, only observable phenomena are considered. The researcher seeks an objective reality; thus, the researcher's role is to find a way to observe the phenomena and remain outside the system. These assumptions underlie the criteria of traditional research.

A Brief History

It is also helpful to see how criteria have emerged as QR has taken a more prominent place in the research domain. I think it will help you to see the historical and chronological evolution of these criteria. Prior to the 1990s, most QR operated from a post-positivist perspective. Consequently, the researchers found themselves in a traditional mind-set. But I think some researchers knew that something was amiss; they just weren't sure quite what.

Some criteria from these early years were generic and meant to apply to all types of QR paradigms, while others were quite specific. Many involved explicit or implicit expectations that QR should be similar to QN. I have organized the information in a chronological fashion.

Prior to 1990

As QR began to take hold, many were unsure how to judge this type of research. Journal editors tended to rely on traditional criteria (described above, associated with experiments and QN), and many journals were reluctant to publish research that did not appear to fit the format of traditional research. In these early days, there were not any journals that devoted themselves primarily to QR. I recall when several of us submitted a QR study to a marriage and family journal. The reviews came back: "We found the study very interesting but did not see it as more than some ramblings from a few people." University researchers were just beginning to explore qualitative approaches. Those in many social science departments were quite reluctant to approve research ideas that did not adopt a quantitative approach to answering questions that generated statistics.

Among the earliest to write about evaluating QR studies were Lincoln and Guba (1985), who tried to develop criteria that were parallel to foundationalist criteria. They wrote about credibility, transferability, dependability, and confirmability. Smith and Heshusius (1986) criticized Lincoln and Guba and commented that Lincoln and Guba adopted the assumption that there is an external reality independent of the researcher. I think, in these early days, many were left wondering whether they should adopt criteria from the traditional scientific perspective, even though what they were doing did not necessarily fit this traditional mode.

By the next decade, the winds of change were in the air, and we began to see alternative criteria based on different assumptions.

The 1990s

During the 1990s, alternative attempts to define criteria begin to emerge. One camp developed criteria that were meant to be comparable to traditional criteria. Trochim (2001), using Guba and Lincoln's four terms, compared them to traditional criteria. Thus internal validity was replaced by credibility, external validity by transferability, reliability by dependability, and objectivity by confirmability. In my view, on closer examination, these criteria are somewhat limited and limiting.

The term *credibility* suggests that the results should be evaluated from the point of view of the participants, and thus they are the only ones capable of judging the credibility of results. (Some refer to this as *member checking.*) I think this seems simplistic. The research is not written for the benefit of the participants. It should be set in a larger context and the interpretation of the term *credibility* expanded. I would agree that the participants may be the only ones to judge the extent to which the researcher explained or captured the meaning of what he saw. However, they are not the only ones to determine the extent to which the researcher's interpretations make sense in a larger context. (See Choudhuri, Glauser, & Peregoy, 2004, who speak about credibility.)

Transferability, akin to *generalizability*, is the extent to which the results can be transferred to other settings. Here, Trochim (2001) suggested that the reader needs to decide whether the results transfer. But he offered no guidance as to how the reader should make such a judgment.

The term *dependability* emphasizes the need for the researcher to account for the ever-changing context within which research occurs. The researcher is responsible for describing the changes that occur in the setting and how these changes affected the way the researcher approached the study. I am not clear what Trochim (2001) meant when he spoke to the ever-changing context of the field. Does he mean the context in which the research is conducted? Does he mean the larger social context?

The term *confirmability* refers to the degree to which results could be confirmed or corroborated by others. I have the most difficulty with this criterion, because it implies an attempt to describe an objective reality. (Some may have used the idea of *triangulation*, introduced earlier.)

These four criteria are typical of some of the earlier attempts to establish criteria comparable to those used in traditional research. Glaringly omitted are comments about the researcher's role and self-reflection. You will see these emerge as you read criteria established more recently.

Lincoln, Lynham and Guba (2011) remind us that in the early days—mid-1990s or so—"we focused on the contention among various research paradigms for legitimacy and intellectual and paradigmatic hegemony" (p. 97). Reilly (2013) states that

> Since my early experiences in learning and becoming a qualitative researcher, the field has undergone a profound philosophical evolution. . . . It is an evolution which questions the fundamental underlying assumptions of the gold standard of trustworthiness and therefore, the utility of member checks. (p. 2)

She echoes my own sentiments precisely. As she speaks of her own crises of representation and educational experiences in the experimental mode, I am reminded of how I went through the same experiences.

During this time, there were essentially two camps—the positivists and post-positivists constituted one group, while those in the postmodern camp were the other group. Post-positivists tried to fit into the mold of traditionalists and so looked for ways that were parallel to traditional research, while postmodernists discarded these ideas and said they were coming from some other place. Each camp wanted to occupy a place of legitimacy. What were they to do?

In the 1990s, many peer reviewers' assessments of QR also followed criteria often used to judge experimental research (Taylor, Beck, & Ainsworth, 2001). Taylor et al. looked at how peer reviewers judged QR and, not surprisingly, found six themes to be essential to the publication of QR: (1) What is the purpose of the study? (2) How does the purpose build on previous research? (3) How thorough is the methodology? (4) How are the findings presented? (5) What are the contributions, implications, and significance of the study? (6) Is the manuscript organized, edited, and well formatted? If you think these criteria sound familiar and represent a traditionalist stance, you are correct.

So you can see that during the last decade of the 20th century, scholars and researchers were struggling with how to evaluate this new kind of research. Almost all accepted the idea that the traditional criteria of objectivity, reliability, validity, and generalizability were not particularly appropriate. Some looked for parallel ideas, while others recognized that alternative criteria needed to be developed. Some hold the view that QR should not be evaluated in the traditional manner but rather should be judged by the user.

The Early 2000s

Before some of the more recent writings, there were attempts to reinterpret evaluative criteria. Some writers discussed such traditional criteria as study design, sampling and data collection, analysis, findings, interpretations, trustworthiness, and implications (Choudhuri et al., 2004). Morse (2003) acknowledged what she called the "uncertain exploratory nature" of QR using a flexible design and emerging findings (p. 837). Yet she suggested that evaluators look for *relevance* (the worthiness of the question and its value), *rigor* (the adequacy and appropriateness of the method used to answer the questions), and *feasibility* (the ability of the researcher to conduct the research; p. 833).

Other approaches asked us to consider rigor by looking at five fundamental considerations: (1) Does the researcher convey reflexivity or the ability to stay open to the participant's experience? (2) Does the researcher show credibility or validity and accuracy (a concept of traditional research)? (3) Is transferability (the ability to generalize) observed (again, a concept from traditional research)? (4) Is there an audit trail? (5) Is there confirmability or objectivity?

In contrast to criteria that build on fairly traditional notions of what makes for good research, others took a somewhat different view. Parker (2003) posed four questions regarding criteria that address issues relating to (1) what is good, (2) who is the audience, (3) what is analysis, and (4) the role of theory. Rather than answering these questions in a predictable manner, he suggested that there are no clear answers (pp. 5–6). Instead, he suggested that we explore three additional issues as well as their exceptions:

1. *How is the study related to existing research?* We know that a study does not exist in a vacuum and that we need to relate our research to existing research. But isn't it possible that there is no existing research out there, and the absence of research may be equally important?

2. *Does the narrative move in a linear fashion to reach its conclusion?* In general, we expect this to happen. Parker suggests that there may be times when a fragmented format is more appropriate, and a traditional format may inhibit innovation.

3. *To whom is the research accessible?* He suggests that at times, issues are complex and arguments difficult to write, thus making writing less accessible.

I find it particularly interesting that Parker (2003) suggested that "the study should make clear by what criteria it should be evaluated" and when the rules should be followed or broken

(p. 6). In encouraging innovation and flexibility, Parker suggested that criteria typically associated with QN are not necessarily appropriate in QR.

Devers (1999) and Hoepfl (1997) agreed that clear criteria are critical but expressed the concern (as I have) that we have been relying on traditional criteria based on positivism. Devers wants criteria to address the voice of the researcher and alternative means of reporting. Denzin and Lincoln (2000) added the ideas of verisimilitude, emotionality, personal responsibility, caring, political praxis, multivoiced texts, and dialogues with subjects. I know you will agree that these ideas bear little resemblance to the criteria I mentioned earlier.

But Parker (2003) warned that using fixed criteria might limit innovation, as it has done with traditional psychological research, and risks making legitimate certain types of QR at the expense of others (see also Elliott, Fischer, & Rennie, 1999). He continued, saying that there really are no overriding criteria that fit a particular situation. He suggested that new research questions call for a new combination of research methods.

Barbour and Barbour (2002) cautioned against using checklists that appeal to credibility and rigor and suggested that some of the most influential papers would not have been published if traditional criteria had been used. They concluded their thoughtful article with the suggestion that qualitative researchers and reviewers should look for suggestions from their own modes of collaboration and look for new ways of collaborating.

Other new ideas are emerging. For example, you will see such criteria as including thick description (details about the setting, participants, concepts), prolonged engagement (this is primarily appropriate for ethnography), reflexivity (consideration of subjectivity and bias—an idea from traditional research), member checking (using respondents to check language—an idea that the researcher is trying to get it right), theoretical richness (incorporation of appropriate theory, which works only if theory is an issue), alternative structure for writing (use of poetry or ethnotheater), and expressiveness (data and analysis should be interesting). Morrow (2007) spoke to credibility/trustworthiness/rigor and validity in a syllabus for a qualitative course in psychology:

> If necessary in your field, give rationale and educate a bit. DON'T do this if your program is accustomed to qualitative research, as you will bore them to tears. The 10th time one reads about Guba and Lincoln's parallel criteria, they will want to cry. If using critical or feminist or other ideological theory, describe authenticity criteria and how you will accomplish them.
>
> Briefly summarize components of rigor that you have already described (self-reflective journal, multiple data sources, immersion in the data, peer research team, etc.).

One final take on criteria for judging QR comes from the United Kingdom. The following list reflects some of the thinking that has emerged as the new century is upon us.

- owning one's own perspective and reflecting on subjectivity and bias
- producing coherent connections between theory and method
- focusing on meaning
- accounting for, and being sensitive to, context
- adopting an open-ended stance on data collection and analysis

- collecting and engaging in depth with rich data
- balancing description of data with interpretation of data
- offering transparent analysis (e.g., grounded in example)
- offering plausible/credible/meaningful (to reader or others) analysis
- offering sense of what is distinct within account of what is shared
- drawing out "resonant"/accessible conclusions (Larkin, Watts, & Clifton, 2006)

It is clear that criteria in the 21st century are not one-dimensional. Patton (2002) has suggested different criteria depending on the type of QR being conducted. He suggested that a traditional, scientific type of QR would involve the expected ideas of objectivity, rigor, generalizability, and triangulation. On the other hand, a study that used social constructivism would look at trustworthiness, reflexivity, particularity, subjectivity, and multiple perspectives, and a study based on critical change would identify the nature of injustice and inequality and issues of power and of taking action. Despite the diversity of views on the feasibility or desirability of criteria, some believe that several criteria need to be developed. However, it is clear that more discussion and debate should be conducted.

To restate the obvious, at this point, I caution you to be careful as you review criteria for judging QR. Several viewpoints are in play. One group contends that we need to return to research that is more scientific, but I believe that is not necessarily the majority viewpoint. Others see the field as still in a state of flux. Freeman, deMarrais, Preissle, Roulston, and St. Pierre (2007) laid out their interpretation of the problem. Savall, Zardet, Bonnet, and Peron (2008) talked about the emergence of implicit criteria. The climate of the world of qualitative research is such that there is increased accountability and standardization and control. The field has become more politicized than it once was. Savall et al.'s premise, like some other voices, is that it is not possible, nor is it desirable, to reach any kind of consensus about what standards should be adopted. Rather, they recommend a continued conversation. They cited the political movement across the United States related to the NCLB initiative and the emphasis on "mandating scientific method into law" as the reason for this discussion (p. 25). They are against this movement because they believe that "top-down efforts such as these to legislate scientific practice and mandate research design threaten to harden the boundaries of what counts as science, to devalue many qualitative research endeavors, and to limit creative research practice of all kinds" (p. 25).

Cohen and Crabtree (2008) reviewed published journal articles discussing criteria for rigorous research. They reported seven criteria that emerged from their research: (1) conducting ethical research, (2) importance of the research, (3) clarity and coherence of the final report, (4) appropriate and rigorous methods, (5) reflexivity and researcher bias, (6) importance of establishing credibility, and (7) importance of verification or reliability. But they pointed to the difficulties with using these criteria for all types of QR: The assumptions underlying QR—whether explicit or implicit—influence the manner in which the research is conducted and reported. As I have argued throughout this book, they concluded that the field is not unified and that reviewers of journals often embrace a kind of generic criteria. Although they reviewed articles in the health field, the points they made are applicable to education and other disciplines.

Paulus, Woodside, and Ziegler (2008) explored what happens to their assumptions about QR when they engage in a dialogic collaborative process:

> Assumptions about research are pervasive, and the need for qualitative research to compete with or position itself in relation to the positivist paradigm remains implicit and all too often unacknowledged. Collaborative research, as we have experienced it, addresses the concern that qualitative research methods need to be more transparent and public. The transparency begins with the researchers themselves, because they first must make the process visible to themselves through dialogue and writing. Through our collaborative process we have demonstrated how dialogue and writing blend to become inseparable parts of a transparent meaning-making process. (p. 239)

Paulus et al. (2008) addressed an important and novel topic: collaboration among researchers. They commented that the collaborative effort transformed some of their fundamental assumptions about QR. I am struck by their acknowledgment that collaboration led them to see findings as part of an ongoing conversation. I think that by making their assumptions explicit to others, they began to question them and changed as a result.

That the issue of judging, quality, and rigor is very much alive can be seen in the report of a two-day workshop held in Norway in 2007 on the topic "Is there a 'legitimation crisis' in qualitative methods?" The workshop, sponsored by the European Scientific Foundation, was aimed at improving the quality of QR. Speakers and presenters were prominent leaders in the field from Europe and the United Kingdom. I report this because it is clear that the issue of quality is not yet resolved (Weil, 2008).

Current Thinking

Since the turn of the century, much interest has been generated in the general topic of quality in QR. As the calendar turned to the 21st century, I wondered whether the issue would become less thorny. But that is not the case. Reilly (2013), teaching in the Applied Human Sciences Department at Concordia University in Canada, observes that trustworthiness "is still the most often cited standard of truthfulness and authenticity for qualitative research across numerous and various disciplines" (p. 1). Educational qualitative researchers Cho and Trent (2006) suggested that although issues about validity in QR have been with us for a long time, the concern has increased with the new century. They used the term *validity* in a general sense and suggested that you can think of the concept of validity in more than one way. A traditional idea of validity is what they called a *transactional approach.* In this approach, a researcher would utilize such techniques as member checking (asking the respondent to confirm what was said), bracketing (putting aside the researcher's views), or triangulation (looking for multiple evidence to confirm a particular idea). These techniques are designed to assist the researcher in making the research "more credible " (p. 322). You will come across a number of these techniques in the literature. In my view, all aim to make QR more objective and legitimate.

These early responses to how to make a study valid have been replaced. I restate again from Lincoln and her colleagues (2011), who suggest that current thinking revolves around two arguments. One is concerned with rigor in the application of a particular method (*research approach*). The other "argues for both community consent and a form of rigor-defensible reasoning" (p. 120). So we have two forms or types of rigor. One is concerned with rigor of method; the other is concerned with rigor of interpretation. According to Lincoln et al., it is the rigor of interpretation that has become most prominent in recent writing. What does this mean, you ask? Can we rely on our co-constructions as a call to action on the part of those participating in the research? Further, "new-paradigm inquirers, however, are increasingly concerned with the single experience, the individual crisis, the epiphany or moment of discovery, with that most powerful of all threats to conventional objectivity, feeling, and emotion and to action" (p. 120). I suspect that is why autoethnography has burgeoned recently.

While there are other turns in this history that are too detailed to consider, we need to return to our original question about validity. How can we rely on what we know? Is it believable? And in today's world, how can we feel that it is safe in acting upon what we learn? So let's try three criteria proposed by Lincoln and her colleagues (2011):

- *Validity as authenticity*. "Objectivity is a chimera: a mythological creature that never existed, save in the imaginations of those who believe that knowing can be separated from the knower" (p. 122).

- *Validity as resistance and poststructural transgression*. Proposed by Richardson by using experimental forms (some of which I have cited elsewhere in this text) of presentation, she seeks to create new relationships. Experimental forms permit a social scientist to create a different kind of social science. Lather also wants to disrupt the status quo.

- *Validity as an ethical relationship*. Connection to research participants is critical here.

Northcote's (2012) criteria involve guiding principles. Does the research contribute to advancement of knowledge or understanding about policies and practices? Does it follow rigorous and transparent practices in the collection and analysis of data? Is the design defensible and credible? Does it acknowledge the excitement of research discoveries?

An alternative idea about validity is somewhat more radical. Called *transformational validity* by Cho and Trent (2006), this approach is concerned with the "value-laden" (p. 324) nature of the research within a social or political context. Thus, validity cannot nor should it be achieved by such techniques as member checking or triangulation. Rather, validity is achieved as the research itself promotes actions. For some who support this notion, then, a more traditional idea of validity is inappropriate. Others who are aligned with this position emphasize a greater self-reflexivity. Cho and Trent concluded that what is needed is a way to demonstrate the credibility of QR to those outside the field as well as a way to begin the social construction of a holistic view of validity.

Doloriert and Sambrook (2011) describe how a traditional business school accommodated an autoethnographic PhD. One author is the student and the other the student's supervisor. The school is located in the UK. This paper explores how they negotiated "within and around" a traditional culture and the associated structures. They use autoethnographic vignettes to tell their story. They acknowledge that there is currently a debate about whether this type of research can be seen as credible. In their paper, they argue that the quality of an autoethnography can be viewed along two dimensions: the relationship with consensus and the context of quality judgment. Since the student received her PhD, you can assume their argument was supported, albeit not without challenges along the way. As you come to the end of your journey learning about QR, I hope you will use this work to make a case for using alternative forms of research to your own institution.

Tracy (2010) pointed to issues of quality as ever changing and "situated within local contexts and current conversations" (p. 837). While she acknowledged the differing views about whether or not to develop criteria at all, she suggested that "criteria, quite simply, are useful" (p. 838). Tracy therefore puts her hand into the criteria pot as well. Is anyone to say that she is correct? Let's look at the criteria she offered. She called them eight "big tent" criteria: (1) worthy topic, (2) rich rigor, (3) sincerity, (4) credibility (we have certainly heard this one before), (5) resonance, (6) significant contribution, (7) ethics, and (8) meaningful coherence. For me, some are more salient than others. What do you think? Her recommendation at the end of the article is critical: "The most successful researchers are willingly self-critical, viewing their own actions through the eyes of others while also maintaining resilience and energy through acute sensitivity to their own well-being" (p. 849).

Similar to Cho and Trent, Koro-Ljungberg (2010) focused her discussion of criteria specifically on validity. She summarized the commentaries about validity in QR and suggested that they include a variety of issues (some of which are included in Tracy's big-tent list). She included such ideas as authenticity, credibility, confirmability, internal coherence, transferability, reliability, and significance. Like Tracy, she suggested that continued discussions about quality are useful so that qualitative researchers are not excluded from current discussions and more mainstream policy considerations.

The debate continues. Some offer alternatives (see Rouse, 2012.) In her presentation for the *Journal of European Psychology Students Bulletin*, Rouse (2012) asks if we are judging by the wrong standards. After commenting that QR comes from different roots than QN, she recommends that we still need to develop common criteria. She presents core principles developed by Yardley in 2011. These are sensitivity to context, commitment and rigor, coherence and transparency, and importance and impact. On the traditional end of the spectrum, Collins, Onwuegbuzie, and Johnson (2012) address criteria for evaluating mixed-methods research. Citing Teddlie and Tashakkori's 2009 work, they point to design components of quality, suitability and fidelity. They continue with other traditional criteria.

I know. Much of this seems quite technical and somewhat abstract. This is how I see it. Many writers do not really think we can have specific and agreed-upon criteria for judging QR. However, in the same breath, they think we need to. I agree with Koro-Ljungberg (2010). We should avoid "external, objectified, over-simplified, and mechanical approaches to validity in qualitative research" (p. 604). Koro-Ljungberg's thoughtful article is somewhat technical and challenging. She made a very strong case for the ethical responsibilities of researchers. I suggest you take note of her suggestion:

> I do not know how to define or capture validity, but I believe that validity is in doing, as well as its (un)making, and it exhibits itself in the present paradox of knowing and unknowing, indecision, and border crossing. Validity can become possible in doing the impossible, allowing possibilities to develop. (p. 609)

Summary

Just as QR encompasses a number of traditions, the criteria for judging and evaluating QR are varied. By the 1980s, criteria began to appear that were patterned after the criteria used for traditional research. Credibility (internal validity), transferability (external validity), dependability (reliability), and confirmability (objectivity) were suggested criteria.

Multiple sets of criteria have recently been presented. Many of those suggestions inform my personal criteria. To what extent does the report contain the researcher's role, convincing arguments, rich detail, and communication? Communication is clarified by attention to the following hallmarks: intriguing opening, engaging style, reflections, integration, rich detail, voices of others, justification, and new meanings.

Guides are simply guides. The reader must choose his or her own criteria, whether self-developed or adopted from others.

CHECK YOURSELF

- Criteria for judging QR continue to expand as the field evolves. There are numerous lists of criteria; no one set has been adopted by all
- Increasingly, review boards recognize that standard criteria suitable for QR may not apply. Some review boards recognize a need to develop alternative criteria; however, by no means do all boards see this. One pragmatic solution appears to be the use of mixed-methods research.
- A backlash reflected in a conservative movement in the United States and other European countries has led some to require more scientific approaches. By no means is the debate settled. My intention is that you become aware of the issues and make a decision for yourself what makes the most sense for you.

KEY DISCUSSION ISSUES

1. There have been more than a hundred different sets of criteria developed to evaluate QR. How confusing is this? I have developed my own criteria. Are you prepared to develop your own set?
2. Criteria differ both by discipline and by research approach. They are also influenced by the researcher's view of how we learn about the world. How do criteria in your discipline compare with those in other disciplines?
3. What are some of the reasons why we cannot agree about criteria to use?
4. Do you think less of research that doesn't seem to have the guideposts often used in QN? Why or why not?

MODULE 14A

Compare Lincoln and Guba's Four Criteria

Purpose: Compare Lincoln and Guba's four criteria—credibility, transferability, dependability, confirmability—with latest ones you can locate in your discipline.

Activity: Select a QR study that has been published in either the *Qualitative Report* or *FQS*, two journals that are devoted exclusively to qualitative studies and that are in the forefront of thinking in this area. Make sure the study represents a completed piece of research. Form groups of three, and then compare Lincoln and Guba's criteria with those you located in your discipline. Decide how they are alike and how they differ. Now, read the study you selected and evaluate to what extent the study does or does not meet the criteria for your discipline. Comment on what the authors might have done differently.

Evaluation: Gauge how students are able to select specific elements from a study to illustrate the extent to which it is judged "good."

MODULE 14B

Learn How to Add Your Voice

Purpose: Learn how to add your voice to what you are doing. By this time, you have begun to think about the field and have some ideas. I would like you to work on developing your own checklist for criteria.

Activity: Using the criteria for good QR as described in this chapter, react to each criterion and indicate what you like and what you would change. Share with the class, if time permits.

Evaluation: Here, you will begin to see how students are evolving and thinking on their own. You should get a range of comments, and we hope that some will be useful as you develop new criteria or adapt what is out there.

REFERENCES

Barbour, R., & Barbour, M. (2002). Evaluating and synthesizing qualitative research: The need to develop a distinctive approach. *Journal of Evaluation in Clinical Practice, 9*(2), 176–186.

Economic & Social Research Council National Centre for Research Methods. (2010). Qualitative methodology journals in the social sciences. *Qualiti*. Retrieved from http://www.cardiff.ac.uk/socsi/qualiti/PubSocMethJourn.html

Cho, J., & Trent, A. (2006). Validity in qualitative research revisited. *Qualitative Research, 6*(3), 319–340. doi:10.1177/1468794106065006

Choudhuri, D., Glauser, A., & Peregoy, J. (2004). Guidelines for writing a qualitative manuscript for the *Journal of Counseling and Development*. *Journal of Counseling and Development, 82*(4), 443–446.

Cohen, D., & Crabtree, B. (2008). Evaluative criteria for qualitative research in health care: Controversies and recommendations. *Annals of Family Medicine, 6*(4), 331–339.

Collins, K., Onwuegbuzie, A., & Johnson, R. (2012). Securing a place at the table: A review and extension of legitimation criteria for the conduct of mixed research. *American Behavioral Scientist, 56*(6), 849–865.

Denzin, N., & Lincoln, Y. (Eds.). (2000). *The SAGE handbook of qualitative research* (2nd ed.). Thousand Oaks, CA: SAGE.

Devers, K. (1999, December). How will we know "good" qualitative research when we see it? Beginning the dialogue in health services research. *Health Services Research, 34*(5, part 2), 1153–1188.

Doloriert, C., & Sambrook, S. (2011). Accommodating an autoethnographic PhD: The tale of the thesis, the viva voce, and the traditional business school. *Journal of Contemporary Ethnography, 40*(5), 582–615.

Elliott, R., Fischer, C. T., & Rennie, D. L. (1999). Evolving guidelines for publication of qualitative research studies in psychology and related fields. *British Journal of Clinical Psychology, 38*(3), 215–229.

Freeman, M., deMarrais, K., Preissle, J., Roulston, K., & St. Pierre, E. (2007). Standards of evidence in qualitative research: An incitement to discourse. *Educational Researcher, 36*(1), 25–32.

Hoepfl, M. (1997). Choosing qualitative research: A primer for technology education researchers. *Journal of Technology Education, 9*(1). Retrieved from http://scholar.lib.vt.edu/ejournals/JTE/v9n1/hoepfl.html

Keller, J. F., Protinsky, H. O., Lichtman, M., & Allen, K. (1996). The process of clinical supervision: Direct observation research. *Clinical Supervisor, 14*(1), 51–63.

Koro-Ljungberg, M. (2010). Validity, responsibility, and aporia. *Qualitative Inquiry, 16*(8), 603–610.

Larkin, M., Watts, S., & Clifton, E. (2006). Giving voice and making sense in interpretative phenomenological analysis. *Qualitative Research in Psychology, 3*(2), 102–120. Retrieved from http://www.tandfonline.com/doi/abs/10.1191/1478088706qp062oa

Lincoln, Y., & Guba, E. (1985). *Naturalistic inquiry.* Beverly Hills, CA: SAGE.

Lincoln, Y., Lynham, S., & Guba, E. (2011). Paradigmatic controversies, contradictions, and emerging confluences, revisited. In N. Denzin & Y. Lincoln (Eds.), *The SAGE handbook of qualitative research* (4th ed., pp. 97–128). Thousand Oaks, CA: SAGE.

Morrow, S. (2007). Qualitative research in counseling psychology: Conceptual foundations. *The Counseling Psychologist, 35*(2), 209–235.

Morse, J. (2003). A review committee's guide for evaluating qualitative proposals. *Qualitative Health Research, 13*(6), 833–851.

National Institutes of Health, Office of Behavioral and Social Sciences Research. (n.d.). *Best practices for mixed methods research in the health sciences.* Retrieved from http://obssr.od.nih.gov/scientific_areas/methodology/mixed_methods_research/section4.aspx

No Child Left Behind Act. (2001). *Elementary and Secondary Education Act.* Retrieved from http://www2.ed.gov/nclb/landing.jhtml

Northcote, M. T. (2012). Selecting criteria to evaluate qualitative research. *Education Papers and Journal Articles.* [Paper 38]. Retrieved from http://research.avondale.edu.au/cgi/viewcontent.cgi?article=1038&context=edu_papers

Parker, I. (2003). *Qualitative research in psychology: Criteria.* Retrieved from http://www.uel.ac.uk/cnr/documents/Parker.doc

Patton, M. Q. (2002). *Qualitative evaluation and research methods.* London, England: SAGE.

Paulus, T., Woodside, M., & Ziegler, M. (2008). Extending the conversation: Qualitative research as dialogic collaborative process. *The Qualitative Report, 13*(2), 226–243. Retrieved from http://www.nova.edu/ssss/QR/QR13-2/paulus.pdf

Phillips, D., & Carr, K. (2009). Dilemmas of trustworthiness in preservice teacher action research. *Action Research, 7*(2), 207–226.

Reilly, R. (2013). Found poems, member checking and crises of representation. *The Qualitative Report, 18,* Article 30, 1–18. Retrieved from http://www.nova.edu/ssss/QR/QR18/reilly30.pdf

Rouse, L. (2012, July). Evaluating qualitative research: Are we judging by the wrong standards? *JEPS Bulletin.* Retrieved from http://jeps.efpsa.org/blog/2012/07/01/evaluating-qualitative-research/

Savall, H., Zardet, V., Bonnet, M., & Peron, M. (2008). The emergence of implicit criteria actually used by reviewers of qualitative research articles: Case of a European journal. *Organizational Research Methods, 11*(3), 510–540.

Smith, J. K., & Heshusius, L. (1986). Closing down the conversation: The end of the quantitative-qualitative debate among educational inquirers. *Educational Researcher, 15*(1), 4–12.

Taiwo, A. (2013). Relational poetry in the expression of social identity: Creating interweaving dialogues. *Qualitative Social Research, 12*(2), 215–228.

Tay-Lim, J., & Lim, S. (2013). Privileging younger children's voices in research: Using drawings and a co-construction. *International Journal of Qualitative Methods,* 12, 52–64.

Taylor, E., Beck, J., & Ainsworth, E. (2001). Publishing qualitative adult education research: A peer review perspective. *Studies in the Education of Adults, 33*(2), 163–179.

Tieken, M. (2013). The distance to delight: A graduate student enters the field. *Qualitative Inquiry, 19*(4), 320–326.

Tracy, S. J. (2010). Qualitative quality: Eight "big-tent" criteria for excellent qualitative research. *Qualitative Inquiry, 16*(10), 837–851.

Trochim, W., & Donnelly, J. P. (2001). *Research methods knowledge base.* Mason, Ohio: Atomic Dog/Cengage Learning. Retrieved from http://www.socialresearchmethods.net/kb/qualval.php

Weil, S. (2008). Conference essay: Is there a "legitimation crisis" in qualitative methods? [31 paragraphs]. *Forum Qualitative Sozialforschung/Forum: Qualitative Social Research, 9*(2). Retrieved from http://www.qualitative-research.net/index.php/fqs/article/view/438

STUDENT STUDY SITE

Visit **http://www.sagepub.com/lichtmanqrss** to access additional study tools, including eFlashcards and links to SAGE journal articles.

Epilogue

Social Science and the Future of Qualitative Research

As you conclude your study of qualitative research (QR), I think it is important that you consider how far you have traveled. I hope you come away with these understandings:

- Social science and its several disciplines have embraced QR as a useful and important vehicle for answering questions and finding new meaning as we explore and understand human behavior and interaction.
- QR is a meaningful addition to traditional quantitative ways of answering questions. It can be used alone or in combination with other ways of knowing.
- QR is a field that is ever changing and developing. It is not a unitary concept or way of doing something. Rather, it is a multifaceted approach.
- There is no right or better way of conducting QR. No single group or individual is the caretaker of the appropriate way to do QR.
- As new ideas are advanced, the field continues to be open to exploring and adapting its processes and procedures. No voice is more privileged than any other in terms of guiding these new ideas.
- QR is useful if it helps provide answers to questions otherwise unknown or if it stimulates us to ask other questions we have not considered previously.
- QR is useful if it moves us to take political and social action in a world that pushes to become more democratic and as oppressed people are able to give voice to their hopes and needs.
- The reflective voice of the researcher is critical in all aspects of QR. Researchers come to a new study with their own knowledge and experiences that will be useful. An individual researcher's thoughts should not be made mute or sanitized in an effort to purify the process or make it more objective.
- You can play a part in the growth and development of the field. Do not leave it for others to do.

Now, for my own thoughts about the future.

The Digital Age

Our parents and grandparents have spoken about the changes they saw in their lifetimes. They pointed to advances from agrarian to industrial to postindustrial to technological societies. I don't think the advances today could have been imagined by our parents, let alone by us. The rise of the digital age, the immediacy of information, the technological advances that facilitate instantaneous information exchange—these are changing the world as we know it. We have only just begun to explore such tools as smartphones or GPS devices. Smaller and smaller chips lead to smaller and smaller devices. The creative minds of individuals challenge us to think in ways we cannot yet imagine, and new apps are being developed that may offer us new ways of doing things. I don't know what to expect next. But I do expect that things will change.

Here are some examples: One challenge is the use of technology to gather data, analyze data, and report results. Cater (2011) used Skype to interview, record, and transcribe data. Shulman (2011) developed Textifier, a program for real-time analysis of Facebook and Twitter discussions. Cordelois (2010) used digital technology (Subcam and Webdiver) as part of her ethnographic observation of the experience of coming home. Erickson (2010) described a documentary study using social media and what she calls *locative technology* (using GPS locators). Jones, Drury, and McBeath (2011) described how GPS-enabled mobile computing can be used to augment qualitative interviewing.

How does that relate to QR? In several ways. We now have available communities and cultures to study that we could not have dreamed of before. It seems so old-fashioned to think about studying impoverished families in Mexico, as Oscar Lewis did in 1975. We now have Facebook or LinkedIn communities to study in real time. We have facial-recognition software that will allow us to identify individuals in various groups. Markham (2011) has written extensively in this arena. She writes about the Internet as a tool, a place, and a way of being.

But we need to be cautious, lest we violate the privacy of the individual or encroach on their personal space and time. Issues related to confidentiality, gaining access, ethics, and informed consent are being addressed. Researchers are currently writing about such issues as what constitutes an open group; what acknowledgement, if any, should be given to group members; and how the information can be transmitted. We need to make sure that we balance the needs of the researcher with needs of the individuals we study. Personally, I err on the side of worrying about individual needs.

Globalization, Political Activism, and Social Justice in Troubled Times

Does a researcher have an obligation or a responsibility to become an activist? Traditionally, researchers who conducted quantitative studies remained objective and remote. They reported findings in a journal but did not advocate a particular viewpoint. Of course, there have always been activists. In 1970, Paolo Freire urged us to think about the teacher, student, and society and proposed new relationships in which the learner was considered the cocreator of knowledge. Radical for some, these ideas led to critical pedagogy and views about social justice. But Freire was the exception. Most researchers adopted a neutral and remote posture.

Some qualitative researchers are interested in pursuing social justice agendas. See, for example, the theme of the 2011 Congress of Qualitative Inquiry agenda (Nevo & Stanfield, 2011), which addresses whether and to what extent qualitative researchers should become activists.

I think this is a very personal decision you make as a qualitative researcher. What motivates one person to become an activist while encouraging another to be an observer is complex. But as the world shrinks and news about those who are oppressed reaches us instantaneously, qualitative researchers might find themselves challenged to take action.

That the world is both larger and smaller remains a given in today's society. It is larger in that we have moved from the privileged position of knowing to a more democratic position of recognizing voices from many and all—from the outmost reaches of the earth. The two billion souls in China who have been silenced are making their voices heard. The oppressed and suppressed in African countries cry out to us. Those in the Middle East mounted the Arab Spring. And the lost souls in the most civilized and wealthiest country—the United States—who live under our very noses without our seeing them are waiting. Elliott Liebow (1967) studied street-corner men back in the 1960s. According to Kelly (2011), quoting Liebow's wife,

> He had a job convincing the folks at CU [Catholic University] that this was a legitimate undertaking and that the technique of participant observation could be applicable within a group in our complex industrialized society. They were rather skeptical. I think he was probably one of the first to apply that method of research to populations within our own society. (para. 5)

In the past, those being studied were just that—subjects of the research. Those in positions of power often looked down on them or patronized them, observed them, and tried to understand them. They looked for people unlike "us" to study. Today we all hope that is not the case. We see these groups in new ways, and we hope that members of diverse groups will be part of the process of knowing and seeing. Krumer-Nevo and Sidi (2012) caution us about "writing about the other" and the risk of portraying the other as different and by inference inferior.

We are guided by our personal ethical and social values both in the way we conduct our research and the use we make of it when we are finished. Although there are institutions and organizations that develop guidelines for appropriate behavior, it is ultimately up to us as researchers to police ourselves.

■ Communicating—The Written Word and Beyond

We are so used to communicating our ideas through the written word. The academy seems to demand it. Professors expect it. Students struggle to find just the right word to say something. But with technology and new apps and devices, the written word is taking a back seat. Twitter expects our communications to be no longer than 140 characters. YouTube lets us tell a story visually. Television news that is available 24/7 depends on the strength of the visual. Words are not enough.

So it is with QR. Through this volume, I have illustrated alternative ways of telling the story. Kip Jones's sensitive film on aging gay men in rural England conveys the message visually. Hilary Hughes's magazine format on the topic of adolescent girls draws the reader in ways that traditional forms of communication do not. Unfortunately, she was not permitted by her university to use that format for her dissertation (Hughes, December 2012, personal communication). Laura Lorenz's photovoice or Gunter Mey's photos provide insight into individuals that mere words cannot.

Telling the story better—that is something we must work to do. It is hard work to write well. I don't mean to ignore the written word. I believe in it. But we need to take responsibility to bring the reader in, to use language in ways that engage the reader while not diminishing the strength and value of the research. Richardson (2013), Ellis (2013), and Bloor (2013) do this so well in their many personal stories. For me, it is ultimately about the story we learn and how we tell it to others. We can use devices, metaphors, fictions as facts, or facts as fictions. We can take lessons from writers of fiction and poetry. Hopefully, faculty and review committees will be open to different ways of writing. The word is important.

I think we will see that universities and journals continue to be open to alternative methods to tell about what we learned. And if our research is to have meaning, we need to communicate to the larger world and to those who might be able to make changes.

Change and Resistance

I recognize that with change comes resistance. The mixed-methods movement has worked out a pragmatic compromise as a way to accommodate a myriad of viewpoints and beliefs. I think this might be a useful alternative in many instances.

The conservative movement still holds to the gold standard of research, the objective nature of research, the post-positivist thinking about what constitutes good research. There are many who still hold these beliefs. Whatever your personal position, I hope you will be able to see that reasonable alternatives exist.

Qualitative researchers continue to seek financial support from government and private institutions. Students and faculty continue to need approval from Institutional Review Boards (IRBs) and editorial review boards that oversee publications. All these institutions need to be educated by the QR community as to what constitutes appropriate and valuable QR approaches.

Are you ready?

References

Bloor, M. (2013). The rime of the globalized mariner: In six parts (with bonus tracks from a chorus of Greek shippers). *Sociology, 47*(1), 30–50.

Cater, J. (2011). Skype—A cost-effective method for qualitative research. *Rehabilitation Counselors & Educators Journal, 4*(2), 3. Retrieved from http://uark.academia.edu/JanetCater/Papers/538835/Skype_A_cost_effective_method_for_qualitative_research

Cordelois, A. (2010). Using digital technology for collective ethnographic observations: An experiment on "coming home." *Social Science Information, 49*(3), 445–463.

Ellis, C. (2013). Crossing the rabbit hole: Autoethnographic life review. *Qualitative Inquiry, 19*(1), 35–45.

Erickson, I. (2010). Documentary with ephemeral media: Curation practices in online social spaces. *Bulletin of Science, Technology & Society, 30*(6), 387–397.

Freire, P. (1970). *Pedagogy of the oppressed*. New York, NY: Continuum.

Jones, P., Drury, R., & McBeath, J. (2011). Using GPS-enabled mobile computing to augment qualitative interviewing: Two case studies. *Field Methods, 23*(2), 173–187.

Kelly, J. (2011, February 26). 44 years later, Tally's Corner is revealed. *Washington Post.* Retrieved from http://www.washingtonpost.com/wp-dyn/content/article/2011/02/26/AR2011022603483.html

Krumer-Nevo, M., & Sidi, M. (2012). Writing against othering. *Qualitative Inquiry, 18*(4), 299–309.

Lewis, O. (1975). *Five families: Mexican case studies in the culture of poverty*. New York, NY: Basic Books.

Liebow, E. (1967). *Tally's corner: A study of Negro streetcorner men.* Boston, MA: Little Brown and Company.

Markham, A. (2011). *Social media, methods, and ethics.* Retrieved from http://www.markham.internetinquiry.org/

Nevo, M., & Stanfield, J. (2011). *Qualitative inquiry and the politics of advocacy.* Walnut Creek, CA: Left Coast Press.

Richardson, L. (2013). Twelve uneasy pieces on research and therapy. *Qualitative Inquiry, 19*(1), 20–26.

Shulman, S. (2011). *JITP 2011: The future of computational social science.* Retrieved from http://www.umass.edu/jitp/Shulman.htm

Glossary

Action research is a **research approach** associated with a group taking action to effect change. Usually, a specific problem is addressed. See also **Participatory Action Research (PAR)**.

Anthropology, a social science discipline, was brought to the U.S. from England and Europe. **Informants** and **fieldwork** and **field methods** are terms associated with anthropology.

Arts-based research is a loose combination of approaches that emphasize the creative and artistic aspect of research, especially in terms of presentation of results. Ethnodrama, poetry, weaving, film, and other artistic outlets are used.

Autoethnography is a **research approach** associated with study of the self and is heavily dependent on **reflexivity**. See also **performance ethnography**.

Biography was a way to discover and describe in narrative fashion the meaning of human interactions. Now, this is known as **narrative**. See also **storytelling**.

Case study is a **research approach** that involves a detailed examination of a particular case. The case can be a program, a business, an organization, or other circumscribed unit.

Coding is the first step in the process of making meaning from the **data**.

Combined qualitative approach includes two or more **qualitative research approaches** in the same design. For example, a researcher might conduct a grounded theory case study.

Constant-comparative method is a concept associated with **grounded theory**. It involves a specific way of making meaning from **data**. It involves open **coding**, axial **coding**, and selective **coding**.

Constructivists believe that reality is constructed by the researcher. See also **interpretists.**

Content analysis is a way of making meaning from the **data**. It involves detailed analysis of the text. Some researchers have described specific ways of doing such an analysis.

Conversation analysis is a way of making meaning from the **data**. It involves a detailed analysis of the interactions between the researcher and **participant**. It can also involve analysis of the interactions between or among the **participants**.

Critical theory/theorists are concerned with a critique of culture and society.

Culture is a system of shared beliefs, values, customs, and behaviors that individuals use to cope with their world and with each other.

Data are the information you collect as part of your research study. In **qualitative research**, data usually take the form of words or pictures.

Discourse analysis is another way of making meaning from the **data**. It is associated with **postmodern** thinking.

Epistemology is concerned with how reality is known.

Ethics/ethical behavior/ethical conduct considers the way in which a researcher addresses all aspects of research. It includes concern for the treatment of **participants** so that no harm shall be done. It also includes treatment of the **data** and results so that information is reported accurately. It includes a set of moral principles or rules, usually enforced by a professional or governing body.

Ethnographic methods are the ways in which ethnographers collect and analyze **data**.

Ethnography involves the study of culture and social interactions of a particular group. Offshoots of traditional ethnography have emerged, including **autoethnography**, photo-ethnography, online ethnography, urban ethnography, public ethnography, and so on.

Evidence–based research is a **research design** that involves results or **data** obtained from experimental research; it is part of the backlash against **qualitative research**. See also **gold standard** and **scientific**.

Experimental design refers to the overall **research approach** for the conduct of traditional quantitative research. True experimental design is the **gold standard** of design. It includes random assignment of **subjects** to treatment and double-blind study. In a double-blind study, the subject does not know which treatment group he/she is in, and the researcher does not know which group received the treatment and which received a placebo.

Feminist research/researchers use a feminist perspective or viewpoint as they conduct research. They pay special attention to issues of power discrepancies and often rely on a political or social agenda. As with other qualitative concepts, there is no single definition or agreement on what constitutes feminist research. Some say only women can conduct feminist research, but not everyone accepts that idea. Topics and those studied often feature women, but that is not a requirement. Feminist research is often combined with **constructivist** or **postmodern** approaches. See also **postfeminist**.

Feminist theory is based on inequality in the treatment of women. It is also concerned with power discrepancies.

Fieldwork/field methods are terms associated with **ethnography** and **anthropology**. They involve extensive immersion into the field for extended periods of time.

Gaining access is a concept that originated with **ethnography**. Components involve identifying **informants**, obtaining permission, initial contact, developing rapport, and exiting.

Generic approach to coding does not involve any specific research process or approach as researchers go about making sense of the **data**.

Generic approach to research does not rely on a specific **research approach**, such as **grounded theory** or **phenomenology**. Instead, a researcher does not have an underlying philosophical or theoretical underpinning. It relies instead on general strategies. Some call it a *noncategorical* or *interpretive* description.

Gold standard is a **research design** that involves experimental research using randomized trials and double-blind design. See also **evidence-based** and **scientific**.

Grounded theory is a **research approach** designed so that theory emerges from the **data**. It was originally developed by Glaser and Strauss in 1967.

Hermeneutics involves the interpretation and close reading of text. It originally referred to interpretation of the Bible.

Informant is a term associated with **ethnography** and **anthropology**. An informant is an individual who is studied by the researchers as they study culture.

Inter-rater reliability/member checks is a concept associated with QN. It involves using two or more raters to provide a value or score for an observed phenomenon; for example, raters who judge a gymnastics event. Some QR use the concept, especially when coding interviews or observations. It relies on the underlying assumption that an approximation of an objective reality can be obtained.

Interpretative analysis is a way to analyze or make meaning of the **data**. It has its roots in **phenomenology**.

Interpretists believe reality is constructed by the researcher. This viewpoint is in contrast to that of a **positivist** or **post-positivist**. See also **constructivists**.

Journals are the accounts that the researchers keep of observations, reflections, and/or thoughts about the research.

Key concepts are derived from the **data** through a process of **coding**, sifting, sorting, and identifying **themes**.

Life history. See **biography**.

Meta-synthesis is the process of combining **data** drawn from many qualitative studies. Its precursor is the meta-synthesis movement in quantitative research. Meta-synthesis in quantitative research involves specific statistical ways of merging results from different studies. Qualitative meta-synthesis relies on more general approaches similar to combining **data** in a literature review.

Mixed-methods research involves combining both qualitative and quantitative approaches in the same study. This is not to be confused with combined qualitative research, which combines two qualitative approaches in the same study.

Narrative analysis is the process of deriving meaning from the **data** by examining the narratives people tell.

Narrative approach/inquiry/style is a **qualitative research** design that involves stories and epiphanies. See also **biography** and **life history**.

Nontraditionalist. See also **postmodernist**.

Ontology deals with the nature of reality.

Paradigm wars refer to conflicting views between **traditionalists** or **post-positivists** on the one hand and **constructivists** or **postmodernists** on the other about the best way to conduct research. Today, one pragmatic compromise to the wars involves **mixed-methods research**.

Participant observation is a concept associated with **ethnography**. It admits that the researcher actively participates in the culture that is studied. Overt observers admit why they are present, but covert observers might try to hide their role.

Participants refers to those studied in a qualitative study. While some researchers use the term ***subjects*** or ***informants*** or *interviewees*, today most prefer this neutral term. **Postmodernists** and **feminists** more likely to use the term *co-participants* to distinguish a more active role of those studied.

Participatory action research (PAR) is an approach in which researchers and participants work as co-researchers to change an organization or system.

Performance/performative ethnography is an arts-based approach that uses a performance (e.g., play, film) to convey results.

Phenomenology is a **research approach** aimed at learning about the essence of lived experience. It is also a philosophy.

Photovoice involves combining the use of photos and social action at a local level.

Positivist/positivism believes that there is an objective reality that can be known by the researcher. This is in contrast to a **constructivist**, who believes that reality is constructed by the researcher.

Postfeminism is a reaction (or backlash) to the **feminist** viewpoint and dominates contemporary media culture.

Postmodernism/postmodernists are concerned with crisis of representation. They reject the objectivity of the **positivist** and **post-positivist**. This is both a philosophy and an intellectual movement. See also **nontraditionalist**.

Post-positivists accept that a true objective reality cannot be known, but an approximation of one can be known by the researcher. See also **traditionalist**.

Qualitative comparative analysis is connected with making meaning from the **data**. It is used in situations where there are multiple cases from which data are collected.

Qualitative data are the words (or visuals) you obtain in your qualitative study.

Qualitative research/researchers study human interactions in natural settings and in the social world.

Qualitative research approach. See **research approach/research design** or **research method**.

Reflective practice is the act of making explicit the researcher's views and assumptions about the world and how it is known.

Reflective researcher is one who reflects on his or her own views, how they influence the research process, and how the researcher is influenced by it. See also **subjectivity**.

Reflexivity is the general stance of thinking about one's views. *Personal reflexivity* is concerned with the researcher's values. *Epistemological reflexivity* is concerned with the researcher's view about how the world is known. *Contextual and ethical reflexivity* deal with the appropriateness of doing research with some groups and informed consent.

Research approach/research design is the underlying philosophical or theoretical basis for the conduct of the research. See also **research method**.

Research method includes the specific ways or tools used by researchers to conduct the study. It usually involves ways of collecting and analyzing **data**.

Research methodology is the specific design a researcher uses. In **qualitative research**, it may be **ethnography**, **grounded theory**, **autoethnography**, **case study**, or one of many others. In quantitative research, it may be **experimental design**, quasi-experimental design, or survey design.

Role of researcher is a concept associated with qualitative research in which the researcher plays a pivotal role in collecting and analyzing data. It contrasts with the researcher role in quantitative research in which the researcher attempts to maintain an objective stance.

Scientific is a label that represents **research designs** based on the natural sciences in which experiments are conducted to test hypotheses. For the past twenty years, the term *scientific* has been considered legitimate in the QR domain as well. (See Brinkmann, 2011, Chapter 1.)

Snowball sampling is a way a researcher selects a group of participants to study. One participant recommends another, and the process continues until the researcher obtains a sufficient amount of data. *Snowball* refers to building up a snowball by adding pieces to it.

Storytelling/narrative is an alternative way of making sense of the **data**. See also **narrative analysis.**

Subjectivity is a term that is in contrast to the objective, neutral, or unbiased stance a researcher may take in designing and conducting research. A reflexive researcher takes a subjective stance out of necessity, since he or she is part of the system rather than outside or removed from the system in which research is designed.

Subjects refers to those who are studied in an experiment. In qualitative research, a preferred designation for those studied is *participant* or *co-researcher*. Some may use the term *informant.*

Symbolic interactionism is a social theory that involves analyzing communication among individuals. It serves as a framework for examining how individuals interact through the meaning of symbols. George Herbert Mead and his student Herbert Blumer are two key theorists.

Themes can be extracted from analyzing **data** through a process of **coding**.

Theoretical sampling/theoretical sensitivity/theoretical saturation are concepts associated with **grounded theory**. It involves selecting samples and analyzing **data** simultaneously until no new information is gained. In practice, most researchers practice only a variation of this idea. It also involves the ability to recognize important elements in the **data** that might contribute to an emerging theory.

Thick description is a concept associated with **ethnography**. The intention is to provide sufficient information about a culture. Clifford Geertz coined the term in his 1973 book *The Interpretation of Cultures*.

Traditionalists. See **post-positivists**.

Triangulation involves the use of three **data** points or three types of **data**. The underlying meaning is that when multiple **data** points yield the same information, that information is more believable or acceptable. It is a concept associated with a **post-positivist** position. It originates from locating a submarine via three data points.

Index

Academic integrity, maintaining, 139
Access, gaining, 102–103, 285
Action research / participatory action research (PAR), 87, 136, 138–140
  distinguishing features, 139
  examples from the field, 140
  history and meaning, 138–139
  special issues, 139
Adolescents, interviewing, 254
Advanced Research Projects Agency (ARPA), 208
Ai Wei Wei, 205
Allen, Mitch, 372
Alternative ethnography movement, 352
Alternative writing presentations, 366–367
Ambrose, Stephen, 318
Among Schoolchildren (Kidder), 358
Analysis of variance (ANOVA), 98
Analytic paralysis, 109
Anonymity, and ethical conduct, 57–59, 77, 128
Anthropology, 5, 100–101
Antonioni, Michelangelo, 16
Appignanesi, Josh, 185
Application software (app), 209–210, 309, 311
Approach/approaches, 99. *See also* Qualitative research approaches
Archival data, 281
Archival information, 305
Arguments, convincing, 382–383
Argyris, Chris, 138
Armstrong, Neil, 318–320
Arts, the, and social sciences, 364
Arts-based research approaches, 140–142
  distinguishing features, 141
  examples from the field, 142
  history and meaning, 140–141
  special issues, 141
Authentic reflection, 116
Autoethnographic narratives, 364–365
Autoethnography, 20, 44, 136, 142–145
  distinguishing features, 143
  examples from the field, 144–145
  history and meaning, 142–143
  reflexivity, role of, 143
  special issues, 143–144

Baddeil, David, 185
Baltimore, David, 64
Basic qualitative research, 88
Behavior, inappropriate, and ethical conduct, 62
Behind Closed Doors (Stark), 71
Benedict, Ruth, 101
Bernauer, James, 164–168
Berners-Lee, Tim, 208
Besten, Den, 305
Bias, 43
Biography, 35, 99, 332
Black, Karen, 198
Blogs (web logs), 22, 211, 371
Boas, Franz, 101
Bochner, Arthur, 143
Bogardus, Emory, 293
Boole, George, 233
Bowen, Murray, 192
Bracketing, 44, 112, 115–116
Brayton, Jennifer, 181
Brinkley, Douglas, 318
Brooks, Christine, 14, 179–183
Brown, Laura S., 181
Browsers, 209
Buffett, Warren, 242, 245
Burnett, Emma, 32
Burt, Cyril O., 65
Buy-in, getting, 139

Capote, Truman, 359
Card catalog, 225

Case study, 6, 118–123, 129
  blogs and beyond, 123
  distinguishing features, 120
  examples from the field, 122–123
  history and meaning, 119–120
  special issues, 120–122
  utility of, 123
  words of caution, 123
Casual individual interview, 250
Categorizing/categories, 328, 330–331
Challenging populations, and focus group interviews, 296
Chattiness, 271
Chenail, Ron, 371
Children
  drawings by, 366, 367 (figure)
  interviewing, 254
  studying, 69–70
Classical ethnography, 281
Clinton, Hillary, 108
Closing questions, 267
Cloud computing, 210
Co-constructed material, 305
Coding/codes, 43, 108, 328–331
Coding rubric, 111
Coleman, James, 86
Collective creation, 349
Colonial other, 102
Combined qualitative research approaches, 83, 85, 92
Comfort zone, leaving, 189–201
Communication, rapid, tools for, 211
Communicating, 399–400. *See also* Writing qualitative research
Comparison/contrast questions, 266
Complex questions, 271
Computer software, data analysis with, 340–343
Concepts, 29, 328–331
Concrete questions, 265
Confidentiality, and ethical conduct, 59, 76
Confirmability, 387
Constant-comparative method, 105, 335–337
Constructionist conception of interviewing, 247, 257
Constructivists, 14, 90
Content (textual) analysis, 215, 337
Context, understanding, 127
Contextual reflexivity, 32–33
Contextual review, 234–235
Conventional content analysis, 337
Conversation analysis, 7, 337
Coresearchers, 146, 247
Cox, Rebecca D., 98
Creation of Fiction to Share Other Truths and Different Viewpoints, The (Vickers), 361
Creative nonfiction, 358–361
Credibility, 386
Creswell, John, 9
"Critical Lede," 143
Critical theory/theorists, 13, 15, 90, 151–152
Cultures and subcultures, study of, 39, 102. *See also* Ethnography
Cutter, Charles, 225
Cyberethnography, 39
Cyberspace, 208
Cycle of fear model, 117

Data, 4, 318
  archival, 281
  collection, using the Internet, 258–260
  interpretation, 62
  managing and analyzing, 309
  ownership and rewards, 62
  preparing and organizing, 327
  reporting, truthfulness and accuracy in, 60
  See also Data analysis; Data gathering
Data analysis, 317–348
  computer software for, 340–343
  narratives or stories, 332–335
  qualitative research approaches and, 335–343
  themes/concepts and, 323–331
  when to conduct, 323
Databases, social science, 229–230
Data gathering, 279–314
  apps for, 311
  focus group interviews, 292–300
  images and visuals, 301–305
  observations, 281–291
  technology, 307–310
  written word (the), 281, 305–307
  See also Interviewing/interviews
Davidson, Judith, 123
Davis, Heather, 37
Decolonizing conception of interviewing, 257
Degas, Edgar, 380
Dependability, 387
Descriptive coding, 336
Dewey, John, 27
Dibbs, R. A., 168–173
Didion, Joan, 359
Diebenkorn, Richard, 136
Digital age, 398
Digital cameras, 213

di Gregorio, Silvana, 341
Direct approach to content analysis, 337
Direct questioning, alternatives to, 256–257
Disciplines
phenomenology and, 113
qualitative research and, 4–6
Discourse, human, 38
Discourse analysis, 124, 337–338
Discovery of Grounded Theory, The (Glaser and Strauss), 90, 106
Disraeli, Benjamin, 383
Dissertation Abstracts International, 230
Distance education, 217
"Do no harm," and ethical conduct, 57
Dorsey, Jack, 208
Double-barreled questions, 271
Dramaturgy, 245
Dude, You're a Fag (Pascoe), 283

Echo probe, 268
Eisner, Elliot, 140
Elaboration, 268
Elites, interviewing, 254–255
Ellis, Carolyn, 142, 282
Emotions, and interviewing, 256
Epistemological reflexivity, 32–33
Epistemology, 14, 36
Epoché, 115–116
Equality of Educational Opportunity (Coleman), 86
E-readers, 213
Ethical issues, 53–80, 128
ethical behavior, 54, 56–57
ethical conduct, 54, 57–64, 76–77
misconduct, 64–66
qualitative researchers' concerns, 66–76
Ethical reflexivity, 32–33
Ethics, 55, 215–216
Ethnodrama, 140, 365
Ethnographers, 45, 281
Ethnographic methods, 14
Ethnographic narratives, 364–365
Ethnographies, 29
Ethnography, 100–105, 128
blogs and beyond, 104
classical, 281
distinguishing features, 101–102
examples from the field, 103–104
history and meaning, 100–101
special issues in, 102–103
words of caution, 104–105
Ethnography movement, alternative, 352
Ethnotheater, 352
Ethnotheatre (Saldaña), 142, 365
Events, and research questions, 30
Evidence-based research, 15
Evocative text, 334
Exemplary case, 121
Experience, essence of, 115
Experimental design, 84
Exploratory study, 150
External validity, 18

Facebook, 207
Facial recognition software, and privacy, 302
Fact or fiction, 127
Faking friendship, 61
Feminism and Geography (Rose), 113
Feminist research, 13, 18, 63, 145–149
definition of, 146–147
distinguishing features, 146
examples from the field, 147–149
history and meaning, 145–146
special issues, 146–147
Feminist researchers, 15, 90
Fiction, 361
Field methods, 14, 101, 358
Fieldwork, 35
Film, performance, 366
First person, 354
Flood, Julie T., 98
Fluid environment, 40
Focus group interviewing/interviews, 280, 292–300
example, 299–300
issues regarding, 294–299
purpose of, 294
Forum: Qualitative Sociology (FQS), 137
Freire, Paulo, 138, 398
Friendship, and ethical conduct, 61
Fundamental qualitative descriptions, 88

Gaining access, 42
Gender, in interviewer and participant, 256
Generalizability, 387
Generic approach
to coding, 196, 336
to research, 89, 336
Generic qualitative research, 88
Getting Lost (Lather), 148
Gibson, William, 208
Glaser, Barney, 106

Glassmeyer, David, 168–173
Globalization, 398–399
Global Positioning System (GPS), 210, 308
Gold standard, 15, 98
Google Maps, 210, 308
Google products, 308
Gossamer walls, 33
Grand tour questions, 264–265
Grounded theory, 6, 87, 90, 105–111, 128, 295, 321
  blogs and beyond, 109
  distinguishing features, 106–107
  examples from the field, 108–109
  history and meaning, 105–106
  special issues, 107–108
  true, determining, 111
  words of caution, 109–111
Groups, types of, 284–285
Guided individual interview, 248

Hardware
  research on, 217–218
  types of, 213
  See also Technology
Hearing, Trevor, 184–188
Hermeneutics, 14, 115
Historical review, 235
"Hot Monkey Sex," 326–327
Hughes, Hilary, 400
Human interactions, 30–31
Humphreys, Laud, 66
Husserl, Edmund, 112

Ideas, communicating. *See* Communicating; Writing qualitative research
Il, Kim Jong, 71
Images and visuals, 301–305
  examples of usage, 303–304
  image manipulation, 303
  image quality, 303
  issues regarding, 302–303
  mapping, 304–305
  purpose of, 302
Imanishi-Kari, Thereza, 64–65
Impure Science (Bell), 64
Inappropriate behavior, and ethical conduct, 62, 77
Inclusion, and ethical conduct, 62–63
In-depth draw and talk methods, 383
In-depth interviewing, 248–250, 261–263, 273–274 (table). *See also* Interviewing/interviews
In-depth study, 44–45
Individual created material, 305
Individual interviewing/interviews, 246
  issues in, 250–260
  types of, 247–250
  See also Interviewing/interviews
Inductive approach, 41, 107
Informal groups, 285
Informants, 40, 247
Information
  archival, 305
  how to get, 127
  search for, 229
  selecting relevant, 231
  using, 234
Informed consent, 59–60, 77, 215–216
Initial coding, 329–330. *See also* Coding/codes
Innovations from the field, 164–189
Inside Higher Education (Smith), 71
Instant messaging (IM), 211
Institutional Review Boards (IRBs), 54, 74–76, 77, 309
Integrative review, 235
Intentional causation, 7
Interaction, human, 38
Internal validity, 18, 385
Internet (the), 205–221
  collecting data using, 258–260
  research related to, 214–215
  tools, 209–212
  See also Social media; Technology
Interpretative analysis, 35
Interpretative phenomenological analysis, 338
Interpretists, 14, 90
Interpretive descriptions, 88
Inter-rater reliability, 44, 60
Interviewing/interviews, 241–278
  adolescents and children, 254
  constructionist conception of, 257
  decolonizing conception of, 257
  dynamic aspects of, 39–40
  elites, 254
  emotions and, 256
  example, 272–274
  guide, 271–274
  in-depth, 248–250, 261–263, 273–274 (table)
  individual, 246–260
  males with limited verbal skills, 254
  neopositivist conception of, 257
  online, 258–259
  participant gender, 256
  postmodern conception of, 257
  purpose of, 246–247
  quality of, 257–258

recording, 253
romantic conception of, 257
setting for, selecting, 252
techniques, developing, 263–271
transcribing, 253
transformative conception of, 257
Intrusiveness, and ethical conduct, 61
I-poems, 333
IRBs (Institutional Review Boards), 54, 74–76, 77, 201

James, William, 183
Jargon or technical language, questions with, 271
Jobs, Steve, 210
Johnson, Steven, 322
Johnson, W. E., 359
Jones, Kip, 184–188, 366, 400
Jottings, 319
Journal of Mixed Methods Research, 22
Journals, 37, 370
open access, online, 370
subscription, online, 371

Kawulich, Barbara, 326
Keefer, Jeffrey, 206
Kershaw, Harry, 189 (figure)
Key concepts, 107, 318
Kidder, Tracy, 358
Knotted image, 304
Kroeber, Alfred, 86

Lahman, Maria, 168–173
Lather, Patty, 20
Lauder, Ronald, 380
Leading questions, 270–271
Learning organizations, 138
Legitimacy, attaining in a scientifically oriented world, 141
Lewin, Kurt, 138
Lewis, Oscar, 39, 398
Liebow, Elliot, 358, 399
Life, exploring experiences of. *See* Autoethnography
Life history, 99, 124. *See also* Biography
"Life in the Social Sciences" (Brooks), 179–183
Life story, 332
Lightfoot, Sarah, 140
LinkedIn, 208
Literature review, 223–240
conducting, 228–233, 238
incorporating, 234–236
organizing, 236
potential limitations of, 227
style of, 235
types of, 234–235
value of, 226–227
when to conduct, 227–228
Lived experience, 114–115. *See also* Phenomenology
Lives of Others, The (film), 129
Lo, Alice, 61
Location tools, 210
Locative technology, 217, 398
Long Interview, The (McCracken), 248
Lorenz, Laura, 173–178, 400

Magazine, 366
Mailer, Norman, 359
Malinowski, Bronislaw, 101
Manet, Édouard, 380
Man Who Mistook His Wife for a Hat, The (Sacks), 359
Mapping, 304–305
Maps, subjective, 366
Maslow, Abraham, 192
Mead, Margaret, 39, 101
Meaning, gaining, 323–325
Member check(ing), 44, 60, 386
Metaphors, use of, 356–358
Meta-synthesis, 92–93
Methodological review, 235
Methodology, 98. *See also* Qualitative research approach(es)
Mey, Gunter, 400
Miller, Jean Baker, 181
Mind Wide Open (Johnson), 322
Mixed methods, 83
Mixed-methods research approaches, 7, 91–92, 149–151, 280
distinguishing features, 149–150
examples from the field, 150–151
history and meaning, 149
special issues, 150
Monet, Claude, 380
Morgan, Lewis Henry, 101
Morse, Samuel F. B., 208

Narrating the Closet (Adams), 364
Narrative, human, 38
Narrative Inquiry (Clandinin), 127
Narrative inquiry and analysis, 6, 99, 124–128, 129, 320, 334, 345
blogs and beyond, 127
distinguishing features, 125
examples from the field, 126–127
history and meaning, 124–125
special issues, 125–126
words of caution, 127–128

Narratives, 45–46
looking at, 324–325
looking for, 332–335
Narrative style, 4
Natural causation, 7
Natural settings, observing in, 281–291
Neopositivist conception of interviewing, 257
Netnography, 39
Neutrality, 269
New elements/topics questions, 266–267
New Journalism, The (Wolfe and Johnson, eds.), 359
NiNucci, Darcy, 343
Noncategorical, 88
Nonlinear, 46
Nonparticipant observations, 282
Nontraditionalists, 86. *See also* Postmodernists
NVivo, 341–342

Objectivity, 385
Observations, 280, 281–291
conducting, 286–288
issues regarding, 284–286
purpose of, 282–284
scenarios for practice, 288–291
Observer role, 288–289
Occasional groups, 285
Online focus groups, 297–299
Online groups, 285
Online interviewing/interviews, 258–260
Online Interviews (Salmons), 310
Online open access journals, 370
Online subscription journals, 371
Ontology, 14, 36
Open access journals, online, 370
O'Reilly, Tim, 209
Others, learning from, 369–372
Ownership, and ethics, 128

Paradigm wars, 14, 19, 90–91
Paris Salon, 380
Participant behaviors, 309
Participant observation, 6, 103
Participant observer role, 290
Participant product, 305
Participants, 6, 67, 247
deciding on, in grounded theory, 108
determining number of, 251
identification of, 250–252
Participatory action research (PAR). *See* Action research / participatory action research (PAR)
Pelias, Ron, 143
People, and research questions, 28–29
Performance ethnography, 87
Performance film, 366
Performative ethnography, 104
Personal reflexivity, 33
Phenomena, 38
Phenomenology, 13, 111–118, 128
as a philosophy and as a method, 114–116
blogs and beyond, 118
distinguishing features, 116
examples from the field, 117
growth worldwide, 113–114
history and meaning, 112
in today's world, 112–114
reinterpretations of, 113
special issues, 116–117
words of caution, 118
Photography, 365
Photovoice, 173
"Photovoice in Practice" (Lorenz), 173–178
Pinterest, 208, 327
Pitt, Brad, 326
Places, and research questions, 30
Poetry, 352, 365–366
Poetry-based research, 140
Political activism, 398–399
Pollock, Jackson, 16
Popularizing Research (Vannini), 366–367
Portraiture, 148
Positive Lives (photographic exhibition), 304
Positivists/positivism, 14
Postfeminism, 147
Postmodern conception of interviewing, 257
Postmodernism, 15, 19, 151–152
Postmodernists, 15, 151
Postmodern observer role, 291
Post-positivism, 19
Post-positivists, 14, 90
Post structural and postfeminist viewpoints, 147
Power, 103, 255
Preliminary codes, 319
Presentation formats, alternative, 141, 364–367
ethnodrama, 365
ethnographic and autoethnographic narratives, 364–365
magazine, 366
performance film, 366
photography, 365
poetry, 365–366
social sciences and the arts, 364
subjective maps and children's drawings, 366
writing presentations, alternative, 366–367

Privacy, 215–216
ethical conduct and, 57–59, 77
facial recognition software and, 302
Probing, 268–269
ProQuest, 230
Publishers, 372

QN. See Quantitative research
QR. See Qualitative research
Qualitative comparative analysis (QCA), 338
Qualitative data, 46
Qualitative data analysis (QDA), 320, 337
Qualitative Inquiry, 22, 137
Qualitative Report, The, 137
Qualitative Research, 137
Qualitative research (QR), 3
basic, 88
challenges of doing, 47
characteristics of, 12
critical elements of, 37–46
dealing with the whole, 42
definitions of, 8–14
disciplines and, 4–6
dynamic nature of, 38–40
evaluating, history of, 386–391
future of, 397–400
growth of, 14–16
human behavior and, 38
in-depth study and, 44–45
inductive nature of, 41–42
innovations and perspectives in, 164–188
misconduct in, 65–66
multiple ways of conducting, 40–41
natural settings occurrences, 42–43
nonlinear nature of, 46
proposal, 189–200
purpose of, 38
questions, 28–31, 154
reasons for, 16
reflexive stance, 27–51
social science and the future of, 397–401
study, planning and conceptualizing, 163–204
theoretical and philosophical foundations of, 18
thinking about, 81–85
topics, 31, 137
validity and, 18–21
See also Ethical issues; Qualitative research approaches; Qualitative researchers; Quantitative research (QN); Questioning/questions; Writing qualitative research
Qualitative research approaches, 6, 14, 81–96, 97–134, 135–159
action research / participatory action research (PAR) , 87, 136, 138–140, 153
arts-based, 140–142, 153
autoethnography, 20, 44, 136, 142–145, 153
case study, 6, 118–123, 129
combined, 83, 85, 92
comparison of, 128 (table), 153 (table)
critical theory research, 151–152, 153
data analysis and, 335–344
ethnography, 100–105, 128
feminist, 63, 145–149, 153
functions of, 100
generic versus specific, 88–90
grounded theory, 6, 87, 90, 105–111, 128, 295, 321
history of, 85–90
interrelatedness of approaches, topics, and participants, 136–138
judging, 377–396
meta-synthesis, 92–93
mixed-methods, 91–92, 153
narrative inquiry and analysis, 6, 99, 124–128, 320, 334
paradigm wars, 14, 19, 90–91
phenomenology, 13, 111–118, 128
postmodernism, 151–152, 153
problems with, 90
selecting, 152–155
summary of, 97–100, 128–129, 152
See also Qualitative research (QR); Questioning/questions
Qualitative Research Café, 85
Qualitative researchers, 4
as instrument, 255
ethical concerns for, 66–76
interpretation by, 41
role of, 43–44, 155, 381
See also Qualitative research (QR)
Qualitative Research Methods (Mack et al.), 103
Qualitative research proposal, 189–200
developing, 191–197
elements of, 193, 197–200
outline, 196–197
writing, 200–201
See also Qualitative research (QR); Qualitative research approaches
Qualman, Erik, 206
Quantitative research (QN)
approaches, criteria for judging, 385
compared with qualitative research, 6–7, 16–17, 99
complementary to qualitative research, 7–8
See also Mixed-methods research approaches

Quasi research designs, 98
Questioning/questions
  closing, 267
  comparison/contrast, 266
  complex, 271
  concrete, 265
  double-barreled, 271
  grand tour, 264–265
  jargon or technical language, 271
  leading, 270–271
  new elements/topics, 266–267
  strategies for, 267–271
  strategies to avoid, 270–271
  types of, 263–270
  See also Interviewing/interviews; Qualitative research (QR)

Rapid communication, tools for, 211
Rapport
  developing, 252
  ethical conduct and, 61
Reader's Theatre, 142
Ready-made, 380
Reality, as interpreted by the researcher, 41
Reductionist process, 115
References, 232
Reflective practice, 35
Reflective researcher, 12
Reflexivity, 16, 31–35, 255
Reflexivity of discomfort, 143–144
Reinharz, Shulamit, 181
Reliability, 385
Repass, Mary, 61
Research
  design, 18, 98
  evidence-based, 15
  methodology, 5, 98
  See also Qualitative research (QR); Qualitative research approaches; Quantitative research (QN)
Research Alive (Carlsen and Dutton), 37
Research Design (Creswell), 149
Research literature review. *See* Literature review
Review boards. *See* Institutional Review Boards (IRBs)
Rewards, and ethical conduct, 62
Rhizome, 304
Richards, Lyn, 341
Romantic conception of interviewing, 257
Rose, Charlie, 242, 245
Rowling, J. K., 243
Rufus Stone, 142, 333, 366, 368 (figure)

Sacks, Oliver, 359
Sallee, Margaret W., 98
Salon des Refusés, 380
Saturated, 106
Saturation, 295
Scientific, 4
Scientific community, misconduct in, 64–65
Search terms, 229
Self, role of, 31–32
Self-reflection, 363, 381
Semi-structured individual interview, 248
Sexual Life of Savages, The (Malinowski), 101
Silent probe, 268
Single question, 269
Skype, 211, 308
Smartphones, 213, 307–308
Sneaky Kid and Its Aftermath, The (Wolcott), 65
Snowball sampling, 6, 250
Social distance scale, 293
Social justice, 62–63, 398–399
Social media, 205–221
  definitions, 206–207
  social networking sites, popular, 207–208
  See also Internet (the); Technology
Social network analysis, 215
Social phenomena, 30–31
Social processes, 30–31
Social Science Research Network (SSRN), 229
Sociological Research Online, 137
Sociosite, 229
Specificity, level of, 8–10
Standardized individual interview, 248
Standards, setting and maintaining, 71–74
Stanford Prison Experiment, 57
Stapel, Diederik, 53, 64
Stevens, J. Christopher, 205
Still life painting, 190 (figure)
Stimuli, using, 269
Story/stories
  looking for, 332–335
  ownership, 126
  retelling, 126
  storytelling, 124
  See also Narrative inquiry and analysis
Stranger Next Door, The (Stein), 58
Structure, and idea communication, 362–364
Structured individual interview, 248
Study, in-depth, 44–45
Studying sideways, 255
Subject, 67, 146, 247

Subjective maps, and children's drawings, 366, 367 (figure)
Subjectivity, 7, 31–32, 36–37
Subjects, 18, 381
Subscription journals, online, 371
Summative analysis, 337
Summerson, Annika, 189 (figure)
Surroundings, observing, 253
Swanson, John Erik, 189
Symbolic interactionism, 39

Tablets, 213
Tally's Corner (Liebow), 358
Taylor, E. B., 101
"Teaching Qualitative Research to Practitioner-Researchers" (Cox), 98
Technology, 205–221, 281, 307–310
  advances in, 208–212
  definitions, 208
  Global Positioning System (GPS), 308
  Google products, 308
  Internet tools, 209–212
  issues regarding, 308–309
  Skype, 308
  smartphones, 307–308
  tools, 216–218
  use of, 308–309, 309–310
  See also Internet (the); Social Media
Textual analysis. *See* Content (textual) analysis
Thematic analysis, 151, 320. *See also* Themes/concepts
Themes/concepts, 11, 45–46, 323–332
Theoretical/conceptual review, 235
Theoretical sampling, 105, 110
Theoretical saturation, 108, 111
Theoretical sensitivity, 107
Theories, and grounded theory, 111
Theory development, 105–111
Thick description, 45
Tools
  Internet, 209–212
  location, 210
  rapid communication, 210
  research on, 217–218
  visual, 210
  ways to use, 216–217
  See also Technology
Total immersion, 103
Traditionalists, 19, 86. *See also* Post-positivists
Traditions, 99
Transactional approach, 391
Transcribing, 338–339
Transferability, 387
Transformational validity, 392
Transformative conception of interviewing, 257
"Transparent Technology" (Dibbs, Glassmeyer, and Lahman), 168–173
"Traversing the Lonely Road" (Bernauer), 164–168
Triangulation, 15, 44, 150, 379, 387
True research designs, 98
Trustworthiness, 195, 378, 379
Tumblr, 208
"Turning Research into Film" (Jones and Hearing), 184–188
Tuskegee Experiment, 64
Twain, Mark, 383
Twitter, 208, 211
Typical case, 120–121

Unique case, 121
Unobtrusive observer role, 289–290
Unplanned individual interview, 250
Unstructured individual interview, 248–250
Unusual case, 121
"Using Qualitative Research to Bridge Research Policy and Practice" (Sallee and Flood), 98

Validity, 21, 391–392
Vannini, Phillip, 366
Verbatim theater, 352
Verifiability, 379
Videography, 301
Virtual community, 219
Virtual learning, 216–217
Visual Methods in Psychology (Reavey), 301
Visuals/images, 281, 301–305
Visual tools, 210
Voight, Jon, 86
von Donnersmarck, Florian Henckel, 129
Vulnerable participants, studying, 69–71
  children, 69–70
  limited English or other challenges, persons with, 70–71

Wait time, 270
Web, the. *See* World Wide Web (WWW)
Web logs. *See* Blogs
Winfrey, Oprah, 243
Wolcott, Harry, 65
Wolfe, Tom, 359
Words, 45–46
Worldviews, inconsistencies in, 150

World Wide Web (WWW), 208
browsers, 209
organizing and analyzing information on, 212
Writing qualitative research, 45–46, 281, 305–307, 349–376
alternative formats, 364–367
creative nonfiction, 358–361
dissemination of, 369–372
fiction, 361
first steps, 351–352
guidelines, 352–358
structure, 362–364
students' examples of, 367–368

YASNS (Yet Another Social Networking Service), 208
YouTube, 207

Zuckerberg, Mark, 207

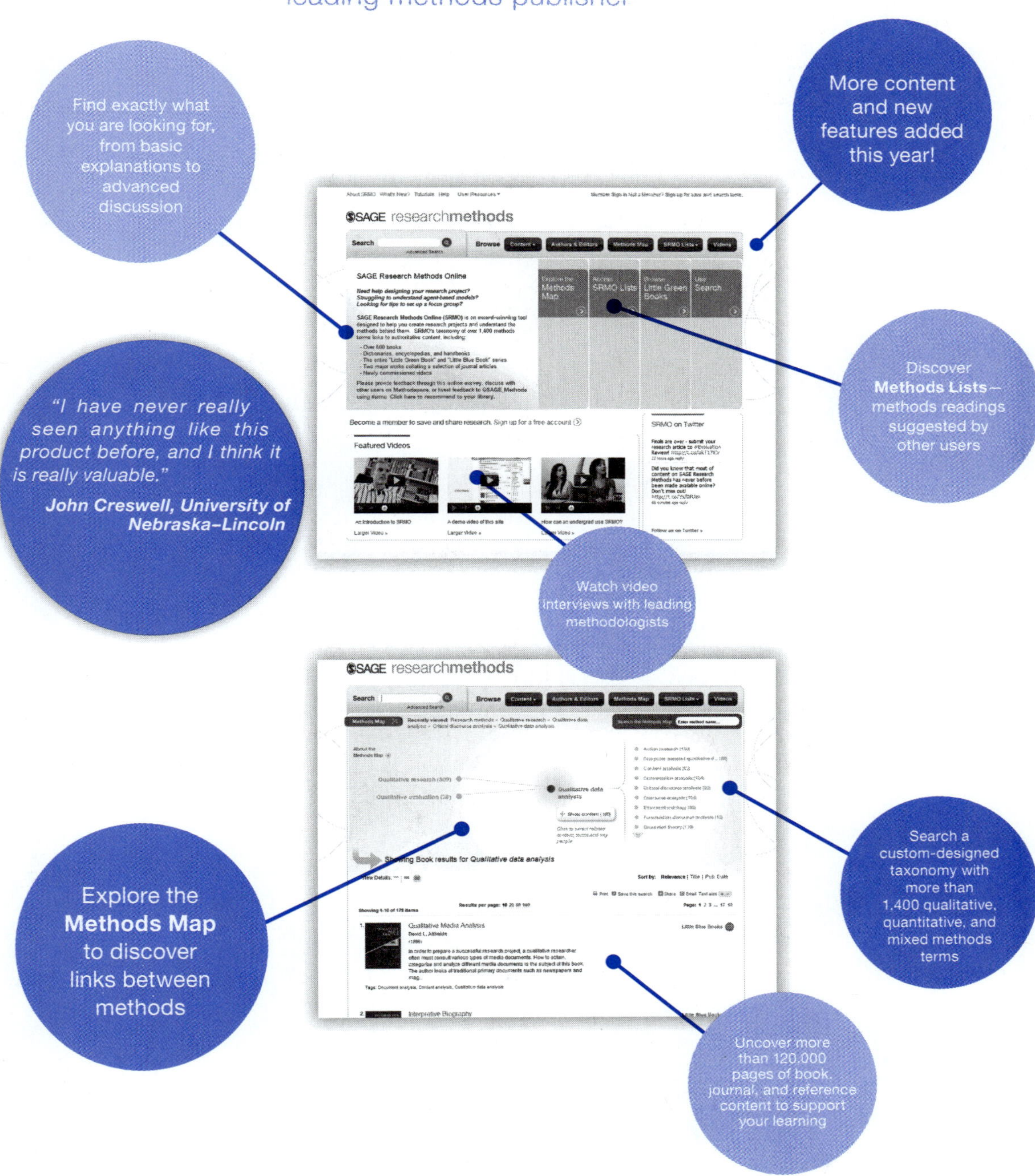
SAGE researchmethods
The essential online tool for researchers from the world's leading methods publisher
Find exactly what you are looking for, from basic explanations to advanced discussion
More content and new features added this year!
Discover Methods Lists— methods readings suggested by other users
"I have never really seen anything like this product before, and I think it is really valuable."
John Creswell, University of Nebraska-Lincoln
Watch video interviews with leading methodologists
Explore the Methods Map to discover links between methods
Search a custom-designed taxonomy with more than 1,400 qualitative, quantitative, and mixed methods terms
Uncover more than 120,000 pages of book, journal, and reference content to support your learning
Find out more at www.sageresearchmethods.com